Praise for Gary Moulton's edite
The Journals of the Lewis and Cla.

"These journals of exploits and courage in a pristine West
have a simplicity and timeliness about them—never failing to
capture the imagination of the ordinary reader or to interest
the historian, the scientist, or the geographer."
—MARY LEE SPENCE, *Montana*

"Superbly edited, easily read."
—LARRY MCMURTRY, *New York Review of Books*

"The journals of the Lewis and Clark expedition are the single
most important account of early western American exploration.
Their interest to specialist and lay reader alike is perennial."
—W. RAYMOND WOOD, professor of anthropology at
the University of Missouri—Columbia

"Masterfully edited and annotated by Gary E. Moulton."
—*St. Louis Post-Dispatch*

"Rich and definitive."
—*Choice*

"Each volume of Moulton's edition renews the
Journals' status as *the* American epic text."
—*Virginia Quarterly Review*

"If the criterion for good editing of an exploratory account is
that it should result in a narrative that is as gripping as an adventure
story, then Moulton's success as editor is unquestioned."
—JOHN LOGAN ALLEN, *Utah Historical Quarterly*

"Meticulous scholarship marks this landmark revision. . . .
Essential to every American history collection."
—*Reference and Research*

"This project compels superlatives. The manner in which
the journals are presented to us here is an exemplary response
to the need which has been felt for a definitive edition
of the journals of the expedition."
—JOHN PARKER, *Minnesota History*

The Lewis
and Clark
Expedition
Day by Day

Gary E. Moulton

University of Nebraska Press
Lincoln and London

The introduction, afterword, and maps originally appeared, in a
slightly different form, in *The Lewis and Clark Journals: An American
Epic of Discovery* by Meriwether Lewis, William Clark, and members of
the Corps Discovery; edited with an introduction by Gary E. Moulton
(Lincoln: University of Nebraska Press, 2003).

Publication of this volume was assisted by a grant from the
Friends of the University of Nebraska Press.

LIBRARY OF CONGRESS CATALOGING-IN-PUBLICATION DATA
Names: Moulton, Gary E., author.
Title: The Lewis and Clark Expedition day by day / Gary E. Moulton.
Description: Lincoln: University of Nebraska Press, 2018. |
Includes index.
Identifiers: LCCN 2017026969
ISBN 9781496203380 (cloth: alk. paper)
ISBN 9781496203830 (pbk.: alk. paper)
ISBN 9781496205292 (epub)
ISBN 9781496205308 (mobi)
ISBN 9781496205315 (pdf)
Subjects: LCSH: Lewis and Clark Expedition (1804–1806) |
West (U.S.)—Discovery and exploration. | West (U.S.)—
Description and travel.
Classification: LCC F592.7 .M689 2018 |
DDC 917.804/2—dc23 LC record available at
https://lccn.loc.gov/2017026969

Set in Minion Pro by Mikala R Kolander.

Contents

Illustrations

Preface

The publication history of works drawn from the journals of the Lewis and Clark expedition has covered more than two centuries. The resulting books were brought forward piecemeal and directed under varying levels of editorial attention. Sergeant Patrick Gass was the first member of the Corps of Discovery to have his journals in print; they were edited and apparently bowdlerized by David McKeehan and published in 1807 (the original journals have since been lost). In 1814 the journals of the two captains were combined with those of Sergeant John Ordway and published as a narrative paraphrase under the direction of Nicholas Biddle and Paul Allen. Later editions of Gass and Biddle were printed throughout the nineteenth century, until Reuben Gold Thwaites published a verbatim edition of most known materials during the expedition's centennial years. One-volume abridgments of Thwaites's eight-volume work followed in the mid-twentieth century while discoveries of previously unknown journals were also edited and published separately as they were found. By the mid-1970s it had become apparent that a new comprehensive edition, capably edited and thoroughly annotated, was needed. Such an endeavor began in 1979, sponsored by the Center for Great Plains Studies at the University of Nebraska–Lincoln with the American Philosophical Society, Philadelphia, published by the University of Nebraska Press, and funded largely by the National Endowment for the Humanities, Washington DC. I was selected as the project's editor.

With the completion of my editorial work on *The Journals of the Lewis and Clark Expedition* in 1999, I undertook a one-volume abridgment of the thirteen-volume edition. That was completed and published in 2003, again with the University of Nebraska Press.

Then I saw a gap remaining in my work with the journals that earlier had followed a publication path through narrative, comprehensive/verbatim, and abridged editions. I had skipped the narrative portion, so enduringly done by McKeehan and Biddle as the first authors of expedition journal–based accounts. I was ready to come full circle back to Biddle. Remembering courses in the American middle period from my graduate school days, I recalled works that might be a model for a twenty-first-century Biddle. Both Abraham Lincoln and the Civil War had received day-by-day studies, so I conceived of similar treatment for the Lewis and Clark expedition.

My method in this undertaking was to use Lewis's journal (when one existed) as the prime source for each day's entry, then to follow with Clark, who often became the principal source because of gaps in Lewis's writing. In cases where one of the two added significant detail or deviated from the basic story line, I noted the difference and named the writer. When the captains separated on independent excursions, I split the narrative accordingly. Otherwise, the captains' journals were blended into a single day's narrative, in which I incorporated the enlisted men's material one by one according to their rank. Like Lewis, some of these men had gaps in their journalizing. Indeed, only Clark and Ordway were consistent writers, with entries for every one of the 863 days of the trip. The enlisted men occasionally added details in their notebooks not found in the captains' journals, so I gave them credit when I included such additions. Moreover, where an enlisted writer digressed, diverged, or disagreed with the basic narrative I had created, I called attention to the variance and named the writer. After blending these various entries into a single day's narrative and completing the book as a whole I turned to separate scientific and collateral work carried out by the leaders and not found in regular entries. Here was work in botany, zoology, geology, meteorology, astronomical observations, and linguistics that needed to be incorporated into my day-by-day narrative. Finally, I reviewed Biddle's published materials in order to discover discrepancies with existing journals, and then I noted such instances of Biddle's supplementary information.

References in this book to "Biddle" relate, of course, to Nicholas Biddle of Philadelphia. Initially disinterested in writing a book about the expedition, he nonetheless visited Clark in Virginia in 1810 and agreed to be the expedition's author/editor, thus replacing Clark, who had inherited the job after Lewis's death. During his time with Clark in 1810, Biddle studied the journals and took detailed notes on queries he put to the captain. Afterward, Biddle took the journals to Philadelphia along with Ordway's notebooks, which the captains had purchased from the sergeant. In Philadelphia Biddle also had the ready assistance of Private George Shannon, who worked as an informant at his side. Moreover, Biddle and Clark carried on an active correspondence while Biddle prepared the work. Biddle asked and got answers to a host of questions about details of expedition events. He then incorporated the information from journals, conversation notes, correspondence, and Shannon's memory into the final two-volume publication, *History of the Expedition under the Command of Captains Lewis and Clark*, published in Philadelphia in 1814, with the assistance of Paul Allen. In the present work when I refer to "Biddle's book" (or similar wording), it is to the publication of 1814. When I use the term "Biddle's notes" (or similar language), it refers to his notes of the 1810 conversations with Clark published in Donald Jackson, ed., *Letters of the Lewis and Clark Expedition with Related Documents, 1783–1854*, 2nd ed., 2 vols. (Urbana: University of Illinois Press, 1978), 2:497–545.

Likewise, references to "Pursh" relate to Frederick Traugott Pursh, originally from Saxony, in present Germany, but in the United States since 1799 and working as a curator and collector for Benjamin Smith Barton in Philadelphia when Lewis learned of him. Lewis hoped to hire Barton as his botanical advisor, but he declined and suggested Pursh to help catalog and identify specimens from the expedition. While Lewis was in Philadelphia in 1807 he employed Pursh to execute drawings of his plants and to assist him in preparing his proposed natural history volume. Lewis turned over his entire botanical collection to Pursh, returned to St. Louis, and apparently never had contact with him again. By late 1809 Lewis was dead, and Pursh had left Philadelphia. Before leaving he turned Lewis's collection over to collaborators who eventually placed the materials in the American Philosophical Society, Philadelphia, where they remained until nearly the twentieth century. Later Pursh found employment in London with a botanical collector who encouraged him to complete his work on American flora. Unknown to his American counterparts, Pursh had carried some of Lewis's collection with him. Descriptions of these specimens and of those that remained in Philadelphia formed a significant part of his book. Ironically, his book, *Flora Americae Septentrionalis* (London, 1814) was published at about the same time as Biddle's and in some ways became the natural history volume that Lewis had proposed. A number of the Pursh items eventually returned to Philadelphia while others, eleven in number, eventually reached Kew Gardens, outside of London. The American collection has since been gathered at the Academy of Natural Sciences, Philadelphia.

Just as the Corps of Discovery needed a "Travelers' Rest" in the Rocky Mountains on trips west and east, I took an "editor's rest" for nearly a decade. In fact, I had begun work on the present book shortly after completing the abridged volume but then laid it aside for the extended period, coming back to it only occasionally. I began work again in earnest in January 2015 and had the book completed by early the next year. After carefully reviewing and revising the finished project I was ready to turn it over to the University of Nebraska Press but waited for an auspicious date. That came on May 14, 2016, when I submitted the manuscript for publication.

It is an honored tradition but also a sincere pleasure for me to recognize and thank those many persons and organizations who assisted in the present work. Once more I am indebted to those people who gave so much of their time and talents to the completion of the comprehensive edition project. Over one hundred persons shared their subject knowledge in numerous fields over the twenty-year effort to complete the project. I benefited anew from their incredible knowledge, as is readily apparent in the following pages. I thank them all again. Moreover, some of the persons and organizations who provided financial assistance to the larger project were willing to aid me once more. Subject and local experts also provided help in answering some vexing questions on matters in their own special fields or geographic areas. Let me name these friends, colleagues, sources, and organizations.

My good friend Samuel H. Douglas III, Whittier, California,

encouraged me in this work and provided funds for me to spend time at Lewis and Clark College, Portland, Oregon, while preparing this book. The college also offered me a scholar-in-residence appointment at the Aubrey R. Watzek Library and access to its outstanding Lewis and Clark book and periodical collection. That collection was ably administered by Doug Erickson and Jeremy Skinner, who guided me to numerous sources in the repository. I also spent a profitable time at the Fort Clatsop National Memorial, Astoria, Oregon, under another residence program. Here again I found excellent assistance from Scott Tucker, superintendent, Rachel Stokeld, librarian, Debbie Wilson, Sally Freeman, Carla Cole, and Chris Clatterbuck.

Locals along the Lewis and Clark trail helped clarify some tricky expedition points. Don Peterson was always a reliable guide around Great Falls, Montana, while Loren Flynn of Lolo, Montana, answered questions about the party's Travelers' Rest campsite. I also reconsidered the identity of Indians at Travelers' Rest when I read Jack Puckett, "Who Were They? An Examination of the Encounter at Travelers' Rest, September 10, 1805," *We Proceeded On* (May 2016): 24–26. Gerry Daumiller of the Montana State Library, Helena, provided a modern place-name in the state. James R. Fazio's *Across the Snowy Ranges: The Lewis and Clark Expedition in Idaho and Western Montana* (Moscow ID: Woodland Press, 2001) helped me find the Corps of Discovery's way in the Idaho mountains. Jim was also kind enough to read the portions of this book that deal with that area and offer very helpful corrections and suggestions. I was put on the right path to follow Ordway's excursion in Idaho when I used Allen Pinkham and Steve Evans's reconstruction of the trip in their *Lewis and Clark among the Nez Perce: Strangers in the Land of the Nimiipuu* (Washburn ND: Dakota Institute Press, 2013). I spent an enjoyable day with Tom Wilson of Astoria, Oregon, and Jim Sayce of Seaview, Washington, tracking down the locations of the expedition's "Dismal Nitch" and "Station Camp."

In the sciences I tapped the knowledge of familiar friends and newfound colleagues. Robert N. Bergantino, Bozeman, Montana, was patience as always when I stumbled at getting expedition latitudes and longitudes right. John W. Jengo, Downingtown, Pennsylvania, saved me countless hours of pouring through his magnificent work on Lewis and Clark's geology, published mainly in the Lewis and Clark Trail Heritage Foundation's quarterly, *We Proceeded On*. He generously read passages from this book that deal with geology and corrected, enlarged, and enhanced that aspect of the work. Robert Kaul of the Division of Botany, University of Nebraska State Museum, Lincoln, helped me with some thorny botany questions, while the work of Scott Earle and James L. Reveal, *Lewis and Clark's Green World: The Expedition and Its Plants* (Helena MT: Farcountry Press, 2003), led me to correct some botanical nomenclature. Finally, Rex Ziak, Naselle, Washington, in his own inimitable way, corrected me on a fish identification, confirmed by Robert A. Hrabik of the Missouri Department of Conservation, Perryville.

Issues of *We Proceeded On* since completion of the journals edition have carried a number of articles that were helpful to me in the present work, while other useful sources have also been published since that time. I list them here (while surely missing some) with thanks to the editors and authors who continue to add to our knowledge and appreciation of the expedition.

Robert C. Carriker, *Ocean in View! O! the Joy: Lewis and Clark in Washington State* (Tacoma: Washington State Historical Society, 2005).

Keith G. Hay, *The Lewis and Clark Columbia River Trail: A Guide for Paddlers, Hikers, and Other Explorers* (Portland OR: Timber Press, 2004).

Robert Heacock, *Wind Hard from the West: The Lewis and Clark Expedition on the Snake and Columbia Rivers* (Liberty Lake WA: Crown Media and Printing, 2015).

Troy Helmick, "The Lewis and Clark Expedition and the Townsend Black Snake," *We Proceeded On* (February 2017): 29–32.

Glen Kirkpatrick, "The Rediscovery of Clark's Point of View," *We Proceeded On* (February 1999): 28–31, 39.

Martin Plamondon II, *Lewis and Clark Trail Maps: A Cartographic Reconstruction*, 3 vols. (Pullman: Washington State University Press, 2000–2004).

Mike Rees, "Ocean in View? A Scientific Analysis of the View from Pillar Rock, November 7, 1805," *We Proceeded On* (May 2009): 22–30.

Ralph Saunders, "Using Modern Technology to Help Solve a 200-Year-Old Mystery: The Search for 'Clark's Canoe Camp' on the Yellowstone," *We Proceeded On* (November 2011): 18–25.

Christopher Steinke, "'Here is my country': Too Né's Map of Lewis and Clark in the Great Plains," *William and Mary Quarterly*, ser. 3, 71 (October 2014): 589–610.

Fred C. Zwickel and Michael A. Schroeder, "Grouse of the Lewis and Clark Expedition, 1803 to1806," *Northwestern Naturalist* 84 (Spring 2003): 1–19.

Closer to home I had the unwavering support of Faye. Although I promised her after completing the earlier works that all our travels would be to places never visited by Lewis and Clark, she graciously joined me on the trail once more. To her I dedicate this book.

Introduction

The president awoke at his residence in the White House on the morning of May 14, 1804, tired and sore from the previous day's journey. It had been a very exhausting trip from Monticello to the capital city for Jefferson, and he called it "the most fatiguing journey I have experienced for a great many years" over a "laborious road as could be travelled." The night's sleep had not entirely rested him, and he still felt the aches of the final fifty-five miles by horseback on his six-feet-two-inch frame of sixty-one years. He promised daughter Martha that he would not forget his age before setting out on a similar trip. In Jefferson's day such cross-country trips required the vigor of youth. Transcontinental travel demanded much more.

Half a continent away, the president's explorers, Meriwether Lewis and William Clark, readied themselves for such a trip. Having spent a winter in camp across from the mouth of the Missouri River in Illinois, the young army officers were anxious to set out. Indeed, Lewis must have viewed the day as the culmination of a decade of delay, for he later called the undertaking a "da[r]ling project of mine for the last ten years." The winter had not been a period of inactivity. At Camp Dubois the officers selected and disciplined their troops and molded a disparate group of men into the Corps of Discovery. They also began to sharpen their skills at the many tasks they would perform over the next twenty-eight months. They made their initial efforts at scientific descriptions and astronomical observations, tested and retested their equipment, visited with Indians, gained advice from seasoned river travelers, and recorded events in rough journal notes. Camp Dubois can fittingly be called the proving ground of the Lewis and Clark expedition. The final days were spent in checking out equipment, packing goods, and adjust-

1. Meriwether Lewis. Portrait by Charles Willson Peale, 1807.
Independence National Historical Park Collection, Philadelphia.

2. William Clark. Portrait by Charles Willson Peale, 1810.
Independence National Historical Park Collection, Philadelphia.

ing loading. Some experimental trips were even made up and down the Mississippi in laded boats. Clark's journal entries grew shorter as excitement mounted to get underway. Finally, on the morning of departure, May 14, 1804, he briskly penned, "fixing for a Start."

Meriwether Lewis and William Clark

Jefferson's choice of Meriwether Lewis to head this important mission grew out of confidence formed from a lifelong acquaintance. Lewis was born in 1774 at the family's plantation, Locust Hill, in Albemarle County, Virginia, a short distance from Monticello. After the death of his father, William, and his mother's remarriage to John Marks, the family moved to Georgia but returned to Locust Hill after Lucy was widowed once more. During his youth Lewis received rudimentary education and seems to have had a keen interest in natural history. Like others of his generation he found his first calling in military service—for young Lewis, militia duty during the Whiskey Rebellion in 1794. Within a year he joined the regular army as ensign, equivalent to a modern lieutenant, and the next year was transferred to the First Infantry Regiment. By 1800, at age twenty-six, he had risen to the rank of captain and probably saw for himself a career in military service. During these years he moved about on various assignments, with no apparent combat experience but with exposure to command, the frontier, and Indians. It was also during this period that he met fellow soldier William Clark, four years his senior and his superior officer for a time. Little is known of that encounter, but it is certain that they struck a deep friendship and it lasted their lifetimes.

Shortly before assuming the presidency Jefferson called Lewis from military duty to become his private secretary, allowing the captain to retain his army rank. It now seems possible that Jefferson selected the young officer not only to groom him for western exploration but also to use Lewis's knowledge of military personnel in order to remove weak links in the officer ranks. During his stay with Jefferson, Lewis had the president's magnificent library at his disposal and he used the opportunity to prepare himself. What Jefferson wanted for the expedition, he confided to a friend, was a person "perfectly skilled in botany, natural history, mineralogy, astronomy, with at the same time the necessary firmness of body & mind, habits of living in the woods & familiarity with the Indian character." He knew that no such person existed but that Lewis filled the latter requirements perfectly and could be sufficiently trained in the former to carry out such duties in the field. With that in mind he sent Lewis to study in Philadelphia with some of the leading scientists of the young republic.

During the return trip to Washington, Lewis took time to ask Clark to join him as co-commander of the expedition, "in it's fatigue, it's dangers and it's honors." Delays in the mail caused some frustration for Lewis, to the point that he had invited another officer, Lieutenant Moses Hooke, to accompany him in case Clark declined. In fact, Clark replied enthusiastically the day after getting Lewis's letter, saying that "no man lives whith whome I would perfur to undertake Such a Trip."

The red-haired Clark was born in Caroline County, Virginia, in 1770. His older brother, George Rogers Clark, was a Revolutionary War hero whose fame might have eclipsed William's were it not for the expedition. Apparently, Jefferson did not know the younger Clark but was well acquainted with his family, in spite of which he consistently spelled the name "Clarke." When Clark was fourteen the family moved to the site of today's Louisville, Kentucky. From there he enlisted in the militia, transferring to the regular army in 1791. He saw actual combat during campaigns in the Ohio valley and rose to the rank of captain, ahead of his junior officer, Lewis. Clark resigned his military commission in 1796 and returned home to Kentucky to help his family. In 1803 he and George Rogers moved across the Ohio River from Louisville and built a cabin near modern Clarksville, Indiana. There he met Lewis as he came down the Ohio.

Clark eagerly accepted the appointment Lewis offered, but a mix-up in Washington denied him a captain's rank. An aggravated Lewis told Clark that his "grade has no effect upon your compensation, which G—d, shall be equal to my own." The leaders hid the fact of Clark's lower rank from their men and throughout the trip shared the command equally. After the expedition Clark brusquely returned the commission. While Lewis signed orders as captain of the First Regiment, Clark occasionally endorsed himself as captain of a Corps of Discovery. Writers have tended to emphasize and even exaggerate the apparent differences in the men's personalities. Lewis appears as the moody, sensitive intellectual, Clark as the pragmatic, less literate frontiersman. These contrasts may be valid and are somewhat borne out in the record, but can be overstated. In spite of the differences, in the twenty-eight months of the expedition, there is no hint of disagreement between them.

Lewis performed most of the expedition's scientific tasks, principally as the party's naturalist and astronomer, and he tended to be absent from the party on intellectual quests. His writing is more technical than Clark's, and he had something of a literary flair. Clark worked primarily as the party's surveyor and his writing is more matter-of-fact. His eccentric spelling, grammar, and punctuation, resulting from a lack of formal education and the loose rules of that era, have accentuated his reputation as a backwoodsman. Yet his vocabulary and phrasing are hardly those of an illiterate man and his prose can be as stirring as Lewis's, if less poetic.

Expedition Underway

The morning of May 14, 1804, dawned cloudy and cool and rain began at nine o'clock, but by afternoon the temperature had climbed to the midsixties and the weather turned fair. At four o'clock, with nearby settlers there to cheer them off, the men fired the keelboat's swivel gun and set out, all in high spirits, according to Clark. The sail was hoisted on the keelboat and the two pirogues fell in as they crossed the Mississippi and started up the Missouri. Lewis was in St. Louis making final arrangements and would ride overland to meet them at St. Charles, a few miles up the river. No great distance was covered that first day; it was a shakedown run and the party traveled less than five miles.

It is unclear how many men were with the expedition at the outset. The captains' apparent indifference to the number of temporary hands may explain discrepancies in the records. These Frenchmen, called *engagés* (engaged men), were professional boatmen who enlisted to pole and pull the heavy keelboat and two pirogues up the Missouri as far as the first winter post. Altogether it appears that forty-two men left Camp Dubois with Clark, organized into three squads of permanent soldiers and two units of temporary personnel. Interpreter George Drouillard was ahead and, like Lewis, would catch up at St. Charles. The permanent party manned the keelboat for the most part, the French *engagés* were in the larger, red pirogue, while the return detachment took the smaller, white pirogue. Alterations were made along the way and in difficult situations everyone helped out where needed.

The party arrived at St. Charles on May 16. The loading in the boats was shifted again, some last-minute supplies were purchased, and other final preparations were attended to. Extra boatmen were also added, including the Frenchmen Pierre Cruzatte and François Labiche, who enlisted as privates in the permanent party, although they may have been with the corps earlier. Both were of mixed-blooded heritage, perhaps part Omaha Indian, so they could assist with interpreting Indian languages as well as translating French. Both were also expert Missouri boatmen. Cruzatte is remembered for his fiddle playing that entertained soldiers and Indians alike, while Labiche took charge of the boats at several critical junctures.

Here, too, at St. Charles was the last chance for social pursuits among townspeople. The men entertained the villagers aboard the keelboat and were welcomed to parties in return. Some of the men went too far in their carousing, so that Clark called a court-martial and charged three of the men for misbehavior. About twenty of the more sober celebrants attended Mass on Sunday, the twentieth. Lewis came in that same evening and the men set out the next afternoon, to the cheers of townsfolk lining the banks. On May 26 the party passed La Charette, a tiny cluster of cabins and the last white settlement on the river. From there they moved into the wilderness, meeting occasional parties of traders heading downriver for St. Louis.

The first stage of the journey, as far as present north central North Dakota, was through country already explored to some extent. Indeed, the captains carried reliable maps of the Missouri to that point. Moreover, some of the French *engagés* had been that far on previous trading ventures and could name incoming streams and prominent landmarks. Curiously, there are no records of daily events by Lewis for this period, from May 1804 to April 1805, except for two short fragments of two days each. Lewis seems to have contented himself with writing scientific notes from his observations. Whether he failed to keep a diary of daily events for the period or whether such notes are lost has never been wholly resolved.

The journey up the Missouri against the current was slow and laborious. Occasionally the men raised the keelboat's sail under a favorable wind, but more often they poled the huge craft or pulled the boats with a tow rope, called a *cordelle*. Toiling in the increasing summer heat, the men were plagued by boils, diarrhea, mosquitoes, and sandbars. Despite their heavy work, the land appeared lush and beautiful to the working hands and expedition diarists universally reported high spirits and enthusiasm. The party reached the mouth of the Kansas River on June 26, and on July 21 they came to the Platte River, a point they had anticipated for some time. The corps was now 642 miles up the Missouri by their reckoning, and over two months out of Camp Dubois, averaging about ten river miles a day. Here the captains decided to spend several days to refresh the men, dry out wet gear, take celestial readings, and bring their maps and journals up to date. They also hoped to meet nearby Indians, but the Otoes and Pawnees were away on buffalo hunts and no conferences were held.

A little over a week later the party had its first meeting with Indians in council. On July 30 in a small grove of trees on some prairie high ground, the expedition formed a camp. They called the site Council Bluff, from the meeting held there with Indians over the next few days. The site is near the town of Fort Calhoun, Nebraska, about fifteen miles north of Omaha. At sunset on August 2 the captains arranged to comply with Jefferson's instructions regarding Indians. That evening a resident trader came into the Council Bluff camp with six Otoe and Missouria chiefs and a meeting was arranged for the next day. Lewis and Clark began the formalities by parading the men, then they passed a ceremonial pipe, demonstrated their weapons, and gave gifts to Indian dignitaries. Lewis brought along an air gun to display American technology, since the weapon could fire off several rounds without reloading. It was a continued source of amazement to Indians across the continent. Out of their trunks came Indian presents—red leggings, fancy dress coats, and blue blankets; ball and powder, tobacco, and whiskey were also handed out. Lewis and Clark also distributed printed commissions for acknowledging chiefs and, of course, Indian peace medals, which were especially prized by the recipients. Indians presented food, tobacco, and native handicrafts.

After the exchanges one of the captains delivered a speech announcing American sovereignty over the new lands, then pled for peace among the Indian tribes, promised increased trade, explained the purposes of the expedition, and requested Indian emissaries to journey to the capital. Now the Indians rose to respond. They apparently approved of what they had heard and promised to heed the good advice. Lewis and Clark perfected such rituals over countless meetings across the continent, but Council Bluff became the initial test of Indian diplomacy, and it apparently went well. At four o'clock that afternoon the party moved on.

Hard physical labor and distance from settlement temptations did not guarantee an end to disciplinary problems. In fact this period marked the most serious breach of order when one of the men deserted. Prior to reaching Council Bluff and finding Indians, the captains dispatched one of the Frenchmen, La Liberté, to find natives and invite chiefs to a council. The Otoes and Missourias arrived, but without La Liberté. After the conference and as the expedition moved upriver, Private Moses B. Reed requested permission to return to the area to reclaim a lost knife. Several days later, with both Reed and La Liberté still out, the captains sent a detachment to apprehend the missing men.

Reed's desertion was a serious offense, punishable by death; La Liberté's action, though not technically desertion since he was a civilian, set a poor example if not treated seriously. Wholesale quitting could endanger the success of the endeavor, if not the very lives of the men if attacked. On August 18 the search party returned with Reed. La Liberté had been captured but true to his name had escaped and was seen no more. Reed was tried, convicted, and expelled. He was also forced to run the gauntlet four times as the men flogged his bare back. Considering the era's military discipline, his sentence was lenient. Some weeks later Private John Newman was arrested for "mutinous expression," tried, punished with seventy-five lashes, and dishonorably discharged. Both men were repentant but were never reinstated to the corps. Nonetheless, they continued with the party until the following spring, doing hard labor, since it would have been virtually a death sentence to cast them adrift in the wilderness.

Near present Sioux City, Iowa, on August 20, a loss of another sort occurred. Sergeant Charles Floyd died, apparently of a ruptured appendix. He was the only member to die on the expedition. His comrades buried him on a bluff and commemorated him by naming Floyd's River in his honor. The medical treatment given him by the captains—probably bleeding with lancets and purging with strong laxatives—was the accepted practice of the day, and a remedy that Lewis learned from Dr. Benjamin Rush in Philadelphia. If used here it would have weakened the sergeant and hastened his death. Patrick Gass was elected sergeant in Floyd's place.

The Middle Missouri

As the men moved on into present South Dakota, they became increasingly concerned about George Shannon, the youngest member of the corps, who had been missing for several days, after he separated to find stray horses. Believing the boats were ahead of him, Shannon hurried on trying to catch up, when in fact the party was behind him. Not until September 11 did they overtake the young man, now weak from hunger after being out more than two weeks. A relieved Clark reflected, "thus a man had like to have Starved to death in a land of Plenty for the want of Bullets or Something to kill his meat."

In late September the corps arrived in the vicinity of present Pierre, South Dakota. Here they encountered a band of the Teton Sioux, or Lakota, Indians, and for the first time their meeting with natives was less than cordial. The Tetons regularly charged tolls of Missouri River traders and now tried their bullying tactics on Lewis and Clark. After some conversation and exchange of gifts, the Indians became surly, demanded more presents, and would not allow Clark to return to the keelboat. The tense situation that followed arose not only from Indian arrogance but also probably from the lack of a Sioux interpreter. Nonetheless, the captains were not ready to submit to payments; their military pride and sense of security required a show of strength. They readied their weapons and made plain their intention to fight—fortunately, the Sioux backed off. Afterward the leaders feared that the Tetons planned a surprise attack and they kept a tight guard until well out of the area. To indicate their irritation, the captains called the island where they camped after the episode "Bad Humored Island." Lewis later called the Tetons "the vilest miscreants of the savage race" and the "pirates of the Missouri." A few days later, on October 8, they reached the earth-lodge villages of the Arikaras in northern South Dakota. Their reception by these sedentary farmers was quite hospitable, and the party remained with them for several days.

Lewis and Clark were the first Americans to evaluate the Great Plains, an area so different from the wooded lands of the East to which they were accustomed. Their conclusions were more optimistic than those of some later explorers who labeled the region the Great American Desert. Between the Kansas and the Platte Rivers they noted a difference in topography, but their impressions did not greatly change. Beyond the Platte, terms like "high and dry" were more frequent than the usual "beautiful and well-watered." Nonetheless, they still considered the plains a virtual paradise. Even on the high plains above the Niobrara River it was the profusion of animal life that caught their attention rather than the terrain, with its absence of trees and unbroken, featureless horizon, and its short grasses and semiarid climate. In fact, they did not use negative terms to describe the plains until they reached their western edge.

The men were fascinated by the region's new and varied animal life. In present northeast Nebraska they spent time hauling barrels of water from the river to a prairie dog hole in order to flush out a live specimen. Such was the work of pioneering naturalists. Besides the prairie dog the captains were the first to scientifically describe coyotes, pronghorns, jackrabbits, mule deer, black-billed magpies, and northern flickers. Moreover, they told of vast numbers of buffalo, the mainstay of plains Indian life. From a vantage point in present central South Dakota, Lewis estimated that one immense herd numbered at least three thousand of the shaggy beasts. It was the captains' return reports of the abundance of beaver that sent eager bands of fur trappers to the farthest reaches of the Missouri's drainage.

As they crossed the Great Plains, Clark was struck by the grandeur of the land and in his own inimitable style declared, "What a field for a Botents [botanist] and a natirless [naturalist]." On another occasion he was moved to write one of his most elegant and descriptive passages:

> The Plains of this countrey are covered with a Leek Green Grass, well calculated for the sweetest and most norushing hay—interspersed with Cops [copses] of trees, Spreding ther lofty branchs over Pools Springs or Brooks of fine water. Groops of Shrubs covered with the most delicious froot is to be seen in every direction, and nature appears to have exerted herself to butify the Scenery by the variety of flours Delicately and highly flavered raised above the Grass, which Strikes & profumes the Sensation, and amuses the mind throws it into Conjecterng the cause of So magnificent a Senerey in a Country thus Situated far removed from the Sivilised world to be enjoyed by nothing but the Buffalo Elk Deer & Bear in which it abounds & Savage Indians

It is important to remember that the men's evaluation of the plains was developed from a river valley perspective. They never ventured far from the rich bottomland—a fact that prejudiced and narrowed their opinions considerably. Nonetheless, twentieth-century biologists have been impressed with the men's perceptions of plains biota and their acute ecological distinctions.

It had been a good summer for the corps. Now, as days grew shorter, trees dropped their leaves and plants and shrubs began to fade. The men watched as migrating waterfowl passed overhead on their southward flights. They saw temperatures dip to the freezing point and frost form overnight. In late October they hurried on to their winter encampment—the most distant outpost in the new lands of a young republic.

Knife River Winter

As the party came up the Missouri River in late October they passed abandoned villages of the Mandan Indians. Such deserted settlements attested to the tribe's weakened state and to the ferocity of their enemies, the Sioux. On October 25 the explorers arrived at the outskirts of the lower Mandan village and were ogled by curious Indians who lined the banks and called for them to come ashore. By their estimate the men were now sixteen hundred miles out of Camp Dubois and 164 days into their transcontinental trip. Winter was near and the captains discovered that the Missouri would soon freeze. They decided, therefore, to make their winter quarters among these friendly folk.

The Mandans and their immediate neighbors to the north, the Hidatsas, were established in five villages at the mouth of the Knife River, where they lived in circular earth lodges. Lewis and Clark estimated their population to be about four thousand persons—the largest concentration of Indians on the Missouri River. The captains found the Mandans in the two lower villages, Mitutanka and Ruptáre, now designated as the Deapolis and Black Cat archaeological sites. Any trace of the villages is now gone, lost to modern construction or to the Missouri's changing course.

The Mandans were primarily horticulturists, growing corn, beans, and squash, and they gathered native plants to supplement their crops. They also turned out for seasonal buffalo hunts to augment their food sources. A peaceful people, they were generous and fair with the American visitors. Fair-skinned, light-haired persons among them led to stories that they were descendants of Welsh travelers who supposedly had wandered to the deep interior of North America. They had lived on the Missouri River since they were first known to Europeans, but they may have come from the Mississippi valley in the distant past. They had moved to the Knife River region after experiencing a devastating smallpox epidemic in 1780–81. The disease reduced their population by perhaps two-thirds in their former villages at the mouth of the Heart River near present Bismarck, North Dakota. In this decimated state they were forced to move north because their Sioux enemies threatened further destruction. For protection they joined the Hidatsas, to whom they were related culturally and linguistically.

To the north were the Hidatsas, or Minitaris to Lewis and Clark, who lived in three villages. The first village, Mahawha, was occupied by the Awaxawis, a people somewhat distinct from their neighbors but considered a branch of the Hidatsas; it is the present Amahami archaeological site, after an alternate name for the band. Lewis and Clark called them by a variety of names, but they are most easily remembered as Hidatsas, with whom they shared much in language and in custom. Above them were the villages Metaharta of the Awatixas and Menetarra of the Hidatsas proper, known today as the Sakakawea and Big Hidatsa archaeological sites.

The three villages roughly approximated the three divisions of the Hidatsas, but such distinctions were disappearing by Lewis and Clark's time because ravages had so decreased their numbers as to consolidate their cultures. The Mandans were joining this cultural pool, and further disintegration of the tribes forced an unexpected homogeneity. The Hidatsas also participated in an agricultural life, and they too pursued buffalo on the plains. More aggressive than their Knife River neighbors, the Hidatsas raided as far as the foothills of the Rocky Mountains in search of martial glory and kinship revenge. As soldiers themselves, Lewis and Clark were impressed with the tribe's warrior societies and military exploits. Moreover, the wide-ranging Hidatsas were excellent informants for the captains' queries about regions to the west.

The Knife River villages in time became the central marketplace on the northern plains—a grand entrepôt of the Missouri trade system. The Mandans and Hidatsas were brokers in an international trade network that disbursed goods over thousands of miles: to the west and southwest with the Cheyennes, Crows, Kiowas, and Arapahoes for horses and mules from the Spanish; to the north and northeast with the Crees and Assiniboines for European manufactured goods coming in from Hudson's Bay; and to the east and southeast with the Sioux for eastern Indian items and additional European manufactures.

The Knife River natives were trading their crops for these goods or acting as distributors. As middlemen in this intertribal network the Mandans and Hidatsas were warehousing horses and guns for distribution to tribes throughout the plains—often marking up prices 100 percent. This intertribal trade continued side by side with the European trade that developed in the 1790s as merchants from the Hudson's Bay and North West companies of Canada came to bargain directly with the Mandans and Hidatsas. Now the Indians were able to increase their store of manufactured goods and solidify their position as the prime traders on the northern plains.

Lewis and Clark arrived among these farmer-hunter-traders with three principal goals based on Jefferson's instructions to Lewis before the expedition began. One goal was to extend American commercial interests into the new territory. In this regard they hoped to shift trade toward enterprises at St. Louis and away from the English in Canada. Another function was diplomatic—to apprise the tribes of the new sovereignty of the United States under the Louisiana Purchase and to explain the purposes of their own mission. They also wanted to establish intertribal peace; for the Mandans and Hidatsas that meant better relations with the Sioux and Arikaras.

It is doubtful the Indians understood the purpose of exploration, nor did they grasp the idea of diplomacy outside of trade. Lewis and Clark looked to trade in the long run; Knife River Indians looked for the immediate exchange of goods. Lewis and Clark wanted to expand U.S. commercial influence as far as possible to compete with Great Britain. The Mandans and the Hidatsas wanted the best goods at the lowest price from the most dependable supplier. Nor were they ready to talk of peace with their traditional enemies without some assurance of security. At this time Lewis and Clark could not provide such guarantees. They did not fully reveal this to the Mandans and Hidatsas, but the Indians were not ignorant of American weakness in this arena. Lewis and Clark were probably too optimistic about what they could do in such a short time, that is, to rearrange trade alliances and lessen enmities that had developed over decades.

Lewis and Clark's final function was ethnographic—to gather information about the tribes in order to increase knowledge. The men obtained their information in a number of ways: by interviewing natives and traders who lived among them, by collecting cultural objects, by reporting on firsthand observations, and by participating in some Indian activities. The captains did their best work in recounting objective matters: describing villages, weapons, food, clothing, and other external aspects. They were not as good at describing ritualistic behavior or subjective matters, and they misunderstood and misinterpreted some activities they observed or participated in. They also missed some important ceremonies and activities because of the time of year when they lived with the Indians.

On November 2, after several days of hunting for the best location, the party began construction of Fort Mandan. By November 20 everyone was inside but work continued for several more days. The fort was located on the east side of the Missouri a few miles below the mouth of the Knife River and nearly opposite the lower Mandan village. The spot is now beneath the river, but a modern reconstruction is not far from its historic location—about fifty miles northwest of Bismarck. Sergeant Gass, a carpenter and perhaps the fort's construction chief, described the structure as roughly triangular, with two rows of huts along each side. The roofs of the huts came off the outer side walls, about eighteen feet high, and descended shed-like toward the center. The picketed front of the triangle served as the fort's main gate, while a small enclosure filled the semicircular point at the rear. That shed was used to house the expedition's supplies, and its flat roof served as the sentry's watchtower.

The stockaded log fort would be their home for five months, during a bitter northern plains winter in which temperatures sometimes dropped to lower than 40° below zero and venturing outside was likely to result in frostbite. Nevertheless, Clark described the party as being in good spirits. On both Christmas and New Year's Day, the explorers had celebrations with music, dancing, and frolic. Moreover, Indians visited the fort frequently and the chiefs, at least, expected to be entertained by the captains. The winter was by no means a period of idleness—hunting, in spite of the fierce cold, was necessary to provide meat. To augment their food, the men built a forge and blacksmiths like Shields were kept busy making war axes and other metal goods to exchange for village crops. The men visited the villages regularly, and some soldiers contracted venereal disease from liaisons with Indian women. York was a particular novelty to these Indians, who had never seen a black man. The Hidatsa Indian chief Le Borgne was so incredulous that he rubbed York's dark skin with his moistened finger, trying to remove the "paint."

Soon after arriving at the Indian villages, the captains hired René Jusseaume as a temporary interpreter. Jusseaume was an independent trader who had lived with the Mandans for about fifteen years but never seemed competent with the tribe's language. Another French-man, Jean Baptiste Lepage, was hired for the permanent party to replace the discharged Newman. Lepage had previously ventured some distance up the Missouri and may have journeyed into the interior, even to the Black Hills of present South Dakota. Because of this he was valuable as an informant and may have aided Clark in preparing his map of the West at Fort Mandan.

Others also joined as permanent members of the Corps of Discovery. A French Canadian trader, Toussaint Charbonneau, was brought in as an interpreter of Hidatsa. He had lived among the tribe as an independent trader for several years and he had two wives from the Shoshone tribe of the northern Rockies. The captains decided to hire Charbonneau and one of the women, Sacagawea, to serve as intermediaries with the Shoshones, whom they anticipated meeting in the mountains. Charbonneau spoke French and Hidatsa, the latter with deficiencies it seems, while Sacagawea spoke Shoshone and Hidatsa. Through this language channel the captains hoped to communicate with Rocky Mountain tribes. Charbonneau has typically been portrayed in negative terms, as a bungler and a wife beater, and Lewis declared him "a man of no particular merit." Clark seems to have thought better of him. At least he fulfilled his obligations to the expedition, however slight.

Sacagawea was born in about 1787 among the Lemhi band of Shoshones. She had been captured by a Hidatsa war party on one of their raids into Shoshone country about 1800, when she was approximately thirteen years old. Her first child, Jean Baptiste, was born at the fort on February 11, 1805, and the infant became the youngest participant in the expedition—carried by his young mother across the continent and back. Sacagawea experienced some difficulty in childbirth, so Jusseaume recommended a folk medication of ground-up rattlesnake rattles to ease her labor. Lewis prepared the potion and administered it to her but doubted its effectiveness, even though the young woman gave birth soon after taking the mixture.

Sacagawea has probably received more attention than any other member of the expedition, save the captains. Time has not diminished her acclaim, and no amount of historical scrutiny has been able to correct distortions about her role in the expedition. Obvious and seemingly trivial items like the spelling of her name and its meaning and pronunciation generate heated debate. The captains' journals clearly give it as "Sacagawea" or some close approximation of that spelling. They state that it meant "Bird Woman," and the name almost certainly comes from the Hidatsa language. Their rendering of the word shows that they pronounced it *Sa-ca-ga-we-a* and probably stressed each syllable equally. Alternate spellings, pronunciations, and translations of the word have had to rely on complicated interpretations that argue against the original records. In fact, almost all of what we know about her is found in expedition journals, and it is very meager material on which to build a legend.

She and her husband, Charbonneau, were hired not as guides but as interpreters. Her services in that capacity among her people and other Shoshonean-speaking Indians in the Rockies were indispensable, while her presence with a baby calmed Indian fears that the party was a war expedition. She did recognize some geographic features when the party reached the region of her girlhood in southwestern Montana. Beyond this, she may have been a pleasant companion, and the baby, called Pomp by Clark, was probably a source of some delight to the travel-weary explorers, but she was by no means the girl guide often depicted in art and fiction.

As spring approached and the ice broke up in the Missouri, the captains prepared to resume their trek westward. They also readied the return party for its departure. Corporal Richard Warfington, with a small squad of soldiers, the remaining French boatmen, and the two expelled men, Reed and Newman, was to take the keelboat back to St. Louis. With them, carefully packed and destined for Jefferson, went the captains' journals completed to that date, tables of observations, letters, maps, a large number of natural history specimens, and live animals: four magpies, a sharp-tailed grouse, and a prairie dog. Only the prairie dog and one of the magpies made it all the way to Jefferson's Monticello. Selected items of the material culture of Plains Indians were also boxed up for Jefferson's inspection. Also included was an "Estimate of Eastern Indians" (those east of the Rocky Mountains), providing all that the captains had learned about Prairie-Plains Indians. It was an incredible array of information about the new lands of the Louisiana Purchase.

Into the Unknown

Just five weeks short of a year after leaving Camp Dubois, the party was set to go, with half a continent to cross before they reached the Pacific. On April 3, four days before the actual departure, an eager and impatient Clark wrote, "we Shall . . . Set out tomorrow." A bracing 28° greeted the explorers on the morning of April 7, but by the time of departure the temperature had climbed to a balmy sixty-four, and a brisk wind blew in to push against their pirogues. Bidding farewell to the St. Louis–bound keelboat and its occupants, the permanent party set out at four o'clock in the afternoon. The Corps of Discovery now numbered thirty-three persons: the two leaders, three sergeants (John Ordway, Nathaniel Pryor, and Patrick Gass), two interpreters (Drouillard and Charbonneau), twenty-three privates, York, Sacagawea, and the infant Jean Baptiste. The end of the season at Fort Mandan marked an important transition. Difficult and potentially dangerous as the route had been thus far, others had ventured here before them and had already mapped the way. From Fort Mandan on, the corps entered country for which they had only Indian and speculative information.

Lewis was in a buoyant mood that afternoon and took to the shore for some exercise in a walk to their night's encampment. The uncounted but faithful Newfoundland dog, Seaman, probably loped along at his master's side. This day Lewis returned to his diary after a long period of infrequent writing; he would keep a steady record until August, when his writing fell off once again. Some of Lewis's best observations and most elegant prose fill the pages of this period. Consider his exuberance at the moment of departure:

> Our vessels consisted of six small canoes, and two large perogues. This little fleet altho' not quite so rispectable as those of Columbus or Capt. Cook were still viewed by us with as much pleasure as those deservedly famed adventurers every beheld theirs; and I dare say with quite as much anxiety for their safety and preservation. . . . The party are in excellent health and sperits, zealously attatched to the enterprise, and anxious to proceed; not a whisper of murmur or discontent to be heard among them, but all act in unison, and with the most perfect harmony.

As the explorers traveled farther west into today's Montana, the terrain became more arid, treeless, and rugged. They had left the midgrass prairies of the northern Great Plains and were moving into a region of sagebrush, juniper, and drought-tolerant short grasses. New animals, like bighorn sheep, were also seen, and the famed grizzly bear made its appearance. The men discounted stories they had heard about the ferocity of the animal. Now out on the plains again, the hunters were anxious to meet one. A limited encounter came on April 29 near the Yellowstone River when Lewis and a companion met two grizzlies, both of which the men wounded. One bear pursued the captain but was so badly hurt that Lewis was able to reload and kill him. The confident captain wrote, "the Indians may well fear this anamal . . . but in the hands of skillfull riflemen they are by no means as formidable or dangerous as they have been represented." Lewis would soon be less assured.

A bear killed on May 5 near the Milk River gave some pause. Lewis wrote, "it was . . . extreemly hard to kill notwithstanding he had five balls through his lungs and five others in various parts he swam more than half the distance across the river to a sandbar & it was at least twenty minutes before he died." The next day when the party saw a grizzly, Lewis commented that "the curiossity of our party is pretty well satisfyed with respect to this anamal . . . [and] has staggered the resolution of several of them, others however seem keen for action with the bear."

The chance for the men of action came on May 14 when six hunters went after a single bear. A volley of four balls ripped into the animal, but it simply charged ahead, took two more rounds from a second volley, and kept coming. One of the balls broke the animal's shoulder, slowing it slightly, but even so it was on them faster than they could believe. The terrified men ran pell-mell toward the river. Two made it to a canoe while the others took cover, hastily reloaded, and fired again. When the bear turned on them, they flung aside their rifles and plunged down an embankment, the grizzly tumbling after them into the water. Finally a rifleman on shore put a round through its brain, killing it instantly. They found eight balls in its carcass.

All the while the less exciting work of the mission went forward. Lewis led a small patrol ahead of the main party on April 25 in order to reach the Yellowstone River and take astronomical readings. For the explorers this spot effectively divided the known from the unknown; as far as they knew no one but natives had ventured beyond this point. They would not reenter lands known to the outside world again until they neared the Pacific Ocean. The boat party came in the next day, and to celebrate the occasion a dram of whiskey was rationed around, Cruzatte brought out his fiddle, and dancing and singing continued through the evening. Two days later they set out again, passing into the modern state of Montana.

On May 14, a few days short of the Musselshell River, Lewis and Clark were both ashore—an unusual circumstance. Charbonneau temporarily had control of the main pirogue when suddenly a squall of wind struck the boat and turned it. Charbonneau, whom Lewis called the "most timid waterman in the world," swung the boat farther around, bringing the wind's full force against the sail and jerking it from the hands of a boatman. The pirogue tilted on its side and began to fill with water, ready to go under. Cruzatte, an expert boatman on board, proved equal to the situation. Threatening to shoot Charbonneau if he did not reclaim the rudder, he also ordered men to bail water and row toward the shore, where they arrived barely above water. All the while Sacagawea, with baby in one hand, calmly bailed water or collected floating items with the other. Lewis, viewing the distressing scene from the shore, shouted orders to Charbonneau but could not be heard. He knew that the endangered boat contained the party's most important articles, including papers, instruments, medicine, and a large share of the Indian trade goods. Realizing the value of the cargo and forgetting himself, Lewis threw down his gun and prepared to jump into the river and swim to the boat, when the folly of the idea struck him. All he could do was stand fretfully by.

In late May the expedition entered the Breaks of the Missouri, a region of broken, dark terrain and impressive geological formations. On the western end of the Breaks lie the spectacular White Cliffs. Lewis's journal passages celebrate the harsh beauty of this rugged land. He was especially struck by white sandstone outcroppings imbedded in black igneous rocks, while erosion created fanciful forms in his mind and enlivened his prose: "with the help of a little immagination and an oblique view at a distance, are made to represent eligant ranges of lofty freestone buildings. . . . As we passed on it seemed as if those seens of visionary inchantment would never have and end . . . so perfect indeed are those walls that I should have thought that nature had attempted here to rival the human art of masonry had I not recollected that she had first began her work."

On May 26 Lewis climbed to the top of a hill and saw what he thought were the snow-capped Rockies for the first time. Despite the prematurity of this sighting, his elation was real, for now he anticipated reaching the headwaters of the Missouri. But a geographic dilemma and a formidable obstacle stood in the corps' way. In early June they reached the Marias River, where they encountered the dilemma. The Hidatsas had not told them of the Marias; the captains had to determine which stream was the true Missouri, knowing that a wrong decision might cost them valuable time and strand them in the Rockies in wintertime. Extensive reconnaissance convinced them that the river to the southwest was the Missouri, although most of the party believed otherwise. After nearly a week the captains' belief was confirmed when Lewis discovered the Great Falls of the Missouri. On June 13, as Lewis walked upstream with an advance party, the men heard a roaring noise and saw clouds of spray that could only come from the falls. They had learned of this place during the previous winter; now they had arrived at the threshold of the Rocky Mountains. Despite their joy, the presence of cascades and rapids presented serious problems, for the canoes and supplies must now be portaged around this barrier. This task would consume an entire month of precious time and test the endurance, patience, and ingenuity of the Corps of Discovery as no other episode to this point.

Portaging the Falls

Lewis called the Great Falls the "grandest sight I ever beheld." His description of it showed his romantic inclinations; he wished "I might be enabled to give to the enlightened world some just idea of this truly magnifficent and sublimely grand object, which has from the commencement of time been concealed from the view of civilized man; but this was fruitless and vain. . . . I hope still to give to the world some faint idea of an object which at this moment fills me with such pleasure and astonishment, and which of it's kind I will venture to ascert is second to but one in the known world." Displeased with his feeble prose, he lay down his pen and longed for the abilities of some great poet or artist.

Clark's survey showed that a diversion of about eighteen miles would be necessary to skirt the falls. The captains had wagon frames constructed on which they placed the canoes to carry supplies. Meanwhile, the men buried the pirogues and excess items to be left behind at a spot they called the Lower Portage Camp, northeast of the modern city of Great Falls. During the portage the men had to endure backbreaking labor, pulling heavy loads across roughened grounds infested with cactus, tormenting their moccasined feet without relief. The exertion was so great that at every rest stop they fell down exhausted. On one trip some ingenious fellows even hoisted a sail over the wagon in order to take advantage of the wind. "This is really sailing on dry land," Lewis commented. Men exempted from this labor hunted for the party's food, but they had to contend with grizzly bears. Occasional heavy rains drenched everyone, and large hailstones injured several; rattlesnakes and mosquitoes were also constant menaces. Sacagawea became ill during this time and there was great fear that she might die. Fortunately, a nearby sulfur spring provided some relief and she recovered.

Complaining of fatigue, the explorers nevertheless revealed extraordinary stamina under such conditions. They could also display amazing coolness in the face of physical peril. A torrent of rain and hail on June 29 caught Clark and a small party near the river. Taking refuge in a ravine, they were deluged by a wall of water running through the gully and were nearly swept into the Missouri. Quick action by Clark, who was waist deep in water himself, saved Sacagawea and her child. Looking back, he saw the water rise to a depth of fifteen feet, carrying everything before it, including some of his valuable equipment. Meanwhile, south of the falls at the party's Upper Portage Camp, Lewis put together the iron-frame, collapsible boat he had designed at Harpers Ferry and carried across the continent. Unfortunately, the lack of pine trees at the falls made it impossible to obtain the tar necessary for waterproofing and the craft simply would not float. The failure of his invention embarrassed Lewis, but the only solution was to construct two more dugout canoes and proceed on.

Shadows of the Rockies

Upriver from the falls the party entered the passage to the Rocky Mountains, passing through the spectacular canyon the explorers called the Gates of the Mountains, near today's Helena, Montana. Beautiful canyon walls did not, however, relieve sore feet and aching muscles. They were now anxiously seeking the Shoshones, but although they saw signs, the Indians were not to be found. Sacagawea began to recognize familiar landmarks; a meeting with her people was now their most urgent concern. On July 25 Clark, leading an overland patrol, reached the Three Forks of the Missouri. Lewis came up with the boat party two days later and found his friend Clark utterly exhausted and quite ill. The explorers remained here for a few days to rest and to tend to blistered feet and sore backs. Since he considered the Three Forks a significant point in western geography, Lewis also needed time to obtain accurate astronomical readings.

The leaders decided to name the three streams the Jefferson, the Madison, and the Gallatin, after the president and his secretaries of state and treasury. The Jefferson, the westernmost stream, seemed most likely to lead them to the Continental Divide, and so they set off up that fork on July 30. Leaving the ailing Clark with the boat party, Lewis pushed ahead with a few men to try to make contact with the Shoshones. On August 12 he finally came to the head of the stream he regarded as the ultimate source of the "heretofore deemed endless Missouri." Atop a ridge at today's Lemhi Pass on the Montana-Idaho border he saw further ranges of snow-capped mountains and realized that the portage to the Columbia would not be so easy as hoped. Despite this discouraging prospect Lewis gave no hint of despair, perhaps because for the first time he tasted waters that touched the Pacific.

Just before crossing the divide Lewis had encountered a lone Shoshone on horseback who fled at his approach, perhaps thinking the men were enemy raiders. On the western side of the ridge the captain entered the valley of the Lemhi River, seeking contact with the Indians. The success of the expedition hinged on a friendly meeting, since Lewis needed assistance if a long overland journey proved necessary. Eventually he was able to meet peacefully with the Shoshones, but they remained apprehensive, fearing treachery. If their misgivings overcame them and they fled, Lewis knew his command might be stranded in the mountains. Consequently, he made every effort to convince them of his good faith, even giving the Shoshone chief his own rifle with which to shoot him if he proved unfaithful.

In the meantime, Clark led the main party up the increasingly narrowing Jefferson. Repeating a mistake made by Lewis, he got diverted on the wrong stream, causing delay and extra effort for the hard-pressed boatmen. In almost comic circumstances, a beaver had chewed down a pole on which Lewis had left a message pointing the correct way along the Beaverhead River. When Clark and party finally reunited with Lewis on August 17, the situation with the Shoshones changed dramatically. The chief, Cameahwait, proved to be the brother or a close relative of Sacagawea, and her services as interpreter helped establish good relations. The captains learned that a long land journey through the mountains would be necessary, for the rivers in the vicinity, although they led to the Columbia, were unnavigable. The Shoshones' description of the route ahead, while dismaying, was informative, and their reports of new tribes to be encountered were important. In spite of discouraging news, the captains anointed the spot Camp Fortunate. It now lies beneath the waters of Clark Canyon Reservoir at the forks of the Beaverhead River. They would stay here until August 24, reconnoitering the area and preparing to surmount the Rockies.

While at Camp Fortunate, Lewis had time to record his impressions of the Shoshones. He found them a poor people despite their riches in horses, an element added to their life after 1700 when they began converting to plains culture. In all, the captain was decidedly complimentary of the Shoshones; he found them "frank, communicative, fair in dealing, generous with the little they possess, extremly honest, and by no means beggarly." By Lewis and Clark's time they were a people of two traditions, digging camas roots and fishing for salmon in the mountains part of the year, then hunting buffalo on the plains at alternate seasons. East of the Rockies they were much abused by their better-armed enemies the Blackfeet and the Hidatsas—Sacagawea's capture by the latter illustrating the oppression. Therefore, they left their mountain fastnesses only under starving circumstances when their over-Rockies food supply of small game, roots, and fish forced them onto the plains to take up buffalo hunts at great peril. The Shoshones welcomed talk of trade with Americans, since they wanted to obtain guns and challenge their oppressors. The captains made promises knowing full well that it would be a long time before such merchandise could reach this remote area. By such promises they hoped the Shoshones would be willing to sell them horses and supplies for their trip through the mountains. Without being entirely deceitful, the leaders did bend the truth because of their critical needs.

On August 18, at Camp Fortunate, Lewis celebrated his thirty-first birthday and penned a reflective passage. Disregarding his considerable achievements, he pledged to redouble his efforts at improving himself and in the future to "live for *mankind*, as I have heretofore lived *for myself*." In the days ahead, the mountains facing them would call for redoubled efforts on the part of every member of the Corps of Discovery. Optimistic and eager to be on the way, Lewis wrote on August 24 that he had had "the inexpressible satisfaction to find myself once more under way." Yet ahead of him and the corps loomed one of the most difficult periods of the entire trip. Having scaled the mountains on a relatively easy ascent, the party now faced the greatest physical challenge of the entire trip—crossing the rugged Bitterroot Range. This challenge called for a carefully calculated strategy, since the most direct route was extremely treacherous, if not impossible. It also called for stamina, courage, and ingenuity—qualities the corps had demonstrated in the past and soon would be called to display again.

Those Tremendous Mountains

Geographical information from the Shoshones about a route to the Columbia River was not encouraging. Clark's reconnaissance of the nearby Salmon confirmed that although the river flowed toward the Columbia, it was unnavigable because of rapids. Moreover, sheer cliffs and precipices along its banks made land travel equally impractical; the perilous stream has earned the nickname "River of No Return." Scarce game and timber unsuitable for canoes were additional deterrents. Evading the direct but dangerous route on the Salmon altogether, the men decided to follow a path along the Bitterroots and come out of the mountains farther to the north. Fortunately, the captains were able to secure the services of a Shoshone Indian guide, Toby, who knew of a route over the ranges. And after a great deal of dickering with their Shoshone hosts, they obtained about thirty horses, not all in the best of shape and fewer in number than needed. Diversion and improvisation at the Missouri's Great Falls were now replaced by avoidance of a treacherous route and dependence on Indian assistance in the Bitterroots. Indian aid and advice were now, and at other times, crucial to the success of the expedition.

The explorers set out northward from the Shoshone encampment on the Lemhi River on August 30, while the Indians traveled eastward toward the Missouri's Three Forks for their seasonal buffalo hunt. The corps followed the Lemhi, a safe portion of the Salmon, and then the North Fork Salmon through difficult terrain along a ridge of the Bitterroots near the Continental Divide. "Horrid bad going," Joseph Whitehouse called it on one of the worst days. On September 3 Toby led them through a pass at the divide near present Lost Trail Pass and they crossed from modern Idaho back into Montana. The next day they came upon a tribe of Indians who, like the Shoshones, may never have seen white men before. At an area later favored by fur trappers who called it Ross's Hole, the auspicious meeting occurred—lucky because the tribe had numerous horses. The party was able to barter for additions to their herd and increase it to more than forty animals—for mounts, for packhorses, and eventually, a few for food.

The Flatheads, more properly called Salish, were much like their Shoshone neighbors, splitting their time between mountains and plains—they too being severely pressed by aggressive plains warriors. In fact, they were at this very time moving to the plains to join the Shoshones for mutual protection in buffalo hunts. Their tribal name appears to come from the Indian sign-language designation, hands pressed against the sides of the head. They did not, however, practice skull deformation, as did coastal Indians the explorers would later encounter. Their language, completely unlike Shoshone, made communication in sign language necessary until a Shoshone captive was discovered among them and Sacagawea brought forward as interpreter. Then followed a laborious line of communication from English to French, to Hidatsa, to Shoshone, to Salish, and then back again. On September 6, with horse trading and customary exchanges completed, the corps headed north along the Bitterroot River while the Salish set out for their Missouri rendezvous with the Shoshones. Calling the stream the Flathead River at first, Lewis eventually named it Clark's River to honor his friend.

Knowing that an even more difficult road lay ahead, the leaders decided to take advantage of clear skies and fair weather and to rest and prepare themselves for the coming trek out of the mountains. On September 9, 1805, they established camp a few miles south of today's Missoula, Montana, on a little stream they christened Travelers' Rest, now Lolo Creek. The camp has likewise been so named. Here they spent two days taking celestial observations, repacking and adjusting loads, hunting game (somewhat unsuccessfully) to replenish their dwindling supply, and resting up for the demanding trip ahead. A passing Indian joined the party briefly and confirmed that a stream to the west was navigable to the ocean and but five days' march ahead. In fact, their trip, marked by incredible hardships, consumed more than twice that optimistic estimate.

Eleven harrowing days in September 1805 were spent on the demanding Lolo Trail. The descent from the Bitterroots via that trail was perhaps the severest physical test of the whole expedition. Winter was already beginning in the high country, and the party struggled through deepening snow. The explorers had to lead their horses along narrow, rocky mountain paths. Some of the horses lost their footing, and one fell to its death and precious supplies and equipment were lost. As winter set in game animals became scarce and the party went hungry before they resorted to eating their packhorses. Toby misled them at one point, costing precious time and adding miles to their hardships. On September 16, one of the worst days, Clark wrote, "I have been wet and as cold in every part as I ever was in my life," and he feared that his thinly clad feet would freeze.

Reaching near-desperation circumstances, the captains decided to adopt a procedure used previously. Clark would press ahead quickly with a small detachment to find open country and make contact with Indians. Setting out with six men on September 18, he arrived two days later at Weippe Prairie, an open area southeast of present Orofino, Idaho. On September 21 Clark sent Reuben Field back with some food supplies obtained from natives to guide the main party in; they staggered in the next day. The long and difficult trip from mountain pass to meadows dashed all hope of a short portage across the Rocky Mountains and ended dreams of an easy passage to the Orient. At the moment those larger consequences were probably forgotten in the face of the immediate accomplishment of coming safely out of the mountains, finding helpful natives, and perhaps obtaining adequate food.

At Weippe Prairie Clark became the first white man to meet the Nez Perce Indians. The captain found them living in two seasonal camps near the prairie where they came to collect a basic food source, camas. Camas roots were sometimes eaten after being steamed and sometimes pounded and formed into loaves. Sergeant Gass thought they tasted like pumpkins. Camas and dried salmon formed the staples of the Nez Perce diet, and these hospitable people graciously shared their supply with Clark and his men. The famished explorers eagerly ate the food, but it proved a mixed blessing since it caused indigestion and diarrhea among the soldiers, who were more accustomed to wild game. They, and the main party later, suffered mightily for several weeks as their systems adjusted to the new diet.

The day after Lewis's arrival, on September 23, the captains held council with Twisted Hair, the ranking chief, while other leaders were away with a war party. Difficult communications followed, for the explorers had encountered another language group. The Nez Perces spoke a variety of Sahaptian, a tongue unfamiliar to Sacagawea or Toby, so conversation reverted to the nearly universal sign language. The usual medals and gifts were passed out and close inquiries were made about the route ahead. The name for the

Nez Perces comes from the French for "pierced noses." The captains called them "Chopunnish," a phonetic spelling of one self-designation, also related to the term piercing. Lewis and Clark noted the tribe's fine horses. The Nez Perces are renowned for their spotted Appaloosas, but there is some dispute about their development of the breed. Nonetheless, after acquiring horses, they too made periodic trips to buffalo grounds. In fact, the Lolo Trail was their ancient route across the mountains.

In their conversations with the Nez Perces, Lewis and Clark discovered that the corps could return to water transport for their passage to the sea, so they quickly set about to locate a camp and begin building canoes. By September 26 the whole party had moved to a spot Clark found with Twisted Hair. Canoe Camp, as it has come to be called, was about five miles west of present Orofino, on the south side of the Clearwater River and opposite the mouth of the North Fork Clearwater, called the Kooskooskee and Chopunnish Rivers by the captains. The explorers remained here until October 7, resting up after the difficult mountain crossing, recovering from bouts with dysentery and from general ill health, and building dugout canoes for the downriver trip.

Roll On Columbia

On October 7 they were ready, and leaving their horses with the Nez Perces to await their return, they set out in five canoes. The Corps of Discovery was now on the long-sought water route to the Pacific. Following the Clearwater and the Snake Rivers, the latter called "Lewis's" in the captain's honor, the corps passed down to the Great Columbian Plain. The party had traveled through a variety of ecosystems previously unknown to Anglo-Americans. From the Great Plains, semiarid and largely treeless yet teeming with game, they had entered the Rocky Mountains, the first whites on record to do so in the region they crossed. In the mountains they found dense forests in many places, where the game necessary for sustenance was scarce and the natives often lived on the edge of starvation. Coming to the Columbian Plain, they again entered a new world, barren of trees like the Great Plains but also barren of game. They shifted from an area inhabited by horseback tribes east of the mountains to one inhabited by tribes who traveled by canoe and subsisted on salmon and roots on the west side.

As they followed these streams they encountered great numbers of villagers living on the river banks, their livelihood dependent on the annual run of fish. Some of these people provided assistance and with some the men traded for food, since game was nearly impossible to find. Tiring of the monotonous diet of fish and roots, the explorers frequently bought dogs to replace the deer, elk, and other game they were unable to obtain. Soon Toby abandoned the enterprise, thinking perhaps his usefulness was ended when he could no longer guide or interpret. Twisted Hair and Tetoharsky, another Nez Perce chief, accompanied the party for several days. On October 16 the corps reached the Columbia, the Great River of the West. They set up camp on a point at the confluence of the Snake and the Columbia and during the next two days the explorers reconnoitered the area. Here they observed the seasonal end of the great salmon run on the Columbia; the numbers of fish Clark found "incrediable to say." Here also they took astronomical observations, met with nearby Yakama and Wanapam Indians (Sahaptian speakers like the Nez Perce chiefs), purchased forty dogs for food, and prepared for the final drive to the sea.

From Indian information the captains expected to find rapids and falls farther down the Columbia, but even the most accurate accounts could not prepare them for the difficulties to come. In one fifty-five-mile stretch, they encountered the most treacherous river conditions of the entire trip. They portaged some of the swirling waters. At other times, eager to reach the Pacific, they plunged directly through the rapids in their ungainly canoes, much to the amazement of Indians who were watching from the shore. On October 23, 1805, the corps entered this spectacular but dangerous stretch of the river, a few miles east of present The Dalles, Oregon. They found a series of three major barriers created by the stream as it cut through the Cascade Range in its descent to the sea. More than a week of demanding physical effort was required to pass through this part of the river. They made a short, successful portage of their first obstacle, Celilo Falls. Local Indians, on the other hand, maneuvered their own heavily loaded crafts skillfully through the high waters.

Expedition boatmen looked on with envy and admiration. In addition to battling the river, the explorers were now set upon by infuriating fleas and irritating body lice, picked up from native huts.

Immediately below the falls were The Dalles, as later travelers named it, comprising two stretches where the river narrowed considerably—the Short and Long Narrows to Lewis and Clark. In spite of the "horrid appearance of this agitated gut Swelling, boiling & whorling," as Clark described it, the party was forced to run the narrow passage since no portage was possible. Under the steady hand of Cruzatte the boats and much of the cargo were guided through the straits to the astonishment of onlooking Indians. Nonswimmers walked on shore carrying what they could of valuable supplies as the boats careened by. That evening the unperturbed Cruzatte played the fiddle as the men danced and entertained locals. The American expedition must have been exceptional amusement for shore-lined natives that fall of 1805.

The area's rapids and falls not only hindered Lewis and Clark but also slowed spawning fish going upstream. As such it became a favorite fishing ground for local Indians. Over time The Dalles became a market center as well, controlled by the Wishram and Wasco Indians whose houses lined the banks. Clark called it "the Great Mart of all this Country." The Wishram-Wasco plank-house villages served as the region's entrepôt for river-traffic trade goods. Pacific Northwest goods found their way up the Columbia to meet over-mountain merchandise relayed from the Middle Missouri by Shoshone traders. On the Columbia dried salmon replaced Dakota corn and jerked buffalo as the principal medium of exchange at The Dalles market.

The Dalles was also a dividing line between language families. Upriver were Sahaptian speakers like the Yakamas and Nez Perces, while at The Dalles and below Indians spoke varieties of Chinook. Although similar linguistically, the myriad tongues along the river were not mutually understood. In time a universal language developed, called the Chinook jargon, which served Columbian natives much like sign language on the Great Plains. Lewis and Clark discovered not only a difference in language and a variation in customs at The Dalles but also a change in attitude near this point. Instances of petty thievery became routine and a source of some irritation to the party. Although the explorers could not understand the cultural backdrop for such activities, the Indians did not consider it dishonorable. The Americans, however, found it troublesome, and possibly dangerous, especially if they lost vital supplies. They were universally scornful of the natives because of this practice. Potentially explosive as the acts of pilfering were, no violence occurred and the expedition moved on.

After a few days' rest and some drying out of supplies at their Fort Rock Camp at The Dalles, the party approached the final barrier, the Cascades of the Columbia, which they negotiated on November 1–2. Here the river passed through a series of chutes and falls with such velocity that it was again necessary to portage some men and equipment. Now somewhat familiar with the routine, the boatmen ran the rapids with little damage to the canoes and without injury to personnel. Lewis and Clark were much relieved at their success. After passing the Cascades the river broadened and the party entered tidewater. On November 2 they passed an imposing formation on the north shore and named it Beacon Rock, a name restored in the twentieth century. Near the mouth of the Willamette River and today's Portland, Oregon, they reentered the world of previously known geography, for boats of George Vancouver's British expedition had come this far up the Columbia in 1792. To the north and south they noticed snow-peaked mountains, some named by Vancouver's party, including Mount Hood, Mount St. Helens, and Mount Rainier. Clark could now check the accuracy of Vancouver's maps, copies of which he carried with him, and add firsthand observations to his own maps.

Evidence of European contact became more apparent as the party moved on; they saw pieces of sailors' clothes and heard occasional English words, most of it salty sailor language. They also encountered a new geographic and climatic zone as they approached the coast. From the relatively dry and barren plateau they moved into the rainy coastal region with its thick forests and fogs. The broad Columbia estuary now opened before them, and Clark exclaimed triumphantly, if prematurely, on November 7, "Ocian in View! O! the joy." He was probably looking only at the waters of the estuary, but in a few days more they did indeed see their long-sought goal. As they worked their way along the Washington side, the men took to carving their names on trees to mark their triumphant transcontinental crossing. Later, copying Alexander Mackenzie, who had crossed Canada in 1793 and inscribed a rock at the conclusion, Clark etched these words on a large pine: "William Clark December 3rd 1805. By Land. U States in 1804 & 1805."

Their satisfaction was tempered by the miserable weather, rain, and wind, which forced them to huddle, wet and cold, on the Washington side of the high waves. The immediate goal was to find a place for winter quarters. Since there seemed to be no really suitable spot on the north side of the Columbia, they looked to the southern shore. Considering whether to winter on the coast or seek some drier spot back up the Columbia, the captains put the question to a vote. Even York, the slave, and Sacagawea, the Indian woman, had their opinions recorded. The final decision was to cross to the south side of the Columbia to seek a location with adequate game and proper timber to build a stockade. After a few days of searching, on December 7 they picked a site on the banks of the Lewis and Clark River, a short distance from today's Astoria, Oregon—4,118 miles from Camp Dubois by their estimate, after 573 days on the trail. Here would be their home for the next 3½ months, until March 23, 1806.

Pacific Coast Winter

Fort Clatsop, named after the local Indians, was the party's third and final wintering outpost. Although the stockade's purposes were similar to those of Camp Dubois and Fort Mandan—protection from the elements, security against assault, and separation from neighboring inhabitants—the temperament of its occupants differed from that of previous winters. The depressing weather, marked by rain, storms, and gray skies, acted on the men's spirits and may have influenced their relations with the natives. Indeed, the journals reflect a dislike, even disgust, with the coastal tribes. Peaceful relations were maintained, but the party did not warm to these people, who were sharp traders, as they had to the Mandans, Hidatsas, Shoshones, and Nez Perces.

Jefferson's original plan included the possibility that the party might meet a coastal trading vessel and return by sea. The captains apparently discarded this idea, but they still hoped that such a ship would enable them to send dispatches and specimens back to guard against accident on the return trip. No ship appeared, so with spring the party packed up, faced east, and began the long trip back to St. Louis. If the winter at Camp Dubois was one of preparation and at Fort Mandan one of anticipation, the winter at Fort Clatsop may well be called the period of reflection. Here Lewis accomplished some of his most important natural history writing, summarizing his observations and discoveries from the Rocky Mountains westward. Here, too, Clark completed an initial draft of his great map of the West, incorporating all he had learned from traders, Indians, and firsthand experience about vast areas only conjectured at before.

After deciding on the location for their fort on December 7, the men set to felling trees and preparing the land for their winter quarters. Axe men found excellent timber nearby. Clark called it the "Streight butifull balsom pine" (probably grand fir) and carpenter Gass declared that it made "the finest puncheons" he had ever seen. By December 12 they had finished three cabins; two days later all seven huts were up with roofs yet to go. Chinking, daubing, and general sealing of openings to keep out the interminable rain kept builders busy for several more days. On Christmas Eve most of the party moved into their huts, but they were soon smoked out, so chimneys were added throughout. The fort was completed by December 30 so the party could retreat to relative dryness. The stockade was about fifty feet square with three huts on one side, four on the other, and an open yard between. The enlisted men occupied three rooms along one row, while across the grounds Lewis and Clark shared a room, the Charbonneau family another, with the remaining two rooms left for storage. Palisades at the front and rear joined the two rows of cabins. The main gate opened to a cleared area and a small rear gate provided access to a nearby spring.

The corps did not starve, but food was neither plentiful nor good that winter. The inability to preserve meat in the damp climate meant that the company lived much of the time on spoiled elk, deer, and small game. The quest for food kept hunting parties out constantly and at ever increasing distances, elk being the chief game animal.

After one productive hunt Lewis commented, "This evening we had what I call an excellent supper it consisted of a marrowbone a piece and a brisket of boiled Elk . . . this for Fort Clatsop is living in high stile." At times the party's provisions were down to only a few days' rations and the captains fretted about their situation. The men, however, seemed wasteful and largely unconcerned about declining food resources. Lewis scolded them for their profligate ways on several occasions. Native plants, dried fish, and dogs were purchased from the Indians, but those seasoned traders demanded high prices and the explorers' store of trade goods dwindled rapidly.

To aid in food preservation the captains set up a camp on the coast where workers boiled seawater to obtain salt. Now called the Saltmaking Camp, it is at Seaside, Oregon, about fifteen miles from Fort Clatsop by way of the party's overland trail. It was initially established by Joseph Field, William Bratton, and George Gibson, but saltmakers varied during its operation, with three men usually present. About four bushels of salt were obtained before shutting it down on February 21. In January Indians brought word of a whale stranded a few miles south of the Saltmaking Camp at today's Cannon Beach. Clark led a detachment of about thirteen men to obtain the meat; Sacagawea insisted on seeing the "monstrous fish" and the ocean, so she joined the excursion, with baby Jean Baptiste. By the time Clark arrived local Indians had stripped the whale and left only the huge skeleton. He was able to purchase a few hundred pounds of meat and a few gallons of oil and returned to the fort four days later.

The men passed their days hunting and dressing animal skins for clothing. Near the end of their stay the men counted over three hundred pairs of moccasins, a seeming abundance of footwear but a number necessary for the return. Routine soldiering duties such as cleaning and caring for equipment also filled their time. It was nonetheless a winter of boredom for the soldiers, but now more disciplined, they were not the raucous lot of Camp Dubois. Undoubtedly they danced to the music of Cruzatte's fiddle, and being young men away from home, they had affairs with local women. The captains, fearing venereal disease and complications with Indians, soon advised against such contacts and the men promised to refrain.

Minor illnesses flourished in the camp because of the dampness and cold, accidents and injuries occurred, and biting insects annoyed the men without relief.

On Christmas morning the captains wakened to shouts and singing from the men. The leaders divided the last of the tobacco to users and gave a silk handkerchief to each of the others. Some special presents were also exchanged. Clark received woolen clothing from Lewis, moccasins from Whitehouse, an Indian basket from Goodrich, and two dozen white weasel tails from Sacagawea. Ordway commented that they had no liquor for toasting "but all are in good health which we esteem more than all the ardent Spirits in the world." Again on New Year's Day another salute resounded through the woods as the men fired their weapons. Lewis thought ahead to January 1, 1807, when he would find himself "in the bosom of our friends . . . [to] enjoy the repast which the hand of civilization has prepared for us." This day he contented himself with boiled elk, cooked roots, and "pure water."

Coastal natives at the mouth of the Columbia were part of a linguistically related group known as Chinooks. The Chinooks proper occupied the north bank of the Columbia across from the expedition's post. Their territory extended some distance up the river and north along the Washington coast to Willapa Bay. The Chinooks occupied villages along the Columbia during the summer fishing season, then moved north to the bay for the winter. The explorers had little contact with them and most of their information about them came from the Clatsops. The Clatsops (also Chinookans) lived on the south side of the Columbia as far upstream as Tongue Point and south along the Oregon coast to Seaside. The Clatsops and the Chinooks proper spoke nearly identical dialects of Lower Chinook. Later the Chinook jargon became a convenient means of communication along the river corridor, even among non-Chinookans.

The trip down the Columbia had perhaps predisposed the party to view their Fort Clatsop neighbors in a negative light. Having experienced petty thefts along the way, the men were weary of the nuisance and were not ready to put up with it at the fort. Indicative of the men's feeling was the password at the post, "No Chinook." Customary civilities were shown to visitors, less frequent here than at

Fort Mandan, but a genuine cordiality was never established. Lewis and Clark found the Clatsops to be gracious hosts on their infrequent visits to Indian lodges, but the Indians seemed to view the contacts not as social gatherings but as commercial encounters.

Local trading practices created a hindrance to ideal relations. The Indians were accustomed to hard bargaining with ship traders who had been coming to their shores to barter for sea otter skins for over a decade. The Clatsops expected the explorers to accept and follow time-honored conventions. Instead, Lewis and Clark thought the Clatsops overcharged for goods they desperately needed. What the Clatsops viewed as good business, the corps saw as gouging transactions directed unfairly at them, especially since they were short of trade goods and in need of basic necessities. Blue beads were the favorite medium of exchange, but the party lacked enough to last a winter of intense haggling. The corps found little of the milk of human kindness among these inveterate traders.

The captains' diplomatic efforts were either slighted or inconclusive at Fort Clatsop. Although the Chinooks, estimated at four hundred persons, were the most influential tribe at the Columbia's mouth, the leaders never ventured across the river for negotiating, and visits from Chinook chiefs were rare and unproductive. Their brief meetings with Chinooks in November while on the Washington side had likewise been inconsequential. Diplomatic ventures with the Clatsops were similarly indefinite. Although only half the size in population as their cross-river cultural kinsmen, the Clatsops should have been the focus of the captains' diplomacy due to their accessibility. The leaders knew personally only one chief, Coboway, however, and they never carried out the round of discussions that had been so customary in the past. Perhaps the value of American interests was not as clear at Fort Clatsop as before, and the men's store of Indian presents had dwindled by this time, especially in the face of intense trading.

Many aspects of the local culture aroused negative reactions from the captains, who were not the wholly disinterested ethnographers they had been before. Chinookan sexual practices provoked a censorious tone not apparent when the men wrote of similar customs among Plains Indians. Lewis commented, "they do not hold the virtue of their women in high estimation, and will even prostitute their wives and daughters for a fishinghook or stran of beads." The leaders noticed, however, that the Clatsops "do not appear to abhor it as a Crime in the unmarried State." Head deformation, a coastal custom quite new to the captains, did not come in for condemnation, however. In infancy Chinookan children were placed in special cradles equipped with a board that pressed against the forehead. Over time the pressure of the board brought about the desired effect, a nearly straight slope of the forehead from the top of the skull to the nose, yielding a pointed look when viewed from the side and a flattened appearance when seen from the front. Clark drew pictures of the cradle and the result of its work in his journal. The look was considered a mark of status, which slaves and non-Chinookans were not permitted to imitate.

Lewis and Clark discovered that resident Indians made rich use of native plant resources. Roots played important roles in the Indian diet, including edible thistle, western bracken fern, rushes, cat-tail, seashore lupine, and most importantly, wapato. Wapato was not indigenous to the Fort Clatsop area but was acquired farther up the Columbia. It grew in swampy places and was harvested by women, who waded into the water, pulled the bulbs loose with their feet, and tossed the floating plants into canoes. The roots were usually cooked, either by boiling or roasting, but sometimes were eaten raw. The enlisted men, used to a diet of buffalo, deer, and elk, probably agreed with Lewis when he described one of the plants as "reather insipid." The greatest part of native subsistence, however, was based on the river's rich and ever recurring resource of running fish. The river provided sturgeon, eulachon, trout, and other fish, but most importantly, salmon, in several varieties. The coastal Indians possessed many skills in this livelihood that the newcomers admired. The captains described in great detail the types of canoes utilized by Chinookans and their dexterous handling of the boats on the Columbia's choppy waves. The explorers also noted the Indian methods of fishing and their use of nets, gigs, hooks, and line, all intricately fashioned from native resources.

At Fort Clatsop the captains had time to reflect on the Indian tribes from the Rockies westward. In their journals they gave careful

attention to native clothing, houses, utensils, weapons, and imple-
ments, and they wrote general descriptions of coastal material culture. They also developed an elaborate document called the "Estimate
of Western Indians" (west of the Rocky Mountains), comparable to
a similar one completed at Fort Mandan for eastern Indians. They
gave extra space in their writing to tribes in the vicinity of Fort
Clatsop. The Wahkiakums and Cathlamets lived on the north and
south sides of the Columbia and to the east of the Chinooks and
Clatsops. They spoke a dialect known as Kathlamet, a part of the
Upper Chinook language, but they differed from upstream Chinookans in several respects and were a transitional group between
those above and below them. Such cultural subtleties either confused the captains or were totally lost on them. South of the Clatsops along the Oregon coast lived the Tillamook Indians, who had
a village at present Seaside and were neighbors to expedition saltmakers. They belonged to the coastal branch of the Salishan language family. As noted by Lewis and Clark, the Tillamooks shared
a number of outward cultural traits with the neighboring Clatsops,
despite language differences.

Dreary as the stay at Fort Clatsop was, the captains did not lack
occupation. Lewis, who had neglected his journals for some time,
returned to writing at Fort Clatsop. On January 1, 1806, Lewis took
up a new journal and continued writing consistently until August
12, when he laid his pen down, ending his record of the expedition.
This new journal contains extensive descriptions of flora and fauna
and the life of local Indians. Nowhere else did Lewis give more time
and journal space to fulfilling the scientific objectives of the mission than in this writing, the product perhaps of enforced leisure
in a strange, new environment. Until late March he devoted the
greater part of journal entries to detailed records, often accompanied by sketches, of animal and plant species observed in the mountains, across the interior, and on the coast, a large portion of them
unknown to science. Perhaps to ensure preservation by keeping a
duplicate record, Clark copied most of the scientific matter almost
verbatim into his own notebooks.

While Lewis wrote, Clark spent the winter months preparing his
maps of the route from Fort Mandan and sorting out geographi-

cal information. Clark drew numerous maps in his journals of this territory and augmented them with larger, more detailed sheets. Neatly executed finished versions showing the route over the mountains and down to the coast were probably completed at Fort Clatsop. As the corps moved into unknown lands, Clark relied heavily on Indian informants for mapping peripheral areas. Indian maps were eagerly sought because they enabled the captains not only to look ahead to country they were to enter but also to look beyond to lands outside their route of travel. Often the maps were no more than rude charcoal drawings on animal skins or stick scratches in the dirt to show rivers and trails with small mounds of earth to represent hills. Indian cartographic concepts were sometimes difficult to interpret and language differences added an extra burden, but native knowledge was essential to Clark's mapping success.

Clark brought all of this information together and at Fort Clatsop he completed a large map of the country west of the Missouri River. The new map was a vast improvement over the map he had sent to Jefferson from Fort Mandan. With great accuracy Clark delineated the avenue of their traverse and filled in the large blank spaces of previous maps. Areas to the north and south of their line of march were sketchier. Clark based his work on outlying lands on knowledge acquired from Indians and traders and on maps the leaders had examined in the East. Lewis and Clark carried the new map back to St. Louis, then Lewis took it on to Washington DC, where a cartographer hastily prepared a finished version for the waiting president. It was the most accurate map then available of the trans-Missouri West.

Homeward Bound

Boredom, sickness, a monotonous diet, and the dreary weather all enhanced the party's impatience to start for home as soon as receding mountain snows were thought to permit their passage. The captains knew that the Nez Perces, with whom they had left their horses, would cross the Rockies to hunt buffalo as soon as the snows melted. They were anxious to secure their horses, cross the mountains themselves, and explore a more direct route from the mountains to the Missouri. They also wanted to carry out a separate exploration of the Yellowstone River. These separate excursions demanded a division of the corps, a plan they settled on at Fort Clatsop.

They had planned to leave on April 1, but eagerness to be underway prompted them to move up the date to March 20; then bad weather and the need to secure additional canoes held them another few days. Lewis and Clark feared that the price the Indians wanted for a canoe would severely deplete their small stock of trade goods and cripple their ability to obtain needed supplies on the way home. The captains succumbed to temptation and violated their long-standing and consistently observed rule against stealing Indian property by sending out a party to take an unattended canoe nearby. They rationalized that the Clatsops had once taken elk shot by expedition hunters before the men could return to claim them.

A few days before leaving, Lewis reflected on the Pacific Coast stay. "Alto' we have not fared sumptuously this winter and spring at Fort Clatsop, we have lived quite as comfortably as we have any reason to expect we should; and have accomplished every object which induced our remaining at this place except that of meeting with the traders who visit the entrance of this river." On March 22 he wrote, "we determined to set out tomorrow at all events." The last morning at Fort Clatsop was similar to so many others at the post since December 7—a steady rain fell and strong winds prevailed, making departure uncertain. At one o'clock the weather cleared and Lewis wrote, "we bid a final adieu to Fort Clatsop." Sluggish muscles strained against the river's current in the five canoes and they made only sixteen miles that first day, camping a few miles beyond modern Astoria, barely a start up the Columbia. St. Louis must have seemed much more than half a continent away, and Virginia, the other side of the world. No doubt tired arms and sore backs were evident that evening, attesting to a winter of inactivity. Any complaints went unrecorded, probably out of elation to be headed home.

Clark's geographical inquiries and mapping at Fort Clatsop required the party to make a stop in the area of present Portland, to seek a river that had begun to figure prominently in their conception of western geography. The natives called it the Multnomah, a name adopted by the captains; it is today's Willamette River. Hidden by a large island, they had missed it on their downriver trip. In fact, they missed it again, but Clark retraced his steps, took a small detachment and an Indian guide, and investigated the stream's lower reaches on April 2 and 3. Indian information became garbled with their geographic theories to the extent that the captains confused the courses of the Willamette and Snake Rivers and gave the former more prominence than it deserves. On Clark's final map he showed the river as coming from much deeper in the continent than it actually does. They were correct, however, in their assessment of the "Columbian valley," the area between the Cascade and Coast Ranges. Lewis declared it "the only desireable situation for a settlement which I have seen on the West side of the Rocky mountains" and capable of supporting fifty thousand persons. On April 6 the party was again on its way.

They were nearly two weeks getting upriver past the Cascades and Celilo Falls. To the wearisome labor of portaging these obstacles again was added the aggravation of bad relations with Indians in the vicinity. Although hunters were out constantly, an occasional elk or deer could not feed hungry laborers. So the explorers had to supplement their hard-won game with dogs, dried fish, and roots from river tribes as before. Again, the natives demanded high prices, perhaps understandable now since fish were late in coming and the Indians were facing hard times. As before, some of them could not resist stealing the explorers' belongings. It was a repeat of the previous year's frustrations. The captains' patience was at low ebb and they threatened violence if stolen goods were not returned. An exasperated Lewis declared the Indians "poor, dirty, proud, haughty, inhospitable, parsimonious and faithless in every rispect." When some Indians made off with Seaman, the captain sent a party of men to recover his dog, with orders to shoot if necessary. Fortunately, no one was killed and Seaman was returned. Sergeant Gass probably summed up the men's opinion in the blunt, sweeping words of an enlisted man: "All the Indians from the Rocky Mountains to the falls of Columbia, are an honest, ingenious and well disposed people; but from the falls to the seacoast, and along it, they are a rascally, thieving set."

Once past the falls they traded canoes for horses and continued their journey by land, making their way up the north side of the

Columbia. On the westward journey the captains had promised to visit Chief Yelleppit of the Walla Wallas and to remain with him for a few days on the way back. They kept their promise and camped among these neighborly people from April 27 to 29 at the mouth of the Walla Walla River. Yelleppit provided much-needed food and entertained the expedition with festivities. The explorers returned the favor in kind—out came Cruzatte's fiddle and the men danced until late in the evening. Yelleppit also loaned them canoes to cross the Columbia and told them about an overland shortcut to the Nez Perces. Because they provided such a contrast to Indians at The Dalles, Lewis called the Walla Wallas "the most hospitable, honest, and sincere people that we have met with in our voyage." On the morning of April 30 they set out guided by a Nez Perce they had met several days earlier. They were anxious to reach his people and recover the horses they had left with the tribe on the westbound trip.

This route took the party over new ground. With their guide's aid and the help of twenty-three horses, they covered the distance between the Columbia and Clearwater Rivers in six days, circumventing the Snake River almost entirely. The cross-country trip followed Indian trails, meandered along the Touchet River, and passed the present towns of Waitsburg, Dayton, and Pomeroy, Washington. Reaching the Snake on May 4, the party crossed over and continued up its north side to the Clearwater, then followed it some distance before crossing to its south side for a better road. They now headed southeasterly, looking for a campsite among the Nez Perces, whose lodges they were passing, hoping to find a spot where game might prove plentiful.

On May 14 the party settled in to a camp on the east side of the Clearwater at the modern town of Kamiah, Idaho, where they would remain for nearly a month. The Nez Perces told them that it would be at least that long before the snows in the Bitterroot Mountains melted sufficiently to allow passage over the Lolo Trail. An impatient Lewis looked to the mountains and wrote of "that icy barrier which separates us from my friends and country, from all which makes life esteemable." Their campsite has come to be called Camp Chopunnish after the explorers' name for the Nez Perces. Except for the two wintering posts, it was the longest encampment of the expedition. They passed their time seeking food, counciling and socializing with the Indians, and obtaining more horses for the next stage of the trip.

The captains also assumed a new and demanding role as physicians. On the westward trip some expedition prescriptions had eased Indian ailments and had, Clark said, "given those nativs an exolted oppinion of my skill as a phisician." Back again, Clark became the natives' "favorite phisician," according to Lewis. During this stay the captain was visited by a host of afflicted persons complaining of a variety of ills, notably rheumatic problems, sore eyes, and abscesses. Lewis was doubtful whether any permanent cures could result, but the immediate benefits were good relations with the Nez Perces, including payment in much-needed foodstuffs. The captains wished that they could indeed cure these "poor wretches."

The captains also mediated a dispute between the local Nez Perce leaders. The previous fall they had left their horses with Chief Twisted Hair. Some more prominent chiefs, Cutnose and Broken Arm, who had then been absent were annoyed with him on returning, thinking that he had assumed too much authority. Twisted Hair had apparently overused the mounts, then, displeased with the criticism, had neglected the horses, and finally let them wander over a considerable area. Now Lewis and Clark did their best to reconcile the squabbling chiefs and sent some men to recover their animals. Tribal horses eventually made up for any lost or damaged ones, bringing the count to sixty-five animals. Some rather fractious stallions were castrated in Indian fashion, which the explorers found superior to their own method.

In councils with local chiefs Lewis and Clark promised that American merchants would follow with trade goods, especially guns, so the Nez Perces could defend themselves against the Blackfeet and other enemies. They also promised, if they should meet the Blackfeet on their eastward trip, to try to persuade them to make peace with the Nez Perces. Their hosts may have been a bit skeptical on this point, but the desire to obtain weapons to match those of their enemies inspired hope. The men found much to admire about their hosts' customs, hospitality, and appearance. At leisure times, the fiddle was once more brought out and dancing and singing ensued;

friendly footraces and competitive games were also a part of camp activities. Camp Chopunnish was by no means a "summer camp," but it was quite a contrast to the most recent winter camp. The traveling ethnographers recorded much about Nez Perce material culture during the forced stay. Food, clothing, and housing of course caught their attention. The horse culture of this equestrian people was also a matter of serious consideration. Finally, the captains tried to explain Nez Perce attitudes, ceremonies, and rituals.

According to the Nez Perces the snow would not be gone from the Lolo Trail until the beginning of July, but the whole party was anxious to start homeward, so they left the valley of the Clearwater "elated," Lewis said, "with the idea of moving on towards their friends and country." On June 10 the Corps of Discovery moved to higher ground on Weippe Prairie. From here they set out on June 15 but soon realized that they could not find their way in the deep snow. Two days later, after caching many of their supplies, they turned back. Lewis lamented, "this is the first time since we have been on this long tour that we have ever been compelled to retreat." They returned to Weippe Prairie and sent to the Nez Perces for guides. Three young men offered to serve for the price of two guns. On June 24 the party set out again; the Indians found the trail easily and they made their way to their old camp at Travelers' Rest. This time they took only six days on the Lolo Trail in contrast to the eleven days of the westbound trip and without a repeat of severe hardships. They spent a few days resting for the next stage of the journey.

Separation and Reunion

At Fort Clatsop the captains had decided to divide the party for an extended time to investigate previously unexplored territory. Each captain would lead a detachment over new ground, eventually reuniting at a predetermined spot, the mouth of the Yellowstone River on the Missouri. On July 3 the two groups went their separate ways. It was the first time during the expedition that they had separated for such a long time and over so great a distance. Lewis admitted, "I could not avoid feeling much concern on this occasion although I hoped this seperation was only momentary." It would be nearly six weeks before these friends were together once again, and there would be much to tell. Without doubt Lewis had the more disquieting news.

Lewis and Clark knew that their outbound route, following the Missouri to its headwaters, had been needlessly roundabout and that there were trails across the mountains that would shorten the journey considerably. This quicker route needed to be examined. Moreover, they wished to discover the northernmost reach of the Marias River, hoping to expand the United States' claims under the Louisiana Purchase. Consequently, Lewis would investigate the shortcut by heading east to the Great Falls of the Missouri, then explore the Marias before returning to the Missouri. Clark's mission was to explore the Yellowstone River. He would travel southeast to the site of Camp Fortunate, then follow the Beaverhead and the Jefferson Rivers to the Three Forks of the Missouri. Part of his group would then take canoes down the Missouri to the Great Falls to meet Lewis's party there, while Clark went overland to the Yellowstone. Thus, Clark's reduced detachment would carry out the investigation of the Yellowstone. The scattered groups would eventually recombine at the Yellowstone's entrance into the Missouri.

On his trip Lewis was accompanied by nine men, volunteers for what was considered the more dangerous assignment, and five Nez Perce guides who left the detachment the next day. With their seventeen horses the party moved north down the Bitterroot River to the vicinity of present Missoula, Montana. From there they headed east across the Continental Divide following the Clark Fork and Big Blackfoot Rivers on a route previously recommended by the mountain Indians. After the Indian name, Lewis called the last stream the "River of the Road to the Buffaloe." Eventually, Lewis and his men crossed the divide over what is now called Lewis and Clark Pass, although Clark never saw it.

By July 13 they were at the old Upper Portage Camp above the Great Falls—one year minus two days since they left this spot. It had taken eleven days of travel to cover the distance; the previous year the corps had labored nearly two months in linking Upper Portage Camp to Travelers' Rest. The new route was also a savings of nearly six hundred miles. The soldiers were delighted after months of meager rations to be eating buffalo again. Lewis was amazed that "there were not less than 10 thousand buffaloe within a circle of 2 miles" about the place. But buffalo country was also bear country, and they were not thrilled at the grizzlies that greeted them at the camp. Some gave the men trouble as the soldiers dug up the cache they had hidden the previous year. Hugh McNeal had a close call with one in which he broke his musket over the beast's head and then spent several hours in a tree waiting for the stunned and angry bear to leave. Memories surely stirred of former battles with bears.

Lewis was disheartened to find some of the materials at the Upper Portage Camp cache damaged by water, including the loss of all the botanical items he had so carefully collected and preserved between Fort Mandan and the Great Falls. Losing several horses, perhaps to Indian thieves, Lewis decided to make the journey up the Marias accompanied by only three of his best men, Drouillard and the Field brothers. Sergeant Gass and the others would await the canoe party from Clark's detachment, then all would portage the Great Falls, recover additional supplies buried there, and finally proceed to the mouth of the Marias to meet the returning Lewis and his detachment. Before departing, Lewis instructed Gass that he should meet him at the Marias about August 5, but if he had not arrived by September 1, that the sergeant should leave to join Clark at the Yellowstone. Lewis was quite aware of the potential danger of the mission.

They set out on July 16, heading north to the Marias and then along its banks to the river's upper forks. After several days' travel the captain began to doubt that the Marias extended as far north as he had hoped. On Cut Bank Creek, near the mountains, they camped from July 22 to 26, the most northern camp of the expedition, about twelve miles northeast of today's Browning, Montana. Here Lewis attempted to take astronomical observations but was frustrated by overcast skies. Thus hindered, Lewis named the place Camp Disappointment. He was further disappointed that the potential for additional American territory was lost, since the Marias did not drain from the north. The four men now turned about to rejoin their companions. The night of July 26 they bedded down along the banks of Two Medicine River. Extra hands warmed themselves at the evening's campfire.

That day Lewis and his men had encountered a party of eight

Blackfeet Indians of the Piegan tribe. Lewis knew that he was in their territory and that they were the avowed enemies of many of the Indians that the corps had befriended. It was the one Indian tribe he had hoped to avoid. Having been spotted by the Indians, however, he believed a retreat might be interpreted as weakness and perhaps invite attack. Moreover, at first Lewis was unsure of the Indians' numbers, as the horse herd in sight seemed to indicate many more than eight. Others might be nearby and cut off any hasty retreat, so he advanced and engaged in friendly sign-language talk. The two parties camped together beneath three cottonwood trees on Two Medicine River.

The next morning the explorers were awakened by the noise of a struggle; one of the Indians had tried to make off with some of the party's guns. Joseph Field, the early morning guard, quickly awakened his brother, Reuben, who pursued the Piegan and stabbed him to death. Another Indian seized the rifles of Drouillard and Lewis, but Drouillard saw him and wrested back his own gun. His shouts and struggles aroused the soundly sleeping Lewis, who took up his pistol and pursued an Indian fleeing with his rifle. He caught the thief and, with pistol at ready, ordered him to lay down the rifle. When the Indian did so, Lewis allowed him to go, denying his men's request to kill the thief.

Failing to obtain the explorers' guns, the Blackfeet rushed to take their horses, hoping perhaps to restore some lost honor. The Indians split into two groups; Lewis pursued one group of two Piegans, while his men went after the rest. One Indian turned to fire on Lewis, who got off the first shot, hitting the man in the stomach. The fatally wounded warrior fired a final shot and Lewis later recalled, "being bearheaded I felt the wind of his bullet very distinctly." Both whites and Indians had had enough. The six surviving Piegans fled north, while Lewis and his men quickly gathered up their belongings and began two days of hard riding back to the Missouri. The fear of avenging Blackfeet warriors spurred them on. At the mouth of the Marias they met the canoes under Sergeant Ordway, who had picked up the men Lewis had left at the Great Falls. Once on the canoes the whole party easily outdistanced any potential pursuit by the Blackfeet.

Clark's trip on the Yellowstone was a good deal less dramatic. He too departed Travelers' Rest on July 3 and took his division by another new route out of the mountains. Going south along the Bitterroot Valley, the group retraced part of the previous year's trek but diverted to cross the Continental Divide at present Gibbon's Pass, giving themselves a straighter shot to their destination. They then proceeded into the Big Hole River valley, following buffalo and Indian trails southeasterly to their old Camp Fortunate, where they arrived on July 8. During this time Sacagawea was able to point the way—one of only two occasions on which she may be said to have served as a guide. The men quickly dug up the goods and canoes they had cached at the camp the preceding year. Although the items were a little water-soaked, they were for the most part undamaged. Especially gratifying to users was the unharmed tobacco, which they immediately put to use, having been without the substance for several months.

From Camp Fortunate the returning explorers journeyed by horse and canoe down to the Three Forks. The summer before it had taken almost three weeks to cover this distance; now they were able to make the trip in as many days. They arrived on July 13, just as Lewis reached the Upper Portage Camp, some 150 miles to the north. At the Three Forks Clark wasted no time. The same day he divided his party, sending Ordway with nine men down the Missouri in canoes to meet the Gass contingent, while he led a party of twelve persons, including the Charbonneau family, east to the Yellowstone. Clark and his group set out through the valleys of the Gallatin and East Gallatin Rivers. The area was a vast landscape of wildlife, with enormous herds of deer, elk, and antelope to be seen in all directions and great numbers of beaver in the rivers. Again following well-worn but confusing trails the party moved through Bozeman Pass and crossed to the Yellowstone on July 15. Along this route Sacagawea was again able to point out an accessible route. Thus Clark remarked that Sacagawea had been of great service "as a pilot through this country."

Traveling along the north side of the Yellowstone the party kept watch for trees large enough to serve as canoes. In the vicinity of present Laurel, Montana, they found cottonwood trees of sufficient size to build canoes and continue their journey by water. While the boatbuilders were at work, Indian prowlers also kept busy—taking twenty-four of the party's fifty mounts. The horse thieves were probably Crow Indians, since the party was in the tribe's hunting territory. Clark decided to split his unit once more. He sent an advance party under Sergeant Pryor with the remaining horses cross-country to the Mandan villages. The sergeant carried a message to a Canadian trader, asking him to induce some Teton Sioux chiefs to go to Washington with the captains. The groups separated on July 24. Shortly after Pryor and his three companions set out, their horses were stolen, again perhaps by stealthy Crows. Pryor handled the emergency admirably. His party killed some buffalo and used the hides to build bowl-shaped "bull boats" such as they had observed among Missouri River tribes. Then they set off down the Yellowstone in pursuit of Clark's party, whom they overtook on August 8.

Clark's trip down the Yellowstone was uneventful. On July 25, near today's Billings, Montana, he arrived at the landmark he named Pompy's Tower after little Jean Baptiste; it is now called Pompeys Pillar. Clark also carved his name and the date on the rock—still visible on this National Historic Landmark. Proceeding on, they arrived at the mouth of the Yellowstone on August 3. There Clark had intended to wait for Lewis, but he found the mosquitoes so intolerable and game in such short supply that he decided to go on down the Missouri, leaving a message for Lewis telling of his move. On August 11 Clark's party met two trappers, the first whites they had seen since April 1805.

Lewis arrived at the Yellowstone on August 7, read Clark's message, and moved on. On August 11 he was the victim of a painful and embarrassing accident. He was out hunting with Cruzatte, an excellent boatman but poor of sight. Seeing a movement that he took to be an elk, Cruzatte fired and hit Lewis in the buttocks. Lewis thought he had been wounded by an Indian, but it proved to be Cruzatte's blunder. The wound, though not terribly serious, was quite painful. In fact, a few days later as Clark was dressing the wound, Lewis fainted. Ever the naturalist, Lewis found energy to discover one last plant, the pin cherry, about which he wrote a lengthy description on August 12, before he lay down his pen. On that same day, a few miles below the Little Knife River in present North Dakota, Lewis and Clark reunited. Clark assumed the remaining writing duties for his ailing comrade.

Hurrying Home

The full party reached the Mandan and Hidatsa villages two days later, where they stayed until August 17. To their dismay the captains discovered that their peace plans for the plains had fallen apart. After they departed, Hidatsa warriors had attacked a Shoshone village near the Rockies, Sioux war parties had attacked and killed some Mandans and Hidatsas, and the Hidatsas had stolen Arikara horses and killed two of the tribe. Hoping to restore their damaged plans the captains persuaded the Mandan chief Big White to accompany them to Washington to see the president. As they departed they left behind Sacagawea, Charbonneau, and little Pomp. Clark offered to take the boy and treat him as if he were his own son, but father and mother thought him too young; they promised to bring him to Clark in a year or so. Here also John Colter took his discharge in order to join two American trappers bound up the Missouri. On their way out they made a brief stop at Fort Mandan and found it nearly all burned down, perhaps the work of prairie fires. The next day Lewis celebrated his last birthday on the trail, his thirty-second; Clark had turned thirty-six on the first of the month.

At the Arikara villages on August 21 the captains faced an awkward situation, for the chief they had convinced on their way upriver to travel to Washington had not yet returned and the villagers had grown suspicious. No other chiefs would agree to go. In fact, though the captains had no way of knowing it, the chief had died of illness in Washington. They smoothed over the situation as well as they could, but ultimately the resulting hostility of the Arikaras would cause a great deal of trouble. On August 30 they met some Teton Sioux, giving them the cold shoulder because of the troubles of 1804. They held a friendly meeting with the Yankton Sioux near the mouth of the Niobrara on September 1, and on September 4 they revisited Sergeant Floyd's grave.

The rest of the downriver journey was made as fast as possible, by men eager to return home. They were now meeting trading parties bound upriver, who gave them the news of over two years, including the fact that many people in the United States had given them up for lost, although "the President of the U. States had yet hopes of us." The traders also sold them some whiskey, which was distributed to the party, the first that had been tasted since the Fourth of July 1805. Lewis was recovering from his wound as they passed the scenes of the toilsome upriver journey, several campsites each day. On September 20, near La Charette, they saw the first cows since leaving the settlements. The next day they reached St. Charles, meeting old friends.

Emerging from the river's mouth on September 23, they briefly visited the camp at Wood River that they had left some twenty-eight months before, then crossed over and reached St. Louis at noon. The citizens, having received advance word, lined the riverfront and cheered. Two days later, at Christy's Tavern, they were treated to a lavish dinner, with eighteen toasts, ending with "Captains Lewis and Clark—Their perilous services endear them to every American heart." The next day Clark brought his journal to an end with the anticlimactic words "a fine morning we commenced wrighting &c."

Expedition Personnel

Members of the permanent party (the thirty-three persons who were members of the expedition party that left Fort Mandan in April 1805 and traveled to the Pacific and back).

Meriwether Lewis, captain

William Clark, captain

William E. Bratton, private

Jean Baptiste Charbonneau (the baby, "Pomp")

Toussaint Charbonneau, interpreter

John Collins, private

John Colter, private

Pierre Cruzatte, private

George Drouillard, interpreter

Joseph Field, private

Reuben Field, private

Robert Frazer, private

Patrick Gass, sergeant

George Gibson, private

Silas Goodrich, private

Hugh Hall, private

Thomas Proctor Howard, private

François Labiche, private

John-Baptiste Lepage, private

Hugh McNeal, private

John Ordway, sergeant

John Potts, private

Nathaniel Hale Pryor, sergeant

Sacagawea, interpreter

George Shannon, private

John Shields, private

John Thompson, private

Peter Weiser, private

William Werner, private

Joseph Whitehouse, private

Alexander Hamilton Willard, private

Richard Windsor, private

York, Clark's slave

Additional personnel

John Boley, perhaps in Return Party

E. Cann, temporary *engagé*

John Dame, perhaps in Return Party

Jean Baptiste Deschamps, temporary *engagé*

Charles Floyd, sergeant, deceased

Jean Baptiste La Jeunesse, temporary *engagé*

La Liberté, deserted party

John Newman, dismissed from party

Paul Primeau, temporary *engagé*

Moses B. Reed, dismissed from party

François Rivet, temporary *engagé*

John Robertson (or Robinson), perhaps in Return Party

Peter (or Pierre) Roi, temporary *engagé*

Ebenezer Tuttle, perhaps in Return Party

Richard Warfington, corporal and head of Return Party

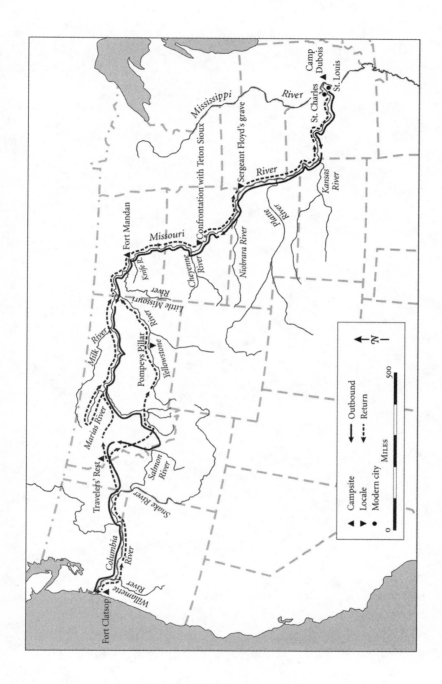

MAP 1. The expedition's route, May 14, 1804–September 23, 1806.

The Lewis and Clark Expedition Day by Day

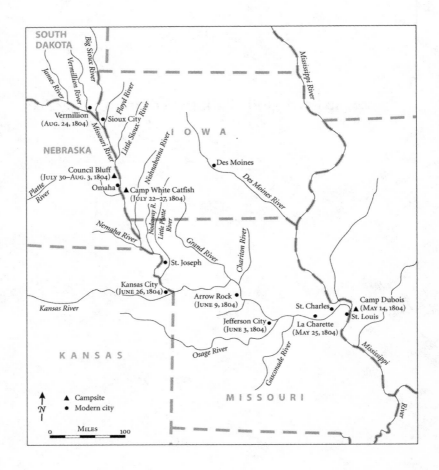

MAP 2. The expedition's route, May 14–August 24, 1804.

CHAPTER 1

Expedition Underway

May 14–August 24, 1804

MAY 14, 1804. At about four o'clock in the afternoon, with a clear sky and temperatures in the midsixties, the men fired the keelboat's swivel cannon and hoisted the sail. As the party's two pirogues fell in behind, the Corps of Discovery crossed the Mississippi River from the wintering camp at the mouth of Wood River in Illinois and began the ascent of the Missouri River and their expedition to the unknown. Well-wishers on shore waved them good-bye. The party, consisting at this time of about forty-two men led by Clark, was divided into three squads: the permanent party manned the keelboat and French *engagés* were in the large, red pirogue, while the return detachment came up in the smaller, white pirogue. In order to test the loading and leave time for readjustments, they advanced less than five miles and made their first camp near Fort Bellefontaine, St. Charles County, Missouri. Lewis remained in St. Louis making final arrangements. Drouillard was also behind on special assignment.

MAY 15, 1804. After a rainy night, Clark had the party underway by nine o'clock. They moved about nine miles up the river and camped below St. Charles at a point called Piper's Landing, after James Piper of the St. Charles district. Here the men adjusted the load of the keelboat, shifting greater weight to the bow.

MAY 16, 1804. After passing coal beds in the vicinity of Charbonnier, the party arrived at St. Charles about noon and saluted spectators who had come down to the river to greet them. While here, extra help was added to the party, including perhaps the Frenchmen Cruzatte and Labiche, who enlisted as privates. The little village, first called Les Petites Côtes (Little Hills), had about 450 inhabitants at the time. It was surveyed in 1787 and still retained a French Catholic flavor despite the influx of American settlers, including Daniel Boone, who moved nearby in the 1790s. In the evening Clark dined at the home of François Duquette, a Canadian who had come to the area eight years earlier and grown prosperous. His elegant home sat atop one of the little hills and was surrounded by orchards and gardens. Clark admonished the men to behave themselves, but it was not to be.

MAY 17, 1804. Three men, Collins, Hall, and Werner, were brought before a court-martial for misconduct. Hall and Werner were charged with being absent without leave and pled guilty. Collins was also charged with being absent without leave, as well as acting improperly at a dance the previous evening and speaking disrespectfully upon returning to camp. He pled guilty to the first charge and not guilty to the other two. The court, made up of Sergeant Ordway and Privates Reuben Field, Potts, Whitehouse, and Windsor, sentenced Hall and Werner to receive twenty-five lashes on their bare backs but recommended clemency, which the captains agreed to. Collins was judged guilty of all three charges and was sentenced to fifty lashes. The punishment was carried out in the evening. None of the enlisted men mentioned these facts in their journals. In the afternoon Clark met with some Kickapoos who informed him of possible warfare between the Sauks and Osages. Drouillard arrived. In the evening the captain dined again with Duquette. The party remained at St. Charles.

MAY 18, 1804. Clark directed the men to shift the loads in the keelboat and pirogues in order to better distribute the weight. Louis Lorimier, a Canadian by birth but now an area trader, came by and brought reports of the Kickapoos he had visited. Lorimier continued on to St. Louis, joined by Drouillard, who carried a letter from Clark to Lewis. Keelboats arrived from Kentucky laded with whiskey and other trade goods. Whitehouse said that some of the men passed the evening in the arms of French ladies who were very fond of dancing. From astronomical observations, the captain gave St. Charles's position, where they remained, as latitude 38° 54′39″ N and longitude 90° 15′07″ W; today it is closer to 38° 46′52″ N and 90° 28′47″ W.

MAY 19, 1804. Strong winds and heavy rains were up during the night. Drouillard returned with cash from St. Louis but had lost a letter from Lewis; it was found the next day. Clark settled payment with some of the men, who then went to a dance in town, but the captain was not able to join them. Nonetheless, he was visited by seven women, and the party remained another day in St. Charles.

MAY 20, 1804. Lewis left St. Louis at noon in the company of Captain Amos Stoddard and Lieutenants Clarence Mulford and Stephen Worrell of the U.S. Army, together with René Auguste Chouteau, Charles Gratiot, David Delaunay, Sylvester Labbadie, James Rankin, and Dr. Antoine François Saugrain, some of the leading citizens of the town. After about an hour's ride through fertile prairies and woodlands, a severe thunderstorm came up, so the group took shelter in an abandoned cabin and had lunch. Eventually they gave up on waiting out the storm and set out in the rain, joining Clark at St. Charles in the late afternoon. Lewis described the little community as having a chapel, one hundred ill-constructed houses, and 450 inhabitants, mostly Canadian French, whom he later characterized as poor, illiterate, and excessively lazy but also polite, hospitable, generous, and harmonious. Most of the party attended church services in the evening while the captains took supper with Charles, or don Carlos, Tayon, the Spanish commandant at St. Charles since 1793. This was their last day in St. Charles.

MAY 21, 1804. After enjoying a final meal with Duquette, the captains led the party out of St. Charles at about three thirty, while inhabitants cheered them from the shore. Meeting a strong wind and heavy rains from the west-southwest, they advanced only a little over three miles before settling in for the night. Drouillard and Willard stayed behind on unknown business.

MAY 22, 1804. While Lewis walked on shore, Clark held the party back to wait for a few of the French *engagés*, who went to St. Charles to complete business matters. They got underway at six o'clock, and after traveling about ten miles they passed Bonhomme Creek in St. Louis County. They also passed a camp of Kickapoo Indians and gave them two quarts of whiskey for four deer. They camped near the mouth of Femme Osage River, St. Charles County, Missouri.

MAY 23, 1804. At the entrance of Femme Osage River, Clark noticed a small community that came to be called Boone's Settlement, near Matson, St. Charles County, Missouri; it was named after Daniel Boone, who came there in 1799. Here they added the Field brothers, Joseph and Reuben, who had been sent ahead to purchase corn, butter, and other provisions. Later, facing hard going, the party passed Tavern Cave, where numerous passers-by had carved their names. Clark added his own. Lewis, out exploring, had a near disaster when he fell nearly three hundred feet from atop a hill above the cave, but he caught himself near the bottom and avoided injury.

On his jaunt Lewis collected a specimen of false indigo-bush that he found in the "moist rich soil" near the mouth of Femme Osage River. This specimen, along with thirty others that he collected below the Niobrara River in the spring and summer of 1804 and sent east from Fort Mandan in April 1805, are now inexplicably lost (see also August 10, 1804). He collected specimens again on August 27, 1806, and one of them is at the Royal Botanic (Kew) Gardens, Kew, England. Seeds of the plant gathered by Lewis and planted in England acquired for a time the designation *Amorpha fruticosa* var. *lewisii*, a name not now recognized. Clark and party camped in either St. Charles or Franklin County, upstream from Tavern Creek. During the evening the captains had the men's arms and ammunition inspected.

MAY 24, 1804. The party encountered a difficult half-mile stretch of the Missouri called the Devil's Race Ground, perhaps later Liffecue Rocks, Franklin County. Here occurred the keelboat's first near tragedy. Choosing what seemed the best way to bypass swift current around the rocks, the boatmen nonetheless ran the boat aground on a sandbar. As it turned crosswise to the current the tow rope broke, and it took the river's full force and tilted perilously on its side. Then the water washed the sand from underneath and set it wheeling downriver until it stuck again in another sandbar. This action was repeated three times before the crew got a rope to shore and steadied the craft. In all they fell back about two miles before they got the boat righted, moved forward again, and finally camped below Washington, Franklin County, Missouri, making about ten miles. Drouillard and Willard came up by land from St. Charles in the evening.

MAY 25, 1804. Progress improved and the party reached the small French village of La Charette, Warren County, Missouri, where they spent the night. It was the westernmost settlement of French and Americans at the time. Clark described the village's few houses as small and the people poor, yet they shared their milk and eggs. The site, near Marthasville, has since washed away. Here the captains met Régis Loisel, who was carrying goods from his post on Cedar Island, Lyman County, South Dakota, which the party would pass on September 22. He also carried a report of the Missouri River tribes to Spanish officials in New Orleans. From him the captains obtained information on the river ahead and news that he had seen no natives after the Ponca Indians who lived near the mouth the Niobrara River in Nebraska.

This day Lewis collected a specimen seed of the ubiquitous cottonwood tree whose cotton-like, drifting seeds frequently clogged the river and troubled boat progress. That specimen is lost, but one collected in August 1806 is at the Academy of Natural Sciences, Philadelphia. The captain noted that pirogues were often made from the tree in spite of the low durability of its soft, light, spongy, white wood, but he knew no other practical use for the wood. In time, especially on the upper reaches of the Missouri where it was the only tree of serviceable size, the party would come to rely extensively on cottonwoods. In discussing sylvan succession on the Missouri, Lewis noted that the sandbar willow was the first to appear as the river formed new lands along its banks and new islands in the stream and lasted two or three years before it was succeeded by fast-growing cottonwoods.

MAY 26, 1804. After an early morning of hard rains and heavy winds, the wind turned favorable and the party moved on. Clark sent Drouillard and Shields ahead on horseback to hunt. The party camped on an island opposite Hermann, Gasconade County, Missouri, having made about eighteen miles. Lewis issued orders establishing squads under the direction of the three sergeants, Ordway, Floyd, and Pryor, while the French *engagés* were to be led by Deschamps and the return party by Warfington. The orders also established the corps' routine and set forth particulars about posts, messes, and general or special duties.

MAY 27, 1804. Canoes arrived from the territory of the Omaha Indians upriver as the party was setting out. Later in the morning the party met four small rafts loaded with furs coming from the Pawnees and Osages. They camped on an island in the mouth of the Gasconade River, Gasconade County, Missouri. The evening was marked by thunder, lightning, rain, and wind. Drouillard and Shields rejoined the party.

MAY 28, 1804. They stayed at the Gasconade River in order to make astronomical observations, but the day was too overcast for successful readings. Clark inspected the French *engagés'* boat and found that a number of items had been carelessly allowed to get wet; the provisions were laid out for an airing. His inspection of arms and other equipment proved more satisfactory. Of the several hunters out, Reuben Field shot a deer.

MAY 29, 1804. Most of the day was spent in making astronomical observations at Gasconade River. The party delayed their departure because Whitehouse was still hunting, or lost, according to Ordway. About four o'clock in the afternoon the boats set out, leaving the *engagés* with the red pirogue to bring him along. They moved about four miles upriver, near the Osage-Gasconade county line.

MAY 30, 1804. After a rainy night the party set out, passing a number of creeks on either side of the Missouri and facing swift water before they landed near Deer Creek and the modern town of Chamois, Osage County, Missouri, traveling some seventeen miles. During the day the men heard gunshots and supposed it was the party's Frenchmen trying to attract Whitehouse's attention. Ordway and Gass noticed the country's vegetation and counted cottonwood, sycamore, hickory, walnut, and butternut trees, plus rushes and grapes.

MAY 31, 1804. Heavy winds from the west forced the party to remain at camp. A French trader from the Osage Indians arrived aboard a raft filled with bear skins and other furs and bound for St. Louis with news for the Chouteaus. One of the Chouteaus had sent a letter to Chief Makes-Tracks-Far-Away (or Big Track) of the Arkansas River Osages in Kansas, informing the tribe that the United States had taken possession of the Louisiana Territory. Big Track refused to believe the news and summarily burned the letter. Clark mentioned that Lewis had gone out into the woods and found "many curious Plants & Srubs." There is no journal by Lewis during this period to indicate any botanizing by the captain, nor is there a record of a plant collection for this day in his shipment of specimens from Fort Mandan in April 1805. The men caught several large rats, probably the eastern woodrat, and Reuben Field got another deer.

JUNE 1, 1804. The party reached the Osage River, forming the border between Osage and Cole Counties, Missouri, and camped a short distance above it. In his extensive "Summary view of the Rivers and Creeks," written during the winter at Fort Mandan, Lewis mentioned that Jean Pierre Chouteau of St. Louis had retrieved some mammoth bones from a spot some distance up the river. The captains inspected the men's firearms and judged them in good order. In the evening the men cut down trees to allow the captains to take astronomical observations. They worked past midnight to obtain accurate fixes at the Osage River and calculated the latitude to be 38° 31′6.9″ N; today its mouth is closer to 38° 35′35″ N.

JUNE 2, 1804. Clark continued with observations and made measurements of the Missouri and Osage Rivers. On top of a point he had climbed to take his bearings he discovered Indian burial mounds that come from the Middle to Late Woodland period, dating to 1000 CE. Whitehouse and Shields came in at sunset, somewhat worn down after having been out for seven days. Nonetheless, they described the country on the north side of the river through which they had passed on horseback in very positive terms. Having inspected the party's firearms, the captains found them in good order.

JUNE 3, 1804. The party held up while Lewis and Drouillard were exploring and hunting. Clark busied himself in astronomical observations despite a cloudy day and an obscure sun. He complained of a bad cold and sore throat. After Lewis returned they took additional readings and got underway at five in the afternoon. They traveled to Moreau River, Cole County, Missouri, just east of Jefferson City, and saw signs of Indian war parties, making about five miles.

JUNE 4, 1804. As the party passed the vicinity of Jefferson City, Clark noticed an abundance of oak, ash, walnut, and hickory trees. He took a walk on the south side of river, passing through a bottom of rushes and nettles. Seeking reported deposits of lead ore, the captain climbed a hill, probably Sugar Loaf Rock of later years, but found none. Lewis brought the boats up under the hill and camped for the night in northwest Cole County, traveling about seventeen miles. The party was kept awake by the singing of a "nightingale," perhaps a chuck-will's-widow, so they named a nearby stream "Nightingale Creek," now Wears Creek. Earlier in the day the rope supporting the keelboat's mast got caught in a sycamore tree and the mast broke.

JUNE 5, 1804. At eleven o'clock, after about five hours on the river, the party met two Frenchmen coming downriver on a small raft from their wintering camp far up the Kansas River. They had caught a great number of beavers during their stay but lost most of the pelts in a prairie fire. They told Clark that the Kansa Indians were now out on the plains hunting buffalo. Clark noticed a projecting rock on which someone had painted a spirit figure or manitou. Biddle would later describe it in his book as "resembling the bust of a man with the horns of a stag." A short distance above this the party passed Moniteau Creek, just east of the Moniteau-Cole county line, named for the pictograph. York went seeking greens for dinner and found native cresses on a sandbar. Wind from behind would have aided the day's travel, but use of the sail was prevented because of the keelboat's broken mast. One of the party found Indian signs and Clark guessed they were those of Sauks on their way to war against Osages. They camped in Boone County, Missouri, across from Sandy Hook, coming about a dozen miles.

JUNE 6, 1804. The men mended the mast and set out about seven o'clock. Clark found Petite Saline Creek, Moniteau County, quite brackish from the many salt licks and salt springs along its banks. The Missouri River's current was rapid, so the party made camp sooner than usual to allow one of the pirogues to catch up. The site was downstream from Interstate 70, Boone County, Missouri. Clark continued unwell, with a sore throat and head ache.

JUNE 7, 1804. They passed another Moniteau Creek, this one on the Howard-Boone county line at Rocheport. Nearby Clark found more pictographs on limestone rocks, which the Indians quarried for the embedded flint. He also found a den of rattlesnakes and killed three. Lewis took men to investigate salt licks and springs up the creek, and after camping at Bonne Femme Creek, Howard County, Missouri, he explored that stream as well. In the evening hunters brought in three black bears—a female and two cubs, according to Whitehouse.

JUNE 8, 1804. After nine miles of travel the party reached Lamine River, Cooper County. Clark noted French reports that lead ore could be found along the Lamine. On a trek with Floyd, the captain described the adjacent land as well timbered; farther out he discovered raspberries, and still farther the plains commenced. The men may have been twelve miles up the Lamine. Back at camp, near the Saline-Cooper county line, Missouri, he found a stash of canteens, axes, pumice stones, and pelts that apparently had been hidden by hunters. The party left them undisturbed. During the day the party met three Frenchmen in two canoes loaded with furs coming from the Big Sioux River of Iowa and South Dakota. The men experienced a hard rain during the night.

JUNE 9, 1804. Shortly after setting out the keelboat got stuck on a snag in the river, but the party was detained only a short time. They passed the area of Arrow Rock, Saline County, and then the boat got caught again. This time the swift current swung the boat around, with its side directly in the path of large trees being carried downriver. With great exertion the men were able to get the craft pulled in to shore, and Clark heaped compliments on the alert crew. They camped near Bluff Port, Howard County, Missouri, thirteen miles from their previous camp.

JUNE 10, 1804. They passed the Little Chariton and Chariton Rivers near Glasgow, Chariton County, Missouri, and camped about five miles above the latter stream. Lewis and Clark walked out on the prairie and Clark described it as rolling, open, and rich, with plenty of water, an abundance of deer, and abounding in hazelnuts, grapes, and plums. Ordway added mulberries, walnuts, hickories, and cottonwoods. Among the hunters, Lewis killed a large buck and Drouillard also killed a deer.

JUNE 11, 1804. The wind was so strong from the northwest that the party stayed in camp and took the opportunity to dry articles, clean weapons, and check provisions. Hunters killed two deer, and Drouillard got two bears. The captains noticed that many small birds were setting and that some eggs had hatched. The men sang and danced in the evening.

JUNE 12, 1804. During the lunch break a raft arrived with Pierre Dorion Sr. on board from the Yankton Sioux. The captains bought three hundred pounds of bear grease from him and sat up late that night querying the old trader. Clark found nothing particularly worthwhile in the information. However, they persuaded him to go upriver with them to the Yanktons to help convince some of the chiefs to visit Jefferson. Whitehouse reported that one of the party was sent downriver with Dorion's boat. It may have been Robertson (or Robinson). The night's camp was near the terminal point of Missouri Highway J, Chariton County, Missouri, some nine miles from the previous camp.

JUNE 13, 1804. After traveling about nine miles, the party reached Grand River at Carroll and Chariton Counties, Missouri, and set up camp. Gass called it as handsome a place as he had ever seen in an uncultivated state. Lewis calculated the latitude at 35° 58′ N; the present latitude of the mouth of the river is about 39° 23′ 05″ N. Clark reported that the Missouria Indians formerly had a large village in the area but had been greatly reduced by attacks by the Sauks and had joined the Otoe Indians on the Platte River in Nebraska, who were also on the decline. The captains walked to a nearby hill for a view of the surrounding country, captured a raccoon, then stayed up until almost midnight taking lunar observations.

JUNE 14, 1804. A thick fog did not detain the party, which set out at six in the morning. In spite of precautions, the keelboat was caught on a shifting sandbar and might have overturned except for the quick work of the men on board. Again, the men's exertions merited Clark's praise. A raft of two canoes with four Frenchmen arrived from trading among the Pawnee Indians at the Platte River in Nebraska, so the party delayed for a few hours while the captains queried the traders. Drouillard reported that he heard a snake making a gobbling noise like a turkey, something that had been mentioned by Indians and confirmed by French boatmen. The party camped in Carroll County, Missouri, opposite Miami, coming about eight miles.

JUNE 15, 1804. Another hard day on the river, with submerged logs imperiling their boats and swift water and shifting sandbars retarding their progress in the area of Malta Bend, Saline County, Missouri. Whitehouse wrote laconically that the men had a dram of whiskey and rowed on. They camped on the north side of the river opposite an old village of the Little Osages and in view of the old village of the Missouria Indians mentioned on June 13. This is the archaeological site Gumbo Point, in the southwestern tip of Saline County. While the party lunched and set up camp, Lewis took astronomical observations. Ordway called it the "pleasantest place I have ever Seen."

JUNE 16, 1804. The party arrived at a spot where James Mackay had placed a fort in his journal and map that Clark used. It was Fort Orleans, established by Sieur Etienne Véniard de Bourgmont in 1723, but the captain found no trace of it. In the evening Clark walked on shore hoping to find timber for oars but found none suitable. The party camped opposite Waverly, Carroll County, Missouri, some ten miles beyond the last camp. Clark complained of ticks and mosquitoes. The captains remarked that they had seen few aquatic fowl on the Missouri but counted abundant wood ducks, a few geese, and a solitary pelican among those observed.

JUNE 17, 1804. The party traveled only one mile before encamping in order to make oars and a tow rope (or *cordelle*) for the keelboat and to rest after hard traveling on the previous day. Clark called it "Rope walk Camp." The men found sufficient timber among ash trees for twenty oars and wove six hundred feet of rope. Clark commented that the area of their encampment was a crossing for Sauk, Ioway, and Sioux war parties looking to attack Osages. Drouillard returned from hunting with two deer, a bear, and a fat, young horse, apparently lost by a war party seeking Osages. The men were greatly afflicted with boils and dysentery, which Clark attributed to the water they were drinking. Clark's own illness continued. The men were also constantly set upon by mosquitoes and ticks, and the French boatmen complained of being underfed; they were used to eating five or six times a day. Clark judged the surrounding country beautiful and rich and noticed a nearby prairie interspersed with timber and rolling lands beyond. The region was well watered and abounded in deer, elks, and bears, some of which the hunters brought to camp.

JUNE 18, 1804. Due to rain and more work required on oars and ropes, the party stayed in camp. Hunters brought in five deer and

Colter killed a bear. In the evening the men jerked the meat and were able to dry some items.

JUNE 19, 1804. After completing work on the oars and other equipment the party set out, leaving Shields and Collins to go ahead with the horses. Along the way Clark noticed abundant raspberries and gooseberries, and when they drew up near Lexington, Lafayette County, Missouri, he discovered a lake with sufficient haws to draw wildlife for food and drink. The captain considered the lands on the north side suitable for settlement and those on the south not as rich but of good quality and well watered. The captains distributed mosquito netting as nighttime barriers against the tormenting insects. They had traveled about seventeen miles.

JUNE 20, 1804. The party set out after a heavy morning shower. York nearly lost an eye when one of the men threw sand into it. Passing Crooked River, Ray County, Missouri, the men caught a glimpse of Shields and Collins but apparently had no contact with them. The captains were up until after midnight taking lunar observations on a beautiful night at their campsite a few miles below Wellington, Lafayette County, Missouri.

JUNE 21, 1804. The skilled boatman Cruzatte charted the safest route through the turbulent waters of Camden Bend, Lafayette County, Missouri, while the crew used the tow rope and anchor to get the heavy keelboat forward. They managed the roaring waters and rolling sands with only slight damage to their craft. Ordway and Drouillard were hunting through "fine Timbered" and "Rich handsome bottom land." They killed a deer and brought it to the river so the party could retrieve it. Clark took an ecological assessment of the region. In the floodplain he noticed cottonwoods and willows, on the next higher terrace he found rich, fertile soils supporting cottonwood, walnut, ash, hackberry, mulberry, basswood, and sycamore trees, then on a gradual rise to the highlands beyond he viewed small streams coming into the Missouri that were dotted with oak, ash, walnut, and other trees, and finally in the distance he saw the treeless prairies. The party camped in Lafayette

County, Missouri, with Camden on the opposite shore, after traveling about seven miles.

JUNE 22, 1804. The bustling of the night guard awakened Clark, as the men secured boats and equipment for a storm that came at daybreak and lasted about an hour. They camped near the Jackson-Lafayette county line, Missouri, and there met Shields and Collins waiting for them.

JUNE 23, 1804. The wind was up and prevented the party from moving forward any great distance, perhaps 3½ miles. Lewis spent the day inspecting arms at the camp near Sibley, Jackson County, Missouri, while Clark walked ahead some six miles in Ray County, Missouri. Clark thought it too far to walk back to the main camp, so he peeled tree bark for a bed, built a fire to ward off mosquitoes and gnats, and settled in. Drouillard joined Clark later with bear meat and venison.

JUNE 24, 1804. As Clark waited for the boats to come up, he watched a snake swim up to Drouillard's deer, which was hung over the river. Clark thought the snake was interested in getting milk from the udder of the doe. He also commented on the great number of bear signs and reckoned that they were seeking the abundant mulberries in the river bottom. The party reached him about eight o'clock, moved on to the Little Blue River ("Hay Cabbin Creek"), Jackson County, Missouri, and camped a short distance above its mouth and the town of Missouri City, making about a dozen miles this day. Whitehouse dubbed the site "hard scrabble Priari." Here they jerked the meat Clark had secured and took astronomical readings.

JUNE 25, 1804. Heavy fog delayed the party a bit this morning. Three miles above their camp Clark noticed beds of coal along the river's banks in Jackson County, Missouri. He also commented on the abundance of plums, raspberries, and crabapples and the numerous deer that were feeding on willows on the shore and on sandbars. They camped opposite the town of Sugar Creek, Jackson County, having come about thirteen miles.

JUNE 26, 1804. A very narrow channel in the Missouri River at the mouth of the Big Blue River, Kansas City, Missouri, called for great exertions to get the boats through—the tow rope broke twice under the strain. Spotting three deer swimming the river, the men in the white pirogue took after them; the boat's riflemen shot all three but lost one to the river's current. Several more deer were taken and the party observed a great number of Carolina parakeets, perhaps the first scientifically noted west of the Mississippi. The party camped just above the mouth of the Kansas River, Wyandotte County, Kansas, at a spot now called Kaw Point.

JUNE 27, 1804. The captains decided to stay at the mouth of the Kansas River for a few days to take astronomical observations, dry and repair the boats (particularly the red pirogue) and equipment, and give the men a break. The men were put to clearing timber so Lewis could get a clear view for his astronomical observations and Clark a straight shot for his measurements. They used the debris to set up a defensive barrier, "Least the Savages would Attempt Comeing in the Night," wrote Whitehouse. While Lewis took his readings, Clark measured the rivers. Lewis calculated the locale's latitude as 39° 05′25.7″ N; the latitude of the mouth of the Kansas River today is about 39° 06′54″ N. Clark gave the width of the Missouri as about five hundred yards and the Kansas as 230¼ yards. Lewis gave space to discussing the Kansas River in his "Summary view of the Rivers and Creeks" and listed fifteen affluents of the river.

JUNE 28, 1804. The men completed more drying of damp goods on this warm, windy day. Clark gave some account of the current state of geographical knowledge of the West when he described the location of the source of the Kansas River being in proximity to those of the Rio Grande, Colorado, and Missouri. As he stated, it was "not well assertaind." The Kansas's most distant headwaters are in east central Colorado, at least within the same state as those of the Rio Grande and Colorado Rivers, but nowhere near the source of the Missouri. The captain also set down notes on the Kansa, or Kaw, Indians, from whom the river derived its name. Although he considered them a fierce and warlike people, he acknowledged that without access to modern weapons they were at the mercy of their rivals, the Ioways and Sauks. He thought the spot an ideal situation for a fort. Hunters were successful at finding deer, and the Field brothers captured a young wolf and brought it back to camp alive.

JUNE 29, 1804. A court-martial was called at eleven o'clock to hear charges against Collins and Hall brought by Sergeant Floyd. The court consisted of Sergeant Pryor, presiding, Colter, Newman, Gass, and Thompson, with Potts as judge advocate. Collins was charged with getting whiskey out of the party's barrel and drunkenness at his post and of allowing Hall to get liquor from the barrel also. Collins pled innocent to the charges but was judged guilty by the court and sentenced to one hundred lashes on his bare back. Hall pled guilty to taking the whiskey and was sentenced to fifty lashes. The captains approved the sentences and the punishment was carried out in the afternoon. An hour later the party was underway and then camped for the night in the vicinity of Riverside, Platte County, Missouri, making a little over seven miles on a short day.

JUNE 30, 1804. The party passed the Platte, or Little Platte, River, Platte County, Missouri, and Clark commented that the area would be suitable for mills since there were reports of falls above its mouth. The men enjoyed bread and bacon, apparently given them by passing traders, and wondered at the abundance of deer, whose tracks Clark said were as plentiful as hogs' around a farm. Hunters killed nine of them. The summer weather took a toll on the men and they became exhausted from their labors in 96° heat. The keelboat's mast broke again before they put up for the night in the vicinity of Walcott, Wyandotte County, Kansas, making ten miles.

JULY 1, 1804. During the night a guard was alarmed by something and had the men up and ready for action, but nothing occurred. Again, excessive heat and exhaustion called for a midday break. Clark observed numerous turkeys on the shore and Drouillard reported seeing pecan trees (now at their northern limit) in Leavenworth County, Kansas. French engagés told Clark that some French people once intended to settle in the area and used a nearby island as grazing land for cattle. The party camped opposite the town of Leavenworth, having traveled about twelve miles.

JULY 2, 1804. The party delayed four hours at midday to make and install a temporary mast for the keelboat. They camped after dark near Weston, Platte County, Missouri, opposite an abandoned Kansa Indian village that had been occupied in the 1740s and 1750s. Clark noted that the French had established a fort in the area. This would be Fort de Cavagnial, active from 1744 to 1764 and located about three miles north of Fort Leavenworth. Clark thought the area an excellent site for a town. The party advanced about twelve miles.

JULY 3, 1804. The party found a well-fed, gentle horse apparently lost by natives and adopted it into their number. Clark indicated that French traders had an establishment for trading with the Kansa Indians near where the party camped for the night, having come about eleven miles. It was somewhat above Oak Mills, Atchison County, Kansas. Ordway called attention to area trees, including pine, black walnut, honey locust, oak, and western buckeye.

JULY 4, 1804. While taking a rest break and some food, Joseph Field was bitten on the foot by a snake. The foot swelled up quite a bit, so Lewis applied a treatment, probably a poultice of Peruvian bark (*cinchona*) in case the bite was from a poisonous species; perhaps a bit of gunpowder was also added to the poultice. The party passed two creeks in Atchison County, Kansas, which they named Fourth of July Creek and Independence Creek in honor of the day. A creek forming the Atchison-Doniphan county line at its mouth still bears the latter name. The men fired the keelboat's swivel cannon in the morning and again in the evening in honor of the day. An extra gill of whiskey was issued to celebrate the day. Clark wrote one of his most descriptive, poetic passages about the plains in his draft entry near where the party camped, in the area of Doniphan, Doniphan County, Kansas:

> The Plains of this countrey are covered with a Leek Green Grass, well calculated for the sweetest and most norushing hay—interspersed

with Cops [copses] of trees, Spreding ther lofty branchs over Pools Springs or Brooks of fine water. Groops of Shrubs covered with the most delicious froot is to be seen in every direction, and nature appears to have exerted herself to butify the Senery by the variety of flours Delicately and highly flavered raised above the Grass, which Strikes & profumes the Sensation, and amuses the mind throws it into Conjecterng the cause of So magnificent a Senerey . . . in a Country thus Situated far removed from the Sivilised world to be enjoyed by nothing but the Buffalo Elk Deer & Bear in which it abounds & Savage Indians.

Ordway called it one of the most beautiful places he had seen in his life; Floyd echoed his praise.

JULY 5, 1804. Clark took note of previous incidents in the area when he studied one of the party's reference books, Antoine Simon Le Page du Pratz's *Histoire de la Louisiane*, published in 1758 and carried by Lewis from the library of Benjamin Smith Barton in Philadelphia. Du Pratz noted that Etienne Véniard, Sieur de Bourgmont, visited the area in 1724 and found numerous Kansa Indians here at that time. Clark speculated that war must have compelled them to move out onto the plains. At dinner near a beaver lodge, Lewis's Newfoundland dog, Seaman, dove in and forced the occupants out. Clark observed grapes, berries, and wild roses as he passed along, and while deer were not as plentiful in this area, he noticed abundant signs of elks. The party camped about ten miles above the previous night's camp. During the day the keelboat hit river obstructions three times but got free undamaged.

JULY 6, 1804. The profusion of sweat that poured from the bodies of the working hands was incredible to Clark. As the captain walked on shore he found light-colored sand mixed with small pebbles and also traces of pit coal. The party spent the night near St. Joseph, Buchanan County, Missouri, but it is unclear whether in Kansas or Missouri. A whip-poor-will perched on the keelboat for a time, so Clark named a stream after the bird, perhaps modern Peters Creek or Walnut Creek, Doniphan County, Kansas.

JULY 7, 1804. Perhaps a bit of homesickness caused Clark to comment that prairies along the riverbanks reminded him of farms with their divided strips of woodland and open field. The captain attributed Frazer's illness to excessive exposure to the sun. Lewis bled him and gave him potassium nitrate to increase his sweating and reduce his fever. The party camped upstream from St. Joseph, Buchanan County, Missouri, but perhaps on the Kansas side in Doniphan County. Someone in the party noticed an eastern woodrat and another person killed a wolf. Ordway, out on land with the horses, did not make it back to camp. Later, after he described a creek to the captain, Clark named it for him; it is probably modern Mace Creek or Mill Creek near the Andrew-Buchanan county line.

JULY 8, 1804. In addition to Frazer, five more men were ill with headaches and boils. Collins, Werner, and Thompson were appointed cooks to their respective squads. Camp was near the mouth of the Nodaway River, Andrew County, Missouri, about twelve miles beyond the previous one.

JULY 9, 1804. Bratton went back to the Nodaway River to mark a tree as a signal to the land party that the boats were ahead. In Doniphan County, Kansas, below Iowa Point, the party passed a spot where either Cruzatte or Labiche had camped with other French river men two years earlier; the explorers camped nearby after traveling about fourteen miles. Being aware of a party opposite the night's camp and finding that it was not their own men, they feared it might be a party of Sioux and went on extra alert. Frazer appeared to have recovered his health.

JULY 10, 1804. It turned out that the party on the opposite shore was from their own group. Clark reported that the men were generally healthy but much fatigued from their daily labors. The captain found Canada wild rye and Indian potato ("wild Potatoes") in the moist soil and floodplains of the Missouri River. Lewis collected a specimen of Canada wild rye on July 27. Lewis killed two from a great number of goslings along the river. The night's camp was in Holt County, Missouri, opposite and near the Nebraska-Kansas border.

JULY 11, 1804. Clark walked on shore in the area of Little Tarkio Creek, Holt County, Missouri, where he found and followed fresh tracks of a horse, finding the animal nearby. He returned to the main party, which had camped opposite the mouth of the Big Nemaha River, which comes in on the Nebraska side of the Missouri just above the Nebraska-Kansas state line, making about six miles for the day. Near here Clark noticed narrow- and broad-leaved willows, probably sandbar and peach-leaved willows. Lewis had collected a specimen of each on June 14 and wrote lengthy descriptions, particularly of the sandbar willow. Floyd reported that "the men is all Sick."

JULY 12, 1804. The party spent the day in camp, resting a bit. Clark took a pirogue and five men up the Big Nemaha about three miles. From an Indian mound he surveyed the surrounding countryside and declared it one of the most pleasing prospects that he had ever seen. Near the meandering Big Nemaha he saw a floodplain prairie that he calculated at fifteen to twenty thousand acres covered with tall grasses such as big bluestem and dotted with trees and shrubs. Lewis collected a specimen of big bluestem on July 27. On the way back to camp Clark gathered grapes and commented on the plums, crabapples, and chokecherries he noticed along the way. Finding a sandstone outcropping along the south side of the Nemaha River near its mouth where native had etched pictographs of animals and a boat, Clark added his own name and the date. The men noticed that deer and bears were getting scarcer and that elks began to appear. Lewis gave the latitude of the spot as 39° 55′ 56″ N; the mouth of the Big Nemaha today is closer to 40° 01′ 33″ N. In the afternoon the captains convened a court-martial for Willard, who was charged with lying down and sleeping while on guard duty the previous night. If convicted Willard could be put to death under existing military rules. Willard pled guilty to lying down but not guilty of going to sleep. He was convicted of all charges and sentenced to receive one hundred lashes on his bare back for each of the next four evenings.

JULY 13, 1804. Clark's field notes for this day were lost in a storm on the morning of July 14 and he had to reconstruct his account of activities from the diaries of the sergeants and from his own recollections. The party passed the Tarkio River, Holt County, Missouri, beyond which Clark observed a grass resembling timothy with seeds like flax. This was probably reed canarygrass, specimens of which Lewis had collected on June 16. The camp for the night was in eastern Richardson County, Nebraska, about twenty miles beyond the last camp.

JULY 14, 1804. Shortly after setting out at seven o'clock the sky suddenly darkened and a storm from the northeast struck the party, nearly ruining the keelboat were it not for the crew's quick-witted action and fast work to get it out of danger. In little more than half an hour all was quiet again and the river turned smooth as glass. The party passed a point in northwestern Holt County, Missouri, where perhaps François M. Benoit or a relative had previously established a post to trade with the Otoes and Pawnees. The men saw their first elk at close range, Ordway's first ever, but both Clark and Drouillard were too far away for their shots to count. Seaman dived in the river and swam after it but was also unsuccessful in the chase. The party made camp after nine miles' travel near the Nemaha-Richardson county line, Nebraska, and near the mouth of the Nishnabotna River coming in from the other side. The river's mouth in 1804 was apparently some miles south of its present location. A number of men were unwell with boils and felons.

JULY 15, 1804. Clark went after elks with Ordway and another man in the morning but apparently was unsuccessful in the hunt. During the jaunt he noted an abundance of cherries, plums, grapes, hazelnuts, and gooseberries. He also noticed hog peanuts and richweed and found the area thickly covered with grass but devoid of timber. The party had entered the eastern margin of the Great Plains, so treelessness would become a more striking phenomenon in the days ahead. Clark came upon the Little Nemaha River, swam it, and waited for the boats to come up, then all camped above the town of Nemaha, Nemaha County, Nebraska, having come about nine miles. In the evening Lewis discovered that his chronometer had stopped again, the third time, but the first occasion since leaving the Wood River camp. He could not account for the malfunction but remembered that it had resumed running accurately after being reset. He decided to make the necessary astronomical observations and set the piece again.

JULY 16, 1804. The party passed an area on the Iowa side that Clark called the bald-pated prairie. He was noticing open prairies that gave way to steep hills along the Missouri River in this area. These hills have drought-tolerant vegetation on the southwest-facing slopes that pick up loess soil from the prevailing northwest winds. Fires assisted in keeping down the growth of trees. In his "Summary view of the Rivers and Creeks" Lewis called the area about the mouth of the Nishnabotna River and bald-pated prairie "one of the most beautiful, level, and fertile praries that I ever beheld." During the noon hour Lewis located a spot to reset his chronometer before the party camped in either Nemaha County, Nebraska, or Atchison County, Missouri, a few miles northeast of Peru, Nebraska, and about twenty miles beyond the previous camp.

JULY 17, 1804. The captains decided to remain at their camp to take astronomical observations and get the chronometer running correctly. During the day Lewis took a ride out to the Nishnabotna River, while Clark tried unsuccessful cures for abscesses on several men. Clark also took time to measure the surface velocity of the Missouri with the party's log line reel that Lewis had purchased in Philadelphia in May 1803 when he was outfitting the corps. The log, which was used to measure the rate of a boat's travel, consisted of a block of wood fastened to a line and run out from a reel. It was also a way to measure the surface velocity of a stream. Clark's calculations this day and the next found the Missouri was moving at fifty fathoms in forty seconds at one point and in thirty seconds and twenty seconds at other points. Thus the Missouri's current was moving at 7.5, 10, and 15 feet per second, or about five, seven, and ten miles per hour. Goodrich caught a couple of very fat catfish, Drouillard killed three deer, and Reuben Field, one. Breezes brought in a swarm of mosquitoes but happily blew them away within two hours.

JULY 18, 1804. Clark noticed that the few trees in the area grew along the watercourses and were predominately cottonwoods, mulberries, elms, and sycamores. Geologic features also caught his attention and he thought he saw iron ore, but it was instead a thin limestone stained with red shale. A stray Indian dog wandered along the bank of the river, but no Indians were sighted. Too shy to come near the explorers, it accepted meat tossed in its direction. The party made about eighteen miles and camped a little below Nebraska City, Otoe County, Nebraska.

JULY 19, 1804. Clark breakfasted on roasted deer ribs and washed them down with coffee. He then walked on shore intending to pace the boat party but instead started following elk tracks into the hills. Suddenly, he lost all interest in elk hunting, being so taken with the view in sight. Before him lay a seemingly boundless prairie covered with grass nearly two feet high and scatterings of timber along the little streams. Later he reflected that as they approached the Platte River sandbars became more numerous and shifting sands increased. The enlisted men gathered a quantity of cherries and added them to the whiskey barrel. Drouillard, out hunting as usual, got two deer, as did Bratton, who also noticed a field of sweet flag. In the evening the party used the last of their butter; they camped opposite and a few miles above Nebraska City, Otoe County, Nebraska, in Fremont County, Iowa, about eleven miles beyond the last camp.

JULY 20, 1804. Bratton swam back a distance to get his clothes and gun that he had left the night before. Clark set out elk hunting again but got a gray wolf instead, perhaps a now-extinct variety. The party passed Weeping Water Creek, Otoe County, Nebraska, and set up camp in Cass County, Nebraska, a little above Spring Creek. Clark remarked on the rich but fire-parched prairies. He was noticing an ecologically important plains phenomenon, that fires, both accidently ignited and purposely set, played an important role in grass renewal and reinvigoration. The captains understood this process.

JULY 21, 1804. Lewis, in one of his infrequent journal entries during this period, wrote a long passage describing the actions of the Platte

River and its relation to the Missouri, into which it drained. He noted the distinct composition of the two streams. What he observed was the sand-rich sediments of the Platte coming out of the Rocky Mountains contrasted with the silt and clay deposits carried by the Missouri. In his "Summary view of the Rivers and Creeks," Lewis declared that "the steady, regular, and incessant velocity of this stream, is perhaps unequaled by any on earth," and he filled several pages with his notes on the river, information gained from traders at St. Louis, at Fort Mandan, and in the party. The captains, with six oarsmen from the party, took a pirogue a short distance up the Platte. Clark remarked on a characteristic of the river that would be noticed repeatedly by generations of observers, its great width and shallow depth. Clark noted the existence of the Elkhorn River somewhat higher on the Platte and soon rejoined the main boat. The party passed Papillion Creek and camped a little above its mouth in Sarpy County, Nebraska, where the horse party joined the men, bringing four deer to the camp; they had come about nineteen miles.

JULY 22, 1804. A few miles farther up and on the opposite side of the Missouri, the men cleared an area, pitched tents, and constructed boweries for their Camp White Catfish, near the Mills-Pottawattamie county line, Iowa. The camp was probably named for the channel catfish that Goodrich caught on July 24. The captains hoped to arrange meetings with leaders of neighboring tribes, particularly the nearby Otoes. During the delay Lewis wrote a long description of his scientific instruments, essentially those he used for astronomical observations.

JULY 23, 1804. At eleven o'clock this morning Clark sent Drouillard and Cruzatte to request any Otoes or Pawnees in the area to come to Camp White Catfish for a meeting. The men carried tobacco as a sign of peaceful intent. Knowing that the Indians were on buffalo hunts, the captain hoped the two men might meet natives who were tending their corn crops. A U.S. flag was hoisted at the river's edge, and around the camp items were spread out to dry. Clark spent part of the day working on the map of the route thus far, one that he planned to send to Jefferson. Gass declared all the men busily engaged in hunting, making oars, dressing skins, and airing out provisions and baggage.

JULY 24, 1804. The party remained at Camp White Catfish. Hunters were out but were largely unsuccessful. The captains were occupied with paperwork, Clark working on the map, Lewis preparing miscellaneous memoranda.

JULY 25, 1804. At two o'clock in the afternoon Drouillard and Cruzatte returned to report no sign of Indians, who they supposed were on the plains hunting buffalo. They had traveled a bit through Sarpy County, Nebraska, crossing Papillion Creek and reaching the Elkhorn River.

JULY 26, 1804. Clark was confined to his tent because of blowing sands from the south. Even that enclosure did not provide protection for his map work, but the rocking boat and swarms of mosquitoes made every choice unsatisfactory. The captain opened an abscess on one man's chest to let it drain; it discharged half a pint of matter. The men easily captured beavers from the abundant supply in the area. They also finished making oars.

JULY 27, 1804. After several days of not finding any Indians, the party departed their Camp White Catfish at half past one o'clock. Their two horses were taken to the southern, or western, shore of the river, as it appeared to be easier going on that side. Clark noticed mounds on the Nebraska side, which he took to be the site of an Otoe village. The mounds were probably natural deposits rather than of native construction. The party camped at Lewis and Clark Landing, north of Interstate 480, Omaha, Douglas County, Nebraska, a trip of about fifteen miles. Whitehouse cut his knee.

JULY 28, 1804. Hunters heard guns being fired during the day. Drouillard came in to the evening's camp with a Missouria Indian who was living with the Otoes. He told the captains that there was a large encampment of Indians farther upriver that included a French trader. The party camped north of Council Bluffs, Pottawattamie County, Iowa, making about eleven miles.

JULY 29, 1804. La Liberté, who may have spoken Otoe-Missouria, was sent ahead with the Missouria Indian to invite Indians to meet the party ahead. This was Willard's unlucky day. He lost his rifle in the Boyer River while returning to the previous camp to retrieve the tomahawk he had forgotten. Fortunately, Reuben Field dived in and brought the gun up. After passing the Boyer River in Pottawattamie County, Iowa, where the men caught three large catfish, they camped with the Washington-Douglas county line, Nebraska, to the west, having traveled about ten miles.

JULY 30, 1804. The corps moved a little over three miles upriver and formed a camp they would call Council Bluff, near Fort Calhoun, Washington County, Nebraska. The spot should not be confused with the town of Council Bluffs, Iowa, downriver and on the opposite side. Here the captains raised a flagpole and prepared to welcome Indian dignitaries. Clark spent some time bringing his map up to date from Camp White Catfish, then he and Lewis walked atop a bluff and observed the country. The surrounding prairies were covered with foot-high grass, then a half mile beyond the bluffs rose and the plains presented an unlimited view, except for the bottomland with its stands of cottonwoods, willows, mulberries, elms, sycamores, lindens, ash, hickories, walnuts, and oaks. Ordway thought it the "prittyset place for a Town" that he ever saw. Lewis's "Summary view of the Rivers and Creeks" declared it an ideal place for an American fort, being so convenient to numerous Plains Indians and superior in many ways to any spot for one thousand miles north along the Missouri. Joseph Field brought in a badger ("*Brarow*," variously spelled) and Lewis wrote a detailed description of the small animal and had it skinned, stuffed, and prepared to send back at the appropriate time. The gray horse the men had found running loose on July 3 died during the night. Clark reported that everything was in prime order and that the men were in high spirits.

JULY 31, 1804. Hunters were out most of the day; the Field brothers brought in three deer but got separated from their horses. They also caught a live beaver, which the party tamed in a short time. Clark completed some map work. No Indians arrived. Floyd reported that he had been ill for several days, but now he thought he had regained his health. Lewis determined the latitude of the Council Bluff camp as 41° 18′01.5″ N; the approximate latitude is 41° 27′14″ N.

AUGUST 1, 1804. Clark celebrated his thirty-fourth birthday by ordering a saddle of venison, elk fleece, and beavertail, with a dessert of cherries, plums, raspberries, currants, and grapes. He gave an account of prairie flora by noting the presence of the wild black ("Blue") currant, western snowberry, and corralberry ("two Kind of Honeysuckle") and then marveled at the abundance of plants and flowers not found on the Eastern Seaboard. He called it a splendid field for botanical study. Only the ever-present, stinging mosquitoes spoiled the scene. Lewis collected a specimen of wild black ("purple") currant this day and western snowberry the next. Drouillard and Colter went after the lost horses. Still no Indians appeared, so the men delayed another day at their Council Bluff camp.

AUGUST 2, 1804. One of the hunters brought in a great egret for Lewis's inspection. The bird received the captain's careful scrutiny and a detailed analysis in his natural history notebook. At sunset a French trader, called Fairfong, came into the Council Bluff camp accompanied by six Otoe and Missouria chiefs. The Indians fired guns to announce their arrival, and the party answered with shots from the keelboat's swivel cannon. A brief welcome and exchange of gifts took place with promises of longer talks in the morning. The captains presented roast pork, flour, and cornmeal, while the Indians gave out watermelons. The Otoes and Missourias spoke similar Siouan languages; they had joined for mutual protection from their common enemies, principally the Sioux. Typical of Great Plains Indians, they followed traditional horticultural practices while adapting to new seminomadic hunting routines with the acquisition of horses. In his "Estimate of Eastern Indians" (probably compiled at

Fort Mandan during the winter of 1804–5), Clark called the Missourias "the remnant of the most numerous nation inhabiting the Missouri, when first known to the French." Repeated occurrences of smallpox that left them vulnerable to attacks by unfriendly tribes made them dependent on the Otoes. Clark contended that the Otoes saw them as inferior and took advantage of them. Lewis estimated the Otoes as numbering about five hundred people and counted the same or less for the Missourias. Whitehouse called them "a handsome stout well made set of Indians."

Hunters had a successful day, bringing in a number of deer, one of which was butchered into quarters—weighing nearly 150 pounds in total. Drouillard and Colter returned with the horses "loaded with Elk," according to Clark. They found the horses about twelve miles south of camp. Two beavers were caught in traps overnight, but one gnawed off its leg and escaped.

AUGUST 3, 1804. After breakfast all gathered under a makeshift awning made from the keelboat's main sail, the corps passed in parade, the pipe of peace was passed, and Lewis delivered a speech to the assemblage. The captain informed the chiefs of the change of authority under the Louisiana Purchase and the desire for peace and friendship, promised increased trade, apprized them of the party's mission, pled for peace among neighboring tribes, and asked for Indian representatives to travel to the nation's capital. The chiefs' response was that they liked what they heard and promised to heed the good advice. Ordway declared that they made "Some verry Sensable Speeches." Clark presented the American response. Lewis then displayed American technology by the rapid, repeating fire of his air gun. The captains also passed out gifts, including gunpowder, whiskey, an American flag, peace medals, and commissions acknowledging the authority of the chiefs, among them Big Horse ("Shŏn gŏ tŏn gŏ"), an Otoe; Hospitality ("We the a"), a Missouria; and White Horse ("Shon Guss Còn"), an Otoe. Some of the gifts were intended for the Otoe principal chief, Little Thief ("We ár ruge nor"), who was not present. Clark took some time to try to sort out in writing his understanding of Plains Indians' language families and ethnic connections. Still with no sign of La Liberté, at four o'clock the party moved ahead about five miles and camped in either Harrison County, Iowa, or Washington County, Nebraska, some miles south of Blair, Nebraska.

AUGUST 4, 1804. Clark noted the constant action of the Missouri River in washing away the banks and carrying off amounts of soil and trees. The threat of snags and sawyers in the river attested to its work. The party passed the remains of an old trading post that Cruzatte had occupied for two years while he traded with the Omaha Indians and camped north of Blair, Nebraska, in either Washington County, Nebraska, or Harrison County, Iowa, a trip of fifteen miles. One of the party, Reed, had gone back for his knife but failed to return in the evening, nor did La Liberté make an appearance.

AUGUST 5, 1804. Lewis killed a bullsnake during the day and added a long description of it to his natural history notebook, along with detailed notes on the least tern. He took time during the noon hour to make astronomical observations. Clark commented on wind and rain but remarked that thunder and lightning were not as common as in the East. He again analyzed the actions of the Missouri River upon its banks and islands and spent a part of the day out reconnoitering but got back to camp by dark. Reed still had not reappeared when the men made camp in Harrison County, Iowa, across from the Burt-Washington county line, Nebraska. Clark suspected that the man had deserted. Whitehouse was blunter, saying, "Read deserted from our party," but his entry may have been written later.

AUGUST 6, 1804. A storm during the night ripped the flag off the large pirogue. Now that he had been absent three days, Clark and others became convinced that Reed had deserted, but the captain still thought La Liberté lost. The party passed Soldiers River and camped about halfway between it and the Little Sioux River, in Harrison County, Iowa.

AUGUST 7, 1804. In the afternoon, the captains sent Drouillard, Reuben Field, Bratton, and Labiche after the deserter Reed with orders to kill him if he resisted. Harsh as it sounds, the order was consistent with military rules of the day. Floyd's response to Reed's action may have been representative when he wrote that the soldier had deserted "with out aney Jest Case." The men sent after Reed were also to seek information from the Otoes about the missing La Liberté and ask some Otoe chiefs to join the party at the Omaha Indian village ahead, where the captains hoped to work out a peace between them and their common enemy, the Sioux. The main party camped a few miles below the mouth of the Little Sioux River, probably on the Iowa side in Harrison County.

AUGUST 8, 1804. Clark walked on shore with Collins, who dispatched an elk. The captain was less successful and blamed the failure of his four shots on his small-caliber rifle, which could not bring down an elk. He also complained of nagging mosquitoes that swarmed at his eyes. As the party passed the Little Sioux River, Clark tried to sort out the geography of the area, the sources of rivers, their proximity to other streams and lakes, and the courses they followed. He may have been querying his French boatmen and the Sioux interpreter Dorion, recalling St. Louis conversations, or consulting available maps. As they passed on, Lewis noticed masses of feathers floating down the Missouri, then discovered a flock of pelicans. After shooting one of the birds, the captain wrote out his customary detailed description in his natural history notebook and estimated that the pouch under its beak held five gallons of water. After about sixteen miles of travel, the party set up camp, probably on the Iowa side, in southwest Monona County, not far above the Harrison County line.

AUGUST 9, 1804. Fog detained the party somewhat, but they still got an early start at half past seven. Beaver signs were plentiful, a turkey was shot, and the mosquitoes worse than ever. The men camped a mile or two south of Onawa, Harrison County, Iowa, making about seventeen miles.

AUGUST 10, 1804. With a hard and favorable wind from the southwest the party was able to hoist sails and get some relief from rowing, pulling, and poling their river craft. From the island camp in Monona County, Iowa, the men could see Blackbird Hill, named after the late chief of the Omaha Indians. In either Monona County, Iowa, or Burt County, Nebraska, Lewis collected a specimen of field horsetail and described it as a species of "sand rush" and a growth of the sandbars and banks of the Missouri. Although thirty other plants had been collected up to this point, all have been lost, so this plant becomes the earliest collected specimen in the Lewis and Clark Herbarium at the Academy of Natural Sciences, Philadelphia (see also May 23 and 25, 1804). The plants were sent east from Fort Mandan in April 1805.

AUGUST 11, 1804. At daybreak the party faced a hard wind from the northwest followed by rain. After the rain, Lewis, Clark, and ten men ascended Blackbird Hill to honor the former Omaha chief and view the countryside. Blackbird had died of smallpox about four years earlier along with upwards of four hundred of his nation. He was a powerful leader and somewhat notorious for his atrocities, and he retained a reputation for wickedness even in death. On a pole the captains fixed a flag with red, white, and blue streamers to memorialize his grave and probably gain favor with the Omahas. The party camped in the vicinity of Badger Lake, Monona County, Iowa, traveling about seventeen miles.

AUGUST 12, 1804. From the shore, a coyote barked at the party as they passed by in the evening, but the men were unable to capture it. Clark compared the coyote's barking to that of a feist dog. Weiser was appointed cook for Sergeant Floyd's detachment in place of Thompson, who may have proved unsatisfactory. The party made about twenty miles and camped in either Monona or Woodbury County, Iowa, near the county line.

AUGUST 13, 1804. The party passed a spot where Mackay had established Fort Charles for the winter of 1796–97. The site is southeast of Homer, Dakota County, Nebraska, but the exact location has not been discovered. Clark may have referred to Mackay's maps or those of his partner, John Thomas Evans, when he noticed the place. The men formed a camp, the party's Fish Camp, a few miles south of Dakota City, Dakota County, or opposite in Woodbury County,

Iowa, making about seventeen miles. From here the captains sent Ordway, Cruzatte, Shannon, Werner, and the *engagé* Cann to the great Omaha village Tonwontonga with gifts and an invitation for village leaders to meet the explorers the next day. Ordway's party had to cut their way through the tall grasses and thick brush on their way up Omaha Creek; they spent the night near Tonwontonga.

AUGUST 14, 1804. Ordway and party returned to the Fish Camp from Tonwontonga to report no sign of the Omahas, who were probably out on buffalo hunts. They found only a burned village, set afire perhaps to destroy the ravages of smallpox that had devastated the tribe in the winter of 1799–1800. Clark commented on the Omahas' situation after the catastrophic epidemic, which may have reduced their numbers to about one thousand people and lessened their power considerably. Clark learned that some Omaha men, faced with the horrible, destructive nature of the disease, killed their wives and children hoping that they would find a better place after death. Lewis mentioned another smallpox epidemic in 1802 that further reduced their numbers, with Clark adding in his "Estimate of Eastern Indians" that they had become a "wandering nation" deserted by traders, deficient in arms, and vulnerable to aggressive tribes.

AUGUST 15, 1804. Clark, with Floyd and nine other men, set up a barrier across a creek and hauled in over three hundred fish, including perch, bass, trout, catfish, and freshwater drums, along with crayfish and mussels. This abundance may have persuaded the party to christen their camp since the thirteenth Fish Camp, where they remained until the twentieth. Dorion led a party to some smoke signals in the distance but discovered only an old fire and no Indians. Several men worked on a new mast for the keelboat, but their labors did not keep them from dancing to the fiddle in the evening.

AUGUST 16, 1804. Lewis with a dozen men went out fishing this time and caught nearly eight hundred fish. An evening breeze helped to drive off mosquitoes and cool the day.

AUGUST 17, 1804. Labiche arrived and reported that the parties sent out in search of La Liberté and Reed were coming in with one of the deserters and with three Otoe chiefs. The men set fire to the prairie near the camp as a signal to other Indians to come in for a meeting. La Liberté, true to his name, had been apprehended but had escaped—never to be seen again. Reed, on the other hand, was under arrest and was now to be tried for a very serious offense.

AUGUST 18, 1804. Reed's trial took place in the morning. He readily confessed that he had deserted and had stolen a rifle, shot pouch, gunpowder, and ammunition. He asked that he be treated as favorably as military rules would allow. The captains sentenced him to run the gauntlet four times while the men flogged his bare back; a portion of that punishment was carried out right then. The Otoes asked that he be pardoned, but after the captains explained military custom, the chiefs appeared satisfied. Reed was also expelled from the permanent party, but he remained doing hard labor until he was sent back with the return party in April 1805. Under a shade tree near the river's edge, the captains queried the Otoes about the origins of the difficulties between themselves and neighboring tribes. Primarily it was a matter of revenge against the Omahas and the Pawnees because of killings on both sides. Being Lewis's birthday, an extra gill of whiskey was rationed to the men, and dancing lasted until late in the night.

AUGUST 19, 1804. The captains prepared gifts for the Otoes and then breakfasted with Little Thief, the principal chief. At about ten o'clock all assembled under an awning while Lewis and Clark explained the message they had sent ahead by Fairfong. Each Indian, including again Big Horse, then made a short speech voicing approval of the captains' aims to bring peace between the Otoes and the Omahas. Afterward medals and certificates were dispersed and the air gun demonstrated. Later a squabble broke out about the distribution of a certificate, but the matter was settled diplomatically and the council broke up after drinks of whiskey. The party became very concerned about Floyd's health. He seems to have taken sick very suddenly and his condition worsened by the hour. York appears to have been a principal caregiver to the sergeant, but all the men cared for him as best they could.

AUGUST 20, 1804. Clark was worn out this morning because he had been up most of the night with Floyd, who grew steadily worse. The party set out after dispensing a few more presents to Fairfong and the Otoes. After a few miles they landed and prepared a warm bath for Floyd, hoping to relieve his pain. Before they could get him ready, he died. As he lay dying Floyd asked Clark to write a letter, but the intended receiver is unknown. Clark mentioned that he died with a great deal of composure. Gass wrote that they made every effort to save him. Modern opinion holds that the sergeant died of a ruptured appendix. Nothing in Lewis's medical chest could have saved him and resorting to their customary remedies, laxatives and bleeding, would have hastened his death. Lewis conducted a funeral service with appropriate military honors (or with ceremonies "as custommary in a Settlement," as Ordway put it), and then the sergeant was buried atop Floyd's Bluff, Sioux City, Woodbury County, Iowa, where a modern monument rises over the Missouri. Gass said that the internment was as suitable as circumstances would allow. Clark wrote warmly of Floyd's devotion and service. The sergeant would be the only member of the corps to die during the expedition. The party moved a few miles farther and camped above the mouth of Floyd River, Woodbury County.

AUGUST 21, 1804. As the party passed the Big Sioux River, Dorion gave an overview of surrounding geography. He laid out the courses of the area's main affluents and reported the navigability of the streams. He also told of a nearby neutral ground where Indians came to quarry catlinite, a red stone used in making pipes; it is in Pipestone County, Minnesota. The party camped south of Jackson, Union County, South Dakota. Clark found a tasty berry on a shrub, the buffaloberry. Lewis collected the plant on September 4 at the mouth of the Niobrara River and characterized the berry as pleasant to taste with an acidic flavor like a cranberry.

AUGUST 22, 1804. While carrying out geologic investigations in bluffs above the Missouri River in Dakota and Dixon Counties, Nebraska, Lewis became nauseated by the fumes of some substance. The bluffs are composed primarily of Cretaceous-age Graneros Shale and Greenhorn Limestone. Here the captain found "alum" (an undetermined substance), pyrite, and melanterite ("copperas"); it may have been the melanterite that caused his illness. August 22 and 23 were banner days for geologic collecting: at least nine mineral specimens were taken this day and six more the next. Clark called attention to "Semented Shels" in the bluffs, which would have been remnants of extinct bivalves of the Greenhorn Limestone. The captains took a vote among the men for a sergeant to replace the deceased Floyd. Gass had the highest number of votes, beating out Bratton and Gibson, so the captains appointed him to the vacancy. The party camped south of Elk Point, Union County, South Dakota, having come about nineteen miles.

AUGUST 23, 1804. Clark killed a fat buck and Joseph Field came in with news that he had shot the party's first buffalo. Lewis took a dozen men to bring the buffalo down to the river. Shooters were less lucky hitting two elks that swam the river in front of the boat; everyone missed what should have been an easy target. Blowing sand hampered Clark's writing, and after about ten miles of travel the men camped in either Dixon County, Nebraska, or Clay County, South Dakota, and spent the evening preparing buffalo meat and venison brought in by hunters.

AUGUST 24, 1804. A short distance upriver Clark noticed fire-damaged bluffs that still retained heat. A day or two earlier the party had passed a spot later called "Ionia Volcano," near the town of Ionia, Dixon County, Nebraska. Later investigations disproved the existence of a volcano and found instead that heat and steam were caused by less dramatic geologic forces. Similar phenomena were occurring here in the Carlile Shale with iron sulfide reactions that released energy in the form of heat. Clark went hunting on shore with York; the captain got a deer and York shot an elk. In spite of being a slave, York was evidently carrying a gun during the expedition. While out Clark again noticed great quantities of buffalo-berries and wrote that they made "delitefull Tarts." A rainy afternoon brought the party into camp near Vermillion, Clay County, South Dakota. In the distance they noticed a high hill and learned that it had supernatural associations for nearby natives. The captains determined to climb Spirit Mound the next day. Again, Lewis found his chronometer defective. It had stopped running just after he wound it, and he could not determine the cause of the problem.

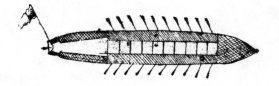

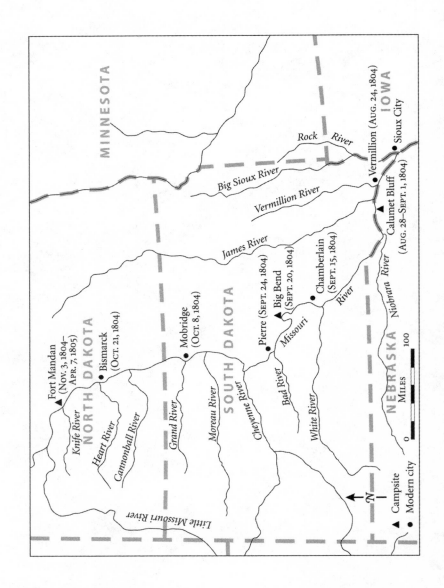

MAP 3. The expedition's route, August 25–October 26, 1804.

CHAPTER 2

The Middle Missouri

August 25–October 26, 1804

AUGUST 25, 1804. In the morning Lewis, Clark, and eleven men set out to climb the mound they had spotted the day before. Seaman was along but became overheated and was led back before reaching the mound. York returned from the trip exhausted by the heat and the fast pace Clark set. Lewis also was affected by the temperature and was still suffering from his exposure to fumes a few days earlier. It took a four-hour, steady march to reach the hill. Clark noted that it was 86° in the afternoon. This was the first temperature reading the captains had taken since May 14, but they would not return to regular, tabled weather observations until September 19.

From the hill the men viewed immense plains all about them, devoid of timber except for scattered trees along the river courses. Equally impressive in their view were the large herds of buffalo and elks. Clark was struck by the symmetry of the hill and thought it might owe its shape to human handiwork except for the soil that composed it. The great confluence of birds atop Spirit Mound was an indication to natives that spirits resided there. Clark found a more prosaic reason: winds blew insects up the slopes and birds arrived to feed on them. On the way back to the boats Clark gathered grapes, plums, and currants, while Lewis collected a specimen of Rocky Mountain bee plant. The main party, having set out at about eleven o'clock, camped near the Cedar-Dixon county line, Nebraska. Clark noted that they had passed a "Bluff of blue earth," probably the bluish-gray Carlile Shale.

AUGUST 26, 1804. The Spirit Mound scouting party got back to the boats about nine in the morning and all set out within an hour, except for Drouillard and Shannon, who stayed behind to hunt for lost horses. Describing a cliff of "white & Blue or Dark earth," Clark was probably viewing white chalk of the Cretaceous-age Niobrara Formation that overlays Carlile Shale in this region. During the day Clark saw what he believed were the remains of an Omaha Indian village established by a band that was dissatisfied with the leadership of Chief Blackbird. His location for the village is questionable and the historical record of Omaha villages is confusing. The party made camp in Clay County, South Dakota, opposite the mouth of Bow Creek, Cedar County, Nebraska, making about nine miles.

AUGUST 27, 1804. Drouillard came in to report that he was not able to find Shannon or the horses, so the captains sent Shields and Joseph Field back to hunt for him. In the afternoon the party landed at James River and were visited by Indians who told them that a large number of Sioux Indians were camped nearby. In his "Summary view of the Rivers and Creeks" Lewis noted Sioux activity on the James River. Pryor, Dorion, and another Frenchman went with two of the Indians in search of the Sioux while the main party moved on toward a rendezvous site called Calumet Bluff. The other Indian, an Omaha boy, stayed with the main party and told the captains that his people had gone to make peace with the Pawnees. After traveling about fourteen miles, the party camped for the night between the mouth of the James River and the town of Yankton, Yankton County, South Dakota. Ordway noticed a mink during the day.

AUGUST 28, 1804. Clark thought that the indisposition suffered by Lewis and himself may have been brought on by the substitution of hominy for bread. A mishap with the red pirogue called for shifting loads and a temporary decision to send the injured boat back with the return party. The party arrived at the Calumet Bluff rendezvous site and set up camp in Cedar County, Nebraska, just below Gavins Point Dam. The Omaha boy joined the Sioux encampment. News of Shannon from Shields and Joseph Field was not good. They had discovered that the young man was ahead of the party rather than behind. Knowing that Shannon was not a first-rate hunter, Clark was especially concerned, so he dispatched Colter to find him.

AUGUST 29, 1804. While at the Calumet Bluff camp awaiting the Sioux, the enlisted men busied themselves making elkskin tow ropes while Clark prepared a speech for the Indians. The red pirogue was repaired, returned to service, and a portion of its load transferred to the white pirogue. At four o'clock Pryor and Dorion arrived with about seventy Yankton Sioux, who set up camp across the river. Among the Indians were three chiefs, so the captains sent over meat, corn, and tobacco and made ready for a council the following day. Pryor had been welcomed by the Sioux, who wanted to carry him to their village on a buffalo robe. Pryor declined and told them that he was not the boat's commander. Nonetheless, the Yanktons offered him dog to eat as a token of respect. The sergeant informed Clark about the nature of the Sioux camps, where he located handsome tipis made of buffalo skins decoratively painted, orderly arranged, and holding ten to fifteen persons each.

The Yanktons were a part of one of three great divisions of the Sioux nation, including Santees, Yanktons-Yanktonais, and Tetons. The Yanktons were a small tribe—Lewis and Clark counted sixteen hundred people along the Missouri and James Rivers—who were in a transitional phase between a village-based, horticultural existence and a nomadic, buffalo-hunting life. They never adopted fully to the nomadic life but went seasonally to the plains to hunt buffalo, more so after acquiring guns and horses in the mid-eighteenth century. One of the men who had visited the Yanktons told Gass that the women were homely and mostly old but that the young men were "likely and active."

AUGUST 30, 1804. In the morning the Yankton chiefs were brought over to the Calumet Bluff camp preceded by dancers and musicians, who went through the camp singing, dancing, and playing their instruments. The captains delivered their standard Indian speech and afterward handed out gifts, giving special attention to high-ranking individuals, to whom they presented commissions and flags. The Yanktons were particularly fascinated by Lewis's air gun and its repeating-fire function. Clark was intrigued by the *akicita*, a warrior society characteristic of the Sioux and other plains tribes, which served not only as battle units in the field but also as a fraternal organization in camp. Its members also acted as civilian police during peacetime. After the ceremonies there was more music and dancing to the drum and rattle, all accompanied by whoops and shouts and interrupted by stories of martial glory and tales of past war deeds. All the while, the American soldiers tossed knives, tobacco, bells, and other small gifts of appreciation to the circle of dancers.

AUGUST 31, 1804. The day continued as before with exchanges of gifts and delivery of speeches. Among the Yanktons, The Shake Hand, White Crane (or White Bear, "Mar to ree"), Struck by the Pawnee (or Arikara, "Par nar ne Ar par be"), and Half Man ("Ar ca we char chi") spoke of the tribe's need for trade goods, especially arms and ammunition. Clark took a Sioux vocabulary and obtained information about the Yanktons from Dorion. Clark also tried to sort out the complicated nature of Sioux tribes and bands. As Dorion and the Yanktons were leaving for their encampment on the opposite side of the river, the captains gave the old trader a bottle of whiskey.

SEPTEMBER 1, 1804. Leaving Dorion and the Yanktons behind, the party set out in the morning. Lewis and Clark went seeking a beaver house reputed to be of enormous size but were disappointed in their search. After about sixteen miles' travel, the party camped on an island between Bon Homme County, South Dakota, and Knox County, Nebraska.

SEPTEMBER 2, 1804. From an island, the men heard hunters Drouillard, Reuben Field, Collins, Newman, and Howard shouting that they needed help to bring in the elks they had killed. The party halted to take breakfast at eight o'clock. After settling in for the day, Clark conducted an elaborate survey of natural wind-blown formations in Bon Homme County, South Dakota, near the party's camp. He believed them to be constructed artifacts similar to ones left by the Mound Builders in the Ohio valley. The *engagés* told him that there were similar phenomena on the Osage, Kansas, and Platte Rivers. Along the bluffs in Bon Homme County or in Knox County, Nebraska, Lewis collected a specimen of prairie sagewort.

He also collected the purple prairie clover and remarked that Indians crushed and wetted its leaves and applied them to flesh wounds.

SEPTEMBER 3, 1804. The men saw signs of Shannon and Colter and decided that Shannon must be ahead of Colter, who had gone in search of the young explorer. Pronghorns, usually called antelopes but also termed "goats" by the party, were seen for the first time. Clark gathered the seeds of three kinds of plums, which he intended to send to his brother, most likely Jonathan. Gass was struck by the endless horizon in view from elevated spots and the "delightful prospects" of the country in sight. The night's camp was in Knox County, Nebraska, probably near the western boundary of the Santee Sioux Reservation, about fifteen miles from the last camp.

SEPTEMBER 4, 1804. By hoisting the keelboat's sail, the party made swift progress for a short time; then the mast broke again. Arriving at the mouth of the Niobrara River, Knox County, Nebraska, they camped for the night. Clark found the Niobrara, which the party called "Rapid River," throwing off sand much like the Platte, only coarser. The captain went up the river for about three miles and spotted the remains of a village once occupied by Ponca Indians.

SEPTEMBER 5, 1804. Shields and Gibson went to the Ponca village on Ponca Creek, but the Indians were hunting buffalo. Clark mistakenly thought the Poncas raised neither corn nor beans, staple crops of Missouri River village Indians. The men saw mule deer, but a description was not posted until September 17. The party camped on "no preserve Island" that lay between southeastern Charles Mix County, South Dakota, and northwestern Knox County, Nebraska. A new mast was constructed.

SEPTEMBER 6, 1804. A short storm kept the men in camp part of the morning, then they set out against a hard wind. Finding the oars and poles of little use, the boats moved closer to shore and the men employed the tow ropes. Colter came in alone, having failed to find Shannon. After about eight grueling miles, camp was established in Charles Mix County, South Dakota, probably a little below the Knox-Boyd county line, Nebraska, on the opposite shore.

SEPTEMBER 7, 1804. The two captains climbed to the top of Old Baldy in Boyd County, Nebraska, and on their descent discovered a village of prairie dogs. After pouring about five barrels of water down one of the holes, the men were able to flush out and catch a live animal. In April 1805 the captains sent a live prairie dog to Jefferson from Fort Mandan, but it is not certain that this is the one. Clark noted but discounted the myth that prairie dog holes were shared with snakes. Lewis and Clark are credited with the scientific discovery of the prairie dog. Shields killed one and the captains had it for dinner. The party made camp at the foot of Old Baldy, about four miles downriver from the Nebraska–South Dakota border.

SEPTEMBER 8, 1804. The party passed a wintering camp of Jean Baptiste Truteau, which the trader had established in 1794–95, after being stopped by Sioux Indians from reaching the Mandans. Truteau's Ponca House was some thirty-four miles above the mouth of the Niobrara River in Charles Mix County, South Dakota. The captains were reconnoitering and hunting during the day. One of the men killed a buffalo and left his hat as a scarecrow to ward off scavengers, but when he returned he discovered the carcass cleaned and his hat carried off. The party camped on an island on the Gregory–Charles Mix county line, South Dakota, having come about seventeen miles; the men were now entirely within South Dakota.

SEPTEMBER 9, 1804. Clark saw so many sandbars during the day that he quit mentioning them. He and York went hunting and York killed a buffalo, as did Lewis and Reuben Field, but Clark failed to get either a pronghorn or a prairie dog that he was seeking. The night's camp was in Gregory County, South Dakota, opposite Stony Point on the opposite shore, a distance of about fourteen miles from the previous camp.

SEPTEMBER 10, 1804. One of the party discovered the fossil remains of a plesiosaur, an aquatic dinosaur of the Mesozoic era, on a hill during the course of the day. Clark measured the backbone of the specimen at forty-five feet. The men camped on an island between Gregory and Charles Mix Counties, South Dakota, having traveled about twenty miles.

SEPTEMBER 11, 1804. Shannon rejoined the party; he had been missing since August 26. The young man thought that the party was ahead of him and pushed on trying to catch up, when in fact the boats were always behind. He had abandoned one worn-out horse, had used up his ammunition, and had lived for the previous twelve days on berries except for a rabbit he had killed by substituting a hard stick for a lead ball in his rifle. Now he was heading downriver hoping to meet another boat and was prepared to kill his horse if forced to. Clark observed that even in this land of plenty a person could starve to death for the want of ammunition. After a day of hard rain that continued into the night, the party settled in just above the mouth of Landing Creek, Gregory County, South Dakota.

SEPTEMBER 12, 1804. With hard winds ahead and sandbars clogging the river, it took three-quarters of the day to make one mile and the party advanced only four miles altogether. At one point the keelboat wheeled around several times and leaned heavily to one side. It took the men's full exertions to keep it righted. Great numbers of sharp-tailed grouse (a Lewis and Clark scientific discovery) were seen along the way, as were prairie dog villages across from camp in Brule County, South Dakota. In the prairies Lewis collected a specimen of rough gayfeather.

SEPTEMBER 13, 1804. Ordway, Pryor, and Shannon went seeking plums but judged them unsuitable. Shannon shot a porcupine and the men ate it for supper and spent the night away from the main party. Lewis also killed a porcupine in a cottonwood tree and enjoyed its meat. He supposed that porcupines were one cause of defoliated trees in the area. Clark commented on the worsening situation of mosquitoes. The party camped in Brule County, South Dakota, having advanced about a dozen miles.

SEPTEMBER 14, 1804. Clark went in search of a volcano that he had learned of from Mackay's accounts of his trip on the Missouri. None were to be found, and the notion may have developed due to the natural burning of bituminous shale. The captains obtained and provided the first scientific descriptions of the pronghorn and the white-tailed jackrabbit and had the animals stuffed. Shields had brought the jackrabbit in for examination. Lewis would later measure a live one's leap at twenty-one feet. Clark named a stream in the area after Shannon, who had stayed there during his absence; the party camped just below its mouth, modern Bull Creek, Lyman County, South Dakota, having come about nine miles.

SEPTEMBER 15, 1804. Lewis and Clark investigated the White River for a short distance from its mouth and found it distributing much less sand than the Platte or Niobrara Rivers. They dispatched Gass and Reuben Field on a longer trip up the stream. Clark declared the area a "butifull Situation for a Town," with its gradual ascents from the river to the heights and a greater quantity of timber than usual at the mouth of the White River. Lewis collected three specimens during his excursion: silky wormwood, spiny goldenweed, and Canada milkvetch. Gray wolves and coyotes sang the party to sleep in Brule County, South Dakota, opposite the mouth of American Crow Creek, Lyman County, South Dakota, about eight miles from the previous camp.

SEPTEMBER 16, 1804. Lewis made journal entries for this day and the next while the party camped near Oacoma, Lyman County, South Dakota. These are two of the few daily entries Lewis is known to have made between May 20, 1804, and April 7, 1805. The captain used his journal space to describe river vegetation, giving particular attention to the bur ("white") oak. He also commented on the vast herds of grazing animals to be seen in every direction. Hunters took advantage of the situation, but the buffalo obtained in the hunt were not suitable for food. Buffalo skins, however, served as useful covers for the pirogues' cargo. The layover was to allow the baggage to dry and to transfer items from the keelboat to the red pirogue. It was also a good time to catch up on making, mending, and washing clothes. With cooler weather arriving, the captains passed out a flannel shirt to each man. The captains finally decided not to send back the red pirogue and the return party under Warfington but to retain the men until spring. Clark noted the western white-tailed deer, a subspecies of the eastern variety with which the captains were familiar; Gibson would get one the next day. The men found a large plum thicket ripe with fruit near the camp. Gass and Reuben Field returned to camp to report on the meandering course and western upriver direction of the White River.

SEPTEMBER 17, 1804. Lewis took six of the best hunters on an excursion, his object being to obtain a female pronghorn since he already had a male. Being unsuccessful in the hunt, he went on to comment extensively about the pronghorn's fleetness and agility. Indeed, he compared the speed of the pronghorn to "the rapid flight of birds [rather] than the motion of quadrupeds." On the outing he noticed dense plum thickets and open country thickly settled with prairie dog villages. Steep, irregular hills fell into deep ravines and above the hills the country leveled off to extensive plains. On new grass—revived from an old fire—Lewis viewed immense herds of animals grazing on lush vegetation. He estimated the number of buffalo at three thousand. One of the hunters killed a magpie, then new to science, and Lewis described it minutely. The men also named a nearby creek, current American Crow Creek, "Corvus" Creek, after the scientific name for crows and ravens, placing the magpie under the same category. The party remained in camp near Oacoma.

SEPTEMBER 18, 1804. Clark obtained the party's first specimen of a coyote, which the men had mistaken for a fox up to that point. The coyote's skin and bones were saved in order to be sent with the return party in the spring and later to be studied by scientists in the East. Lewis noticed the first Canada geese on their return from the north. The party camped a few miles northeast of Oacoma, Lyman County, South Dakota, a distance of about seven miles for the day.

SEPTEMBER 19, 1804. Clark walked on shore to find the trail the Sioux used in crossing the Missouri River in this area. The captain called it the Sioux Pass of the Three Rivers because of the proximity of Crow, Wolf, and Campbell Creeks on the east side of the Missouri, Buffalo County, South Dakota. Here he also found the remains of camps used by the Indians during the crossing and he noticed an abundance of prickly pear cacti. The captains returned to keeping weather observations. Having begun the practice in January 1804, they quit it on May 14 for unknown reasons when they started upriver. A good day on the river brought the party forward about twenty-six miles, where they made camp near the mouth of Counselor Creek, Lyman County, South Dakota, and west of Big Bend Dam.

SEPTEMBER 20, 1804. While the main party made its way around the Big Bend, or Grand Detour, of the Missouri, Drouillard and Shields went overland with the party's horse to hunt and await the main group's arrival. Clark measured the narrowest strip of land across the bend as one and one-quarter miles and the distance by water around the bend as thirty miles. The captain reckoned the party to be 1,283 miles out of the Illinois camp of 1803–4 at this point. Observing dark earth along the bluffs of the Missouri, some journalists reasoned that the substance gave the river its color and texture. This soil, they noticed, dissolved like sugar and was washed into the stream with every rain and carried along the river's course into the Mississippi. Reuben Field brought in a female pronghorn and the captains got a chance to make comparisons with the male of the species. Again, they saved the skin and bones for study in the East. The party spent the night under a pleasing, shiny moon on the Big Bend, a few miles southwest of the Hughes-Hyde county line, South Dakota, after making another good distance of about thirty miles.

SEPTEMBER 21, 1804. During the night the sandbar on which the party camped began to give way as the Missouri River made one of its periodic changes in composition. The guard sounded an alarm and the party quickly jumped in the pirogues and made for shore in the moonlight. The action came just in time, as the men watched the camp disappear into the river's swirling waters. The party established a second camp nearby and at daylight proceeded on around the bend. Clark commented on the smaller size and numbers of catfish in the area, and he delighted at the pronghorns skipping across the plains. Pronghorns and elks were in the rutting season and buffalo were just ending theirs. On September 19 and this day Lewis gathered a number of specimens in the Big Bend area: broom snakeweed, aromatic aster, fourwing saltbush, slender flowered scurfpea, lanceleaf sage, and rubber rabbitbrush. A specimen of broom snakeweed is one of less than a dozen from the expedition that are housed at Kew Gardens, England. Lewis noted the aromatic scent of the rabbitbrush and rightly observed the pronghorn's preference for it. Coming ahead about eleven miles, the men found a secure camp on an island attached to the shore in Hughes County, South Dakota, east of Joe Creek.

SEPTEMBER 22, 1804. In spite of a thick fog, the party got underway by seven o'clock. The corps reached their "Cedar Island," later Dorion Island No. 2 (now submerged by Lake Sharpe), and inspected the remains of Régis Loisel's Fort aux Cedres, which he had built about 1800 in order to trade with the Tetons. The explorers measured the cedar stockade and judged it a sizeable establishment, measuring about 70 feet square with a 13½-feet-high wall enclosing it. Clark observed traces of temporary Indian shelters nearby, left by those who had come to trade with Loisel. Here the men found dog-travois poles suitable for setting poles for the boats. They camped in Hughes County, South Dakota, nearly opposite La Roche Creek and a short distance above the Stanley-Lyman county line on the opposite side.

SEPTEMBER 23, 1804. Clouds of smoke to the southwest gave evidence of Indians but none were seen immediately. Reuben Field had a creek named for him, a procedure the captains adopted for naming physical features across the continent; it is present Medicine Knoll Creek, Hughes County, South Dakota. After the party established a camp for the evening, three Sioux boys swam from the opposite side to inform the captains that two large encampments of their tribe lay ahead. The boys had set the prairie afire to signal the explorers' approach. Lewis and Clark sent gifts of tobacco for the chiefs and requested meetings for the next day. The captains remarked on the dry air and were struck by the speed at which water evaporated. The camp was in Hughes County, South Dakota, just below the mouth of Antelope Creek on the opposite side.

SEPTEMBER 24, 1804. As the party moved on the captains began preparing for meeting the Teton Sioux Indians, selecting clothes and gifts for the occasion. Perhaps it was not a good omen when Colter reported that his horse had been stolen. The party met Indians on shore who wanted to come on board, but all they received was a stern lecture from the captains about the missing horse. Either Labiche or Cruzatte spoke to them in the Omaha language, which was similar to Teton Lakota, but little was understood. Later in the day one of the Teton chiefs, Buffalo Medicine, came to visit as the men moved into camp just above the mouth of Bad ("Teton") River, Stanley County, South Dakota, opposite Pierre. Clark went to shore to meet him and participate in a smoking ritual. Dorion served as an interpreter.

The Teton Sioux are speakers of the Lakota dialect of the Siouan language and are sometimes known simply as the Lakotas. Being one of several divisions of the Sioux people, they themselves are further divided into seven groups, one of which, the Brulés, numbering about nine hundred people according to Lewis, the party met here. In expedition times the Tetons were living on both sides of the Missouri River, but by the mid-nineteenth century they had moved entirely to the west. Their aggressive, martial spirit was well known even by this time. Already they had become a classic plains people, living a nomadic existence in lodge-pole-framed tipis and depending on horseback hunting and the buffalo chase. It was important that Lewis and Clark establish good relations with this powerful Missouri River tribe.

SEPTEMBER 25, 1804. The day dawned fair and crisp as the party arranged to meet the Tetons in council. The men raised a flagstaff and put up an awning to provide shade on the sandbar opposite the mouth of Bad River. The greater portion of the party remained aboard the keelboat, while the captains and a contingent awaited the Indians' arrival. About eleven o'clock, Black Buffalo ("Un ton gar Sar bar"), the principal chief; Partisan ("Torto hon gar"), the second chief; and Buffalo Medicine ("Tar ton gar wa ker"), the third, arrived with a couple of warriors. At noon the customary rituals began with passing the pipe, parading the party, and giving gifts. Black Buffalo received a red coat and a cocked hat adorned with a feather. Lewis delivered his customary speech, interpreted by Dorion but haltingly, it seems.

After the ceremonies the Indians were invited on board the keelboat to see the marvels of modern American technology, including probably a demonstration of the air gun and a display of scientific instruments. After sharing a bit of wine, Partisan feigned drunkenness and became troublesome. Clark tried to get the Tetons off the keelboat and back to shore, but when he landed the pirogue Indians grabbed the boat's rope. At the same time Partisan demanded more gifts and became insulting, to the point that Clark drew his sword and roused the men with him, while Lewis ordered those on the keelboat to ready their arms and load the swivel cannon. All the while, Tetons on shore strung their bows, steadied arrows, and cocked guns. It was a tense situation. At this point Black Buffalo intervened, took the pirogue's rope and returned it to Clark, then ordered his men out of the way. Clark offered his hand to Black Buffalo, but it was refused; nonetheless the three chiefs returned to the keelboat to spend the night. The party moved about a mile upriver and anchored off an island that the captains called "Bad humered" Island, later Marion Island, opposite Pierre.

SEPTEMBER 26, 1804. The men moved the boats about 4½ miles upriver and anchored at a spot where women and children from a nearby Teton village could come aboard and where the chiefs could extend hospitality to the crew. The camp was about four miles north of Fort Pierre, Stanley County, South Dakota. Clark gave a somewhat negative physical description of his visitors; he judged the women nice enough but not handsome. Ordway on the other hand declared them "verry handsome, & friendly." The captain also thought the women almost slaves to their husbands and noticed that polygamy was practiced in the tribe. Nor was he impressed with the outdated weapons of Sioux soldiers. Clark also noted the village's constabulary force, made up of distinguished soldiers who policed the village with diligence and great authority. Clark observed about twenty-five prisoners taken in a raid upon the Omaha Indians, and he saw that Sioux warriors displayed sixty-five Omaha scalps. The captains insisted that the Omaha prisoners be returned.

Lewis and a few of the party went on shore with the chiefs, but after some time had passed Clark became nervous and sent one of the sergeants to look after them. The sergeant, probably Pryor, discovered plans being made for a dance that evening that the captains attended, after being carried ceremoniously to the village on decorated buffalo robes. In the council lodge they were greeted by about seventy of the leading men, smoked the peace pipe, and shared the most delicate parts of dog meat and pemmican. In the center of the lodge was four hundred pounds of buffalo meat as a gift to the Americans. Clark noticed that flags of Spain adorned the lodge alongside the flag that he had earlier presented to Black Buffalo. The captain gave a vivid description of the evening's events as men and women danced, musicians beat out rhythms on the tambourine and drum, and warriors displayed their battle trophies. It was midnight before the festivities ended. The captains were offered women, but they refused.

SEPTEMBER 27, 1804. The Teton chiefs requested that the captains and party remain another night, as more of their tribe would be arriving. The captains obliged and remained at the camp north of Fort Pierre. Much visiting between camp and village took place during the day. Gass, one of the visitors, provided a graphic description of the village, its lodges and occupants, and the events of the day. Clark observed the Tetons' practice of cutting their arms as a symbol of grief when a friend or relative died. The evening's festivals were a repeat of the previous night's activities, with dancing and displays of battlefield honors. On returning to the keelboat a mishap occurred when one of the pirogues struck the cable to the keelboat's anchor, causing its loss. Clark alerted the men, hoping to rescue the anchor, but in the excitement he alarmed the Indians, who suspected treachery and called out their forces on shore. Soon some two hundred heavily armed men were at the river's edge ready for battle. It took a little time to explain the confusion and calm the situation. No one slept well that night and tensions remained high as guards were posted on both sides. Cruzatte, who spoke the Omaha language, discovered from the tribe's prisoners that the Tetons possibly had hostile intentions toward the corps; this information caused renewed alertness, which the party tried to mask.

SEPTEMBER 28, 1804. The party spent a portion of the morning searching for the keelboat's anchor without success—it had buried itself in the muddy Missouri. Difficulties of a more significant sort then occurred. After breakfast, the captains were getting the chiefs off the boat when some warriors on shore grabbed the keelboat's rope. Black Buffalo, who had remained on board intending to go a bit farther upstream, was enlisted to intervene. He informed Lewis that the men holding up the party wanted more tobacco and that Partisan wanted a flag and some tobacco also. Lewis, disgusted at the delay, at first resisted, but finally Clark threw a twist of tobacco to Black Buffalo and readied the fuse on the swivel cannon. Black Buffalo gave the tobacco to the men and jerked the rope from their hold. The party took off.

Later they heard from Buffalo Medicine that the difficulties were instigated by Partisan. The captains sent a note to the Tetons explaining that the party was prepared for hostilities but desired peace. Knowing their relations with surrounding tribes and perhaps recalling the party's difficulties with them over the last few days, Clark described them in his "Estimate of Eastern Indians" as "the vilest miscreants of the savage race, and must ever remain the pirates of the Missouri." After substituting heavy stones for the lost anchor, the men camped in the middle of the river on a sandbar about three miles above Oahe Dam between Stanley and Hughes Counties, South Dakota, having come about six miles. Clark complained that he was ill from lack of sleep.

SEPTEMBER 29, 1804. After the party set out, Partisan called from shore and asked for a ride upriver to the next Teton village. The captains refused the chief's entreaties. Partisan then offered women, but to no avail. Later the captains allowed him a ride across the river in one of the pirogues. After passing an abandoned Arikara village, the party camped for the night on a sandbar between Stanley and Sully Counties, South Dakota, about 3½ miles above Chantier Creek, Stanley County, and about eleven miles ahead for the day.

SEPTEMBER 30, 1804. During the day's journey, Indians came to the shore and asked the captains to join them for a meal. Clark explained the party's poor treatment by the Teton band below and refused the requests but did send tobacco to resident chiefs as a token of goodwill. Black Buffalo was handing out tobacco as well and admonishing good relations with the explorers. Later in the day the keelboat caught on a log, turned, and begin filling up with water. The crew got the boat righted, but the incident so frightened Black Buffalo that he decided to abandon the enterprise. He informed Lewis and Clark that they had seen the last of the Tetons. The captains gave him a blanket, knife, and tobacco, shared a smoke, and sent him on his way. After traveling about twenty miles, the party camped on a sandbar in Sully County, South Dakota, just below the mouth of Cheyenne River on the opposite shore.

OCTOBER 1, 1804. A cold, hard wind blew throughout the night and was still up when the party set out in the morning. Stiff winds and numerous sandbars forced a delay of several hours later in the day, but they made about sixteen miles. Along the route the captains noticed that ash and poplar leaves were fading and turning yellow, as were those of shrubs. In his field notes Clark observed that sharp-tailed grouse were booted and that the shape of their feet enabled them to walk on snow. They passed abandoned Arikara villages below the mouth of the Cheyenne River, testifying again to the ferocity of the Sioux who had pushed the Arikaras out of the region. Clark was mistaken that the river and the Cheyenne Indians derived the name from the French word for dog, *chien*; he would later discover the mistake and correct himself. The captains had an opportunity to visit with French trader Jean Vallé, who had a trading post a few miles above the mouth of the Cheyenne River.

He told them about the Cheyenne River, the Black Hills of South Dakota, and Cheyenne Indians. The party camped on a sandbar in sight of Vallé's post in either Dewey or Sully County, South Dakota.

OCTOBER 2, 1804. Vallé boarded the keelboat for a short ride upriver. Later in the day an Indian tried to get the party to come ashore, but the captains refused his entreaties. Since he was looking to trade, they told him of Vallé's establishment downriver. Worrying about the Tetons, the captains put the men on guard and no hunters were sent out. Whitehouse, perhaps overly concerned about Indian attack, declared that the captains were determined to keep going and that the men were "determined to fight or dye." But all was peaceful at camp on a sandbar just above Plum Island (now submerged), with Sully County, South Dakota, on the east, and Dewey County on the west. Being on alert, however, they dubbed the island "Caution."

OCTOBER 3, 1804. An Indian carrying a turkey came to shore in the afternoon and four others soon joined him, but if the captains had any conversation with them they did not record it. On examining their store of goods, the men saw that mice had cut into bags, gotten to the corn, and damaged cloth and paper. They had difficulty finding a passable channel in the river, so landed on a sandbar for the night near the line of Potter and Dewey Counties, South Dakota, making about eleven miles. The captains sent out men to find a route through the sandbars for the next day.

OCTOBER 4, 1804. The party had to drop back three miles to find a channel deep enough to permit the keelboat's passage but still gained twelve miles for the day. More Indians called for the men to come ashore, and one even "skipped" a ball across the boat's bow. Another swam to the boat asking for gunpowder, but the captains simply handed out tobacco and moved on. They found another abandoned Arikara village ("La ho catt") on Dolphees Island (now submerged) that had been deserted about five years but still had a perimeter palisade and seventeen lodges standing. The party camped on a sandbar just above the village, between Dewey and Potter Counties, South Dakota. During these first days of October Lewis collected specimens from the semiarid, northern sector of the Great Plains that he was entering, including fragrant sumac, silver sagebrush, white sage, Rocky Mountain juniper, long-leaved sage, and fire-on-the-mountain.

OCTOBER 5, 1804. A slight frost occurred during the night, but the temperature was in the midfifties by late afternoon. Snow geese and brants were flying south—another sign of winter's approach. Shooters took four pronghorns from a herd crossing the river. Ordway pronounced it "Sweet Good meat." Near the mouth of Swift Bird Creek Clark located an island covered with Canada wild rye. The party refreshed themselves with a shot of whiskey each before settling into camp in Potter County, South Dakota, in an area later inundated by the Oahe Reservoir.

OCTOBER 6, 1804. Passing an abandoned Arikara village, Clark took time to inspect the characteristic earth lodges of Missouri River village Indians. Inside one he found a number of domestic items and a bullboat, a craft made by stretching buffalo skins over a hemispherical frame. In nearby gardens he discovered three kinds of squashes; the men gathered some. Shields got an elk nearby and Lewis and Clark counted birds, noticing geese, swans, brants, ducks, sharptailed grouse, and magpies but few gulls or plovers. After making about fourteen miles the party camped here at the mouth of Swan ("Otter") Creek, Walworth County, South Dakota.

OCTOBER 7, 1804. At the mouth of the Moreau ("*Sur-war-kar-ne*") River, the party saw another abandoned Arikara village of about sixty lodges, very similar to the one of the day before. Two Teton Indians who were on their way to find Arikaras met the party and asked for food. Clark gave them venison. Near the Moreau River the men saw the tracks of a grizzly ("white") bear and killed a badger ("Brarrow"). They stripped the badger for its skin and bones to ship back East with other items the captains were collecting. One man killed a mule deer—the largest doe Clark had seen. Moving on, the party made camp near Mobridge, Walworth County, South Dakota, having traveled about twenty-two miles.

OCTOBER 8, 1804. Near the mouth of Grand ("We-har-too") River, the men finally came to an occupied Arikara village on later Ashley Island. Here they met Joseph Gravelines, who had lived among the Arikaras for a number of years and proved a useful interpreter for the corps. The Caddoan-speaking Arikaras were established in three villages at the Grand River in Corson and Campbell Counties, South Dakota. They were Great Plains Indians in transition from sedentary horticulturalists to seminomadic horseback hunters who lived in earth lodge villages and carried on extensive trade with men like Gravelines and with neighboring and nomadic natives. In his "Estimate of Eastern Indians" Clark calculated that the tribe had between two thousand and three thousand people at the villages. He also wrote forcefully about their difficult situation with the "lawless, savage and rapacious" Teton Sioux, who "rob them of their horses, plunder their gardens and fields, and sometimes murder them, without opposition." The corps established camp between Oak and Fisher Creeks, Corson County, South Dakota, where they would remain until October 11. Lewis determined the latitude of the mouth of the Grand River as 45° 39′ 05″ N; it is now nearer 45° 34′ 40″ N.

OCTOBER 9, 1804. A council with the Arikaras was put off due to rain, wind, and cold weather. The captains did meet briefly with the three village chiefs—Kakawissassa or Lighting Crow, Pocasse or Hay, and probably Too Né or Whippoorwill. There is some confusion about the last person, whose name is also given as "Arketarnarshar" (variously spelled). His name may be a title ("village chief") rather than an eponym, and he is probably the Arikara who went with Lewis and Clark to Washington DC in 1806. They also met Pierre-Antoine Tabeau, another trader among the Arikaras who also served as interpreter and informant for the captains. The Arikaras marveled at York, the first black man they had seen. York apparently enjoyed the attention and declared to inquisitive Indians that he had once been a wild animal who was caught and tamed by Clark. Then he demonstrated feats of strength. As customary, the men raised a flagpole in preparation for the next day's council.

OCTOBER 10, 1804. After breakfasting with Gravelines and Tabeau and then delaying for a time so Pocasse and Too Né from the upper villages could get there, the council eventually got underway about one o'clock in the afternoon, beneath an awning with the U.S. flag overhead. The officers passed out gifts (an American flag, red coats, cocked hats, and medals to the chiefs), made their usual speeches, and demonstrated modern technology by shooting the air gun. Again, York was a source of interest and he apparently made the most of it, exhibiting himself a little too much in Clark's estimation. Ordway visited the Arikara village and viewed about sixty earth lodges compactly arranged. He also found a considerable crop of corn, beans, pumpkins, squashes, watermelons, and tobacco. Warmly accepted in one lodge, he enjoyed a bowlful of beans and corn and three more servings of different foods before returning to camp. Gass also made a visit and provided a detailed description of a typical Plains Indian earth lodge.

OCTOBER 11, 1804. Another council with the Arikaras gave the chiefs an opportunity to respond to the captains' speeches. Kakawissassa thanked the officers and said he was ready to follow their advice and be open to peaceful relations with neighboring tribes and to trade with Americans. After the meeting, the party set out upriver, taking Kakawissassa and other chiefs with them a short distance to other Arikara villages. They camped a few miles above Fisher Creek, Corson County, South Dakota. Ordway reported that cooks found no wood nearby, so they looked elsewhere for kindling but had an axe stolen in the process. Nevertheless, Gass declared them the "most friendly and industrious" Indians he had met, as well as the "most cleanly." Despite apparent poverty, the Arikaras shared their food with the American visitors. Among the food offerings, Clark enjoyed a flavorful species of native beans, the hog peanut, that the Indians took from the underground stores of mice or voles.

OCTOBER 12, 1804. At Pocasse's lodge the captains began another meeting with the Arikara leaders. The chief presented the captains with seven bushels of corn, leggings, a robe, tobacco twists, and seeds of the tobacco plant. Lewis obtained a specimen of Arikara tobacco, a species that may be extinct. Pocasse, and later Too Né at the third village, reiterated Kakawissassa's sentiments of the previous day. Pocasse voiced hesitancy at visiting Washington, being concerned about his safety when passing through Sioux territory. Clark took time to estimate and evaluate the Arikaras. He judged them "Dirty, Kind, pore, & extravegent," possessing a pride that kept them from begging but ready to accept gifts and exchange goods. Although generally peaceful, the tribe could field from five hundred to six hundred warriors, now somewhat reduced in numbers by Euro-American diseases and warfare with the Sioux. Clark thought the men tall and well proportioned, the women small and industrious. Their clothing, though simple moccasins, leggings, waist flaps, and buffalo robes, was neatly decorated with fringe and colored beads.

Expedition soldiers traded energetically with the natives, who mostly wanted red paint but settled for anything the explorers had. One member of the party got a pair of moccasins for a pin hook, while other small articles bought buffalo robes. The Arikaras also offered women to the men as a token of esteem, but the captains refused despite repeated entreaties. York was another matter and seems to have participated in sexual liaisons at the insistence of native men who admired his color and his strength and offered their wives and sisters to him. Biddle described the man's sexual adventures in Latin in his notes but spelled it out plainly in his book. Taking one of the chiefs (probably Too Né) with them, the party continued on accompanied by the fiddle and the sounding horn. Two "Handsom young" women (according to Clark) followed the explorers. The party camped about ten miles above the previous camp but on the opposite shore in Campbell County, South Dakota.

OCTOBER 13, 1804. Newman was confined for "mutinous expressions." The party's journalists are silent about the extent of his remarks or the conditions of his confinement. At noon nine members of the corps convened for court-martial proceedings against Newman. The private pled not guilty but the court judged him guilty in every particular and sentenced him to seventy-five lashes on the bare back and to be expelled from the party. The captains concurred and further ordered him out of the regular enlisted men's pirogue, set him at hard labor during the remainder of his time with the party, released him from guard duty, and deprived him of his arms and ammunition. The physical punishment was to take place the next day.

Earlier in the day the party passed Spring ("Stone Idol") Creek, and Clark related a legend that provided the party's name for the stream. Opposite the creek Clark observed two stones resembling human figures and another that looked like a dog. The story concerning the features was a classic Romeo and Juliet story of two lovers whose parents would not permit them to marry. The man came with his dog to this point to mourn and his lover followed. They all turned gradually to stone but were able to live on grapes for a time. Clark fittingly observed great quantities of grapes in the area. The party camped about a mile south of the North Dakota state line in Campbell County, South Dakota, having come about eighteen miles.

OCTOBER 14, 1804. The party carried out Newman's punishment in the afternoon. The Arikara chief with them, Too Né perhaps, became very upset at the beating. When Clark explained the reason for the whipping, the chief replied that he had also found it necessary to take corrective action. The Arikaras, however, never inflicted corporal punishment, even on their children, but Too Né had put persons to death. Afterward the party moved on about a dozen miles and camped a few miles above the state line in Emmons County, North Dakota. Along the way the captains noticed that all the trees except cottonwoods had dropped their leaves.

OCTOBER 15, 1804. The party passed a number of Arikara hunting camps and were warmly received when they visited the occupants. The hunters offered meat while the explorers handed out fishhooks and beads. Farther on, at a small Arikara village of about ten lodges, they established camp in Emmons County, North Dakota, near Fort Yates, on the opposite side. Lewis and Clark visited the village, smoked, and shared food with the leading men. Again, the Indians were quite taken with York and in jest he would scare children who followed him. Village women were openly affectionate with the men.

OCTOBER 16, 1804. The two Arikara women who had followed the party since October 12 begged to go along with the corps. Clark did not record his reply, but the women are not heard of again. A short distance from their camp the party passed an abandoned Cheyenne village, dating to an earlier period when the Cheyennes had occupied sites along the Missouri before adopting a nomadic life and moving onto the plains. Clark again called them "Chiens," still thinking their name derived from the French word for "dog"; later he would learn otherwise. While Lewis walked on land with the Arikara chief, Clark observed Indian boys in the water killing pronghorns as they swam the river. Other Indians along the banks would shoot the "goats" with bows and arrows and keep the animals confined to the river, where they were easier to kill. Clark counted fifty-eight pronghorns killed and lined up along the shore. One of the party on shore with Lewis took advantage of the situation and killed three of them. After they arrived at camp about two miles above and opposite Big Beaver Creek, Sioux County, North Dakota, and about fourteen miles from the previous camp, Indians came in shouting and singing and bringing food. Corps members joined the revelry.

While out this day and the next Lewis collected more vegetation, including creeping and common junipers and silver-leaf scurfpeas, the latter used by natives in a decoction to wash their wounds. The captain also captured a live poorwill, which he kept for a few days, observing its languid behavior. On a freezing morning he plunged his penknife into the bird and noted that it lived for nearly two hours after the operation. The poorwill is one of the few birds that go into a state of torpor similar to hibernation, a fact that was not verified until the 1940s.

OCTOBER 17, 1804. This day was Clark's turn to stroll the river's edge with the Arikara chief. He also had Gravelines along, who interpreted the many stories the chief related about turtles, snakes, and a rock that could tell everything. Regrettably Clark did not include the stories in his notebook. The captain also learned from the chief that the numerous pronghorns crossing the Missouri were headed toward their wintering spot in the Black Hills. In the spring, they would return to the plains. Clark was also gathering geographic information from Gravelines, who was familiar with the country. Hard headwinds detained the party until about ten in the morning and camp was not made until dark a few miles below the mouth of the Cannonball River, Sioux County, North Dakota. The party witnessed the passage of snow geese and pronghorns making their way to the Black Hills.

OCTOBER 18, 1804. At the Cannonball River the men discovered numerous stones that gave the stream its name and collected one as a substitute for the keelboat's lost anchor. Two unidentified French traders coming downriver reported that the Mandans had robbed them of traps, tools, and furs. Being employed by Gravelines, they traveled with the corps for a time. The party's hunters had an easy time with finding prey: pronghorns, deer, and elks were readily killed. At one point they saw nearly 250 elks. The night's camp was a short distance above Rice Creek, Morton County, North Dakota, and about thirteen miles beyond the last camp.

OCTOBER 19, 1804. On a walk Clark saw more than fifty-two buffalo and three gangs of elks in one sighting. To the east the captain viewed a number of cone-shaped hills, one of which was probably modern Sugarloaf Butte, whose height Clark estimated to be ninety feet. The party's Arikara informant told the captain that the calumet bird, the golden eagle, lived in crevices in the hills that were formed by water pressure from above. The chief further informed Clark that the abandoned Indian village near the hills was formerly occupied by Mandan Indians, the party's first encounter with remnants of the tribe's former homelands. Traveling about seventeen miles, they set up the night's camp near the hills in Morton County, North Dakota, and a short distance from the mouth of Apple Creek on the opposite side.

OCTOBER 20, 1804. Consulting his copies of John Thomas Evans's maps, a traveler who had visited this area in 1795–96, Clark went in search of the "remarkable places" Evans had depicted. He witnessed instead more abandoned Mandan villages, which had been unsuccessfully fortified against enemy attack. Unrelenting assaults eventually drove the Mandans north in search of security. Near the mouth of the Heart River, the former Mandan center, he probably saw On-a-Slant Village, which has been the source of intensive archaeological investigation in the twentieth century. After about a dozen miles the explorers established camp below the mouth of Heart River, Morton County, North Dakota, and a few miles south of the town of Mandan. During the day Cruzatte wounded a grizzly bear but dropped his rifle and tomahawk in a rush to leave the scene. He was able to retrieve his weapons later, only to be chased by a wounded buffalo. Clark noticed fresh grizzly tracks on his walk and measured them as three times larger than human footprints. He also observed that wolves were the constant companions of buffalo herds, seeking out the accident prone or vulnerable ones who fell behind.

OCTOBER 21, 1804. At daybreak snow began to fall and continued throughout the morning. The captains gained additional information about Plains Indian culture from their Arikara informant. Clark observed a lone tree on the plains near the Heart River and learned that it had withstood the ravages of prairie fires and had obtained religious significance to the Mandans. It was also used in Mandan rituals, especially the annual Sun Dance (Okipa) ceremony, where participants endured great physical pain by lancing their back or chest muscles, inserting bone skewers through them, and then attaching cords to the bone and linking them to the tree. As they danced around the tree and fell back on the cords, the skewers would eventually break through the muscles and skin and the dancer would collapse. Attendants and friends would care for the wounds and the dancer would receive great acclaim for his courage and endurance. After coming about seven miles the party camped at or above Mandan, Morton County, North Dakota.

OCTOBER 22, 1804. Clark awakened in the middle of the night with a severe pain in his neck, so extreme that he was unable to move. Lewis applied a heated stone wrapped in cloths, which gave Clark some relief, but he continued to have spasms of pain throughout the day. Sometime after their early departure, the men came upon a dozen Tetons who were apparently on their way to or returning from attempts to steal horses from the Mandans. The corps refused to share food or hospitality with them. Hunters brought in a buffalo bull and related that they had seen a herd of three hundred buffalo without a single cow in the group. French trappers in the party were catching several beavers every night, perhaps with the hope of gaining profits in St. Louis on their return. Clark noted another abandoned Mandan village on the east side of the river somewhat above and across from Square Butte Creek. It is now called Double Ditch and is a North Dakota State Historic Site in Burleigh County. The men camped farther north in Oliver County near the Oliver-Morton county line, having come about twelve miles.

OCTOBER 23, 1804. Another early morning snow indicated winter's approach. More deserted Indian villages were passed, some with smoldering campfires. The day continued cloudy and cold as the party moved ahead about thirteen miles and reached camp near Sanger, Oliver County, North Dakota. Men eagerly ate the abundant buffaloberries they found near the camp.

OCTOBER 24, 1804. Clark was still feeling the effects of neck pains, although they were easing some. The captain identified another abandoned village as a Hidatsa one, although he used the contemporary term for the tribe, Minitaris, which he would spell a number of ways. At noon the captains met one of the Mandan chiefs in his hunting lodge. The Arikara chief came forward and all had a ceremonial smoke and cordial discussions. For the night, the party camped about two miles below Washburn, McLean County, North Dakota, having made about seven miles.

OCTOBER 25, 1804. The way ahead proved difficult, as sandbars clogged the river and made locating the main channel nearly impossible. The party was also slowed down by frequently getting beached and by meeting hazardous riffles. Clark learned (probably from one of the Frenchmen or from the Arikara chief) that the Sioux had lately stolen a number of Hidatsa horses and on their way home had joined a party of Assiniboines, who killed them and took the horses. Moreover, a French trader, Ménard, who had lived among the Mandans and Hidatsas since the 1770s, had recently been killed by the Assiniboines as he was making his way north to British trading posts on the Assiniboine River in Canada.

Mandans now became numerous along the river's edge, lining the shores and shouting greetings to the party. Several Indians came in to visit the corps in the evening when the men set up camp in Oliver County, North Dakota, south of the Mercer-Oliver county line, about eleven miles above the previous one. Among the visitors was a son of a late Mandan chief. Clark was surprised that he had cut off the end joints of some of his fingers. The captain learned that this was a common practice, along with scarring the body, to denote grief for the deceased. Reuben Field complained of an aching neck and Cruzatte had pains in his legs; Clark confided in his journal that his pain persisted also.

OCTOBER 26, 1804. Leaving the Arikara chief with some Mandans, the party took on two of the tribe's chiefs from the first Mandan village, or at least they appeared as chiefs to Clark at the time. The Coal, whose Mandan name Clark gave as "Sho-ta-har ro-ra," was apparently an Arikara by birth who had been adopted by the Mandans. He was a rival to Black Cat, whom the captains considered the Mandans' head chief. The other person, Big Man, Le Grand, or O-he-nar, may have been an adopted Cheyenne prisoner. In later lists The Coal and Big Man appear as secondary chiefs or head men. The free trader Hugh McCracken also appeared with another man, having come to the village about a week or so earlier to set up trade.

With Clark's pain increasing and committed to having one of the officers at the boat at all times, the captains decided that Lewis should visit the first Mandan village, Mitutanka. Later known also as the Deapolis archaeological site, it was located a short distance above the party's camp in Mercer County, North Dakota, south of Stanton, about eleven miles from their last camp. The Mandans were typical Great Plains Indians village dwellers, being agriculturalists for the most part but resorting to horseback hunting on a regular basis. Additionally, they had become adept middle managers in the Missouri River trading system. From their villages near the mouth of the Knife River they carried on an extensive intertribal trade in several directions and over many miles. Euro-Americans from Canada and out of St. Louis were adapting to this existing trade network, adding important manufactured goods to the pre-European trading lists. In his "Estimate of Eastern Indians" Clark counted 1,250 people in the two Mandan villages and called them "the most friendly, well disposed Indians inhabiting the Missouri. They are brave, humane and hospitable."

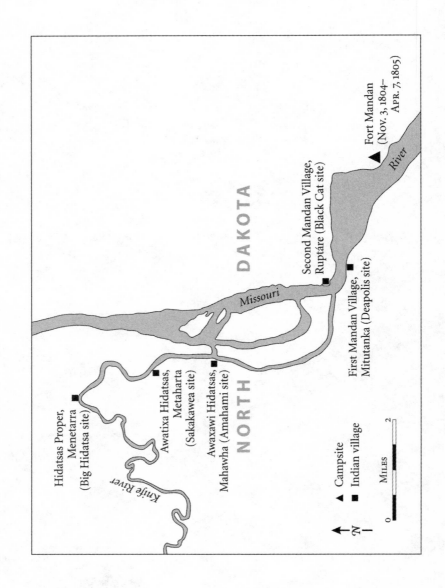

MAP 4. The expedition's route, October 27, 1804–April 6, 1805.

CHAPTER 3

Knife River Winter

October 27, 1804–April 6, 1805

OCTOBER 27, 1804. After getting an early start, the party passed Mitutanka, where the men spent a brief time before moving ahead to establish a camp opposite the mouth of the Knife River and modern Stanton, Mercer County, North Dakota. Clark walked up to the village and smoked with some leading men but was unable to share a meal due to his illness. Upon returning to the keelboat, he sent tobacco as a sign of friendship and respect and perhaps as a way to mollify the Mandans, who were disappointed that he did not eat with them. At Mitutanka the party met René Jusseaume, a free trader who had lived with the Mandans for about fifteen years and who had a wife and children at the village. Jusseaume told Clark that he had once worked for his brother, George Rogers Clark, but William Clark considered the Frenchman cunning and insincere. Despite his deficiencies in the language, Jusseaume served as Mandan interpreter for the captains. Jusseaume was still at the villages in the 1830s but apparently remained unskillful in Mandan. Later in the day Lewis visited the second Mandan village, Ruptáre; it has been designated the Black Cat archaeological site after its chief.

In the evening Lewis sent twists of tobacco to the three Hidatsa Indian villages to the north. Grouped along the Knife River, the inhabitants of three upper villages of the Hidatsas shared a common culture but saw themselves as quite distinct from one another. Lewis and Clark were aware of these divisions and tried to make allowances for the differences in their negotiations with them. Viewed from south to north, the first Hidatsa village was Mahawha, called the Amahami archaeological site after an alternate name for the band, which was occupied by the Awaxawi Hidatsas. The inhabitants of Mahawha were the most distinct of the three Hidatsa divisions and were known to the captains by a number of names, among them Ahnahaways, Shoes, and Watersoons. The captains counted about two hundred people here. The middle village, Metaharta, is known as the Sakakawea archaeological site, because this was where the captains found the Shoshone woman, Sacagawea; it was the village of the Awatixa Hidatsas. Farthest north were the Hidatsas proper, who lived at Menetarra, the Big Hidatsa archaeological site. The captains grouped these two villages in their count and numbered about twenty-five hundred people living in them. Like the Mandans, the Hidatsas were Siouan speakers.

Members of the five villages had come together at the Knife River settlement for mutual protection against their common enemies, the Sioux and Arikaras. Lewis and Clark called the Hidatsas by a number of names that they learned from traders and informants at St. Louis and along the way. Most often they used the French term Gros Ventres or its English equivalent, "Big Bellies," which derived from the Plains Indian sign-language gesture, or some version of "Minitaris," the Mandan designation for the Hidatsas. Although both the Hidatsas and the Mandans were late arrivals at the Knife River, generally settling there in the late 1780s, the two groups appear to have had a long association at other sites lower on the Missouri River. Like their allies, the Mandans, and other Great Plains Indians, the Hidatsas practiced horticulture and participated in the hunt, principally for buffalo. In his "Estimate of Eastern Indians" Clark declared them "in their customs, manners, and dispositions . . . similar to the Mandans." While the Hidatsas joined the Mandans in the rich trade brought to the villages, the Hidatsas appear to have had the stronger military tradition. They carried out raids as far as the Rocky Mountains against Shoshones and Salish and attacked enemies at other distant spots. Indeed, it was on one such raid against the Shoshones that Sacagawea was captured and brought to the Knife River settlement.

OCTOBER 28, 1804. A hard wind out of the southwest prevented meeting the Indians in council, but some of the leading men came to the party's camp. Black Cat, apparently the principal chief of Ruptáre and of the Mandans as a whole, was able to come to the

camp because he did not have to cross the river, as would the Mitutanka chiefs. He was an important visitor and one who could advise
the captains about village leaders and the political situation of the
Knife River settlement. Some Hidatsa leaders were able to reach the
camp, so the captains made arrangements for a general council of
all the village leaders for the next day. Lewis, Clark, and Black Cat
walked upriver for a distance looking for an acceptable spot to build
the party's winter fort but were unsuccessful. The party remained
at the camp opposite Stanton.

OCTOBER 29, 1804. The captains shared breakfast with the elderly
headman of the Hidatsa village Menetarra, The Grape (known by
many names, among them Caltarcota). The old man had relinquished authority to his son, Man Wolf Chief, who was now with a
war party traveling to the Rocky Mountains to fight the Shoshone
Indians. Despite his age and diminished authority, The Grape still
played an important role in village life. After breakfast an awning
was erected and sails from the boats were adjusted to keep the wind
down, and the proceedings got underway. The captains made the
usual speeches and passed the peace pipe among the Mandans, the
Hidatsas, and the Arikara chief who had come upriver with the
corps. Gifts were also distributed and the air gun demonstrated
before the council broke up. Later in the day the prairie caught fire
and killed a woman and a man who could not escape; others were
severely burned. One boy, apparently of European parentage, escaped
the flames. Assigning magical powers to the boy's luck, some Indians thought he had been saved because he was partly white. Clark
pointed to more prosaic reasons. His mother had thrown a green
buffalo robe over him and the fire did not burn through the hide.
Apparently she was the woman lost to the conflagration.

Clark now had enough information from this day's council and
his previous interview of The Grape to develop a list of villages and
principal men. For Mitutanka, the first Mandan village, he listed Big
White (Sha-ha-ka, or Sheheke) and Little Crow (Ka-goh-ha-mi or
Little Raven); at Ruptáre, the next Mandan village, he noted Black
Cat (Pass-cop-sa-he) and Raven Man Chief (Car-gar-no-mok-She)
as chiefs. For the three Hidatsa villages, Clark counted Mahawha as

the third village overall, an Awaxawi Hidatsa village led by White Buffalo Robe Unfolded (Ta-tuck-co-pin-re-ha); the fourth village was Metaharta of the Awatixa Hidatsas, with Black Moccasin (Omp-se-ha-ra) and Little Fox (Oh-harh) as leaders; and farthest north was the final village, Menetarra of the Hidatsas proper, led by Le Borgne (One Eye), principal chief of the Hidatsas. Again, the party remained at the camp opposite Stanton.

OCTOBER 30, 1804. Tribal leaders who had been absent from the previous day's meeting came to the camp to hear the captains' words. Perhaps a little perturbed, Clark complained that these natives did not understand the process of regular councils. Their late arrival and apparent restlessness during the discussions were not reassuring behavior to the captains. Later Clark gathered eight men from the corps in the small pirogue and went searching upriver for a good location for the winter fort. He found one spot about seven miles above the camp that seemed inviting, but it proved to be too far from water. Informants discouraged him about the prospects above the party's camp: both wood and game were scarce in that direction. The captain decided that he would have to seek a location to the south with better access to water, wood, and game. For the time being the party remained at the camp opposite Stanton. In the evening the men entertained the natives with their dancing, and Clark gave each man a dram of alcohol.

OCTOBER 31, 1804. Black Cat invited the captains to Ruptáre to hear his reply to their speeches. Clark, two interpreters (Jusseaume probably being one), and perhaps others were received with great ceremony. The captain was seated on a robe beside the chief and then was honored when the chief wrapped a highly decorated robe over his shoulders. Elders from the village were seated in a circle inside Black Cat's lodge and joined in the occasion as the peace pipe was passed from hand to hand. Black Cat acknowledged the captains' words and spoke of his desire for peace. He looked forward to a time when his young men could hunt the prairies without fear of attack and the village women could work the fields without anxiety. He promised that his second chief and some leading men would accompany the Arikara chief back to his village to smoke the peace pipe and try to settle their differences. As a demonstration of his sincerity, Black Cat returned traps that had been stolen earlier from French trappers. Clark replied to Black Cat in a positive manner and returned to the party's camp. Along the way he met White Buffalo Robe Unfolded and Little Crow and invited them to the camp, where they talked and smoked for about an hour. Later Big White arrived dressed in clothes that the captains had given him; he had come to see the white men dance. Members of the corps were happy to oblige him and continued playing, singing, and dancing until ten o'clock that night.

NOVEMBER 1, 1804. In spite of a hard wind from the northwest, the trader McCracken left early en route to one of the British trading forts on the Assiniboine River, carrying with him a letter and documents from the captains to Charles Chaboillez, the North West Company factor on the Assiniboine River. Lewis and Clark wanted to apprise British officials of their presence at the Mandans and present their credentials, especially Lewis's passport from Edward Thornton, chargé d'affaires in Washington. That document was to ensure their passage across the Rockies and into country that was outside the boundary of the Louisiana Purchase. Big White, Big Man, and another chief from Mitutanka arrived at the corps' camp about ten o'clock and stated their intention to make peace with the Arikaras. In the evening Lewis and Clark went out from their camp, Lewis to Mitutanka to get corn and Clark in search of a location for their winter fort. The majority of the party remained at the camp opposite Stanton.

NOVEMBER 2, 1804. Clark located the spot for the party's winter fort, which the captains named in honor of their neighbors, Fort Mandan; they would remain here until April 7, 1805. Four men in Clark's party, Whitehouse apparently among them, set to work felling trees and readying the spot for the fort while Indians looked on. The captains considered themselves to be approximately 1,609 miles from their starting point at Wood River in Illinois. The site is about fourteen miles west of Washburn, McLean County, North

Dakota, but the Missouri's changing course may have washed a portion of the spot away. On November 16 the men moved into their
huts; four days later the captains occupied theirs, but some cabins
were not fully completed until November 27. Exterior work was not
entirely finished until about Christmas. Gass and Whitehouse provide the best descriptions of the fort, which was roughly triangular
in shape and about sixty feet in length on each side. It had four huts,
each fourteen feet square, facing each other on two sides with shed-
like roofs that descended into the fort from an eighteen-foot wall
on the exterior. A picketed entrance faced the Missouri. At the rear
angle the men built two huts for holding provisions and gear. Lewis
visited Mitutanka to let the chiefs know where the party planned
to winter; he returned in the evening with eleven bushels of corn.

NOVEMBER 3, 1804. The fort's foundation was established, cabins
began to go up, and the French *engagés* were dismissed. Although
some Frenchmen continued with the party at the fort, they were
off the expedition payroll. Some probably wintered with the Mandans and Hidatsas, while others returned to the Arikara villages,
and at least a few of the French boatmen returned with the expedition's keelboat in April. Jusseaume and his wife and child moved
to the fort, while another Frenchman, Lepage, was hired to replace
the discharged Newman. He thus became a member of the permanent party destined for the Pacific. Six hunters were sent downriver, but Gass estimated that they may have had to travel thirty to
forty miles to find good hunting. Little Crow had his wife carry in
a sixty-pound load of dried buffalo meat to the explorers. Lewis
and Clark gave her an axe and some tokens in appreciation. The
captains celebrated the establishment of Fort Mandan by giving a
dram of alcohol to each man in the party.

NOVEMBER 4, 1804. The Hidatsa-speaking French trader Charbonneau visited Lewis and Clark. He had been on a hunting trip
and now informed them that he had two Shoshone wives. This was
important information because the captains knew that they would
need the aid of the Shoshones when they reached the Rockies and
had to switch from canoes to horses. A person from that tribe who

could speak the language and relay information to the officers would be an indispensable addition to the party. The captains hired Charbonneau immediately and enlisted the services of one of the wives. Of course, Sacagawea was the one chosen for the trip.

NOVEMBER 5, 1804. The party began raising the two rows of huts that would serve as the winter's living quarters. The men chose the largest cottonwood timber they could find in the area. They also dug a latrine. At one of the Mandan camps below Fort Mandan the Indians captured one hundred pronghorns by fashioning an elaborate drive line and herding them into a sturdy pen from which they could not escape. Lewis spent the day writing, but not in a regular journal such as Clark's, or at least not in one that is now known to us. Clark suffered with his recurring rheumatism. The captains learned that Assiniboines had arrived at one of the Hidatsa villages (probably Metaharta) and many more were expected soon.

NOVEMBER 6, 1804. The captains were awakened by the sergeant of the guard to witness an aurora borealis. The streaks of light and changing colors fascinated the officers. Gravelines and the Arikara interpreter, along with La Jeunesse and Primeau, two of the French boatmen formerly with the party, set out for the Arikara villages. Gravelines had agreed to accompany the Arikara chief Too Né (perhaps the one here at the Mandans) to Washington DC in the spring. The trip was accomplished, but Too Né died in Washington in 1806.

NOVEMBER 7, 1804. Work continued on the huts in the fort.

NOVEMBER 8, 1804. Jusseaume informed the officers that traders from the Hudson's Bay Company would be coming to the Indian villages the next day. Villagers came round to watch the men work on the fort. The men were pushing their labors to make sure they finished the cabins before winter set in.

NOVEMBER 9, 1804. A hard frost lay about the camp this morning. Under difficult circumstances, noted but not elaborated on by Clark, work continued on building the huts inside the fort compound. Hunters were out, and the party was feeling the want of fresh meat. Indians passed the camp with "flying news" and brought with them a long-tailed weasel, which Clark briefly described; it was then unknown to science. Although the cottonwoods along the Missouri were not the best for building a fort, the trees served the Indians as a feed supplement for their horses. While normally the horses grazed on prairie grasses, during the winter the Mandans brought the animals into their lodges and fed them on the soft bark of cottonwoods.

NOVEMBER 10, 1804. It was probably The Coal who brought a side of buffalo meat to the captains, who gave him and his family small items in consideration. The family had crossed the river in a bull-boat and Clark noticed that the wife carried the boat on her back up to the next village when they departed.

NOVEMBER 11, 1804. Two unnamed members of the party cut themselves with an axe. Charbonneau's two Shoshone wives came to the fort.

NOVEMBER 12, 1804. Big White arrived for a visit and as was the custom his wife came bearing food, on this occasion one hundred pounds of meat, which she carried on her back. These were welcome provisions since the party's hunters had not returned. The captains gave her and her child small presents, including a small axe. Jusseaume was probably the interpreter who told Clark a Mandan creation story and the tribe's recent history. The accounts of the elders related that the tribe came out of a village below a lake. They lived in several villages lower on the Missouri River, but smallpox had reduced their numbers to an extent that they were not able to defend themselves against the Sioux. They moved farther up the Missouri and lived with the Arikaras for a time until difficulties between the two groups forced them on north to join the Hidatsas. Being a military man, Clark took note of the fighting forces the Knife River villages could raise. He counted about 350 fighting men for the Mandans and nearly 700 for the Hidatsas. Clark must have felt confident in the captains' recent negotiations, since he declared that these tribes had been at war with the Arikaras until the captains were able to bring about peace. Clark also gained information about the Crow Indians, relatives of the Hidatsas.

NOVEMBER 13, 1804. Lewis took six men upriver to gather stones for the fort's chimneys. Black Cat arrived with a chief of the Assiniboines, The Crane, Che Chark, or La Grue. Clark noted that the Assiniboines lived to the north and traded with the British on the Assiniboine River. The tribe consisted of three bands and could raise from six hundred to one thousand warriors. Clark wrote unfavorably about them in his "Estimate of Eastern Indians," describing them as "descendants of the Sioux, and partake of their turbulent and faithless disposition: they frequently plunder, and sometimes murder, their own traders." In the same manner the Assiniboines came to the Mandans to trade, although they occasionally warred against one another. For trading visits the Mandans had developed an adoption ceremony that allowed enemies to become temporary fictive relatives. The ceremony was to occur this night.

Ordway reported that Lewis returned in the evening with his party "much fatigued." The men's boat got stuck on a sandbar, and they were forced to be in ice-cold water for about two hours to free the boat. Finally out of the freezing water, their clothes froze tight on their legs; one man received a bit of frostbite on his feet. A taste of whiskey revived their spirits.

NOVEMBER 14, 1804. Clark noted that only two Indians visited the fort, a fact significant enough for comment. It was due to the adoption ceremony and dance of the previous night with the Mandans and the Assiniboines. Getting anxious about the hunters and feeling the want of meat, the captains sent one man by horseback to find out the reason for the delay.

NOVEMBER 15, 1804. The men continued work on the huts in the fort until after midnight. Drouillard arrived from the camp of the party's hunters, who were some thirty miles south of the fort, saying that their pirogue was loaded with meat. The captains sent a runner to tell them to return to the fort without delay. No Indians visited the fort.

NOVEMBER 16, 1804. Tree limbs bore a heavy frost this morning. Although the fort's huts were not completed, the men moved in. The Assiniboines visited the Hidatsa villages north of the Mandans but ill feelings surfaced over the loss of some horses. An Indian who visited the fort related the information, but it is unclear who stole the horses, the Assiniboines or the Hidatsas. The visitor wanted to trade four buffalo robes for a pistol, but the captains refused. The men stayed up late filling in the chinks between the logs of their huts to keep out winter's chill.

NOVEMBER 17, 1804. The frost of the day before fell from the trees in the afternoon like a shower of snow. More Indian visits and much work about the fort filled the day, particularly raising a meat and smoke house. The Arikara chief, perhaps Too Né, gave Lewis a specimen seed of Canada columbine and told the captain that tea made from the plant was a strong diuretic and also that Indian women chewed the seeds and rubbed their hair with them as a perfume.

NOVEMBER 18, 1804. Black Cat came for a visit with lots of questions and with his wife carrying a "back load" of ears of corn. First he was curious about the party's clothing and accouterments. Perhaps more important were the things he had to relate. At a Mandan council, the Indians decided to overlook recent problems with the Assiniboines and Crees until they could see how the captains' negotiations played out. Black Cat remembered earlier traders from St. Louis, such as John Evans, who promised guns and ammunition but never delivered. Clark tried to reassure the chief and explain that it took time to put the new trading patterns from the United States in operation. Before noon one of the Frenchmen of the party arrived with a fat elk.

NOVEMBER 19, 1804. The hunters came in about three o'clock in the afternoon with welcome provisions of thirty-two deer, twelve elks, and one buffalo. All were stored or hung in the fort's newly completed smokehouse. Running ice in the Missouri had detained the men until now. Clark received but did not relate a number of Indian stories.

NOVEMBER 20, 1804. Lewis and Clark moved into their huts. The Mandans who came for a visit were very curious about the fort. They told the captains that the Sioux above the Cheyenne River had been threatening to attack them. Arikara Indians had visited the Sioux carrying a peace pipe, but instead of hospitality they received a beating and had their horses stolen. Part of the Sioux displeasure with the Arikaras had to do with a peace between that tribe and the Mandans that was initiated by Lewis and Clark. It may have been Charbonneau with one of his wives who brought four horses loaded with meat to the fort.

NOVEMBER 21, 1804. The men were in high spirits as they began collecting stones for the chimneys and readied to finish the fort. Drouillard was probably less cheerful, since he injured his hand. Other tasks of the day included arranging and organizing equipment.

NOVEMBER 22, 1804. Pryor was sent to Ruptáre for one hundred bushels of corn from Jusseaume, but it turned out to be less corn than promised. About ten o'clock in the morning Clark learned that an Indian was about to kill his wife. The threats grew out of an incident the previous week because she had slept with Sergeant Ordway, for which the husband had already beat and cut her. Clark attempted to calm the situation and directed Ordway to give the man some gifts. The captain further explained to the husband that no one had touched his wife except Ordway, who had the man's permission, and that members of the party were careful not to have relations with married women. Finally, Clark ordered the men to have nothing to do with the woman in the future. Black Cat arrived during the confrontation and lectured the husband. Husband and wife then left, the man being dissatisfied with the outcome. Ordway was silent on these matters in his journal. Black Cat stayed at the fort and told Clark many stories that also went unrecorded.

NOVEMBER 23, 1804. The men gathered more stones, apparently for the fort's chimneys. Others were employed in making a rope to pull the keelboat up on the bank. Several of the men, however, had bad colds and Shields suffered with rheumatism.

NOVEMBER 24, 1804. Illnesses continued but work went on. Split logs were raised to cover the huts. Men finished the strong multi-cord elkskin rope for hauling the keelboat to shore.

NOVEMBER 25, 1804. Lewis took Charbonneau, Jusseaume, and six men with him to visit Knife River villages while the rest of the party worked to cover the huts and fill the chinks. While Lewis and the interpreters went on horseback, the rest of the detachment took a pirogue up the Missouri. The huts were largely completed, but work remained on the roofs, which was completed on November 27. Two Hidatsa chiefs, Black Moccasin and apparently Red Shield, visited the fort—the first Hidatsas to travel down to the party's encampment. Clark gave them special attention and presented them with several gifts, but he felt the want of an interpreter during the meeting. Since the interpreters were with Lewis, Clark had to make do.

NOVEMBER 26, 1804. A hard northwesterly wind that deepened the cold caused work to come to a near standstill at the fort. Lewis visited with Hidatsas at their villages, but it is not clear at which villages he spent time.

NOVEMBER 27, 1804. Lewis returned to the fort with two chiefs and a leading, unidentified man from the Hidatsa villages. Mar-noh-toh, or The Big Stealer, and Man-nes-sur-ree (also Man-se-rus-se), or Tail of Calumet Bird, who had earlier been listed as subsidiary chiefs at Metaharta, now had disquieting news for the captains. They related that they had learned from the Mandans that the explorers were going to join the Sioux against them. The activities around the fort—with interpreters and families moving inside—seemed to confirm their worst suspicions. Lewis tried to allay these fears and convince the Hidatsas of the Americans' friendly intent. Despite these fears and misgivings, Lewis was received cordially by all, except

Mar par pa par ra pas a too (also Maw-pah-pir-re-cos-sa too), or Horned Weasel, a head man of Menetarra who relayed a message to Lewis that he was not at home. The captains' efforts were further undermined when one of the British traders, Baptiste Lafrance of the North West Company, spread bad rumors about the corps. Lewis complained firmly to François-Antoine Larocque and Charles McKenzie, principal men of the company, about Lafrance's conduct. Difficulties seemed to fade with the evening light and the Indians enjoyed themselves as the explorers danced around the campfires, with *engagé* Rivet showing considerable flair.

NOVEMBER 28, 1804. The Missouri River was filling up with floating ice. The snow that began at seven o'clock continued all day but did not prevent Black Cat from visiting. He joined the Hidatsa chiefs in viewing the curiosities of American manufacture and probably obtained gifts like those distributed to his neighbors. Before departing the captains had a serious talk with the chiefs about the British traders' practice of distributing medals and flags. The symbolic nature of these gifts was not lost on the captains, and they declared that such emblems of authority were the prerogative of Americans and that the chiefs should not accept them. With no elaboration, Ordway indicated that a jealousy between Jusseaume and Drouillard had flared up.

NOVEMBER 29, 1804. Another night of snow brought its depth in the woods to over one foot. When Larocque came to the fort, the captains confronted him about the distribution of the medals and flags. Larocque denied having made such gifts but agreed to keep his conversations with the Indians confined to trading matters. Pryor dislocated his shoulder when he was taking down the mast on the keelboat. It took four attempts before the shoulder was reset, but apparently not fully, since he suffered from the accident throughout the trip.

NOVEMBER 30, 1804. Disturbing news about a Lakota Sioux attack against a Mandan hunting party in which one man was killed reached the captains and stirred them to action. Within an hour of receiving the news, Clark gathered twenty-three volunteers from the corps and set out to enlist Indian supporters to repel a possible attack. The captains agreed that a show of force would demonstrate that the United States would aid allies and oppose those who challenged the peace plan they were trying to establish. Clark crossed the ice-covered Missouri River and marched to the first Mandan village, where he found the inhabitants alarmed at the appearance of his battle-ready troops. The leading men of the village brought the captain into a lodge, where he explained the nature of his undertaking, that is, to assemble a force large enough to withstand an attack and then punish the offenders so they would not war against American allies again

Clark deemed the Mandans reluctant to take up the fight, and they begged off because of the deep snows, the severe weather, and the distance the perpetrators would have now put between themselves and their pursuers. The Mandans counseled patience and wanted to wait until spring to seek revenge. Moreover, the chiefs added that they understood that several Arikara warriors were with the Sioux in the attack. This was unsettling news to Clark since it would undermine the captains' efforts to establish an accord between the Mandans and the Arikaras. He spent some time trying to reverse this opinion, explaining that bad seeds may have been among the attackers but that their action was probably not approved by the Arikara leadership. After two hours of deliberations, Clark recrossed the Missouri to the fort. A round of rum must have been small consolation for a day of numbing cold and meager results.

DECEMBER 1, 1804. Work on the fort continued as pickets were set up around a portion of the exterior. An Indian visitor informed the captains that seven Cheyenne and three Arikara Indians had arrived at the Mandans for trading. It must have eased Lewis and Clark's apprehensions about the presence of Arikaras so close to the events of the previous day when they learned that the Mandan chiefs had forbidden their tribesmen to harm the visitors. Clark also noted the arrival of George Henderson of Hudson's Bay Company from the Assiniboine River in Canada, who was there to compete with North West Company traders in exchanges with Hidatsas in the area.

DECEMBER 2, 1804. Several Mandan chiefs brought four of the Cheyennes to the fort. The captains gave them their standard speech for Indians and presented them with a flag and tobacco. They also asked the Cheyennes to relay a letter to the traders Tabeau and Gravelines at the Arikara villages, asking them to intercede in case any hostilities were developing among the Arikaras and Sioux. Others gifts were distributed as the natives departed.

DECEMBER 3, 1804. The father of the young Mandan killed by the Sioux on November 30 brought dried pumpkins and pemmican to the party and was given small gifts.

DECEMBER 4, 1804. Another cold, cloudy, windy, raw day. Black Cat and two young chiefs visited the fort and spent the day. Clark intimated that the captains were finding the interpreter Jusseaume to be "assumeing and discontent'd," reinforcing Clark's initial estimate of the man in October. The leaders continued to use his interpreting services in spite of their low opinion of him. Biddle added a paragraph in his book about Mandan religion that is not found in expedition journals. He wrote that the tribe's whole religion consisted of the belief that one great spirit presided over their destinies, one they looked to for healing, attributing "great medicine" to anything they did not understand.

DECEMBER 5, 1804. Two traders from the North West Company informed the captains that they would be setting out with additional men for their fort on the Assiniboine River in a couple of days. More Indians came by and brought gifts of pumpkins. The men built a platform on the smokehouse for guards to walk on and be able to see beyond the fort's walls.

DECEMBER 6, 1804. A Mandan and his wife brought meat to the fort and Clark noticed his clothing of buffalo-skin moccasins, pronghorn-skin leggings, and a buffalo robe—rather light attire when the temperature was a mere 10° above zero at eight in the morning. The fourteen brass rings on his fingers made an impression on the captain, who noted the Mandan fondness for ornamentation. With the weather so cold, little work was accomplished on the fort. Clark went hunting with sixteen men, and some got frostbitten.

DECEMBER 7, 1804. During the night the Missouri blocked up with ice measuring 1½ inches thick. When Big White brought news of buffalo nearby, Lewis mounted a hunting party of fifteen men and killed fourteen of the shaggy beasts, but wolves shared in the hunt and only five bison were brought back to the fort. Part of the loss was due to Indian custom, which dictated that any animal seen without an identifying arrow or marker on it was fair game for the finder. Fleet-footed natives beat the party to several downed buffalo. The Indians were also more successful in the hunt because they had well-trained horses that moved close to the buffalo but stayed free of horns or charging strays. Three men in the party reported frostbite. Later the men celebrated and warmed themselves with a taste of rum passed around by the captains.

DECEMBER 8, 1804. Clark made his own excursion to the buffalo, again with fifteen men, and had better luck than on the previous day's hunt. The party killed eight buffalo and one deer, brought in a cow and a calf, and left some of the men to tend the rest and ward off wolves. Frostbite again afflicted some of the hunters, one severely, and York's feet and penis were slightly frostbitten. The hunters shared a drink of rum, courtesy of Clark. A sun dog, or parhelion, appeared twice as the sun's rays reflected off ice crystals in the atmosphere.

DECEMBER 9, 1804. Taking full advantage of the buffalo, Lewis set out with eighteen men, including Gass, and four horses to bring in as much meat as possible. Part of the hunting party led the horses back in the evening, loaded with buffalo meat, while Lewis stayed with the rest at his hunting camp. At noon two chiefs brought in more meat. Two interpreters, perhaps Jusseaume and another person, went to the Indian villages.

DECEMBER 10, 1804. Lewis returned at noon but left six men to continue work on the buffalo. He had experienced an uncomfortable night in the cold with only a small blanket for cover. The temperature at eight o'clock was 10° below zero, so it must have been considerably colder during the night. Due to the cold, guard duty at the fort was rotated hourly. The captains passed out heavy blanket coats to each man who needed one. One of the Mandans who had been wounded in the fight with the Sioux on November 30 came to the fort for medical attention.

DECEMBER 11, 1804. Ice in the atmosphere created more sun dog images. All hunters returned to the fort, some a little frostbitten, but with three horses loaded with buffalo meat. Black Cat came by for a visit.

DECEMBER 12, 1804. As another guard against the cold northern winds, Clark lined his gloves with three-inch lynx, or bobcat, fur. A Hidatsa Indian from Mahawha brought a pronghorn to the fort that he had killed nearby. Clark made a point to record the Mandan word, *kóke*, for the animal, which he called a cabri or antelope. The captains did not think it wise to send hunters out to hunt under the severe winter conditions. Clark thought that the party might acclimate themselves in time and then be hardy enough for outdoor excursions. Nonetheless, the captain took time outside to measure the width of the ice-bound Missouri and found it five hundred yards across. Although the party's huts were warm and comfortable, Ordway noted that the guards who stood out in the weather suffered mightily and had to be relieved every hour.

DECEMBER 13, 1804. Atmospheric conditions made it impossible to get an astronomical fix on their site. In spite of the cold and such impediments to the captains' scientific work, Clark called it "a fine day." And, incredibly, there was some visiting back and forth. A couple of men from Ordway's squad went to Mitutanka and bought back some corn and beans in exchange for some paint and a few rings and other goods. One of the North West Company traders came down from Menetarra. Joseph Field killed a buffalo cow and calf within a mile of the fort and an Indian brought a pronghorn to the captains.

DECEMBER 14, 1804. Clark took a party hunting some eighteen miles to the south. The buffalo were too poor to bother with, but the hunters killed two deer, set up camp, and hoped for better results the next day. Fourteen Mandans crowded into Ordway's room for a meal while Big White visited with Lewis.

DECEMBER 15, 1804. With no buffalo in sight, Clark set out for the fort hoping to encounter buffalo along the way. He sent hunters along both sides of the Missouri on the way back, but their efforts were unsuccessful and they arrived at the fort empty-handed. Clark found several Indian chiefs at the fort awaiting his return, among them Big White and Big Man. Ordway and a couple of men went to the Mandan villages. Given that the temperature was near zero, they were surprised to discover the Indians playing their hoop and pole game, skimming flat stone rings around a yard with sticks in a contest similar to modern hockey. The sergeant noticed the players keeping count but could not discover the scoring system. At each lodge the men were welcomed and fed; they found the occupants very friendly.

DECEMBER 16, 1804. The moon made a hazy appearance through the night's frosty atmosphere. Hugh Heney of the North West Company, along with Larocque of the same firm and George Bunch (or Budge) of Hudson's Bay Company, came to the fort during the day. Heney carried a letter from Chaboillez expressing his desire to cooperate with the explorers, probably in response to Lewis's letter to him of October 31. Heney also showed the captains the root of the narrow-leaved purple coneflower and described its use as a cure for snakebites and rabies. Gass and a couple of other members of the party went for a visit to the two Mandan villages, where they were treated very kindly.

DECEMBER 17, 1804. Heney was quite obliging after spending a night at the fort, even providing the captains with sketches of the country between the Mississippi and Missouri Rivers in North Dakota and drawings of lands to the west that he had obtained from natives. Heney was also informative about various Siouan groups. Word came in that more buffalo had been sighted, and the Americans were invited by neighborhood chiefs to join in a hunt the next day. Another bitterly cold night required changing the fort's guard every hour. At eight o'clock in the evening the captains recorded a temperature of 42° below zero.

DECEMBER 18, 1804. Heney and Larocque departed as seven hunters from the party set out in pursuit of buffalo. The captains provided the traders with a sled built by Gass to haul goods to their encampment. Finding the weather severely cold, the party's hunters soon returned, having seen only pronghorns. Clark, perhaps inspired by Heney's information, began a small map of the connections of the rivers beyond the line of the corps' march. Spotty relations among resident traders surfaced, and Clark had to serve as arbitrator to a dispute. Apparently Black Cat had taken Charbonneau's horse under the impression from Lafrance that Charbonneau owed him the animal and it was the chief's to take. Clark had Jusseaume serve as the intermediary, and he was able to retrieve the horse.

DECEMBER 19, 1804. Clark continued to work on his map, while the men worked on the fort's pickets. Working hands had to be shifted between the cold outdoors work and the warmth of the cabins. Only about half the party could be working outside at a time.

DECEMBER 20, 1804. A moderate day at Fort Mandan; a temperature of 24° allowed further building around the fort.

DECEMBER 21, 1804. The Indian who had tried to kill his wife on November 22 came to the fort to make amends with one of the party's interpreters, unnamed by Clark. Lewis provided medicine for a child who suffered from an abscess on his lower back. The woman who brought the child offered as much corn as she could carry for the medical treatment.

DECEMBER 22, 1804. A number of Indian women came to the fort to sell corn for small items. Ordway identified the favored items as magnifying glasses, beads, buttons, and "articles pleasing to the

Eye." Gass and Whitehouse also counted old shirts, awls, and knives. Among the group were men dressed as women, perhaps male transvestites, who were to be found among plains tribes. Given the general name of "berdache," from a French term that connotes a male homosexual, the men may have been cross-dressers. Clark was rather matter-of-fact about them. In his postexpedition notes Biddle elaborated that boys who showed feminine inclinations were raised as girls and sometimes married men and performed wifely duties. The captains were able to obtain the horns of a bighorn sheep and Clark provided a description of the items and noted the Mandan name for the animal, "*Ar-Sar-ta*." The party may have seen a bighorn sheep as early as April 26, 1805, and Lewis wrote a description of the animal from specimens obtained by Clark, Bratton, and Drouillard on May 25, 1805.

DECEMBER 23, 1804. A great number of Indians ("of all descriptions," wrote Clark) arrived at the fort for trading. Little Crow also arrived, having loaded his wife and son with trade corn. Lewis distributed gifts while Little Crow's wife boiled a stew of squashes, beans, corn, and chokecherries. Although the Mandans considered the dish a special treat, Clark declared it merely palatable. The Mandans were growing fond of visiting the fort and especially enjoyed spending the night at the enclosure.

DECEMBER 24, 1804. More Indian visitors arrived, some for trade, some out of curiosity. The captains gave a two-inch strip of sheep skin to each of the chiefs in this group, quite a gift considering that the Indians valued the skins over a fine horse. The party finished exterior work around the fort and started on a blacksmith shop. In the evening the captains distributed flour, dried apples, pepper, and other goods in anticipation of Christmas fare.

DECEMBER 25, 1804. Christmas Day opened with a bang as three squads of soldiers and Frenchmen from the party fired off their weapons before daylight. The captains gave out a little rum, raised an American flag above the fort, and had the cannons fired. While some men hunted, others cleared out one of the cabins and danced away the evening until nine o'clock, when the fort fell into "peace & quietness," according to Ordway. The wives of Jusseaume and Charbonneau looked on but apparently did not join the dancing.

DECEMBER 26, 1804. An unusual day as the temperature moderated and no Indians came to visit, nor had any the day before, leaving Lewis able to enjoy a game of backgammon. Larocque sought the services of Charbonneau to assist in interpreting the Hidatsa language. The trader also reported that small parties of Hidatsas were coming back to their villages. They had pursued Assiniboine horse thieves as far as the Souris River in Canada, and one group of Hidatsas had acquired eight horses for their efforts.

DECEMBER 27, 1804. Indian visitors were impressed by the party's forge and bellows and the iron products the blacksmiths were able to fashion in the nearly completed blacksmith shop. Shields and Willard were the smiths.

DECEMBER 28, 1804. Hard winds and drifting snow left Clark to report that nothing remarkable happened.

DECEMBER 29, 1804. Becoming accustomed to a Mandan winter, Clark considered the temperature of 9° below zero unimpressive. Perhaps even less so Knife River residents who came by for a visit. They also brought items for the smiths to repair in the now-finished blacksmith shop. One expedition hunter killed a wolf and saved the skin for the traders, who would pay as much for it as for a beaver skin.

DECEMBER 30, 1804. Again Indian visitors noticed the party's ironworks. Ordway was intrigued with the food products the Mandans used for trade. In addition to the usual corn, beans, and squashes, they brought a sort of bread made from a mixture of parched corn and beans and fashioned into round balls.

DECEMBER 31, 1804. Blowing snow and sand created little hillocks around the fort. Interest in the ironworks brought orders for repairs on native axes and hoes. Corn was the immediate means of payment.

JANUARY 1, 1805. Celebrations for the New Year began early in the day when the men fired two cannons. Lewis gave each man a glass of "good old whiskey," according to Gass, followed by another round from Clark. Afterward several of the party made their way to Mitutanka, where the chiefs had asked them to join in dancing. The men took along the party's fiddle, tambourine, and sounding horn. Upon entering the village the men fired a round from their guns and started playing their instruments, marched to the center of the village, reloaded their weapons and fired again, then began dancing. Again, as on November 27, it was probably Rivet who demonstrated the fanciest steps. Then the men moved from lodge to lodge, enjoying the warmth of buffalo robes and their fill of corn as they showed off their dancing form.

Later in the day Clark walked up to the village but not for dancing. He was there for diplomacy because of an unknown misunderstanding between the party and the Indians of the village. Clark hoped to make matters right. At the village Clark found everyone enjoying the dancing explorers, so he had York show his dancing talents. These much amused the crowd, who found York's abilities exceptional for such a large man. The captain visited the lodges of the various chiefs to find out why they had been making unfavorable remarks about the Americans. The chiefs replied that the comments were made in jest, so the issue was dropped. As Clark was preparing to leave Mitutanka, Little Crow and Black Man arrived to report a mission they had been on to return an Atsina girl to her tribe. It seems that some Awaxawi Hidatsa, perhaps White Buffalo Robe Unfolded, had taken the girl and that a party of 150 Atsinas was on its way to extract vengeance or rescue the girl. Little Crow had been detailed to return the girl and smoke the pipe with the offended Atsinas and restore peace. His mission had been successful. Clark got back to the fort with most of the party, but half a dozen remained at Mitutanka. While the captain was away, Black Cat and his family brought meat to the fort.

JANUARY 2, 1805. A number of the party went to Ruptáre for dancing, performing for Black Cat in his lodge and probably elsewhere. Lewis, Gass, and perhaps Jusseaume joined them later and returned to the fort in the evening. Indians arrived at the fort with corn for blacksmithing services on their axes and bridles.

JANUARY 3, 1805. Eight men were hunting, but only a single jackrabbit and a wolf seem to have been the result of their efforts in the snow, or perhaps one old bull. Indians visited, one of whom, a Hidatsa, was looking for his wife, who had sought refuge from abuse at the fort.

JANUARY 4, 1805. Hunters out and Indians in, including Little Crow, who received a handkerchief and two files for his friendliness. Clark became ill in the latter part of the day.

JANUARY 5, 1805. While Clark worked on his map, Indians came by to have their axes mended by the party's smiths. Clark also took time to describe a ceremony at Mitutanka, now known as the Buffalo Calling Ceremony. The captain did his best to explain a custom that must have seemed very foreign to him. Relating this ritual in his history, Biddle reverted to Latin to describe the activities but was explicit in his notes, the reverse of similar accounts of October 12, 1804. As elder men formed a circle and smoked a ceremonial pipe, the young men of the village offered their wives as sexual tokens to older, respected villagers. The purpose of the ritual was to allow the younger men access to the spiritual power and hunting skills of the older men by using the wives as agents for the transfer. By having intercourse with his wife after she had relations with an elder, a young man could tap the power for himself. As Clark explained it, "all this is to cause the buffalow to Come near So that They may kill thim." Now the young men could possess the hunting prowess of tribal elders. One member of the party had attended the ceremony the previous evening and was offered four women. Seeing the novelty and usefulness of the corps' equipment and their skills at working iron, some Mandan men may have hoped to access the explorers' powers as well as the hunting success of their own elders. In his notes Biddle wrote, "White men . . . are generally preferred by the Squaws because they will give probably some present and for other obvious reasons."

JANUARY 6, 1805. Clark continued working on his map, uninterrupted by the few Indian visitors. Bratton trapped a fox that had gained access to the fort through a hole it had made in the pickets; it was after the bone pile of the party's butchers.

JANUARY 7, 1805. Big White, having returned from a hunt, stopped by the fort and provided the captains with a map of the country showing the drainage of the Yellowstone River and its subsidiaries coming in from the south. Big White described the river valley as very hilly, covered with timber, and crowded with beavers. Expedition hunters brought four deer and two wolves back to the fort but had suffered much from the cold for their efforts. Clark continued to work on his map, incorporating Big White's information along with that of traders as well as his own observations and speculations. He considered estimating the distance to the Great Falls of the Missouri but then left the space blank where he would have put the number of miles. It was perhaps Biddle who added the interlineation "800."

JANUARY 8, 1805. With only a few Indians at the fort, Ordway went to one of the villages, probably Mitutanka.

JANUARY 9, 1805. While other Indians were hunting buffalo, Little Crow stopped by for breakfast with the captains. One Indian came to the captains much distressed because he had sent his son to the fort and he was now not to be found.

JANUARY 10, 1805. One hunter from the party had separated from his comrade during the previous day and spent the night out. Worried about his welfare, five men prepared to find him but he came in and informed the party that he was able to make a fire and keep "tollarable comforable," in Ordway's words. It is unclear whether the thirteen-year-old boy that Clark mentioned as having his feet frozen was the youngster being sought on the previous day. The boy had been hunting with others and had spent the night outside without fire and with only a small robe, thin pronghorn-skin leggings, and buffalo moccasins for covering. The mercury dropped to 40°

below zero during the night. Despite their medications, including soaking his feet in cold water, the captains had to remove the boy's toes on January 27 and 31. In his book Biddle expanded on Clark's account to note the careful attention and considerable affection shown the boy, by both his father and villagers in general, in spite of the fact that he had been a prisoner and adopted by his parents "out of charity." Clark was amazed that another person who had stayed out, also without fire and with light clothing, did not seem affected by the severe cold.

JANUARY 11, 1805. The Field brothers, Shannon, Collins, and perhaps Whitehouse were hunting. Black Cat and The Coal spent the night at the fort. One of Charbonneau's wives was ill, perhaps Sacagawea, now far along in her pregnancy. Some of the party went to observe a war dance at Mitutanka. In his book Biddle may have been describing this "medicine dance" under January 8. This time he did not resort to Latin in noting the sexual overtones of the ceremony.

JANUARY 12, 1805. The Field brothers and one other hunter returned with a sleigh loaded with two elks. Lewis noted "luminus rings about the moon" late in the evening; he probably saw the refraction of light created by ice crystals.

JANUARY 13, 1805. Clark observed a great number of Indians heading south to hunt and noted that their custom of sharing buffalo meat in common left the tribe more than half the year without adequate food. Their horticultural products, principally corn and beans, were kept in reserve in case of attack. This fear of attack by their Sioux enemies also forced them to hunt in large groups, and they stayed in constant fear of being ambushed. Clark thought he saw half the Mandan nation en route to the hunt. Charbonneau and another Frenchman had been hunting, perhaps in the Killdeer Mountains to the west or at Turtle Mountain to the north on the Canadian border, and now returned somewhat frostbitten on their faces but with meat. Charbonneau reported that George Bunch of Hudson's Bay Company, a resident at one of the Hidatsa villages, had been making derogatory remarks about the Americans. The interpreter also related a rumor that the North West Company intended to build a fort at Menetarra village. And he further said that Le Borgne had spoken disparagingly about the corps but indicated that if the captains would give him a flag he would come to the fort. Lewis carried out astronomical observations and obtained a latitude reading of 47° 18′ 30″ N for Fort Mandan; the site is closer to 47° 16′ 52″ N.

JANUARY 14, 1805. More Indians moved down the ice-strewn river to catch the hunting party that had preceded them. The captains detailed Pryor and five men to join them. In the evening Shannon, one of the hunters, returned to report that Whitehouse's feet were frostbitten and that he was unable to walk. Before coming back Shannon and Collins killed a buffalo bull, a wolf, two porcupines, and a jackrabbit. Several of the men had contracted venereal disease from Mandan women, perhaps from participating in the Buffalo Calling Ceremony of previous weeks.

JANUARY 15, 1805. Lewis worked from midnight to three in the morning in order to obtain astronomical observations during an eclipse of the moon. He was hampered somewhat by clouds, eventually to the point that he was not fully confident of his observations. Nonetheless, he was able to get some readings and thought he was as accurate as could be under the conditions. (Lewis's longitude readings for Fort Mandan are found at January 28, his latitude calculation at January 13.) Some Hidatsa head men joined Mandans at the fort for a pipe-smoking ceremony. The captains tried to alter the Hidatsas' unfavorable impressions of Americans by giving them special attention.

JANUARY 16, 1805. With about thirty more Mandans arriving at the fort (among whom Clark counted six chiefs), the Hidatsas had an opportunity to state their displeasure to a wider audience and called the Mandans liars for telling them that they would be killed if they came to visit the Americans. Clark did not record the Mandans' response or the discussions that must have grown out of these remarks. Seeing Snake (or perhaps named Rattle Snake), a Hidatsa war chief about twenty-six years old, also arrived with another man and his wife. In order to honor another of their infrequent Hidatsa visitors, the captains demonstrated the expedition's air gun and fired the cannon. Seeing Snake gave Clark a map of the Missouri "in his way," which meant that the chief drew charcoal lines on an animal skin or placed lines in the earth to represent the river's course.

Seeing Snake also related unsettling news that he intended to go to war against the Shoshones in the spring. Clark spoke strongly against the war threats and pushed the American policy of peace. Taking a long view, the military man Clark reviewed the destruction of war, both its economic and human impacts. Clark advocated trade with the Shoshones for the horses the young man sought, but his most convincing arguments were that the "Great father" would not be pleased at such actions. The captain also told Seeing Snake that he and Lewis had obtained promises of peace from all the Indian nations they had visited on their way up the Missouri, although he confided that he was doubtful of the Sioux acceptance of that message. Seeing Snake promised to advise his tribal members to refrain from war with the Shoshones until an accord might be worked out and that he would hold off on his own war excursions. Little Crow arrived later bringing corn. Four expedition hunters returned, apparently with no meat but with Whitehouse. Although Whitehouse's feet were a little frostbitten, he was not in as bad a condition as feared.

JANUARY 17, 1805. A hard north wind with the temperature at zero did not discourage some Indians from visiting the fort.

JANUARY 18, 1805. Larocque and McKenzie came to the fort with several Hidatsas. More hunters returned with a badger and wolf skins, and they reported that Pryor's party had killed three elks, four deer, and two porcupines.

JANUARY 19, 1805. Larocque and McKenzie left the fort but sent three horses back to the party's hunting camp to retrieve meat that hunters had obtained. Jusseaume's wife returned to her village. Lewis measured ice on the Missouri at three feet thick on its most rapid part.

JANUARY 20, 1805. A misunderstanding took place between Jusseaume and Charbonneau. Clark had York give tea and a fruit stew
to one of Charbonneau's wives (perhaps Sacagawea, who was only
a few weeks away from delivering her baby). Apparently this had
caused a rift between the interpreters, but details of the argument
are lacking. Perhaps these problems had influenced Jusseaume's
wife to return to her village the previous day. Gass and some of
the party went to the Mandan villages and were given a portion of
a buffalo head to eat. The Mandans explained that consuming it
would please the buffalo spirit and cause other buffalo to come in
and offer themselves as food. Whitehouse thought that the Indians
had strange ideas and were ignorant of Euro-American customs but
"quick & Sensible in their own way."

JANUARY 21, 1805. Other than noting Indian visitors, Clark simply penned, "nothing remarkable," then added that one man had a
severe case of syphilis ("pox"). Ordway noted that all the hunters
had arrived with three horse-loads of meat. It was probably a couple of these returned hunters who took their wolf skins to North
West Company traders to get tobacco. They were able to get three
feet of twisted tobacco for each skin.

JANUARY 22, 1805. In attempting to free the keelboat and the pirogues
from the ice, the men discovered that at one point the Missouri's
ice was eight inches thick and then a second shelf was about three
feet thick. They were able to cut through the ice at one point but
were able to release only a gusher of water and none of the boats.

JANUARY 23, 1805. Besides four inches of new snow, Clark reported
only that the events of the day were "common." The men came up
with another means of employment by making sleds for the Indians in exchange for corn and beans.

JANUARY 24, 1805. Jusseaume and Charbonneau seem to have rec-
onciled. Hunters out for the day returned empty-handed.

JANUARY 25, 1805. A band of Assiniboine Indians arrived at the Knife River villages for trading, led by "Fils de Petit Veau" or "Son of the Little Calf," as Clark gave it, or "Petit Vieux," according to Larocque. Charbonneau and a member of the party set out for Mahawha, apparently where the Assiniboines had settled. Work continued on cutting the boats out of the ice and on cutting and splitting wood to be used as a substitute for coal, now used up.

JANUARY 26, 1805. Indian visitors shared a meal with the captains. One unnamed man in the party became violently ill with pleurisy. Clark bled him and utilized other remedies at his disposal, perhaps purging him and greasing the man's chest.

JANUARY 27, 1805. Clark bled the man with pleurisy again, while Lewis amputated the toes on one foot of the boy who suffered frostbite during the night of January 9–10. Charbonneau returned from his visit to the Assiniboines, who were returning to their own camps. He brought three of Larocque's horses with him since the trader feared that the Assiniboines, whom he considered "great rogues," might steal them. The men were still trying to bring the boats out of the grasp of the Missouri's ice. Others were cutting prairie grass for hay to be used in the blacksmiths' kiln.

JANUARY 28, 1805. The man with pleurisy was improving, while Jusseaume was quite unwell. Indians were at the fort attempting to get the party's blacksmiths to make war hatchets or battle-axes for them. Clark drew a picture of the most desired model in his journal notebook. Lewis's astronomical observations yielded two readings for Fort Mandan's longitude, 99° 22′ 45.3″ W and 99° 26′ 45″ W; the approximate longitude of the site is 101° 16′ 44″ W.

JANUARY 29, 1805. Clark gave the ailing Jusseaume salts to act as a laxative. A new strategy was devised to free the boats. Men were sent to collect stones and stack them near the boats, where they would be heated, melting the ice around the encrusted crafts and freeing them. The plan fell apart when the stones broke up under the heat.

The party's smith began preparations to set up their forge in order to mend the Indians' war hatchets. Clark explained that this was the only way to obtain the needed corn for the party.

JANUARY 30, 1805. Gass went upriver seeking different kinds of stones that might hold up better to the heat. He returned with some likely looking pieces, but they worked no better. The men gave up on that plan. Larocque came to the fort and found the captains prepared to answer his request to accompany the corps westward. They turned him down.

JANUARY 31, 1805. Two inches of new snow fell during the night. More toes were removed from the boy who had frostbitten his feet earlier in the month. Jusseaume's health was improving, but now Drouillard had come down with pleurisy. Clark bled him and gave him sage tea, and he seemed to be better. Five expedition members led two horses down the river to hunt.

FEBRUARY 1, 1805. Hunters brought back only a single deer to the fort. The Hidatsa chief Seeing Snake brought corn to the party and wanted a war hatchet made. He also stated his intention to go to war against the Sioux and Arikaras as revenge for their having killed a Mandan some time ago. The captains refused his request for this mission just as they had dissuaded him from a horse-stealing venture to the Shoshones in mid-January. The young man accepted the advice and in the evening set out instead in pursuit of his wife.

FEBRUARY 2, 1805. Hunters killed another deer. Jusseaume was still ill and one of Charbonneau's wives, perhaps Sacagawea, who was a little over week from delivering his child, became sick. Larocque left the fort, probably disappointed at being turned down in his request to accompany the corps.

FEBRUARY 3, 1805. The blacksmithing operation got underway, but few Indians visited the fort. Lewis became alarmed at the condition of the boats, now firmly sealed in the ice and becoming burdened with snow. The nature of the river's ice made releasing the boats particularly difficult, as the ice lay in strata. As soon as an upper stratum was broken away from the boats, water rushed in over the next layer and made it nearly impossible to break that barrier, now underwater. The use of axes had been totally unproductive, and heating stones to melt the ice also proved impractical since the stones shattered under the heat. As a last resort, the captains determined to try breaking the frozen shield by attaching iron spikes to poles and thrusting these tools against the ice. Optimistically, they prepared a windlass and an elkskin rope to draw the keelboat up on the bank as soon as it was freed.

FEBRUARY 4, 1805. As Clark was absent from the camp February 4–13, Lewis took up the journal-writing chores. The meat supply being low, Clark set out down the icy Missouri with sixteen men of the party (including Gass and Joseph Field) and two unnamed Frenchmen, three horses, and two sleighs to hunt. The party traveled about twenty-two miles, a few miles below Washburn, McLean County, North Dakota, but found no game and went hungry. Many Indians visited the fort and reported that the villages were also suffering from want of meat. Buffalo had not been seen for several weeks. Shields killed two deer in the evening, but both were very lean.

FEBRUARY 5, 1805. Indians brought corn in trade for blacksmithing work, desiring particularly war axes and buffalo-hide scrapers. Lewis was somewhat amused at the war instrument of choice; it was the same one Clark had mentioned and pictured on January 28. Evaluating it as a military man, he judged it wanting in several ways. The thin blade, seven to nine inches in length and four and three-quarters to six inches wide at its widest part, was particularly long in proportion to its handle of fourteen inches, making it unwieldy and its stroke uncertain and easily avoided. Moreover, the short handle lessened the impact of the weapon's blow, especially since it was frequently employed from horseback. An older instrument Lewis considered even more inconvenient. Clark added a drawing of it in his journal notebook. Its blade was similar to that of an espontoon (an officer's staff with a metal, spear-point head), with the addition of small holes in its elongated triangular shape. It too suffered from the defect of a short handle, according to Lewis. On the hunting excursion Clark broke through the ice and soaked his feet and legs but apparently suffered no serious injury. The men killed a deer and two buffalo bulls early enough in the morning to provide the hunters with breakfast, but only the deer was worth eating. Three more deer were killed later in the day. Clark found the uneven ice difficult going and blistered his feet on the rough edges of the hardpack.

FEBRUARY 6, 1805. Lewis had another sleigh built in anticipation of the hunting party returning with meat. A number of Indians visited the fort, among them Big White, The Coal, Big Man, Hairy Horn, and Black Man, who smoked with Lewis and then left. Lewis was surprised at this action, because they usually "pester us with their good company the balance of the day." The blacksmiths received a considerable quantity of corn for their labors at the forge. Lewis was quite pleased at the situation and confessed that the party may have had no other way to obtain the needed corn from the natives. Not only were war hatchets a popular item but the Indians came requesting a variety of wares fabricated from the party's sheet iron, including arrow points and instruments for scraping and dressing buffalo skins. Lewis even permitted the smiths to dismantle a damaged stove for its iron. The men obtained from seven to eight gallons of corn for pieces of iron of about four inches square. The Indians seemed pleased at the exchange. Shields killed three pronghorns in the evening. Although meager, Clark's hunters managed to bring in more game, including deer, elks, and buffalo.

FEBRUARY 7, 1805. More Indian visitors. The sergeant of the guard had disturbing news for Lewis. Charbonneau's wives had made a habit of opening the fort's gate during the night and admitting visitors. Lewis ordered a lock for the gate and instructed that only those Indians attached to the fort would be permitted to remain overnight in the enclosure and that the gate would remain locked from sunset to sunrise. Clark's party increased their meat supply considerably and all were working at either hunting or preparing meat.

FEBRUARY 8, 1805. Black Cat visited the fort, providing Lewis an opportunity to evaluate the man. The captain judged him a man of integrity, firmness, intelligence, and lucidity. Indeed, he had those admirable qualities to a greater extent than any Indian Lewis had met thus far. Given those traits, Lewis thought that with a "little management" the chief could be made a useful agent for American objectives at the Knife River villages. Black Cat gave Lewis a bow and apologized for not having a shield ready to present. The chief's wife also gave the captain two pairs of moccasins. In response, Lewis gave Black Cat some small shot, six fishing hooks, and two yards of ribbon and gave his wife a small mirror and a couple of needles. Black Cat told Lewis that his people were suffering severely from want of meat and that he himself had not had any for several days. After dining with Lewis, Black Cat returned to his village. Clark sent Charbonneau, an unnamed member of the party, and two Frenchmen with three horses loaded with the best meat back to the fort, now some forty-four miles away. What the horses could not carry, he had collected, loaded on sleighs, and taken to a log enclosure where it would be protected from wolves who had earlier joined ravens and magpies in devouring a portion of the take. Clark proceeded to the mouth of the Heart River but located little game there, although he could see small groups of buffalo on the hills. Lewis noted that the "Black & white & Speckled woodpecker," perhaps the yellow-bellied sapsucker, had returned to the Knife River area.

FEBRUARY 9, 1805. McKenzie arrived at the fort. Howard, who had gone to one of the Mandan villages, probably Mitutanka, returned to the fort late in the evening after the gate was shut and instead of calling the guard to admit him, he simply scaled the back wall. An Indian looking on repeated the trick, and Lewis called the native to task for the action. Having frightened the Indian, Lewis eased the situation by offering him tobacco. Howard was put under arrest and given a court-martial for his offense. Lewis was particularly disappointed in Howard, an experienced soldier who was here setting a bad example for the younger men. He was judged guilty of disobeying orders and sentenced to fifty lashes, but the court recommended leniency, and Lewis forgave the punishment. The buffalo Clark had seen on the hills about the Heart River proved to be useless for meat. Moreover, the captain was now some sixty miles from the fort and packing any meat that distance would be difficult and probably unproductive, so he abandoned the area and worked his way back to about forty miles south of the fort.

FEBRUARY 10, 1805. The wind-chill factor was especially apparent to Lewis. McKenzie left the fort while Charbonneau returned with one of the Frenchmen who had gone with Clark. The Frenchman reported that he had left the hunters' three horses with two men and a supply of meat about eight miles down the river. The horses were heavily loaded and unable to negotiate the ice, so Lewis ordered some men to prepare for a trip to the spot with two small sleighs. He also sent two men, one being Drouillard, to bring the horses back to the fort by land. Clark's party killed some elks and deer and what meat was useful was stored in the holding pen. Joseph Field, along with Clark, got his ears somewhat frostbitten.

FEBRUARY 11, 1805. The party detached to retrieve the meat and bring back the horses set out early. About five o'clock in the evening at the fort Sacagawea delivered "a fine boy," in the words of Lewis, who was involved in the birth of Jean Baptiste Charbonneau. Sacagawea's labor was tedious, and she was in great pain during the procedure. Lewis surmised that the cause of the difficulty was that this was her first child. During the process Jusseaume suggested a remedy. He informed Lewis that he had frequently administered a potion that included small pieces of the rattle of a rattlesnake and that it had never failed to produce results. Lewis found a length of rattle and gave two rings to Jusseaume, who added the crushed parts to water. Sacagawea drank the liquid, and Lewis later learned that within ten minutes she had her baby. Lewis was skeptical of the cause-and-effect relationship here but thought it worthy of further experiments. Clark began his return to Fort Mandan but stopped short when he realized that several of his men were nearly out of their moccasins and that the loaded horses were lagging behind.

FEBRUARY 12, 1805. Lewis set the smiths to making horseshoes and others to preparing gear for a trip with sleighs to meet the hunting party in order to aid those bringing back the meat. The men the captain had sent out the previous day to get the meat left by Charbonneau came back to the fort about the same time as Drouillard arrived with the horses. The horses were quite worn down and Lewis tried to revive them with moistened meal, but the animals would have none of it. The captain was surprised that they preferred cottonwood bark, which was their accustomed winter food in the Indian villages. So intriguing was this discovery that Lewis pondered the reasons. He concluded that Knife River Indians' opponents— Arikaras, Sioux, and Assiniboines—so frequently stole the villagers' horses that they were forced to keep the animals in their earth lodges during the night. The only food for them there were tender branches of cottonwoods that women harvested. The horses had become accustomed to the bark and favored it over feed that the Americans offered. Lewis was further amazed that the animals seemed to thrive on this scanty diet, especially given that the Indians seemed to be hard riders and severe masters.

The hunting party set out early for the fort, but Clark sent one man in pursuit of a gang of elks and that hunter got three and went on in to the fort. The captain noticed that the ice had smoothed over due to the rising and falling of the river as partial thaws occurred. He also reflected on the abandoned Mandan villages at the mouth of the Heart River, of which he showed eight on his map of the area. He considered Sioux attacks and the ravages of smallpox the reasons for their abandonment. Clark arrived at the fort a little after dark. During his absence, his hunters had killed forty deer, nineteen elks, and three buffalo, according to the captain. In spite of the number of animals killed, Lewis noted the poor quality of their flesh and the competition of the wolves, who took a good proportion of the meat. Lewis lamented the speed with which wolves could devour a hunter's kill.

FEBRUARY 13, 1805. Black Cat visited the fort and received a hatchet such as the one under demand from the party's smiths. Whitehouse reported that Shields was at work shoeing horses so they could be used to bring in the meat obtained by Clark's party. Clark spent a portion of the day bringing his journal up to date, recounting his hunting excursion.

FEBRUARY 14, 1805. Drouillard, Frazer, Goodrich, and Newman took horses and sleighs to retrieve more of the meat. While on the trip they were attacked by over one hundred Sioux, who robbed them of two of their horses. An Indian who was with expedition members offered the other horse, perhaps fearing (according to Clark) that the explorers would resist. The soldiers also had to give up their knives but were not harmed. It seems that there was a debate by the Sioux about whether to kill them, but two of the warriors opposed the action, so the men were set free.

FEBRUARY 15, 1805. Lewis set out at sunrise with twenty-four men, including Ordway and Gass, to find the Sioux who had robbed four men of the party the previous day. Big White arrived at the fort later and told Clark that all the young men from Mitutanka and Ruptáre were hunting and the villagers had very few guns. Nonetheless, Lewis was accompanied by several Indians armed with bows and arrows, spears, battle-axes, and a couple of fusils (a type of musket). At the place where the horses were taken, the party found Indian moccasins but no sign of the horses. After a trip of about thirty miles the men located abandoned lodges where they spent the night. Several of the party had sore feet from the long march over the rough ice. One of the Indians with Lewis returned to the fort somewhat snowblinded by the bright reflections of the sun off the ice and snow. A hunter from the fort killed a large red fox.

FEBRUARY 16, 1805. Howard returned to the fort from Lewis's party with his feet somewhat frostbitten; the Indians in the party also went back. Howard reported to Clark that the Sioux who had committed the robbery were so far ahead of Lewis that they could not be caught. Nonetheless, Lewis and the others went about six miles farther and thought they had located the perpetrators when they saw smoke coming from some abandoned lodges. The captain disbursed his force and made ready to storm the lodges but found the place deserted, the Sioux having withdrawn the previous day after setting fire to one lodge; thus the smoke. Ordway sounded the horn and brought up waiting soldiers. Lewis also discovered that the Sioux had taken the remainder of the meat that the robbery victims had been seeking. The men gave up the chase, and some turned to hunting, gaining a deer and a wolf in the outing.

FEBRUARY 17, 1805. The Coal and his son brought about thirty pounds of dried buffalo meat and tallow to the fort. McKenzie also visited the post, perhaps to inquire about his horse that had been one of the animals taken by the Sioux. Any conversation about the horse went unrecorded, but the issue arose again on April 3 as the party prepared to leave the Knife River villages. Lewis's party continued hunting and used a driving strategy that yielded ten deer and four elks.

FEBRUARY 18, 1805. More Indian visitors arrived at the fort and McKenzie left. Clark spent a good part of the day working on his list of subsidiary streams of the Missouri and Yellowstone Rivers above the Knife River villages. He had been collecting this information from Indians and traders who visited the fort. Now the leisure days of winter provided a good time to develop and reflect on his list. The party's store of meat at the fort was exhausted. Lewis's party gained more meat and the captain decided to return to the fort on the next day.

FEBRUARY 19, 1805. The party's blacksmiths were busy filling orders for battle-axes and mending others brought by Indians who paid with corn. Using one of their horses for hauling and putting fifteen men to pull the other sleigh, Lewis's party headed for the fort, while sending four hunters ahead. From the hunters' success, the party added six deer and an elk to their sleighs.

FEBRUARY 20, 1805. Little Crow arrived early this morning, and it was perhaps this chief who informed Clark of the death of an elderly Mandan. Clark had earlier learned from the deceased man that he was 120 years old and that he had requested his grandchildren to dress him in his best robe and set him on a stone on a hill facing his old village downriver when he died so he could join his brother there in an underground spirit village. Clark commented that he had observed several Mandan men of a very old age, while the labor of the women shortened their lives. Lewis's party spent another day moving toward the fort and hunting along the way.

FEBRUARY 21, 1805. The men used a rare sunny day to air their clothes. Big White and Big Man visited the fort and told the Clark that several of their men had made a pilgrimage to a sacred stone about three days' travel from the villages. This stone, on Medicine Hill at Medicine Rock State Historic Park, Grant County, North Dakota, was a source for inspiration and foretelling the future. These men had gone to find out what the next year held for them. The Mandans informed the captain that Knife River Indians made regular visits to the hill as demonstrated by the remains of pictographic paintings and petroglyphic carvings. Clark also learned that the Hidatsas had a similar place to visit. Lewis returned with two sleighs loaded with meat. After determining that he could not overtake the Sioux robbers, Lewis gathered what meat was left at the deposit Clark had made earlier and set his men to hunting along the return route. In two days the captain and his hunters killed thirty-six deer and fourteen elks, but many of them were unfit for consumption. In all, the men brought back about three thousand pounds of meat.

FEBRUARY 22, 1805. The rain that began at noon quickly turned to snow and continued for about an hour before clearing up. Two hunters that Lewis had left behind came in to report that they had killed two elks and hung them up out of reach of wolves. The other members of Lewis's party spent the day resting, while their comrades worked at the boats. The Coal visited the fort, as did many others. Clark declared that these Indians came from the "three nations in our neighbourhood," indicating that he considered there to be three tribes at the Knife River: Mandans, Hidatsas, and Awaxawi Hidatsas at Mahawha. The last was a group that the captains always considered somewhat distinct from the other two Hidatsa villages.

FEBRUARY 23, 1805. A warm day provided opportunity for the men to work at getting the pirogues free from ice. Layers of ice separated by ice-cold water made the work difficult and uncomfortable. Nevertheless, the men were able to free the white pirogue and nearly got the red pirogue loose. Indians came for a visit while Jusseaume and family went to Mahawha. The father of the Indian boy whose toes were frostbitten during the night of January 9–10 came with a sleigh to take his son home. The men worked at the ice with axes and iron-tipped poles.

FEBRUARY 24, 1805. Work continued from early morning on cutting loose the red pirogue and the keelboat. The pirogue was finally freed and readied to be drawn out of its encasement, while the keelboat was somewhat loosened with the aid of pry-bars. In the process of working on the keelboat it started to leak, but the problem was noticed in time to seal it. Several Indians stopped by and Jusseaume and family returned to the fort.

FEBRUARY 25, 1805. With the aid of a winch the men were able to haul the two pirogues to the upper bank of the Missouri along a road of rollers they had built. They also tried the same operation on the keelboat but the elkskin rope proved too weak and broke several times. They had to content themselves with leaving it in the water but at least somewhat free of ice. Black Moccasin, perhaps White Buffalo Robe Unfolded, and others arrived at the fort. They came with their women carrying meat. At least one of the visitors requested one of the corps' famed war axes for his son. Bunch, the Hudson's Bay trader, also visited. The son of Black Cat and a number of others asked to spend the night at the fort, a request the captains granted.

FEBRUARY 26, 1805. The whole day was spent in getting the keelboat completely free of the ice and up on the bank. By doubling the rope and utilizing the windlass, the men succeeded. Just as the task was completed Clark watched the ice give way in huge pieces behind them. All the while visiting Indians observed the party's efforts.

FEBRUARY 27, 1805. The men spent the day preparing tools for work on canoes that would be taken up the Missouri in the spring. Clark was amazed at one Indian visitor who he declared was the largest man he had ever seen. The captain also began drafting a map of the Missouri River and its affluents, perhaps a preliminary draft or an existing version of his map of 1805.

FEBRUARY 28, 1805. Gravelines and at least two other Frenchmen arrived from the Arikara villages with letters from Tabeau. They were accompanied by two Arikara Indians who brought welcome news that the Arikaras had determined to follow the captains' plans for intertribal peace. In fact, the Arikaras wished to visit the Mandans and talked of settling nearby in defense against their common enemy, the Sioux. Less welcome was news that several Sioux bands were forming together with intentions to attack the Knife River Indians and kill every white person in the vicinity. The captains passed this information to the Mandans, emphasizing particularly the peace overtures of the Arikaras. The Mandans responded positively to Arikara peace offers. Gravelines or another Frenchman also brought saccacommis (bearberry) and narrow-leaved purple coneflower for the explorers. Lewis obtained specimens of bearberry and coneflower at Fort Mandan; the coneflower specimen is lost. The coneflower was a gift of Hugh Heney, who had described the plant on December 16 but now provided further medicinal uses for it, particularly for mad-dog bites and snakebites. Clark collected the plant on March 21.

Tabeau's letter informed the captains that Murdoch Cameron, a trader on the Minnesota River in modern Minnesota, was arming the Sioux in order for them to carry out revenge on the Chippewa Indians for killing three of Cameron's men. This affair was outside the captains' immediate concern, but it did not bode well for establishing their plan for peace, because Cameron's weapons could also be used against the Arikaras, Mandans, Hidatsas, and other Missouri River tribes within the scope of the captains' interest. Tabeau also had more positive news. He reported that the Teton chief Black Buffalo and his band were inclined to follow the captains' peace policy.

Gravelines also reported that the Sioux who had robbed the party of horses on February 14 had stopped at the Arikara villages on their return. Apparently the Sioux had debated among themselves whether they should kill the expedition members, but before they made a decision the explorers had gotten away. They said that if they met any more Americans, they would kill them immediately. The Sioux got a cold reception from the Arikaras and scolding for their conduct. Sixteen men were sent about five miles upriver to make a camp and begin building from four to six canoes for the trip on up the Missouri. These vessels would replace the keelboat, which was to be sent back to St. Louis. The builders returned in the evening having located trees of suitable size for the boats.

MARCH 1, 1805. While the men built canoes, made ropes, fashioned battle-axes, repaired Indian guns, and prepared buffalo meat, Clark continued working on his map. Canoe builders drew two days' rations and set out for their camp near the river to do their work.

MARCH 2, 1805. A fair day found all the party engaged in routine activities. Ice in the river was breaking up in places, signaling perhaps the coming end of winter. Larocque arrived at the fort after recently returning from North West Company posts on the Assiniboine River in Canada; he brought trading merchandise for the Knife River villages. He reported that the head of the North West Company, Simon McTavish, had died and that the company had combined with the X Y Company (also known as the New North West Company). The X Y Company had been formed a few years earlier by disgruntled North West men. Now with the death of McTavish the divisive issues faded and the companies could recombine. The Coal and several other Indians also visited the fort.

MARCH 3, 1805. Ducks passing up the Missouri gave another indication of winter's end. Black Cat, perhaps Raven Man Chief, and a Hidatsa Indian came by for a short visit. Clark gave them the information he had learned from Gravelines and the Arikaras on February 28. Canoe builders came to the fort for more provisions.

MARCH 4, 1805. Black Cat and Big White arrived with a small gift of meat. Perhaps it was McKenzie of the North West Company who came by for a horse and requested silk of three colors for Chaboillez's "woman" at the company's post in Canada. Assiniboine Indians who had visited the Mandans earlier for trading returned but this time for raiding the Hidatsas' horse herd. The Hidatsas fired at them, but it was not clear if any Indians were wounded.

MARCH 5, 1805. The day saw a number of Indian visitors and also a Frenchman with an Indian on the way to the Arikara villages with correspondence for Tabeau.

MARCH 6, 1805. The Hidatsas set the plains on fire, causing a smoky haze throughout the day. The purpose of setting the prairie fires was to burn off the winter's dead grass, promote spring growth, and hasten the return of buffalo. The Assiniboines who had stolen Hidatsa horses returned them. Little Fox visited the fort. Shannon cut his foot while using an adze. It may have been Drouillard who accompanied Gravelines to one of the Knife River villages, probably Mitutanka. Water running over the Missouri's icy covering made the river crossing difficult.

MARCH 7, 1805. The Coal came to the fort with a sick child. Clark gave the youngster Rush's pills, a strong laxative. Charbonneau returned to the fort in the evening and reported that the Hidatsas whom he had been visiting, probably of Metaharta village, had returned to their homes from hunting. He brought gifts from Chaboillez of the North West Company's Assiniboine River establishment that included pieces of various cloths, corduroy pants, vests, balls, powder, knives, and tobacco.

MARCH 8, 1805. Greasy Head, probably a Hidatsa, and an unnamed Arikara came to the fort and gave Clark information about the Indians of the Rocky Mountains. A Hidatsa stole Black Man's daughter, but the Mandan father went to the young man's village and retrieved her.

MARCH 9, 1805. Clark set out from the fort to see how the men were coming along with building canoes for the trip west. Along the way the captain met Le Borgne, grand chief of the Hidatsas, with four other Indians on their way to Fort Mandan. This was a fortunate encounter because the captains had been wanting to visit with him since they arrived at the Knife River. Clark asked him to go on, perhaps with Charbonneau, while the captain finished his inspection of the canoe-building operation. Clark found work on the canoes going well but the materials for their construction unsatisfactory. On his way to the fort he delayed at Ruptáre, where he shared a pipe with the attentive and friendly chief Black Cat.

At the fort Le Borgne was greeted with guns fired in his honor, and Lewis presented him with a peace medal, a gorget, clothes, and a flag (perhaps remembering the chief's request for one in January). The captain also demonstrated the use of the air gun, quadrant, and telescope. Biddle related an episode in his notes and book that is not found in expedition journals. He wrote that Le Borgne told Lewis that some foolish person had declared that there was a man of black color living at the fort, and he wanted to know the truth about it. Lewis sent for York, who surprised Le Borgne by his appearance, so much so that the chief spit on his fingers and tried to rub paint off the man's body. Being unsuccessful at erasing his blackness, Le Borgne was even more surprised when York removed his cap to display his uncommon hair. Clark got back to the fort just as Le Borgne was leaving for Menetarra, some distance to the north.

MARCH 10, 1805. Black Moccasin of Metaharta and White Buffalo Robe Unfolded of Mahawha visited the fort, and while Black Moccasin left during the day, White Buffalo Robe Unfolded spent the night and gave Clark accounts of his tribe. He informed Clark that the Awaxawi Hidatsas had earlier lived about thirty miles below their present village but were so oppressed by the Assiniboines and the Sioux that they were compelled to move closer to their Hidatsa kin, eventually to the mouth of the Knife River where they lived now. At this location they had intermixed with their Hidatsa relations and with the Mandans. Having been so decimated by their enemies they now could raise only fifty men. He also told Clark that the Mandans had also been more numerous at one time and had occupied nine villages about the mouth of the Heart River. They too had been harassed by the Sioux, who totally wiped out one village, and those who had escaped the Sioux were otherwise devastated by smallpox. Biddle added a paragraph in his book about marital relationships in the Knife River villages that is not found in expedition journals. He used Le Borgne as an example of both revenge and forgiveness when two of his wives proved unfaithful. One he killed, but the other he let go with her lover.

MARCH 11, 1805. The captains decided that two more canoes would need to be built in order to haul the party's provisions upriver. They may have given this directive to one of the builders who was returning to the camp after securing more provisions. Without any clear explanation about the circumstances, Lewis and Clark were convinced that Charbonneau had been "Corupted" by the British traders at the Knife River. They gave him a night to decide whether he wanted to accompany the corps under the terms previously settled on.

MARCH 12, 1805. The slight snow on the ground had all but disappeared. Charbonneau decided not to go with the corps. Perhaps it had to do partially with the captains' duty requirements for the trip and his own demands for certain perquisites, since he indicated that he was not willing to stand guard duty, demanded the freedom to leave the enterprise if he became "miffed with any man," and wanted to be able to bring along as many provisions as he desired. The captains judged his demands unacceptable and released him from their verbal commitments.

MARCH 13, 1805. Along with McKenzie a number of Indians visited the fort, most seeking war axes. Realizing that the blacksmiths would soon be leaving, villagers placed steady demands on their time, until the smiths had hardly a moment away from their forges.

MARCH 14, 1805. McKenzie left but many Indians remained at the fort. The captains set all the hands to shelling corn, a provision for the trip as well as ready nourishment. Ordway alone indicated that Gravelines was to take Charbonneau's place, but it is unclear if this was to be only for the remaining time at the Knife River or for a longer duration. Charbonneau moved outside the fort and settled into a nearby lodge.

MARCH 15, 1805. A sunny day provided opportunity to dry the party's goods, clothing, and parched meal and to further prepare corn. Curious Indians were much interested in the party's goods, spread out for all to see.

MARCH 16, 1805. Joseph Garreau, who had lived many years with the Arikaras and Mandans, gave Lewis a demonstration of how the Indians made beads. Garreau told Lewis that the Arikaras and Mandans had learned this art from Shoshones whom the Arikaras had taken prisoner. Lewis wrote a long description of the process in Clark's journal, while Clark merely commented that the captains received the demonstration. An Indian complained that Whitehouse had struck his hand for "behaving badly" while eating with a spoon.

MARCH 17, 1805. Charbonneau, who apparently was in the process of moving his goods across the river and returning to Metaharta village, changed his mind and sent one of the Frenchmen of the party to apologize for his behavior. He said that if the captains would accept him back he would go with the party on the terms the captains had specified. In fact, Charbonneau, probably through Labiche, had asked two days earlier to be excused for his "Simplicity" and returned to service. Now the captains agreed and Charbonneau was set to go. Werner lost his tomahawk and Ordway blamed the loss on Indian pilfering.

MARCH 18, 1805. Clark spent the day dividing the party's goods into eight parts to be distributed among the two pirogues and six canoes for the trip. During the day he was to learn that some days earlier a party of Cree and Assiniboine Indians had been killed by about fifty Sioux near the British trading establishments on the Assiniboine River. Parenthetically, Clark credited the assault to Murdoch Cameron as revenge for the death of three of his men at the hands of Chippewa Indians who were somewhat allied with the Crees (an incident reported to the captains on February 28). Although the captains had reinstated Charbonneau on the previous day it became official on this one. Clark was ill during the day. A couple of canoe builders came to the fort for provisions. Lewis was busy collecting plants, probably from the natives, to send back to Jefferson, particularly the narrow-leaved purple coneflower that he had learned about on February 28 that was supposed to be useful for curing mad-dog bites and snakebites.

MARCH 19, 1805. Big White and Little Crow visited the fort, as well as a man and his wife with a sick child. Clark ministered to the youngster. It must have been disheartening to the captains when they learned that two Hidatsa parties were off to war and that another party would follow shortly. Their plans for peace were falling apart before them. Gass came to the fort from the canoe-building camp and reported that the work was completed and that he needed men to help drag the boats to the river, which was about 1½ miles from the camp.

MARCH 20, 1805. Clark visited the Mandan villages while inspecting the canoes. He took all the men who could be spared from the fort and had them carry four of the craft to the river in preparation for them to be floated down to the fort when the river cleared. Taking a break from moving the canoes, Clark smoked a pipe with Big White and some elder Mandans.

MARCH 21, 1805. The remaining two canoes were taken to the river. Clark then returned to the fort with all but three of the men, Gass being among them, who were left to finish work on the boats. On his way back Clark collected "Pumice Stone, burnt Stone & hard earth" along the hillsides after noticing indications that the hills had been on fire. The pumice and "burnt stone" were probably clinker, while the "hard earth" or "hard Clay" were lithified claystones. At the fort he put the collected materials in the smiths' furnace and noticed that the clay turned to "Pumice Stone," more likely a substance resembling volcanic rock and similar in appearance to true pumice. He also collected narrow-leaved purple coneflower and recalled that it was supposedly a cure for snakebites and rabies. The captain noted that Heney (his earlier informant about uses of purple coneflower) thought the plant grew along the courses of the Big Blue or Little Blue Rivers of the present state of Missouri.

MARCH 22, 1805. It was apparently Man Wolf Chief of Menetarra who arrived at the fort with many other Hidatsas. He had been away with a war party in October when the captains met his father, The Grape. Now the captains acknowledged him as second chief of Menetarra, after Le Borgne, and gave him a peace medal, beads, and clothing. In further recognition of his status he was allowed to spend the night at the fort and members of the party danced in the evening, which Clark acknowledged as typical amusement for the men. The traders Larocque and McKenzie also stopped by the fort and spent the night. Without elaboration Clark noted that Jusseaume was "displeased."

MARCH 23, 1805. After breakfast Larocque, McKenzie, and the Indians left the fort. Soon after the guests left, the captains were visited by Le Borgne's brother, who gave them a vocabulary of the Hidatsa language. The captains also counted The Coal and a number of other Mandans, including perhaps Raven Man Chief, as visitors during the day.

MARCH 24, 1805. In a brief entry, Clark simply penned, "prepareing to Set out." Nonetheless, Indian visitors showed up as usual. Men were sent to help bring the canoes downriver, but the boats were not fully corked nor ready. Others were building cages for live animals being sent to Jefferson: four magpies, a prairie dog, and a sharp-tailed grouse.

MARCH 25, 1805. A flock of swans returned to the Knife River area. Clark reported few Indians at the fort, perhaps because the ice was breaking up in the river, making it more difficult for villagers to cross the Missouri. The moving ice almost carried away or destroyed some of the new canoes that men were bringing to the fort. With a fair day at hand, Lewis took astronomical observations while the men continued with preparations to head west.

MARCH 26, 1805. Opposite the fort, the ice-choked Missouri ran heavy with broken slabs, causing problems with bringing the canoes down from the building camp. As the men were floating them down the river, drifting ice slabs looked to overcome the canoes and damage them. Quick work by the boatmen saved them from being impacted.

MARCH 27, 1805. The captains had the pirogues and the new canoes, now all at the fort, corked, pitched, and tarred to seal up leaks, which were especially evident in the wind-shaken cottonwood canoes. Lewis noticed the first insect of spring, a large black gnat.

MARCH 28, 1805. Few Indians visited the fort, probably because many were at the riverbank hoping to snare dead buffalo that floated by among the slabs of ice. Bison that had broken through the ice and drown provided an important source of meat for Knife River natives. Clark discovered that the Indians relished decomposing meat. The men worked at making oars and poles.

MARCH 29, 1805. The natives busied themselves along the river and on the ice slabs, jumping from one sheet to another to catch the floating bison. Clark was struck by their dexterity, as some ice segments were no larger than two feet square. During the day Indians set the plains on fire much as they had earlier in the month in order to burn off the winter's dead cover and stimulate the growth of new grass, thus providing forage for their horses and attracting wandering buffalo. An obstacle in the Missouri above the fort broke away and ice rushed down the river in great quantities, causing the river to rise thirteen inches in twenty-four hours. The increasing appearance of insects was an indicator of annoyances to come.

MARCH 30, 1805. In the closing days at Fort Mandan, Clark found all the party in high spirits and "perfect harmony." Hardly an evening went by without music and dancing. The men were generally healthy except for venereal disease that they had contracted from Indian women. Lewis carried out more astronomical observations.

MARCH 31, 1805. Ice thinned in the river.

APRIL 1, 1805. Along with thunder, lightning, and hail, rain poured forth—the first of any consequence for several months. Rain continued through the night. The captains had the boats put in the river. Clark wrote briefly of the numbers and composition for the returning keelboat and for the permanent party in two pirogues and six canoes heading west. It was much the same as the final arrangements on April 7.

APRIL 2, 1805. The captains spent most of the day writing, some of their efforts going into bringing journals up to date or otherwise preparing letters. Clark stayed up late attending to pen and paper. He now decided to send expedition journals to the president with the returning party. Although there is uncertainly and debate about which notebooks and manuscripts were sent, they seem mostly likely to have included the following: notebooks now known as Codices A, B, and C at the American Philosophical Society, Philadelphia, which include Clark's entries from May 14, 1804, to April 7, 1805; and perhaps a part of Clark's field notes at the Beinecke Collection, Yale University, New Haven, Connecticut, which in their entirety covered the period from December 13, 1803, to April 3, 1805. A portion of Clark's field notes, or perhaps all sixty-seven sheets, were sent to his brother, Jonathan Clark, in Louisville, Kentucky. Mandans killed twenty-one elks some fifteen miles below the fort, but the animals were so meager they were hardly fit to eat. Raven Man Chief was miffed that the captains were not paying enough attention to him and returned to his village after having spent ten days at the fort.

APRIL 3, 1805. Being anxious to leave, Clark declared that the party would set out the next day. The actual departure was on April 7. Larocque and McKenzie came to the fort. The visit was not entirely social since McKenzie wanted payment for two horses on loan to the explorers. Clark agreed to pay him for at least one of the animals, which was lost during the Sioux robbery on February 15.

The captains filled containers with articles bound downriver for the president. In four boxes, a large trunk, and three cages the captains packed an incredible array of items that they had collected to this point. Examples of plains animal life were numerous: skins and bones of pronghorns; horns, tail, and ears of a mule deer; a marten's skin; the bones of a coyote and a white-tailed jackrabbit; skins and bones of badgers; horns of a bighorn sheep; skins of a weasel and red squirrels; various mice and insect specimens; and the skin of a grizzly bear. The boxes also contained products of Plains Indian material life, including a Mandan bow and a quiver of arrows, an ear of Mandan corn, a carrot of Arikara tobacco, Hidatsa and Mandan buffalo robes, buffalo robes with depictions of Indian battles, and examples of Mandan pottery. One box had over sixty mineralogical specimens the captains had collected up to Fort Mandan. At an unknown date the specimens were transferred to the Academy of Natural Sciences, Philadelphia, and were integrated into the general collections. Only three specimens today can be definitely linked to the expedition. The same box contained sixty plant specimens, the first thirty of which are now missing from the Lewis and Clark collection at the Academy of Natural Sciences. Finally, the cages contained living animals, including a prairie dog, four magpies, and a sharp-tailed grouse. Only the prairie dog and one magpie reached Jefferson alive.

APRIL 4, 1805. Brant passed upriver. Lewis commented at length on the force and constancy of the wind, which blew across the plains unobstructed by trees and which hampered navigation on the river. Probably sensing how engaged the party was in preparations for setting out, Larocque and McKenzie bid farewell. Packing and loading continued, especially of the keelboat destined for St. Louis.

APRIL 5, 1805. Equipment, provisions, and "stores" were loaded into the two pirogues and six canoes that would face the Missouri River's current the day after next. Ordway declared the party "ready for a start." Mandans came to the fort for a visit. And Gass gave a critical review of sexual practices among the natives:

> We ought . . . to give some account of the *fair sex* of the Missouri; and entertain [readers] with narratives of feats of love as well as of arms. Though we could furnish a sufficient number of entertaining stories and pleasant anecdotes, we do not think it prudent to swell our Journal with them; as our views are directed to more useful information. . . . It may be observed generally that chastity is not very highly esteemed by these people, and that the severe and loathsome effects *of certain French principles* are not uncommon among them. The fact is, that the women are generally considered an article of traffic and *indulgencies* are sold at a very moderate price. As a proof of this I will just mention, that for an old tobacco box, one of our men was granted the honour of passing a night with the daughter of the headchief of the Mandan nation. An old bawd with her punks, may also be found in some of the villages on the Missouri, as well as in the large cities of polished nations.

APRIL 6, 1805. A flock of cedar waxwings arrived at Knife River, and after obtaining one Lewis wrote a long description of the familiar bird. More Mandans came by and reported the arrival of numerous Arikaras at an abandoned village across the Missouri. The captains sent an interpreter, probably Gravelines, over to see if any of the chiefs would join the returning keelboat and continue on to meet the president in Washington DC.

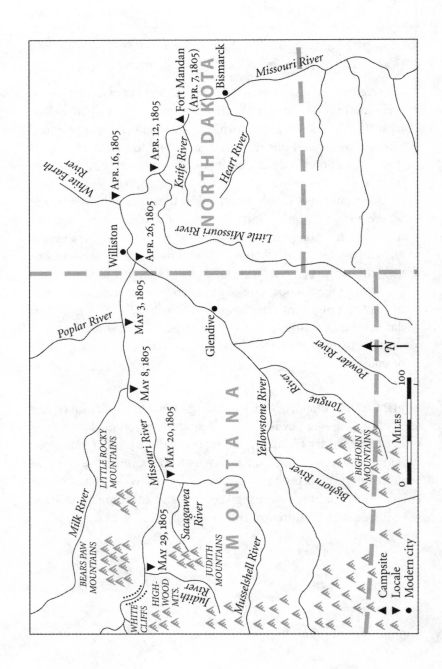

Map 5. The expedition's route, April 7–June 2, 1805.

CHAPTER 4

Into the Unknown

April 7–June 2, 1805

APRIL 7, 1805. Again, as on May 14, 1804, the party prepared for a four o'clock departure, now under a strong headwind on a fair day. Although it was a brisk 28° at sunrise, by midafternoon the temperature had climbed to the midsixties. The party was newly divided, first into a crew that would manage the keelboat for its return trip down the Missouri to St. Louis. Led by Corporal Warfington, this return party counted the two discharged soldiers, Newman and Reed, and Warfington's regular squad of Boley, Dame, Tuttle, White, and perhaps Robertson, but the exact membership of the boatmen is uncertain. Gravelines was also on board, as was an Arikara Indian, both bound for the Arikara villages. Even less certain are the identities of other passengers on the keelboat and in an accompanying canoe, noted simply as "Frenchmen." The permanent party now formed the Corps of Discovery, heading west in two pirogues and six canoes. Numbering thirty-three persons, the corps consisted of the two captains, three sergeants, twenty-three privates, Drouillard, York, Charbonneau, Sacagawea, and her baby. And of course, there was Lewis's Newfoundland dog, Seaman. A Mandan Indian also joined the group with a promise to accompany the party to the Shoshone Indians and there work for better relations between the tribes, but he left the party two days later. Contemplating the departure from Fort Mandan, Lewis took a view to the past and wrote optimistically of the future:

> This little fleet altho' not quite so rispectable as those of Columbus or Capt. Cook were still viewed by us with as much pleasure as those deservedly famed adventurers ever beheld theirs; and I dare say with quite as much anxiety for their safety and preserva-

tion. we were now about to penetrate a country at least two thousand miles in width, on which the foot of civillized man had never trodden; the good or evil it had in store for us was for experiment yet to determine, and these little vessells contained every article by which we were to expect to subsist or defend ourselves . . . entertaing as I do, the most confident hope of succeading in a voyage which had formed a da[r]ling project of mine for the last ten years, I could but esteem this moment of my departure as among the most happy of my life. The party are in excellent health and sperits, zealously attatched to the enterprise, and anxious to proceed; not a whisper of murmur or discontent to be heard among them, but all act in unison, and with the most perfect harmony.

Before the departure, Gravelines returned to the fort with Raven Man (Kakawita), a chief of the Arikaras whom the captains apparently had not met earlier, and three others of the tribe. Raven Man informed the captains that he came to discover the Knife River Indians' attitude about his tribe settling near them and also to visit with the Assiniboines and Crows about a move in their direction. The Arikaras sought mutual protection among friendly tribes against the common enemy, the Sioux. The captains welcomed this alliance and assured him of the United States' goal of stopping Sioux aggression. They presented him with a certificate, a small metal, and other items in recognition of his status. Raven Man also brought a letter from Tabeau informing the captains that some Arikara chiefs wanted to visit Washington and that he wanted to load some men and pelts on the keelboat. Lewis and Clark readily assented to this plan, as it would add manpower and firepower to the boat and act as a deterrent to possible Teton attacks.

Having had no exercise for several weeks, Lewis took to the northeast shore and walked as far as Ruptáre village hoping to see Black Cat. Finding the chief away and the boat party under Clark still downriver, the captain retreated about two miles to the evening's camp across from Mitutanka, in McLean County, North Dakota. For the night and possibly for some time to come, Lewis and Clark slept in a large, buffalo-hide, Indian-style tipi along with Drouillard, Charbonneau, Sacagawea, and the baby. The rest of the party probably stayed in canvas tents, arranging themselves into various and unknown groupings.

APRIL 8, 1805. Lewis again walked on shore and found Black Cat at his village. After smoking a pipe with him, the captain proceeded on about four miles and waited for the party. Later Clark and the boat party passed Ruptáre and the villagers flocked to the river to watch the little flotilla pass by. Clark also had a visit with Black Cat and received a pair of moccasins from the chief. The boats came up to Lewis about noon, but one was behind in distress having filled with water and soiled some goods, including a bag of biscuits and about thirty pounds of powder. This was the only loose gunpowder on the boats, but the captains still considered it a serious loss and spread it out to dry, hoping to rescue some. In weather notes the captains gave an accounting of birds observed at Fort Mandan, including magpies, ravens, undesignated woodpeckers, golden eagles ("*calumet bird*"), and sharp-tailed grouse ("Prairie Hen or grouse"). After lunch the party moved to the night's encampment in McLean County, North Dakota, a mile or so below Garrison Dam and about three miles for the day. While encamped the Mandans brought to the captains an Indian woman who wanted to accompany one of the men on the trip. They refused.

APRIL 9, 1805. The corps got an early start and had breakfast after some traveling. After eating, the Mandan Indian accompanying the party decided not to go on and left for home. Lewis observed snow geese passing up the river and noticed the slight difference between the white and blue genetic morphs of the species. The captain also noted the workings of the northern pocket gopher, which established hillocks from its subterranean diggings much like the southeastern pocket gopher with which Lewis was familiar from South Carolina and Georgia. The gopher's mounds were equivalent to nearly ten or twelve pounds of loose earth. Along the river's bluffs Lewis saw horizontal strata of lignite coal ("carbonated wood"). Over millions of years immense quantities of accumulated plant material in the area underwent physical, chemical, and biological alteration to become vast lignite coal reserves. Those and other deposits compose the Bullion Creek and Sentinel Butte Formations. Farther out broken hills appeared to have been on fire and showed considerable signs of lignite coal, which catches fire and fuses overlying clay to superficially resemble volcanic substances (now referred to as "paralava").

At lunch, Sacagawea sought out Jerusalem artichokes, which Lewis described. Lewis also related a method she used to rob the driftwood stashes of meadow mice in order to retrieve the hog peanut. When Clark took a turn on shore, he saw what may have been Richardson's ground squirrel. And he noticed a mosquito—a pest that would torment the party unmercifully in days to come. In fact, Ordway wrote that "the Musquetoes begin to Suck our blood this afternoon." Clark also sighted boxelder, elm, and cottonwood trees and red osier dogwood bushes, in addition to prairie flowers and two species of junipers, Rocky Mountain juniper, an upright tree found on hillsides, and creeping juniper, a low, dwarf species. On the unsteady pirogue, Lewis complained that he could hardly write. Along the way the party passed Hidatsa wintering and hunting camps and Snake ("Miry") Creek, McLean County, North Dakota. The party camped again in McLean County, a few miles southwest of Garrison, having made about twenty-three miles by the captains' estimate.

APRIL 10, 1805. Not out of range of Hidatsas, Indians gathered on shore to watch the party pass. Clark saw a herd of pronghorns but was unable to get a clear shot at one. Spring prairie grasses attracted geese, which were feeding in the bottomlands. Mosquitoes renewed their annoying tactics. From the tops of the river hills, Lewis described a level, fertile plain without a solitary tree or shrub to be seen except in low, moist areas protected from the ravages of prairie fires. About dozen or so miles into the day's route, Lewis saw a bluff on fire and smelled the sulfurous content of the Sentinel Butte Formation on the edge of the Badlands in Mercer County, North Dakota. During the course of the day, the party overtook three French hunters who had set out ahead of the corps in order to trap beavers. They had taken twelve animals since leaving the Knife River villages. Lewis called the beaver skins the best he had ever seen. The Frenchmen joined the corps for a time in order to protect themselves against any Assiniboines who might be patrolling the area and looking for bounty or trouble. Finding the current of the Missouri somewhat moderate, the party moved on with comparative ease, making about eighteen miles. They camped above the later site of Fort Berthold, McLean County, North Dakota.

APRIL 11, 1805. The river party set out early while Clark and Drouillard hunted on shore. Clark noticed that prairie grasses were greening up in the sandy soil of glacial till. After making a few miles the boats stopped for breakfast and Clark and Drouillard arrived, bringing a welcome deer to the morning's repast. It was especially gratifying as the party had been without fresh meat for several days. The men discovered that the Hidatsas had so effectively hunted a wide area around the Knife River villages that game was difficult to obtain. Lewis was happy to find that the gunpowder soaked in the accident of April 8 was drying and the damage was not as great as supposed. Salty springs feeding into the Missouri were strong and bitter to the taste and acted as a purgative to drinkers. Evaporating waters produced a salty crust on the ground, and Lewis noticed the abundance of clusters of the white substance. As whooping cranes, ducks, geese, gulls, and brant passed overhead the party reached the night's encampment a few miles below the mouth of the Little Missouri River, McLean County, North Dakota, having traveled about nineteen miles. Across from camp they spotted a hunting party, perhaps Hidatsas, but the wide river prevented them from crossing for a visit.

APRIL 12, 1805. At the mouth of the Little Missouri River, a few miles above the previous day's camp, the party set up camp early so the captains could engage in scientific work. Lewis took astronomical observations and carried out some botanical collecting, while Clark noted wildlife and observed geologic features of the country. It was also an opportunity for the men to rest a bit, and ten men went out to hunt for fresh meat. The hunt was not successful and only a single deer was brought in. Before arriving at the campsite, Lewis had the men maneuver the white pirogue and the canoes to the south side of the Missouri in order to avoid a bank that was falling in on the opposite side. Unaware of Lewis's action, the red pirogue did not follow suit and passed dangerously near the hazardous shore, causing the captain anxious moments. Watching the near catastrophe from a distance, he decided not to shout orders and relaxed only when the boat got by without incident.

Lewis's astronomical observations were unsatisfactory, as the evening proved too cloudy after the thunder and rain of the afternoon, so he took time for other activities. He gathered a small quantity of wild onions on the plains and collected a specimen of creeping juniper. The captain labeled the juniper "No. 2," indicating that he had collected another plant earlier without noting it in his daily journal. This specimen and all the others that he collected between Fort Mandan and Upper Portage Camp were lost in a cache at the White Bear Islands near Upper Portage Camp when water seeped in and destroyed the plants before Lewis returned to the spot on July 13, 1806, to recover his goods. Lewis found the plant in its natural habitat of dry, rocky, open hillsides, and he wrote a short description of the specimen. He compared it to common box but considered the juniper more attractive and better suited for garden edgings and walkways.

Lewis wrote a detailed description about the size, course, and character of the Little Missouri River and noted that its course had been placed too far to the southwest on Clark's Fort Mandan map in relation to the Killdeer Mountains in Dunn County, North Dakota. Lewis gained information from Lepage, who had been on the river previously. In the river's bottomlands he observed cottonwood, elm, ash, willow, and boxelder trees, while he described the underbrush as thick with red osier dogwoods, buffaloberries, and chokecherry bushes. His evaluation of the land about the Little Missouri was quite positive: "the soil appears fertile and deep, it consists generally of a dark rich loam intermixed with a small proportion of fine sand."

Clark too had time for excursions, during which he killed a white-tailed jackrabbit and observed magpies, grouse, western meadowlarks, and crows. Along the Little Missouri he witnessed the results of weathered glacial till and rocks brought in by glacial ice, one being

Knife River flint that had probably been carried to the spot by the Missouri River's action. He also noticed the remains of Hidatsa and Assiniboine hunting camps. When examining the canoes Clark discovered that mice had gotten into the bags of corn and parched meal.

APRIL 13, 1805. Disappointed at his inability to get a longitudinal fix at the Little Missouri, Lewis directed the party to set out. With a favorable wind at their back until midafternoon, the men raised sails on the white pirogue to ease their labors. Considered the more trustworthy of the two pirogues, this vessel carried the scientific instruments, papers, books, medicine, and most of the gifts for Indians and its occupants included the captains (when not on shore) and Sacagawea, her child, and her husband. In fact, Charbonneau was steering the boat when a squall of wind hit the pirogue and turned it sideways into the wind, frightening the Frenchman to the point that he lost control and brought the boat nearly to going under. At the same moment that the wind settled, Lewis ordered Drouillard to take control of the boat and drop the sails, which he did quickly and corrected the situation. Reflecting on the circumstance, with three nonswimmers on board plus the woman and child, Lewis declared that had the boat overturned these persons would probably have been lost, as the waves were high and the shore was more than two hundred yards away.

The French hunters who were with the party were so successful in beaver trapping that they decided to stay near the mouth of the Little Missouri as the corps moved on. As Clark surveyed the surrounding area he found forty-three temporary Indian lodges, which he supposed were Assiniboine camps. Lewis saw buffalo and elks at a distance from the river and buffalo carcasses along the shore, probably drowned from falling through the ice during the winter. Enormous bear tracks near the remains indicated the presence of grizzly bears feeding on the fallen. Lewis declared the men's desire to meet the grand beast, as they had heard many stories of its strength and ferocity from Indians and were anxious to try out their weapons on the formidable animal. Indeed, Lewis belittled the Indians' abilities against the bear with their bows and arrows and inferior weapons with which they had little skill. Lewis noted a phenomenon unknown to him from the East: that here Canada geese built their nests in trees. Overhead he observed bald eagles, kestrels ("sparrow hawk"), brants, and geese. The party camped in Mountrail County, North Dakota, near a spot later called Fort Maneury Bend, having made about twenty-three miles.

APRIL 14, 1805. Mineral deposits of the Sentinel Butte Formation caught Lewis's attention, and he mentioned salts, coal, and pumice-like rocks but may have been incorrect in naming sulfur, since the rocks of this area contain little of the substance. He also noted the mineralized groundwater and its discoloration. On Clark's rambles he discovered more Indian lodges, presumably Assiniboine, with discarded metal hoops from rum or whiskey barrels. Clark described in some detail the composition, decoration, and positioning of Assiniboine buffalo-hide tents. Lewis wrote a bit on Assiniboine drinking habits and the tribe's trade with British fur companies, also noting with Clark that their hunters had left the area devoid of wildlife. While the bottomlands through which the party passed were broad, moist, and somewhat timbered, the uplands were broken, devoid of trees, and given to grassy knobs. Lewis considered the plants on the hilltops and noted sages, hyssops, wormwoods, and southern-woods, with which he was familiar, as well as junipers and plants new to him: big and silver sagebrushes. Magpies and a great horned owl also caught his attention, and he noted the slight differences between this owl and its eastern variety. The party lunched near a prairie dog ("burrowing squirrels") village. Above that Lewis declared this the highest point to which any white man had ascended, except Lepage, who may have hunted a few miles upriver. Close by they passed Bear Den ("Sharbono's") Creek, entering the Missouri near the Dunn-McKenzie county line, North Dakota. The party camped across and a little above the creek in Mountrail County, after coming about fourteen miles.

APRIL 15, 1805. As Lewis walked on shore, Clark directed the boat party following a rule that both not be absent from boats at the same time. In Lewis's six-mile jaunt spring presented itself with the cry of the chorus frog. Trees began to show green coloration in spite of ground that was frozen to a depth of nearly three feet. The captain also commented on the call and behavior of the sharp-tailed grouse ("Grouse or *prarie hens*"), which he compared to the familiar ruffed grouse from the East. Later in the morning Clark took a turn on shore, climbed to a high point, and surveyed the Missouri River valley as far as he could see—a beautiful, open, fertile plain, he called it. But subsidiary streams of the great river he deemed brackish and unfit for use. He also found more temporary Assiniboine camps near the Little Knife River where native hunters had set up pens or compounds to catch pronghorns; hence he called the river "Goat Pen Creek" on expedition maps. Lewis must have queried Clark about the pens, as his journal has a more extensive description of the structures than Clark's. The corps camped several miles beyond the mouth of the Little Knife River and on the opposite side in McKenzie County, North Dakota, about twenty-three miles above the previous camp.

APRIL 16, 1805. The captains' comments on the landscape continued as usual. Lewis found petrified wood and theorized that it had been created by actions of the Missouri River. It is more likely that the wood petrified in the Paleocene epoch and rolled down hills or drifted to this point. He also observed lignite coal of the Bullion Creek Formation and discussed its proximity to other substances. Beavers were more abundant and their work on willows and cottonwoods was everywhere apparent. Few ducks were sighted, but mallards and blue-winged teals were seen. Lewis noticed his first bat. Ordway observed piles of ice along the shore—about four feet high—carried down during the spring thaw. He also saw trees greening and grass rising on the plains. After passing White Earth River the party camped a little above Beaver Creek but on the opposite side in McKenzie County, North Dakota, after traveling about eighteen miles.

APRIL 17, 1805. With an early start the corps managed to make twenty-six miles—quite a feat going upriver against a strong current, but a steady southeast wind helped carry them westward. Clark spent the day on shore and did not return to camp until after six o'clock. He saw the remains of more Assiniboine camps and numerous wildlife, including a curlew, new to science. From the boat Lewis counted immense herds of buffalo, elks, and pronghorns and scatterings of deer and wolves. Lewis killed one buffalo, but it was so poor that he took only the tongue; another one proved equally inedible. A catch of three beavers provided the meat that the men relished. Lewis especially savored the tail and liver. Catfish caught this day may have been added to the evening's meal. They camped again in McKenzie County, North Dakota.

APRIL 18, 1805. A beaver caught with a leg in each of two traps nearly caused a fracas between two unnamed members of the party who each claimed the bounty. Clark was again out, now accompanied by a slightly ill Charbonneau, plus Sacagawea and the baby. With a less helpful wind, the men were forced to resort to the tow lines, pulling the boats upriver. Lewis walked along with them. In the early afternoon the headwind became so strong that the men were forced to abandon their labors and wait it out. Finding buffalo hair caught in a rosebush, Lewis surmised that it would make an excellent wool, as it was finer than that of sheep and also more silky and soft. A flock of pelicans passed overhead. Camp was not obtained until dark, in Williams County, North Dakota, after about thirteen miles.

APRIL 19, 1805. A strong wind from the northwest kept the party in camp. The captains remarked that beavers in this area appeared more abundant, larger, fatter, and with a thicker, darker fur than any they had previously seen. Berry bushes were in bloom.

APRIL 20, 1805. Reversing positions, Lewis took to land while Clark remained with the boat party. Ever the botanist, Lewis counted cottonwoods, boxelders, ash, elms, willows, rosebushes, honeysuckles, snowberries, red osier dogwoods, gooseberries, currants, serviceberries, and sagebrushes on his ramble. He also noted the remains of an abandoned Indian camp with a burial scaffold still standing. Although it stood about seven feet off the ground, the contents had fallen through to the ground so Lewis was able to get a look.

He viewed a woman's body wrapped in buffalo skins and a bag of belongings that included a pair of moccasins, a bit of red and blue earth, beaver claws, a bluejay, dried roots, braided sweetgrass, Indian tobacco, and utensils. The contents also included dog travois and harnesses. Nearby he saw the carcass of a dog and presumed that it was killed to accompany its owner to an afterlife. He wrote that sacrificing horses or dogs for the deceased was a common Plains Indian custom. He knew of no instances of human sacrifice. On the river it was hard going. with heavy winds and choppy water, so little distance was made. A collapsing cliff stirred up water and almost capsized the canoe Ordway oversaw. Blowing sand created a thick fog and further inhibited progress. After about six miles the corps landed in Williams County, North Dakota; the men laid out provisions to air and dry.

APRIL 21, 1805. Still chilly with a frost in the morning, on this day Ordway found water frozen in buckets near the campfire. At different times the captains were with separate hunting parties, taking deer, beavers, otters, and buffalo. The four buffalo calves they took were especially delicious, and Lewis compared them to the best veal he had ever tasted. A hard wind in the evening forced a halt; nevertheless the party made over sixteen miles and camped opposite the Little Muddy ("*White earth*") River, McKenzie County, and nearly opposite Williston, North Dakota.

APRIL 22, 1805. Again the wind was up and the men were put to the tow ropes, while the captains went ashore to examine the country around the Little Muddy River. They found saline deposits so widespread as to nearly color the earth white. Probably based on Indian information, the captains speculated that the river might be navigable to its source, that being near the Saskatchewan River or perhaps at least as far as 50° N. This was an optimistic estimate, perhaps based on a hope that the Louisiana Purchase might extend into that region and gain territory for the United States. In fact the river's source and course are some distance from the present Canadian border. Lewis also gave attention to geologic features of the Missouri River valley, noting that the broken hills displayed large masses of broken rocks, including granite, flint, limestone, freestone, and petrified wood that would make excellent whetstones. The large rocks are glacial erratics while smaller ones are derived from the Canadian Shield and from lower Paleozoic formations to the west. From a bluff Lewis had a vast view of the Missouri River valley, unhampered by timber and revealing enormous herds of buffalo, elks, pronghorns, and deer feeding on a boundless pasture. A buffalo calf attached itself to Lewis, who took a stroll in the evening. It stayed with him until the captain returned to the boat. After eleven miles the party camped a few miles above Williston, on the opposite side in McKenzie County, North Dakota.

APRIL 23, 1805. With a wind so violent and the river so turbulent, Lewis was barely able to get the boats into a safe spot without serious accident. Even so, some canoes took on water that damaged provisions. Those were taken out to air and dry while the party waited out the windstorm. It was five in the evening before the boats were launched again but even with this late start the corps made over thirteen miles for the day. Clark was out hunting in the morning—upon returning he found the party huddled against the wind. He commented on the impeding force of the winds and its ability to slow progress. The captain had killed three mule deer along with other animals, and his use of the term *mule deer* may have been a first for this expedition discovery. Another first for the season was the sighting of a robin. The party camped on the north side of the river in Williams County, North Dakota.

APRIL 24, 1805. The wind kept up its tempest and forced the party to stay off the river. Rising water reached the small canoes and wet articles before they could be unloaded and brought to safety. Hunters were out nonetheless and brought in buffalo, deer, and elk meat. One hunter also brought in six coyote pups. Members of the party complained of sore eyes, which the captains attributed to the fine particles of blowing sand that permeated everything. They ate, drank, and breathed the dust. Lewis even blamed the malfunction of his pocket watch on the invasive irritant.

APRIL 25, 1805. Moderating winds allowed the party to set out at an early hour but icy-cold water caused oars and paddles to freeze over. Seaman, who had been out all night, returned to camp and eased Lewis's worries for his dog. Having been forced ashore by heavy winds at midmorning, Lewis decided to take a small party and push ahead by land on the south side of the Missouri to the mouth of the Yellowstone River while Clark and the boat party followed the twisting river to that point. He took Ordway, Drouillard, Joseph Field, and one other man with him. From an eminence Lewis could follow the tree line of the Yellowstone to its entrance into the Missouri. The party applied varied spellings to the French name of the river, Roche Jaune. From his perch the captain viewed a country teeming with wildlife. As he pushed on, buffalo, elks, and deer were so gentle that the men could pass near them without arousing them to run. The men killed and dressed buffalo, carried meat with them to the Yellowstone, and hung other pieces for later use and out of the reach of wolves. They also took half a dozen eggs out of a goose's nest. Lewis and his small party moved two miles up the Yellowstone and made camp.

Meanwhile Clark pushed forward with the boats but rising winds forced an early stop. In the evening the winds lulled, so the boats set out again and made over fourteen miles on a difficult day but did not reach the Yellowstone. Clark's party camped on the north side of the Missouri in Williams County, North Dakota, about eight miles from the Yellowstone. Gass and other writers observed the lack of dew and rain in the region. The sergeant, or his editor, thought the phenomenon might be caused by the absence of timber, stating the later-discredited idea that rain increased where trees grew or were planted.

APRIL 26, 1805. Lewis sent Joseph Field up the Yellowstone River to explore as far as he could and still be back by evening, while two others were directed to bring in meat secured the previous day. The captain took another man, probably Drouillard, with him about two miles to the mouth of the Yellowstone. Along this course of the river and at the conjunction with the Missouri, Lewis viewed a heavily timbered terrain of cottonwoods, elms, ash, and boxelders.

On the sandbars and in the undergrowth were willows, and in the low bottoms, rosebushes, red osier dogwoods, and serviceberries. On the higher bottoms he reported more willows, along with gooseberries, chokecherries, currants, and honeysuckle bushes. Hyssop covered open areas that bordered the hills and was a favorite food of ungulates. Sandbar willows were also a choice food of these animals as well as nourishment for grouse, porcupines, jackrabbits, and cottontails.

Toward noon Lewis heard the report of guns and sent Drouillard to have some of Clark's party come ahead and retrieve meat from the previous day's hunt. That evening in camp at the mouth of the Yellowstone, the captains ordered a dram of alcohol for each person in celebration of reaching this important point in their exploration. Out came the fiddle, and the party spent the evening, as Lewis described it, "with much hilarity, singing & dancing, and [forgetting] their past toils." Joseph Field returned from his excursion up the Yellowstone and gave a report of the country that was very similar to the captains' descriptions of the Missouri valley. Field may have been the first member of the party to sight bighorn sheep but could not get a shot at one, so he brought back a large horn that he picked up on his walk.

Lewis repeated geographic information that he had received from Indians about the courses and sources of western rivers, including the Missouri and Yellowstone. While generally accurate, a good deal was a mixture of speculation and miscommunication. Lewis failed to get a fix on the party's location, but Clark was more successful in measuring the widths of the two rivers (520 yards for the Missouri, 858 for the Yellowstone) and in generally surveying the point. He thought the area a prime situation for a fort. Examining the point he saw many dead buffalo on the riverbanks, most stripped of their meat by scavengers, and he speculated that they had been drowned while crossing the ice during the winter or had collapsed in exhaustion after attempting to swim the wide and rushing rivers. During the day Seaman sighted a pronghorn crossing the Yellowstone, jumped in, drowned it, and brought it back to shore. Clark, like Lewis, wrote of the varied wildlife and reported "beaver is in every bend." The enlisted writers calculated that the party was

1,888 miles from the mouth of the Missouri and 279 miles beyond Fort Mandan.

APRIL 27, 1805. Lewis spent part of the morning trying to get coordinates at the intersection of the two rivers but was again unsuccessful. He then walked ahead of the boat party and wrote favorable descriptions of the landscape. He also deliberated on the best site for a fort or trading establishment in the area. Unable to rejoin the main party, he killed a goose for lunch and noted that the party killed only what was necessary to feed themselves. With wildlife so abundant, he thought that two good hunters could easily supply a regiment. Getting the boats underway after breakfast, Clark and party were forced to halt when heavy winds came up before noon and were not able to resume the upriver labors until four in the afternoon. Camp was made in Roosevelt County, Montana, a mile below and opposite the village of Nohly, Richland County.

APRIL 28, 1805. Contrary to days past, the winds proved favorable, so sails were raised on the boats, which eased the men's labors and added twenty-four miles to their trip. In another switch, Clark walked on shore with Charbonneau while Lewis managed the boats. Both men commented on the continuing variety of mineral deposits, particularly the great quantities of lignite coal and salts that covered the land to such an extent as to make it appear that snow or frost had blanketed the ground. Four grizzly bears were sighted in the evening, and a rifleman may have wounded one. The corps camped in Roosevelt County, Montana, near and opposite Otis Creek.

APRIL 29, 1805. On shore Lewis had the party's first encounter with a grizzly bear. He and a walking companion came on two of them and wounded both; one took off but the other pursued Lewis some seventy or eighty yards. It was so badly wounded that the captain was able to outdistance it, reload his rifle, and finish it off. It was a male of about three hundred pounds. Lewis took space in his journal to describe it and speak of its ferocity. He was much impressed by reports that the bear could take multiple hits and keep coming, but he again disparaged this Indian information, saying that the natives had inferior weapons to meet this foe. Using a famous phrase he may have come to regret, he wrote, "but in the hands of skillfull riflemen they are by no means as formidable or dangerous as they have been represented."

Lewis viewed abundant wildlife in all directions, particularly the dominant plains ruminants—deer, elks, pronghorns, and buffalo—and the ever-present wolves who preyed on inattentive grazers. The captain noted that wolves in packs of six, eight, or ten were particularly keen on pronghorns that they caught swimming clumsily across rivers and easily dispatched. Seaman had taken one in just such a situation. Much harder to catch on the plains, one of the swift runners had to be singled out and worn to exhaustion by alternating hunters from the pack. In his notes for this date Biddle related that curiosity got the best of pronghorns on some occasions. From a prone position hunters could wave an object and entice the curious creatures to come close enough to shoot. Clark spotted bighorn sheep during the day but shooters were unable to kill one given its swiftness over difficult terrain. Whitehouse wrote that Sacagawea informed the men that bighorns were common in the Rocky Mountains. On the plains Ordway saw a stray horse that had gone feral. After Lewis returned to the boats, Clark went out for a time. Both men noted abundant lignite coal through the region, part of the Tongue River Member of the Fort Union Formation. Clark explored a stream about three miles above its mouth and named it "Martheys river" in honor of "the Selebrated M. F.," whose identity remains unknown. It is now Big Muddy Creek in Roosevelt County, Montana, above which the party camped, having come about twenty-five miles.

APRIL 30, 1805. Although the wind blew hard all night and into the day, the corps pushed on and made about twenty-four miles in the face of it. The lack of timber continued to catch the attention of the captains, but Clark could still call the bottomlands extensive and fertile. Clark walked ahead with Charbonneau and Sacagawea and, though not mentioned, certainly her baby. Sacagawea brought the captain a currant that she said had a delicious flavor and was abundant in the Rocky Mountains. The buffalo currant she picked

is not found in the Rockies but is very similar to the golden currant of the area. After their return, Lewis went out for a time and
killed what he thought was the largest elk he had ever seen. It measured five feet, three inches from the point of its hoof to the top of
its shoulder. The men ignored the large herds of buffalo swimming
across the Missouri—they had meat enough, Ordway conceded.
Camp was in Richland County, opposite and near present Brock-
ton, Roosevelt County, Montana.

MAY 1, 1805. Catching a favorable wind, the crew raised the sails
and set out at a good pace at sunrise. But one canoe became separated from the flotilla because of heavy winds and high waves and
spent the night apart from the group. Whitehouse, who was in the
detached boat, reported suffering a miserable, cold night without
covering. The main party had to cut short the day after about ten
miles and camped in Roosevelt County, Montana, in the vicinity
of later Elkhorn Point. Shields complained of rheumatism. Shannon killed an American avocet and brought it for Lewis to examine.
Already known to science, the bird nevertheless earned a lengthy
description from the captain in both his regular journal and his scientific notebook. Clark added a shorter account of the bird to his
own journal. Positive descriptions of the country continued, marking it as abundant in wildlife, fertile, and heavily timbered in the
river bottoms.

MAY 2, 1805. Heavy winds continued through the night and snowfall
greeted the party at sunrise. The inch of white covering contrasted
sharply with greening vegetation and flowering plants. The winds
kept the party in camp until about three o'clock in the afternoon,
which gave time for an advance of only four or five miles. Along
with the regular diet of deer, elks, and buffalo, the party also secured
three beavers, with a meat that Lewis relished. He especially liked
the tail boiled and compared it to Atlantic cod. It could easily make
a meal for two men, the captain conceded. One of the men shot an
Indian dog that had been stealing the party's food. While out hunting Joseph Field noticed a piece of scarlet cloth hanging from a tree
limb and brought it back for inspection. Lewis speculated that it

had been left to honor a personal deity by a native hunter and noted that Plains Indians often left prized articles in this way, hoping to obtain relief from illness or hunger, success in hunting or cultivating crops, or advantage in battle or wanting to honor friends or relatives. He also remarked that Indians called the incomprehensible "big medicine" and that it was under the power of "the great spirit." The party camped in Richland County, Montana, in the vicinity of the crossing of Montana Highway 480.

MAY 3, 1805. It being cold and icy, the party delayed setting out. A kettle left out had a quarter inch of ice on top and snow clung to hilltops. Two miles into the trip Lewis noted a bundle of bushes tied together and standing on end, perhaps a native memorial. Facing hard winds, the crew pushed on and found Clark waiting with a freshly killed elk for lunch. Clark continued his walk while Lewis stayed with the boat party and observed the scenery from a river point of view. While mineral deposits decreased, the wildlife was as ample as ever, and due to the large numbers of porcupines a passing stream was named in the animal's honor; it is now Poplar River, Roosevelt County, Montana, a few miles above the party's camp, reached after traveling some eighteen miles for the day. Clark went a few miles up the Poplar, and on the excursion he waded the stream, counting 112 steps to cross it. It reached the Missouri some 2,000 miles from its mouth by the captain's calculations, providing a name, "2,000 Mile Creek," for the Redwater River, McCone County, Montana, across from the Poplar. As optimistic as he was at the Little Muddy River, Lewis thought the Poplar more robust and extensive than it is. The porcupines there were so nonchalant and clumsy that he got close enough to poke one with his espontoon.

MAY 4, 1805. The red pirogue demanded repairs in the morning after an accident to its rudder as it landed the day before. Despite a hard wind against them, the morning was not as cold as on the previous day and the snow and frost were virtually gone. Grasshoppers were seen this day. The sky was so obscured that Lewis was not able to get a fix on the latitude of Poplar River. The country was greening up and wildlife was as thick as ever. Having more than enough meat on hand, Lewis walked by vast animal herds without firing a shot and was hardly noticed. During his jaunt he saw several Indian hunting camps and described one extensively. It was apparently a Blackfeet war lodge that served as fortification, shelter from weather, base for scouting, supply depot, and message board. Lewis thought it at best an "imperfect shelter." Clark named a nearby creek "Indian Fort Creek," later Nickwall Creek, McCone County, Montana; the party camped above it and on the opposite side in Roosevelt County, making another eighteen miles. Joseph Field was sick with fever and dysentery. Lewis gave him a dose of Glauber's salts (sodium sulfate), a laxative, and drops of laudanum (tincture of opium) to help him sleep.

MAY 5, 1805. The white pirogue developed its own rudder problems after running into a submerged tree. It was easily fixed by securing rawhide around the broken part with nails. A harvest of meat was on the plains for the taking, and Lewis allowed that buffalo provided "fine veal and fat beef" along with other favorites like venison and beaver tail. He deemed elk and pronghorn inferior and less appealing. Buffalo carcasses along the shore showed the work of wolves and bears. Overhead the captain noted snow geese, brants, and Canada geese and discussed their distinctions, callings, and behavior. He gave close attention to the snow goose, even counting the sixteen feathers of its tail. Since Clark happened onto a den of young wolves, Lewis took an opportunity to discuss the two species, coyote and gray wolf. The coyote, which the men usually called the "prairie" or "small wolf," was not able to take a deer alone so it hunted in packs of ten or twelve or took smaller game near its burrow. Lewis called gray wolves "faithfull shepherds" of buffalo herds and seldom saw the shaggy beasts without a trailing pack.

More interesting, perhaps, was the grizzly bear that Clark and Drouillard dispatched. It was extremely hard to kill. Despite five bullets to its lungs and another five in various parts, it swam to an island in the Missouri River and took at least twenty minutes to die, roaring all the while. Clark reckoned that it weighed five hundred pounds but Lewis was willing to add another hundred. It measured

8 feet, 7½ inches from nose to hind feet, 5 feet, 10½ inches around the breast, and 3 feet, 11 inches around the neck. Its claws were 4⅜ inches long, with five on each foot. Most impressive was his mouth, ten times the size of the black bear's. The men boiled the meat for oil and grease to save for future use, getting about six gallons of the grease. Ordway and Whitehouse thought Joseph Field's illness worse, Gass thought he had improved. Ordway's canoe nearly capsized from a bluff collapsing on it. After lunch the party was treated to a couple of ounces of liquor, then camped southeast of present Wolf Point, Roosevelt County, Montana, a trip of about seventeen miles from the last camp.

MAY 6, 1805. With favorable winds on a pleasant day, the party set out early and made about twenty-five miles, passing several creeks, the most prominent being Wolf Creek, Roosevelt County, Montana, before settling into camp in McCone County, a few miles southwest of Oswego. Sprinkles of rain fell in the afternoon but lasted only briefly. Lewis noticed mineral deposits along the way, particularly salts formed where groundwater and surface water had evaporated; they were sodium sulfate, sodium bicarbonate, and magnesium sulfate. The captain also speculated on the reach of the streams and the country through which they passed, which he thought would be "level low dry plains." He further surmised that they got their water in the spring, discharged it quickly into the Missouri River, and then faced a lack of rain through much of the rest of the year. Lewis saw a grizzly swim the river ahead of the party, but it was out of reach. Then he recorded his memorable observation about the grizzly: "I find that the curiossity of our party is pretty well satisfyed with rispect to this anamal, the formidable appearance of the male bear killed on the 5th added to the difficulty with which they die when even shot through the vital parts, has staggered the resolution of several of them, others however seem keen for action with the bear; I expect these gentlemen will give us some amusement sho[r]tly as they soon begin now to coppolate." Clark walked on shore and killed two elks. Hunters took only the best meat from animals, and it was easy to keep the party fed from the abundance of wildlife within easy reach. Beavers peeked out from holes they had burrowed along the banks of the river as the boats passed. Joseph Field was still unwell.

MAY 7, 1805. In spite of a fine morning and an early start, the party was compelled to stop before noon due to high winds. Indeed, a steersman in one of the small canoes proved inadequate to the task and nearly sunk one boat. It was brought ashore, unloaded, and dried out. Within a couple of hours the flotilla was underway again. Lewis called the country on the north side of the river one of the most beautiful plains he had seen. It set some fifty or sixty feet above the river bottom, then leveled out as far as could be seen. Hilly on the south, the land soon became level. Seeing only bald eagles and no ospreys ("fishing hawks") or kingfishers ("blue crested fisher"), Lewis concluded that the eagles must feed on the carcasses, otherwise fish would attract the other birds. The turbid texture of the Missouri made such fishing impossible, he decided. Clark was out hunting at least part of the day. The party camped in either McCone or Valley County, Montana, depending on shifts in the river, southwest of present Frazer, having traveled about fifteen miles.

MAY 8, 1805. With a gentle breeze from behind, the party set out early only to be soon overtaken by dark clouds and light rain but not sufficient to delay progress. At noon they had lunch at the mouth of the Milk River, Valley County, Montana. Lewis took a jaunt about three miles up the river, finding it from 150 to 200 yards wide, gentle, deep, and probably navigable for some miles. As with other significant streams that entered the Missouri from the north beyond Fort Mandan, the captain speculated that the Milk might reach the Saskatchewan River in Canada. In fact, it rises in the mountains of Glacier National Park, in northwestern Montana, and flows northeast through southern Alberta before returning to the United States and meeting the Missouri River. The river retains the name given it by the corps due to its color, which Lewis called "a peculiar whiteness, being about the colour of a cup of tea with the admixture of a tablespoonfull of milk." Both captains concluded correctly that this was the stream that the Hidatsas called "the river which scoalds at all others." Clark scaled a height on the south side and got a commanding view of the Milk River valley for fifty or sixty miles. He judged it a beautiful level plain with large herds of buffalo on both sides of the river. To the south he saw the Milk River Hills that rise nearly seven hundred feet above the Missouri's floodplain.

Lewis noted the abundance of wild licorice in the area but failed to mention that Sacagawea had gathered some on the excursion with Clark. He also did not note that she gave Clark a specimen of Indian breadroot to eat. Lewis called it "white apple" after the *engagés'* name for the plant, "*pomme blanche*." It is also called prairie turnip and scurfpea. Lewis collected a specimen at some unknown date but probably not this day. The captain provided a detailed description of this scientific discovery and added ethnobotanical information. He noted that the root formed an important part of the diet of Missouri valley natives. Although they ate it year round, they particularly liked it during the harvest season, from mid-July to the end of autumn. After collecting the roots, the Indians would strip the rind, string them on cords, and dry them in the sun or over fires. A well-dried root would keep for several years in safe storage. The dried plant was eaten boiled or roasted, or it was pounded to a fine powder and used to thicken soups. Additionally it was mixed with buffalo grease and berries to make a sort of pudding. Grizzly bears fed on the root, too, using their long claws to dig it from the earth. To Lewis it was tasteless, but he thought it might serve chefs as a replacement for truffles in gravies or ragouts. In his excursion Clark saw a goat skin that an Indian had stripped of its hair. Lewis worried that it could be the work of Assiniboine Indians who might cause trouble for the corps. Clark had also seen smoke and Indian lodges up the Milk River. Although Clark mentioned that they camped early, the party made about twenty-eight miles and settled in a mile or two above Fort Peck Dam, Valley County, Montana.

MAY 9, 1805. With a favorable wind, sails went up and the party moved on. Lewis was amazed at the dry bed of today's Big Dry Creek, Garfield County, Montana—a streambed nearly as wide as the Missouri without a single drop of running water. He walked up it a few miles and climbed an elevated point to view its course and condition. He could see that it supported little timber along its valley and that its bed was composed of a light brown sand. That alluvium is from the Fort Union Formation, Hells Creek Formation, and Fox Hills Sandstone. The captain also noticed calcium, or sodium carbonate–rich, silt and selenite of the Bearpaw Shale. From a buffalo cow he salvaged the necessary pieces for Charbonneau's "*boudin blanc*" (white sausage). This was a "white pudding" highly prized by the party and the Frenchman's specialty. With a gourmet's interest Lewis described the preparation in great detail. Charbonneau first removed about six feet of the lower gut, then compressed the flesh with his hands, emptying its contents. Taking other portions of the buffalo, he tied off one end of the tube and skillfully stuffed it to its limits with delicacies before tying off the other end. After quickly dipping it in the Missouri, he first boiled then fried it with bear's oil until brown and ready to be eaten. Buffalo were easy to obtain and so gentle that the men threw sticks or clubbed them out of the way.

Fallen timber for several acres along and back from shore showed the work of beavers of the previous season. Lewis saw stumps nearly as big around as a man. A bit of anxiety set in as the captain noticed that the Missouri was not getting any narrower, but it was getting shallower, clearer, and more crowded with sandbars. He longed to get a view of the Rocky Mountains. The captain killed four willets ("plover") in the evening—a bird new to science—and wrote a scientific description, noticing the eye, head, beak, neck, feathers, and wings as well as coloring and song. He compared it to birds in the East with which he was familiar. He added nearly the same description to his zoological notes. After traveling about twenty-four miles the party made camp in Valley County, Montana, a few miles above the present town of Fort Peck, at Duck Creek, the party's "Werner's River" (after expedition member Werner).

MAY 10, 1805. A short day's travel of under five miles due to heavy winds and choppy water brought them into camp in either Garfield or Valley County, Montana, on a site now inundated by Fort Peck Reservoir. An Indian dog wandered into camp shortly after the party landed, so hunters were sent out to look for Indian signs. Lewis was concerned as he knew this to be the country of the Assiniboines, whom he considered "a vicious illy disposed nation." To be certain of their readiness the corps' weaponry was inspected—all in good order. Hunters returned in the evening reporting no sign of Indians, but they brought fresh kill, including white-tailed deer, mule deer, buffalo, and beavers. They also sighted more mule deer and bighorn sheep. One man who must have stayed behind caught a number of fish. Lewis commented on the frequency of boils and abscesses among the party, particularly Bratton, who was unable to use his hand due to a sore. Eye problems also persisted. For the abscesses Lewis applied a damp, warm poultice to the sore, while he mixed a solution of zinc sulfate and lead acetate for injured eyes. Both remedies he probably learned directly from Benjamin Rush in Philadelphia or from medical books prior to setting out on the expedition.

Having specimens of deer before him, Lewis wrote a detailed description of the mule deer, comparing it to the more common white-tailed deer. The most distinguishing characteristic was its long ears, hence the common name. He measured the ears of one large buck as eleven inches long, and 3½ inches wide at its widest. The mule deer he declared fully a third larger and the male particularly large, yielding another distinctive feature, the difference in size between the male and female. He examined and compared the hair, antlers, eye, rump, and tail, the latter eight to nine inches long with black hair covering the final three inches; hence the animal's other appellation, black-tailed deer.

MAY 11, 1805. Heavy winds and high waves were not the only obstacles to a safe passage on the Missouri; the banks were constantly falling in. Lewis wondered that the party's canoes were not occasionally swallowed up by the tremendous disgorging of earth into the river. Indeed, they had a number of hairbreadth escapes from such events. The loose black loam carried a portion of sand so that it broke off easily from its riverside mooring and dissolved like sugar in the steady current. Clark was hunting with other men and returned to camp with specimens of the ponderosa pine and dwarf cedar for Lewis to describe. Lewis collected a specimen of ponderosa pine on October 1.

Bratton returned to camp ahead of Clark—on the run, yelling

as he came, out of breath, and with a story. Something over a mile away he had shot a grizzly, which turned and chased him a considerable distance but was slowed due to its wound. Lewis quickly gathered seven men and went in search of the beast. They located its blood trail and followed it to a hiding place in thick brush. Two shots to the skull finished it. Lewis called it a "monstrous beast," though not quite as large as the one taken on May 5. On examination, they found that Bratton had shot it through the lungs; nevertheless the bear had pursued the soldier nearly one-half mile and then had returned more than double that distance, dug a bed about two feet deep and five feet long, and seemed fully alive when they located it. It being so hard to kill, Lewis declared that the grizzly "intimedates us all." He went on to confess that "I do not like the gentlemen and had reather fight two Indians than one bear." There was no other way to kill a grizzly with a single shot than to hit it squarely in the brain, but that organ was protected by bone and muscle. It took two men to carry the fleece (fatty meat along the backbone) and hide back to camp. The fleece yielded eight gallons of oil. More prosaically, Lewis mentioned a new sagebrush, perhaps black sagebrush, from Piney Buttes of Garfield County, Montana. In the bottomlands he saw greasewood, a species new to science, wrote a brief description, and christened it "fleshey leafed thorn." He collected a specimen on his return trip, July 20, 1806. The party camped at a spot now inundated by Fort Peck Reservoir, Garfield County, making about seventeen miles.

MAY 12, 1805. Wanting some exercise, Lewis walked on shore while the boat party set out early on a calm, clear morning. Armed with his rifle and espontoon, Lewis felt confident he could face a grizzly bear, especially if he met one in the woods or near water where he had a chance of escape. He felt less confident on the plains, so he decided to act only defensively if he met one. In his jaunt Lewis noticed scatterings of ponderosa pines and Rocky Mountain junipers on the tops of hills on the north side, while on the south he saw only junipers. In hollows and gullies he met the frequently seen chokecherry, which he compared to his familiar sour cherry. The captain even tried out Latin terminology on the species, identifying it as "*pentandria monogynia*," a plant having five stamens and one pistil. Ripening in July, the berries remained on the plant until the end of September with bears and birds feeding on them. Natives of the Missouri valley made great use of the chokecherry, eating it straight off the plant or pounding and mashing it, then boiling it with meat and with hog peanuts and Indian breadroots. They also dried the berries and formed them into small cakes for winter nourishment.

In this area Lewis noticed a change in soil composition and color. The base of the hills and river bottoms continued with their usual rich, black loam while higher up the earth took on a light-brown color, was of poor quality, and was mixed with a coarse white sand. Lewis was viewing an area where the Missouri River cuts across a preglacial drainage and where lighter-colored formations over-lie the darker Bearpaw Shale. The wind came up about noon and drove the party into camp in Garfield County, Montana, on a site now inundated by Fort Peck Reservoir, after proceeding about eigh-teen miles. At sunset it began to rain and continued moderately until midnight.

MAY 13, 1805. The wind continued its blustering until the after-noon, when the party set out, leaving hunters behind to catch up later. Lewis noticed that the Missouri's water was becoming pro-gressively clearer and concluded that they would see a change in the country as they moved on. Clark, out with the hunters, killed a mule and a common deer, while others took more deer and elks. The lat-ter were taken mainly for their hides to make clothing. Lewis was also reserving skins for the outer covering of his iron-framed boat, which he anticipated assembling at the falls of the Missouri. The captain had the boat constructed in the spring of 1803 at Harpers Ferry, present West Virginia, while he was requisitioning arms for the corps. Devised by Lewis, it was a lightweight, collapsible water-craft designed to be used in the shallow waters of the upper Mis-souri. Again, the party camped in Garfield County, Montana, on a site now inundated by Fort Peck Reservoir, making a scant seven miles. They passed two creeks on the south side during the day, probably Sheep and Crooked Creeks, Garfield County.

MAY 14, 1805. On the first anniversary of their leaving the Wood River camp in Illinois, the party had a day of adventures. In the evening the men in two rear canoes saw a large grizzly in the open and not far from the river. Six of them, all good hunters according to Lewis, went after it. They were able to get within rifle shot of the bear by concealing themselves behind a rise. Four of them opened fire while two kept their weapons ready in reserve. Hit in several places, including two shots to its lungs, the bear nonetheless was up and charging them in an instant, with jaws agape and teeth exposed. Now reserve riflemen fired with one round, breaking the charging bear's shoulder but slowing it only momentarily. Without time to reload, the men took off toward the river. Two men grabbed the canoe while others tried to conceal themselves as best they could while reloading and firing again. The shots served only to point the bear to their location, and it took off purposely after two of them, who dropped their rifles and other encumbering items and dived into the Missouri from the riverbank. The enraged animal plunged in after them and nearly caught one man. Luckily a man on shore had a good shot and finally finished the bear with a round to the head. When the men butchered it, they found eight balls had passed through the five-hundred-pound behemoth. This proved to be an old bear, useful only for its skin and several gallons of oil. And certainly useful for storytelling for some time to come.

Lewis had his own story of exciting events. While Charbonneau was at the rudder of the white pirogue a sudden squall of wind struck the vessel's sail from the side. Instead of putting the boat into the wind, the Frenchman turned it against the wind's full force, causing the sail to be jerked out of control and putting the pirogue in a perilous position. On shore Lewis and Clark fired their guns and yelled orders to correct the situation but to no avail—their shouting was not heard. They could only look on in horror. Indeed, Lewis forgot himself and was flinging off clothes and preparing to jump in the river to swim to the sinking boat when he realized the folly of such action. Being so far from the pirogue and facing high waves and frigid water, he would surely have died in the effort. He confessed that would have mattered little if the boat had been lost. The white pirogue contained what Lewis called "every article indispensibly necessary . . . to insure the success of the enterprize." For what must have seemed an eternity the boat was on its side taking in water. When finally the sail was under control and the boat righted, Cruzatte at the bow had to threaten to shoot Charbonneau in order to get him to allow Cruzatte to take command of the rudder. At the same time he ordered the occupants to bail water, Cruzatte and two others rowed the boat to shore, arriving barely above water. All the while, as Clark related, Sacagawea calmly collected articles that floated within her reach. Safely on shore, the boat was quickly unloaded and salvage operations were begun.

Later writing about the event, Lewis was still shaken as he reviewed what might have happened. Indeed, this event was almost a repeat of the white pirogue's near disaster of April 13, again with Charbonneau, whom Lewis called "the most timid waterman in the world," as the culprit. The incident has left historians to wonder why the Frenchman was at the rudder at all. When things settled down, the men downed a drink of grog or a shot of spirits. More routinely, the party passed three streams during the day—Sutherland ("Gibson's," after Gibson of the party), Valley County, Montana, and "Stick Lodge" and "Brown Bear Defeated" (Hell Creek and Snow Creek, both in Garfield County, Montana)—and camped in Valley County, a few miles above and opposite Snow Creek and under present Fort Peck Reservoir, some sixteen miles beyond the last camp. The enlisted men reported a hard frost overnight that even froze moccasins left by the fire.

MAY 15, 1805. After a brief rain shower, articles from the previous day's near accident with the white pirogue were set out to dry. The cloudy, damp day gave little chance for repairing the wet items but at least they were saved from further deterioration. In spite of the previous day's difficulty with the grizzly, hunters took on another one but only wounded it; there were no reports of being chased. The party remained at the camp of the day before.

MAY 16, 1805. The men spent the better part of the day drying and repacking the white pirogue's damaged items. Lewis was relieved that the loss was not as great as he had at first anticipated. Medicines received the greatest injury, some entirely destroyed. Other losses included seeds, a small quantity of gunpowder, and a few cooking utensils that fell overboard and sank in the river. Now the captain acknowledged Sacagawea's contribution for saving items: "the Indian woman to whom I ascribe equal fortitude and resolution, with any person onboard at the time of the accedent, caught and preserved most of the light articles which were washed overboard." Before setting out two men fired on a mountain lion that was burying a half-eaten deer. In honor of the sighting, the party named the camp "Panther Camp." A grizzly shredded Labiche's coat that he had left on the plains. Not leaving until four in the afternoon, the party made only seven miles and camped on the north side of the river in Phillips County, Montana, according to the captains but on the south, in Garfield County, as shown on expedition maps and as given in the enlisted men's journals; both spots are now under Fort Peck Reservoir.

MAY 17, 1805. Not having the wind at their backs, the men utilized the tow rope for the better part of the day. The firm ground along the shoreline provided sure footing for the laborers. The river was narrowing, with only a scattering of cottonwoods along its edges while willows dominated the sandbars. Passing two creeks during the day, the captains christened them "Rattlesnake" or "Bratton's" Creek, for Bratton of the party (Timber Creek, Phillips County, Montana), and "Burnt Lodge Creek" (Seven Blackfoot Creek, Garfield County, Montana). The latter got its name when the guard roused the party during the night because a large tree was on fire and dangerously close to one of the party's lodgings. The occupants moved to a safer spot. In fact, shortly after they moved a portion of the tree collapsed at the very spot vacated and blowing embers caught the lodge on fire, but no one was harmed. After coming more than twenty miles, they camped a short distance above Seven Blackfoot Creek. While Clark was out in the evening he was nearly bitten by a rattlesnake. Another rattler similar to Clark's was killed and brought to Lewis for examination; it was a prairie rattlesnake, a subspecies new to science. He perceived it to be smaller than those of the East and went on to describe its colorings and composition, even counting 176 scales on its belly and 17 on its tail. Clark also saw a fortified Indian site, which the captains supposed was a Hidatsa war party encampment.

MAY 18, 1805. Facing a hard headwind, tow ropes were a necessary aid to the men at oars, paddles, and poles. The corps passed their "Wiser's Creek," named after Weiser of the party, now Fourchette Creek, Phillips County, Montana. It was an uneventful day with the usual count of wildlife and standard comments on the country. Rosebushes were in bloom, and the brown thrasher made an appearance. The deer taken now were as prized for their value in fashioning leggings and moccasins from their skins as for their meat. A slight shower was not even sufficient to thoroughly soak their clothes, yet it was the first downpour since leaving Fort Mandan that could really be called rain. They camped in Garfield County, Montana, a few miles upstream from the present Devils Creek Recreation Area, a trip of about twenty-one miles.

MAY 19, 1805. Heavy fog greeted the party after a cold night that kept them from setting out until eight o'clock. The thermometer at sunrise read 38°. The men again made use of tow ropes attached to the boats; they found the river rapid, crooked, and choked with upended timber. Another encounter with a grizzly marked the bear as determined and nearly as indestructible as ever. Clark with two hunters shot one through the heart, yet it was able to run almost half a mile before it collapsed. When one of the boat party shot a beaver, Seaman jumped into the river to retrieve it but was bitten in the leg. The bite cut an artery, and Lewis was hard pressed to stop the bleeding. Even after he stemmed the flow, the captain thought the wound might yet take the dog's life. From a height Clark saw the Musselshell River emptying into the Missouri and some forty or fifty miles farther on he viewed the Little Rocky Mountains. They camped in either Phillips or Garfield County, Montana, a few miles below the mouth of the Musselshell, another twenty-mile day.

MAY 20, 1805. The party set out early and by eleven had traveled about seven miles to reach the mouth of the Musselshell, where they would spend the night on its upstream side in Petroleum County, Montana. They ate breakfast along the way at a small stream they dubbed "Blowing Fly Creek" (earlier Squaw Creek, now Nancy Russell Creek, Garfield County, Montana) and struggled to keep the flies out of their food. The captains had heard of the Musselshell from the Hidatsas, whose anglicized name they now used and which it retains. Lewis related other Hidatsa information about the source and course of the river and the likelihood that they would find the area well timbered. The captain saw only what he had been seeing for some time: a scattering of scrubby pine and dwarf cedar on hilltops and a country devoid of timber but instead covered with short grass, aromatic sages, and prickly pears. Like other streams entering the Missouri, the Musselshell's river bottom supported good stands of cottonwoods. It measured 110 yards wide and was 2,270 miles above the mouth of the Missouri by the captains' calculations. Hunters reported a stream about five miles above the Musselshell's mouth and the captains decided to name it after their Shoshone interpreter, Sacagawea. After being called Crooked Creek in earlier years, the river has been restored to the name the captains gave it. Shields located a spring a few miles farther up the Missouri that fascinated Lewis, who had seen only one other since leaving Fort Mandan. Two large owls also caught his attention, probably the Montana horned owl as on April 14. From his observations at the mouth of the Musselshell Lewis determined the latitude as 47° 00′ 24.6″ N; today its mouth is closer to 47° 27′ 02″ N.

MAY 21, 1805. Lewis called it "a delightfull morning" as the party set out, again utilizing tow ropes. The captain gave his customary descriptions of the country: fertile soil, short grass, prickly pears, "not a stick of timber," and the usual mineral elements. Not seeing the normal number of sharp-tailed grouse ("growse or praire hen"), he conjectured that they might be away from the river and out on the open plains at this season. A hard wind came up in the evening blowing a continuous cloud of sand and dust and preventing the party from cooking, eating, or sleeping. Several articles were blown off the boats and lost. Nonetheless, they pushed forward some twenty miles. After finding their first spot unsuitable, they retreated into shelter in present Phillips County, Montana, at a site now inundated by Fort Peck Reservoir.

MAY 22, 1805. The wind had not abated in the morning, causing a late start at around ten o'clock, again using the tow ropes for assistance. Having mentioned the shortage of sharp-tailed grouse on the previous day, Lewis spotted a number of them near a stream he named "Grouse Creek," now Beauchamp Creek, Phillips County, Montana. In his shoreline walk Lewis commented that wildlife was not as abundant as below the Musselshell River. Fishing was also less productive since leaving the Mandan villages, but the men were catching an occasional channel catfish of two to five pounds. Hunters killed a grizzly without incident, and the party stopped to render its fat. Lewis commented incorrectly that he thought they were out of the range of black bears since he had not seen their tracks, which were easily distinguished from the grizzly's by the length of the claw prints. The party camped in Phillips County, just below present CK Creek (Lewis and Clark's "Teapot Creek" of the next day), having traveled about sixteen miles.

MAY 23, 1805. A severe frost came up during the night and ice covered the edges of the river; the party found their oars and paddles frozen over. Gass thought the ice on the river's edge to be as thick as window glass. The chill did not inhibit worrisome mosquitoes, and abundant wild roses were in bloom. They passed today's CK ("Teapot") Creek, Phillips County, Montana, just a mile above their camp. Fifteen yards wide, it exhibited a curiosity that Lewis found with the Missouri's affluents: dry at the mouth but with running water farther up. Like others in the area it was strongly salinated and undrinkable. Lewis drank a bit as an experiment and found it mildly purgative and painful to his bowels. Not far above CK Creek Lewis located a prairie dog village, although no other journalist mentioned it and expedition maps place one farther up. Nonetheless, the captain added observations about the animal. He was particularly astonished at its ability to go without water. Lewis may have been the first to report this phenomenon, which is typical of some arid-land rodent species that obtain water through their food. The captain also thought that prairie dogs closed their burrows in the fall and did not emerge until spring. In fact, black-tailed prairie dogs (the species here) do not usually hibernate but sometimes stay underground for several weeks during extremely cold weather. Lewis also noticed Douglas fir among the pine trees, here at its northeastern limit in the United States; it grows more commonly farther west and in mountains. Strawberries were in bloom, and they saw the first kingfisher of the season. At lunch a cooking fire got out of control, set woods ablaze, and destroyed one man's shot pouch, powder horn, and rifle butt. They made about twenty-seven miles and camped a little below the mouth of Rock Creek, Phillips County, Montana.

MAY 24, 1805. Frost again this morning created a one-eighth-inch-thick coating on water standing in containers. Foliage on cottonwoods had been destroyed by the cold, but the trees were putting out second buds. Lewis conjectured that the high country through which they were passing was a part of the Black Hills. Giving the hills a larger extent than they deserve, the captain's erroneous concept was carried over onto Clark's postexpedition maps and not corrected until the 1850s. Members of the party got relief from the tow ropes when an advantageous wind blew in from the southeast and countered the river's opposition. Given that help, they made over twenty-four miles and camped in either Fergus or Phillips County, Montana, about three miles above where U.S. Highway 191 crosses the Missouri River. The party passed a number of streams coming into the Missouri, most notably Rock Creek ("North Mountain Creek"), Phillips County, and Sand Creek ("Little Dog Creek" after a nearby prairie dog village) and Armells Creek ("South Mountain Creek"), Fergus County. "North Mountain" refers to the Little Rocky Mountains, while "South Mountain" relates to the Judith Mountains. Wildlife numbers seemed to be decreasing, especially beavers, whose declining presence appeared to keep pace with the lack of timber. Six men and two canoes were left behind to get the meat of a buffalo that Clark killed, but they did not rejoin the party at camp.

MAY 25, 1805. The party set out about eight o'clock, after the men who were left behind the day before caught up. With another strong headwind, they again resorted to tow ropes. Drouillard was able to get a bighorn sheep and later in the day Clark and Bratton killed one also. This was the party's first specimen, but of a species already known to science. Nevertheless, Lewis examined and described the animal. He gave it a full discourse, noticing its general dimensions, habits, horns, eyes, nostrils, teeth, hoofs, tail, hair, hide, and coloring, and compared it to deer, goats, and common sheep. He was especially impressed by its dexterity at seemingly inaccessible places on the hillsides, where it bounded with ease. Clark copied Lewis's extensive notes on the bighorn almost verbatim into his own journal. Gibson discovered the problems with climbing steep, rocky places when he dislocated his shoulder in an attempt. Gass and Whitehouse say it was reset without difficulty; the captains did not mention the accident. The party saw their first skunk in some time, as well as the eastern kingbird. Buffalo were scarcer, and Lewis feared it might mean an end to a favored delicacy—Charbonneau's white "puddings" (*boudin blanc*, or white sausage). The party was now entering the Missouri River Breaks region, where sandstone, limestone, and coal are part of the Judith River Formation, with black rock of the Claggett Shale underlying it. The party camped in Fergus County, Montana, a few miles below present Cow Island Landing Recreation Area and about eighteen miles from the last camp.

MAY 26, 1805. Oars and paddles were little used this day, only to keep the boats close to shore and aid the men pulling tow ropes. They continued to see temporary Indian camps at timbered points along the way. Lewis noticed numerous faults in the late Cretaceous formations along the river. The faulting occasionally exposes Claggett Shale, but most of the rock belongs to the Judith River Formation. On a walk Clark saw the distant hills to the north and south as on previous days and open country with only small stands of pine and spruce. He wrote, "this Countrey may with propriety I think be termed the Deserts of America, as I do not Conceive any part can ever be Settled, as it is deficent in water, Timber & too Steep to be tilled." And Lewis called it "truly a desert barren country." Later in the day Lewis climbed an elevated point to get a long-range view of the party's prospects. From his point Lewis thought he was see-ing the Rocky Mountains for the first time and wrote emotionally,

> while I viewed these mountains I felt a secret pleasure in finding myself so near the head of the heretofore conceived boundless Mis-souri; but when I reflected on the difficulties which this snowey barrier would most probably throw in my way to the Pacific, and the sufferings and hardships of myself and party in them, it in some measure counterballanced the joy I had felt in the first moments in which I gazed on them; but as I have always held it a crime to anticipate evils I will believe it a good comfortable road untill I am compelled to believe differently.

On his way back Lewis killed a fat buffalo and came within inches of stepping on a rattlesnake but stabbed it with his espontoon before it could strike. During the day the party passed Cow ("Windsors") Creek, Blaine County, Montana, named for the party's Windsor, and Bird Rapids, which they called "Elk" or "Elk Fawn" rapids after an elk and her fawn that swam through the waves as they approached. The men doubled up in the boats and at the ropes to get through the rapids. Nearby they found a cottonwood bottom and camped in Fergus County, Montana, where they butchered Lewis's much appreciated buffalo. They had come about twenty-three miles.

MAY 27, 1805. Another hard headwind prevented the party from setting out until ten o'clock. Still traveling through the Missouri River Breaks, Lewis noticed that the river cut a deep, narrow chan-nel, and he saw only occasional level land on which "two or thre[e] impoverished cottonwood trees will be seen." The country contin-ued broken and barren with spotty showings of pines, spruces, and creeping junipers on the hills. Lewis observed stones along the river that are derived from fractured sandstones and concretions of the Judith River Formation. In perceptive detail he noted particularly the thickness and color variability of the formation's rocks, includ-ing descriptions of resistant layers of sandstone alternating with layers of vulnerable siltstone and shale. Bearpaw Shale caps some of the river hills. After about fourteen miles the party camped in

Fergus County, Montana, near dead cottonwoods to serve as wood for fires, but the trees provided a scant supply. Whitehouse said the spot was an old Indian camp.

MAY 28, 1805. Riffles and rocky points were becoming increasingly hazardous. As the river surged around a point its velocity increased considerably and brought danger to boats and occupants. The slender elkskin ropes that doubled as lifelines were constantly exposed to the elements, quickly rotted, and became weak. Lewis knew that if the ropes gave way the boats would be swept into deeper water, tipped over, and dashed to pieces. Every precaution was taken to avoid such accidents. Finding native items, the captain thought they might have belonged to Atsina Indians. Passing though smoke, the captains surmised that Indians may have set the plains on fire to move wildlife toward them. The party passed a large creek with running water that they named for Thompson, current Birch Creek, Chouteau County, Montana. Here the Missouri River opened up and islands dotted the widened channel. They camped in Chouteau County, opposite Dog Creek, Fergus County, the party's "Bull Creek," and about twenty-one miles from the previous camp.

MAY 29, 1805. During the night a large buffalo bull swam from the opposite side of the river, used the white pirogue as a landing spot, and then tore through the camp, coming within inches of some of the men. The guard tried to divert it, but instead it swung toward sleeping soldiers and again came within inches of trampling them. Then it headed directly for the captains' tent before it was turned by Seaman, apparently revived from the beaver bite of May 19. By this time, with the buffalo safely gone, the camp was in an uproar, with rifles at ready and generally confused. With the guard's explanation, things quieted down, and everyone went back to bed. In the morning they discovered that the bull had broken York's rifle in the pirogue as well as damaging the boat's blunderbuss. Lewis criticized York's for not securing his gun, but he was happy that there had been no serious injuries. Considering the problems befalling the white pirogue, he wondered if it was not "attended by some evil gennii."

Within 2½ miles after departing camp, the explorers arrived at the mouth of the Judith River, Fergus County, Montana. It still bears the name that Clark choose for it, although the name does not appear in his journal; it is found only on his maps and in Lewis's journal. For a time they may have called it the "Big Horn River," perhaps because of Lewis's doubts about the propriety of naming streams after girls in the states. Julia (or Judith) Hancock, of Fincastle, Virginia, would become Clark's wife in 1808. He may have met her as early as 1801 while visiting an army friend nearby when she was not quite ten years old. We may never know why Clark chose to name the river after her from this brief and innocent encounter, but he returned to Fincastle after the expedition, and she became his bride. Just above the Judith Lewis counted evidence of 126 Indian lodges, while Clark noticed another large encampment on the opposite shore. Sacagawea examined moccasins left behind and declared them not of her people, but perhaps from the Blackfeet. Lewis thought they might be Atsina footwear.

Farther on the party passed an immense heap of buffalo carcasses, which Lewis believed were the remains of animals driven over the ledge in traditional buffalo hunts. Clark killed a wolf with his espontoon as it scavenged among the offal, and journalists noted the stench. Lewis took time to explain the buffalo-jump process. Fleet young Indian men disguised themselves in buffalo robes and head pieces and took hidden positions near a precipice while others drove the animals in that direction. When close, the young men jumped up, frightened the charging beasts, and funneled them toward the ledge, then hurriedly took safety at prearranged spots as the lead bison plunged over. It was dangerous work. Lewis's accurate description of the action was probably obtained from the Mandans or Hidatsas during the winter at Fort Mandan. It is likely that here, however, he was seeing winter-kill bison pushed downriver by spring floods and jammed against the shore, rather than a buffalo jump, since the area's topography does not fit known jumps. Above this spot they stopped at a stream they called "Slaughter River" (inspired by the dead buffalo), then camped above it and on the opposite side in Chouteau County, Montana, coming almost eighteen miles. It is now Arrow Creek, the boundary between Fergus and Chouteau

Counties. Later the captains poured liquor for the men, perhaps a half pint, and some became a little tipsy.

MAY 30, 1805. The party waited until eleven o'clock to set out due to rain and high winds. Rain was an unusual occurrence, and Lewis commented on the lack of it and the dryness of the air. In experiments the captain found that a tablespoon of water evaporated in thirty-six hours when the temperature was at most 66° during the day. His inkwell frequently dried out and his sextant's seasoned case had shrunk. It was difficult going this day. Along with the impediments of a rapid current, numerous riffles, and the river's rocky outcrops, a narrow shoreline made footing unreliable for boat pullers. The recent rain also made the shore muddy and slippery and added to their difficulties. Tow ropes broke several time during the day, at least once on the ill-fated white pirogue. And the men had to watch out for falling earth and stones from the steep banks. The party passed a number of temporary Indian hunting camps, which Lewis thought were Hidatsa or Blackfeet dwellings. From the Hidatsa villages to this place, he declared that no permanent Indian establishments existed. They made a scant eight miles and camped in Chouteau County, Montana, a little above Pablo Island and nearly opposite Sheep Shed Coulee.

MAY 31, 1805. The corps was entering the White Cliffs area of the Upper Missouri River in Chouteau County, Montana, a scenic portion of the river that has delighted travelers to this day. During the glacial period, ice forced the Missouri River to cut a new channel through the late Cretaceous formations of Claggett Shale, Eagle Sandstone, and Marias River Shale. The most conspicuous of these is the nearly white sandstone of the Virgelle Member of the Eagle Sandstone, hence the region's designation. Without the covering of solid materials, the sandstone erodes and forms incredible shapes that have gained impressive names. Moreover, dark igneous rocks (shonkinite) resist erosion and flank the river in near-vertical sheets (dikes) that resemble walls, which have also been given storied names. In other circumstances circular protective iron-rich concretions overlay the creamy-white, weakly cemented, erodible sandstone and form columns, pulpits, toadstools, pedestals, and other picturesque features. The fantastic size, shape, and contrasting shades of light and dark have fascinated travelers for generations. Lewis was so impressed that he became his most poetic in portraying the wonders before him:

> The hills and river Clifts which we passed today exhibit a most romantic appearance. . . . The water in the course of time in decending from those hills and plains on either side of the river has trickled down the soft sand clifts and woarn it into a thousand grotesque figures, which with the help of a little immagination and an oblique view at a distance, are made to represent eligant ranges of lofty freestone buildings, having their parapets well stocked with statuary. . . . As we passed on it seemed as if those seens of visionary inchantment would never have and end; for here it is too that nature presents to the view of the traveler vast ranges of walls of tolerable workmanship, so perfect indeed are those walls that I should have thought that nature had attempted here to rival the human art of masonry had I not recollected that she had first began her work.

Beautiful scenery did not ease the boatmen's labors. The river's obstructions and difficulties continued and made hard work for weary haulers. On shore the men faced slippery footing, while mud tugged at their moccasins and forced them to go barefooted over sharp rocks. Otherwise they were compelled to be nearly up to their armpits in cold water pulling the boats. Impressed by their dedication, Lewis wrote, "in short their labour is incredibly painfull and great, yet those faithfull fellows bear it without a mumur." In fact, Clark found shore-side going so laborious that he returned to the boats. They stopped at noon, and the captains gave the men a well-deserved dram of alcohol.

Whitehouse noted that the captains collected the horns of two bighorn rams killed this day in order to take them back east. Again, the white pirogue's "evil gennii" was at play when the boat's hemp tow rope broke and sent it spinning. In this situation it nearly overturned; Lewis was sure that it would one day go under. The captain noticed a stand of limber pine, new to him and far from its nearest and typical location in the Little Belt Mountains. He also witnessed cliff swallows ("small martin") building their mud nests in niches on rock walls. Traveling about eighteen miles, the party camped above the mouth of Eagle ("stone wall") Creek, Chouteau County.

JUNE 1, 1805. The river cliffs were not so high and the country leveled out. To the north they could see the Bears Paw Mountains and to the southwest, the Highwoods. Wildlife was diminishing—they killed only a bighorn and a mule deer. Lewis viewed chokecherry and currant bushes, while rosebushes and prickly pears were numerous and in full bloom. The party camped in Chouteau County, Montana, in the vicinity of present Boggs Island, making about twenty-three miles.

JUNE 2, 1805. Violent winds and a slight shower blew in during the night, but a fair morning gave the party an early start. In spite of the river's steady current and strong winds, the men found good footing on shore as they pulled the boats forward. Lewis set out with some men in search of elk skins to cover his iron-framed boat, which he thought might be needed soon. In fact, that work would not get underway for another three weeks. The hunters were successful in killing six elks, two buffalo, two mule deer, and a grizzly. Before it was dispatched the grizzly took after Drouillard but then turned on Charbonneau, who fired his gun in the air as he raced for cover and hid among thick bushes. Drouillard finally killed the bear with a shot to its head. Being too late to examine the Marias River, they settled in across from its mouth in Chouteau County, Montana, making about eighteen miles. In the evening the captains took lunar observations. Lewis named the Marias on June 8 upon returning from a reconnaissance of the stream.

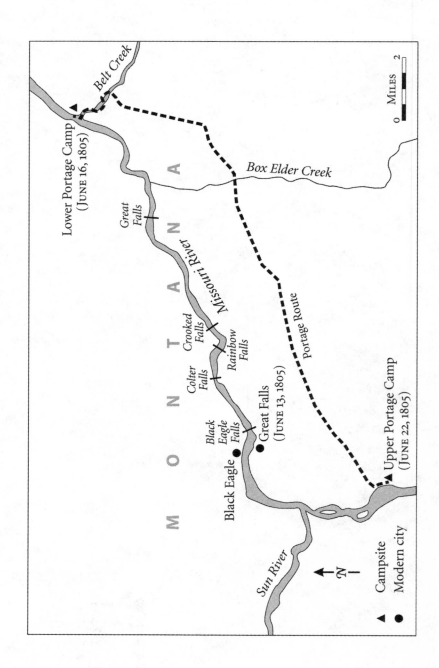

MAP 6. The expedition's route, June 3–July 14, 1805.

CHAPTER 5

Portaging the Falls

June 3–July 14, 1805

JUNE 3, 1805. The party crossed the Missouri and made a new camp on the lower side of the Marias River. They remained here until June 12. The captains now faced a dilemma: which of the two rivers was the true Missouri, the one coming in from the north or the one from the south? Spring runoff had swollen the Marias (coming from the north) to nearly the size of the main stream and made the determination difficult. This was more than a routine geographic question, and Lewis penned his anxieties: "to mistake the stream at this period of the season, two months of the traveling season having now elapsed, and to ascend such stream to the rocky Mountain or perhaps much further before we could inform ourselves whether it did approach the Columbia or not, and then be obliged to return and take the other stream would not only loose us the whole of this season but would probably so dishearten the party that it might defeat the expedition altogether." The captains decided to take time here to investigate the rivers in order to make the correct decision about which stream to follow. They dispatched two canoes with three men each to investigate. Pryor led a party going up the Marias, while Gass managed a crew up the Missouri. Whitehouse said he was with Gass. At the same time they sent parties to examine the immediate area, get views of the rivers from high points, and return with reports by nighttime.

Lewis and Clark also ascended the heights above the rivers to check the courses of the streams. From a vantage point they got "an extensive and most inchanting view." Wildlife abounded, with uncountable buffalo "tended by their shepperds the wolves," pronghorns, and elks. The ground was clothed with a rich green covering and dotted with prickly pears. Along the river bottoms they saw chokecherries, currants, gooseberries, and wild roses. It was a beautiful day. To the south stood the Highwood Mountains and beyond them the Little Belt and Big Belt ranges covered with snow. Returning to camp, the captains noticed the Teton ("Tansey") River, a tributary of the Marias. At camp they measured the widths of the two rivers, the Missouri 372 yards across and the Marias 200, but deeper than the Missouri. In fact, the Marias had all the characteristics of the main stream, with its rolling manner, color, and consistency, convincing almost the entire party that it was the true Missouri, except for the captains, who found themselves in the distinct minority. The captains were particularly baffled that the Mandan and Hidatsa Indians had not told them of the Marias and weighed their earlier determination that the Indians' *"river that scolds at all others"* was the Milk River, against what they were seeing here. Finding the large falls reported by Indians would be the determining factor.

Those who had remained at camp had been busy making clothing from animal hides. Lewis viewed their bruised and mangled feet caused by walking over rough and rocky ground in poor moccasins or barefooted. He also saw their diminished state but judged them still cheerful in spite of their difficulties. The river parties returned without convincing evidence about which river was the main stream and which the tributary. The Field brothers on a land excursion up the Missouri also brought inconclusive reports. Given the uncertainty, the captains decided to make excursions of their own. Lewis would go up the Marias with Pryor, Drouillard, Shields, Windsor, Cruzatte, and Lepage, while Clark would lead Gass, the Field brothers, Shannon, and York on the Missouri. It was agreed that they would travel a day and a half or longer if necessary to answer the question. The captains shared a drink of grog with the men and prepared for an early departure. Lewis filled a haversack and confessed that it was the first time in his life that he had ever prepared such a load. The captain took an astronomical observation and determined the latitude at the mouth of the Marias as 47° 24' 12.8"N; today it is nearer 47° 55' 48" N.

JUNE 4, 1805. Taking an early departure, Lewis started up the east side of the Marias. From a high point he watched the Bears Paw Mountains to his north and the Highwood Mountains to the south and plotted their positions. He also sighted Square Butte ("Barn Mountain") south of Geraldine, Chouteau County, Montana. As far as Lewis could see the country was a dry, level, open plain to the foot of the Rockies. In spite of the dark, rich soil the captain was surprised that the grass was just high enough to conceal the ground. The party was in the heart of the shortgrass prairie eco-system of the Great Plains. Here, too, they were troubled by the abundance of prickly pears that cut through their moccasins and pierced their feet. "Brown Curloos," probably a long-billed cur-lew, were numerous, and Lewis took a few lines to describe them. He also counted three species of sparrows and made notes on McCown's longspur ("small bird . . . resembles the lark"), which "add much to the gayety and cheerfullness of the scene." He concluded that the abundance of grasshoppers accounted for the numerous winged creatures. Buffalo, wolves, elks, and foxes were also seen in great numbers.

Having walked some eight miles, the captain directed the party back toward the Marias seeking refreshing water. At the river they viewed two mule bucks, Drouillard shot them, and they paused for a late breakfast near noontime. As they moved on, Drouillard killed four deer, which the men stripped, taking enough meat for their supper. As they passed Sheep Coulee, Chouteau County, oppo-site them, Lewis described the Marias as forty to sixty yards wide, deep, and with a strong current and a turbid appearance—in fact, the same appearance as the Missouri except for the difference in size. Its bottomlands were "one emence garden of roses," well tim-bered and displaying salts, coal, and other mineral substances. These deposits as well as other formations were from Claggett Shale, Eagle Sandstone, and Marias River Shale. The party ascended the bluffs but found the going so difficult that they came back down to the river and traveled though the Marias's bottomlands at the foot of the bluffs. Soon they located a spot for the night some miles above Sheep Coulee on the opposite side. Before settling in they killed a badger, a beaver, and a mule deer. It rained during the evening and doused them considerably, only adding to the discomfort of the chilly night air. They made about thirty-two miles.

Clark and party followed the south fork, the Missouri, along a narrow ridge that separated the Teton River from the Missouri on the main stream's west side. Later called *Cracon du Nez* (bridge of the nose) by French rivermen, the ridge is now a part of Rowe Bench. They stopped at Shonkin Creek ("Snow River" on expedition maps) for a meal. Clark observed much the same landscape and animal life as Lewis but had the additional greeting of prairie dogs ("barking Squirel"). They made camp about a mile and a half upstream from Carter Ferry, Chouteau County. Near camp Joseph Field was chased by a grizzly bear and could not use his wet gun. After the bear nearly caught the explorer, the shouts and shots of Field's comrades frightened it and drove it away. Clark's party covered more than thirty miles.

JUNE 5, 1805. With a chill still in the air Lewis donned his blanket coat, and at sunrise the party set out upriver. At eight miles they passed a dry Black Coulee ("Lark Creek"), Chouteau County, Montana. Lewis was astonished at the amount of water the soil could soak up, as he observed large dry creek beds across the plains. The men climbed the river's bluffs and made their way through the plains. To the northwest, some eighty miles distant by his estimate, the captain saw the Sweetgrass Hills ("tower Mountain" for one majestic peak) on the Montana-Alberta border. Again, as the day before, the men counted the abundant wildlife of the grasslands: buffalo, wolves, foxes, pronghorns, and a large colony of prairie dogs ("barking squirrels"). They killed a prairie dog apiece as insurance for supper. Lewis witnessed a flock of greater sage-grouse and sent Shields to get one, but he was unsuccessful. The captains' weather diaries noted the appearance of nighthawks and turkey vultures. Before establishing camp, hunters killed five elks and a mule deer and then the group settled in on the east side of the Marias River a few miles downstream from Highway 223, Liberty County, Montana. Lewis declared roasted prairie dog "well flavored and tender."

Clark's party also experienced a cold and wet night with a little snow. They watched buffalo try to cross the Missouri, but they were stopped by swift water. Three grizzlies came close to camp. The men killed all three and ate part of one. Continuing along the west side of the Missouri, Clark spied the Little Belt range of mountains to the south. From a ridge Clark viewed the southwest, upriver course of the Missouri and noted that its width, depth, and rapidity continued as far as he could see. He felt no need to go farther and turned back, following a course that took him to the Teton River, where hunters killed two elks; the men ate the bone marrow of the animals. From there they traveled on, seeing elks, deer, beavers, pronghorns, mule deer, wolves, and a bear. Clark carved his name on a tree. The night's camp was north or northwest of Fort Benton, Chouteau County, Montana, on the Teton River.

At the main camp the party was busy making moccasins, leggings, and other clothing. Goodrich took a considerable quantity of fish, among them catfish. Ordway noted that with the abundance of meat there was little inclination for the men to fish.

JUNE 6, 1805. Lewis was convinced that the Marias pointed too much to the north for it to be the party's route to the Pacific, so he decided to start back to the main camp the next day after he got a latitude reading. Due to overcast skies he had been unable to get a fix the day before. Pryor and Windsor went upriver to find a high point and get a bearing on the river's course as far as they could. Lewis and the rest of the party set about making rafts to descend the river after those two returned and observations were completed. About noon Pryor and Windsor returned and confirmed the river's northern course. After lunch all set out on the rafts but quickly found the crafts unsafe, even causing some water damage to their baggage. They abandoned the rafts and took to the land. They also had to leave the five heavy elk skins that Lewis had intended to use as cover for his iron-framed boat. Swinging packs over their shoulders, they trekked across the open plains but soon faced a rainstorm and cold winds. They came back to the river to set up camp at Black Coulee ("Lark C."), Chouteau County, Montana, killing two buffalo along the way and harvesting the meat for dinner and the next day's meals. Without shelter, they looked toward an uncomfortable night.

Clark's party also faced a raw, cold, windy day. They continued along the Teton toward the main camp, killing seven deer for their skins and arriving at camp about five o'clock. The captain expected to find Lewis, but he had not arrived. The excursion party was exhausted after their long march over difficult terrain. Everyone enjoyed a dram of liquor.

Ordway noted that Joseph Field had a bear encounter on his way back to camp with Clark's party. Field was attacked by "an old hea bear" (apparently a grizzly), but his gun misfired, and he looked to be overtaken and attacked. Fortunately, his fellow soldiers heard the gun's report and rushed to his aid. Their volleys turned the bear and saved Field from a certain mauling.

JUNE 7, 1805. As Lewis had expected, his party spent a "disagreable and wrestless night." They were ready to get out of their wet beds at an early hour and get underway toward the main camp, in spite of facing more rain and hard, cold winds. As they walked along, Lewis was again amazed at the slick gumbo that resisted saturation and made sure footing hard to find. Formed from glacial till and Claggett Shale, the gumbo is not only slippery but very sticky as well. In fact, Lewis slipped while walking along a bluff and was saved only by using his espontoon for support. He looked down a craggy slope some ninety feet to view what would have been his descent. Within minutes he heard a voice cry out, "Good god, captain, what shall I do?" Turning around he saw that Windsor had slipped and fallen and was hanging over the bluff, holding on with his left arm and leg but in difficult straits. Lewis saw the fear in his face and his precarious situation and thought he might lose his grip any moment and slip off into the abyss. The captain disguised his own fears and tried to calm the soldier with soft words and reassurances. He told him to take out his knife and dig a hole for his right foot and then raise himself to his knees. Now he directed him to remove his moccasins and come forward on his hands and knees using his knife and rifle for support. Both men were much relieved when Windsor was on top again.

The party returned to the Marias River and continued their route along its edge or in its shallowest parts. They knew that the steep ravines would make overland travel impossible. Trudging along in mud and chest-high water, they continued the hard march until late in the evening, making only eighteen miles. They encamped in an abandoned Indian stick lodge that gave them some protection from the elements. It is not certain where the party camped along the Marias, but it was in Chouteau County several miles from the river's mouth. For dinner they roasted the best meat from six deer they had killed during the day. Lewis curled up on some willow boughs to enjoy a well-deserved rest. "So much will a good shelter, a dry bed, and comfortable supper revive the sperits of the waryed, wet and hungry traveler," he wrote.

Clark recorded a morning temperature of 40° at the main camp. Rain continued all day, but hunters were able to get two buffalo, an elk, and a deer on a dreary day. Ordway decided that Lewis's absence was due to the weather and to the muddy, slippery condition of the terrain.

JUNE 8, 1805. Rain throughout the night and until ten this morning did not delay Lewis's party's departure. After an early breakfast they were on their way at sunrise along the Marias's river bottoms and in mud and water as the day before. Before noon the sun broke through and little songbirds in river-lined trees took up a chorus "very gay and sung most inchantingly." Lewis counted brown thrashers, robins, doves, goldfinches, blackbirds, wrens, and perhaps finches as well as unnamed others.

Lewis confessed that the whole of his party to a man was convinced that the Marias was the true Missouri. He disagreed and decided to name the stream for "Miss Maria W—d," that is, after his cousin Maria Wood, and call it "Maria's River." It is now named the Marias River, Chouteau County, Montana. Writing in a romantic vein, Lewis penned, "it is true that the hue of the waters of this turbulent and troubled stream but illy comport with the pure celestial virtues and amiable qualifications of that lovely fair one; but on the other hand it is a noble river; one destined to become in my opinion an object of contention between the two great powers of America and Great Britin with rispect to the adjustment of the North westwardly boundary." The captain went on to extol the river's commercial value in fur-bearing animals, its fertility, and its beauty: "one of the most beautifully picteresque countries that I ever beheld, through the wide expance of which, innumerable herds of living anamals are seen, it's borders garnished with one continued garden of roses, while it's lofty and open forests, are the habitation of miriads of the feathered tribes who salute the ear of the passing traveler with their wild and simple, yet s[w]eet and cheerfull melody."

Lewis and party reached the main camp about five in the evening, very exhausted. Here he discovered Clark awaiting his return with some anxiety for his safety, since they had been gone two days longer than arranged. The captain and his men enjoyed a dram while Clark plotted the courses of the two rivers as far as they had traveled on them. With their firsthand surveys completed, Lewis wrote that he "began more than ever to suspect the varacity of Mr. Fidler or the correctness of his instruments." The captain had access to a copy of London cartographer Aaron Arrowsmith's map of 1802, partially based on information from Peter Fidler, surveyor for the Hudson's Bay Company. Fidler's information about the lands south of Canada was from a Blackfeet Indian, and it became garbled on the surveyor's maps and in his comments. Lewis was trying to fit the scene before him and evidence from reconnaissances of the last few days onto a map based on secondhand knowledge that had been misinterpreted.

Before Lewis's arrival Clark penned his uneasiness for the captain and his party since they were overdue to return. In the meantime he had the main party check their weapons and sent several hunters out. Given a return of fair weather at midmorning, he had baggage and stored items brought out to air and dry. Later he wrote a detailed account of Lewis's courses and distances on the Marias and estimated that the captain had been 77½ miles up the river.

JUNE 9, 1805. The captains decided to deposit the red pirogue at this point, plus all excess heavy baggage along with items like salt, lead, and gunpowder. Thus they hoped to lighten the load of the remaining boats. This would also allow the seven men from the red pirogue to help move the other watercraft. The leaders sent some men to dig a cache for the deposit and put Cruzatte in charge since he was acquainted with such operations. The men were able to finish the work before evening. It was located on the high plains above the Missouri and between it and the Teton River. Lewis described the design and construction of the cache in his journal. Hunters killed one of the largest buffalo so far; it took eight men to bring in the meat.

Reviewing their maps and other pre-expedition sources, comparing the various reconnaissances of the rivers, and considering Indian information, the captains came fully to the conclusion they had arrived at earlier: that the south fork was the true Missouri. Lewis laid out all the particulars in a long passage assessing the rationale for choosing the south fork. He again reassessed Fidler's data as a part of this review and reflected on what he understood of it. The captains further made their decision based on the strong prospect of finding waterfalls on the south fork, which would confirm Indian information about the Missouri. They found confirmation as well in the lay of the land, the clarity of the water, and the distribution of mountains as related by Indian informants. Lewis let the party know the leaders' determination but found that only he and Clark held that opinion, while the remainder opted for the north fork as the Missouri. He penned their objection: "They said very cheerfully that they were ready to follow us any wher we thought proper to direct but that they still thought that the other was the river and that they were affraid that the South fork would soon termineate in the mountains and leave us at a great distance from the Columbia." It did not help the captains' position that Cruzatte, an old Missouri waterman and skilled navigator, agreed with the majority.

Acknowledging the divided opinion, the captains decided to send a small, swift party ahead up the south fork (Missouri) until they found the falls, the determining factor. Recognizing Clark as the better boatman of the two, Lewis would lead the land party. They decided to wait a day or two more to allow time to repair damaged weapons, particularly the broken mainspring of Lewis's air gun, and give the captain opportunity for astronomical observations. Feeling ill earlier in the day, Lewis took a dose of salts and improved by evening. With others he listened to Cruzatte's fiddle and watched the men sing and dance "in the most Social manner," according to Clark. A dram of alcohol revived the party, said Ordway.

JUNE 10, 1805. Shields repaired the mainspring of the Lewis's air gun while others hauled out baggage and merchandise to air and dry on this fair day. Lewis heaped praise on Shields, noting that although he had not obtained regular training at gunsmithing, he was able to make extensive repairs on expedition weapons. In addition he was a good hunter and an excellent waterman. The captains decided to leave more supplies at this place, particularly gunpowder and lead, which they secreted near the camp. They also selected the articles to go in the large cache prepared the day before: these included axes, an auger, planes, files, chisels, a cooper's howel or plane, tin cups, two muskets, beaver traps, and blacksmith's tools such as bellows, hammers, and tongs; also flour, parched meal, pork, salt, and several animal skins. The cache also contained superfluous clothing and extra baggage "of every discription." Gass thought the items may have weighed one thousand pounds. The men hauled the red pirogue onto a small island at the mouth of the Marias River, secured it to trees, and covered it with brush. Lewis branded several nearby trees.

Lewis was sick again but determined to set out overland the next day, leaving Clark to complete the deposits and follow him by water. In this regard, the party pulled the canoes on shore, made any necessary repairs, and began loading them. Lewis told Drouillard, Joseph Field, Gibson, and Goodrich to prepare for the overland trip with him. Noticing an unfamiliar, small bird, Lewis wrote the first, lengthy description of the white-rumped shrike, considering its morphology and comparing it to known species. Sacagawea was sick in the evening, so Clark bled her. This was the beginning of an illness that would continue until June 20. Given the limited descriptions of her illness, the best possible explanation seems to be that she had a pelvic infection, perhaps exacerbated by a sexually transmitted disease.

JUNE 11, 1805. Although still weak from his illness, Lewis swung a pack over his shoulder and set off with his party along the northwest side of the Missouri. Along the way they fell in with a gang of elks and killed four of them. They took a portion of the meat and skins and hung it up to be seen from the river and available to the river party as they came by the next day. The captain was disappointed that he could not enjoy the elk feast because his illness returned, now with violent stomach pains. The pain increased during the evening with the addition of a high fever. Finding Lewis unable to go farther, the party camped at a point later called *Cracon du Nez* (bridge of the nose), where the Teton and Missouri Rivers come especially close to one another, a few miles northeast of Fort Benton, Chouteau County, Montana, having made about nine miles. Having brought no medicine with him, Lewis concocted a brew by boiling choke-cherry twigs until the mixture became a "strong black decoction of an astringent bitter tast." He drank a pint at sunset and repeated the dosage an hour later. By ten he was entirely free of pain, his fever had broken, and he had a mild sweat. He slept comfortably. In the meantime, Goodrich went fishing and caught several dozen fish of two varieties, saugers and goldeyes. The captain provided the first scientific descriptions of each species.

Clark at the main camp made another list of items buried in the cache that fairly matched Lewis's inventory of the day before. The party spent the day completing the deposit and repairing weapons. Sacagawea was still ill, so Clark bled her again, which seemed to provide some relief.

JUNE 12, 1805. Feeling revived from his illness, Lewis took another drink of his decoction and set out at sunrise with his party. Moving away from the steep ravines along the river, the party pushed out onto the plains and by nine o'clock had traveled twelve miles. They then turned back toward the river seeking water and something to eat for breakfast. On the open plains the buffalo were too wary for hunters to get within rifle shot. Closer to the river's timber they encountered two grizzlies and killed them both at first firing, a feat not accomplished to this point. Again they hung up unused portions for the river party, and Lewis left a note for Clark letting him know of their progress. Now back on the high plains after a two-hour diversion, they saw a land awash in animal life: wolves, pronghorns, mule deer, immense herds of buffalo, and great numbers of prairie dogs. From a high ridge, they viewed multiple ranges of the Rocky Mountains covered with snow. The sight gave the captain some pause: "this was an August spectacle and still rendered more formidable by the recollection that we had them to pass."

After another twelve miles, they struck the Missouri again and found a suitable spot to camp among a small grove of cottonwoods. Although early, Lewis, still weak from his illness, decided to rest. In spite of his weakened state the party had traveled about twenty-seven miles altogether. The camp was in Chouteau County, Montana, a short distance upstream from Black Coulee. On the way to camp hunters killed a buffalo, a pronghorn, and three mule deer, saving the best parts for later use. While entering notes on the day's events Lewis ate a hearty dinner, enjoying the fish caught the day before. Going fishing himself, the captain used Goodrich's bait to catch more than a dozen fish in a few minutes. He finished the day's entry comparing the plains ("broad leaf") and narrowleaf cottonwood trees and measuring the footprint of a grizzly at 11 inches long (exclusive of its claws) and 7¼ inches wide, "a formidable impression."

Clark and the main party set out up the Missouri at eight o'clock. Sacagawea was so sick that Clark moved her to the covered and cooler part of the pirogue. The captain described the lower blackish clay bluffs along the river, composed of the dark-gray to black Marias River Shale. Above that the earth turned a brownish yellow filled with coarse gravel, the result of glacial till. Rattlesnakes were numerous and one explorer unintentionally grabbed one reaching for a bush. Fortunately he was not bitten. Another soldier had a felon or whitlow (a finger infection), while another man complained of a toothache. Sacagawea fared the worst; Clark declared her as sick as he had seen her. He gave her some unnamed medicine. The main party camped about five miles downstream from Fort Benton, Chouteau County, after making about eighteen river miles.

JUNE 13, 1805. After a breakfast of venison and fish, Lewis's party set out at sunrise, ascending the river's heights to the level plains. The captain claimed he could see fifty to sixty miles across the plains and witnessed more buffalo than he had ever seen in a single viewing. With the river bending to the south, the party shifted their trek in that direction to avoid missing the falls they were seeking. Lewis sent hunters to the right and left of his line to obtain meat while he went on. Alone and ahead, the captain suddenly was "saluted with the agreeable sound of a fall of water" and a little farther on he saw a spray of water arising from the plains. He walked directly toward that point and soon heard "a roaring too tremendious to be mistaken for any cause short of the great falls of the Missouri." Reaching there at noon, Lewis hurried down a hill to gaze on "this sublimely grand specticle." He estimated the river to be about three hundred yards wide at the falls, two hundred of which formed "the grandest sight I ever beheld" as the water broke against the rocks some eighty feet below and then flew back up to a height of fifteen or twenty feet before it was caught in the continual downpour. The spray of water produced a beautiful rainbow, which, for Lewis, added "not a little to the beauty of this majestically grand senery." The captain read his description, then looked again at the falls and was dissatisfied with his words; he was about to scratch it out when he decided that he could do no better than to pen his first impressions. Nonetheless, he wished he had the skill of an artist or the facile pen of a better writer so that he "might be enabled to give to the enlightened world some just idea of this truly magnificcent and sublimely grand object, which has from the commencement of time been concealed from the view of civilized man." Lewis may have drawn a picture of the scene but no such piece has been found. "I hope still to give to the world some faint idea of an object which at this moment fills me with such pleasure and astonishment, and which of it's kind I will venture to ascert is second to but one in the known world."

The captain decided to set up the day's camp here on the north side of the river at the Great Falls, combined today with Ryan Dam, Cascade County, Montana. He planned to send one of the men to Clark in the morning, informing him of his find and ending any lingering doubts about this being the true Missouri. Hunters came in with a part of the meat of three buffalo cows. After a rest and refreshment, the men returned to the kill to bring in the rest of the meat and prepare it for the river party. In the meantime, Lewis turned back downriver to locate a spot where the boats might land in preparation for an overland journey. In his short jaunt he saw a river laced with rapids and unnavigable; a landing spot would have to be farther downriver. Returning to camp, he found the others waiting and Goodrich holding half a dozen cutthroat trout (new to science; its specific name, *clarki*, honors the captain) and other fish. Lewis wrote a short description of the new species. The captain called the evening meal "sumptuous": "buffaloe's humps, tongues and marrowbones, fine trout parched meal pepper and salt, and a good appetite; the last is not considered the least of luxuries."

Before retiring the captain tried to sort out color variations of local bears. He decided that the "Brown, the white and the Grizly bear" were the same species with only color differences. He had seen cream-colored bears and reddish-brown ones but confessed that he had never seen a "grizly bear." From the claws that Indians had shown him and that he had compared to others, he was convinced that there was only one species, the grizzly bear. The black bear was not found in this country, he concluded.

Sacagawea, with the main party, was as sick as ever. Clark gave her a dose of salts, perhaps hoping that a bowel movement would relieve her stomach pains. Whitehouse was also ill, and three others had medical complaints. The party passed Shonkin Creek ("Snow River") and camped in the vicinity of Bird Coulee, Chouteau County, having traveled about thirteen miles.

JUNE 14, 1805. Lewis sent Joseph Field with a letter for Clark telling him of the discovery of the falls of the Missouri. Lewis also ordered Field to stay close to the river and look for a suitable landing point and staging area to begin the portage around the falls. The captain set one man to building a scaffold and collecting wood to dry meat for use during the portage, while the others went to collect what meat was left from the previous day's buffalo kill. They came back shortly to report that wolves had devoured most of the meat. Lewis decided to hike upriver a few miles to investigate the river and return by lunchtime, so with gun and espontoon he set out.

Passing a river strewn with rapids, after about five miles he came to a falls of about nineteen feet that he named Crooked Falls, a name it still retains in Cascade County, Montana. After a brief viewing, he was ready to return but heard a roaring noise ahead and proceeded on. Within a few hundred yards he was again "presented by one of the most beatifull objects in nature, a cascade of about 50 feet perpendicular streching at right angles across the river." Lewis was so taken with Rainbow ("Handsom") Falls that he could not decide which was the more beautiful, this one or the Great Falls of the day before. He settled for calling this one *"pleasingly beautifull"* and the other *"sublimely grand."* While debating the issue in his mind and walking on he discovered another cascade about a half mile farther on. Colter Falls, so named then and now, had a drop of about fourteen feet for Lewis but is submerged today. Conceding that anywhere else this would be extolled for its beauty, the captain noted that here among such competing cascades it barely made an impression. He decided against returning as soon as he had planned but went on in search of more falls. After about 2½ miles of following a rapid-rich river, he made his final discovery, Black Eagle Falls, with a cataract of twenty-six feet. Without a distinctive expedition name, it later acquired its present name but was diminished in size in order to accommodate Black Eagle Dam. Taken with the majesty of the moment, Lewis called it "much the greatest I ever behald except those two which I have mentioned below."

Beyond these falls Lewis saw a calmer river, and climbing a nearby hill he had a grand prospect of the Missouri River and its valley. He viewed a beautiful and extensive plain through which the river flowed from the south and southwest out of snow-clad mountains. On its western side he noticed the Sun River about four miles above him, conspicuous by the line of trees following its meandering course. On the plains and all along the Missouri's valley he gazed on immense herds of buffalo while vast numbers of geese settled on the river's "watry bosome." He determined to continue his walk to the Sun River, which he reasoned must be the one that the Mandans and Hidatsas called *"medicine river."*

Seeing a herd of "at least a thousand buffalo," Lewis decided to kill one and leave it for his return should he have to spend the night there. He selected one, shot it through the lungs, and watched it slowly die, neglecting to reload his rifle. So distracted, he did not notice a grizzly that had come within twenty paces of him. Raising his gun to shoot he quickly recognized his negligence and saw the bear moving briskly toward him. Looking around he saw not a bush or tree for protection, and he had no time to load his weapon. Now the bear moved toward him at full speed with mouth agape. Lewis took off in a dead run for the river some eighty yards distant. He decided to get into the river where he could stand while the bear would have to swim; then with his long espontoon he might be at an advantage. In the water, Lewis turned and waited for the assault, but the bear declined combat and sauntered off. Lewis could not account for the bear's strange behavior. Out of the water he quickly reloaded and "determined never again to suffer my peice to be longer empty than the time she necessarily required to charge her."

The grizzly experience did not deter Lewis from his mission to visit the Sun River. He found it a handsome stream, about two hundred yards wide, clear, deep, and gentle. Having examined it to his satisfaction, he began his return at about six thirty with twelve miles to go. Along the way he saw an animal, perhaps a wolverine, that he first thought a wolf. He tried to shoot it but apparently missed. While examining the animal's burrow, he was charged by three buffalo bulls. The captain decided that "all the beasts of the neighbourhood had made a league to distroy me." Moving on he passed the buffalo he had killed earlier in the day but decided not to spend the night there, partly because "the succession of curious adventures wore the impression on my mind of inchantment; at sometimes for a moment I thought it might be a dream, but the prickley pears which pierced my feet very severely once in a while, particularly after it grew dark, convinced me that I was really awake." Arriving at his small party's camp he discovered that the men were very worried about him and were planning a search for him in the morning. Greatly fatigued, he took a hearty supper and enjoyed a good night's rest.

Clark considered Sacagawea's illness dangerous. She had complained all night and was particularly ill this morning. Others also continued in pain: two with toothaches, two with tumors on their hands, and one with a tumor and slight fever. These men spent the night ashore, and one of them killed a buffalo that served as the party's breakfast. The river's current was swift and made progress difficult; some of the canoes frequently took in water. Whitehouse saw buffalo carcasses in the river and thought they might have been killed in the falls. About four o'clock Joseph Field arrived with Lewis's message and news that the falls were about twenty miles ahead. Lewis also related that the river party might have to land some five miles above the falls and rapids to establish a point for the portage. Making about ten miles, the river party set up camp near the entrance of Black Coulee, Chouteau County.

JUNE 15, 1805. When he awoke, Lewis discovered a large prairie rattlesnake nearby, killed it, and counted 176 scuta on its abdomen and 17 on its tail, the same as the one of May 17. The captain sent his men out to bring in more of the meat obtained by Drouillard the day before and continue the drying operation. He spent the day resting from the previous day's exertions and got in a little fishing. He caught a number of cutthroat trout, as did Goodrich, who also added some channel catfish to the count. Phenological remarks in the captains' weather diaries noted that deer were giving birth and that grizzlies were mating. In the evening Joseph Field returned to report that the river party had arrived at rapids some five miles below and would delay until Lewis arrived. From his survey of the river, Lewis had concluded that the north side of the Missouri would be difficult as a portage route given its deep ravines. He considered the south side the best option. He ordered Field to go back to Clark in the morning and have him send some of his men to retrieve the dried meat that the land party had prepared.

Clark and party were already experiencing difficulties in river travel, facing a rapid current and dangerous spots. The work of moving the boats was incredibly fatiguing, which Clark described in admiring terms: "the men in the water from morning untill night hauling the Cord & boats walking on Sharp rocks and round Sliperery Stones which alternately cut their feet & throw them down, not with Standing all this dificuelty they go with great chearfulness." During the day the river party passed Highwood Creek ("Shields River," after Shields of the corps), Chouteau County, Montana. The enlisted journalists called it "Strawberry River." In this area Clark noticed red bluffs mixed with black stones and elsewhere a white clay that when mixed with water reminded him of wet flour. He was seeing the reddish-brown sandstone and shale of the Kootenai Formation and the dark siltstone and shale of the Blackleaf Formation. The "white clay" was probably a bentonite bed of the Black-leaf. Arriving at a particularly bad rapid late in the evening, Clark decided to go no farther in the dark. They camped a little below and opposite the mouth of Belt ("Portage") Creek, Cascade County, having come about twelve miles.

Sacagawea was still sick and now dispirited. Clark applied poultices of Peruvian bark to her pelvic region, her main area of pain, and she gained some relief. It did not last. In the evening she felt worse and would not take any medicine. Her husband, Charbonneau, even asked to return. It is unclear if he intended to take his family back to the Mandan-Hidatsa villages.

JUNE 16, 1805. Joseph Field left Lewis early to secure men from the main party to assist in carrying meat they had acquired. He returned by noon with workers, and all set out for the main party with about six hundred pounds of dried meat and several dozen dried trout. They reached Clark about two o'clock. Lewis told Clark of his investigation of the river ahead and of his determination that the south (or east) side furnished the best route for a portage around the falls. Clark had already sent two men over to examine that side of the river and now most of the party moved across as well, about a mile below Belt ("Portage") Creek, Chouteau County, Montana, where wood was available. This became the party's "Lower Portage Camp," a staging area for the month-long portage of the Great Falls. Clark resolved to seek and survey a portage route in the morning. The captains selected six men to find timber large enough to build wheels for two wagons to transport the party's canoes and goods on the route that Clark would establish.

Lewis took four canoes up to Belt Creek from the north (or west) side to find a place where they could get them onto the plains and ready for the portage. Gass said, "This business was attended with great difficulty as well as danger, but we succeeded in getting them all over safe." One of the small canoes was left behind to shuttle from one side of the Missouri to the other. Lewis particularly wanted to use it to get water from a sulfur spring about two hundred yards from the river on the north side opposite Belt Creek. He believed that the sulfur water might serve as a cure for Sacagawea's illness.

The captains decided to leave the white pirogue and superfluous goods in a cache and substitute the iron-framed boat for the shallow waters ahead. The two men sent to examine a possible portage on the south side returned in the evening to report that the way out of Belt Creek to the plains would be difficult and impractical. The captains disagreed: "g[o]od or bad we must make the portage," they declared. Lewis was convinced from his earlier reconnaissance that it should be on the south side.

When he arrived at Clark's camp, Lewis found Sacagawea extremely ill and very weak. Clark had been unable to get her to take medicine, but Charbonneau, "finding her out of her Senses," convinced her to take it. Clark was unimpressed by Charbonneau's attitude toward his wife and wrote, "if She dies it will be the fault of her husband." Lewis discovered that her pulse was barely perceptible, irregular, and sometimes racing and that her fingers twitched. He was deeply concerned for her welfare in both a compassionate way and as a practical matter. He sympathized with her condition but also realized that she provided the best hope for a favorable encounter with her Shoshone people for the acquisition of horses. He gave her two doses of barks and some opium and found her pulse improved, stronger, and more regular and that the nervous, twitching symptoms had subsided. He also had her drink some of the sulfur water he had acquired from across the river. Although feeling better in the evening, she still complained of stomach problems, so Lewis applied poultices of Peruvian bark and administered laudanum. He diagnosed her problem as having an obstruction in her menses flow. The captain decided to stay with her while Clark made the portage survey. Meanwhile Lewis would take some celestial observations and get everything ready for the portage at Clark's return.

JUNE 17, 1805. Clark set out early with five men, among them Willard, Colter, and perhaps Joseph Field, to survey a portage route around the Great Falls. The six men of the day before were directed to prepare four sets of wheels for two wagons, including couplings, tongues, and bodies to transport the canoes and baggage. Lewis noticed that some of the elk skins he had saved for his iron-framed boat were damaged, so he sent two hunters after elks. The balance of the party he set to unloading the white pirogue and preparing it to be left behind. Completing that, the men took five of the small canoes up Belt Creek about 1¾ miles to be laid out in the sun to dry. At that spot there was a gradual ascent to the high plains, whereas elsewhere the banks were far too steep to accomplish the haul. Rapids and rocks blocking the creek's entrance made the going tough even for this short distance. In fact, one of the canoes overturned and nearly injured its crew.

The party found one cottonwood tree just below Belt Creek that was large enough to make wagon wheels of about twenty-two inches in diameter. Lewis wrote with some relief that "I do not believe that we could find another of the same size perfectly sound within 20 miles of us." Although soft and brittle and not perfect for wagon construction, cottonwood trees were the only timber available to them. They made two axletrees out of the mast of the white pirogue, but its quality was also questionable. Above the river on the plains, Lewis saw vast herds of buffalo, and he witnessed bison carcasses drifting down the river and being mangled by cataracts and rapids. Earlier he had watched animals at the river suffer a similar fate. Forward ones were pushed from narrow paths by those behind and sent tumbling into the raging stream with little possibility of escape.

Sacagawea seemed to be improving, but Lewis continued his course of medication of the day before. Her fever had lessened, her pulse was more regular, and she was eating again. Lewis permitted her to eat some boiled buffalo meat and a soup made from the same. He was optimistic about her condition and thought her on the way to recovery.

Clark and his five men went up Belt Creek for some distance, hoping to find a spot to get the party onto the plains with a straight shot toward the Sun ("Medicine") River on the opposite side. But they found Belt Creek becoming narrow, rapid, and shallow with steep banks. Only one spot less than two miles up the creek provided the gentle slope to the plains that the party needed. Up on the plains they came to deep ravines and creek beds, and finally turning north toward the Missouri they heard the roaring sounds of the falls; then the captain "beheld those Cateracts with astonishment." Trying to get the dimensions of the Great Falls, Clark nearly slipped and was certain that he would have been "Sucked under in an instant." For lunch the men stopped at a spring with shady willow trees. Clark marked his name and the date on one and added the height of the falls. Moving along the south side of the river, the little party halted a short distance below Crooked Falls and camped in Cascade County, Montana.

JUNE 18, 1805. All hands at the Lower Portage Camp were employed in bringing the white pirogue on shore and hauling it to a hiding place among a thick bunch of willows a little below the camp. Once in place they secured the boat tightly and covered it with bushes and driftwood to keep it out of the sun. Lewis selected a spot for the cache and sent three men to prepare it. He had those who had moved the pirogue begin inspecting, repairing, airing, and packing all the goods to be moved overland. The captain took a close look at his unassembled iron-framed boat and found all the parts in place except for one screw, which he knew Shields could make. The hunters of the day before returned without the desired elk skins but with ten deer. Lewis preferred elk skins even to buffalo hides since the former were more durable and strong and resisted shrinkage. Nevertheless, viewing buffalo across the river near the sulfur springs, he sent hunters after them with orders also to bring back more mineral water. Wagon construction was completed in the evening, and they appeared ready for the road, according to Lewis.

During the day Lewis took time to describe a native plant he called a "goosberry." From his morphological notes it is clearly the squaw, or western red, currant, not a gooseberry, which is distinguished by prickles on its stem. The captain also noted the presence of numerous grasshoppers, which he deemed responsible for the low grasses in the area. He was probably seeing blue grama or buffalograss.

Sacagawea was recovering fast, sat up for most of the day, and went for a walk. This was her first venture out for some time, and she seemed to take it without difficulty. She was eating heartily, showed no fever, and suffered no pain. Lewis continued his medication of before but added a dose of fifteen drops of sulfuric acid at noon to serve as a tonic.

With an early start Clark and party quickly passed Crooked Falls and reached Rainbow ("Handsom") Falls. Clark measured the height of its fall as forty-seven feet, eight inches and the Missouri's width as 473 yards. From there the group moved upriver about one mile and reached Giant Springs, Cascade County, Montana, which the captain called the largest spring he had ever seen and perhaps the largest in the United States. The spring discharges over 150 million gallons of water a day. Clark pointed out that its clear-blue cast colored the Missouri for nearly one-half mile downstream. Passing several rapids Clark missed or ignored Colter Falls but measured Black Eagle Falls at twenty-six feet, five inches.

As they moved on a herd of buffalo crossed the river above the falls. Some were caught in the rapid waters and, half drowned, barely made it to shore. The men killed one of the cows, took the choicest parts of its meat, and ate opposite the Sun ("Medicine") River in a small grove of trees. Moving on, the men found Sand Coulee Creek ("Flattery Run") upstream from a group of islands where they camped. Less than a mile northeast of the creek, the corps would establish their "Upper Portage Camp," where they stayed until July 13, and the islands became the "White Bear Islands" due to numerous grizzlies on them. The men killed seven buffalo and a calf crossing from the islands and saved as much meat as they could. While hauling in a load, Willard attracted a grizzly from the islands and was pursued for some distance before the bear abandoned the chase. Clark and three others set out after the bear, fearing that it might attack Colter, who was still out. Indeed, they found Colter in the water, having been chased there by the grizzly. The bear retreated when they arrived, so Clark was not able to get a clear shot at it.

JUNE 19, 1805. Lewis sent several men across the river after the deer meat that hunters had secured the day before. They found it still safe from roving wolves. He also sent Drouillard, Reuben Field, and Shannon across the river with instructions to go ahead to the Sun River searching for elks. The captain reasoned that since there was more timber on that side, there should be more elks. The party at camp completed the cache. Lewis spent part of the day fishing, catching several saugers but no cutthroat trout or catfish. Otherwise he managed the packing for the overland trip to come, had the iron-framed boat cleaned and greased, and took care of mundane matters like waxing the stoppers of the gunpowder canisters. The men were likewise looking ahead to land travel over difficult terrain, so they set to mending moccasins and generally preparing themselves for the hard labor ahead. At dusk Seaman began to bark and act anxious. As a caution Lewis ordered the sergeant of the guard to take extra care against possible Indian pilfering. Seaman may actually have been barking at a buffalo bull that had failed to swim the river, was swept down near the camp, struggled free, and raced away. Lewis calculated a latitude at the lower camp of 47° 8′59.5″ N; it is probably closer to 47° 36′36″ N.

Sacagawea was much better and able to gather "white apples" (Indian breadroot), which she ate raw along with some dried fish. All of this was done without Lewis's knowledge or consent. Soon her fever returned and her illness came back. Lewis reprimanded Charbonneau in very strong language, since the captain had given him strict instructions about her diet. He gave her doses of potassium nitrate (saltpeter) in order to produce perspiration and lessen her fever, and then thirty drops of laudanum to provide a restful sleep.

Clark and party went on to the White Bear Islands in search of the offending grizzly of the day before but did not find it. The captain decided to investigate Sand Coulee Creek ("Flattery Run") above their camp; he found it dry except for some back water from the Missouri. Making further investigations of the area, he did not return to camp until late in the evening. He decided that the best route for the portage would be from the Lower Portage Camp to the lower point of one of the islands. A windy day brought with it a little accident, as part of Clark's notes were swept away, blown helter-skelter, and not to be found. He either retained or rewrote his survey of the course of the Missouri River and his suggested route for a portage around the Great Falls from Belt Creek to the White Bear Islands (Upper Portage Camp). His distance estimate for the route was 17¾ miles and forty-six poles.

JUNE 20, 1805. With work done on the cache and preparations completed for the portage the main party had little to do except wait for Clark's return and get his recommendation for the way ahead. Lewis was a little worried about Clark's delay—an absence longer than he had expected. He sent four hunters across the river after buffalo, which were easier to take on that side given the nature of the terrain. He wanted to lay in a supply of dried meat while they had the opportunity to hunt. Once on the move all hands would be employed in hauling efforts. Two hunters returned in the evening having killed eleven buffalo, eight of which were in good order. Lewis immediately sent men to bring in the meat. A few returned with about half the meat while others stayed to finish the butchering job and protect the remainder. The captain was amazed at the number of buffalo that came to the river, many of which drank at the mineral spring. He was unsure whether they preferred the mineral water or drank it out of convenience. Sacagawea was free of pain and fever and on the way to full recovery. She went walking during the day and took in a little fishing.

Clark had his men cut stakes to set up along the route that the portage party would take on the portage from the lower camp to the upper. Meeting rain on the first part of their journey back to the main camp, the men experienced a fair afternoon. Arriving at Box Elder Creek ("Willow Run"), Clark determined that it could not be negotiated by the party's wagons owing to its steep banks. He sought a way around it but as it was getting late he gave up and headed for the main camp. They arrived late in the evening to find that Lewis had moved the boats almost two miles up Belt Creek to a spot the captain considered a good place to ascend to the plains and begin the cross-country trek. A good portion of Clark's final notes of this day were copied from Lewis's entries of July 4 and 11 (see below). Ordway and Whitehouse gave a summary of the events of Clark's party in their journals.

JUNE 21, 1805. Lewis had most of the men moving baggage onto the plains above Belt Creek. One of the canoes was hoisted onto a wagon and was also taken onto the plains, then loaded with baggage. He wanted to get an early start on the initial portage trip tomorrow. Lewis had determined that he would go to Upper Portage Camp in order to prepare the iron-framed boat, help unload supplies as they were brought in, and generally look after camp matters. The first load would include the boat's assembly parts and scientific instruments. Moreover, he had the baggage of Gass, Joseph Field, and Shields separated and packed for the first trip. These men would stay with Lewis and help assemble the boat and maintain the camp. Lewis was already beginning to worry about his "leather boat." Would they find the proper wood, bark, skins, and most importantly, pitch to seal it? For the latter he was mentally trying to concoct mixtures of available materials to use as substitutes. Clark echoed his concerns. Whitehouse provided the best description of the boat in his entry for the day.

Lewis took time from portage preparations to describe "a species of fishing ducks" that he thought the same as he knew in the East. It was either the female red-breasted merganser or the female common merganser. He also enumerated local trees, "what little there is," including cottonwoods, willows, and boxelders, while the undergrowth consisted of rosebushes, gooseberries, currants, honeysuckles, and red osier dogwoods. Lewis reported that the inner bark of the latter was used by *engagés* as a mixture with tobacco.

JUNE 22, 1805. Leaving Ordway, Goodrich, York, Charbonneau, Sacagawea, and her baby behind to look after the remaining baggage, the party set out toward the Upper Portage Camp at the White Bear Islands carrying what the wagon with canoe atop could handle. Clark was the guide on this first crossing. At Box Elder Creek ("Willow Run"), the only place for water along the route, they stopped for lunch and made repairs on the wagon, taking two hours for the work. The cottonwood timber was not holding up to the task, so the men substituted willow wood, hoping it would better take the strain. It was after dark when they found themselves within a half mile of their destination and needing to abandon their wagon as the tongues had broken down. Each man gathered as much baggage as he could carry and moved on to the camp "much fortiegued," wrote Lewis. More than tired, they were also injured from the sharp points of prickly pears stabbing through their moccasins. Owing to the difficulty of this initial trip, Clark related that the captains determined to use every available man ("Cooks & all")

on subsequent trips. After reaching camp they built fires for dinner but discovered that the meat that Clark had left for them from
the previous day had been devoured by wolves. They slept soundly,
nevertheless. At the base camp Ordway reported that York killed
a buffalo out of a large herd crossing the Missouri, and Charbonneau took a pronghorn.

Lewis was not entirely distracted from his scientific work during
the crossing. He noticed long-billed curlews ("large brown curloo"), now setting and laying eggs in an exposed situation. He also
provided a morphological description of the western meadowlark,
a bird new to science, which he compared to his familiar eastern
meadowlark ("oldfield lark").

JUNE 23, 1805. Lewis selected a spot under some shady willows to
begin assembling his iron-framed boat. Clark returned the short
distance to the abandoned wagon and brought it up with the canoe
and baggage from the place they had left them the day before, then
all breakfasted on the scanty supply of meat that remained. Afterward Clark and party started the return journey to Lower Portage Camp to prepare for another trip. Lewis had his men clear
the area to form their camp and start assembling his iron-framed
boat. Gass measured the boat as 36 feet long, 4½ feet long, and 2
feet, 2 inches deep. The clearing completed, the captain sent Gass
and Shields after timber for the boat while he went downriver in
the canoe with Joseph Field to the Sun River in search of hunters
(Drouillard, Reuben Field, and Shannon) sent out on June 19. Gass
said his party was seeking wood to form into "thin shaved strips"
for lining the iron-framed boat.

Arriving at the Sun River, Lewis and Field walked up the north
side, hollering for their companions as they went. Some five miles
up the river they discovered Shannon, who had killed deer and buffalo and had acquired and prepared about six hundred pounds of
dried meat. But he had killed no elks. He had no idea of the whereabouts of Reuben Field and Drouillard, since he had parted with
them on June 19 and had not seen them since. It being late, the captain decided to stay at Shannon's camp on the opposite side of the
Sun. The men built a hastily prepared raft and moved across the

river—about eighty yards wide at this point. Lewis filled out his day's entry with an account of Clark's events of the day, which information he obtained when the two men regrouped. In fact, Lewis reported that Reuben Field returned to the lower camp and told Clark that he was worried about Shannon's absence. Clark was silent on this matter, but Ordway and Whitehouse noted it.

After breakfast Clark started toward Belt Creek with the wagon in tow. He had the men stick poles in the ground as guides for future crossings and altered somewhat the way as he went. His final measurement was 18¼ from Lower Portage Camp to Upper Portage Camp. He arrived at the lower camp in time to take two canoes to the top of the ridge at Belt Creek. He found the men double-soling their moccasins in order to guard against the sharp spikes of prickly pears. Recent rains had softened the ground, which was then torn up by buffalo herds. Now hardened, it made the going even more difficult. Clark recounted the task in graphic terms:

> the men has to haul with all their Strength wate & art, maney times every man all catching the grass & knobes & Stones with their hands to give them more force in drawing on the Canoes & Loads, and notwithstanding the Coolness of the air in high presperation and every halt, those not employed in reparing the Cou[r]se; are asleep in a moment, maney limping from the Soreness of their feet Some become fant for a fiew moments, but no man Complains all go Chearfully on— to State the fatigues of this party would take up more of the journal than other notes which I find Scercely time to Set down.

In spite of these difficulties and distractions Clark noticed currants along the route and prairie birds in immense numbers.

JUNE 24, 1805. Thinking that Drouillard and Reuben Field might be higher up the Sun River, Lewis sent Joseph Field in that direction with orders to go at least four miles and then come back to Shannon's camp whether he found them or not. In the meantime the captain walked down the south side of the river while he sent Shannon across to descend it on the opposite side, collect the party's canoe, meet him at the Missouri, and take him across to the east (south) side. Having accomplished this, Shannon returned to his camp in the canoe to meet Joseph Field upon his return. The soldier was to collect his dried meat and bring it ahead to the White Bear Islands camp. When Lewis arrived at the upper camp, he found Shannon and Field there as well as the portage party, "wet and fatigued." Lewis gave them each a dram of alcohol. Reuben Field was with this party, and he related his activities with Drouillard. Drouillard was still at their temporary camp with the dried meat they had prepared. Lewis also learned that Gass and Shields had found little suitable timber for the iron-framed boat and were making do with willow and boxelder wood, cottonwood being entirely too soft and brittle for the intended purpose. Lewis gathered some pine driftwood hoping it would yield pitch to seal the boat's seams. He took Frazer from the portage party to stay at the upper camp so he could sew hides to cover the boat. Doubtless the captain learned from the men that "the Indian woman is now perfectly recovered."

Clark was up early at the lower camp to supervise bringing the last canoe out of the water to dry. He had the baggage divided into three groups, one of which men backpacked to the five canoes that had been taken about two miles up Belt Creek, pulled ashore to dry, hauled up the embankment, moved out on the plains, and readied for transport. The portage crew then set two canoes on the wagons and set out. Clark went with them for about four miles and then returned. He explained that his feet were sore from several days on the rough plains. Slight showers in the morning were followed by darkening skies by six, then a hailstorm was succeeded by rain that lasted about an hour.

Ordway and Whitehouse related the work of this second portage. At Box Elder Creek the men were detained a short time to refresh themselves and repair a broken wagon tongue. Within three miles of the upper camp the men were hit by hard rain and had to work their way through holes half-filled with water. Hot, thirsty men lapped up rain caught in puddles. The wind gave them some assistance in moving the wagons, and they hoisted a sail on the largest canoe to take advantage of it. Whitehouse said it equaled four men pulling on ropes. Ordway termed it "Saleing on dry land in

everry Since of the word." They arrived wet and tired and appreciated Lewis's offer of a drink.

JUNE 25, 1805. Lewis got the portage party underway to the lower
camp and sent Frazer in the canoe for Drouillard and his dried meat
and Joseph Field up the Missouri to hunt for elks. Later he ordered
Gass and Shields to the largest of the White Bear Islands in search
of bark and timber for the iron-framed boat. Field returned about
noon and reported that he had encountered some grizzlies and was
chased by one. In his escape he jumped down a steep bank, bruised
and cut himself, and bent his gun in the fall. Fortunately, the bank
hid him from the bear, and he came back to camp. Lewis counted
the man lucky, as this was his second narrow escape from grizzlies;
the first was on June 4. A few hours later Gass and Shields returned
with only a small quantity of wood for the boat and a report that no
more was to be found. On their excursion they had killed two elks
and brought back the skins and part of the meat. Even later Frazer
and Drouillard came in, bringing about eight hundred pounds of
dried meat and one hundred pounds of tallow.

Lewis described the Upper Portage Camp as being in a "pretty
little grove." The captain noted either foxtail barley or squirreltail
("wild rye"), eighteen or twenty inches high, a "very handsome grass"
with a fine, soft "beard." He also saw great quantities of field mint,
young blackbirds beginning to fly, and painted turtles ("water ter-
ripens"). Being unsuccessful at fishing, he decided that there were
no fish in that part of the river.

At the lower camp Clark was unwell, probably with diarrhea
("looseness"); Pryor was also sick. The captain took a little coffee for
breakfast, which he called a rarity that he had not tasted since winter. He directed that more supplies be put out to dry and that Charbonneau begin cooking for the portage party, soon to return. The
party gathered driftwood for fire. In spite of his illness, Clark saw
beauty about him. He witnessed a country of "romantick appearance," with the river enclosed by high, steep bluffs that were cut by
deep ravines, sheltering a scattering of trees along its border. He saw
only a solitary cottonwood against the horizon. He considered the
plains' soil here inferior to lands farther down the Missouri, yet it

yielded great quantities of chokecherries, gooseberries, red and yellow berries, and red and purple currants. He also noted the "hard red and redish brown earth Containing Iron" of the lower Cretaceous Kootenai Formation, with its reddish color coming from oxidized iron compounds. Fishing paid off in trout, mussels, goldeyes, catfish, and perhaps suckers. The portage party, worn out as usual, arrived about five o'clock and quickly set to repairing their damaged moccasins and preparing new loads for an early start in the morning. They took two canoes up the hill from Belt Creek and onto the plains. Despite their fatigue, the men lifted their bone-weary bodies to the tunes of Cruzatte's violin until ten o'clock, to "shake a foot . . . dancing on the green," as Lewis put it. "All Chearfullness and good humer," according to Clark.

JUNE 26, 1805. Mosquitoes harassed the men at the upper camp but work went on. Joseph Field and Drouillard took one of the canoes up the Missouri in search of elks. Frazer started sewing skins together for the iron-framed boat covering. Gass and Shields went to the other side of the river, still in search of wood and bark to line the boat. Lewis assigned himself as cook for these men and for those coming from the lower camp with the next load. He collected wood and water, boiled a good quantity of buffalo meat, and made each man a suet dumpling "by way of a treat." By four o'clock Gass and Shields were back with a better supply of wood than previously, but it was still inadequate. They had some cottonwood bark, but Lewis thought it too soft and brittle. He preferred the tough, strong bark of the peach-leaved willow. The men also brought the skins of seven buffalo they had killed and the choicest meat. Lewis decided that he might have to be content with buffalo hides if elks were not found.

The portage party arrived at the upper camp late in the evening with two more canoes on wagons loaded with baggage. Ordway viewed innumerable buffalo as they made their way to the upper camp, the plains "black with buffalow," he said. Whitehouse related that "I can without exaggeration say, that I saw more Buffalo feeding—at one time, than all the Animals I had ever seen before in my life time put together." Whitehouse came in to the upper camp overworked and overheated. Unwittingly, he drank a great deal of water and became extremely ill. Lewis observed a quickened pulse in the soldier and bled him "plentifully," after which he felt somewhat better. The captain did not have medical tools and so improvised with his penknife for the operation. "It answered very well," he indicated.

Clark inventoried the loads in the two canoes as they set out: parched meal, pork, biscuits, portable soup, gunpowder, lead, axes, miscellaneous tools, merchandise, and clothes. He ended the list with "&c. &c."—et cetera, et cetera. The captain gave Pryor, still ill, a dose of salts. He detailed Charbonneau, one of the nonportage persons, to render buffalo tallow and pack it in kegs. He sorted out the items that remained to be cached: kegs of pork and flour, two blunderbusses, ammunition, and Lewis's desk and books. He also mentioned depositing "lumbersom articles" that could be left behind. In recounting events at the lower camp Lewis added other items that were cached, specifically, specimens of plants and minerals collected from Fort Mandan to this point. In fact, these specimens were not deposited there but at the upper camp and on the return trip were found to be mostly lost to water damage (see July 13, 1806).

JUNE 27, 1805. The portage party set out early for return to the lower camp to get the final canoe and remaining baggage. Whitehouse was still sick, so he remained behind. Later, when he was feeling better, he joined Frazer in sewing skins together for the iron-framed boat. Gass and Shields worked on fitting horizontal bars into sections of the boat, but the wood was so crooked that they made little progress. Lewis continued as cook so others could concentrate on their tasks. Unlucky elks wandered too close to camp and were killed by the men. In the afternoon a storm set in with thunder, lightning, and hail. Lewis reported in the weather diary that the hailstones would bounce ten to twelve feet high. He measured some at seven inches in circumference and weighing three ounces. Gass watched the ground turn white as snow.

Drouillard and Joseph Field returned in the afternoon having killed nine elks and three grizzlies. One of the bears was the largest that Lewis had seen, and he compared its skin size to that of an ox. Its forefeet measured nine inches across, and the hind feet 11¾ inches long (not counting the claws) and seven inches wide. The hunters acquired it by a bit of deception. They noticed bear tracks on their way, followed them to a place where the animal was concealed, climbed a nearby tree, and began hollering to get its attention. Soon enough, it came out and headed their way, and Drouillard was able to get it with a single shot to its head. Lewis noted that grizzlies do not climb. A grizzly had come close to the camp during the night and had scavenged thirty pounds of buffalo suet hanging on a pole. So many bears were in the neighborhood that Seaman was barking nervously all night. The captain noticed the "soft red stone" of the Kootenai Formation in the bluffs and gullies, which leached out and colored the river.

Ordway and three others separated from the main portage party and returned by way of the Missouri's falls. The sergeant could not resist stopping for a while to admire the cataracts. At Giant Springs he relished the "finest tasted water" he had ever drunk, and so clear he was certain he could have seen a pin at the bottom. They lunched about noon on the hump of a buffalo bull they had shot. Nearing the mouth of Box Elder Creek they experienced a hard rain and hail, so violent that the men crawled under a shelving rock for protection. The sudden storm caused the creek to surge and threaten their safety, so they abandoned the spot and walked through driving rain and hail. The men could hardly stay upright against the torrents. They arrived at the lower camp just after the main portage group. Ordway and one other man decided to use the cache for a sleeping spot and spent the night there.

Clark declared Pryor in better health. The captain put the finishing points on a rough draft map of the Missouri River up to Fort Mandan and completed a table of distances to that point. He intended to leave the map at the lower camp. It is unclear what map Clark was working on, and it is apparently lost. At four o'clock the portage party returned from the upper camp. In the evening hard rain and hail set in, lulled for about an hour, then followed with more rain and hard winds. In his weather diary remarks Clark reported that the men saved themselves from hailstone injury by covering their heads or by ducking under canoes. Nevertheless, two men were knocked down while others had exposed parts bruised. Clark passed around a drink of grog. Later he watched buffalo cross the river, get caught in the rapids, and then be carried over the falls to be mangled below.

JUNE 28, 1805. Lewis had everyone working on his iron-framed boat: Drouillard shaving elk skins, Joseph Field making cross stays, Frazer and Whitehouse working various skin coverings, and Gass and Shields finishing horizontal bars. Lewis found that without sufficient elk skins he had to substitute buffalo hides to cover one section. Too tough to shave, the buffalo hide had to be singed. Lewis thought it would answer his purpose. In the meantime, the captain prepared dinner for the portage party, who were to arrive in the evening. Later he sent Gass and Shields to the islands after more willow bark for the boat. Realizing that grizzlies were too much for a single man, he decided to always send at least two persons on any mission. Although no bears had invaded the camp, they had come close during the night, only to be diverted by Seaman, on the alert. Nonetheless, Lewis had the men keep their weapons close at hand.

At the lower camp Clark sent the remaining canoe with baggage up the embankment from Belt Creek, worked on final allocations for the cache, and made repairs on one of the wagons. With the cache completed and covered, the party loaded the wagons with the remaining baggage and set out for the upper camp. As usual, it was a difficult pull to the high land above the creek. When the party arrived at the canoe already in place above the creek, Clark realized that they had too much baggage for a single trip, so they left heavy ammunition boxes and pork and flour kegs for another trip. They went on with what they could take on the two wagons, reaching Box Elder Creek so late that Clark called a halt and made camp for the night. It was an uncomfortable situation, with little water in the creek, showers in the evening, high winds at dark, and then more rain that drenched the unready explorers. Clark passed out a dram of liquor.

JUNE 29, 1805. After an early morning shower, the day turned fair, at least somewhat. Having not seen Giant Springs, Lewis decided to visit the site, since he could be spared from the upper camp. Giving orders to keep work going, he set out with Drouillard across the plains. They were soon overtaken by violent winds and heavy rains accompanied by thunder and lightning. Lewis expected a hailstorm, so they took safety in a little gully with overhanging rocks, but no hail appeared. Nonetheless, as the men sat waiting they were thoroughly drenched. When they reached the springs Lewis thought it as grand as Clark had related and the largest fountain he had ever seen. Like others, he reported clear, clean, cold water. In fact, he gloried in the scene: "it [Giant Springs] may well be retained on the list of prodegies of this neighbourhood towards which, nature seems to have dealt with a liberal hand, for I have scarcely experienced a day since my first arrival in this quarter without experiencing some novel occurrence among the party or witnessing the appearance of some uncommon object." After enjoying the scene for about twenty minutes, Lewis became aware of his wet clothes and chilled condition and decided to return. He and Drouillard had killed a buffalo on the way out and now took choice pieces for dinner. Lewis especially relished the tongue and hump of a fat buffalo, which he called "great delicasies." At the upper camp he was surprised to find that the portage party had not arrived and blamed the delay on the wet, muddy condition of the prairie.

With more rain in the morning Clark declared it too wet to take the wagons forward. He sent most of the party back after the baggage left the day before at the ridge above Belt Creek. Leaving one man in charge of the items there at Box Elder Creek, he went ahead with York, Charbonneau, Sacagawea, and the baby by way of the Great Falls and the river. The captain wanted to add to his notes about the river and make up for any deficiencies in his accounts. Shortly after they arrived at the river, a dark, threatening cloud appeared, so Clark looked anxiously for shelter. The little party raced for a deep ravine about one-quarter mile away. Under a shelving rock they found protection from a harsh rain that increased in violence as they waited. Suddenly their hiding place became a target of roaring water as the ravine filled with a menacing onslaught. Clark grabbed his rifle and shot pouch in his left hand and lifted himself out of the ravine with his right, pushing Sacagawea and the baby ahead of him. Charbonneau, already on top, was pulling her as well but occasionally froze up and was of little help. Reaching the top, they found York "greatly agitated, for our wellfar." Indeed, before Clark could get out the water was up to his waist; it was ten feet deep by the time he reached the top and quickly rose to fifteen feet. Lewis, hearing about it later, called it a "current tremendious to behold." Clark directed the group to get back to the Box Elder Creek camp as quickly as possible since they were all thoroughly soaked. The captain was particularly concerned about the baby and Sacagawea, who had only recently recovered from her severe illness. He feared a relapse. He had everyone take a bit of liquor from York's canteen. In the haste and confusion Clark lost his compass, fusil (a type of musket), tomahawk, umbrella, shot pouch and horn with gunpowder and ammunition, and moccasins. He considered the loss of the compass the most serious, as they had no other large one. Sacagawea lost her baby's mosquito netting and his clothes.

Back at camp Clark found the party that had gone after the supplies at Portage Creek. Experiencing the same weather conditions as Clark's group, they had abandoned their loads in the prairie after their wagon broke down and ran for shelter toward the camp at Box Elder Creek. Along the way they were severely beaten by the hard hailstones. One man had been knocked down three times, while others were bruised and bloody. They found nowhere to hide, as the creek was up nearly six feet. Later in the day the weather cleared, and Clark gave them a little grog as consolation. Ordway appreciated some warm soup and a dry bed.

JUNE 30, 1805. At the upper camp Frazer and Whitehouse kept up work on binding skins for the iron-framed boat, Gass and Shields worked on the bark lining, and Joseph Field stayed with making cross braces. Lewis and Drouillard rendered tallow and took care of cooking duties. By evening most of the preparation work on the boat was completed. Lewis had the bark and hides immersed in water to be readied for the boat by morning. It had taken twenty-eight elk skins and four buffalo hides to complete the covering. Lewis still worried about elements for the boat that were not available in the area. He had other worries as well. In spite of this activity the captain was becoming anxious about the party's forward progress.

With three months having passed since leaving Fort Mandan, he realized that they would not make it back there within the year. He was even doubtful that they could reach the ocean and return to the Shoshones in that time. He was also concerned that the portage party had not returned from the lower camp. Despite these concerns, Lewis remained ever the naturalist. He listed the common nighthawk ("large goatsucker") as abundant in the area. He killed one and found it the same as the bird he knew in the East. He noted that the bird laid its eggs in the open plains without a nest. He had not seen "small goatsuckers," the common poorwill, in this vicinity, nor had he seen bats or whip-poor-wills.

Clark, on the prairies at Box Elder Creek, sent a party back to the abandoned wagon that carried the supplies from Belt Creek and had been left on the plains yesterday. Five persons stayed behind at the Box Elder Creek camp, two to hunt, two to go to the Great Falls, and one to cook. The hunters were back by ten o'clock, loaded with meat. The men sent to the abandoned wagon returned with its baggage, so Clark dispatched four men to return, make repairs to the wagon, and bring it in. Others took whatever baggage they could carry to the opposite side of Box Elder Creek, as the water had gone down and permitted passage. The two men sent to the Great Falls in search of articles lost in the previous day's torrent returned. They had found Clark's compass near the mouth of the ravine, but no other items were located. They told Clark that the place where he had hidden from rain and hail was filled with huge rocks. At eleven o'clock the captain had a party move a load of baggage forward to a designated waypoint ("6 mile Stake"); they returned in the evening. Clark saw huge herds of buffalo in every direction and counted perhaps ten thousand in a single sighting.

JULY 1, 1805. Grizzlies prowled the upper camp during the night, provoking Lewis to either kill them or drive them away. The plan was to go after them on White Bear Islands the next day. Work continued on Lewis's iron-framed boat. Frazer and Whitehouse began sewing the leather skins to its outer sections, Shields and Joseph Field collected wood for a fire to make tar, and Gass worked with willow strips ("way strips") that would be used for lashing purposes.

Drouillard and Lewis completed rendering tallow and obtained about one hundred pounds. By evening the skins were attached to the boat and Lewis had the watercraft's sections set in water. He was elated that everything was ready to start putting the sections together but still worried about the quality of the lashing material. Bringing the necessary items together for the boat's readiness had been a major hindrance to its completion. Lewis's attention to the boat ("a novel peice of machinism") had consumed his time at the upper camp, and the addition of cooking kept him "pretty well employed." A warm day increased the annoyance of mosquitoes.

Clark's party set out early with the last load from the temporary camp at Box Elder Creek. They reached the upper camp at three in the afternoon. They were unable to pick up the baggage deposited the day before at a forward waypoint, and they were too exhausted to return for it that evening—that would wait until the next day. The captains offered a dram of alcohol and a relaxing evening to the portage crew. Lewis assigned Bratton to join others in making tar the next day and selected other men to help put the captain's favorite boat together. Without naming him, Clark related that one man was very sick and exhibited swollen and marred legs. Clark brought his journal up to date a bit with notes on Lewis's events but in a much abbreviated form.

JULY 2, 1805. After an early rain, the captains sent men after the remaining baggage at the interim waypoint. Shields and Bratton worked at the tar kiln, Pryor and Gass prepared willow strips, and others began putting the iron-framed boat together. The latter project took about three hours, then interior finish work became the task of four men. At about two o'clock the party sent after the baggage returned. For all purposes, the portage of the Great Falls of the Missouri River could be called accomplished. In understated terms, Lewis declared everyone "well pleased that they had completed the laborious task of the portage." Perhaps as a reminder of their force, Clark acknowledged that they could hear the roar of the falls many miles above them. Considering the constant wind from the southwest, Lewis theorized that chilled, heavy winds glided off the snowy ranges of the Rockies, then mixed with the lighter, warm

winds of the plains and moved through the wide, untimbered country. Not wholly convinced of his theory, he decided to test it when
he viewed wind action on the other side of the range.

In the afternoon the captains led a party of twelve men to the largest of the White Bear Islands to hunt for offending grizzlies. They
found an almost impenetrable thicket of willow bushes where the
bears hid. They broke up into parties of three or four in search of
the bears but found only one. This one made an assault on Drouillard, who shot it through the heart and slowed the beast, giving
him time to hide. The bear lumbered away, but the men were able
to follow its blood trail to where it had collapsed and died. This
young, male bear weighed about four hundred pounds. The bushes
yielded no others. A less weighty nuisance was caught in the party's stores. Lewis gave his usual detailed, morphological description of the pack rat, or bushy-tailed woodrat, which was new to
science. The captain had frequently seen the rats' nests, but this
was his first chance to examine one. Clark drew a map of the falls
and the party's portage around them at this day's journal entry.
It occupies a spread across two pages with detailed notes on each
of the falls and physical features along the Missouri. Lewis copied
the map in his journal entry of July 4.

JULY 3, 1805. All hands were hard at work: making or attempting
to make tar, attaching skins to the iron-framed boat, cutting and
fitting bark for the boat's interior, and hunting for buffalo in order
to obtain a supply of pemmican for the trip ahead and hides to
cover baggage in the boat and canoes. Men not otherwise engaged
made moccasins to replace the ones worn out on the plains. Ordway indicated that a good pair lasted only two days on this rugged
terrain. Indians (probably Hidatsas) had told them that they would
leave buffalo country after passing the falls. Lewis did not look
forward to the loss, knowing that the party might occasionally go
hungry. He also regretted that he would be deprived of Charbonneau's "'white puddings" (*boudin blanc*, or white sausage). True to
predictions, hunters over the last three days had killed only a single buffalo along with some pronghorns, beavers, and otters. Gass,
McNeal, and other unnamed men who had not seen the falls and

Giant Springs headed downriver on that excursion. The sergeant rated Crooked Falls the most beautiful. Lewis was discouraged with progress on the boat since work at the kiln had yet to yield any tar and without it the boat would not seal properly. He decried his blunder in using a needle that left ragged-edged holes in the boat's covering that binding thongs would not fill, thus opening additional points for leakage. He still hoped that the boat could be completed the next day. Clark copied Lewis's conjectures of July 2 about winds coming off the Rocky Mountains. The captain placed three detailed maps of the falls in his journal at this day's entry.

JULY 4, 1805. Lewis bemoaned that there was still no tar from the kiln, a serious loss for completing the boat. In fact, the iron-framed boat was ready by four in the afternoon except for sealing the seams. Clark completed his maps of the Missouri River from Fort Mandan to the upper camp, which the captains intended to cache at this site to avoid losing them on the long trip west. Looking that direction, Lewis saw mountains entirely covered in snow and glistening in the sun and guessed that from their appearance the Rockies had gained the name "Shining Mountains." Considering the trip to come and unsure of Shoshone friendship or assistance, the captains decided not to send a canoe back to St. Louis from this point as they had earlier contemplated. Such a move would cut their numbers too thin and might discourage the remaining members of the party. In fact, the captains had not told the men of this plan and said nothing now. With great confidence in his corps, Lewis wrote, "all appear perfectly to have made up their minds to suceed in the expedition or purish in the attempt. we all believe that we are now about to enter on the most perilous and difficult part of our voyage, yet I see no one repining; all appear ready to met those difficulties which wait us with resolution and becoming fortitude."

During the party's time in the Great Falls area they had heard a repeated noise that the military man Lewis described as "the discharge of a piece of ordinance of 6 pounds at the distance of three miles." At first thinking it was thunder, the party heard it even on clear, calm, and cloudless days. Lewis thought he might be able to find its source if he had time and believed that it might come from winds blowing from caves such as those in Virginia. The sound was heard by later visitors to the area, but no clear explanation has been established for the sonic anomalies. Clark largely followed Lewis in describing the phenomenon in his entry of June 20.

It being Independence Day, the captains passed a bottle and all enjoyed a bit of revelry. Lewis described the evening's festivities in glowing words:

> our work being at an end this evening, we gave the men a drink of sperits, it being the last of our stock, and some of them appeared a little sensible of it's effects the fiddle was plyed and they danced very merrily untill 9 in the evening when a heavy shower of rain put an end to that part of the amusement tho' they continued their mirth with songs and festive jokes and were extreemly merry untill late at night. we had a very comfortable dinner, of bacon, beans, suit dumplings & buffaloe beaf &c. in short we had no just cause to covet the sumptuous feasts of our countrymen on this day.

JULY 5, 1805. To get the iron-framed boat as dry as possible workers erected a scaffold, turned its underside to the sun, and built fires underneath. Lewis had a couple of men pound charcoal to mix with beeswax and buffalo grease with the idea that the composition could be used to make the boat watertight. Beyond this serious problem, the captain found that the boat met all his expectations: it was light (eight men could easily carry it), strong (capable of loading eight thousand pounds along with its crew), and elegantly formed. But the sealing issue persisted. As the boat dried the cracks and holes opened even more.

Buffalo came near the camp during the day, but Clark and a dozen hunters were not able to secure any because the bison caught their scent. Expedition hunters then went in pursuit and got three of them. Two wolves and three pronghorns were also killed. The captains allowed three men who had not seen the falls to visit and take in that magnificent scenery before the party departed the area. Upon returning they reported an abundance of buffalo around the falls. Ordway and Whitehouse said the men could have killed hundreds if they had wanted since they were penned against high cliffs. The captains decided to send hunters after them the next day.

JULY 6, 1805. Rain and hail fell during the night, accompanied by thunder and lightning. At daybreak a heavy storm came through dropping hailstones the size of "musket balls," according to the captains. The party cooled their drinks with the ice. On the negative side, the weather kept Lewis's iron-framed boat wet in spite of all efforts to shield it. The rain and hail also delayed applying the grease-and-coal composition. The after part of the day turned clear and calm. Four hunters set out for the falls after the reported herds of buffalo. Lewis mentioned a "remarkable small fox," the swift or kit fox, then unknown to science. It resided in burrows on the prairies and was so alert to predators that the captain had not obtained a specimen. Clark caught a few small fish during the day.

JULY 7, 1805. Finishing the iron-framed boat was further delayed by cloudy weather, but small fires were kept going to dry it out. Lewis's sealing composition was ready to apply but rain in the evening prevented its application. Hunters went out to gather more hides to cover the boat's baggage. At camp men dressed skins for clothing, which wore out quickly when the men worked in the river or under the present damp conditions. Whitehouse indicated that he was one of the tailors. Clark gave the ailing York a dose of "tartar emettic," a compound of ingredients meant to induce vomiting. The medicine had its intended effect and York started to feel better by the end of day. Lewis allowed that he had not used the medicine before except in cases of intermittent fever. The hunters sent to the falls the day before returned with three buffalo hides, along with skins of two pronghorns, four deer, and three wolves. Lewis was a bit disappointed in the results. Hunters from this day's outing were even less successful, having killed but a single elk. Lewis had one of the men fashion some sacks out of the wolf skins to carry his scientific instruments when going by land. Mosquitoes and blowing flies tormented the party.

JULY 8, 1805. Given the delay in finishing Lewis's iron-framed boat and the lack of work to keep everyone engaged, Clark took a party, including Ordway, to the falls in order to complete his calculations of the waterfalls and river widths. This was also an opportunity for more hunting. The captain measured the Sun ("Medison") River as 137 yards wide at its mouth and the Missouri just above at 300 yards wide at its narrowest part. Above the falls it was 1,440 yards wide and then varied from one fall to another. Clark's hunters killed three buffalo, two pronghorns, and a deer. The immense herds of the previous days had now passed on. Clark and party came back to camp in the evening.

A warm day at the upper camp brought renewed efforts on the boat. It was now dry enough to get its first coat of Lewis's sealing composition. Lewis admitted that the coating improved the look of the boat, giving it the appearance of being one solid craft. He hoped it served its purpose of sealing openings in the hide covering. He gave it a second coat to be sure. Gass announced that the party called the boat the "Experiment." Whitehouse kept at his tailoring task. A hunter in Clark's party brought in a small female fox that Lewis gave descriptive scrutiny. The captain called it a "kit fox" showing that he knew the swift fox's common name, but it was new to science. One of the men also brought him a "living ground squirrel," a thirteen-lined ground squirrel, for which he provided the first detailed, scientific description. Mosquitoes were as troublesome as ever.

JULY 9, 1805. The morning was fair and pleasant, the canoes were corked and put in the water, and the iron-framed boat was finally launched. "She lay like a perfect cork on the water," Lewis bragged. He directed that seats be fitted and oars prepared for the watercraft. Loading the canoes got underway and everything seemed ready for departure. Weather did not oblige—heavy winds and rain required unloading the canoes, getting some baggage wet in the transfer. Adding to the discouragement, Lewis observed that his sealing composition had separated from the boat's covering hides and it was leaking profusely. The captain confessed that it "mortifyed me not a little." He knew that he needed pitch to seal the leaks but that obtaining it was impossible. He was further vexed when he saw that the hides that still had some hair kept the composition and sealed almost perfectly, while those that had been scraped and singed clean did not seal properly. "But to make any further experiments in our present situation seemed to me madness; the buffaloe had principally deserted us, and the season was now advancing fast," he lamented. He relinquished all hopes for his "favorite boat" and ordered that it be sunk in water to soften the hides for removal and ready it to be disassembled and cached the next day. Castigating himself further, he regretted that he had singed the skins and hides too closely; otherwise they would have answered his purpose. at least until they reached pine country, where they could have obtained the required pitch and tar. Gass may have put it most succinctly: "Therefore for want of tar or pitch we had, with all our labour, to haul our new boat on shore, and leave it at this place."

Now a new dilemma faced the captains: how to convey all the supplies and baggage that the iron-framed boat was to carry. Hunters had reported that timber in the river bottoms was much better a few miles farther on and large enough to make canoes. Lewis confided that if they found trees of sufficient size they would indeed be fortunate; he had not seen any large enough since leaving the Musselshell River. They estimated that they would need two additional canoes to replace the load intended for the ill-fated boat. The captains decided that Clark would set out overland early the next morning with ten of the best workmen to begin the building. Lewis and the remainder of the party would disassemble the boat and deposit it along with other items. They would then start transporting the party's baggage in the six small canoes to the canoe-making camp. After the captains agreed on this procedure they announced their intentions to the corps. Clark's group began sharpening axes and preparing other equipment for the work in order to get an early start.

JULY 10, 1805. Clark and party crossed over early and set out upriver by land, seeking a spot that contained trees large enough for canoes to replace the lamented iron-framed boat. Clark had Pryor, four wood choppers, two "Involids" (counting perhaps Bratton), and a man to hunt. At the same time Ordway went ahead with four canoes and eight men (including Whitehouse) to take the first load of baggage as far as where Clark would locate. Clark proceeded about 8 miles and estimated that the spot was 23¼ miles by river from the portage's upper camp. This camp, known generally as "Canoe Camp," is in Cascade County, Montana, on the north side of the Missouri River, a few miles east of Ulm. Here Clark found two trees that he thought large enough to serve as canoes. After cutting them down, one proved hollow and split at one end while the other was too wind damaged to use. Taking down others, the men found them to be even less worthy and returned to the first trees, which could serve the purpose with some adjustments. The woodworkers were hampered by poor axe handles—thirteen were made and broken during the course of this one day. They substituted chokecherry wood for the preferred hickory, which was not to be found in this country. They were also tormented by irritating mosquitoes, and they did not receive supplies from the Ordway's boat party, which was delayed along the way by high winds. Indeed, the captains' comments in their weather diaries for July 10–13 are brief: "wind violent all day."

Lewis set men to work disassembling his iron-framed boat and had it ready to cache in about two hours. He also deposited some papers and a "few other trivial articles" and had the wagon wheels buried in another pit. With little to do, the captain took in some fishing but with meager results. Most of Lewis's entry for the day is a recapitulation of Clark's and Ordway's events, revealing that the writing must have taken place after the parties reunited on July 13. Lewis took an astronomical observation and determined a latitude for the upper camp as 47° 03′10″ N; it is closer to 47° 27′23″ N.

JULY 11, 1805. With nothing to do but wait for Ordway to return with the canoes taken to Clark's canoe-making camp, Lewis sent a small party to hunt. In the evening they brought back a good quantity of buffalo meat. Lewis noticed "grey Eagles" and compared their size to the bald eagle with which he was familiar. He thought the bald eagles in this region were smaller than those in the East. His "grey" eagle being considerably larger than the local bald one, he concluded that it was a distinct species. Opinions differ as to the bird Lewis wrote of here, perhaps a golden eagle or an immature bald eagle. The captain also heard again the strange noises like artillery that he had mentioned on July 4.

Understanding that Bratton was unable to work at canoe-building, Clark sent him to meet Ordway's party coming upriver in canoes. Apparently Bratton had a "whitlow" on one finger, which is a painful infection. The soldier returned in about two hours to report that one of the canoes was some three miles behind. It arrived about one o'clock. The river party had killed a buffalo along the way, so Clark sent Pryor with three men to collect the meat. They killed another one and brought the meat of both back to camp. At sunset the remaining three canoes arrived, were unloaded, and started back to the Upper Portage Camp to get more baggage. Whitehouse went ashore during the upriver trip and stepped on a very large prairie rattlesnake, which bit him on his leggings. The private shot it and measured it as 4 feet, 2 inches long and 5½ inches in circumference. No one else reported the incident. Ordway related that on the return journey they floated about eight miles until high winds drove them to shore for the night. The tormenting mosquitoes at Clark's camp were now joined by pesky gnats.

JULY 12, 1805. Still waiting for Ordway's return with the canoes, Lewis decided to send Gass with three men to join Clark in the work at the canoe-making camp. He deemed the remaining men sufficient to load the rest of the baggage and take the six canoes upriver. The captain was getting anxious to be on the way. Ordway and party were detained by high winds until about two in the afternoon and arrived at the upper camp so late that Lewis decided to delay the final exit from the upper camp until the next day. The invalid Bratton arrived during the day and made a quick turnaround with the axes he had been sent for in order to speed the canoe building. Lewis described the belted kingfisher ("blue crested fisher"), a bird with which he was familiar but one that he had seen infrequently along the Missouri River. Lewis and party were bothered by the same pests as Clark's group: mosquitoes and gnats. The buffalo gnat did not sting, Lewis acknowledged, but groups of them swarmed their eyes and were a constant nuisance.

Clark had all hands at work at daylight either forming the canoes or drying meat for the voyage ahead. Gass and the three men from the upper camp arrived later in the morning. Pryor put his shoulder out of place the day before while carrying a heavy load of meat. The sergeant was experiencing a great deal of pain. Hunters brought in three deer and two otters. The sight of beautiful passenger pigeons did not distract from the constantly annoying mosquitoes and gnats.

JULY 13, 1805. Greeted by a clear, calm morning, Lewis had the remainder of the baggage loaded into the six canoes and assigned a two-man crew to each. Ordway revealed that he was again in charge of the flotilla, and Whitehouse said he was in one of the boats. Lewis "bid a cheerfull adue" to the Upper Portage Camp at White Bear Islands, where he had been since June 22, and set out by land with Lepage, Sacagawea, and the baby. Charbonneau had taken Lepage's place in a canoe, as the soldier was ill. Along the way Lewis passed what may have been a Blackfeet Indian sun dance lodge and gave it a careful description. Gass had noticed it on his overland trip the day before. The captain knew that it was not a family dwelling, since it was 216 feet in circumference. It had probably been built for "some great feast, or a council house on some great national concern," he speculated. This was the first such structure he had seen. Commenting on buffalo killed by hunters, Lewis also reflected on the party's nutritional needs: "we eat an emensity of meat; it requires 4 deer, an Elk and a deer, or one buffaloe, to supply us plentifully 24 hours. meat now forms our food prinsipally as we reserve our flour parched meal and corn as much as possible for the rocky mountains which we are shortly to enter, and where from the indian account game is not very abundant."

The fair weather was fickle, and Ordway soon encountered the high winds that had vexed his progress on previous trips. Two of his canoes took on a considerable amount of water, so the canoeists moved the boats to shore. They returned to the water later in the evening but had to camp several miles short of their objective. On the other hand, Lewis reached the canoe-making camp by nine in the morning and found the mosquitoes and gnats even more troublesome than those at the upper camp. Knowing he would not get a minute's sleep without it, he sent a man back to the canoes for his netting. The runner got back a little before dark. Clark reported that the canoes were completed.

JULY 14, 1805. A warm, fair morning was spoiled only by ever-pestering mosquitoes. In the evening the two new canoes were launched. One was twenty-five feet in length, the other thirty-three feet and about three feet wide. Lewis walked out a distance, climbed a hill, and got a "commanding view of the country." From there he took directions and distances to prominent points in the Rocky Mountains from twenty-five to two hundred miles away. He viewed a country generally level but with a gentle, undulating appearance and a region "destitute of timber except along the water-courses." The grass on the plains was a scant three inches high but alive with innumerable grasshoppers and small birds that fed on them. At camp he saw sand rushes and stinging nettles. On returning to camp he found that Ordway and his river party had arrived about noon and had unloaded their canoes. Now, except for the construction of some oars, poles, and miscellaneous items for the canoes, the party was set to be underway the next day.

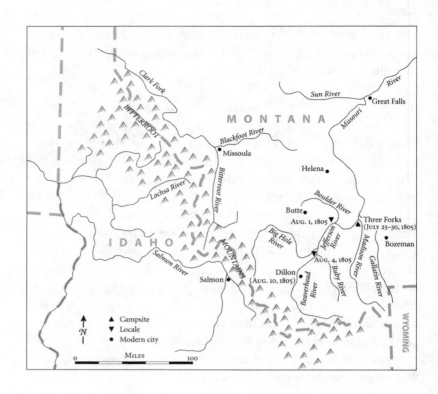

MAP 7. The expedition's route, July 15–August 9, 1805.

CHAPTER 6

Shadows of the Rockies

July 15–August 9, 1805

JULY 15, 1805. Rising early after a rainy night, the captains assigned loads to the canoes—now eight in number—and found them heavily loaded despite having deposited items at several points from the Marias River to the present canoe camp. Lewis complained that they could not get the men to leave unnecessary items behind and that they added "bulky articles of but little use or value to them." By ten o'clock the party set out, having been in the Great Falls area since June 2, when they reached the mouth of the Marias. Lewis walked ahead and killed two elks, one of which the party ate as they came upriver to the spot. Potts and Lepage, who were on sick call, went along with the captain as he continued by land on the east side of the Missouri. In time they came to a stream that Lewis named "Smith's River" (a name it retains, after Robert Smith, Jefferson's secretary of the navy), entering the Missouri from the east near Ulm, Cascade County, Montana. Crossing to the west side, Lewis viewed numerous herds of buffalo as he traveled southward upriver.

In time Lewis moved away from the meanderings of the river to shorten his path but kept the Missouri in sight. He described native plants such as prickly pears, sunflowers, lambsquarters, mock-cucumbers, scouring rushes, and Mexican docks. He also noticed Square Butte ("Fort Mountain") some ten miles to the west in Cascade County. Given its appearance the captains decided to give it the descriptive name. The captain noted its features, which are formed on the lower two-thirds from late Cretaceous Virgelle Member of the Eagle Sandstone and Telegraph Creek Formation, while the top is composed of basaltic sill. Finding a timbered spot, he halted and waited for the canoes to catch up. It being late when the party re-formed, they made camp a few miles southwest of Ulm. From his land-side view Lewis calculated that the party had made about twenty miles. The river men, Ordway, Gass, and Whitehouse, estimated it as twenty-six miles. Drouillard wounded a deer near camp, and Seaman pursued it into the river and brought it back. Clark also abandoned the canoes during the day but found it difficult to map the courses of the zigzagging Missouri from shore.

JULY 16, 1805. Without naming him, the captains sent Ordway back several miles to retrieve an axe that he had carelessly left behind. Ordway admitted to the negligence. Not long after setting out the party passed about forty small shelters made of willow brushes, which the captains supposed had been made by Shoshones less than two weeks earlier. Evidence of horses was also apparent. These signs raised Lewis's hopes that they might meet the Indians soon. Coming from behind Clark saw the shelters and farther on more indications of Indian lodges, but from an earlier period. Drouillard's buffalo provided a midmorning's repast for Lewis and his men. Always interested in expanding his palate preferences, the captain tried an Indian style of preparation of the animal's "small guts" by cooking it without any cleaning or other preparation. He found it very tasty. This would be the party's last fresh buffalo meat until July 9, 1806.

Lewis separated from the main party, taking Potts, Lepage, and Drouillard with him along the northwest side of the river in order to find a spot to make astronomical observations. They entered the Big Belt Mountains, which Lewis incorrectly thought were composed of "hard black grannite." Following the Missouri, the captain and his little party made camp near Half-Breed, or Lone Pine, Rapids, Cascade County. Nearby he noticed a large rock some four hundred feet high that he called "Tower Rock," a formation south of Hardy, Cascade County. Making a difficult ascent, the captain had a clear view of a country crowded with immense herds of buffalo on the plains below. A fat elk served for supper. The captain spent an uncomfortable night tormented by mosquitoes, having forgotten his mosquito netting. He berated himself for his neglectfulness and promised "in my wrath" not to be guilty of such carelessness again. Clark and party wended their way up the twisting Missouri. The captain noted the variety of foliage, including cottonwoods, willows, boxelders, red osier dogwoods, chokecherries, gooseberries, serviceberries, currants, and sumacs. Clark and company also camped in Cascade County, several miles behind Lewis, having made about twenty-three miles.

JULY 17, 1805. Observing sunflowers in bloom, Lewis commented on uses that Indians of the Missouri made of the plant, particularly those who did not raise corn. Sunflower seeds were made into bread or used to thicken soups, he wrote, and then described the process. Here too the captain witnessed the transition from eastern cottonwoods ("broad leafed") to the western species ("narrow leafed"), while noting that aspens lined the river. And he noticed the small berries that Clark noted the day before (perhaps copied from Lewis), conceding that he preferred the golden ("yellow") currant to all others. He followed his note on taste preference with several lines of morphological data. He gave similar attention to the western serviceberry, comparing it to an eastern variety, probably juneberry, that he knew. The river party caught up with Lewis about eight o'clock, and all took breakfast together.

Having heavily loaded canoes, the captains ordered to shore all men who were not actively engaged in moving the boats. Getting around Half-Breed Rapids required double manning the canoes, leaving some heavy articles behind, and considerable hard towing. The abandoned items were retrieved after successfully getting the canoes through. Not being able to negotiate the river's edge, the on-shore walkers were forced farther inland, compelling them frequently to cross and recross the Missouri. The only wildlife they saw during the day were bighorn sheep. Again Lewis alluded to "black grannite" rocks, but the mountain material is composed of Adel Mountain volcanics without granite. Finding a place with sufficient wood for fires, the party camped a few miles downstream from the Dearborn River, Lewis and Clark County, Montana, having come about eleven miles.

JULY 18, 1805. On an "immencely high and nearly perpendicular clift" (now Eagle Rock), Lewis saw a large herd of bighorn sheep bounding with ease along its precipitous slopes. The captain was certain that no other animal could negotiate these cliffs; thus the sheep were safe from predators. But not safe from Clark, apparently, since Whitehouse reported that the captain killed one. Just over two miles from camp the party passed "Dearborn's river," coming in from the west and named after Secretary of War Henry Dearborn, a name it retains in Lewis and Clark County, Montana. Anxious to meet Shoshones in order to gain information about the way ahead and secure horses if necessary, the captains decided to send a small party ahead. They feared that the sound of their hunting weapons might scare off Indians, send them into the mountains, and defeat their chance for a rendezvous. Accordingly, Clark set out with Joseph Field, Potts, and York along the west side of the Missouri. The advance party found an Indian road that led them through the mountains, took them away from the river, and saved several miles of following the meandering Missouri. Clark's route is unclear because he did not keep separate traverse notes or make detailed maps for this period, and the location of his camp for the night is unclear. For the period of Clark's absence (July 18–27) Lewis added a narrative of his co-commander's events each day in his own journal. It may be that Lewis was keeping field notes of his exploring during this time and then combined the separate events into his regular journal after they reunited.

Facing a stronger current than the day before, the river men were obliged to use towing ropes as well as oars and setting poles to advance the canoes. In the evening they passed Little Prickly Pear Creek, Lewis and Clark County, which Lewis named in honor of Sergeant Ordway. For several days the captain had noticed a species of flax growing in the river bottoms. His detailed morphological description of blue flax may have caused Pursh, after the expedition, to name the plant in his honor, *Linum lewisii*, based also on a specimen Lewis collected on July 9, 1806. The captain also saw roundleaf harebell, a plant similar to flax that prompted a short description. His party camped above Holter Dam, Lewis and Clark County, having made about twenty-one miles.

JULY 19, 1805. Getting an early start, the party faced a river of increasing velocity and occasional rapids. The sight of snow on high mountains did not ease the constant heat in the river valley. Lewis's river party now entered an area that the captain christened the *"gates of the rocky mountains,"* now known as Gates of the Mountains, roughly midway between Holter and Hauser Dams, Lewis and Clark County, Montana. Estimating the cliffs' height at twelve hundred feet and calculating the distance through the area at about six miles, Lewis was struck by the "dark and gloomy aspect" of "vast collumns of rocks mountains high." He looked with pleasure at fine springs that burst out from rock interstices. With a narrow shoreline that hardly provided space for footing, the party was fortunate that they could move the boats with oars, since tow ropes and setting poles would not function here. In fact, it was late in the evening before they could locate a spot wide enough to establish a camp.

With Clark absent from the river party and without reliable expedition maps for the area, it is difficult to determine Lewis's campsite. It seems to have been a short distance downstream from Upper Holter Lake at a point where a small drainage entered the Missouri from the east, providing room for twenty-nine persons, some twenty-two miles from the day's starting point. Here the explorers found ponderosa pine, and Lewis noted what he took to be granite and "flint of a yelloish brown and light creemcolourd yellow." The gates are formed of light to medium gray Mississippian-age Mission Canyon Limestone. Near the upper end of the gates Mississippian Lodgepole Limestone occurs and weathers to a light gray or yellow-buff color. There is no granite or flint here. Leaving buffalo behind, Lewis noted only bighorn sheep, pronghorns, beaver, and otters.

Clark and party continued along the Indian path in the mountainous terrain. Falling in with a gang of elks, the men killed two and cooked the meat over a fire of dried buffalo dung for a late breakfast. Clark saw several Indian camps and evidence of native presence. He noticed that bark had been peeled from pine trees; Sacagawea later informed Lewis that Indians did this in order to obtain sap and the soft part of the wood for food. Clark's route and camp for the day are again difficult to determine due to the lack of traverse notes and route maps. Nor was the going easy, as they walked across sharp fragments of rocks that bruised and cut their feet. Moreover, prickly pear spines pierced thick moccasins and added to the painful passage. Clark reported pulling seventeen spines out of his footwear.

JULY 20, 1805. Facing an unusually strong current, the main party under Lewis resorted to tow ropes whenever they could find footing along the narrow shore. In time the valley widened and cottonwoods, pines, and aspens bordered the river. Lewis found a black currant that he considered even more flavorful than the yellow one of July 17. In fact, it was the same plant, the golden currant, with its many color phases. Meeting a substantial creek coming into the Missouri from the west side, the captain named it "Pott's Creek" after expedition member Potts, now ahead with Clark. Reconciling the captains' journals and maps with present geography remains difficult through this region. The captain's "Pott's Creek" may be Towhead Gulch, Lewis and Clark County, Montana. Seeing a fire to the west, Lewis was not sure if it was set by Indians as a warning about the party's presence or accidently by Clark. He later discovered that it was set by Indians who had noticed Clark's party.

In the evening Lewis found part of an elk that Clark had left for the river party along with an account of his movements. Later he camped on the east side of the Missouri between Soup and Trout Creeks, Lewis and Clark County, making about fifteen miles. Abundant prickly pears barely allowed a spot to lie down. About the camp Lewis noticed a "distinct species of woodpecker," but he could not get a specimen of it. It was Lewis's woodpecker, named for the captain and more fully described by him on May 27, 1806. Clark moved his party through a valley some six miles from the Missouri until they found an Indian path that took them back to the river. The ever present prickly pears pestered the men, punctured their moccasins, and hampered their progress. Sharp stones on their path also slowed them. Clark may have camped above Beaver Creek, Broadwater County, Montana.

JULY 21, 1805. Another day against a strong current with the men at tow ropes, aided occasionally by setting poles. "Our progress was therefore slow and laborious," wrote Lewis. Unable to fly, two trumpeter swans fell victim to expedition guns; a third one escaped. The captain saw Canada geese afloat with their young in great numbers. Seaman caught several during the day. Lewis thought the young geese excellent fare but the older ones unfit for use. Sandhill cranes were also sighted, and although they were known to science the captain provided a bit of information about their habits. He also saw two blue grouse ("dark brown") and compared them to ruffed grouse, with which he was familiar. The captain provided fuller descriptions on August 1, 1805, and March 3, 1806. Coming out of the closed-in, mountainous terrain, the party now entered a wide, beautiful, and extensive plain. The river, too, spread out to nearly a mile in width, crowded with islands. Rich, black soil promoted grasses from eighteen inches to two feet high in expansive river bottoms. The main party camped near the Lewis and Clark–Broadwater county line, Montana, after coming about fifteen miles. During the day they passed a large creek that Lewis decided to name for Pryor, but on Clark's map of the area it is labeled "Potts Valley Creek," showing again the difficulty of identifying geographic features in this region. It is probably Spokane Creek, Lewis and Clark County.

Clark and his men's feet were so cut and bruised that he decided to delay and wait for the canoes to catch up to his advance party. He also intended to hunt and provide some meat for the main party. Nonetheless, they did go three miles farther, hoping to find Indians, but then turned back and made camp a mile below the previous one in the vicinity of Beaver Creek, Broadwater County. The captain was struck by the beauty and abundance of plant and animal life in the Missouri River valley.

JULY 22, 1805. The multiple-ribboned river with its many small islands made it difficult for Lewis to lay down the party's course, so he went on shore to better follow its windings. On one large island he found an abundance of onions ("white crisp and well flavored"), which he gathered for later cooking. He stopped there to await the canoes and then had breakfast with the river party. Afterward he passed to higher ground on the west side and soon came to Beaver Creek, Broadwater County, Montana. Geographic confusion persisted as Lewis first named the stream for Pryor, crossed that out, and substituted "white Earth Creek," while Clark listed it as "Pryors

Vally R or C" on his map. Waiting for the canoes to catch up, Lewis shot an otter, which sank to the bottom. The river was so clear that Lewis could see to its eight-feet depth, so he jumped in and retrieved the animal. The canoes had taken different channels through the islands, but all came together for lunch there with Lewis. The captain set his thermometer out during the meal and inadvertently left it behind when travel resumed. He sent Ordway back for it and found that it registered 80°—the warmest day except for one that summer. Sacagawea "cheered the sperits of the party" when she told them that she remembered this area from her childhood. The men now anticipated seeing the head of the Missouri, "yet unknown to the civilized world." Moving ahead (now with the boats) Lewis saw geese, cranes, and "small birds common to the plains," including a small plover that may have been either the mountain plover or the upland sandpiper. Lewis had seen the bird earlier but had been unable to collect one. He also listed the abundant plant life in the area: willows, boxelders, cottonwoods, red osier dogwoods, rosebushes, honeysuckles, greasewoods, southernwoods, sages, and sumacs, as well as a multitude of berries and currants.

Late in the evening the river party caught up with Clark's group. The men joined the canoes and all moved ahead a short distance to camp, apparently on an island on the east side some miles above Beaver Creek, Broadwater County, coming about twenty miles upriver. Lewis found Clark exhausted and his feet suffering from cuts, blisters, and bruises and his men much the same. Clark had opened the blisters the night before and now was in some pain. Regardless, he insisted on renewing his journey the next day and decided to take the Field brothers and Frazer with him. Charbonneau also asked to be on the trip and was added to the advance party. Not knowing that the parties had recombined, Drouillard remained apart from his comrades.

JULY 23, 1805. As the river party took canoes to water, bending to tow ropes and pushing at setting poles, Clark and his men began their jaunt up the west side of the Missouri. About ten o'clock Drouillard appeared. Not finding the corps' camp, he had spent the night alone. He now presented the party with five deer, part of which had been left by Clark's men. The river was still littered with small islands, so finding the best channel was chancy, and forward movement was slowed by the river's swift current. Irritating mosquitoes made the hard work even more frustrating. Furthermore, poling proved difficult against smooth stones in the riverbed, so Lewis had gigs and wire attached to pole ends to prevent slippage. The captain noticed sediments of middle to late Tertiary age and a "red slate" (actually shale) on the bluffs. Wide bottomlands were thinly timbered, but willows harbored a thick undergrowth of rose and currant bushes. Farther out the plains stretched to the base of mountains some eight to twelve miles away.

Passing a large creek on the east side, Lewis named it in honor of Whitehouse, now Gurnett Creek, Broadwater County, Montana. Clark labeled it "Ordway's Creek" on his map but corrected it to Lewis's designation. Following his botanical bent, Lewis listed thistles, onions, and a "species of garlic," which was probably short-styled onion, with its distinctly garlic odor. He also collected seeds of the blue flax, which he found in abundance in the bottomlands. Lewis must have killed the two-feet-long black snake ("black . . . as jet itself") he described, since he counted 128 scuta on its belly and 63 on its tail. It was most likely a melanistic phase of the western terrestrial garter snake. The captain ordered an early halt for lunch to dry some articles. He had small flags hoisted on the canoes in case Indians saw the party and were frightened that they were native enemies. After about twenty-two miles the party camped on an island near Townsend, Broadwater County. Clark had advanced about twenty-five miles and also camped in Broadwater County.

JULY 24, 1805. Early on the party passed a "remarkable bluff of a crimson coloured earth," as Lewis termed it, south of Townsend, Broadwater County, Montana. Gass related that Sacagawea told the men that Indians used the coloring for paint. The exposed rocks belong to the upper part of the pre-Cambrian Greyson Shale. Penetrating deeper into the mountains, Lewis commented that they "seem to rise in some places like an amphatheater one rang above another as they receede from the river untill the most distant and lofty have their tops clad with snow. the adjacent mountains com-

monly rise so high as to conceal the more distant and lofty mountains from our view." To the east he viewed the Big Belt Mountains
and to the west, the Elkhorns. Lewis could not understand the lack of
falls or rapids in such mountainous country, in spite of Sacagawea's
assurances that they would find none. Nevertheless, small rapids and
riffles were a constant annoyance to the boatmen. Lewis described
the work of beavers building dams across small channels between
islands, causing the river to alter its course, drying the dammed
area, and sending the beavers to new worksites. The captain blamed
beavers for the island-strewn river through this region. The party
found a pronghorn skin left by Clark's men and took a deer for themselves. They sighted a bear but could not get a clear shot at it. They
also saw signs of elks but encountered none. The same was true of
buffalo, and Lewis lamented that he would not be able to enjoy his
"white puddings" until they returned to buffalo country. Cranes,
geese, mergansers, and curlews abounded, as did snakes about the
river. Lewis mentioned bullsnakes, garter snakes, and the melanistic
western terrestrial garter snake of the day before. The party's ever-
present pests bedeviled them and reached biblical proportions in
Lewis's estimation: "our trio of pests still invade and obstruct us on
all occasions, these are the Musquetoes eye knats and prickley pears,
equal to any three curses that ever poor Egypt laiboured under,
except the *Mahometant yoke*." The boatmen faced incredible labor
moving canoes upriver and ended each day extraordinarily fatigued.
To encourage them in their labors Lewis occasionally joined the
men in the work and allowed that he had learned to "*push a tolerable good pole*." The main party camped a few miles north of Toston,
Broadwater County, Montana, after traveling about twenty miles.

Clark woke to a fine day and followed an Indian road up Crow
Creek, Broadwater County. The party encountered a horse, "fat and
very wild," but could not get near it. They turned back toward the
river, found a deer, and killed it for a meal. Clark's advance party
camped somewhere north of Trident, Broadwater County.

JULY 25, 1805. The strong river current and riffles hampered the
party's progress, but they got on "tolerably well," said Lewis. Perhaps not so well, since Whitehouse revealed that the men had to

double up to get the canoes through some rough spots. The soldier cut his foot on sharp stones while towing one of the boats. A grizzly escaped hunters, perhaps because bears here were more willing to run than those met earlier in the trip, the captain surmised. The men were able to take a pronghorn, and the captain noticed that the animals were gathering in small herds except for solitary males. The fleet pronghorn preferred the plains to the woodlands and would dash out of timber and head for open land, where its speed provided safety. The party passed out of a wide valley and were again hemmed in by hills and rocky cliffs. Out of these rocky crags springs burst forth that offered cold, clear water. Lewis described the cliffs as lighter in color than previous ones, and he noticed smooth, small limestones in the riverbed, perhaps carried there from above. The captain witnessed the Lombard thrust fault that cuts through the bluffs, while Mission Canyon and Lodgepole limestones of the Madison Group occur upstream. Later they passed a large creek that Lewis named in honor of Sergeant Gass; it is either Crow Creek or Warm Springs Creek, Broadwater County, Montana. Gass made no comment about the naming. Coming about sixteen miles, the river party camped just north of Toston Dam, Broadwater County.

A short walk brought Clark's party to the Three Forks of the Missouri, where three rivers converge to form the Missouri near the Broadwater-Gallatin county line. The captain sized up the three and concluded that the "north" or west fork (Jefferson River) presented the most likely stream for the party's route to the Rocky Mountains. After a breakfast of ribs from a buck killed the day before, Clark began his ascent of the Jefferson along its west side. He wrote a note to Lewis informing him of route he was taking. About six or eight miles along their route, the small band passed Willow Creek ("Pholosophy River"), Gallatin County. The captain was amazed at the number of beavers and otters that inhabited area streams. Clark's campsite was on the north (or west) side of the Jefferson some twenty to twenty-five miles from its mouth. The explorers were exhausted, particularly Charbonneau, whose ankle had given out. Blistered feet punctured with prickly pear spikes added to their misery. Thankfully, night breezes blew away tormenting mosquitoes.

JULY 26, 1805. River as usual: strong current and frequent riffles that required towing ropes and setting poles. Oars proved useless along this section of the river except to move the canoes from shore to shore to find the best channel. Shortly into the day the party passed a creek that Lewis named in honor of Private Howard, now Sixteenmile Creek, the boundary between Broadwater and Gallatin Counties at its mouth. Here the valley widened again, revealing fertile bottomlands in a greensward setting. Crowded with islands, the Missouri varied from 2 to 250 yards wide; including islands, the full width was three-quarters of a mile in places. The captain noticed "a species of grass" (needle-and-thread grass) with a sharp barb that penetrated the men's moccasins and cut their feet; he collected a specimen on the return trip, July 8, 1806. Seaman suffered greatly, constantly biting and scratching at the irritants. Prickly pears and yellow pincushion cactus caused more pain. Lewis gave both grass and cactus his usual morphological attention. He found the note that Clark had left the preceding day with the discouraging news of no Indian encounters. One of Lewis's men brought him an Indian bow, but it was similar to those of tribes already met, without indicating Indians nearby. They camped near an elevation later called Eagle Rock (not to be confused with the one of July 18), Gallatin County, making from sixteen to eighteen miles.

Clark decided to leave the ailing Charbonneau with Joseph Field, whose feet were badly damaged, while he, Frazer, and Reuben Field marched on. He wanted to reach the top of a mountain some twelve miles ahead to get a long view of the river valley and the way forward. With much difficulty they reached the top by eleven o'clock. From there he saw the course of the Jefferson River for about ten miles and viewed the "middle fork" (Madison River) to the east. Now satisfied that he was on the right path to the Rockies, he turned back and found an Indian road to follow. Stopping at a spring, the men drank deeply of its cold water. Clark regretted the act, since he thought that the excessively cold water brought on an illness that would persist for days. Then his small entourage passed through a valley in scorching heat with blistered feet punctured by sharp prickly pear spines. Returning to the invalid colleagues, Clark ate little of the deer killed by Joseph Field. In spite of the pain and fatigue, he was determined to examine the Madison River. In crossing the Jefferson River at a large island, Charbonneau was nearly swept away in the strong current, but Clark retrieved him. Being a nonswimmer, the interpreter was fortunate to have someone nearby and alert. Clark's party made camp on Willow Creek ("Philosophy River"), Gallatin County, a few miles above its entrance into the Jefferson.

JULY 27, 1805. Lewis watched as the men exerted themselves to the fullest against a strong current and saw them tire quickly under the strain. On the cliffs above, he viewed bighorn sheep leap effortlessly along precipitous mountain slopes. Within a few miles the valley opened to an extensive and beautiful prairie, and they came to the entrance of the "southeast fork" (Gallatin River). They halted for breakfast while Lewis took a walk up the Gallatin about a half mile. Climbing a high cliff, he could view the course of the river for nearly seven miles. In this extensive plain he could also see the "middle fork" (Madison River) divide into several streams and then some fourteen miles beyond. Between these two rivers he glimpsed the Madison Range of mountains in the distance with its snow-clad heights. Near the junction of the two rivers Lewis noted an elevated greensward of about two acres that would be perfect for a fort. He also looked to the "southwest fork" (Jefferson River) for some twelve miles, finding it more serpentine than the other two and passing through a similarly beautiful country. From his height Lewis said he drew the courses of the rivers and their connections at the Three Forks, but no such drawing by the captain is known to exist. His information was probably incorporated into Clark's map of the area. About this time Lewis determined to name the three streams in honor of the nation's leaders (names the rivers retain): for Secretary of the Treasury Albert Gallatin, for Secretary of State James Madison, and "in honor of that illustrious peronage Thomas Jefferson President of the United States." Lewis returned to the main party for breakfast, then led them up the Jefferson nearly two miles, passing the junction of the Madison with the Jefferson, and made camp on an island in Gallatin County; they would remain here until July 30.

Lewis found Clark's note informing him of his intended excursion up the Jefferson. The captain agreed with Clark that the Jefferson was the correct way into the mountains. He called the Three Forks "an essential point" in western geography and was determined to remain there until he could get an accurate fix on its latitude and longitude. He had all the canoes brought to shore and unloaded and the baggage stored safely away. He then released some men to hunt while he examined the Madison River. On his walk he saw mallards with their young and currants and gooseberries in great abundance. He gave particular attention to the swamp currant, which he called a "large black gooseberry." He also recognized the mud nests of cliff swallows ("small martin") attached to smooth rock walls and sheltered by overhanging outcrops. Hunters returned with six deer, three otters, and a muskrat and reported that they had seen great numbers of pronghorns and signs of beavers, otters, deer, and elks.

Clark spent an uncomfortable night with a high fever and "akeing in all my bones." Not feeling much better in the morning, he nevertheless determined to trek overland to the Madison River from his spot on Willow Creek. Accordingly he set out "in great pain" some eight miles across the prairie to the Madison. Here again the excursion party found no fresh signs of Indians, so they worked their way downriver to the Three Forks. At about three o'clock Clark arrived at the main camp, "very sick with a high fever on him and much fatiegued and exhausted. . . . [with] frequent chills & constant aking pains in all his mustles," as Lewis characterized him. The captain's debilitated state further convinced Lewis to remain a few days at the Three Forks. Lewis learned that his friend had not had a bowel movement for several days, so had him take a dose of "Rushes pills" (a strong laxative), which he had "always found sovereign in such cases." He also had him rest and bathe his feet in warm water.

Learning of Clark's unsuccessful search for the Shoshones, Lewis began to worry about the expedition's chances of achieving their goals. Horses were essential to getting over the mountains, so they must find Shoshones or other Indians to provide the mounts and point the way. Lewis expressed his anxiety in poignant terms:

> we are now several hundred miles within the bosom of this wild
> and mountanous country, where game may rationally be expected

shortly to become scarce and subsistence precarious without any information with rispect to the country not knowing how far these mountains continue, or wher to direct our course to pass them to advantage or intersept a navigable branch of the Columbia, or even were we on such an one the probability is that we should not find any timber within these mountains large enough for canoes if we judge from the portion of them through which we have passed.

Nevertheless, Lewis's optimism pushed through, and he still hoped for the best. Considering Clark's condition, Lewis decided he should now go ahead, "taking a tramp myself in a few days to find these yellow gentlemen if possible." He was also confident that if Indian nations could subsist in the mountains, the Corps of Discovery could manage as well.

JULY 28, 1805. It was a day to catch up, dry baggage, and rest at the Three Forks. Lewis had a shelter built for the ailing Clark's comfort. He had been sick again during the night but seemed to be improving this morning as his medicine took effect. Lewis sent two men to examine the Gallatin River while others went in search of provisions or set to making and mending their leather clothes. Whitehouse indicated that he was the principal tailor. The captain thought the Three Forks area a likely spot for a trading establishment. He saw sand rush growing vigorously in the three rivers' floodplains, while grasses of the plains were lush and able to provide good pasture for horses and cows. A refreshing shower cooled the evening and may have driven away the annoying mosquitoes and gnats. Hunters returned with eight deer and two elks, while the excursion party reported that the Gallatin was wide, rapid, and filled with islands but sufficiently deep for canoe travel. Lewis calculated a latitude at Three Forks of 45° 24′ 54″ N; the area is closer to 45° 55′ 44″ N.

Lewis indicated that they were camped on the spot where Hidatsa warriors attacked a Shoshone group five years earlier. The Shoshones, including Sacagawea, tried to escape up the Jefferson River about three miles, where they hid in the woods. The Hidatsas found them, killed four men, four women, and a number of boys, and made prisoners of four boys and several women. Sacagawea was captured as she was trying to cross the river at a low spot. She was taken back to the Hidatsa villages where Lewis and Clark found her. Lewis probably got this account from Sacagawea and Charbonneau through one of the French speakers in the party. He ended the story with this assessment of Sacagawea: "I cannot discover that she shews any immotion of sorrow in recollecting this event, or of joy in being again restored to her native country; if she has enough to eat and a few trinkets to wear I believe she would be perfectly content anywhere."

JULY 29, 1805. Hunters turned out in the morning and soon brought in "four fat bucks." Lewis commented that hunters had killed no mule deer in the area and that the deer here were a western variety ("longtailed red deer") of the familiar eastern species. They also brought the captain a young sandhill crane yet unable to fly, which pecked fiercely at him until he finished his examination and let it go. He noticed other birds about the camp, such as belted kingfishers and mallards. He had not seen wood ducks since leaving the Great Falls, but he was mistaken that its range did not extend to the Rockies. Grasshoppers and crickets were common on the plains, as were the small birds that fed on them. The captain identified what was probably the western harvester ant and gave it some morphological attention. Clark was better this day—his fever had decreased and his appetite had returned, but he was still weak and complained of general achiness. Lewis had him take some Peruvian bark as a precaution. Soldiers in camp kept up their work on making and mending clothing. Lewis called them "leather dressers and taylors."

JULY 30, 1805. With Clark feeling much better and Lewis's astronomical observations completed, the corps was ready to be on the way again. Canoes were reloaded, and the party set out south up the Jefferson River. Walking on the east side of the river, Lewis began his search for the Shoshones. He had with him Charbonneau, Sacagawea, and two men on sick call, and although not counted, undoubtedly Sacagawea's baby. At about 4½ miles they came to a spot that Sacagawea identified as the place where she had tried to hide from the Hidatsas but was found and taken captive. They waited there until Clark arrived with the boat party and had lunch.

Afterward Lewis passed to the west side of the Jefferson and went forward on his own. He saw numerous beavers and their dams situated in little backwaters of the river. The captain moved up to the high plain to avoid these areas, but just to get away from them he had to wade waist high in water and trudge through muddy terrain. In fact, Lewis confided that he would have rejoined the boats but the way back to the river was so difficult that he decided to go on by land. He eventually found a place to get near the river and perhaps meet the boats but found no tracks of men pulling canoes. He was convinced that the main party was behind him, so he fired his gun and whooped but got no response. As it was getting dark, he decided to settle in just as a duck landed near him and provided supper. He went looking for a spot to avoid mosquitoes, found willow brush to form a bed, built a fire of driftwood, and enjoyed his duck. Constantly annoying mosquitoes ruined a good night's sleep, and he was briefly awakened by some animal—probably an elk or grizzly bear, he thought—running over a stony bar near him. Nevertheless, he stayed warm and comfortable near his large fire, but Gass called it a "howling wilderness." The main party under Clark proceeded about thirteen miles up the Jefferson and camped just below the mouth of Willow Creek and near the Broadwater-Jefferson county line, Montana. They were about two miles below Lewis.

JULY 31, 1805. "Impatiently" waiting for Clark and the boat party, Lewis recorded the time as seven o'clock and wondered where they were. He decided to wait another hour before concluding that they were ahead of him. Just as he was ready to move on Charbonneau appeared, walking along the shore. Lewis learned that the canoes were behind, slowed by the rapid current and twisting river. Soon the canoes arrived and all joined for breakfast, after which Lewis again set out alone. The Jefferson River, now 90 to 120 yards wide, was crowded with small islands and was as swift as ever. Passing Willow Creek, which joins the Jefferson in Gallatin County, Montana, the captains decided to name it the "River Philosophy." Brimming with beavers and otters, it came out of the Tobacco Root Mountains and fell, multimouthed, into the Jefferson.

Returning to the boat party, Lewis found that Drouillard had discovered a grizzly in some bushes. The wily bear was able to escape, although the captain was certain they had it surrounded. With animals scarce nothing was killed this day, and the party lacked fresh meat. Lewis berated his men: "when we have a plenty of fresh meat I find it impossible to make the men take any care of it, or use it with the least frugallity. tho' I expect that necessity will shortly teach them this art."

The captains were leading a somewhat weakened crew. Two men had severe boils, one a bad "stone bruise," one a dislocated arm (perhaps Pryor), and a fifth (Gass) had injured his back when he fell over the gunwale of one of the canoes. Gass experienced a great deal of pain trying to work in canoes, so he was selected to go with Lewis the next day on his renewed search for Shoshones. Drouillard and Charbonneau were also to join the advance party. Charbonneau begged to go and promised that his ankle was sufficiently healed to permit the march. Lewis had doubts but indulged him. Noting fertile bottomlands with black, rich soil yielding bulrushes and cattails, Lewis termed the uplands poor and sterile, producing prickly pears, sedges, and needle-and-thread ("bearded") grass. The party camped a little above Antelope Creek, near the Gallatin-Madison county line, making about eighteen miles.

AUGUST 1, 1805. As arranged, Lewis, with Drouillard, Charbonneau, and Gass, left the boat party about eight o'clock in search of Shoshones. They walked along the north (or more generally, west) side of the Jefferson River, Jefferson County, Montana, entering the Tobacco Root Mountains. Clark recommended a route to Lewis, having seen the course of the river on July 26 from a high vantage point. It proved to be a mistake and took the little party along Boulder River ("R. Fields Creek," after Reuben Field of the party) and out of their way. They made a difficult return of eleven miles to the Jefferson in the heat of the day and arrived at two o'clock, exhausted and quite thirsty. Lewis had taken a dose of Glauber salts (a laxative) before setting out in the morning because of several days of diarrhea. This had further weakened him and made the walk even more difficult. He was elated when they reached the river and got a refreshing drink, and he and Drouillard each shot an elk. The men ate a good part of it and left the rest for the boat party. Having regained some strength, they marched on for about six miles and camped above Cardwell, Jefferson County, having come altogether about seventeen miles. Lewis had remembered his mosquito netting and so found the pests less troublesome this evening. During the day Lewis saw a flock of "black or dark brown phesants" and wrote the first description of the blue grouse, a bird new to science, noting its distinctive features. In the mountains he noticed a pinyon jay ("blue bird") and provided enough information to identify this new species.

Clark and the main party took the canoes through this section of the Jefferson, where high cliffs rose up on either side. Clark viewed limestone rocks that are dominantly of the Mission Canyon and Lodgepole Formations and sandstones of Pennsylvanian through Cretaceous age. The river was becoming shallower and swifter, increasing the men's labors. The captain killed a bighorn sheep, on which the party dined, and later they found Lewis's elk meat and ate the last of it. Clark saw a grizzly feeding on berries but was unable to get a shot at it. Ordway and Whitehouse reported that the tow line on Clark's canoe broke and sent the boat reeling and slamming against rocks. Fortunately, it did not overturn and everyone was safe. Only Whitehouse among the journalists noted that it was Clark's birthday. He also confessed that he left his pipe tomahawk behind and much regretted losing a favorite smoking instrument. The boat party made camp opposite of Boulder River, Madison County, coming some thirteen miles. Some miles back they had passed South Boulder Creek, naming it "Frazier's Creek," after Private Frazer of the corps. The Field brothers killed five deer in the evening.

AUGUST 2, 1805. Lewis's advance party set out at sunrise and crossed the Jefferson River about five miles above their camp, going from Jefferson County to Madison County, Montana, in order to shorten their route. Up to their waists in the rapid river, they crossed it at a spot about ninety yards wide. Soon after the crossing, Gass lost the captain's tomahawk in thick brush. The sergeant did not mention the incident in his journal. Not finding it, Lewis consoled himself that "accedents will happen in the best of families." The river meandered through a treeless but beautiful, level plain. Lewis considered the land "tolerable fertile," consisting of a "black or dark yellow loam" covered with grass from nine inches to two feet high. The men gorged on currants, gooseberries, and serviceberries, which were ripe and "in full perfection." The captain was particularly fond of the golden currant and serviceberry. He made morphological notes on his two favorites. He had collected the golden currant on July 29; he would get another in mid-April 1806, along with the serviceberry. The later currant specimen is at Kew Gardens, England. He also described the construction of beaver dams. The party saw numerous deer and pronghorns but only tracks of elks and no recent indications of Indians. Buffalo bones and old dung were seen, but Lewis had given up all hope of finding the shaggy beasts in the mountains. At sunset they camped in the vicinity of Waterloo, Madison County, having come about twenty-four miles. The day's heat was nearly suffocating, but at night they needed two blankets to stay warm. Lewis felt fully recovered from his illness and was ready to be off again in the morning.

The boat party under Clark met the same river difficulties as in past days, facing a strong current that required the men's utmost exertions on poles and tow ropes. Clark took to shore and saw several rattlesnakes on his walk. He also noticed prairie dog villages, as well as mallards, mergansers, and Lewis's woodpecker. Ordway and Whitehouse added golden eagles and their nests atop dead trees. They passed a small creek that was later named "*birth* Creek," probably by Lewis in honor of Clark's thirty-fifth birthday on August 1; it is Whitetail Creek, Jefferson County. The party camped below Big Pipestone ("Panther") Creek, Madison County, making fifteen to seventeen miles. Reuben Field of the boat party killed a mountain lion the next day; thus the party's name for the creek. In the evening Clark complained of a severe pain on his ankle, which he reasoned was caused by an insect bite or a boil. Whitehouse mentioned a pain in his shoulder.

AUGUST 3, 1805. Up and out before daylight, Lewis and party continued their route through Madison County, Montana. At eleven o'clock they halted for a couple of hours to breakfast on Drouillard's doe. Along the river's bottomlands the captain witnessed "deep holes as if rooted up by hogs," which possessed "excellent terf or peat." He also mentioned mineral salts that he had seen elsewhere on the Missouri River. Faulting and other natural changes on the Jefferson River caused swamps and peat bogs to form. The salts—sodium sulfate, sodium bicarbonate, and magnesium sulfate—gathered here from runoffs of the Big Hole and Ruby Rivers. Lewis gazed at the heights of the Tobacco Root Mountains on either side of the Jefferson River valley, lightly covered in timber. The prevalent species was limber pine on the hills while along the river course he saw narrowleaf cottonwoods. Undergrowth consisted of small willows, snowberries ("honeysuckle"), rosebushes, currants, and serviceberries. He wrote a short description of scrub birch. Along with noting the usual plains and riparian animals, Lewis called attention to longbilled curlews and northern suckers (*"bottlenose"*). Traveling about twenty-three miles, the advance party camped above the mouth of the Big Hole River, Madison County.

Clark again left the boat party for a bit of hunting and secured a deer. He saw tracks that he took to be those of Indians because the large toe was pointed inward. Shallow, swift waters necessitated hauling the canoes over rocks and gravel in many places, and the river became more rapid and island-strewn as the day wore on. The men were in the water half the day. Clark counted the same diversity of wildlife as Lewis: deer, elks, pronghorns, and bears in the bottomlands, while at the river he noted beavers, otters, geese, ducks, and curlews. Making thirteen miles, the boat party camped near Waterloo in either Jefferson or Madison County.

AUGUST 4, 1805. At four miles into the day, Lewis's advance party reached the Big Hole ("Wisdom") River, coming into the Jefferson from the west. Farther on the Ruby ("Philanthropy") River comes in from the east and forms the "Forks of the Jefferson," Madison County, Montana. Lewis spent a good deal of time investigating the area and these streams, but Charbonneau's complaints about his

leg slowed the party considerably. It appeared to Lewis that Indians had destroyed what little timber there was along the river by
setting fires in the bottoms. For the captains the main stream, the
Beaverhead River, remained the "Jefferson" and would be the one
they followed from this point. Lewis saw the bed of the Ruby as so
obstructed by gravel bars and islands that it would be impossible to
navigate, so he left a note on a pole advising Clark to take the middle
fork (Beaverhead). He considered that stream deeper, gentler, and
more likely to be navigable into the mountains that seemed to be its
source. Lewis and his men refreshed themselves on some venison
and then set out to explore the Big Hole River until at least noon
the next day, then to cross overland to the Beaverhead and follow
it to the forks or at least until they linked up with the main party.
They camped on the Big Hole River near the Madison-Beaverhead
county line, having come about twenty miles.

Clark brought his party up to Lewis's camp of August 2 and found
Lewis's note telling him that he had seen no trace of Indians in the
area. With a sore ankle caused by a boil, Clark stayed with the canoes
and witnessed closely the work of the men: "the method we are
compelled to take to get on is fatigueing & laborious in the extreen,
haul the Canoes over the rapids, which Suckceed each other every
two or three hundred yards and between the water rapid oblige to
towe & walke on Stones the whole day except when we have pole-
ing men wet all day Sore feet &c." Even under these conditions, the
party made about fifteen miles and camped in the vicinity of Silver
Star, Madison County.

AUGUST 5, 1805. Lewis sent the ailing Charbonneau with Gass back
to the Beaverhead River, to a downstream point about seven miles
distant, directing them to proceed "at their leasure" and remain there
until he and Drouillard returned from their reconnoiter of the Big
Hole River. Lewis and Drouillard stayed on the west side of the Big
Hole for about four miles, then waded across and continued for
another 1½ miles. Finding a high point, the explorers climbed with
some difficulty to the top and obtained a commanding view of the
valley through which they had passed. From here they could also
see the course of the Beaverhead for some twenty miles before it

disappeared into the mountains. Given his panoramic view, Lewis was more convinced than ever that the Beaverhead offered the best route forward for the corps. He could also see a place where the Beaverhead came within five miles of the Big Hole and decided to cross there and then make his way to Gass and Charbonneau. The descent was as hard and treacherous as the climb. In fact, Drouillard missed a step and took a fall, injuring his fingers and leg. After a short delay he was able to go on. They rested again and quenched their thirst at the Beaverhead, which Lewis declared still navigable. Here Lewis spotted an Indian road but no fresh tracks. Avoiding great bends in the river, the two men took as direct a route as possible, returning to their comrades. Lewis described the soil of the plains as "meager" and mixed with gravel, producing only needle-and-thread grass, sedges, and prickly pears. Because this area receives only about ten inches of rainfall a year, a rich soil cannot develop, so the uplands are composed principally of sand, clay, and soft sandstone. Gravel was deposited by adjacent rivers when they flowed at a higher elevation. In moister areas Lewis encountered a more fertile soil with fine grass and rushes.

Nearing the rendezvous point in the dark Lewis whooped his presence but got no response. Gass and Charbonneau had missed the appointed place (which Gass did not mention in his journal), necessitating two hours of extra trekking for Lewis and Drouillard in the dark through thick brush of spiny greasewoods and prickly pears to locate them. After traveling about twenty-five miles this day, the captain and Drouillard were happy to eat Gass and Charbonneau's meager meal of meat—the only meat they had eaten this day. The four made camp on the Beaverhead River a few miles above the mouth of the Ruby River, Madison County, Montana. Lewis fell asleep quickly and slept soundly until morning.

Facing a straighter but more rapid river, Clark and party pushed ahead under the usual difficulties. The captain sent the Field brothers to hunt, and soon the party was able to breakfast on a deer supplied by them. Reaching the Forks of the Jefferson about four o'clock in the afternoon, Clark missed Lewis's note about the practicality of the Beaverhead River and instead decided to ascend the Big Hole River, which seemed to point in their intended direction. Incredibly, a beaver had carried off Lewis's instructions, which were placed on a green pole. Gass later indicated that he had planted the pole. They went about one mile upriver from the forks, cutting their way through thick, low-hanging willows, and camped northwest of Twin Bridges, Madison County, making about nine miles. The men were exhausted and weak from their labors and wished the water travel would end so they could go by land. Clark's foot was increasingly painful, and he was running a slight fever.

AUGUST 6, 1805. Setting out with nothing to eat, Lewis sent Drouillard into the woods to get a deer and had Gass go toward Ruby River with orders to be on the lookout for the main party in case they came up that way. Lewis and Charbonneau continued down the Beaverhead toward the forks. About five miles above the forks Lewis heard men whooping to the west and turned toward the noise. When he reached them he learned that Clark had not found his note directing them to take the Beaverhead but had taken the Big Hole River instead. Clark had already met Drouillard and was making his return to the forks with the intention of following the correct stream. It had been a disaster on the swift Big Hole. One canoe had overturned, soaking everything, including a vital medicine box. Moreover, several articles were lost, including a shot pouch, a powder horn, and other rifle gear, never to be found. Two other canoes had filled with water, damaging their contents. Whitehouse was thrown (or jumped) out of one canoe, and as it swung about in the torrent it ran over the top of the man. Lewis was certain that if the river had been two inches shallower the boat would have crushed him. Nevertheless, he was injured and "was near breaking my leg," wrote the soldier. Parched meal, corn, Indian gifts, and many valuables were soaked in the swift waters of the Big Hole. Lewis's first priority was to get to a spot to examine and dry everything. They found a good place and camped on the Jefferson River opposite the mouth of the Big Hole, Madison County, Montana. It was here that the captains decided on names for the three streams at the Forks of the Jefferson River. They called the middle or main fork "Jefferson (Beaverhead) River," while christening the rapid stream "Wisdom (Big Hole) River" and the placid one "Philanthrophy (Ruby) River."

They honored Jefferson "in commemoration of two of those cardinal virtues, which have so eminently marked that deservedly selibrated character through life," wrote his protégé Lewis.

Now secure, the party examined the contents of the canoes. Lewis was quite proud that the canisters of powder had remained intact and the contents dry, "not in the least injured," although some had been underwater more than an hour. Prior to the expedition the captain had devised a method of storing gunpowder in lead canisters so that when the lead was molded to shot, the balls corresponded exactly to the amount of gunpowder inside. Hunters were sent out and returned with a welcome supply of three deer and four elks. While on the Big Hole Clark had sent Shannon to hunt, but he had not returned when Drouillard arrived. Clark then sent Drouillard after the young man while the main party made its way back to the forks. Drouillard came into camp this evening absent Shannon. The captains blew the sounding horn ("trumpet") and fired rifles but got no reply. Lewis feared that Shannon was lost again, as he had been in late August and early September 1804. Clark's ankle was still quite painful.

AUGUST 7, 1805. All the soaked items from the canoes were set out to dry. In surveying the cargo the captains decided that they could do without a canoe, so one was drawn up into the thick brush and secured so that rising water would not get to it. They would go ahead with seven canoes. Lewis did some routine maintenance on his air gun and found that it fired as fine as ever. By one o'clock the baggage was dry enough to reload and move on. Clark again took charge of the boat party and began ascending the Beaverhead River, while Lewis and Gass stayed behind to take astronomical observations. They would join the main party in the evening. Clark put the latitude of the mouth of the Big Hole as 45° 02′ 21.6″ N; it now is nearer 45° 33′ 44″ N. Lewis and Gass were quite rain soaked by the time they reached the camp above the entrance of the Ruby River, Madison County, Montana, about seven miles from their previous camp.

The captains had sent Reuben Field in search of Shannon but nighttime brought no news. They suspected that Shannon had pursued game up the Big Hole River and was awaiting their arrival, unaware that it was not the route of choice. Drouillard brought a deer into camp in the evening. Flying pests persisted—horse flies, deer flies, and blow flies principally. The party was consoled somewhat by the disappearance of gnats and by smaller swarms of mosquitoes.

AUGUST 8, 1805. With one less canoe, there were more men available to hunt, so the captains sent out four this morning. Game being scarcer, more hunters were required to supply the party. Finding the Beaverhead River, here thirty-five to forty-five yards wide, deeper and gentler below the Big Hole River, the party could travel faster but were thwarted in efforts to get ahead by a crooked river with many bends. The work of moving the canoes was done almost entirely with setting poles. Lewis enumerated the plant species in the bottomlands, including probably mountain thermopsis ("buffaloe clover"), Nuttall sunflowers, rushes, sedges, and wild ryes. He gave morphological attention to a species like "timothy," which was probably northern reedgrass or stream foxtail. Passing the Ruby River, Lewis speculated that it headed with the Madison River in snowy mountains to the southeast, the Gravelly Range; in fact the Madison heads in the Yellowstone Plateau in northwestern Wyoming. Having made about eight miles, the party camped a few miles above the Ruby River, Madison County, Montana. Cloudy skies in the evening prevented Lewis from getting lunar observations.

At noon Reuben Field returned and reported that he had been up the Big Hole River several miles and found no trace of Shannon. Two hunters also came back about the same time, having each killed a deer and a pronghorn. Other hunters brought in a deer in the evening. The boil on Clark's ankle discharged a "considerable quantity of matter" but still was swollen, inflamed, and painful. Sacagawea recognized a high point in the plains, which she said was near a summer retreat of her people, the Shoshones. She said the Shoshones called it "beaver's head" (Beaverhead Rock) from its resemblance to the animal's head. She assured the captains that they would find the Shoshones on this river or on one near its source. Given the size of the Beaverhead at this point Lewis was certain that the Indians could not be too distant. Stating that it was "all important" to find Sacagawea's tribe, Lewis determined again to go ahead with a small party seeking the Shoshones. He was emphatic: "in short it is my resolusion to find them or some others, who have horses if it should cause me a trip of one month. for without horses we shall be obliged to leave a great part of our stores, of which, it appears to me that we have a stock already sufficiently small for the length of the voyage before us."

AUGUST 9, 1805. Lewis set out early on his own to a point he thought the canoes would reach by eight o'clock, where they would meet for breakfast. While waiting he caught up with some of his writing, "which I conceived from the nature of my instructions necessary lest any accedent should befall me on the long and reather hazardous rout I was now about to take." Deciding that the party would not reach him, he turned back a mile and met them for breakfast, bringing two geese to the meal. While they were halted, Shannon arrived and related that he had thought the party was ahead of him on the Big Hole, so he spent a day seeking them up that river. Finally convinced that the river was not navigable, he turned back to the forks and followed the Beaverhead to find his comrades. Although he had not faced the starving conditions of his separation in 1804, he was still a bit worried during his travels. Nevertheless, he had gathered information about the Big Hole, which he relayed to the captains.

After breakfast Lewis "swung my pack and set out." This time he was accompanied by Drouillard, Shields, and McNeal. Clark emphasized that he would have taken the trip had he been able to walk. He called the boil on his ankle "a rageing fury." Lewis's party took to the west side of the Beaverhead River, and with Beaverhead Rock in sight, the men made their way across the plains. About eight miles above their starting point they waded the river, continued up the east side, and made camp northeast of Dillon, Beaverhead County, Montana, having come about sixteen miles altogether. They had killed two pronghorns along the way and harvested enough meat for the night's supper and the next morning's breakfast. Looking at a river laced with islands, crooked, rapid, rocky, and shallow, Lewis wondered whether the boat party would be able to advance in such a stream and if so, under what incredible labors. Indeed, the difficulties allowed them to move a mere five miles directly while going fourteen on the river. Gass alone related that at lunch they had to haul out a leaking canoe and caulk it. They camped near the Madison-Beaverhead county line.

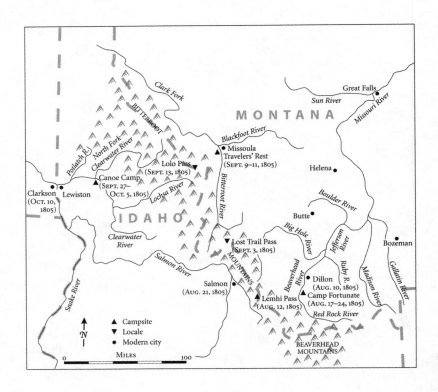

MAP 8. The expedition's route, August 10–October 10, 1805.

CHAPTER 7

Those Tremendous Mountains

August 10–October 10, 1805

AUGUST 10, 1805. Lewis and the advance party set out early and continued along the east side of the Beaverhead River, Beaverhead County, Montana. After passing Blacktail Deer Creek ("McNeal's Creek" on expedition maps, after McNeal of the party), they found an Indian road and followed it. The captain sent Drouillard after a deer while he and the other men waited under a rock cliff. Because of the large number of prairie rattlesnakes at the place, Lewis called it "rattle snake clifts," a name it retains. It is about ten miles southwest of Dillon, Beaverhead County. By noon Drouillard returned with the best meat of three deer he had killed. They ate a hasty lunch and got back on the Indian road leading toward the Tendoy Mountains. As it had the day before, the Beaverhead continued to be divided by islands, rapid, rocky, crooked, and shallow. As he neared the mountains Lewis noticed it was less circuitous but even more rocky and rapid. Lewis was amazed that the Missouri and Jefferson Rivers could still be navigable at this distance. He hoped the Columbia River would demonstrate the same characteristics and provide "a communication across the continent by water."

Continuing their route along the Indian road, about fifteen miles from Rattlesnake Cliffs they arrived at an open valley where the Beaverhead River divided into the Ruby River from the east and Horse Prairie Creek from the west. The captain made a quick examination of the two and decided that neither would allow navigation of the party's canoes. Here also the Indian road forked, following each of the streams. Lewis sent Drouillard on one and Shields on the other to find which appeared the most used. In his pursuit of Shoshones Lewis wanted to take the road most traveled. Leaving a note for Clark, Lewis advised that the main party wait here until he returned from his reconnaissance. Remembering the difficulties at the Big Hole River, this time he put the note on a dry willow pole. Drouillard and Shields recommended that they proceed up Horse Prairie Creek to the west and into the mountains, but Lewis made a quick trip up Red Rock River before he made the decision to follow their recommendation.

Hemmed in by the rough rocks and steep cliffs of the Tendoy Mountains, the advance party followed the mile-wide valley of Horse Prairie Creek to the west. Something over four miles into the trek, they entered an extensive plain about ten miles long and five to six miles across, "forming one of the handsomest coves." Given as both "Snake Indian Cove" and "Shoshone Cove" by the captains, the village of Grant, Beaverhead County, lies in the middle of it; nearby the men camped. With few trees in the area, they built a fire of willow brush and cooked a deer. Lewis broke down the day's tramp of thirty miles: ten to Rattlesnake Cliffs, fifteen to the forks of the Beaverhead River, and five on Horse Prairie Creek.

The main party under Clark reached Beaverhead Rock by following the very crooked Beaverhead River. The task of moving canoes through these shallow waters was extremely difficult. A hard rain and hail hit the party in late afternoon, which drenched them all. They tried to protect themselves with willow bushes. A single deer from this day and a three-day-old one served as meager meals for hungry boatmen, "which goes hard with us as the fatigues is hard," wrote Ordway. Whitehouse allowed that "we are content with what we can git." The party camped south of Beaverhead Rock, having made four miles directly but moved thirteen miles by water.

AUGUST 11, 1805. The Indian road that the advance party had been following disappeared this morning. Lewis decided to head toward a pass some ten miles to the west in hopes of finding it again. While Lewis and McNeal moved away from Horse Prairie Creek and onto the plains, the captain sent Drouillard on his north along the creek and Shields to the south looking for the Indian path. If the men found such a road they were to signal with a hat on the end of a rifle. After moving along in this way for about five miles Lewis saw an Indian on horseback coming toward them. Using his telescope for a closer look, he was certain by the man's dress that he was a Shoshone. Lewis was overjoyed. Now if he could only get close enough to convince him that they were white men and not enemies, he knew he could make contact with the tribe. Lewis and McNeal started toward him; when they were within a mile of one another the Indian stopped. The captain also halted and removed his blanket to signal that he wanted a meeting. He had learned that waving a blanket in the air, then laying it out on the ground was a universal sign among Missouri and Rocky Mountain Indians for a gathering. It did not work. The Indian kept his distance and seemed to be watching Drouillard and Shields coming up on either side, lending an air of suspicion to the encounter. The men were too far away to hear Lewis, and the captain feared that any signal he made would be mistaken for some sinister purpose.

Lewis quickly took some trinkets and trade items out of his pack, laid his gun aside, and slowly advanced with his offering. When he was within two hundred paces, the Indian turned his horse about and began to move away. Lewis called out, "tab-ba-bone," which he had learned (probably from Sacagawea through Charbonneau) meant "white man." Perhaps lost in the shuffle of multiple languages, it is unclear what the word actually meant to the lone horseman, but it was unpersuasive. He kept looking over his shoulder at Drouillard and Shields, so Lewis signaled for the men to halt, but only Drouillard saw the command—Shields continued to advance. Tantalizingly, the Indian halted again and turned about as if to wait for Lewis. The captain repeated "tab-ba-bone," held up his trinkets, and opened his shirt to show the color of his skin, but to no avail. When the captain was within one hundred paces of the man, he wheeled about, gave his horse the whip, and was gone. Lewis's heart sank since "with him vanished all my hopes of obtaining horses for the preasent." He was also upset at the men, particularly Shields, whom he blamed for bungling the encounter, and reprimanded them for their inattention. He sent the two men back after items he left behind while pursuing the Indian.

Lewis and the three men now began to follow the horseman's tracks, hoping they might lead them to a Shoshone camp. Seeing that the route led toward some high hills, Lewis reasoned that any

Indians camped there would see them from a distance and flee. The men rested a spell and ate breakfast while Lewis displayed an assortment of trinkets on a pole in case any Indians came to them. Rain with some hail pelted the men and soaked them a bit, but they were soon underway, following the Indian's tracks. After several miles the traces were lost in an array of hoofprints. Having traveled about twenty miles altogether, or about ten miles from their previous camp, the men settled down near the northwest end of Shoshone Cove, Beaverhead County, Montana. Lewis attached a small U.S. flag to a camp pole—one that he had had McNeal carry since they met the Indian.

Clark and the main party passed an island that the captain called "3000 mile Island," that being the distance he calculated it was from the mouth of the Missouri River. It has since disappeared due to changes in the Beaverhead's course. The river displayed its usual characteristics, requiring the men to be in the water a good part of the day hauling the canoes through riffles and shallow waters, while mosquitoes tormented them. The boatmen killed a beaver with a setting pole and tomahawked several otters, while hunters killed three deer and a pronghorn. They camped about halfway between Beaverhead Rock and Dillon, Beaverhead County, having come about fourteen miles on the river and about five directly.

AUGUST 12, 1805. Lewis sent Drouillard out at first light to find the route that the Indian of the day before had taken. He found and followed the horseman's tracks for a distance, then returned to Lewis, who now determined to move in that direction, hoping to locate a Shoshone encampment. The men were still along Horse Prairie Creek, moving through the Beaverhead Mountains. Dividing the men as he had the day before, the captain sent Drouillard to his right and Shields to his left with orders to look for an Indian road or fresh horse tracks. After about four miles of travel Lewis encountered some small lodges of willow brushes and discovered a road that the explorers followed to Bloody Dick Creek, where they ate the last of their venison. Along the way Lewis saw an animal of "the fox kind" and different from any that he had seen. Drouillard got a shot at it from 130 yards, but even wounded it escaped. From Lewis's description, the animal was possibly a wolverine. He also saw several "heath cock" and compared them to the common chicken and the sharp-tailed grouse; they were sage grouse. Again, they failed to get a specimen.

After lunch a short climb brought them to Trail Creek, where the road was plainly visible and Lewis "did not despair of shortly finding a passage over the mountains and of taisting the waters of the great Columbia this evening." Indeed, at four miles farther the road took them

> to the most distant fountain of the waters of the mighty Missouri in surch of which we have spent so many toilsome days and wristless nights. thus far I had accomplished one of those great objects on which my mind has been unalterably fixed for many years, judge then of the pleasure I felt in allying my thirst with this pure and ice cold water . . . two miles below McNeal had exultingly stood with a foot on each side of this little rivulet and thanked his god that he had lived to bestride the mighty & heretofore deemed endless Missouri.

After resting the men walked to the top of the dividing ridge and viewed "immence ranges of high mountains still to the West of us with their tops partially covered with snow." Descending to the west, Lewis located a bold, running creek and here "tasted the water of the great Columbia river," probably on Agency Creek. Lewis and his advance party had crossed the Continental Divide at Lemhi Pass and gone from Beaverhead County, Montana, to Lemhi County, Idaho. After a short halt the men continued to follow the Indian road, which led them over steep hills and into deep basins. They camped for the night at a spring near Agency Creek, having come about twenty miles, according to Lewis. Along the way Lewis noticed a "deep perple currant," the Hudson Bay currant, gave it a short description, and offered a negative review of its fruit.

Clark and the main party got underway early, facing a swift and increasingly shallow Beaverhead River, which forced them into the hard work of hauling canoes over rocks. Clark called it "emencely laborious," weakening the men by requiring them to be constantly in water. The men complained and asked to go ahead by land, but

Clark said "I passify them." Other than to encourage them, we do not know his methods; the liquor was gone. They camped a few miles below the mouth of Blacktail Deer ("McNeal's") Creek and north of Dillon, Beaverhead County, having come forward a mere four miles while traveling about twelve miles on the twisting river.

AUGUST 13, 1805. Leaving Agency Creek, Lemhi County, Idaho, the advance party followed the Indian road for about five miles to a large creek, perhaps Pattee Creek, and crossed it. Coming over a hill Lewis saw a heavily timbered valley through which he supposed a river must run. It was the Lemhi River, which he would encounter later. Moving through a plain parallel to the valley, the men saw two women, a man, and some dogs on a height above them. Lewis was sure that they saw him, and they appeared to be waiting for the explorers. Arriving within about a half mile of them, the explorers halted and Lewis dropped his gun and pack, unfurled the flag, and advanced slowly alone. The women took off, but the man waited until Lewis was within a hundred yards from him before he too fled. All the while Lewis was repeating his Shoshone word, "tab-ba-bone," but without success. He hurried to the top of the hill but could see nothing of them. He tried to tie a handkerchief filled with trinkets on a dog and send it after its owners, but the dogs refused his entreaties and ran off. Lewis's comrades joined him, and they tracked the Indians, who were following the same road the explorers had been pursuing.

Along the way, the captain could not resist some botanizing. He had been viewing Rocky Mountain ("white") maple, either skunk-bush sumac or poison ivy ("shumate of the small species"), and common snowberry ("honeysuckle"). He gave a brief morphological description of the snowberry, comparing it to the western snowberry ("small honeysuckle of the Missouri"). Lewis's specimen of the common snowberry, collected at an unknown date, is housed at the Charleston Museum, Charleston, South Carolina. The captain also noticed three types of cacti: plains prickly pear, pincushion cactus, and brittle prickly pear. The last he called "the most troublesome plant of the three."

Only a mile farther on their route the men encountered three females. One of the women fled, while an old woman and a girl of about twelve huddled together. Lewis laid down his gun, walked toward them, and saw that they were quite afraid. He took the woman's hand, lifted her up, gave his Shoshone greeting, "tab-ba-bone," and raised his shirt sleeve to reveal his skin color. That seemed to soothe them, so the other men came up. Lewis gave the woman some beads and other items and had Drouillard ask her in sign language to call back the woman who had run away. The captain feared that she might alarm the camp and send Shoshones to attack them before they could explain their peaceful intentions. The old woman was able to get the other one back. Lewis gave the woman who had returned some trinkets and painted her face with vermillion, which he had learned was a sign of peace among the Shoshones. When all were composed Lewis indicated through Drouillard's sign language that he wanted to meet the tribe's chiefs and head men at their camp. The women acceded, and they set out on the road the explorers had been following.

After they had traveled about two miles, a party of about sixty mounted warriors came rushing toward them at full speed. Lewis again advanced slowly alone, leaving his gun behind and unfurling the flag. A few of the Indians quickly learned about the Americans from the women, who displayed their gifts, and the situation quieted. Now the Shoshones came forward and embraced Lewis "very affectionately" in their traditional way, which the captain explained was to put a left arm over your right shoulder, set their left cheek against yours, and shout loudly, "âh-hi´-e, âh-hi´-e," which the captain took to mean "I am much pleased," and in modern Shoshone means "thank you." All came together, hugging and painting with grease until Lewis confessed that he was "heartily tired of the national hug." They then gathered in a circle and Lewis offered a pipe while the Shoshones respectfully removed their moccasins. After smoking awhile, Lewis distributed some trifles. The recipients seemed especially pleased with the blue beads and vermillion. Finding a chief, Lewis told (again through the gesticulations of Drouillard) of their friendly intentions and promised a full explanation when they reached the Shoshone camp. The principal chief among them, Cameahwait ("Ca-me-âh-wait"), made a short speech to the warriors, after which Lewis presented him with a flag as an emblem of peace.

As they moved toward the Shoshone camp Lewis learned that the Indians had thought them to be their enemies, perhaps Atsinas, and had come prepared for battle. Most carried bows, arrows, and shields, but a few had small guns of European origin. Four miles farther on they reached the Shoshone camp, about seven miles north of Tendoy, Lemhi County, on the east bank of the Lemhi River. The explorers were escorted into a lodge that had been prepared for the meeting by young Indians sent ahead. Seated on green boughs and prong-horn skins, the Americans were requested to remove their moccasins, as had the Shoshones. Cameahwait lit a pipe, made a speech, and then presented the pipe in each of the cardinal directions. He then gave the pipe to Lewis, who took several draws before it was passed to others. Lewis then explained the object of their mission and afterward distributed what few, small gifts he had. As it was getting late, Lewis told Cameahwait that they had had nothing to eat. The chief could only offer berry cakes, so the explorers made a meal of them. Lewis learned that the Shoshones had been attacked by the Atsinas in the spring and that about twenty of their number had been killed or taken as prisoners. They had lost horses in the fight and their lodges had been destroyed. They were now living in makeshift willow brush enclosures. In spite of the loss, Lewis observed a great number of horses and was confident that the corps could obtain enough pack animals to get them over the mountains if they were forced to go by land.

After eating Lewis walked down to the Lemhi River and learned from Cameahwait that it discharged into another, larger stream, the Salmon River, about a half day's march from the encampment. The captain then got some disquieting news about the Salmon. From the junction of the rivers there was little timber, the Salmon was confined between inaccessible mountains and was very rocky and rapid, and the way was impassible by land or water. Lewis hoped that the description was exaggerated in an effort to get the Americans to linger awhile. Nevertheless, looking around Lewis saw no trees large enough to convert to canoes. Indeed, they were barely fit for fuel. Upon his return to camp an Indian called to Lewis and shared some food, a morsel of boiled pronghorn and a piece of roasted salmon. This was the first salmon that he had tasted and it convinced him that they were on waters that linked to the Pacific. Late as it was, the Shoshones celebrated the explorers' arrival and began dancing. By midnight Lewis was exhausted and went to bed, leaving his comrades to dance on. He was awakened several times during the night by the revelry.

Clark and party spent another day hauling boats in the cold, shallow waters of the Beaverhead River. The men worked most of the day dragging the canoes but in spite of their hard labors advanced only five miles on the twisting stream. They camped a few miles southwest of Dillon. Earlier they passed Blacktail Deer ("McNeal's") Creek, Beaverhead County, where Clark noticed a limestone cliff of the Mississippian-age Madison Group; it is shown on one of his maps as "rock Clift." At Dillon it is known as "Clark's Lookout." Hunters brought in a single deer.

AUGUST 14, 1805. Lewis decided to stay a day at the Shoshone camp in order to give Clark time to get to the forks of the Beaverhead River. He also hoped to be able to obtain more information about the area and the way ahead. Having had little to eat for some time, he sent Drouillard and Shields hunting. The Shoshones furnished horses for the explorers, who were joined by a number of young men. Lewis noted that the Shoshones hunted pronghorns from horseback with bow and arrows. Since the pronghorns were so fleet and hardy, it was impossible for a single rider to catch one. The Shoshones had therefore developed a tactic of wearing the animals down with multiple horses until the exhausted animals could be caught. Lewis discovered that forty to fifty hunters would spend half a day in such pursuits and not get more than two or three pronghorns. The captain watched one such hunt that lasted about two hours and yielded nothing but unhappy hunters and horses dripping with sweat. Drouillard and Shields were likewise unsuccessful. Elks and deer were either not available or too elusive for Indian hunters with only bows and arrows. Running down pronghorns on horseback seemed to be the only recourse.

Lewis asked Cameahwait to tell him about the geography of the country. In fact, it may be Clark who obtained this information on August 20, with Sacagawea serving as interpreter. Lewis then copied it into his journal sometime later, meaning that Lewis must have done his journal writing after the events of this period. (See below for where this apparent copying ends.) Enlisting Drouillard as interpreter, the captain praised him for his ability with the Indian sign language that enabled the communication. Cameahwait drew the course of the Lemhi River on the ground, showing a divide not far away. That division may be Hayden Creek and the Lemhi River itself, which merge near Lemhi, Lemhi County, Idaho. The chief then indicated that the Lemhi flowed into a much larger stream, the Salmon River, about ten miles distant. From the confluence the new stream continued to the northwest for a day's march, then turned west. Cameahwait heaped mounds of sand on either side of the Salmon and told Lewis that they represented "vast mountains of rock eternally covered with snow." He also related that perpendicular cliffs hemmed the river so closely that there was no passage along the shore. Moreover, the bed of the Salmon was obstructed by sharp rocks in a raging river, and the mountains were inaccessible to man or horse. Cameahwait told Lewis that none of his people had been beyond this impossible stretch of the Salmon. Lewis then asked about alternate routes, but the chief could only recommend old men for that information. Lewis also learned that "persed nosed Indians," Nez Perce Indians, had informed Cameahwait that the river "ran toward the seting sun and finally lost itself in a great lake of water which was illy taisted."

The captain soon found an elderly Indian informant with knowledge about the country to the southwest. This man gave an equally negative account of that way out the mountains. He said that the explorers would be obliged to climb steep mountains that lacked game of any kind and would possibly face a fierce and warlike nation of Indians. After getting out of the mountains they would have to cross a dry, parched, sandy desert with no food for man or horse and devoid of water. It seems likely that the informant was describing the area of southwest Idaho between the Snake and Owyhee Rivers where a band of Shoshones or perhaps Bannocks or Northern Paiutes lived. He painted a dismal picture in the extreme. He advised

Lewis to put off his journey until spring, when he would lead the party. Lewis thanked him and said this direction took him farther to the south than he wanted to go. Nevertheless, he gave the man a knife for the information. Lewis deduced from this that the rivers of which the man spoke were southern tributaries of the Columbia River, but that hypothesis was wrong, as was his idea that following the Owyhee toward its source would take him to either the Pacific or the Gulf of California.

Lewis returned to Cameahwait and asked what route the Nez Perces took over the mountains to reach the Missouri River. The chief said they used a road to the north, but he described it in unfavorable terms. He said the Nez Perces suffered excessive hunger, as there was no game in that part of the mountains, and that the route was so thickly covered with timber that it was nearly impossible to get through. Lewis was hardly daunted by this negative report:

> knowing that Indians had passed, and did pass, at this season on that side of this river to the same below the mountains, my rout was instantly settled in my own mind, povided the account of this river should prove true on an investigation of it, which I was determined should be made before we would undertake the rout by land in any direction. I felt perfectly satisfyed, that if the Indians could pass these mountains with their women and Children, that we could also pass them; and that if the nations on this river below the mountains were as numerous as they were stated to be that they must have some means of subsistence which it would be equally in our power to procure in the same country.

He also learned that there were no buffalo on the west side of the mountains, that elks, deer, and pronghorns were few, and that the people subsisted principally on fish and roots.

The captain spent the rest of the day smoking and conversing with informants, trying to acquire as much information as possible about the country. They told Lewis that they could reach the Spanish in ten days, but he found the Shoshones not overly friendly with the Spanish. Their main complaint against them was that the Spanish would not provide them with firearms. This put them at a great disadvantage with their Blackfeet, Atsina, and Hidatsa enemies, who could get weapons from French, English, and American traders. In consequence of this handicap they were nearly defenseless against constant attacks by their "bloodthirsty neighbours to the East." In order to avoid the harassment they were forced to spend at least two-thirds of the year in the mountains, living on scant rations without meat and with only small portions of fish, roots, and berries. Cameahwait, "with his ferce eyes and lank jaws grown meager for the want of food," declared that would not be the case if the Shoshones had guns; then they could get to the plains and hunt buffalo, defend themselves adequately, and not be compelled to hide in the mountains. "We do not fear our enemies when placed on an equal footing with them," he told Lewis. The captain told him that the Arikaras, Mandans, and Hidatsas had promised to cease making war on the Shoshones and that he would endeavor to get the same promise from other tribes. He also maintained that after the explorers returned home, traders would be coming to supply them with "an abundance of guns and every other article necessary to their defence and comfort" in exchange for beaver, otter, and weasel skins. Lewis found them delighted with this information. This is apparently the place where Lewis stopped copying Clark's entry of August 20 into his own journal entry for this day (see above for the spot where the apparent copying begins).

Lewis asked Cameahwait to request the Shoshones to go with the explorers to the forks of the Beaverhead to meet Clark and the main party. The captains also asked that the Indians bring about thirty spare horses to carry the party's baggage into the mountains. Lewis indicated that once together he wanted to trade for horses in order to get the party to accessible rivers for the trip to the coast. Cameahwait exhorted his people on these matters and gave the welcome news that they would be ready to accompany Lewis in the morning. Drouillard estimated the tribe's horse herd at four hundred animals, most of them in excellent condition. Indeed, Lewis declared that they would "make a figure on the South side of James River or the land of fine horses." A number of horses carried Spanish brands and wore Spanish bridles, bits, and other gear. Shoshone warriors kept one or two horses tied to their lodges during the night in order to be ready to defend the tribe at a moment's notice. In

spite of the extreme poverty that Lewis viewed, he found the Shoshones a happy people, full of merriment and ready to dance again
until late in the night.

With so many in Clark's party stiff and sore from the hard work
of moving boats on the Beaverhead River, the captain decided to
delay a bit and have breakfast before moving on. Even so, they
got underway by seven o'clock. Meeting the same struggles as in
days past, the boat party advanced seven miles and camped about
ten miles southwest of Dillon, Beaverhead County, Montana, and
downstream from Rattlesnake Cliffs. Several men were injured in
the hauling work, so Clark spent time at the setting pole. The Field
brothers killed four deer and a pronghorn, while Clark got a "fat
Buck" in the evening. Without additional explanation Clark confided that he "checked our interpreter [Charbonneau] for Strike-
ing his woman [Sacagawea] at their Dinner." Lewis called Clark's
action "a severe repremand" to Charbonneau.

AUGUST 15, 1805. Up early, Lewis declared that he was "hungary as
a wolf." A scant meal of flour and berries the day before hardly sustained him, and he found that McNeal had only about two pounds
of flour left. He had the soldier divide it and make a kind of berry
pudding with half, saving the rest for the evening. The four explorers breakfasted on this while also giving a portion to Cameahwait,
who called it "the best thing he had taisted for a long time." Lewis
tried to hurry the Shoshones along but learned that a rumor had
spread that the explorers were in league with Atsina Indians and
sought to deceive and destroy the Shoshones. Lewis tried to cajole
them by assuring them of his honesty, by promising future visits
from traders if they cooperated, and by questioning the bravery of
doubters. He also explained that the boats at the forks of the Beaverhead were loaded with merchandise. Cameahwait boasted of his
own bravery, mounted his horse, and challenged followers to mount
and join him. Six or eight men accepted the challenge and smoked
a pipe with Lewis to seal the bargain. Lewis complimented himself
for questioning their courage: "to doubt the bravery of a savage is
at once to put him on his metal." The captain had everyone pack up
quickly so as not to lose the moment, and they were off a little after

noon. Older women cried out as they left and called on the gods to protect their warriors. Before traveling far, the party was joined by ten or twelve more horsemen and later by nearly all the men and some women of the village. Lewis thought this action demonstrated the fickle nature of the Shoshones (or Indians in general), who acted on the spur of the moment and quickly shifted from depression to cheerfulness: "they were now very cheerfull and gay, and two hours ago they looked as sirly as so many imps of satturn."

The party of explorers and Shoshones stopped at the spring near Agency Creek where Lewis had camped on August 12 to have a smoke and let their horses graze. Lewis commented that the Shoshones were very fond of smoking but were limited in the pleasure because they did not cultivate tobacco. Lewis purchased horseback rides for himself and his men but soon tired of riding without stirrups and returned to walking, hiring an Indian to carry his pack. About sunset they reached Shoshone Cove and camped on the south side of Horse Prairie Creek, a few miles west of Grant, Beaverhead County, Montana. Drouillard had separated earlier to hunt but returned after dark empty-handed. The explorers finished the last of their flour.

Clark and the main party continued as usual, now facing a cool wind from the southwest, which added a chill to the cold water of the Beaverhead River that they worked in. They passed Rattlesnake Cliffs and later Grasshopper Creek, Beaverhead County, which the captains named for Willard of the party. The men complained of their hard labors and the bitter-tasting, poor deer meat that was supposed to sustain them. Clark could offer only a buck that he killed that day and some trout taken by others. Ordway mentioned that Sacagawea gathered serviceberries. While on shore hunting and fishing the captain was nearly bitten twice by rattlesnakes. Advancing about seven miles without a tree in sight, the party camped near some abandoned Indian brush lodges just below the mouth of Gallagher Creek, Beaverhead County.

AUGUST 16, 1805. Still with nothing to eat, Lewis sent Drouillard and Shields to hunt. The captain asked Cameahwait to keep his young men back, as their noise scared game. This request frightened some Shoshones who were still suspicious of the explorers, so they followed the American hunters. Lewis knew that if he tried to prevent this he would simply arouse further suspicions, so he kept quiet. In fact, a number of fearful Shoshones turned back. Within an hour everyone was on the road again. After they had traveled awhile an Indian horseman came racing back, and Lewis feared the worse. For a moment he thought that by some unfortunate coincidence the hunters and Indian followers had stumbled onto Shoshone enemies and confirmed Shoshone fears. As it was, the rider had good news. One of the hunters had killed a deer. In an instant, riders raced toward the kill. Lewis, riding with a Shoshone, got caught in the dash and his on-board Indian companion kept whipping their horse so as not to miss the feast. At the same time Lewis was pulling back on the horse, so his riding companion leaped off and raced on foot toward the fallen deer. At the spot, Lewis witnessed the starved Shoshones "tumbling over each other like a parcel of famished dogs each seizing and tearing away a part of the intestens which had been previously thrown out" by Drouillard. Lewis nearly lost his appetite at the scene:

> each one had a peice of some discription and all eating most ravenously. some were eating the kidnies the melt and liver and the blood runing from the corners of their mouths, others were in a similar situation with the paunch and guts but the exuding substance in this case from their lips was of a different discription. one of the last who attacted my attention particularly had been fortunate in his allotment or reather active in the division, he had provided himself with about nine feet of the small guts one end of which he was chewing on while with his hands he was squezzing the contents out at the other. I really did not untill now think that human nature ever presented itself in a shape so nearly allyed to the brute creation. I viewed these poor starved divils with pity and compassion.

The captain had McNeal take a quarter of the deer and give the rest to Cameahwait to be divided among his people. They ate it all with little cooking. Moving forward to find wood for a fire, they found that Drouillard had killed a second deer, and the previous scene was repeated. Soon the explorers built a fire, ate an ample share, and gave the balance of the meat to the Shoshones, who consumed nearly every part, "even to the soft parts of the hoofs," Lewis observed. Drouillard now joined them with a third deer and more meat was consumed.

After the feast explorers and Indians moved on to the lower part of Shoshone Cove. Along the way Shields killed a pronghorn and again the meat was shared. Nearing the place where they were to meet Clark with the main party, Cameahwait insisted on halting. He then had shawls ("tippets") placed around the necks of the Americans to give them a Shoshone appearance. Lewis thought this further revealed Shoshone suspicions of treachery and that the act was to give the explorers an Indian appearance, so they all would share if harm reached them. To instill confidence Lewis gave up his cocked hat. The other explorers followed his example and "were so[o]n metamorphosed" into Indians. All now hurried along toward the forks of the Beaverhead with an Indian carrying a flag to announce them. Within two miles of the appointed spot Lewis could clearly see that the boat party had not arrived. Seeing the unoccupied place as well, the Shoshones began to slacken their pace and pull back. Lewis was anxious to restore confidence no matter the cost, so he handed Cameahwait his rifle and offered his life if he was lying. His companions also gave up their guns.

Lewis turned to another stratagem to gain Shoshone confidence. He sent Drouillard along with a Shoshone to the forks to retrieve the notes that he had left for Clark. At their return Lewis assured Cameahwait that the notes were from Clark informing that he was near and that Lewis was to wait for him here. The captain asked the chief to send one of his men with one of Lewis's to meet Clark while he and the two others would remain with the Shoshones. Cameahwait agreed and one of his young men volunteered for the mission. Lewis promised the man a knife and some beads as a reward. He wrote a hasty note to Clark, which Drouillard and the Indian were to take in the morning. Earlier he had stressed to Cameahwait that they had with them a woman of his own tribe who had been taken prisoner by the Hidatsas. Through her Lewis declared that he would be able to explain his mission fully. His men told skeptical Shoshones that the main party also had with them a black man with curly hair. This excited their curiosity, and they seemed as anxious to see this "monster" as they were to view American merchandise. Nevertheless, Lewis still observed restlessness and lingering doubts among the Shoshones.

As night came on, Cameahwait and a few others slept near Lewis, while the rest secreted themselves in distant spots among the willow bushes. Their fears were not entirely allayed by Lewis's actions. The captain had his own fears and conjectures. Had Clark found the river too difficult and simply halted at Rattlesnake Cliffs? If so, Lewis would surely lose the Shoshones, who would abandon him and flee to the mountains, never to be found. As he considered the possibilities, his worries increased "that they would spread the allarm to all other bands within our reach & of course we should be disappointed in obtaining horses, which would vastly retard and increase the labour of our voyage and I feared might so discourage the men as to defeat the expedition altogether. my mind was in reality quite as gloomy all this evening as the most affrighted indian but I affected cheerfullness to keep the Indians so who were about me." The captain slept little that night as he mulled over these matters. He considered the importance of the expedition equal to his own life, and its fate now seemed to "depend in a great measure upon the caprice of a few savages who are ever as fickle as the wind."

The men of the main party woke to a cold morning tired, sore, and chilled, so again they delayed leaving, had breakfast, but still got underway by seven o'clock. Trying to equalize the work, Clark shifted men among the canoes. He found the going somewhat easier than the day before. The captain found an abundance of serviceberries and currants in a walk with Charbonneau and Sacagawea. Ordway revealed that they shared a bucketful of berries with the men. Gass said they dubbed the place "Service-berry valley." Clark also noticed mountain thermopsis, which Lewis called "buffaloe clover," perhaps noting bison-grazing preference, and Clark, "long leaf Clover," for its long leaflets. With few trees along the river, the captain counted only limber pines and Rocky Mountain junipers on the slopes above the Beaverhead. Clark climbed a hill for a view ahead and saw the forks of the Beaverhead. The party camped about four miles below the forks. Lewis and the Indians may have just missed hunters from Clark's party who came to the forks in search of game.

AUGUST 17, 1805. Soon after his early rise Lewis sent Drouillard and his Indian follower downriver in search of the main party and Shields out to hunt. He assigned McNeal to cook the remainder of the previous day's meat, which the two men shared with Cameahwait. Within two hours another Shoshone who had followed Drouillard came back to report that more white men were on their way. All were elated at the news and Cameahwait gave Lewis the inevitable Shoshone "fraturnal hug." Soon Clark and an advance party appeared; the rest of the party hauling the canoes arrived at noon. The men received the universal Shoshone hug, or as Ordway related, "they take us round the neck and Sweze us in token of friendship." With all in place a delighted Lewis wrote, "we had the satisfaction once more to find ourselves all together, with a flattering prospect of being able to obtain as many horses shortly as would enable us to prosicute our voyage by land should that by water be deemed unadvisable."

Finding a level, grassy spot, explorers and Shoshones formed a camp at the forks of the Beaverhead River, Beaverhead County, Montana. Here the party would remain until August 24, and the spot would acquire the name "Camp Fortunate." The canoes were unloaded and one of the large sails was converted to a canopy to provide shade for a gathering. About four o'clock all came together and a council was begun using the interpretive skills of Sacagawea and Charbonneau and some unacknowledged French speaker from the party. The captains gave their standard speech about the purposes of their mission, about future trading possibilities, and about the strength and goodwill of the American government. They emphasized that since no trade could take place until the explorers had returned safely home, it was important that they receive as much aid as possible from the Shoshones to ensure positive results. Most important in this regard was the sale of horses to get them over the mountains and hasten their return. Cameahwait thanked them for the good words but was sorry that they did not have guns with them to trade. The Shoshones would wait patiently for the firearms.

The chief indicated that there were not sufficient horses to move the explorers' baggage to the mountains at this time. He promised to return to his village the next day and encourage his people to bring pack animals to their aid. The captains were pleased with the promises. Cameahwait told Clark that his name was "*Too-et-te-con'l*," meaning "Black Gun" and that his war name was "*Ka-me-ah-wah*," or "Come & Smoke." In fact, as a sign of friendship he gave Clark his war name.

Lewis confided that the council could not last too long, since "to keep indians in a good humour you must not fatiegue them with too much business at one time," so he turned from diplomacy to other matters. Hunters had killed four deer and a pronghorn, so a good portion of the meat was passed around. The captains asked Cameahwait to point out chiefs among them, and they awarded different-sized peace medals to those of varying ranks. Cameahwait received the largest one and also a uniform coat, a shirt, a pair of scarlet leggings, a twist of tobacco, and other small items. They also handed out paint, moccasins, awls, knives, beads, and magnifying glasses to Shoshones in attendance. All appeared pleased with the gifts and astonished at aspects of the party, particularly the white men, the canoes, Lewis's dog, Seaman, and York.

Earlier in the day Lewis described the meeting of Sacagawea with her people as "really affecting," particularly the encounter between Sacagawea and a Shoshone woman who had been captured with her by the Hidatsas but who had escaped and returned home. And though both captains noted it, they made little of the fact that Cameahwait was Sacagawea's brother. Indeed, the leaders gave greater attention to the benefits of her interpretive skills, which allowed significant sharing of information. Later Biddle expanded on this moment in his book and wrote an intimate account of the meeting between Sacagawea, her relatives, and her people:

> they had not gone more than a mile before captain Clarke saw Sacajawea, who was with her husband one hundred yards ahead, began to dance, and show every mark of the most extravagant joy, turning round him and pointing to several Indians, whom he now saw advancing on horseback, sucking her fingers at the same time

to indicate that they were of her native tribe. . . . A woman made her way through the crowd towards Sacajawea, and recognising each other, they embraced with the most tender affection. The meeting of these two young women had in it something peculiarly touching, not only in the ardent manner in which their feelings were expressed, but from the real interest of their situation. They had been companions in childhood, in the war with the Minnetarees [Hidatsas] they had both been taken prisoners in the same battle, they had shared and softened the rigours of their captivity, till one of them had escaped from the Minnetarees, with scarce a hope of ever seeing her friend relieved from the hands of her enemies. . . . After this the conference was to be opened, and glad of an opportunity of being able to converse more intelligibly, Sacajawea was sent for; she came into the tent, sat down, and was beginning to interpret, when in the person of Cameahwait she recognised her brother: she instantly jumped up, and ran and embraced him, throwing over him her blanket and weeping profusely: the chief was himself moved, though not in the same degree. After some conversation between them she resumed her seat, and attempted to interpret for us, but her new situation seemed to overpower her, and she was frequently interrupted by her tears. After the council was finished, the unfortunate woman learnt that all her family were dead except two brothers, one of whom was absent, and a son of her eldest sister, a small boy, who was immediately adopted by her.

In the evening the captains queried Cameahwait about the geography of the country and a way out of the mountains. The captains received a repetition of information that Lewis had obtained earlier, that is, an impossible passage by water and a very difficult one by land. The captains then agreed on a plan of action for the next several days. Clark was to select eleven men, carrying tools for making canoes, arms, and other necessary items, and set out for the Shoshone mountain camp in the morning. He was to take Charbonneau and Sacagawea with him, leaving them with the Shoshones, whom they were to persuade to come down to the forks with horses for the transfer of the explorers' baggage into the mountains. Clark was to proceed on with his eleven men, find a suitable place along a navigable river (if such existed), and begin making canoes for the voyage to the west. In the meantime Lewis would bring the party and its baggage to the Shoshone mountain camp. The captains calculated that by the time all was in place at that camp Clark would be able to report whether they would continue their journey by land or by water. If by land, then they would need to purchase all the horses the Shoshones would spare, and if by water, then to hire Indians to help carry supplies to the canoe-building point. Clark was to send a runner back to Lewis with news of conditions ahead as soon as he had made a clear determination. They apprised the party of their decisions. As he settled in for the night, Lewis mused that he was certain there was not much game ahead. For this and other reasons he was strongly convinced that they must get underway as quickly as possible.

AUGUST 18, 1805. While Clark was preparing to get underway, Lewis spread merchandise out to barter with the Shoshones for horses. Clark could use the animals to carry baggage on his excursion and others would serve to pack meat that hunters would bring in. He soon obtained three good horses, for which he gave a uniform coat, a pair on leggings, a few handkerchiefs, three knives, and other small items, all of which he estimated to be worth about twenty dollars. The Shoshones seemed pleased with the exchange. The enlisted men were able to get another horse for an old checked shirt, a pair of old leggings, and a knife. Whitehouse emphasized Shoshone poverty and stressed that they had few weapons, not even knives or tomahawks. Otherwise he found them "tollarably well dressed" and wearing beads and earrings. Lewis gave two horses to Clark, who got underway about ten o'clock. He was accompanied by the Shoshones except for two men and two women who stayed with Lewis and the main party. Before he left Clark gave a couple of his old coats to some lesser chiefs who were miffed that they had not received the same gifts as Cameahwait. Lewis also promised that if they significantly aided the explorers in their trip over the mountains he would give them more. They seemed satisfied with this promise. From this day until August 26, when Lewis quit writing, he typically ended his entries with a recounting of Clark's excursion activities, indicating that Lewis must have written these notes sometime after August 29, when the captains reunited.

Clark set out at about ten o'clock for his excursion. Only a few of the names of the eleven men he had with him can be confirmed. Gass was with the party, perhaps Pryor, and Collins, Colter, Cruzatte, Shannon, and Windsor. Moving through a mist of rain, cold weather steadily increased during the day. They generally followed Lewis's earlier route into the mountains but on a more direct line and camped near Red Butte, about eight miles west of Grant, Beaverhead County.

After Clark's departure with his Shoshone retinue, Lewis had all the baggage and stores opened and aired. He also began separating the goods into parcels for horseback travel. He had rawhide soaked in water to be cut into strips and used for lashing the packs and securing them to horses. Rain in the evening interrupted the packing work. In a departure from his usual routine of descriptive journal writing, Lewis ended the day with an introspective passage:

> This day I completed my thirty first year, and conceived that I had in all human probability now existed about half the period which I am to remain in this Sublunary world. I reflected that I had as yet done but little, very little indeed, to further the hapiness of the human race, or to advance the information of the succeeding generation. I viewed with regret the many hours I have spent in indolence, and now soarly feel the want of that information which those hours would have given me had they been judiciously expended. but since they are past and cannot be recalled, I dash from me the gloomy thought and resolved in future, to redouble my exertions and at least indeavour to promote those two primary objects of human existence, by giving them the aid of that portion of talents which nature and fortune have bestoed on me; or in future, to live for *mankind*, as I have heretofore lived *for myself.*

AUGUST 19, 1805. Up at daylight, Lewis sent three hunters in search of game. Others were detailed to make clothing, construct packsaddles, or load baggage. Checking their nets, the men found no fish but did catch a beaver in a trap. Later in the day they built a fishing net out of willow brush and hauled in a large number of trout (probably cutthroat) and a "kind of mullet," a northern sucker, which Lewis noted on August 3 but described more fully this day. Hunters returned in the evening with two deer.

Lewis set aside a good part of the day and several pages in his journal to write a lengthy essay on the Shoshones. He was struck by their poverty but amazed at their cheerfulness in the face of it. He found them fond of gambling, boastful, and egotistical, bragging of war deeds probably never performed, but also "frank, communicative, fair in dealing, generous with the little they possess, extreemly honest, and by no means beggarly." He emphasized that a chief's authority and influence were limited and were exerted by his power of persuasion and by the force of his character. The office was not hereditary and Lewis was unable to discover any ceremony of installation. Individualism seemed to reign. Lewis further characterized the Shoshones as "deminutive in stature, thick ankles, crooked legs, thick flat feet and in short but illy formed" and with a darker complexion than Mandans or Hidatsas. Both genders wore their hair loosely over their shoulders, while men occasionally braided theirs with leather thongs. Now, in mourning for losses to the Hidatsas, their hair was cut short. Cameahwait had his cut particularly close to his head. Men wore robes, leggings, shirts, shawls, and moccasins, while women dressed in robes, chemises, moccasins, and occasionally short leggings. Both men and women ornamented themselves with seashells, blue and white beads, and leather collars decorated with colored porcupine quills. They wore earrings but did not pierce their noses, nor did they tattoo themselves, although the women occasionally added a mark to their foreheads.

The captain counted about one hundred warriors among them and perhaps three times that number in women and children. In fact, he was surprised at the number of children in a tribe so pressed for resources. He saw few old persons and perceived that they were not treated with tenderness or respect. He observed male dominance in the family setting and concluded that husbands could dispose of their wives and fathers their daughters as desired. Multiple wives were not uncommon, and the women were not necessarily sisters, as was usual among other tribes. Wives were acquired by the presentation of horses or mules to the father, who often gave infant daughters to grown men. Girls stayed with their family until they reached puberty, or about thirteen or fourteen years of age, when they were presented to their husband as previously arranged along with a dowry sometimes equal to the suitor's initial offering. Lewis reported that Sacagawea had been thus promised before she was taken by the Hidatsas and before reaching puberty. Her appointed husband was still living among this band, had two other wives, and was nearly twice her age. He claimed her as his wife but relented because she had a child by another man.

Possession of horses was a man's point of pride. He would feel disgraced if he had to walk any distance but left his wife and daughters on foot if he had only enough horses to carry himself and his goods. In spite of recent losses of horses to the Hidatsas, Lewis counted about seven hundred with the band, with about forty colts, and a number of mules. Shoshone armaments included bows and arrows, lances, shields, and a type of club or cudgel ("pog-gar'-mag-gon'"). Lewis described them more fully on August 23. They fished principally for salmon using wears, gigs, and hooks. They snared wolves and foxes.

Shoshones were very lenient with their children, particularly their boys, who were given free rein in their actions. Disciplining boys by whipping, they thought, broke their spirits and was a punishment from which they would never recover. Women did not receive equal respect, and they were compelled "to perform every species of drudgery." Lewis cataloged a list of women's duties: collect wild plants, attend to horses, cook meals, dress skins, fashion clothes, collect wood and make fires, build lodges, and pack travel goods. "In short the man dose little else except attend his horses hunt and fish," he declared. The captain discerned that women's chastity was not highly regarded among the Shoshones and that husbands would readily offer their wives for the right price. But Lewis considered the Shoshones more respectful of their women in this regard than other Plains Indians he had met. The captains admonished the men to be careful in their encounters with Shoshone women so as not to cause jealousy. Lewis was not certain if his young men could comply with this request, as "some months abstanence have made

[them] very polite to those tawney damsels." Lewis had Sacagawea and Charbonneau inquire about venereal disease among the Shoshones and whether they had discovered a cure. He found them infected with it, but he could not learn of a remedy. Knowing that the Shoshones were so detached from Euro-American contact, he thought it strong proof that venereal diseases were native to the continent. He did concede that smallpox and other communicative diseases were acquired from tribes that had more consistent contact with the wider world and transmitted it to remote regions.

The Shoshones moved seasonally from their mountain fastnesses to the Missouri River valley. From the middle of May to the first of September they resided in the mountains with access to salmon-filled rivers, which formed their principal subsistence. As the fish died off, the tribe moved to the Missouri buffalo country, adapting Plains Indians' hunting practices. There they joined other bands or tribes in order to increase their numbers and add to their strength. Without these allies they would be subject to attacks by better equipped and more aggressive enemies. In fact, they delayed descent as long as possible, often living on meager resources rather than face annihilation on the plains. As soon as they acquired a good stock of dried meat they would retreat to the mountains. Lewis construed that the Shoshones were now preparing for such a transition to the Missouri and expected to meet allies at the Three Forks. The captain took an astronomical observation at noon and calculated the latitude as 44° 37′57.4″ N; the site of Camp Fortunate is approximately 44° 59′36″ N.

Clark continued his trek into the mountains with Shoshones. They followed Horse Prairie and Trail Creeks, Beaverhead County, Montana, to the dividing ridge at Lemhi Pass. Along the way Cameahwait pointed out a place where a number of his people had been killed a year earlier. Before reaching the pass they met an Indian with two mules, who offered one to Clark, who was on foot. It was a generous offer since mules were particularly valued. Lewis noted that a good mule could not be obtained for less than three or four horses. He thought their mules of superior quality. Clark gave the man a waistcoat in exchange for the mount. They camped on Pattee Creek, Lemhi County, Idaho.

AUGUST 20, 1805. Lewis sent out two hunters in the morning and put others to the tasks of the day before: making clothing and packing supplies. The captain walked the area to find a spot out of sight of Indians that could be used for a cache. Finding one, he set three men to digging while another he placed on watch with orders to signal the workers if any Indian came near. By evening the cache was completed and goods were ready to deposit, but packsaddles and other gear needed more attention. Lewis also prepared for the cache an assortment of medicines along with specimens of plants, minerals, and seeds that he had collected since the Great Falls. He regretted the absence of nails and boards for constructing packsaddles, so substituted leather thongs for the former and for the latter cut off the ends of oars and refashioned plank boxes. The goods in those boxes were transferred to rawhide sacks. This retrofitting provided the party with about twenty packsaddles. In the meantime, Shoshone women were engaged in making and repairing the explorers' moccasins. Lewis declared that the "Indians with us behave themselves extreemly well." In the evening the hunters returned empty-handed. Drouillard had tracked a beaver that got away with his trap and brought the animal back as the only game for the day. Goodrich caught several dozen trout.

Lewis returned to his lengthy essay on the Shoshones. The Shoshone robe was the same for both genders. It was draped over the shoulders and hung loosely to the knees; in cooler weather it was tied about the waist. It became a covering at bedtime. Although it was fashioned principally from the skins of pronghorns, bighorn sheep, or deer, the Indians preferred buffalo hides. In any case the hair was left on. Finished elk skins were more common in the summer. Lewis particularly admired the men's shirts, calling them a "commodious and decent garment" that hung nearly to the thigh and ended with the tail of the animal from which it was made. The hem was occasionally fringed and ornamented with porcupine quills. Collarless, a square opening admitted the head and neck while the sides were heavily fringed, as were the undersides of the upper portion of the sleeves. Shoulder straps displayed elaborate colored quill and bead work. Made from the same materials as the robe, the shirts were shorn of hair. Leggings were typically fashioned from the dressed skins of pronghorns. Fitting tightly about the legs, these too were fringed and highly decorated with quills along the sides and sometimes set off with tufts of hair of enemies killed in battle. They were fashioned in such a way as to cover buttocks and front, thus not requiring a breechcloth. Indeed, Lewis found them "more decent in concealing those parts than any nation on the Missouri."

Lewis declared the shawl ("tippet") of the Shoshones "the most eligant peice of Indian dress I ever saw." The collar, about four or five inches wide, was formed from an otter skin and ornamented with oyster shells. To it were attached from 100 to 250 little rolls of weasel ("ermine") skins. Sewed together with native grass used as a textile fiber, they were arranged so as to conceal the connections and give the furs their fullest display. At the ends of the tails small bundles of black fringe made for a beautiful contrast to the white fur. The finished piece hung nearly to the waist. Lewis thought the animals must be abundant and easily available to the Shoshones based on the number of shawls he had seen. In fact, Lewis was so enthralled with the piece that he wore one for his portrait made after the expedition by Charles B. J. F. de Saint-Mémin, perhaps the one he received from Cameahwait on August 16.

After an early start Clark encountered many Indians on his way to the Shoshone camp, relocated about four miles north of Tendoy, Lemhi County, Idaho, near where Kenney Creek joins the Lemhi River. Before reaching the camp Cameahwait requested a brief halt and a ceremonial smoke. On entering the camp Clark found that a lodge had been prepared for him that was superior to the brush lodges of the villagers. The captain participated in more ceremonies and explained the purposes of the explorers' mission. He also requested horses for Lewis at the forks to help him reach this point. Further, he related his objective to find a navigable river leading west and asked for a guide. Cameahwait received these words, probably through the interpretive skills of Sacagawea, Charbonneau, and a French speaker in the party. The Shoshones could give Clark and party only a few salmon and some dried chokecherries to eat. While a number of Shoshone men set out to hunt pronghorns, Clark enlisted an old man as a guide and set out on his mission to find a navigable river. The guide would later be identified as "Toby," and he would later lead the full party on their long excursion to the north. Clark did not have much luck getting information from the Shoshones about the route. He left Cruzatte to buy a horse and then catch up, and Charbonneau and Sacagawea to return to Lewis with the Indians. Making about eight miles along the Lemhi River, Clark and party camped in the vicinity of Baker, Lemhi County. Gass revealed that five Indians came along and spent the night.

AUGUST 21, 1805. A cold morning. One-quarter inch of ice formed in standing water in the canoes, wet deer skins were frozen stiff, and Lewis's ink froze in his pen. Frost covered the bottomlands, giving the appearance of new snow. In his weather diary, Lewis stated his astonishment that the temperature could climb 59° between sunrise and four o'clock without noticing the transition. The captain sent out hunters, hoping to get meat before the Shoshones arrived. He sent Drouillard separately by horse to hunt at Shoshone Cove. The remainder of the men continued in packing and preparing operations. By evening everything was ready for the trip or for depositing in the cache. After dark he had the items to be cached moved to the appointed spot and felt sure that the Shoshones were unaware of the activity. Without the return of hunters, the men ate some pork and corn that Lewis distributed.

Late in the evening Drouillard returned with a fawn he had killed and "a considerable quantity of Indian plunder." The "plunder" called for some explanation, which Lewis provided. While hunting in Shoshone Cove, Drouillard came upon an Indian camp with several Shoshones, among them a young man and three women. He spoke to them for a time in Indian sign language, then they collected their horses and saddled up. Drouillard likewise fetched his horse, which he had loosed to graze, leaving his gun unattended. When Drouillard had gone a distance after the animal, the young man seized his gun, and all galloped off toward the mountains. Drouillard took off after them. The horses of the two women wore out in the chase, and the young man returned to help them. Drouillard rode in and convinced them by signing that he had no intention of harming them but only wanted his gun. He caught the young man momentarily off guard, moved in beside him, and seized his gun. They wrestled with it a bit, then, the Indian realizing he would lose it, turned it over and emptied the gunpowder in the pan, making it briefly ineffective. Drouillard returned to the Indians' camp and gathered up the items that they had hastily abandoned, which amounted to some animal skins, dried serviceberries, chokecherry cakes, various roots, and some flint (probably obsidian). Lewis's description of the roots allows identification of them as edible valerian, bitterroot, and western spring beauty (see June 25, 1806). The captain learned that bitterroot was boiled for use and tried some, but found it "naucious to my pallate." He gave it to the Shoshones, and they ate it heartily. He preferred the western spring beauty root, which he thought tasted like Jerusalem artichoke. This was all reported in the next day's entry.

Lewis resumed his essay on the Shoshones. Usually made of deer, elk, or buffalo skins shorn of hair, the moccasins of men and women were much the same. In winter they made them with the hair on the inside, similar to those of the Mandans and Hidatsas. Occasionally they ornamented them with porcupine quills, while dressy ones had the skins and tails of skunks. Women's robes were similar to men's and worn in much the same way. Their chemises were loose and hung to the middle of the leg. A nursing women's garment had an opening at the sides. Sleeves were open underneath nearly to the elbow and then fringed and ornamented below with red cloth and beads. The opening provided easy release from the sleeve, which was thrown back over the shoulder. The upper front of the chemise was decorated with colored porcupine quills, and it was here that women displayed their finest work. A dressed leather belt secured it at the waist. Women's leggings, without fringe or decoration, reached to the knees and were secured by garters. Lewis had not seen beads displayed as necklaces on adults, but children sometimes worn them this way. Both men and women did wear them on earrings, mixed with triangular-shaped pieces of oyster shells . Men wove beads into their hair along with bird wings and tails. They particularly admired golden eagle feathers for their hair and also added them to the manes and tails of their horses. Neither gender pierced their noses. Seashells that they obtained in trade from friends and relatives to the west formed part of their clothing decorations.

Shoshone warriors, or those acknowledged as brave men, wore grizzly-bear-claw collars. The claws were decorated with beads near the point where the thick end was strung with leather thongs and tied about the neck. The killing of a grizzly bear was so esteemed by the Shoshones that it was equated with killing an enemy. Lewis allowed that given their inferior weapons, it must be a frightful undertaking. Elk antlers were generally worn around the neck by women and children. Sweetgrass, which grew abundantly in the area, was braided and also worn around the neck, usually by men. Another collar was formed of a leather thong and dogbane and covered with colored quills. Men wore headbands from fox or otter skins. Lewis considered Shoshone clothes "as descent and convenient as that of any nation of Indians I ever saw."

Clark renewed his trek with Indians for about five miles to their camp, where he smoked with them. Gass indicated that this was the place where Toby lived. It was on the Lemhi River, a few miles southeast of Salmon, Lemhi County, Idaho. Clark went to the place where they had erected a fishing weir across a channel of the Lemhi in a way to catch fish both coming and going. Lewis drew a picture of the device at his journal entry of this day, again indicating that he copied Clark's notes about his trip, at least after August 29, when the captains reunited. Lewis also wrote extensively about these weirs, but not from Clark's notes, which have no account of the device. Clark gave a brief description of the Shoshone fishing pole and gig. Returning to the Indian camp, Clark was offered salmon and chokecherries for the party. One Indian brought the captain a tomahawk (apparently Drouillard's) that he said he found, but which Clark thought he had stolen. Clark sent Collins and an Indian ahead to find Cruzatte, who had been left with the Shoshones at their main camp to purchase a horse but in coming forward had missed them and gone ahead. When Collins and Cruzatte returned they informed Clark that the Lemhi forked a few miles below and that the river coming in from the southwest was the larger of the two. In time Clark decided to call the Lemhi "East Fork of Lewis's River" and the other, the Salmon River, "West Fork of Lewis's River." After traveling about twenty miles altogether, Clark and party passed the fork and camped on the east side of the

Salmon River, a few miles north of Carmen, Lemhi County, below the mouth of Tower Creek.

Clark wrote his own brief account of the Shoshones, in part apparently taken from Lewis's more extensive writing but also based on his own observations: "Those Indians are mild in their disposition appear Sincere in their friendship, punctial, and decided. kind with what they have, to Spare. They are excessive pore, nothing but horses   there Enemies which are noumerous on account of there horses & Defenceless Situation, have Deprived them of tents and all the Small Conveniances of life. . . . The women are held Sacred and appear to have an equal Shere in all Conversation, which is not the Case in any othe nation I have Seen. their boeys & Girls are also admited to Speak except in Councils."

AUGUST 22, 1805. Lewis sent men to finish camouflaging the cache, which could not be done in the dark the previous night. Others were employed in making and repairing moccasins, while Whitehouse fashioned leather shirts and trousers ("overalls"). Before noon Charbonneau, Sacagawea, and Cameahwait arrived with about fifty men and unnumbered women and children. The Shoshones set up camp nearby. After they settled in Lewis called the chiefs and warriors together for a second counsel. He passed out more gifts, particularly to minor chiefs who had assisted in bringing help to Camp Fortunate, as promised. Having no meat Lewis did the best he could with beans and boiled corn. Cameahwait said he wished to live in a country that could provide such food, so Lewis promised that it would not be long before they could live outside the mountains and grow corn, beans, and squashes. Lewis gave the chief some dried squashes to eat, and Cameahwait declared them almost as good as the sugar that Sacagawea had given him.

Late in the evening the men dragged the river and brought in over five hundred fish, most of them trout. Among them Lewis found for the first time nearly a dozen of a "wh[i]te species of trout" and provided the first description of the steelhead trout. He distributed a good portion of the fish to the Shoshones and was able to purchase five good horses for about six dollars each in merchandise, which he considered reasonable. He deemed the Shoshones very orderly and honest. They borrowed knives, kettles, and other goods from the men and always returned them.

Clark and party continued down the Salmon River, passing mountains so steep that "it is incredible to describe." At their bases fallen rocks formed a solid bed of brown and white fragments for miles. The captain was viewing brown rocks that belonged to the Precambrian Belt Group of Tertiary Challis Volcanics. The white rocks are sandstones of the Carmen Formation and rhyolites of the Challis Volcanics. The Shoshone horses moved agilely along the cliffs and hillsides, not slowing the party and hardly missing a step. Passing Indian encampments, the party alarmed some of the occupants at North Fork Salmon River ("Fish Creek"), who were unprepared to meet white men. In fear, some offered gifts while others ran away. Toby was able to pacify them, and Clark gave them some small items. They reciprocated with berries and fish for the explorers. Nevertheless, a number of women and children cried in fear the whole time Clark remained. While there Gass noticed them making "a kind of bread" of sunflower seeds and lambsquarters, pounded and mixed with serviceberries. Along the way, the men attempted to gig fish but without success. A few miles beyond the mouth of the North Fork Salmon River they camped for the night on an island on the only wide, level spot they could find on the Salmon, in Lemhi County, Idaho. Clark learned (probably from Toby) that a road led up the North Fork and by following it (by way of Big Hole Pass) one could reach the Missouri. In his own naturalist studies Clark observed and described a "Bird of the wood pecker kind," one that bears his name, Clark's nutcracker.

AUGUST 23, 1805. With little to show for past hunts, Lewis sent two hunters out early with orders to widen their search to the southeast. Lewis knew that he had to provide for the Shoshones as well as his party, and his supplies of corn and flour were nearly depleted. He needed the meat of large game. In fact, he reminded Cameahwait of their situation, so the chief sent out his own hunters. Lewis got to watch one hunt in which Shoshones pursued a mule deer nearby, finally rode it down, and brought it to camp. It was the largest he had ever seen, almost as large as a doe elk. Shoshone hunters added another mule deer and two pronghorns. Lewis observed that the meat was not evenly divided among the Indians: some families received a large portion, others none. This was not customary for Indians, Lewis thought, so he asked Cameahwait about it. The chief explained that since meat was so scarce, hunters reserved it for themselves and their families. In the afternoon expedition hunters arrived with two mule deer and three common deer. Lewis distributed the meat of the three deer among families that appeared to have none.

Lewis had wanted to set out for the mountains this day, but Cameahwait asked him to delay, as more Shoshones were expected to arrive. He also wanted to bargain for more horses, but the Indians refused to do so until they had returned to their mountain camp. The captain had the canoes unplugged, weighted down with stones, and sunk in a nearby pond. The Shoshones promised him that they would not disturb the boats, and he considered them too lazy to take the trouble to raise them anyway. By three o'clock the other Shoshones arrived, about fifty men, women, and children. Lewis learned that they were actually on their way to the buffalo country, and those already at Camp Fortunate who were supposed to help Lewis into the mountains seemed anxious to join them. They said they would be back soon to assist in the transfer, but Lewis decided to set out in the morning with or without them. He sent two hunters ahead to Shoshone Cove to kill game, having them leave the meat on the route they would follow.

Returning to his Shoshone study, Lewis focused now on utensils, tools, and weapons. The Shoshones had few metal weapons or tools, only a few indifferent knives, some brass kettles, iron and brass armbands, a spear or two, and iron and brass arrow points, which they obtained from Crow Indians on the Yellowstone River in exchange for their horses. Bridle bits and stirrups they obtained from Spaniards. They often used flint in place of iron, particularly for knives and arrow points. They seemed to have no axes nor hatchets but used stone or elk antlers for cutting wood. Spoons were fashioned from horns of buffalo or bighorn sheep. The captain thought their bows unremarkable. Made of cedar or pine, or less often of elk or buffalo horn, they were similar to Plains Indians' bows, while the arrows were more slender than plains types.

Shoshone shields were made of buffalo hide, "perfectly arrow proof," and about 2½ feet in diameter. Painted with various figures, their edges were decorated with feathers and leather strips. The Shoshones made a ceremony of fashioning their shields, investing them with power in the rituals. After obtaining the hide of a two-year-old bull buffalo, a feast was prepared for older warriors and magicians ("jugglers"). A round hole was dug in which stones were placed and then heated to red hot. Water was thrown on the stones, creating a hot steam over which the green hide, flesh down, was stretched by those in attendance. As the hair loosened it was removed, and the hide was allowed to contract to the desired size. When removed from the steam it was repeatedly pounded over several days by barefooted stomping while feasting also continued. Finally, the old men and magicians declared it finished and able to withstand the arrows or even bullets of their enemies.

Mentioned earlier, Lewis described the "poggamoggon" (a kind of club or cudgel) as a weapon with a wooden handle covered with leather and about twenty-two inches in length. At the end a stone of about two pounds was wrapped in leather and attached to the handle, while a leather strap at the other end fit about the wrist. Able to inflict a serious blow, it was a formidable weapon. Shoshones also used a kind of armor formed of many layers of pronghorn skins united with glue and sand. It was sufficient to stop an arrow. Otter skins seemed the preferred article for making quivers, which were made deep enough to protect arrows from inclement weather. Blunt arrow points and a piece of seasoned wood were used to make fires. Lewis was astonished at how quickly a fire could be kindled using these primitive tools.

Clark and party advanced with great difficulty along the Salmon River. Large, sharp, loose rocks hindered them at every step. With little space between the rising hillsides and the river, the horses also found the going rough. Moreover, the previous night they had eaten the five salmon Indians had given them, and only a goose was killed this morning. At four miles they had to take the horses into the river. Soon they found the river confined to a very narrow channel, strewn with rapids and allowing no place to walk the horses. Clark decided to take Toby and three men on down the Salmon to see if it continued in this manner. He left the other eight men, including Gass and probably an ailing Pryor, to hunt and fish near the mouth of Dump Creek, Lemhi County, Idaho. The sick sergeant improved during the evening. For twelve miles Clark followed a small "wolf" path, which required clamoring over huge rocks to get ahead. Eventually they reached Indian ("Berry") Creek, Lemhi County, coming in from the north side. They halted there about two hours, caught some small fish, added some berries, and had lunch. The river to this point was one continual rapid, making passage by loaded boats impossible. Clark surmised that portaging around the rapids was equally out of the question given the inaccessibility of the terrain. He saw only great risk to men and horses. Moreover, feeding the party in this area would be extremely difficult with little but berries to sustain them and only a single bear track in sight. As he moved on he found the river even more twisting, demanding more crossings back and forth, a necessity that would add more danger for the whole party if they took this route.

Clark related the dreary and disheartening news about the way ahead: "the water runs with great violence from one rock to the other on each Side foaming & roreing thro rocks in every direction, So as to render the passage of any thing impossible. those rapids which I had Seen he said was Small & trifleing in comparrison to the rocks & rapids below, at no great distance & The Hills or mountains were not like those I had Seen but like the Side of a tree Streight up."

On reaching Squaw Creek, about a half mile above Indian Creek, Toby told Clark that by ascending it they would find a better road and miss a considerable bend in the Salmon River. Following it for several miles, they came to a flat about three miles above Shoup, Lemhi County, where on a ridge Clark got a view of the river for a great distance. Lewis gave this account of Clark's view of the Salmon River and Toby's commentary.

It continued it's rout to the North for many miles between high and perpendicular rocks, roling foaming and beating against innumerable rocks which crouded it's channel; that then it penetrated the mountain through a narrow gap leaving a perpendicular rock on either side as high as the top of the mountain which he beheld.

that the river here making a bend they could not see through the mountain, and as it was impossible to decend the river or clamber over that vast mountain covered with eternal snow, neither himself [Toby] nor any of his nation had ever been lower in this direction.

Clark was now perfectly satisfied with the impossibility of this route by water or by land. His little party returned to Squaw Creek and camped, probably near the mouth of Papoose Creek, which joins Squaw Creek, Lemhi County.

Reading later of Clark's difficult trek and negative report, Lewis penned his own discouragement in this day's entry: "the season is now far advanced to remain in these mountains as the Indians inform us we shall shortly have snow; the salmon have so far declined that they are themselves haistening from the country and not an animal of any discription is to be seen in this difficult part of the river larger than a pheasant or a squirrel and they not abundant; add to this that our stock of provision is now so low that it would not support us more than ten days."

AUGUST 24, 1805. As a group of Shoshones set out toward the Three Forks, Lewis noticed what he thought were spare horses among them. He asked Cameahwait to inquire whether they were willing to trade surplus ones. Answering affirmatively, they wanted to see what the captain had to offer, so he brought out battle-axes that were made at Fort Mandan. They were willing to bargain for these and also for expedition knives. The captain was able to obtain three horses and a mule. For each horse he gave an axe, a knife, a handkerchief, and a little paint. For the mule he had to add another knife and handkerchief, a shirt, and a pair of leggings. Even paying nearly double the price of a horse for the mule, Lewis considered it a "great acquisition." With horse trading ended, he directed the party to prepare to leave. The corps now had nine horses and a mule, plus two horses that Lewis had hired. He gave Charbonneau some items to use to purchase a horse for Sacagawea and the baby. With expedition pack animals loaded and Shoshone women carrying excess baggage on theirs, at noon the party started up Horse Prairie Creek, Beaverhead County, Montana, for Shoshone Cove and the mountains with their Indian companions. Viewing the heavily laded animals, perhaps twenty in all, Lewis decided that they would need more than twice their number of horses for the trip in the mountains. Nevertheless, he was elated: "I had now the inexpressible satisfaction to find myself once more under way with all my baggage and party." An obliging Shoshone offered Lewis his horse to ride, and the captain accepted so he could better manage the march.

Lewis's party was making good headway until a Shoshone rode up to tell the captain that one of the expedition's men was ill and could not go on. While the party halted Lewis rode back to find Weiser very sick. He sent Ordway, who had stayed with him, after water, while he administered essential oil of peppermint, a digestive stimulant to expel gas, and laudanum to relax him. Within half an hour Weiser was able to ride Lewis's horse, and they rejoined the party. In the meantime the Shoshones had unloaded their horses and turned them out to graze; the explorers followed their example. With daylight left but seeing that it was too late to regroup, Lewis had the party make camp near the mouth of Medicine Lodge Creek, a few miles east of Grant, Beaverhead County. The party had made barely six miles. Goodrich was able to get a few fish in the evening, but Drouillard returned from his hunt with nothing. With few provisions to share, Lewis asked Cameahwait to have those Shoshones who were not helping with the transfer go ahead the next day so he would not have to provide food for extra persons.

Returning to his discourse on the Shoshones, Lewis used Cameahwait's name as an example of how Indians went by different names during their lifetimes. The captain noted that Cameahwait meant "*one who never walks*," but the chief told Lewis that when he became a warrior he was known as "Too-et'-te-con'-e," meaning "*black gun*," as he told Clark on August 17. Lewis learned that personal names changed after important events in one's life, particularly valor in warfare. He heard that killing an enemy was less significant than taking his scalp, and if another removed the scalp or struck the dead person first the honor accrued to him. The act came to be called "counting coup." Lewis realized that among the Shoshones as well as other tribes bravery, especially in battle, was esteemed. To become distinguished in an Indian group, exemplary war deeds were imperative. Lewis found this to be such a strong and enduring principle that he knew he faced an incredible obstacle in establishing peace among warring tribes. Indeed, when he brought up the matter of peace to the chiefs at Fort Mandan, he found ready acceptance by those who had already obtained recognition, but a young man looking ahead asked how his nation would acquire chiefs without warfare. Lewis saw that he could conceive of no other way to elevate a person to leadership.

Lewis came back to Shoshone weapons. What few guns they had were used in warfare, while bows and arrows were intended for hunting. Being so rich in horses, the Shoshones distinguished themselves in their horse gear. Lewis described their halters and saddles. The former were made from flexible rawhide or woven from buffalo hair and left on the horse at all times. They were exceptionally long and trailed on the ground even when riding. Saddles were made of wood and covered with rawhide, much like Spanish ones. A piece of buffalo hide served as the saddle blanket and occasionally a hide was tossed over the saddle as well. Stirrups of wood and leather were used by older men and women. Young men frequently used nothing more than a small leather pad on the horse, secured by a rope around the animal. They often painted their horses, cut their ears into various designs, and decorated the manes and tails. Lewis considered them excellent horsemen who were extremely adept at roping. The captains saw few wild horses and those appeared to have been abandoned or runaways. With a nod to his naturalist work Lewis noted that the Shoshones possessed skins of the mountain goat, but so worn that he could not get a good impression of the animal. The captains never saw a live goat at close range.

Clark continued down Squaw Creek, Lemhi County, Idaho, with his three men and the guide, Toby. When they reached its mouth, Clark cut his name in a pine tree and the group had a breakfast of berries and rested about an hour. They followed the Salmon River to the point where the remainder of his detachment waited, arriving about four o'clock. Along the way Clark slipped and bruised his leg on a rock. Clark sat down to write Lewis and describe the alternatives facing the corps. He gave his co-commander three options. His favored plan was to procure as many horses as possible from the Shoshones (at least one per person), to hire Toby as a guide, and to proceed by land to a point where they could access a navigable stream to the Columbia River. They would have to depend on what game they could procure by hunting or use their horses for food as a last resort. His second plan was to divide the party, sending one to attempt the Salmon River by canoe with what provisions they had while the remainder went by land along the Salmon on horseback, taking provisions to the canoe party as they were able. Knowing the country as he did, Clark was certain this would not work. The final plan was equally untenable. One party would go north on horseback while another would descend to the Missouri, collect provisions, and follow the Sun River back into the mountains to reunite. Someone, probably Clark, crossed that scheme out as being entirely too impractical. He reiterated his attachment to the first plan. It was the one they would follow. Clark dispatched Colter with the message, then moved the party about two miles farther up the Salmon and made camp in Lemhi County, a few miles southwest of the mouth of the North Fork Salmon River. "Poor and uncomfortable enough, as we had nothing to eat and there is no game," wrote Gass.

AUGUST 25, 1805. Lewis with the main party and their Shoshone helpers set out at sunrise through Shoshone Cove toward the mountains. Ordway called it a "level Sandy plain or desert." Not following his request of the day before, those Shoshones not engaged in assisting the move stayed on. Riding on the edges of the column, they stirred up some pronghorns and chased them for a good distance, but killed none. While crossing Shoshone Cove, Frazer fired his musket at some ducks in a pond. The shot ricocheted off the water and came close to hitting Lewis. The captain learned that about six years earlier the Shoshones had suffered a severe defeat by the Hidatsas in the cove. After about seven miles they all halted for a meal. Expedition hunters came in with three deer, the greater part of which Lewis shared with the Shoshones.

During the lunch halt, Charbonneau casually remarked to Lewis that he expected they would meet the Shoshones the next day coming from their mountain camp on their way to the Missouri. This was alarming news to Lewis. Even more startling was the interpreter's report that Cameahwait had sent a few young men ahead to tell the tribe to meet him the next day and that the combined group would then leave the explorers and go to hunting grounds on the Missouri. Sacagawea gave Charbonneau this information early this morning, but he had waited until the afternoon to tell Lewis. Lewis was infuriated that Charbonneau did not have the sense to see the consequences of this plan. The captain let his anger out in sharp words to the man.

Lewis acted quickly to alter this plan and get the Shoshones to wait until the party was well into the mountains, and until the captains could acquire more horses. He called the chiefs together, passed the pipe, and then recounted their pledge to assist the party to the mountain camp. He said that if he had not received that promise he would have made other plans, which would mean that white traders would never come to them. He reminded them of his own promises, of their fulfillment, and of his generosity in sharing food. Lewis questioned their honor. He finished by saying that if they intended to keep their word, they must send men to counter the previous order and have the Shoshones at the mountain camp await their arrival. Two of the lesser chiefs agreed and said that it was done at Cameahwait's orders. Cameahwait, silent for a time, finally said that he was acting in behalf of his starving people, who needed the meat that the Missouri plains provided. He promised to countermand the order and sent a young man ahead for that purpose. Lewis gave the chief a handkerchief to seal the promise. The captain called together all the Shoshones who were assisting in the transfer and gave each a note that promised payment when they reached their destination for each horse that carried baggage. They seemed satisfied with the bargain. After reloading, the group moved along Horse Prairie Creek until late in the evening and made camp on Trail Creek, Beaverhead County, Montana, above its mouth with Horse Prairie Creek, making about fifteen miles. Hunters rejoined the party with another deer, which Lewis gave to women and children, but he went without supper himself.

Clark and party set out early and reached the small Shoshone camp at the North Fork Salmon River. They halted there for about an hour and received a little boiled salmon and some dried berries. This hardly satisfied the explorers' hunger, but Clark acknowledged that the Shoshones had given as much as they could spare and were kind in spite of being extremely poor. From there they continued their return trek by the same route they had followed on the outbound excursion. An ill Windsor slowed them a bit. Late in the evening they camped at the same place they had camped on August 21. Clark sent out hunters in several directions. A few Indians passed by and Toby was able to get a couple of salmon. By adding small fish the explorers caught and a beaver from Shannon, they made a good supper. One hunter saw a gang of elks on the opposite side of the river, but not in range. Other hunters had seen only a single deer and also brought in nothing.

AUGUST 26, 1805. On a cold morning Lewis found ice a quarter inch thick on open water in containers. The party collected the horses and set out at sunrise up Trail Creek, "with our big coats on and our fingers ackd with the Cold," as Ordway put it. They were soon at Lemhi Pass and the little rivulet they counted as the head of the Missouri River. They crossed the ridge into Idaho and halted to take lunch and graze the horses, where Lewis viewed "fine green grass" watered by a spring. Elsewhere he saw only dry grass scorched by the sun. The captain passed out a pint of corn to his Shoshone bearers, which they pounded and made into soup. He noticed that one woman had tarried behind and let someone else bring up her packhorses. When Lewis inquired about her, Cameahwait nonchalantly replied that she had stopped to give birth and would be along shortly. In about an hour she appeared with her newborn as if nothing out of the ordinary had happened. The incident set Lewis to speculating on birthing practices of the "aborigines of North America." He disparaged the idea that Indian women's ease of giving birth was the result of carrying heavy burdens, since here horses bore the heavy loads. He also belittled the notion that "pure and dry air, an elivated and cold country is unfavourable to childbirth," since these were the very conditions of the Shoshones. Lewis believed that the lack of difficulty was a "gift of nature." He claimed that it was a rare occurrence for a Shoshone woman to have problems in childbirth.

In fact, he had heard that Indian women who were impregnated by white men had a more difficult time. If true, he believed it supported his opinions.

Lewis turned to botanizing. He had noticed Shoshone women collecting the root of a "fennel." From his careful, detailed, and lengthy description, scientists have identified it as Gairdner's yampah, a plant new to science. He thought it had an anise flavor. In moist meadows he saw Nuttall sunflowers, and besides brief morphological notes, he offered a bit of ethnobotany. He described how Shoshones collected the plant's seeds, which were ripe at this time of year, and pounded and rubbed them between stones to create a cornmeal-like consistency. It was one of their favorite foods.

After lunch the party continued along their route to the Shoshone camp. Young men on horseback met them as they approached the village. Cameahwait had requested that they fire their weapons as they approached, so Lewis lined the men up and ordered a discharge of two rounds per person. The young Shoshones seemed pleased at the demonstration. Arriving at about six o'clock, Lewis found thirty-two brush lodges in the village, located about four miles north of Tendoy, Lemhi County, Idaho, where they had moved on August 20. He was led to a large tent lodge that had been prepared for him in the center of the encampment. Colter had arrived a short time earlier carrying Clark's letter describing the country ahead and advising a plan of action. Reading the report of the treacherous Salmon River, Lewis thought it foolish to consider taking the Salmon route, accepted Clark's plan for land travel, and began bargaining for horses for the trip. He informed Cameahwait of the decision and his need of twenty more horses. The chief appeared pessimistic when he reminded Lewis that Hidatsas had stolen many of their horses in the spring but said he hoped for the best from his people. When Lewis asked about a guide, Cameahwait recommended Clark's guide, Toby, as the most knowledgeable about the route. With that settled for the evening, Lewis had the fiddle brought out and dancing began, much to the delight of the Shoshones. A worried Lewis did not wholeheartedly join in the festivities since he "feared that the caprice of the indians might suddenly induce them to withhold their horses from us without which my hopes

of prosicuting my voyage to advantage was lost; however I determined to keep the indians in a good humour if possible, and to
loose no time in obtaining the necessary number of horses." This
ends Lewis's regular journal-keeping until January 1, 1806, except
for a few scattered entries before that date. There is no definitive
explanation for this gap.

A fine morning greeted Clark and his party but missing horses
detained them until nine o'clock, when Toby and four men found
the strays. For breakfast they had a little salmon and beaver left
over from the previous night. The captain sent three men ahead to
hunt. The remainder worked their way back to an Indian camp they
had visited on August 21, on the Lemhi River, a few miles southeast of Salmon, Lemhi County. Clark's party remained there until
August 29. The Shoshones gave them two salmon and one of the
men shot a salmon in the river. Hunters came in empty-handed,
so the few fish had to suffice for supper, or as Clark put it, "not one
mouthfull to eate until night." Clark believed that if the Shoshones
had any more to spare they would have shared it with the explorers. During the day the captain noticed great numbers of a "large
Black grass hopper," perhaps Mormon crickets, as well as jackrabbits and eastern short-horned lizards, but few birds except for possibly passenger pigeons.

AUGUST 27, 1805. Information for the main party is taken from the
journals of Ordway and Whitehouse, absent Lewis's writing. On
this beautiful morning the men hoisted a large flag, and Lewis gave
one to Cameahwait and another to a lesser chief. The captain settled with the women who had helped transport expedition baggage
to the village from Camp Fortunate and began to trade for horses.
Ordway observed that Shoshone women were mostly employed in
gathering and drying seeds for food. Nuttall sunflower seeds were
stone ground into meal. He reported that the Shoshones killed few
deer but relied largely on freshwater salmon, which they gigged with
poles. Expedition hunters brought in four deer and had gigged eight
or ten salmon weighing seven or eight pounds each. Lewis was able
to buy eight or nine horses from reluctant sellers demanding high
prices. Charbonneau bought one for a red cloak. Ordway calculated

that Lewis was getting most of them for about three or four dollars' worth of merchandise. He speculated that the price would be going up. In the evening the Shoshones entertained the party with a dance. While the men danced, women sang. Ordway found the Shoshones easygoing and contented with their lives. They loved to gamble and played the widespread Indian hand game that consisted of tossing a small object from one hand to the other, then wagering about which hand held the piece.

Clark sent most of the men out to hunt. A small salmon from one of the men and another from the Shoshones provided a scant breakfast. A young man came in from the Shoshone village to report that Lewis would join him about noon. Clark contrasted the contented Shoshones who were fishing at this spot with little to show for their efforts and no other game to sustain them with his own party, "hourly Complaining of their retched Situation" and worried about starving in this country without game. The captain was able to buy another two salmon from a Shoshone for supper, as the hunters brought in nothing but a fish. Lewis did not arrive.

AUGUST 28, 1805. About nine o'clock Lewis renewed his trading efforts. As predicted, the prices for horses went up. He was able to get five or six more, bringing the total to twenty-five, "most of them with sore backs," according to Ordway. Hunters brought in nothing; others were employed in making packsaddles. Two Shoshones from another band to the south arrived, so the chiefs and head men called a council in the evening for the arrivals.

As he had the day before, Clark reported frost on the ground. The Shoshones caught several salmon and gave the explorers a couple. Clark was able to purchase two more and that provided food for the day, since hunters were able to find nothing. He also bought some fish roe for three small fishhooks from "these pore but kind people." The captain allowed that salmon was pleasant enough but not very nourishing. The diet "weaken me verry fast and my flesh I find is declineing." About forty Indians passed by during the day. The captain sent Gass to the main party to find out if Lewis was coming. The sergeant returned late in the evening with a letter from Lewis explaining the situation of the main party. Lewis wanted

Clark to join him and help with the horses. He let Clark know that he had purchased twenty-two mounts. Gass called it twenty-three, perhaps counting Charbonneau's horse, and then added the two with the scouting party to make twenty-five total, confirming Ordway and Whitehouse's number. Clark had the men construct three packsaddles.

AUGUST 29, 1805. About eight o'clock a number of Shoshones of this band arrived who had been absent for some time. They had lost one man, who had been scalped, but they could not identify their attackers. Relatives wailed as they came into the village. Ordway and Whitehouse related Clark's dismal findings from his excursion. They emphasized the lack of game on his route. They also revealed the dilemma in getting horses: the Shoshones wanted guns, powder, and ammunition for the animals in order to defend themselves, but the corps had no weapons to spare. Nonetheless Lewis was able to obtain two more horses. The explorers planned to leave the next day with what horses they had, now twenty-seven in number, according to enlisted journalists.

More frost on the ground with winds from the south. Clark left Gass and another man and took the rest of the scouting party back to the main party at the Shoshone village. When the little party reached the place at about one o'clock they found Lewis busily engaged in trying to buy horses. Clark then made his pleas. He spoke of the advantage it would be to the Shoshones to help the explorers expedite their journey so they could return in order to assist them in the buffalo country. The captains still hoped to get a horse for each member of the party. Clark had to pay dearly for a horse he bought: a pistol, one hundred rounds of ammunition, gunpowder, and a knife. Since the animals were accustomed to frequent moves between pastures, Clark knew they would not thrive on grass they would find in the mountains. Moreover, they could not count on them being able to bear heavy loads. Clark was elated to find that hunters had killed two deer, since he had not eaten meat for the past eight days. Back at the temporary camp Gass got a lesson from the Shoshones in making fire with sticks. He wrote admiringly of their water-tight baskets.

AUGUST 30, 1805. At the main camp at the Shoshone village Clark accepted that they could buy no more horses. He had given his fusil (a type of musket) to one of his men who had sold his musket for a horse. Gass later estimated that the party's herd cost about $100 in goods. The captains had wanted one for each person in the party, thirty-three in all, but had to settle for twenty-nine horses (Ordway and Whitehouse count thirty), many of them young, unaccustomed to packs, and in poor condition. Unsatisfactory ones would serve as food, Clark conceded. With trading done and horses loaded, the corps got underway, now heading down the Lemhi River, Lemhi County, Idaho, led by Toby, who was accompanied by his three (or perhaps four) sons and another Shoshone. At the same time they headed north, the Shoshones left their village and moved toward hunting grounds on the Missouri River. The party made about twelve miles and camped on the Lemhi below Baker, Lemhi County, and short of the Shoshone fish weirs where Clark had stayed August 26–29. Gass said the main party camped within a mile of his place, where they found a good spot for grass. During the day a hunter got three deer.

AUGUST 31, 1805. Setting out at sunrise, the party soon reached Gass's camp at the fish weirs, collected Gass and his fellow soldier, bought some salmon from Shoshone fishers, and continued their route on the Lemhi River, Lemhi County, Idaho. They stopped three hours at Carmen ("Sammon") Creek on the Salmon River to let the horses graze. An Indian on horseback was surprised by the explorers and rushed ahead to warn a Shoshone camp of approaching enemies, but they must have met Clark on his earlier excursion, as they were not frightened. The party took a diversion at Tower Creek and followed a road upstream for about four miles, where they camped in Lemhi County, having made twenty-two miles by Clark's estimate. They found some old Indian lodges for shelter. Hunters killed a deer, a goose, and a grouse.

SEPTEMBER 1, 1805. The party got an early start over rugged hills where they passed the heads of numerous small streams on their cross-country trip to the North Fork Salmon River. Whitehouse

called one descent "nearly as Steep as the roof of a house." At one
sharp ascent a horse fell over but was not injured. Clark sent two
men ahead to purchase fish from Indians; they were able to purchase
about twenty-five pounds of dried salmon and fish roe. Hunters and
fishers brought in a deer and four salmon. Abundant serviceberries and chokecherries along the route provided a supplement. Gass
also observed creeping Oregon grape bushes. One man shot a bear
but was unable to retrieve it. In the afternoon, the party faced rain
and a little hail; the rain returned in the evening. Clark reported
that their Shoshone companions, except for Toby, left them. One
of Toby's sons came back the next day. Gass related that York's feet
became so sore that he took to a mount. The party camped near
the mouth of Hull Creek, a few miles south of Gibbonsville, Lemhi
County, Idaho, having made about twenty miles.

SEPTEMBER 2, 1805. Continuing along the North Fork Salmon
River, the party came to a large creek coming in from the east,
Dahlonega Creek, at Gibbonsville, Lemhi County, Idaho. Toby told
the captains that it led back to the Missouri River. This was probably the way Toby had told Clark about on August 22. Indeed, this
way would have taken them to another trail that would eventually
get them over the Continental Divide at Big Hole Pass and back
into Montana. By this route they also could have connected with
established Indian trails and followed a long but comparatively easy
road to the north. They chose the shorter, more direct route along
the North Fork Salmon. It was a disaster. Here they lost a convenient road and had to hack their way through a tangled mass under
tall trees and take rocky slopes with constant danger of horses slipping over the sides to their destruction. As it was several fell, some
turned over, and all were slipping and cutting their shoeless feet on
sharp rocks. One horse was crippled and two simply gave out. Ordway and Whitehouse called it a "dismal Swamp," and Whitehouse
deemed it "horrid bad going." Gass declared it "the worst road (if
road it can be called) that was ever travelled." Toby supplied some
encouragement when he promised a fair plain the next day. From
Dahlonega Creek they made a mere five to seven miles through this
risk-filled terrain to camp in the area of Quartz Creek, northwest of

Gibbonsville. It was late at night before the last of the party dragged in, leaving behind the load of the crippled horse. With no game in sight, only a few grouse were taken by hunters. Gass reported that one of Toby's sons rejoined the explorers.

SEPTEMBER 3, 1805. Clark declared the horses "very Stiff" this morning. Just as likely the members of the party were bone weary and aching as well. The captain sent two men back with a horse to retrieve the abandoned baggage of the crippled horse, which made the party late getting away. He described the country ahead on the North Fork Salmon much like the day before: thickly timbered, heavily overgrown, and with high hills and rocky slopes. Since the hills came to the water's edge the explorers were forced to the heights. Here again they faced an incredibly difficult route, with horses and explorers constantly in jeopardy on slippery slopes. Ordway was certain that one horse was nearly killed in a tumble. Clark summarized the day: "over emence hils and Some of the worst roade that ever horses passed." Nor were they able to find game to nourish themselves. Clark got four grouse and hunters brought in five more. Those with a little corn provided a meager supper. Some of the men threatened to kill a colt, Ordway reported. Gass lamented, "to add to our misfortunes we had a cold evening with rain," or as Whitehouse put it, "So we lay down and Slept, wet hungry and cold." Where the party camped and the route by which they got there remains a highly debated topic. Most likely they crossed the Continental Divide west of Lost Trail Pass and entered Ravalli County, Montana, where they camped in the Bitterroot Mountains. Clark called one accident a "great misfortune" when the party's last thermometer broke, but his weather table has the accident occurring on September 6.

SEPTEMBER 4, 1805. The party awoke to find everything soaked and frost on the ground. They delayed in order to get moccasins and baggage covers thawed but got underway by eight o'clock. Again, the route of the day is unclear. The party apparently ascended Saddle Mountain and came down into the valley between the forks of Camp Creek, Ravalli County, Montana. Ordway noted that snow came up over their moccasins and "our fingers aked with the cold." Clark was at the front of the column and saw several bighorn sheep. Hunters killed a most welcome deer ("to our great joy," exclaimed Gass), which the party eagerly ate. At the forks of Camp Creek they found a Salish ("Flat head" or "Tushepau") Indian village, which Clark estimated at thirty-three lodges, eighty men, and four hundred people. He also counted five hundred horses among them.

The Salish welcomed the explorers, draped white robes about them, and smoked in recognition of their arrival. A weary Clark confessed that the "Chiefs harangued untill late at night." The captains decided to camp here for a few days, rest the party, trade for horses, and query the Salish about the route ahead. The spot is in the valley now called Ross, or Ross's, Hole, east of Sula, Ravalli County, and probably on Camp Creek near its entrance into the East Fork Bitterroot River. The explorers' use of the term "Flathead" for these people is puzzling since the Salish did not practice head deformation like coastal peoples. "Tushepau" is a possible corruption of a Shoshone term for the tribe, meaning "people with shaved heads." The Salish, like the Shoshones, were rich in horses but poor in weapons; thus they faced the same threats from better-armed enemies, such as Blackfeet, when they descended to the Missouri valley on buffalo-hunting excursions. Clark found them friendly, well-dressed, stout, and of light complexion. Later Gass called them "the whitest Indians I ever saw." Ordway thought they spoke "as though they lisped or have a bur on their tongue. We suppose they are the welch Indians." The sergeant was recalling the myth that some interior Indians were descendants of a legendary Welsh traveler. The Salish are speakers of a branch of the Salishan language family.

SEPTEMBER 5, 1805. The corps' large flag was hoisted, and a council of chiefs and warriors was held in the morning. Passing through six languages with the help of a Shoshone boy among the Salish, Clark found it a time-consuming effort to make his points. Like Ordway the day before, Clark found Salish speech "a gugling kind of languaje" with a throaty sound. Giving their typical address, the captains explained the nature of their mission and their destination and asked about buying horses. Clark considered Salish horses excellent and during the day was able to purchase eleven and traded seven of their inferior animals for better ones. This made about forty horses in all for the corps. The captains acknowledged four chiefs and presented them medals as tokens of recognition. In return they were given a dressed badger skin, as well as otter and pronghorn skins. Having little food themselves, Salish women nonetheless gave the party berries and roots to eat. Ordway witnessed ravenous Indian dogs eat several of the party's moccasins. Clark noticed that Salish men braided their hair with otter skins intertwined and let it hang forward over their shoulders. Women wore loose shoulder dresses that hung to their ankles, tied off with a belt about their waist and covered with a robe. Their few ornaments were similar to those of the Shoshones. Ordway considered them "the likelyest and honestest we have seen." Clark learned another term for the tribe, "Eootelash-Shute," which may represent a Salish term for "those down below." He also heard that they had some 450 lodges among their several bands. Hunters brought in a deer or two.

SEPTEMBER 6, 1805. Clark was able to buy two more horses, then took a vocabulary of the Salish language as the men redistributed the loads on the extra horses. Ordway counted forty good packhorses and three colts. Four horses were left free of loads for hunters. It rained constantly until noon, so the party did not get underway until about two o'clock. At the same time the Salish set out to meet the Shoshones at the Three Forks of the Missouri. The explorers crossed the East Fork Bitterroot River, Ravalli County, Montana, soon after setting out, and then traveled cross-country to wade Cameron Creek coming in from the north. Apparently they climbed the heights and skirted Sula Peak on its north side, then turned west along Spring Gulch and descended to East Fork Bitterroot and followed it to their camp for the night near and across from Laird Creek. Clark gave the day's travel distance as ten miles. The captains ordered guards for the horses, fearing that the new arrivals might try to find their former owners or the Salish might sneak in to take some back. Hunters brought in two grouse only, so the party had to settle for those and a little corn and some berries for supper. From this date the party began calling the East Fork Bitterroot River, and later the

Bitterroot River "Clark's River"; as the captain said, "I was the first white man who ever wer on the waters of this river."

SEPTEMBER 7, 1805. A dark, drizzly day confronted the party as they followed the East Fork Bitterroot River to its junction with the West Fork, forming the Bitterroot River, at Conner, Ravalli County, Montana. Along the way they passed several creeks coming in from the west, mostly unnamed by the explorers but found on Clark's map of the area and noted in his course and distance table, including McCoy or Tin Cup, Rock, and Lost Horse Creeks. At noon, one of the hunters brought in two deer, which Gass called "a subject of much joy and congratulation." Whitehouse was more expansive: "Our party seemed revived at the success that the hunters had met with, however in all the hardship that they had yet undergone they never once complained, trusting to Providence & the Conduct of our Officers in all our difficulties." Clark saw two horses but judged them wild as elks. A hunter returned without his horse, which had broken loose during the night. Searching for a suitable spot, the party did not make camp until late in the evening, finally settling down southwest of Grantsdale, Ravalli County, on the east side of the Bitterroot, near the mouth of Sleeping Child Creek, having made about twenty-two miles.

SEPTEMBER 8, 1805. Several creeks joined the Bitterroot River from the east as the corps moved north, including the Skalkaho, Gird, Willow, Soft Rock, Birch, Spoon, and Willoughby. Two hunters joined the party at noon with an elk and a buck. The party delayed about two hours to let the horses graze. Later Drouillard got another deer and Clark a grouse. Clark judged the valley to be "pore Stoney land," while he looked up to the snow-clad mountains on each side. To the west was the Bitterroot Range and to the east, the Sapphire Mountains. The captain noticed the brittle prickly pear, which Lewis had identified on August 13. He was particularly aware of its "Strong Thorns," which punctured the explorers' feet. Along the way they found two lame mares and a colt. A cold, hard rain hit the explorers when they camped south of Stevensville, Ravalli County, Montana, on the east side of the Bitterroots, after traveling about twenty-three miles. They turned out the horses on good pasture.

SEPTEMBER 9, 1805. Lewis returned to writing this day and the next. Continuing on the Bitterroot River, which Lewis called the "Flathead," showing that they had not completely determined to name it after Clark, the captain described trees and plants along the watercourse. He mentioned ponderosa ("longleafed") pine, Engelmann spruce, probably Douglas fir ("resembleing the scotch furr"), and black ("narrow leafed") cottonwood along with honeysuckle and rosebushes in the underbrush. On September 2 he had collected trumpet honeysuckle, and on the return trip he took more specimens of this species new to science. Lewis commented on a "white gravley soil," which may be moderately saline soils of the Burnt Fork fan, clay layers in Tertiary sediments exposed in cutbanks, or the thin wash of light-colored Tertiary clay.

The party waited until noon for a breakfast of leftover meat from the day before and three geese taken by a hunter this morning. One of the hunters brought the captain a "redheaded woodpecker," which may have been that very bird or perhaps a pileated woodpecker. It was the first Lewis had seen since leaving Illinois. As they were setting out again, Drouillard arrived with two deer. Having crossed the Bitterroot to its west side, "as deep as the horses belleys," wrote Ordway, they reached a creek that Toby said would be the point of departure from the northbound Bitterroot. Moving about two miles above the creek's mouth, they set up camp on its south side and called it "Travellers rest," now Lolo Creek, near Lolo, Missoula County, Montana. They had come about twenty miles. The party remained here until September 11 and made it a stopover on the return route, June 30–July 3, 1806.

Querying Toby about the Bitterroot River, Lewis could not obtain conclusive information about the connections of rivers but learned that as far as the guide knew the stream continued north until it merged with another large river. Indeed, the Bitterroot meets the Clark Fork River just west of Missoula, Missoula County, and emerges as the Clark Fork from that point. Toby related that a person might pass to the Missouri valley in four days using that river's route to the east. In fact, Lewis would use a portion of the Clark Fork and then take a subsidiary stream, the Blackfoot River, as his return route to the Missouri in July 1806.

SEPTEMBER 10, 1805. With a fair morning, the captains dispatched all the hunters. They sent two of them north on the Bitterroot River to find the junction with the Clark Fork that Toby had told them about. Lewis surmised that the Clark Fork continued north along the Rocky Mountains until it turned west to join the Fraser ("Tachoo-chettessee") River. The captain was conflating information he had gained from the exploration of Alexander Mackenzie with his own exploration and the information of Toby and others. Mackenzie, as well as Jefferson, Lewis, and Clark, believed that the Tacoutche-Tesse was either the Columbia River itself or a major affluent. The Clark Fork beyond the Bitterroot River flows northwest to Lake Pend Oreille, in northern Idaho, and from there the Pend Oreille River flows into the Columbia.

In the evening one of the hunters, Colter, returned from his excursion up Lolo ("*travellers rest*") Creek with three "Flathead" Indians. These may have been Nez Perce Indians rather than Salish (Toby was unable to converse with them), whom the captains usually called "Flathead," but recent research has leaned toward their Salish identity. The captains seem to have used the Flathead term broadly for Rocky Mountain Indians. The Indians had been alarmed at Colter's arrival and prepared for battle, but he was able to calm them by laying down his gun and signing friendship. Now Toby also gained information from them by way of Indian sign language. The Indians were in pursuit of enemies, perhaps Shoshones, who had stolen twenty-three of their band's horses. Being in a hurry, two of them took a little boiled venison and some trinkets and went on their way. The other one decided to stay with the corps, act as a guide, and provide access to his tribe to the west. He tantalized the captains with stories of approaches to the sea and trips made there by his relatives, where they encountered white men. He said it would require six days' travel to reach his people. The captains took astronomical observations and gave the latitude of the Travelers' Rest campsite as 46° 48′28″ N; it is approximately 46° 44′58″ N. Hunters brought in four deer, a beaver, and three grouse.

SEPTEMBER 11, 1805. On this day Clark began a field journal in addition to his regular notebook; it is known as the elkskin-bound journal and extends to December 31. It is believed that he put his standard notebook aside during this time and copied his entries from the elkskin-bound journal into it at convenient times, perhaps even as late as the winter of 1805–6 at Fort Clatsop. Lewis discontinued his writing again. The loss of two horses delayed them from leaving Travelers' Rest until three in the afternoon. The party now began their westward journey on the Lolo Trail, named for some long-forgotten French Canadian trapper after the expedition's time. Clark called the "Flathead" Indian "restless," and he soon separated from the corps. The captains selected their four best hunters and sent them ahead, but they brought nothing in that evening. The party camped near Tevis and Woodman Creeks, Missoula County, Montana, at some old Indian lodges, having made about seven miles. Ordway called attention to pine trees whose bark had been peeled and noted that natives ate the inner part. Considered a survival resource today, it was an important food to mountain Indians. The sergeant and Whitehouse, perhaps copying one another, noticed a large tree painted with figures that also had a grizzly bear hide hanging from it. Whitehouse supposed it to be a place of worship.

SEPTEMBER 12, 1805. Getting an early start, the party soon passed Woodman Creek, Missoula County, Montana. Clark noticed an Indian encampment nearby with an Indian sweat lodge. Staying on the north side of Lolo Creek the party traveled through a thickly timbered country. The captain counted lodgepole ("Short leaf") pine, ponderosa ("long leaf") pine, Engelmann ("Spruce Pine") spruce, and probably Douglas fir. The captains faced the dilemma of whether to stay away from Lolo Creek and take a "most intolerable road" or follow the creek and fight the dense undergrowth and fallen timber. They took to higher ground on an Indian road with fewer obstructions but with numerous climbs, deep ravines, and no access to water. Coming down a steep hill they made camp east of

Lolo Hot Springs, Missoula County, having covered twenty-three miles by Clark's estimate, or over seventeen by Ordway's and White-house's counts. Reaching the spot about eight o'clock, Clark indicated that some did not arrive until ten. Ordway said they "could not find a level place to Sleep"; Clark declared, "party and horses much fatigued." They found little food for their horses. The captain noted the same phenomenon as Ordway had the day before: natives used the inner bark of pine trees as food. Hunters got perhaps four deer and a grouse.

SEPTEMBER 13, 1805. While Clark moved ahead with the party, Lewis stayed behind with four men to hunt his lost horse and a colt. Continuing on Lolo Creek, Clark came to Lolo Hot Springs, Missoula County, Montana. Natives had dammed up a spot for bathing, so the captain stuck his finger in the water and "at first could not bare it in a Second." Its temperature has been measured at 111°F. Nonetheless, several men drank the hot water and washed up a bit. Whitehouse said it had a sulfur taste. Clark described the rocks in the area as "hard Corse Grit." The springs emerge from granitic rocks of the Cretaceous-age Idaho batholith. With several roads leading away from the springs, Toby took a wrong turn and led the party about three miles "through intolerable rout," until they got back on the correct road for another four or five miles to reach a spot where the horses could graze and where the party could wait for Lewis and his men to catch up. Seeing Lolo Creek dammed up by beavers, Clark must have been disappointed that they saw none of the animals. After Lewis joined them, they climbed the heights, crossed from Montana into Idaho County, Idaho, near Lolo Pass in the Bitterroot Range, and went down Pack ("Glade") Creek to Packer Meadows. Here they camped at the lower end of the meadows, covering twelve miles by Clark's count. Hunters got a few grouse, and Shields a mule deer. Clark killed a distinctive grouse with a black tail; this could be either the female spruce grouse or the blue grouse.

SEPTEMBER 14, 1805. A cloudy day, with rain and hail in the valley and snow gathering on mountain tops. Leaving Packer Meadows the party crossed a high mountain and reached the joining of

Bushy Fork and Crooked Fork, Idaho County, Idaho. Clark listed trees along his route: Engelmann spruce, lodgepole ("pitch") pine, subalpine fir, and western larch ("Hackmatack & Tamerack"). From here they crossed Bushy Fork and again ascended a steep mountain, generally following Crooked Fork from a distance to the south and east for about nine miles. Passing through an "almost inaxcessible" route, Clark reported the fatigues of men and horses as exceedingly severe. They tripped over fallen logs and trudged up and down steep mountain paths. Toby had missed the main trail and took the party down toward the Lochsa River, which would force a difficult climb back to the ridge the next day and add miles to the distance covered by their aching limbs.

Coming down from the heights they encountered another stream joining Crooked Fork that they called "Colt Killed" or "Killed Colt" Creek, later White Sand Creek but now Colt Killed Creek, Idaho County. It was near here that a fat colt fell victim to their hunger, "which eat very well," in Ordway's opinion. It was that or Lewis's portable soup, not a favorite with the party. Beyond the confluence of the two creeks, the emerging stream is the Lochsa ("Flathead") River. The party camped on the north side of the Lochsa about two miles below Colt Killed Creek, at Powell Ranger Station, Idaho County, opposite a small island where they set their horses to graze. They made about seventeen miles on a difficult day. Two men who had gone after Lewis's horse rejoined the party with the stray. Clark declared the mountains they crossed this day much worse than those of the day before.

SEPTEMBER 15, 1805. Staying on the north side of the Lochsa River, Idaho County, Idaho, the party faced the usual terrain: steep inclines, rocky surfaces, and thick underbrush. At about four miles they found an Indian fishing place, probably Whitehouse Pond, named much later for the expedition member. Near here they located an Indian trail, left the river, and climbed northward toward the ridge to regain the Lolo Trail. Clark described the route up Wendover Ridge as "winding in every direction," because they had to "pass emence quantity of fallen timber." During this incredibly grueling climb, horses lost their footing, slipped, and rolled down the hill.

Some were severely injured, but to the explorers' amazement none were killed. It took nearly ten men to restore one from its accident. One packhorse carrying Clark's writing desk fell, turned over, and careened down the mountain for a considerable distance before crashing against a tree. The desk shattered, but unbelievably the horse seemed to shake it off. About halfway up Wendover Ridge the party located a spring where they stopped to refresh themselves and rest the horses. It took two hours to get everybody together at the spot. Even portable soup for lunch may have been welcomed. Struggling to the top, they reclaimed the Lolo Trail and established camp there after dark near the Idaho-Clearwater county line, having come about twelve miles. Finding no water, they settled for a spot with snowpack nearby. Two of the hurt horses gave out and had to be abandoned. The party dined on their hunters' two grouse, the last of the colt from the day before, and unpalatable portable soup. Nonetheless, Whitehouse wrote, "[we] lay down contented." Clark concluded, "the road as bad as it can possibly be to pass."

SEPTEMBER 16, 1805. Three hours before daylight it began to snow and continued all day. In fact, the snow was four inches deep by morning and by nightfall measured six to eight inches. Whitehouse noted that some of the men had no socks, so they wrapped rags around their bare feet before putting on their moccasins. Before the party set out Clark saw four mule deer but was unable to kill any, as his rifle misfired seven times. He was quite surprised at the malfunction since his weapon had never failed him this way before. He determined that the flint was loose. Without breakfast, the party set out. Clark took point position in the day's march in order to mark the way; he found it very difficult to find the road's faint traces. The party halted at the top of Spring Mountain, Idaho County, Idaho, to warm up, dry out, and let the horses rest and graze. They ate a little portable soup. Gass contended that the route was "over the most terrible mountains I ever beheld." Passing through a thickly timbered country, Clark counted eight "different kinds of pine." He was probably using the general term "pine" for conifer evergreens. The trees include lodgepole pine, Douglas fir, subalpine fir, Engelmann spruce, whitebark pine, grand fir, and mountain hemlock. At lower elevations trees would also include ponderosa pine, western white pine, and western redcedar. The captain was more plainspoken and graphic than ever about his discomfort and distress: "we are continually covered with Snow, I have been wet and as cold in every part as I ever was in my life, indeed I was at one time fearfull my feet would freeze in the thin mockersons which I wore . . . to describe the road of this day would be a repitition of yesterday excpt the Snow which made it much wors to proseed as we had in maney places to derect our Selves by the appearence of the rubbings of the [Indians'] Packs against the trees."

After taking a break in midafternoon, Clark decided to race ahead with another man to find a suitable spot for the party to camp. At six miles they located a likely place, built fires, and waited for their fellow explorers. The campground was less than Clark had hoped for, as it barely provided space for the party to lie down. It was getting dark before they all finally arrived, wet, cold, and worn out. Hunger gnawed at the travelers, so a second colt was sacrificed to their cravings. The camp was not far from a rock mound later called Indian Post Office (not mentioned by any expedition journalist), perhaps on Moon Creek, Idaho County, and about thirteen miles from their previous camp, by Clark's reckoning.

SEPTEMBER 17, 1805. During the night the horses had scattered, so the party kept busy rounding them up until one o'clock. It seems that the mare of the colt killed the day before led four other horses back to a previous point on the trail. Other pack animals were spread out in the mountains. Snow was falling as they finally got underway, and it dropped off trees as they passed, making them wet and miserable all day. Again, the journey was a repeat of the previous day: high hills, deep ditches, and a "road excessively bad," wrote Clark. Two horses stumbled and hurt themselves. The afternoon warmed up but made the trail a soggy, slippery mess. Hunters killed a few grouse along the way, but the birds were scant provisions for hungry explorers. One of the hunters chased a bear for a distance but was unable to get it. Another colt, Clark related, "being the most useless part of our Stock he fell a Prey to our appetites." After making twelve miles, they made camp near a spot Whitehouse called a

"Sinque hole full of water." A possible spot, now designated "Sinque Hole," is near Indian Grave Peak, Idaho County, Idaho, but like so many other points along the expedition route, the exact location is contested.

SEPTEMBER 18, 1805. Clark separated from the main party this morning with six men, including Reuben Field and Shields, to find a way out of the mountains and locate a place where they could hunt game and provide for the balance of the party when they caught up. Lewis took up writing again in order to record events of the trailing party in Clark's absence. He continued his journal until September 23, when they reunited, then stopped again. The timing of his renewed writing seems to lend weight to the idea that Lewis had indeed quit his journal writing (rather than losing his notes) during this period, only to pick it up during a period of separation. Lewis was ready to get the party underway early, but a negligent Willard had let his packhorse stray and delayed departure. Eventually Willard was sent on his own to collect the animal but was unsuccessful and rejoined the party late in the afternoon. Lewis's party made about eighteen miles and camped. The place is generally assumed to have been a few miles west of Bald Mountain, Idaho County, Idaho, but some researchers opt for a point considerably farther to the west, near Sherman Peak or even west of there at Sherman Saddle, Idaho County. What was left of the previous day's colt had been consumed at breakfast, so out came portable soup for supper, using melted snow to cook with. Lewis lamented that their guns were of little help in a country empty of game except for small grouse and squirrels.

Clark, perhaps writing after the expedition, penned the distress that convinced the captains to send him ahead: "The want of provisions together with the dificuely of passing those emence mountains dampened the Sprits of the party which induced us to resort to Some plan of reviving ther Sperits." Moving forward about twenty miles, Clark stood atop perhaps Sherman Peak and viewed open prairies beyond. It must have been discouraging when he wrote, "no Sign of deer and nothing else." Lightly loaded and proceeding at a fast pace, the leading party made about thirty-two miles and camped at Hungery Creek, a name retained from Clark's designation, near the mouth of Doubt Creek, Idaho County.

SEPTEMBER 19, 1805. With no stray horses to hunt down, the main party under Lewis set out shortly after sunrise. Six miles into the day they reached the edge of a ridge and "to our inexpressable joy discovered a large tract of Prairie country," Lewis excitedly wrote. Gass was even more exultant: "When this discovery was made there was as much joy and rejoicing among the corps, as happens among passengers at sea, who have experienced a dangerous and protracted voyage, when they first discover land on the long looked for coast." This may be the same prairie that Clark had seen from Sherman Peak the day before. With Toby telling them that they could reach the place by the next day, Lewis declared that the party's spirits were revived by the news that game could soon be had.

Climbing up and down the treacherous cliffs for another six miles, the party reached Clark's Hungery Creek, Idaho County, Idaho. Whitehouse said the trip "made the Sweat run off our horses & ourselves." Following Hungery Creek, they took a road on a narrow, rocky path along the edge of precipices that were extremely dangerous. Lewis emphasized that "in many places if ether man or horse were precipitated they would inevitably be dashed in pieces." In fact, Frazer's horse fell from the road at one point, rolled with its load nearly one hundred yards, and plunged into a creek. To their astonishment, when the horse was relieved of its load, it got up and within twenty minutes was on the road again with loaded packsaddles in place. Lewis called it "the most wonderful escape I ever witnessed." Coming eighteen miles over a very bad road, the party camped on Hungery Creek, a few miles beyond Clark's camp of the previous night. Worn out from the extreme labor of the day, the party had only portable soup to nourish them. In spite of their discouragement, Gass voiced a faintly optimistic note about "some hopes of getting soon out of this horrible mountainous dessert." Lewis observed dysentery among several men and also witnessed "brakings out, or irruptions of the Skin." The ailments were symptoms of early stages of malnutrition due to their poor and restricted diet.

Clark's leading party got an early start out of their Hungery Creek camp. They found a horse in a glade at about six miles, killed it, had a portion for breakfast, and then hung the remainder up for the main party. The spot is now memorialized as "Horsesteak Meadow." They followed Hungery Creek for some distance before leaving it to cross steep ridges and work their way over dense fallen timber. They reached Eldorado Creek, Idaho County, Idaho, followed it for a few miles, climbed another mountain, and at dusk made camp at Cedar Creek, near Lewis and Clark Grove, Idaho County, covering perhaps twenty-two miles. Along the way Clark killed two grouse and spotted a few other birds, including blue jays, black-shouldered kites, crows, ravens, and hawks, but these were limited.

SEPTEMBER 20, 1805. Taking up scientific work in spite of his arduous labors on the trail, Lewis wrote morphological descriptions of birds he had been seeing. The varied thrush was already known to science but was new to him. He wrote a longer description of it on January 31, 1806. He noted that it fed on the berries of the Cascade mountain-ash, which he had seen on September 2. Lewis collected specimens of this new shrub on September 2 and June 27, 1806. The captain also observed and described Steller's jay and perhaps the gray jay. He was impressed by their calls: "chă-ăh, chă-ăh" for Steller's jay and the "mewing of the cat" for the gray jay. He deemed Lewis's woodpecker common to the area. With only brief descriptions, he noted three grouse species, all unknown to science at the time: the blue grouse ("large black"), spruce grouse ("dark uniform color"), and the female spruce grouse ("brown and yellow"). He would return to these birds at his leisure during the winter at Fort Clatsop.

Lewis's main party was detained until ten o'clock by trouble with their horses. Breakfast was a handful or two of "peas," according to Ordway, perhaps hog peanuts carried from Fort Mandan, mixed with a little bear's oil or grease. "We finished the last morcil of it and proceeded on half Starved and very week," said the sergeant. At about two miles they found the remains of the horse that Clark had left for them. They halted a little later to relish the meat, "much to the comfort of our hungry stomachs," Lewis allowed. The captain also found a note from his fellow officer informing him that the advance party would proceed as quickly as possible to the prairies that both had seen from the heights. At lunch Lepage's packhorse was discovered missing, so Lewis sent the man back after it; he returned during the afternoon without it. Lewis considered it a serious loss since some valuable merchandise and all his winter clothing was aboard the animal, so he sent two of the best woodsmen after it and moved ahead with the rest of the party. Following the same hard road as Clark's party for about fourteen miles, they camped on a ridge between Dollar and Sixbit Creeks, Idaho County, Idaho.

Lewis ended the day's entry with more attention to scientific matters. He noticed that the soil became more fertile as they left the mountains and that a "gray free stone" appeared in many places along the trail. The short growing season and high rate of erosion in the mountains produces rocky material with little humus. And in forested areas the decomposition of evergreen needles creates an acidic condition in the soil. Both forces work against a soil that Lewis would count as fertile. His gray freestone is actually granitic rock of the Cretaceous-age Idaho batholith, which breaks off in slabs and shows up on the surface. The captain also enumerated several plant species, including mountain huckleberry (new to science), western trumpet honeysuckle, possibly Sitka alder (if so, then new to science), common snowberry ("honeysuckle which bears a white bury"), chokecherry, and western redcedar ("Arborvita").

Clark reported proceeding through a country "as ruged as usial." Coming over a low mountain the advance party reached the forks of Lolo and Eldorado Creeks, crossed the former, and followed it. On one of the expedition maps Clark called modern Lolo Creek "Collins Creek" for the expedition member. After facing more difficult terrain, they descended the mountains to Weippe Prairie, Clearwater County, Idaho, where they found a number of Indian lodges. Getting within a mile of the encampment, Clark met three Indian boys, who ran away. The captain was able to approach two of the boys, gave them ribbons, and sent them to their village. A man from the village came out to meet the party and then escorted them to the village, taking Clark to the lodge of the chief, who was absent with others on a war mission. Clark learned that the chief would not be back for two weeks or more. Only a few elderly men remained in the village, along with women and children. The women, although frightened, offered small pieces of buffalo meat, dried salmon, berries, and camas bread and soup. Clark reciprocated with a few trinkets. The captain then went with a chief to his village some two miles away on a branch of Jim Ford Creek about a mile southwest of the town of Weippe. Being treated kindly, Clark decided to spend the night here, after making about seventeen miles.

Clark's advance party had reached a village, or seasonal camp, of Nez Perces, whom the captains would call "Choppunish" or "Pierced Nose" Indians. The designation for the tribe comes from the French words for "pierced nose." Clark called the men large and portly and the women small and handsome. He thought they dressed similar to the Salish, but with more shells, beads, brass, and copper. He noticed a difference between the Nez Perce language and that of the Salish. The languages are indeed unrelated: Salish belongs to the Salishan language family, while Nez Perce is Sahaptian. Like other mountain tribes they were rich in horses and used them in periodic hunts to the Great Plains in search of buffalo. They were also noted horse breeders and may have developed the famed Appaloosa breed. They stored immense quantities of camas, which they gathered on prairies like Weippe and which formed an essential part of their diet. The captains referred to the plant, then new to science, by several terms, most often a form of "quamash," from the Nez Perce word for the plant from which the name "camas" derives. Clark briefly described one method the Nez Perces used to cook the plant. The captain diagnosed his illness of the evening as being brought on by eating too freely of fish and the roots.

SEPTEMBER 21, 1805. It was eleven o'clock before the main party got underway. Scattered horses again caused the delay. They left the ridge they had been moving along and came to the junction of Eldorado and Sixbit Creeks, Idaho County, Idaho. Following Clark's lead over the same difficult terrain, Lewis declared the road so obstructed with fallen timber that "it was almost impracticable to proceed in many places." They passed Clark's camp of September 19 on Cedar Creek and pushed on to Lolo Creek, which they followed on its west side for about one mile and established camp in Clearwater County, Idaho, having come about eleven miles. Here they found a small open space with adequate grazing for their horses. Remembering the delays of previous days, Lewis ordered the horses hobbled in order to get an early start the next day and reach the prairies ahead. Hunters got a few grouse and Lewis killed a coyote, which together with the balance of the horse meat from the day before and a few crayfish they had caught made a "hearty meal," according to Lewis. The captain confessed, however, that he did not know where the next meal was to be found. Indeed, he saw himself growing weak for want of food, and his men also complained of the lack.

Clark awoke to a beautiful morning and sent hunters for deer. The captain stayed with the chief in order not to arouse suspicions about their conduct. He also wanted to gather as much information "by signs" as possible about the river and country ahead. The Nez Perce informed him that a greater chief named "twisted hare" (Twisted Hair) was fishing nearby at a river (Clearwater) and that a little below his camp another river came in (North Fork Clearwater). At a great distance two large rivers merged (perhaps the Snake and Columbia) and beyond that was a great fall of water (probably Celilo Falls). He also told of "white people" who lived at the falls, from whom the Nez Perces acquired beads and brass. Clark was also visited by another chief, and they all shared a smoke. He gave trinkets to each man. The hunters returned empty-handed, so Clark tried to buy as much food as he could with the few items he had carried along.

At the same time that Clark and his five men set out to the Clearwater River and Twisted Hair's fishing camp, Reuben Field and an Indian started back up the trail to inform Lewis of the advance party's situation. Along the way Clark's party met a Nez Perce coming from the river and hired him to guide them to Twisted Hair for the price of one of the men's handkerchiefs. They did not reach the chief until nearly eleven o'clock at night. Clark called him "a Chearfull man with apparant Siencerity." The captain gave him an Indian peace medal, smoked with him until past midnight, then settled in for the night. The camp was on the Clearwater River, which the captains would eventually call "Kooskooskee," about one mile upriver from

Orofino, Clearwater County. Considering the country about him, Clark called it "a leavel rich butifull Pine Countrey badly watered, thinly timbered & covered with grass." He was describing an open parkland with widely scattered ponderosa pine trees interspersed with drought-tolerant grasses. The dominant grasses of the area are Idaho fescue and bluebunch wheatgrass.

SEPTEMBER 22, 1805. In spite of Lewis's clear instructions to hobble the horses, an unnamed negligent soldier did not comply and then pled ignorance of the order. Having the delay of rounding up horses again, the main party did not get underway until eleven thirty. Two and a half miles into the march Reuben Field from Clark's advance party met them. His supply of dried fish and camas bread was a welcome repast for the hungry explorers, who halted for the meal. Gass thought the camas bread tasted like pumpkin bread. Soon the two men who had gone back to find a lost horse on September 20 arrived. They had found the horse and regained its baggage but then lost the animal along with the horse they had taken with them. They carried the packhorse items to the camp on their backs. After another 7½ miles they arrived at the more easterly of the two Nez Perce villages on Jim Fork Creek, Weippe Prairie, southeast of the town of Weippe, Clearwater County, Idaho. Lewis penned his elation at the moment: "the pleasure I now felt in having tryumphed over the rocky Mountains and decending once more to a level and fertile country where there was every rational hope of finding a comfortable subsistence for myself and party can be more readily conceived than expressed, nor was the flattering prospect of the final success of the expedition less pleasing." Gass was more straightforward: "arrived in a fine large valley, clear of these dismal and horrible mountains." The party was met by several of the men but women and children fled. Lewis was surprised at their flight, since he thought Clark's presence for the last couple of days should have convinced them of the explorers' peaceful intentions. Lewis again ended his writing, not to return to his journal until another separation of the party on November 29.

Clark took a short tour of the river, then met Twisted Hair coming to him in a canoe from his island camp. He returned with the chief, had a brief visit, then joined his men. He sent out hunters but left one man in charge of their possessions while he turned back to the Nez Perce village with Twisted Hair and his son to meet Lewis. Along the way he met Shields, who had killed three deer. He took a small piece of the meat and exchanged his horse for the soldier's fresh one. That was a mistake, as the horse threw him three times and injured his hip slightly. The captains reunited in the evening. Remembering his own problems with Nez Perce fish and roots, Clark cautioned the newly arrived party to eat moderately. Clark learned that the Indians had stolen Reuben Field's shot pouch, knife, cleaning cloth, compass, and striking steel. The captains were hampered in recovering the items by the lack of an interpreter. All conversation came by way of sign language. Clark got Twisted Hair to draw a map of the river west from his camp. Using a white elk skin he delineated the Clearwater to where it was joined by the North Fork Clearwater River, then on to a large fork (probably the Snake River), which he said was "2 sleeps," then to a large river (probably the Columbia River) that was "5 sleeps." At the falls (perhaps Celilo) he placed a large establishment of white people and great numbers of Indians. Clark got a similar account from other Nez Perces.

SEPTEMBER 23, 1805. The captains assembled the chiefs and head men and informed them of their mission "to inculcate peace and good understanding between all the red people," wrote Clark. They gave peace medals to lesser chiefs, a flag and a shirt to Twisted Hair, and a knife, a handkerchief, and a small piece of tobacco to each. They also left a flag and handkerchief for the absent "grand Chief." The captains also brought out trade items to purchase raw and dried camas, camas bread, hawthorn berries, and dried fish. Red cloth and blue beads seemed the Nez Perces' most desired items. In the evening the party moved to the other Nez Perce village and bought as many items as their weakened horses could carry. Some of the men traded a few old tin canisters for dressed elk skins to make shirts. One unnamed soldier was left behind to find his horse. Lewis and two men were very sick this evening and Clark's hip was especially painful due to his falls from horseback the day before. Twisted Hair invited the captains into his lodge, which was nothing more than some pine bushes and bark. He presented dried salmon to eat. A little rain in the evening lasted about half an hour. The Nez Perces—who seemed to be constantly around the party all night—were engaged in storing food for the winter, particularly camas.

SEPTEMBER 24, 1805. Awakening to a fine morning, the captains sent Colter to find the horses lost in the mountains and to bring up some items left behind. By ten o'clock they were underway toward the Clearwater River by Clark's earlier route. A few Nez Perces tagged along. At sunset they reached the island where the captain had met Twisted Hair and made camp on another island, later China Island, about a mile upriver from Orofino, Clearwater County, Idaho. Lewis's illness had become severe; he was barely able to ride a gentle horse. Others were also so sick that they were laying by the roadside trying to regain their strength or were being helped onto horses to be brought to camp. Clark gave the sick men Rush's pills, a strong laxative, in the evening. The sick men may have been suffering the same illness Clark had experienced earlier, which was probably due to the radical change in diet and eating bacteria-laded salmon. In the evening hunters brought in four deer and two salmon.

SEPTEMBER 25, 1805. Illness had become a general complaint among the party, extending even to two hunters that Clark had left at the Clearwater on September 22 while he went to join the main party at the Nez Perce village. Perhaps because of their illness the men had killed only two bucks. Clark set out down the Clearwater River on horseback with Twisted Hair and two young men to find trees large enough to build canoes. Traveling along the north side, they crossed Orofino ("rock dam") Creek, Clearwater County, Idaho, and soon reached the North Fork Clearwater River (which eventually they called "Chopunnish"). They halted here for about an hour, during which time one of the young Nez Perce men gigged six salmon. Two of the fish were roasted and eaten right away. While here at the forks, two families came by in canoes that were loaded with their possessions. Clark admired the long, steady, and nearly square-sided craft. He then crossed to the south side of the Clearwater and made his way through thick bottomlands of pine trees.

He was gratified to see ponderosa pines large enough for the party's canoes. Clark then returned to the island camp to find Lewis sick as ever and several others (including Gass) also suffering. He apparently gave them Glauber salts, a laxative, and tartar emetic to induce vomiting. The man left behind on September 22 returned with his lost horse. He had hired some Nez Perces to find it. Hunters furnished only a small mountain lion and a grouse for the day.

SEPTEMBER 26, 1805. The corps decamped their island location, followed the Clearwater to its fork with the North Fork Clearwater, crossed to the south side, and established a spot that has come to be called Canoe Camp, a name not used by expedition writers. It was about five miles west of Orofino, Clearwater County, Idaho. They would remain here until October 7, building canoes for their journey to the coast. Axes were brought out and distributed to builders in anticipation of beginning work the next day. Clark found the axes too small for the canoe work but had to settle for the tools at hand. In addition to Lewis's illness, others had taken sick on the way to the new camp. Clark administered his usual purgative and emetic remedies. The captain confessed that he was feeling a little unwell himself. They purchased some fresh salmon from Nez Perces. Two chiefs and their families came with the party and camped nearby.

SEPTEMBER 27, 1805. All men who were able were divided into five work crews and set about felling pine trees for the canoes with their inadequate axes. Some workers became ill, and hunters also came in ailing. The hunt had been unsuccessful. Colter returned having found only one of the horses lost in the mountains along with a canister of shot, but he also brought half a deer; the rest he had given to Nez Perces. The meat went to feed the party's sick. Clark bought some fresh salmon, perhaps from several Indians who had come upriver to visit. Clark singled Lewis out as being very sick but counted nearly all the men unwell. Gass reported that he was feeling better. Toby seemed well enough and spent his time making flint arrowheads.

SEPTEMBER 28, 1805. Clark described the general bowel complaint as "a heaviness at the Stomach & Lax." Some of the early sufferers were getting better. The other universal complaint was directed at the limited diet of dried fish and camas roots. With nothing killed this day, it looked as if the unwelcome and insufficient victuals would continue. The party's best hunter, Drouillard, was also ailing. Those who were not on sick call tended to the canoes. Several visiting Indians left, but not before one old man informed Clark that he had been downriver, where he had seen white people at a fort and had gotten white beads. The captain discounted the story.

SEPTEMBER 29, 1805. Drouillard must have revived, at least enough to allow him to kill two deer, while Colter got another. Those who were able kept at the canoes. Lewis was still very sick, and others in the party had the ubiquitous stomach distress. A cool morning was followed by a warm afternoon.

SEPTEMBER 30, 1805. A fine morning brought good news of men recovering from the raging intestinal disorders of the last several days. In fact, Clark could report that everyone was at some kind of work except for two of the very sickest. Nevertheless, the men's illness hampered progress on the canoes. Ordway explained that "the party So weak that we git along Slow with the canoes."

OCTOBER 1, 1805. Clark had all baggage brought out to sort, dry, and inspect. He separated some favored trade items (particularly beads) in order to buy foodstuffs. They had little to eat except some dried fish, which the men complained had the same effect as a dose of salts, a laxative. The men continued building the canoes. They set fires on some of them to burn out the center and speed the work of creating dugout canoes. Gass called it "the Indian method." Several Indians came by for a visit, some perhaps from as far away as the Snake River. Hunters were again unsuccessful. Lewis's health was improving.

OCTOBER 2, 1805. Clark sent Frazer and Goodrich back to the nearest Nez Perce village with an Indian and six horses to purchase a supply of dried salmon and camas bread. "We have nothing to eate," he deplored, and what they had was giving them "violent pains in the bowels." The captains gave some gifts to the Indians who had visited the day before, including handkerchiefs, pieces of ribbons, and small bits of tobacco, and to two principal men, a ring and a brooch. Clark tried his hand at hunting in the hills but got nothing. Other hunters killed only a coyote. With no other option, they were compelled to kill one of the party's horses. They used a portion of the meat to make soup for the sick men. A hungry Ordway expressed that "we eat the meat as earnest as though it had been the best meat in the world."

OCTOBER 3, 1805. It was a fine, cool morning with an easterly wind. The party's general health was improving and work on the canoes progressing. The Indians who had been visiting Canoe Camp left early, but others came to take their place.

OCTOBER 4, 1805. Clark caught an Indian taking tobacco from the party's stash, and then the fellow was upset that the captain would not give him any. This was unusual, since the corps had little or no trouble with natives during their time with the Nez Perces. Three more Indians arrived, probably from the Snake River area. Frazer and Goodrich returned with dried fish and camas roots from their trading venture: not exactly the most welcome sight, since the food seemed to be the cause of their abdominal distresses. With the previous day's horse meat consumed, they were back to the distasteful fish and roots. Ordway and Whitehouse revealed that some of the men bought a "fat dog" and roasted the meat. Lewis was improving and even walked a bit.

OCTOBER 5, 1805. Counting thirty-eight horses, the captains had them collected and branded and the fore part of their mane cropped for identification. They may have marked the animals with Lewis's branding iron, which bore the inscription "U S Capt. M Lewis." It was discovered in the 1890s near The Dalles, Oregon, and is now in the possession of the Oregon Historical Society, Portland. The animals were delivered to Twisted Hair's relatives, who were to care for them in the party's absence. Clark gave the men some trinkets and got a promise they would safeguard the horses. Expedition men launched two canoes and found that one leaked a little. Lewis seemed to have relapsed and was not feeling as well this day. As usual, hunters brought in nothing, so the party turned again to fish and roots. Clark confessed that the captains' supper of boiled roots "filled us So full of wind, that we were Scercely able to Breathe all night." The captains' latitude reading at Canoe Camp was 46° 34′ 56.3″ N; it is nearer 46° 30′ 05″ N.

OCTOBER 6, 1805. During the night the men dug caches to bury items they would not take on the river voyage, primarily saddles. The pits also hid extra gunpowder and ammunition. All the canoes were finished in the evening and put in the river. Clark now began to experience the same stomach and bowel ailments as other members of the party. He credited his discomfort to a diet of fish and roots. The captain applied the name "*Kos kos kee*" to the Clearwater River, an uncertain Nez Perce term that the men usually spelled "Kooskooskee," or some close variant.

OCTOBER 7, 1805. In spite of his illness Clark had to manage preparations for the trip, or as he put it, "obliged to attend every thing." The canoes, four large and one small vessel, were loaded and ready to go. The party included its regular expedition members plus Toby and his son. Not to be found were the two chiefs who had volunteered to go with them. Twisted Hair was to be joined by Tetoharsky, whose name was not mentioned until May 4, 1806, and who is known only by references in expedition journals. Clark was missing his pipe tomahawk; nevertheless the party set out about three o'clock and during the twenty-mile trip encountered ten rapids. At other points they had to haul the canoes through shallow water, but mostly the river was deep and the current gentle, according to Clark. Whitehouse was less sanguine, reporting that waves were quite high at the rapids and that the boats took in quite a bit of water and struck several large rocks. In fact, the captains' canoe hit a sharp rock at one of the rapids and sprung a leak. They were able to repair the damage at camp that night near Lenore, Nez Perce

County, Idaho, opposite Jacks Creek ("Canister Run"). They light-
ened the load of one canoe by burying two canisters of gunpowder. The Nez Perces had told the captains that after they reached the
Snake River they would have no more river difficulties until they
came to the falls, probably Celilo Falls, Klickitat County, Washington, and Wasco County, Oregon.

OCTOBER 8, 1805. Part of the morning was spent reloading and
repairing canoes, but the party got underway by nine o'clock. They
passed fifteen rapids and four islands during the eighteen- to twenty-
one-mile trip, taking in some water with the high waves. Passing
a number of Indian encampments, they discovered Twisted Hair
and Tetoharsky at one and took them on board after a ceremonial
smoke. They also bought some salmon and a couple of dogs. Near
the entrance of the Potlatch River ("Colter's Creek," after the member of the party), Nez Perce County, Idaho, the canoe that Gass was
steering hit a rock, spun around, hit another, and almost turned
over. The impacts opened a gash on one side and the bottom, waves
washed over the side, and the boat began to fill with water. Swimmers escaped, but nonswimmers hung on to the canoe until help
arrived. Fortunately the river was only waist deep at this point.
Clark had one of the other canoes quickly unloaded, and together
with the small craft and an Indian canoe, got all the goods transferred, the nonswimmers saved, and the crippled canoe brought
to shore. Thompson was slightly injured, and all the boat's contents were soaked. A tomahawk and some small items were lost in
the confusion. The captains had everything laid out to dry and put
guards on watch to protect the merchandise. Although Clark cautioned that the Indians were likely to steal from the party, he conceded that they had been very helpful during the canoe's distress.
The party spent two nights here below the mouth of the Potlatch
River, a few miles from Spalding.

OCTOBER 9, 1805. A cool morning was followed by a cloudy day,
which was not conducive to drying wet articles from the previous
day's river accident. Repairing the injured canoe called for installing
braces inside and adding strength to the damaged sides and bottom.

Clark felt sure that it could be ready by the time its load had dried. He put Pryor, Gass, Gibson, and Joseph Field to work on it and by one o'clock it was finished. "Stronger than ever," bragged Clark. Since its baggage was still damp, the captains decided to spend another night on the Clearwater River. Lewis was still recovering from his illness. Busy with the canoe, the captains did not notice until later that Toby and his son had disappeared. They were last seen running up the river.

Lewis and Clark could not account for Toby's departure, especially since he had not been paid for his services. The captains asked Twisted Hair to send a man on horseback to retrieve them so Toby could be paid, but the chief declined. He said Nez Perces would steal whatever payment the Shoshone man received, so it would be a useless gesture. Clark understood, as he had had his spoon stolen during the day, but it was later returned. Indians flocked to the expedition camp and all "were very mery this after noon," dancing to the fiddle, Clark observed. The party witnessed one woman who appeared mad, singing and offering small gifts to persons and if refused, hissing and cutting herself "in a horid manner." Ordway offered a graphic description: "[she] took a Sharp flint from hir husband and cut both of hir arms in Sundry places So that the blood gushed out. She Scraped the blood in hir hand and Eat it, and So continued in this way about half an hour then fainted or went in to a fit Some time then came too by their puting water on hir and Seemed to take great care of hir." Whitehouse mentioned that Clark gave her some small gifts, which seemed to please her.

OCTOBER 10, 1805. On a fine morning the party was underway once more, getting off by seven o'clock. They soon passed Catholic Creek, joining the Clearwater River from the north, and some miles farther Lapwai ("Cottonwood") Creek coming in from the south at Spalding, Nez Perce County, Idaho. A few miles beyond they came to Hog Island and a series of very bad rapids. The party landed near a Nez Perce village of eight lodges to plan a strategy for proceeding. The first two canoes got through without trouble, but the third hung up on a rock, and it took the party an hour to get it loose. The boat came out of the incident almost unscathed, receiving only a small split on the side, which was quickly repaired. While there the captains purchased fish and dogs from local Indians, had lunch, and then moved on. A few miles farther on, they observed an Indian who had formed a pond, thrown heated rocks into the pool, and created a hot bath. Below that they reached the Snake River, with Lewiston, Nez Perce County, on its east side, and Clarkston, Asotin County, Washington, on the west. Initially calling it the "*Ki-moo-e-nem*" River, they later realized that it was the river they had first called "Lewis's" River, a combination of the Lemhi and Salmon. Only much later would they learn that the Snake was the dominant stream and the Lemhi-Salmon subordinate.

Gaining information from Nez Perces, Clark described tributaries of the Snake River and Indians along its course beyond their reach. The party set up camp on the north side of the Snake River above the mouth of the Clearwater, Whitman County, Washington, opposite Clarkston, making about twenty miles. Without a clear explanation, Clark mentioned that a misunderstanding had taken place between Charbonneau and the Field brothers. There may have been some joking that got out of hand. Food was still a constant source of concern. Clark confessed that "all the Party have greatly the advantage of me, in as much as they all relish the flesh of the dogs." Several of the animals were bought to add to the usual fare of fish and roots. Biddle added in his book that Nez Perces had great numbers of dogs but never ate them and that they ridiculed the explorers as "dog-eaters." The captain ended the day's entry with a short description of Nez Perce clothing, accessories, games, hunting, fishing, diseases, and customs. Admiring them in some ways, he found them generally to be selfish.

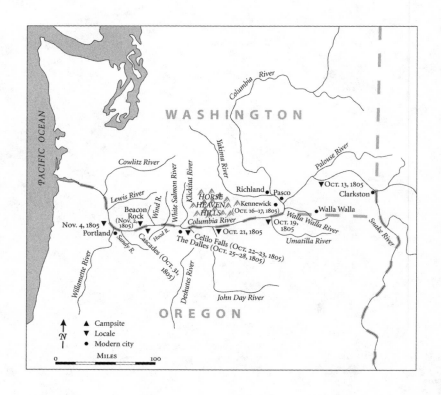

MAP 9. The expedition's route, October 11–November 14, 1805.

CHAPTER 8

Roll On Columbia

October 11–November 14, 1805

OCTOBER 11, 1805. Stopping at a Nez Perce village on the Snake River about six miles from their camp, the corps bought all the fish they could and seven dogs. Here Clark noted an uncommon sweat lodge. It was built underground, and a small hole at the top admitted hot stones, which occupants splashed with water to keep up steam and heat. Ordway noticed beads, trinkets, and copper kettles that must have come from white traders. At another village they purchased dried cherries, camas roots, five dogs, and a few fish. They ate some of the dogs for lunch. Gass noted that the meat-hungry men preferred dog to fish. Gass also mentioned "stones of a round smooth kind" in the river. These pebbles, cobbles, and boulder-sized stones from the confluence of the Snake and Clearwater Rivers to near the mouth of the Palouse were pre–Glacial Lake Missoula flood deposits. During the day, the party passed nine rapids by Clark's count, which Indians used for fishing spots and where they built houses to accommodate them while they fished. Now they were away hunting pronghorns. At a Nez Perce and Palouse fishing site, they camped near native lodges and got more dogs and fish. The site is below Almota Creek, in the vicinity of Almota, Whitman County, Washington, about thirty miles from the last camp. Near the lodges Clark found graveyards that were marked with upright sticks placed over the graves. When revisiting this place on May 6, 1806, Clark described the burials in more detail and somewhat differently.

OCTOBER 12, 1805. In the morning the explorers bought all the provisions that the natives would sell, then set out. After passing through swift water and bad rapids for thirty miles, the party reached one rapid that they had been told by natives was very difficult. They landed and decided to get a closer look at it before they attempted a run. They found it long and dangerous, with many turns and exposed rocks. One of the party's small canoes followed an Indian boat through, but the rest remained in camp to make the run the next day. Camp was in the vicinity of present Riparia, Whitman County, Washington. Now entering the Great Columbian Plain, Clark described a landscape quite dissimilar to the wooded mountains to the east. Nearly devoid of trees, the area offered little firewood. The dark, rugged stone that Clark noticed is Miocene-age basalt of the Columbia River Basalt Group.

OCTOBER 13, 1805. With an early morning rain, an overcast sky, and a hard wind from the southwest, the party delayed facing the rapids until nine or ten o'clock. Lewis led the first group through without incident, and then others followed, also without injury. Nonswimmers carried light articles and scientific instruments overland. Clark declared they would prefer to make portages around such obstacles, but the season was late, and they felt the pressure of time. They passed the Tucannon River ("Ki-moo-e-nimm," a Nez Perce term), Columbia County, Washington, and the Palouse River ("Drewyers River," for Drouillard), the boundary between Franklin and Whitman Counties, Washington. Less than ten miles east of the Palouse River the corps entered a region impacted by the Pleistocene-epoch Glacial Lake Missoula floods, and they would follow the floods' path to the sea. These colossal events would find expression in geologic descriptions of expedition writers. At the Palouse they found a great fishing area, with housing timbers piled up and a place established for depositing fish. After making about twenty-three miles, the corps camped in Franklin County opposite Ayer, Walla Walla County, Washington. Two Indians on horseback, perhaps Palouses, joined them, along with perhaps two others. Giving Sacagawea recognition without naming her, Clark wrote, "The wife of Shabono our interpetr we find reconsiles all the Indians, as to our friendly intentions a woman with a party of men is a token of peace."

OCTOBER 14, 1805. At about 2½ miles into the day the party passed a large rock they called "Ship Rock" due to its resemblance to a ship's hull, now called Monumental Rock, Walla Walla County, Washington, northeast of Magallon. It is an outcropping of the Lower Monumental Member of the Saddle Mountains Basalt. At twelve miles they reached a very bad rapid that two canoes negotiated with difficulty, while a third under Ordway and steered by Drouillard got stuck, started to fill, was vacated, and lost important articles to rushing water. Although other articles were saved, Clark lamented especially the loss of loose gunpowder. After the canoe was hauled to shore, powder in lead canisters was found safe, and other items could be redeemed. The men took wood from an Indian lodge for a fire to dry soaked articles. Clark explained that the corps tried not to take items belonging to Indians, even wood, but felt compelled here to break that rule since they found no other wood. Twisted Hair and Tetoharsky accepted the act. In fact, one of them had dived in the river and saved cargo of the endangered canoe as he swam to shore. The night's camp was on an island in Franklin and Walla Walla Counties, across and downriver from Burr Canyon and about fifteen miles from the last camp.

OCTOBER 15, 1805. Returning hunters reported no signs of wildlife. On an excursion Lewis viewed a range of mountains some sixty miles to the south and southeast. He probably saw part of the Blue Mountains of southeastern Washington and northeastern Oregon. Without getting the wet items from the day before completely dried out, the party set out at about two o'clock. They passed eleven islands and seven rapids during the twenty-mile day—some of them hazardous. In fact, the Nez Perce chiefs with the other Indians went ahead to a particularly bad rapid and waited to show the party a possible passage. All camped just above Fishhook Rapids ("bason Rapids" on an expedition map) in Franklin County, Washington. Again they found Indian shelters and appropriated boards for campfires. On examination, Clark found the rapids an even more serious impediment than the Indians had indicated. Shallow spots exposed large rocks through a channel that was crooked and narrow.

OCTOBER 16, 1805. They passed through Fishhook Rapids with only one accident. Bringing up the rear, Pryor's canoe hit a rock and got stuck, but three canoes came to the rescue, with the only injury being wetted articles. At fourteen miles they came to another bad rapid, perhaps present Five Mile Rapid, Franklin and Walla Walla Counties, Washington. This time they decided to unload the canoes and portage three-quarters of a mile. Five Indians, perhaps Palouses, came by land to meet the corps. The captains smoked with them, gave them tobacco, and sent them to inform villagers of the explorers' arrival. They had come about twenty-one miles.

Reaching the confluence of the Columbia and Snake Rivers, Clark saw a country devoid of timber on level plain in every direction except for the Horse Heaven Hills to the southwest, in Yakima and Benton Counties, Washington, and beyond them the Cascade Range. The party set up camp at a point between the Snake and Columbia in Franklin County, just southeast of Pasco and at the site of Sacajawea State Park. Here a great number of Indians came in, including the Nez Perce chiefs who had gone ahead to assure locals of the party's peaceful mission. One chief from a nearby village arrived at the head of two hundred men, singing, beating drums, and dancing. The procession formed a circle around the corps and continued in song and dance. The captains gave out gifts according to rank, presenting a principal chief, Cutssahnem, with a large peace metal, a shirt, and a handkerchief; others received lesser items. Here the party was meeting primarily two groups: Yakamas ("Chimnapams") and Wanapams ("Sokulks"). The Yakamas lived in the vicinity of Pasco on both sides of the Columbia and the Wanapams farther up the Columbia, on the west bank. Their belonging to the same Sahaptian language family as the Nez Perce chiefs made communication possible and contact friendly. Walla Walla, Umatilla, and Palouse Indians also lived in the area, all part of the Plateau Indians cultural group. With the help of Twisted Hair and Tetoharsky the explorers were able to procure seven dogs and some fish. One Indian gave Clark about twenty pounds of dried horse meat.

OCTOBER 17, 1805. The captains took lunar observations in the morning. Later an old chief with several men and women came to the camp with dogs and fish to sell. The party bought all the dogs they could get but declined the out-of-season salmon. Hunters went out in search of greater sage-grouse ("Pheasent," "Prairie Cock"), a species new to science, which Clark described as the size of a small turkey and which fed on grasshoppers and sagebrushes. Catching several, Gass deemed them "good eating." Lewis took a vocabulary of the Yakamas and Wanapams. The captains detected similarities between their languages and that of the Nez Perces, also Sahaptian speakers.

In the afternoon Clark took two men and a small canoe to examine the Columbia about ten miles above the camp. Along the way he saw numerous Indian mat lodges and everywhere salmon drying on scaffolds. Seeing an incredible number of fish dying in the rivers, Clark could not explain the phenomenon. He was seeing salmon at the end of their annual migration, having laid and fertilized their eggs. Natives took advantage of the situation to gather dying fish. The captain also wondered where the natives got the timber to build their scaffolds, since there were no trees of any consequence to be seen for miles. On his excursion Clark entered one of the mat lodges and found a man preparing food. He was splitting driftwood with an elk antler wedge and a carved stone mallet. He placed stones on a fire to heat, then transferred them to a basket of water containing a salmon. Laying the cooked fish on a woven platter, he offered Clark a serving, then prepared dishes for each explorer. Clark called the meal delicious. At a distance the captain was shown the Yakima ("Tape-ett") River, which meets the Columbia at modern Richland, Benton County, Washington, but being late he had to return to camp without reaching it. Clark was followed by three native canoes with about twenty men. He found the camp swarming with Indians while Lewis and the men dressed skins, mended clothes, and put weapons in order.

Having been with Indians much of the day, Clark put down his observations. Their lodges, framed by poles fifteen to sixty feet in length, were about six feet high, with flat roofs, of rectangular shape, and covered with large bulrush (tule) mats. Clark saw few horses, canoes being the main means of transportation. Although generally their clothes differed little from those of Indians he had met earlier along the Snake River, Clark noticed that the women of the Columbia did not wear ornamented, long skirts but rather tied leather pieces around their hips and drew them up under their legs in girdle fashion. The item was quite revealing. The captain also counted other clothing and ornaments and noted social customs. Labor seemed more equally shared by men and women than he had found among other Indians, and he did not find them practicing polygamy. He thought them comparatively content with life, mild and friendly, and venerating old age. The women tended toward corpulence and were short with broad faces, dark eyes, and coarse black hair. Eye problems were universal, with a degree of blindness among them. Bad teeth were also quite common, which Clark attributed to the grinding effect of sand in the native diet of fish and water plants. The most striking physical feature, however, was a flattened head, here encountered for the first time. Lower Columbian tribes placed infants in special cradles with an angled board that compressed the forehead and created the desired effect: a forehead broadly flattened from a front view and pointed upward when viewed from the side. This head deformation marked the person as a member of the group, was considered a sign of distinction, and was not allowed for slaves.

OCTOBER 18, 1805. The captains held a council with Indians who came to the camp, explained the purpose of their mission, and gave out gifts. Cutssahnem drew a map of the Columbia River above their location, identifying tribes living along it and streams that flowed into it. Clark incorporated the information on maps in his journals. The captains determined the latitude at the junction of the Snake and Columbia Rivers as 46° 15′13.9″ N; today it is closer to 46° 11′34″ N. Deciding that fish were out of season and provisions might be harder to come by along the way, the party stocked up. They purchased forty dogs using trinkets such as bells, thimbles, pins, wire, and beads for exchange. The Indians appeared satisfied with the bargain.

Everything being ready by noon, the corps set out again, still accompanied by Twisted Hair and Tetoharsky. Passing Indian villages of the now familiar mat lodges, all were amazed at the incredible number of dried and drying fish scaffolded along the shore. The "black rugid rocks" that Clark noticed are in the area of Wallula Gap and are mostly exposures of the Frenchman Springs Member of the Wanapum Basalt, a part of the Columbia River Basalt Group. Reaching the Walla Walla River, Walla Walla County, Washington, the party set up camp south of its entrance into the Columbia and short of the Washington-Oregon line, having come about twenty-one miles. The captains learned from their Nez Perce companions that the "great Chief of all the nations about" lived nearby and wanted the explorers to stay with him. Clark was a little perturbed that he had not gotten the information earlier, especially since the chief had wood to offer. The captain sent the Nez Perce men back to ask the chief to join them for the night. Late in the evening he came in with twenty of his tribesmen, offered mashed berries as a gift, and set up camp nearby. Clark may have seen Mount Hood of the Cascade Range, in Hood River County, Oregon, earlier in the day.

OCTOBER 19, 1805. Yelleppit, a chief of the Walla Wallas (or Walúu-lapams), with two or three other chiefs came into camp this morning, bringing fish. Clark characterized Yelleppit has "a bold handsom Indian, with a dignified countenance." He thought him to be about thirty-five years old, possibly five feet, eight inches tall, and well proportioned. Yelleppit wanted the party to linger a few days, but the captains promised a longer stay on the return trip (see April 27, 1806). The captains went through their practiced routine, expressing their desire for peace and handing out Indian peace metals and gifts to dignitaries. By nine o'clock the corps was on its way. A short distance beyond their camp, the party passed the modern border between Oregon and Washington. Indian villages along the shore and on islands had scaffolds loaded with drying salmon. The natives would often hide in their lodges at the sight of the explorers. Along the way Clark spotted Hat Rock, Umatilla County, Oregon, giving it the present name. The captain gave the feature recognition on his maps; it is an outcropping of the Pomona Member of the Saddle Mountains Basalt. Arriving at a very bad rapid, the party delayed and adjusted loads in the canoes while Clark went ahead to investigate the country.

Taking the two Nez Perce chiefs, Charbonneau, Sacagawea, and the baby with him, Clark found a high point to reconnoiter the river. From this position the captain thought he saw Mount St. Helens, but it was more likely Mount Adams, Yakima County, Washington. The party came on with difficulty but without accident. Clark visited one village of five lodges of perhaps Umatilla Indians, near present Plymouth, Benton County, Washington, with not a person in sight. These people may be the "Pish-quit-pahs" of April 25, 1806. When he entered one lodge he found thirty-two persons in great agitation, crying and wringing their hands in fear. They gained their composure when Clark offered small gifts and had the Nez Perce chiefs explain their peaceful intentions. The local Indians seemed to believe that the explorers "came from the clouds . . . and were not men." They were further pacified on seeing Sacagawea, and many joined an impromptu meeting as Lewis and the others arrived. Again without naming her, Clark acknowledged Sacagawea's important presence with the party: "the sight of This Indian woman, wife to one of our interprs. confirmed those people of our friendly intentions, as no woman ever accompanies a war party." Making thirty-six miles, the party camped, apparently at Blalock Island, in the vicinity of Irrigon, Morrow County, Oregon. A number of Indians, probably Umatillas and Cayuses, came into camp, passed the pipe with the captains, and enjoyed fiddle tunes by Cruzatte and Gibson. Clark described their clothes as similar to those seen earlier, except they were less modest. He noticed that the women's exposed breasts were large, pendulous, and illy shaped.

OCTOBER 20, 1805. After dog for breakfast, then a smoke with the principal Indian visitors (with perhaps another two hundred in the gathering), the party got underway. Rapids and huge black rocks of the Columbia River Basalt Group were soon choking the river. Clark noted the American white pelican on the wing and the double-crested cormorant on the river, while the enlisted men added crows and ravens. He killed two gulls and four mallards. Clark examined an Indian burial vault made of boards augmented by canoe parts. It rose about six feet off the ground and was sixty feet long and twelve feet wide. Inside he found numerous skeletons, and at one end a circle of human skulls on a mat. More recent remains were still wrapped in leather robes, awaiting decay and transfer to the main part of the vault. He also found baskets, bowls, robes, skins, utensils, and various trinkets. Outside he saw horse skeletons, which he thought were sacrificed for the dead. As they moved on, they encountered the familiar round of rapids, islands, lodges, and drying fish. The appearance of European trade goods increased as they moved toward the coast. After about forty-two miles they camped in the vicinity of present Roosevelt, Klickitat County, Washington, and found not a single stick of wood to make a cook fire.

OCTOBER 21, 1805. Still without wood, the explorers skipped breakfast and proceeded on. Passing several Indian villages, they stopped at a promising one and were able to get enough wood to cook breakfast. Called "Met-cow-wes" by the party, the Indians were probably Umatillas, but some sources suppose they were Methows. The party found them in Klickitat County, Washington, west of Roosevelt. They were similar in language, dress, and custom to the natives the explorers had lately been meeting. Clark noticed people wearing European clothes and carrying cloth blankets. The explorers were received with kindness and closely examined. Besides wood, the party purchased roots, fish, and acorns.

Every rapid now demanded careful inspection, and nonswimmers were sent to portage dangerous ones, while skilled boatmen navigated unpredictable passages. At the end of one particularly difficult rapid they reached the present John Day River, the boundary between Gilliam and Sherman Counties, Oregon, which the captains named for expedition member Lepage. Along the way Clark observed "large rocks Stringing into the river." The rocks are part of the middle Miocene Grande Ronde Basalt and Frenchman Springs Member of the Wanapum Basalt, both part of the Columbia River Basalt Group. The party camped in Klickitat County, in the vicinity of the modern John Day Dam, having made about forty-two miles. In the evening Collins gave the party a little beer that he had made from moldy camas bread obtained earlier from the Nez Perces.

OCTOBER 22, 1805. Within nine miles or so of leaving camp the explorers came to a large stream they eventually called "Towarnahiooks" (variously spelled), after a Chinookan term meaning "enemies," perhaps referring to Paiute Indians to the south. The Deschutes

River forms the line between Wasco and Sherman Counties, Oregon, where it reaches the Columbia. The party landed above the Deschutes so the captains could examine it. The two men soon separated, with Clark heading straight to the river while Lewis took a more circuitous route. While out, Lewis discovered a plant being harvested by natives; it was probably wapato, an important element of the Columbian diet. Along the way and heading back, Clark counted numerous Indian lodges and saw again a river filled with rapids, compressed channels, and obstructive rocks. The Indians were the captains' "E-nee-shurs" (variously spelled), the historic Teninos, a Sahaptian-speaking people.

About six miles beyond the Deschutes, they discovered the first pitch of their "Great Falls of the Columbia River," Celilo Falls, near Wishram, Klickitat County, Washington, and Celilo, Wasco County, now inundated by The Dalles Dam. The area was a great meeting place and trading site for Columbia Indians and a dividing line between Sahaptian and Chinookan language groups. On the north side the Wishram Indians exploited the vast resources of the Columbia River. The captains called them "Echelutes" (variously spelled), and along with the Wascos to the south they were the first Chinookan speakers the party encountered. Both were part of the Plateau Indians cultural group. The captains found a native guide to lead them to a spot where the party could safely make a portage. They chose a route on the Washington side and established camp at the modern city of Wishram near villages of Wishram Indians, after traveling about nineteen miles. They unloaded the canoes and brought the baggage to camp, assisted by locals with their horses. Clark observed narrow channels in the river revealing a "hard black rock." The route through Celilo Falls and the Short and Long Narrows (see below) is dominated by the Frenchman Springs Member of the Wanapum Basalt, but faulting in this area has also exposed the Priest Rapids Member of the Wanapum Basalt and the older Grande Ronde Basalt.

The explorers bought wood, fish, and a dog for supper from Wishrams, whom Ordway and Whitehouse thought were "verry troublesome about our Camp." Some of the party found a suitable channel for the canoes on the opposite side of the river, which required only a short portage for the boats. At the Wishram lodges Clark observed salmon "neetly preserved." The fish were thoroughly dried, then pounded with stones to a fine state before being placed in salmon-skin-lined baskets made of beargrass and bulrushes. After the baskets were secured, they were pressed down, then bundled into groups of twelve, weighing nearly one hundred pounds a stack. Preserved this way, the fish would be good for several years. Clark learned that the leaders of the villages were hunting, so no meeting was held. He noted that no Indians lived on the south side of the Columbia at this point because of fear of attacks by Paiutes ("Snakes"). The river provided a barrier of protection. Farther on they would find Wasco Indians on the south side.

OCTOBER 23, 1805. After an early breakfast, Clark led most of the men to the south side of the river above the falls and started portaging the canoes the 457 yards around the first barrier. From there it was in and out of the river, taking advantage of what seemed to work best, even lowering the boats by elkskin ropes at one drop. One canoe got loose when the rope broke, but Indians caught it as it whizzed by, forcing the captains to buy it back. Gass called it a terrifying place, with the river foaming through numerous channels obstructed by huge rocks. In all, the river dropped thirty-seven feet, eight inches over a distance of twelve hundred feet at the falls, by Clark's measurements. By three o'clock the work was done, with all the canoes safe at the Wishram camp. The men were not so lucky—they were covered with fleas (or perhaps lice), which they had picked up at an Indian camp at the head of the portage. They stripped naked during the work to keep the pests out of their clothes and more easily rid themselves of the nuisance. What Clark took for sea otters were probably harbor seals, a species new to science. He got a shot at one but could not recover it.

Twisted Hair and Tetoharsky, the Nez Perce chiefs, told the captains that they had learned that Indians in the next village intended to kill the party. Arms and ammunition were examined and put at ready. When the natives left them earlier than usual in the evening, it seemed to confirm the reports. The party kept their customary guard, but the Nez Perce chiefs appeared uneasy. A confident

Whitehouse bragged, "we are not afraid of them for we think we can drive three times our nomber." Since they could not get any good fish from the locals, some of the sick men who had stayed in camp purchased eight small, fat dogs. Clark thought most of the party had become fond of dog meat out of habit. Gass called it "a strong wholesome diet." The captains were struck by the design, beauty, and functionality of native canoes. Clark commented that "these Canoes are neeter made than any I have ever Seen and Calculated to ride the waves, and carry emence burthens." Lewis exchanged the party's smallest canoe for one of the Wishram variety. He had to add a hatchet and trinkets in the trade. The party remained at the Wishram camp of October 22.

OCTOBER 24, 1805. Twisted Hair and Tetoharsky's concerns carried over to this day, and they were ready to head home, particularly since they were out of their language range and of less value to the party. The captains convinced them to stay for two more days and help make peace with Indians below the falls. They also needed them to report threats by the locals. While Lewis and three men went across the river to view the falls, Clark set out downriver with the rest of the party. Within a little more than two miles, Clark reached the Short Narrows of the Columbia, where the river was constricted from a width of about two hundred yards to a narrow channel of forty-five yards for about one-quarter of a mile. In spite of what Clark described as a "horrid appearance of this agitated gut Swelling, boiling & whorling in every direction," he determined that Cruzatte's boatmanship could get them through. The captain sent all who could not swim to transport precious articles such as papers, guns, ammunition, and other valuables by land while the boats raced through. Indians perched on rocks to watch the spectacle, and "to [their] astonishment" (according to Clark) the party got safely through.

Below the Short Narrows Clark was surprised to see the first wooden structures they had encountered since leaving Illinois. The Wishram plankhouses were about thirty by twenty feet and sunk about six feet below the surface, with perhaps four feet rising aboveground. The roof's ridgepole was supported by three strong timbers, while corner posts held up the structure. The roof was covered with white cedar bark, while gables, eaves, and side walls were secured with split boards. Carpenter Gass called them "tolerably comfortable houses." Clark noticed small openings in the walls aboveground that he took as a place for shooting arrows at attacking forces. Three families typically occupied a house, with as much as half of the space given to the storage of dried fish. Inside Whitehouse saw copper teakettles, beads, and other manufactured items. He also saw a mixed-race child with fair skin and rosy color at one place. Nearby Clark counted 107 stacks of dried fish with a total weight he calculated at ten thousand pounds. The party camped below the Short Narrows in the vicinity of Horsethief Lake State Park, Klickitat County, Washington, near a village of Wishram Indians. In the evening a chief arrived at camp; he was presented with an Indian peace metal and other gifts, a council was held, Cruzatte played the violin, and the enlisted men danced, to the delight of the natives.

OCTOBER 25, 1805. Lewis and Clark walked to the spot that Indians told them was a very difficult point in the river. They had reached the third obstacle along this stretch of the Columbia, the Long Narrows, a channel about five miles in length that cuts through the easily eroded zone of the Priest Rapids Member of the Wanapum Basalt. Again, portaging the canoes seemed impossible, so they unloaded them, put the best boatmen aboard, and began the run through the "bad whorl & Suck" (as Clark put it). As before, Indians crowded the scene to view the show while shore-side men stood ready with ropes to rescue endangered men and boats. In spite of "Swelling and boiling in a most tremendious maner," the first three canoes got through without mishap, but the fourth took in water, while the fifth was slightly drenched. Clark sighed with relief after everyone came safely through the worst part. Everything was reloaded and the party set out. The unfortunate canoe of the last run now hit a rock and was in danger of foundering but escaped without damage.

The party landed when they saw Twisted Hair and Tetoharsky with an area chief and his entourage and smoked a friendly pipe. The unnamed chief appeared to be about fifty years of age and of pleasing appearance. He was presented with an Indian peace metal and probably heard the customary speeches. After a parting smoke Twisted Hair and Tetoharsky left the party on horses they had purchased from the passing Indians. The captains gave "our two faithful friends" some gifts as they separated. Moving on, the corps arrived at Mill ("Que-nett") Creek, at the modern city of The Dalles, Wasco County, Oregon, and formed a camp at a point of rocks that they eventually called "Fort Rock Camp," or the like. The captains considered it an ideal defensive location and a good base for hunting. Accordingly, Drouillard shot a deer and Clark, a goose, and the captain remarked, "Suped hartily on venison & goose." Here they would stay until the morning of October 28. Clark viewed "falls mountain," Mount Hood, again.

OCTOBER 26, 1805. Half a dozen men were sent hunting, while others laid out articles to air and dry or drew up the canoes and worked on repairing the rock-scarred hulls. Fleas, or more likely body lice, in the men's clothing were impossible to get rid of without stripping naked and killing the pests in the infested garments. They suffered much without a change of clothes. In the evening two chiefs and fifteen men came to camp from the opposite side in a small canoe and gave foodstuffs as gifts. The captains presented each chief with a small Indian peace metal, a red silk handkerchief, an armband, a knife, a painted pin, and a comb. They gave the son of one a tin gorget tied with ribbon. Cruzatte entertained them with his violin, and York danced to a lively tune—soon others joined in. The two chiefs and a few Indians spent the night. Ordway and Whitehouse observed the captains making language studies and comparisons. Hunters returned with five deer, four gray squirrels (a variety new to science), and a goose. Half of one deer was shared with the visitors. One of the guards caught a steelhead trout, which, when cooked in a little bear's oil, Clark declared "one of the most delicious fish I ever tasted." The hunters reported a rocky, broken country, thinly timbered with pine and white oak, but with elk and bear signs in the woods. High above whooping cranes flew in great numbers.

OCTOBER 27, 1805. Cryptically and without further explanation Clark wrote that he had "some words with Shabono [Charbonneau] our interpreter about his duty." Hunters brought in four deer, one pheasant (or grouse), and a squirrel. More Indians came in to join the others who had spent the night and to enjoy the hunters' catch. All was not well, however, as some Indians became perturbed at not being allowed to go through the party's goods that were exposed to dry. The captains took a vocabulary of the Indians in attendance, and Clark was struck by the difference in language between groups living within only six miles of one another. He noticed that the Teninos ("E-nee-shurs") at Celilo Falls were understood by those upriver, while the Wishram-Wascos ("E-che-lutes") at the narrows spoke a language similar to those downriver. Here he was seeing an extreme example of the language shift from Sahaptian to Chinookan at the falls and the narrows. Clark also identified a people he called "Che-luc-it-te-quars" (variously spelled), which was probably the term "he is pointing at him," rather than a name for an Indian group (see also April 14, 1806). Since all practiced head deformation on infants, he gave them the general denomination "Flathead Indians." The visiting chiefs departed in the evening.

OCTOBER 28, 1805. The party loaded the canoes and set out at about nine o'clock. At four miles they landed at a village of eight houses in Wasco County, Oregon, a few miles below The Dalles. Noting a difference in speech, Lewis took a vocabulary. Clark called the Indians "Chil-luckdit-te-quaws," as before, but they were probably the familiar Wishram-Wascos. The captain went into one house and saw a British musket, a cutlass, and brass teakettles. Manufactured trade goods were becoming ever more common as they neared the coast. They purchased five small dogs, dried berries, and "white bread made of roots" (probably camas). The dogs may have been spared another day when a hunter killed a deer. A heavy wind came up and forced the party into an unpleasant but safe camp in Wasco County, having made only a little over four miles. Indians soon arrived with items to sell. Clark marveled again at how easily they maneuvered their canoes through winds and waves. He also admired their craft work in decorating the boats and in making watertight baskets of western redcedar.

OCTOBER 29, 1805. Off at daylight, the party landed on the north side at a seven-house village in Klickitat County, Washington, a little above Lyle. Visiting the home of a chief they had met earlier, the explorers were greeted with pounded fish, camas bread, hazelnuts, and dried berries; they offered each woman of the house a brace of ribbons. Experiencing such a warm reception, the captains dubbed it "Friendly Village." While there the chief had his wife bring trophies of his war exploits, including a medicine bag containing fourteen fingers he had removed from slain enemies, then decorated. Clark was somewhat surprised—he was more accustomed to a display of scalps. As the chief returned the grisly items to their pouch, he exclaimed his war deeds to all. After breakfast, the party purchased twelve dogs, four sacks of fish, and some berries and proceeded on. At four miles they stopped at a village of eleven houses just below the Klickitat River, the party's "Cataract River" (variously spelled), named for its reputed falls. After a smoke and conversation, they bought four more dogs and set out again, soon passing a large, rocky island they called "Sepulchar [sepulcher] Island" from the number of burial vaults on it; it was later named Memaloose Island, Wasco County, Oregon. Farther on they passed Hood River, Hood River County, Oregon, the party's "River Labiche," after the expedition member, and noticed a country still rocky and broken but thicker in timber. They were also seeing houses on the south side for a change, perhaps those of White Salmon or Klickitat Indians, here given the generic name "Flatheads." On the opposite side was the White Salmon River ("Canoe Creek"), the dividing line between Klickitat and Skamania Counties, Washington. They camped in Skamania County, a little above the mouth of the Little White Salmon River, their "Little lake C," after traveling about thirty-five miles (or somewhat less, according to the enlisted writers).

OCTOBER 30, 1805. After a skimpy breakfast of venison, the party set out. They passed a number of small creeks cascading from the heights in the area of Viento, Hood River County, Oregon. Viewing stumps in the river, Clark conjectured that the Columbia had been damned at some point in the past. He was seeing the results of the Bonneville landslide that came from the north side and damned the river. The event created the Cascades of the Columbia and has been dated at around 1450 CE (see also April 14, 1806). They stopped for lunch at Wind River on the Washington side, in Skamania County, a stream the explorers called both "New Timbered River" and "Crusats River," after Cruzatte of the party. Viewing California condors ("Buzzard," now nearly extinct), Lewis shot one of the large birds but did not describe it until February 17, 1806. Clark noticed Oregon ash and red alders (new to science) growing together, trees that here reach their eastern-most distribution limits in southern Skamania and western Klickitat Counties. The captain also counted Sitka spruces, black cottonwoods, ponderosa pines, and Oregon white oaks in timbered lands on both sides of the river.

After traveling about fifteen miles they camped nearly opposite present Cascade Locks, Hood River County, on an island below Stevenson, Skamania County, until November 1. Just below the camp was the "Great Shute" (variously spelled), the Cascades of the Columbia, now inundated by Bonneville Dam. Clark took two men and followed an old Indian path about three miles to the cascades. He determined that they would have to carry their important items about 2½ miles around them, while the canoes could be dragged over rocks. In the meantime Lewis and five men had visited a nearby Chinookan Indian village, probably the "Y-eh-huh Village" of April 11, 1806. While the inhabitants were generous with nuts, berries, and fish, they provided little information. Ordway and Whitehouse reported that Indians came to the camp and said they thought that the explorers had "rained down out of the clouds." It was a wet, disagreeable evening, but they found ash wood made a tolerable fire.

OCTOBER 31, 1805. On this cloudy, rainy morning Clark set out along the north side of the river with Cruzatte (the most experienced waterman) and Joseph Field to examine the cascades and accompanying rapids. Taking Indian paths, they passed flea-infested, abandoned houses and cemeteries with highly decorated burial vaults. Clark found the vaults of uniform size, about eight feet square and five feet high, with sloping roofs to shed water and a door on the east side. Inside he saw bodies, sometimes as many as four side by side, wrapped in skins and tied off with cords of grass and stripped bark, all lying in an east-west orientation. Other vaults contained bones stacked four feet deep. Attached to the structures were all sorts of trinkets along with brass kettles, frying pans, seashells, and bits of cloth and hair. Carved human figures also adorned the vaults, some old and worn and nearly shapeless. On the surfaces, particularly the doors, were paintings of animals and geometric markings. While Clark called the work "curious ingraveing and Painting," Biddle with his interlinear comment supposed it to be "Hieroglyphics." Clark wondered if the carved figures were worshiped by the Indians. He thought not, since in native homes he had seen them treated more as ornaments than objects of adoration. Some vaults had rotted away and collapsed and were covered with moss.

After a few miles the captain sent Cruzatte back to examine a rapid while he and Field went on about ten miles from their camp to Beacon Rock, a late Pleistocene, eroded volcanic neck in Skamania County, Washington, just above the town of Skamania. It was called Castle Rock for many years, but Clark's name was restored in 1916. Along the way Clark and Field passed Bradford ("Brant") Island, Multnomah County, Oregon, and Hamilton ("Strawberry") Island, Skamania County. The rapids began at the island on which they were camped, where the channel narrowed, dropped off about twenty feet, and was littered with large and small rocks (the "Grand Shute"). Clark said the water surged "with great velocity forming [foaming?] & boiling in a most horriable manner." At a mile lower another large rapid stirred the river into huge waves. Farther on they found a path that the Indians used as a portage around a particularly difficult portion of the cascades. Rock slides from the north side added to obstructions in the river, which were again the result of the Bonneville landslide. With a long view downriver, Clark concluded that he had finally come to the end of the rapids at Beacon Rock and returned to camp. In fact, on one map Clark noted that the rapids ceased at the point between Bradford and Hamilton Islands, and there he witnessed the effects of tidewater. Although not reported by Clark, enlisted writers indicated that the men moved two canoes pass the cascades, making a portage of about a mile. At some points they used rollers, at other times they were in the water, hauling them over huge rocks. Gass called it "the most fatiguing business we have been engaged in for a long time." Indians came in during the evening and camped nearby.

NOVEMBER 1, 1805. The men began the work of taking the small canoe and all the baggage the 940 yards around the cascades along a slippery, rocky path. They noticed that the Indians of the previous night carried their loading the whole 2½ miles of the portage in order to avoid a second drop and rapids in the river. The remaining expedition canoes were brought along by sliding them on poles from rock to rock. Three canoes were badly damaged and demanded a delay for repairs, so the party camped in Skamania County, Washington, above Bonneville Dam and near the present community of Fort Rains, being only partway along the portage. Somehow the captains worked in time to take astronomical readings.

Clark visited a nearby Indian village and received nuts, berries, and dried fish from the villagers and bought one of their brimless hats. He noticed that the construction of the houses was very similar to those he had seen earlier. The structures, about thirty-five to fifty feet by thirty feet, housed from four to six families. Here again he saw carved human figures conspicuously placed about the interior that he supposed were ornaments rather than venerated objects. Seeing many manufactured objects in the households, Clark speculated that they came from trade with natives farther downriver and not directly from Europeans. The Indians' knowledge of Europeans he found scanty, and they had little of value to entice traders to the region—pounded fish, beargrass, and roots being their principal commodities. What they especially sought in trade were beads, particularly blue and white ones. While Clark thought the Indians of the Columbia valley generally healthy, he noticed tumors, weak eyesight, and bad teeth among them. He found them generally small, and the women homely, with swollen legs and thighs. He considered them dirty in the extreme, both in personal hygiene and in cooking practices. And he saw head deformation universally applied to women, and all with pierced noses.

NOVEMBER 2, 1805. Nonswimmers completed the remaining 1½-mile portage carrying about half the baggage, while boatmen ran the canoes through the rapids with the rest. The boats were only slightly damaged—one struck a rock and three others took in water. After all was secure the party rested a bit and took breakfast. They got around rapids at Hamilton Island, Skamania County, Washington, and passed Beacon Rock, also in Skamania County, where the Columbia widened and the thickly timbered Cascade Range appeared on both sides of the river. Just below Beacon Rock stood a village of nine houses called "Wah-chel-lah" by the party and occupied by Watlala Indians, an Upper Chinookan–language people, who belonged to the wider group from the area known as Cascades Indians. Beyond Beacon Rock Ordway and Whitehouse noticed waterfalls, perhaps Multnomah Falls and others, coming off the cliffs in Multnomah County, Oregon. Farther on they passed another landmark, Phoca Rock, Skamania County, named by Clark using the harbor seal's scientific name. It is composed of Grande Ronde Basalt and represents a compact landslide block that fell to its present location. The captain calculated its height at one hundred feet, when in fact it rises only thirty feet out of the river. From Beacon Rock they traveled on a smooth, gentle stream more than two miles wide. They had breached the last of the rapids. Having come over twenty miles from the cascades, the party camped near Crown Point, Multnomah County, Oregon, perhaps below at Rooster Rock. Among the waterfowl brought to camp by hunters was a lesser Canada goose, an expedition scientific discovery.

NOVEMBER 3, 1805. A thick fog detained the party until ten o'clock. Clark walked on the southern side of the river while the boats moved on. Along this route the corps passed the highest point on the Columbia reached by Lieutenant William Broughton of George Vancouver's expedition of 1792. They had returned, for the first time since April 1805, to a country previously explored by Europeans. Coming to a river he attempted to cross, Clark found it layered with quicksand and impassable, so he hailed a canoe and landed below its mouth. He and Lewis went up their "Quick Sand River," present Sandy River, Multnomah County, Oregon, about a mile and a half.

They found it much like the Missouri's Platte River in Nebraska with its coarse sands and strong current. The sand here is derived by erosion of mudflows (lahars) from Mount Hood, including material from a major eruption in 1781–82, and containing abundant volcanic ash. Opposite the Sandy they viewed the Washougal ("Seal") River, Clark County, Washington. Landing on "Diamond Island" (later Government and McGuire Islands, opposite Portland, Multnomah County), they decided to camp and send out hunters. Fowlers had their choice of birds: swans, geese, brants, cranes, storks, gulls, cormorants, and plovers. Harbor seals were also abundant. Clark said the party had a "Sumptious Supper" of the three swans, eight brants, and five ducks that hunters brought back. During the evening an Indian man, his wife, and three children came into camp with a "Snake" woman. Sacagawea tried to talk with her but without luck. The woman may have been a Paiute or from another Shoshonean-speaking tribe whose language was unfamiliar to Sacagawea.

NOVEMBER 4, 1805. The party set out at eight thirty under a cloudy sky on a cool morning. Overnight the tide rose eighteen inches. Shannon went ahead on foot to find game on the island where they camped. He met them at the other end with a buck. The main party landed at a village of twenty-five houses near the site of Portland International Airport, Multnomah County, Oregon. Clark counted about two hundred men in the village of the "Skil-loot nation," a term meaning "look (at him)," which the captain misinterpreted as an ethnonym. Often spelled "Skil-lute" by the party, they were Chinookan Watlalas. The captain saw fifty-two canoes banked at the village, some quite large. A villager they had met earlier invited them to his lodge and gave them roots that Clark described as "about the Size of a Small Irish potato which they roasted in the embers until they became Soft." Called "Wap-pa-to" by the natives and "Sa-git ti folia" or "common arrow head" by Clark, it was wapato (or arrowhead), an important foodstuff to Chinookans. The captains described it more fully on March 29, 1806. Clark liked its taste and bought four bushels of the tubers for the party. The captains also purchased two fat dogs. Seven miles farther on they reached a large island, their "Image Canoe Island," that is today separated into Hayden and Tomahawk Islands, Multnomah County. Clark went on shore in Clark County, Washington, to examine an open prairie where he found Oregon white oaks, Sitka spruces ("Spruce pine"), bigleaf maples (new to science and called an "Ash" in Clark's second entry), black cottonwoods, various pine trees, and Oregon crabapples (new to science). Here in the Columbia Gorge the party passed an ecological transition from the dry ponderosa pine–white oak forests on the east to the moist Douglas fir–western hemlock–Sitka spruce forests to the west.

Clark rejoined the main party at lunch and was visited by several canoes of Chinookans "dressed for the purpose" in scarlet and blue blankets, sailor's jackets, trousers, shirts, and hats of European make. The Indians carried war axes, bows and arrows, a sword, muskets, pistols, and tin flasks for gunpowder. They were fully vested in European trade goods. Clark found them "assumeing and disagreeable" but smoked with them and treated them civilly. In spite of that, someone stole the very pipe tomahawk that he had been smoking with them. The explorers searched every man but did not find the item. Incredibly, "one of those Scoundals" stole a blanket coat ("Cappoe," or capote) while they were looking for the tomahawk. Clark called them "thievishly inclined." They recovered the coat and the Indians departed, as did the corps. Farther on they met two canoes with a dozen men. The larger canoe was highly decorated with painted figures and wooden carvings of men and animals. Ordway and Whitehouse heard one of the Indians use English curse words. Weaving between islands, Sauvie ("Wappato") Island, Columbia County, Oregon, being the principal one, the party encountered numerous canoes of Chinookans, "constantly about us, and troublesom," and noted their villages in passing. Sauvie Island reaches from the Willamette River at Portland to the Lewis River at Clark County on the Washington side. Clark also got a view of Mount St. Helens, in Skamania County, Washington. After making twenty-nine miles, the party camped near the entrance of Salmon Creek, Clark County, not shown on expedition maps.

NOVEMBER 5, 1805. Kept awake by noisy waterfowl, the corps also contended with rain during the night until they rose. They set out early and made their way by Bachelor ("Green bryor," for the Pacific blackberry) Island, Clark County, Washington, viewing a channel of the Lewis River, the boundary between Clark and Cowlitz Counties, Washington, the party's "Chahwahnahiook" River, variously spelled. Here too they found a Cathlapotle ("Quathlapotle," variously spelled) Indian village of fourteen houses known as "Nahpooitle." The Cathlapotles were an Upper Chinookan–language group living on the Columbia and lower Lewis Rivers in Clark County. Seven canoes from the village came out to trade and stayed with the explorers for a few miles. The party halted for lunch at Deer Island, Columbia County, Oregon, so named by the party, as well as "E-lallar" Island, from the Chinookan term for deer. A few miles farther on they landed and made camp near Prescott, Columbia County, and opposite and below the Kalama River, Cowlitz County, having come over thirty miles. Clark calculated that they had come sixty miles in a direct route from the Sandy River, through a "fertill and a handsom valley . . . Crouded with Indians." Indeed, the area through which the corps now passed had one of the densest Indian populations in western North America. Less crowded this evening, Clark wrote that this was the first night they had been entirely clear of Indians since arriving on the Columbia River. Rain continued, even increased, falling on a party who were already wet, cold, and miserable.

NOVEMBER 6, 1805. Setting out early on a cool, rainy morning, the party soon passed the Cowlitz River at Kelso and Longview, Cowlitz County, Washington, the party's "Coweliskee" here interlined by Biddle and named by the captains on the return trip. Clark almost overlooked Mount Coffin, "a remarkable Knob" that he passed at Longview just downstream from the mouth of the Cowlitz River, but he mentioned it as an afterthought at the end of his journal entry. The captain thought it 80 feet high, but it is closer to 225 feet and was a volcanic unit of the Eocene-age Cowlitz Formation. It was quarried and leveled at the beginning of the twentieth century. Indians came out in canoes and traded their wapato, salmon, and beaver skins for five small fishhooks.

Continuing downriver, Clark viewed hills and mountains cov-

ered with western redcedars (*"Arber Vitea,"* "white Cedar"), California rhododendrons (*"red Loril"*), red alders (new to science),
and willows, while the undergrowth included rushes, bulrushes,
nettles, and cattails. In fact, the woods and undergrowth were so
thick that hunters had trouble making any headway and killed no
game. Passing one large island, Crims Island, Columbia County,
Clark may have named it "Fanny's" on the return trip in honor of
his sister Frances. Biddle inserted the name here. The party overtook two canoes of Indians going downriver to trade. One Indian
spoke a little English and said that a "Mr. Haley" traded with them
and was fond of one of the women in his canoe. "Haley" may have
been Captain Samuel Hill of Boston, skipper of the brig *Lydia*, who
came to the area in April or July 1806 after the corps had left. Coming about twenty-nine miles, they had difficulty finding a level spot
to camp but eventually moved enough rocks to create a suitable
space in southwestern Wahkiakum County, Washington, on the
point later called Cape Horn and near the upper end of Puget ("Sturgeon") Island. Here they built large fires and tried to dry their wet
clothes and bedding and kill the fleas they collected at every Indian
village they visited.

NOVEMBER 7, 1805. Thick fog and heavy clouds blocked the explorers' view but did not deter them from setting out about eight o'clock
along the rugged, hilly northern shoreline. Passing modern Puget
Island, the party met two canoes of Indians, who guided them to
their small village of four houses. These Wahkiakums traded fish,
wapato, dogs, and otter skins for fishhooks. Living on the north
side of the Columbia in the area of present Wahkiakum County,
Washington, they shared the culture of Chinookan people generally but were most closely associated with their cross-stream neighbors, the Cathlamets. Clark compared the Wahkiakums to their
upriver neighbors. He noticed differences in their language (essentially a form of Upper Chinook) and house architecture but similarities in their canoe styles and the men's clothing. The women's
attire differed enough to demand more attention and greater space
in Clark's journal, particularly a piece he called a "petticoat" made
from softened bark strands of the western redcedar. When stand-

ing the garment modestly covered the wearer, but otherwise it was quite revealing. He found the Wahkiakums short, ill-shaped, and bearing the familiar flattened foreheads, while Whitehouse characterized them as dirty and indolent.

After an hour or so of trading and resting, the party set out again, guided by a native dressed in a sailor's outfit who proved his worth in navigating them around islands and into the main channel. From a nearby island other Wahkiakums canoed out from their seasonal camps to trade their usual items of animal skins, wapato, and fish. Farther on the party landed at another village of seven houses near present Skamokawa, where they bought fish, wapato, and a dog. Clark also purchased two beaver skins to make a robe to replace his rotting one. From here the island-strewn river widened considerably and mountainous country continued on either side. After traveling thirty-four miles the explorers had difficulty finding a suitable camp along the rocky shore until they discovered a place large enough to accommodate them near a prominent rock column. In the evening Indians who had come with them from Skamokawa were caught stealing and were evicted from camp. Later one of the manned canoes that had separated from the main party in the morning's fog rejoined the main group. It was here at present Pillar Rock that Clark penned his famous phrase, "*Ocian in view*! O! the joy." The anticipation was real, but not the sighting. The captain was actually seeing the broad estuary of the Columbia.

NOVEMBER 8, 1805. More clouds, rain, and wind greeted the explorers in the morning. They continued along the northern shore, observing Cathlamet Bay on the southern side. Passing two villages, they stopped at a third, flea-infested one and were overtaken by three Indians in a canoe wanting to sell salmon to the party. Moving on, the explorers hugged the shoreline and turned into Grays Bay, called "Shallow Bay" by the party, and had lunch, after which they took advantage of the outgoing tide to pull them toward the coast. But the river's swells made progress difficult at best and dangerous to the point of foolishness. Moreover, Reuben Field, Weiser, McNeal, and Sacagawea were suffering greatly from seasickness. The captains therefore thought it prudent to set up camp early, even at this unwelcome spot of unlevel terrain, small space, and salty water near Frankfort, Pacific County, Washington. Gass estimated that a straight line to here from their previous camp would be nine miles, but their distance around the bay to this point was more like twenty. A straight shot in unsteady canoes would have been suicidal. During the evening the captains conjectured on the possibility of Euro-American trading stations in the vicinity but thought it more likely that trading vessels came in at regular intervals, as was the case.

NOVEMBER 9, 1805. High tides moved in upon the party's camp but did not overtake them as they clamored toward high ground. The canoes, however, began to fill with water, so the men hastily unloaded the boats and were able to save them all. Stuck in their cramped camp until the afternoon, the explorers were exposed to the elements and then got drenched as the flood tide returned with heavy winds and huge waves. More rain and high tides added to the misery, as did the southwest winds, which brought more water on the soaked explorers. A rising tide in the afternoon carried floating trees of enormous size to shore and endangered the canoes again; all hands worked frantically in the adverse situation to save the stricken vessels. Adding to their misery, diarrhea plagued some of the party due to the use of salt water, since fresh water was not to be found. In spite of all the unpleasantness or perhaps to cheer himself, Clark declared the party upbeat and anxious to proceed.

NOVEMBER 10, 1805. It rained as usual during the night and into the morning, but the wind lulled enough to encourage the party to load the canoes and set out. They made a good ten miles, maneuvering in and out of coves and niches, before the wind rose up and forced them back two miles to find a suitable landing space. Settled in on a pile of drift logs, they unloaded the canoes and waited for the winds to abate and the river to settle. When all appeared calm they quickly reloaded the boats and moved ahead, only to be pushed back by high waves to another unsteady situation on drift logs below a steep cliff with barely enough room for all. Making only about ten miles, at least here they found fresh water from a rivulet. The spot is east of the modern town of Megler, Pacific County, Washington, in the vicinity of Cliff Point, where they remained until November 12. This locale, along with the nearby next camp, is called "Dismal Nitch" after Clark's term for the combined area. He defined their miserable situation this way on November 15: "this dismal nitch where we have been confined for 6 days passed, without the possibility of proceeding on, returning to a better Situation, or get out to hunt, Scerce of Provisions, and torents of rain poreing on us all the time." In spite of being wet through and through, the party worked at drying out bedding and blankets for the night. The evening's meal was little more than dried, pounded fish that they had bought at Celilo Falls. Harbor porpoises, ducks, seagulls, and sea otters enlivened the day's scene but did not lessen the misery.

NOVEMBER 11, 1805. A stormy, wet day kept the party in camp, although Joseph Field and Collins were sent to hunt. They returned with nothing but information about high, steep hills, thick undergrowth, and fallen timbers that hampered their hunt. Fishing upriver by other members of the party yielded better results. The camp itself was scarcely livable. Constant rain loosened rocks from the hillsides immediately to their backs and showered the exposed explorers with small stones. The canoes bobbled in the waves, the party's baggage was scattered among the huge drift logs, and the party spread out wherever they could find a dry spot on the hillside or among the logs. The captains were surprised when five Cathlamets managed to make it to the camp through strong winds and high waves in a canoe loaded with salmon. The party had met Cathlamets at the marshy islands along the way, but their permanent settlements were across the Columbia River from the Wahkiakums, with whom they shared a similar culture and language. The captains traded fishhooks and trifles for thirteen fish, probably bull or Dolly Varden trout. Clark found the Indians "badly clad"—one in an old sailor's jacket and pantaloons that he said he got from white people who lived a short distance down the Columbia. Clark was amazed at the natives' nautical skills. He watched in admiration as they crossed the five-mile width of the Columbia through the highest waves imaginable; he called them the best canoeists he had ever seen.

NOVEMBER 12, 1805. A tremendous thunderstorm came in at three o'clock in the morning and continued with rain, hail, and lightning for three hours, until light broke forth for a brief spell; then the weather returned to its usual dark, stormy pattern. During the night one of the canoes broke loose and was carried downriver but was found undamaged. The men secured them as well as they could by sinking and weighting them down with rocks to keep them from being dashed to pieces against the rocks. By early afternoon the party's location became untenable, as high winds and hard rains pounded their encampment and shook the rocks and trees on which they lay. Using a calm spell at low tide, they moved a short distance to a welcoming spot downriver, beyond Cliff Point and within Hungry Harbor, that they had missed on the previous excursion. Clark lamented their situation and declared that anyone viewing the party would be moved to sympathy seeing how wet, cold, and miserable they were. But he felt comforted knowing that the party was in good health. Again, disappointed hunters found the going too difficult and returned to camp empty-handed except for some salmon. Hoping to find a way out of their confinement, Gibson, Bratton, and Willard braved the rolling river in a canoe fashioned in the Indian way. But their canoeing skills did not match those of the natives—they were tossed about as so much driftwood and barely made a mile before returning.

NOVEMBER 13, 1805. A bit of fair weather during the night must have raised the party's spirits. At morning Clark decided to ascend the mountainous country behind him in order to get a clear view of the river and country ahead. He made only three miles in his wet, exhausting climb through a maze of fallen timber and thick undergrowth of shrubs, herbs, ferns, and mosses. Along the way he noticed devil's club and used its branches to pull himself up the steep climb but cut his hand on the thorny stems of his climbing aid. Sitka spruce, the region's dominant species, towered overhead, mixed with western hemlock and western redcedar that are so much a part of the Sitka spruce vegetation zone. He also noticed red berries of the bunchberry but found their taste insipid. Lewis collected a specimen on June 16, 1806. From the height Clark saw winds churning up the river and creating high waves near the camp, but clouds obscured a more distant view. Upon returning to camp he dispatched Colter, Willard, and Shannon in the Indian canoe around the point to find a safe harbor to relocate the party. Again, the evening's meal consisted of pounded fish and the catch of the day. At day's end Clark worried about the possible impact of cold weather on the raggedly clad party.

NOVEMBER 14, 1805. The party was stuck and without defense against the wind-borne water and heavy rains that seemed to come at them from every direction. During the night one of the canoes was damaged by being dashed against rocks during high tide. At about ten this morning Wahkiakums, who seemed to glide through the high, rolling waves with ease, came for a visit. While two women waited in the canoe at a distance, three men came ashore and reported that they had seen Colter, Willard, and Shannon. At about this time Colter returned by land, having broken the lock on his gun, and disclosed that these very Indians had stolen a gig and basket from him. Considering how they had been welcomed, Clark was incensed that they would steal from the party. He demanded that the women bring the boat to shore and return the pilfered items, but it took the threat of gunfire to get the loot back. He then ordered them all out of camp.

Colter informed the captains that he and his comrades had gone as far as possible with the canoe against the waves and that Willard and Shannon had gone ahead on foot. Colter also brought good news. He explained that it was only a short distance around the point to a good harbor with a beautiful and spacious sand beach. Lewis decided to leave the main party and go by land to see if the reports of white traders in the vicinity were true. He also wanted to compare the terrain with maps from George Vancouver's 1792 travels in the area, particularly to discover Vancouver's Baker ("Haley's") Bay. Drouillard, Joseph and Reuben Field, and Frazer joined the captain. At three in the afternoon they set out in one of the large canoes, manned by five others who would drop them at Colter's spot and return to camp. The canoe party returned at dusk, having dropped Lewis and party at the appointed spot and with their boat now half filled with water. The river did not give up its ways to newcomers so easily.

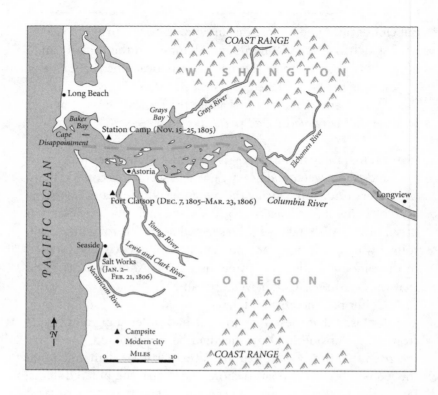

MAP 10. The expedition's route, November 15, 1805–March 22, 1806.

CHAPTER 9

Pacific Coast Winter

November 15, 1805–March 22, 1806

NOVEMBER 15, 1805. Experiencing a pause in the morning's constant rain, Clark prepared the party to set out, only to be disappointed when heavy winds raised swells in the river, making it impossible to proceed. A test run in an empty canoe convinced the captain that more waiting was necessary. Again he bemoaned the situation and counted the eleven days without relief from rain for little more than two hours at a time. Confined to their wet situation, the men could not hunt, nor could the party retreat or go forward. A break finally came in the afternoon when the sun broke through and provided a chance to dry bedding and baggage and to check the condition of arms and ammunition. By three o'clock the winds abated and the Columbia calmed. The party quickly loaded the canoes, paddled around Point Ellice, the party's "blustering Point" or "Point Distress," entered Baker ("Haley's") Bay, and moved to the new camp suggested by Colter.

The spot has become known as "Station Camp" and is just west of present McGowan, Pacific County, Washington. Nearby the party found a small creek of fresh water and an Indian village of thirty-six huts, known as "Middle Village," now abandoned except for the ever-present fleas. Shannon with five Indians met Clark here and informed him that he had seen Lewis about ten miles farther on. Lewis had sent him back to warn Clark of native thievery, which Shannon and Willard had experienced the previous night when their rifles were stolen from under them as they slept. Being disarmed, the men were unable to force the return of their weapons and feared them lost to the Indians. It was only Lewis's timely arrival with his party that convinced the Indians to relinquish the stolen goods. Clark warned Shannon's accompanying Indians that similar behavior would result in swift punishment.

Clark noticed that these Indians spoke a different language, that they came from the north, and that they called themselves Chinooks. The Chinooks occupied the north bank of the Columbia River from the area of Grays Bay to Cape Disappointment. Their name, Chinookan, is now applied to the broader linguistic and cultural area of the Columbia River. The Chinooks followed seasonal settlement patterns, occupying fishing villages along the Columbia during the summer before moving north to Willapa Bay for the winter. This probably accounts for the party having met so few of them at this time of year. After Clark landed he declared this the party's farthest point by water. Immediately before him he could see the line from Cape Disappointment to Point Adams where the river met the ocean—he had a full view of the incredible tempest at the mouth of the Columbia. He knew it would be foolish to take the party's small craft into such a torrent of dangerous waters. The captain consulted Vancouver's maps and compared them to the topography in his sight. Some of the maps' features were not apparent to him, so he laid out the scene on his own maps. The men used lumber from the old village to build shelters for their stay.

NOVEMBER 16, 1805. A clear and beautiful morning provided an opportunity to lay out the party's belongings to air and dry. It also gave Clark a chance to take celestial observations. He set the party's latitude at 46° 19′ 11.1″ N; the approximate position of Station Camp is 46° 14′ 47″ N. After Shannon's Chinooks left, Clark dispatched several men to find elks, deer, or fowl to bolster the party's dwindling provisions. Indians came by in a canoe loaded with wapato while others wandered into camp by land. Clark smoked with the visitors but did not extend a cordial welcome. One of the members of the party was violently sick with a cold, which Clark attributed to his having laid in his wet clothes for several nights. In the evening the hunters returned with two deer of good size but poor quality, one crane, and two ducks. York also brought in two geese, five brants, and three snow geese. Clark's entries indicate that they moved the campsite two miles west, but none of the other journalists mention it.

Gass viewed this place as the culmination of the party's journey, and he (or his editor) wrote in elegant terms of the achievement. "We are now at the end of our voyage, which has been completely accomplished according to the intention of the expedition, the object of which was to discover a passage by the way of the Missouri and Columbia rivers to the Pacific ocean; notwithstanding the difficulties, privations and dangers, which we had to encounter, endure and surmount."

NOVEMBER 17, 1805. A fair but cool and windy morning greeted the explorers. Clark noted that the tides, rising to 8½ feet, brought huge swells that broke forcefully against the sandy shore before the party's camp. Six hunters went out in search of food. At one in the afternoon Lewis and his party returned to camp. Lewis's route took the captain and his men around Baker Bay to Cape Disappointment and then northward along the coast. He saw the area where vessels came in to trade, but none were there. There is no account of the captain's activities for these days, nor is there a map of his route. Clark's brief notes and those of the enlisted men who were not with him serve as the source for Lewis's journey.

Several Chinooks followed Lewis back to camp, offered items for sale, and presented the captains with the root of the seashore lupine ("liquorice"). Someone, perhaps Lewis, interlined the Chinookan name for the plant, "*cul-wha-mo*" (variously spelled). The Chinooks prepared the plant's rhizome by roasting or boiling and pounding it. Clark found it like common licorice in taste and size. The captain commented on the natives' trading practices. He thought it unwise to accept gifts from them because they were greedy, demanded greater gifts in return, and were never satisfied with an offer. The hungry explorers were surely pleased when their hunters brought back deer, ducks, and brants. They had seen signs of elks but none to shoot. Later in the day a Chinook chief, probably Comcomly, came by for a visit. Clark took a moment to comment briefly on the local tribe. He counted four hundred persons inhabiting the bay, who lived principally on fish and roots. The low numbers probably reflected the season of their absence from the area. He found them well armed with fusils, lightweight, smoothbore muskets that were able to take down birds, deer, and elks. At day's end, Clark called for volunteers to follow him to the ocean the next morning. Pryor, Ordway, the Field brothers, Shannon, Colter, Bratton, Weiser, Charbonneau, and York signed on.

NOVEMBER 18, 1805. At daylight Clark set out with his party of volunteers. Labiche either took the place of Bratton or was added; otherwise the party remained as formed the previous day. Their overland route, shown as a dotted line on map 91 in the *Atlas of the Lewis and Clark Expedition* and on Clark's journal map of the area, took them northwest along the eastern shore of Baker Bay to the Chinook River. The area was alive with waterfowl and the bottomland filled with alder and grand fir ("balsam") trees. At the river they found a Chinook hut with four women and some children. One of the women was covered with scabs, sores, and ulcers, which the captain attributed to the effects of venereal disease. He was able to hire two women to transport the men across the river in a canoe in exchange for fishhooks. Now they followed the shoreline through boggy wetlands to Wallacut ("Chinook") River, where they found the remains of a whale on the beach near some Chinook huts. The men made a fire and lunched on brants and plovers that Labiche had shot as they came along. Reuben Field killed a California condor ("Buzzard") near the whale's carcass. Clark gave its weight as twenty-five pounds and measured its wings from tip to tip as 9½ feet. The captain later discovered a flat fish or flounder shaped like a turtle that he carefully examined; it is the grampus or Risso's dolphin, a cetacean rather than a fish. Clark pictured it in his elkskin-bound field journal.

After lunch the men crossed the Wallacut in an old canoe that they found near the huts. In coves along the bay Clark noticed cliffs of siltstone and coarse-grained sandstone. Coming around the bay near the tip of Cape Disappointment, the men discovered a small island in a deep cove and were informed by Chinooks that this was the spot where traders anchored and loaded peltries they had obtained from the natives. Clark declared it a fine harbor for large ships. Nearby, Clark saw Lewis's name blazed on a tree and added his own, with the date and the inscription "by land"; several of the men followed suit. From here the party continued south around the bay on Cape Disappointment, which at its point hooks back toward the northeast. After reaching the farthest extent Clark crossed the narrow neck at the point and stood gazing at the open ocean, pounded by the mighty Columbia. Nearby and to the north he saw McKenzie Head on the cape, and across the expanse of water he viewed Point Adams. At a distance farther south he could see Tillamook Head, which he would visit in January. Turning back north, the men followed the western shoreline, climbed McKenzie Head, came down the north side, and camped in Fort Canby State Park, Pacific County. The men supped on brants and pounded fish, and Clark declared them satisfied with the day's excursion. Some of the men expressed to Clark a desire to go back upriver to Celilo Falls or the narrows for their winter camp.

At the main camp hunters disbursed into the woods while others traded with Chinooks for dried salmon and wapato. The hunters returned with one deer, a squirrel, a hawk, and a flounder, the last being deposited by the tide. Lewis took notes on the Chinook language.

NOVEMBER 19, 1805. After peeling off the wet blanket that had covered him during the night, Clark sent two men ahead to hunt while he gathered the others to follow. He caught up with the hunters and shared Joseph Field's one small deer for breakfast, calling the roasted venison sumptuous. The men continued through rough country up the coast for about nine miles to the area of present Long Beach, Pacific County, where they found a sandy beach. Here Clark again marked his name and the date on a tree and copied the inscription on his journal map, "W. Clark 19th Novr. 1805." Along his northward jaunt he saw a dead sturgeon and the backbone of a whale and then turned back toward the cape. Moving south, he climbed the highlands on North Head, Pacific County, and looking north some twenty miles by his estimate to a point of highland named Cape Shoalwater, he named it for "my particular friend" Lewis. He learned that the Chinooks inhabited all the area through which he had passed. He also noticed what he termed "Some curious Deer," the Columbian black-tailed deer, which Lewis described on February 19, 1806, as having characteristics of both the common and the mule deer. The party now struck out overland to the east, toward the mouth of the Wallacut River, secured the canoe they'd left behind, and camped on the east side of the river, a mile of so northeast of present Ilwaco, Pacific County. Chinooks came and went at the main camp, one large group composed of fifteen men and a woman. Admiring the waterproof, redcedar and beargrass hats of the Chinook men, one man gave an old razor for one. Contrary to the party's general impression, Whitehouse called the Chinooks handsome people.

NOVEMBER 20, 1805. The able hunter Labiche set out to get brants for breakfast, while Joseph Field and Colter went after elks. The Frenchman came back with eight large ducks. Clark's party retraced the route to the main party at Station Camp. Finding no Indians with canoes to hire at the Chinook River, the party made a raft, which Reuben Field used to cross over and secure a small canoe that the men had spied near a Chinook hut. Three Chinook Indians joined the party's procession and offered Clark sturgeons and wapato. Others also came along and added to the many Indians that Clark found at the camp, among them two chiefs, Comcomly and Shelathwell. The captains presented them with peace medals and a flag. Lewis and Clark were both struck by a beautiful robe of sea otter skins worn by one of the Chinooks and tried to buy it. They were unsuccessful until Sacagawea yielded her blue-beaded belt for the purchase. The next day the captains gave her a blue cloth coat for the belt and beads.

NOVEMBER 21, 1805. While most of the Chinooks left the explorers' camp, other Indians came in. The visiting Chehalis ("*Chiltz*") were a Salish-speaking people living in Grays Harbor and Pacific Counties on the southern Washington coast. They lived adjacent to the Chinooks, whose culture they shared. From across the Columbia came Clatsops, also a people of the Chinookan cultural stock, who occupied territory along the river from Point Adams to Tongue Point and south along the Oregon coast to Tillamook Head, all in Clatsop County, Oregon. The Clatsops and the cross-river Chinooks spoke dialects of the Lower Chinook language. All were part of the Northwest Coast cultural group. While visiting with these Indians Clark watched brants fly south but without the familiar snow geese among them. At noon it began to rain and kept up moderately all day, while the flood tide raised the river and almost overtook the camp. Nevertheless, the captain marveled at the temperate climate on the coast. Given the present severity of the weather and the restless river, the captains delayed plans to start back. Even now they began to consider whether they should spend the winter on the coast or retreat to a more favorable spot upriver.

A wife of one the Chinook chiefs, perhaps Delashelwilt's wife, came to camp with six young women relatives whose sexual services to the men she hoped to trade for trinkets. Clark noticed that Chinookans did not look negatively on such sexual practices and accepted barter in human flesh as a normal part of life. Perhaps that accounted for the venereal disease that Clark found so common among them. And this particular group of women may have been the ones that gave venereal disease to several in the party. Delashelwilt's wife brought them to Fort Clatsop in March 1806, but Lewis ordered the men to have no encounters with them that time. But on this occasion the captains gave the men ribbons for the young women, saving their more precious commodities to trade for necessities. The explorers were already realizing what hard traders the coastal people could be, as they had to pay exorbitant prices for salmon, sturgeons, cranberries, edible thistle, and wapato, as well as for baskets, hats, and mats.

Clark thought the Indian women's faces were handsome enough but considered their squatty bodies badly shaped. He put his most critical eye to their legs and thighs. Tying strands of beads and decorated strings around their lower legs, the women cut off circulation, which caused swelling and disfiguration above. They also pricked images and figures into the flesh of their legs and decorated their bodies with other tattoo-like symbols. Clark saw one woman with a sailor's name, "J. Bowmon," tattooed on her arm. Indeed, women without body markings were considered lower-class creatures. With their hair laying loosely on their shoulders and back, the women threaded-in strands of the favored blue beads, which they also used in necklaces and earrings, while they also fashioned brass wires into rings and bracelets. The coastal women copied the "petticoat" style of their upstream neighbors. The men favored the red, blue, and white Hudson's Bay robes and old sailors' outfits. They also wore robes fashioned from the skins of local animals—sea otters, beavers, elks, deer, foxes, and bobcats—and bartered with neighbors for the pelts of the mountain beaver, which they highly prized. Gass wondered how they managed in the winter with only these small robes and no moccasins or leggings. Clark found the men homely and just as physically repugnant as the women. Men and women alike had the flattened foreheads so common to the culture and so distasteful to the Americans. Like others of the Columbia River culture, the coastal natives depended on the rivers, from which they harvested fish with their nets and gigs. Roots formed another principal part of their diet, including seashore lupine and edible thistle, which they traded for wapato from villagers to the east. Chinookan men had some good fusils that they used for hunting deer, elks, and birds, but fish and roots remained the staple foodstuff of coastal people.

NOVEMBER 22, 1805. A miserable night led into a wet morning as immense waves from the Columbia River joined constant heavy rain and nearly deluged the camp, forcing some of the party to move their shelters. Clark cried out, "O! how horriable is the day." The whole day continued with torrents of rain and the river's lash of water. One canoe was badly split as it was tossed about, while the party huddled in shelters, soaked and sulking. The captains purchased wapato with brass armbands and rings, which the Chinook women favored. Generally, however, they kept the natives at a distance.

NOVEMBER 23, 1805. With clearing weather hunters set out and returned with three bucks, four brants, and three ducks; those who stayed in camp worked on the damaged canoe. The clear day gave opportunity for the men to mark trees. Lewis marked a tree with the branding iron that carried his name and rank and then added the date. Clark also carved his name and date into a tree, while members of the party set their initials in the bark. Clatsops came over in the evening and demanded high prices or blue beads for their sea otter skins. To test their trading practices, Clark offered one Clatsop his watch, a handkerchief, red beads, and an American coin for a sea otter skin, only to be rebuffed with demands for the "Chief beads," the highly sought after blue beads. Clark thought the Clatsops were the remainder of a much larger group that was reduced by smallpox or another infectious disease. He also thought them more honest than the Chinooks and not given to petty stealing. Gass noticed one Clatsop man with the reddest hair he had ever seen, his skin fair and freckled. He may have been the Clatsop known as Jack Ramsay, who visited Fort Clatsop on December 31.

NOVEMBER 24, 1805. The captains spent time in the morning making astronomical observations. The party also took advantage of the fair weather to dry wet bedding, clothing, and the like. Hunters brought in but a single brant. In the evening Chinooks arrived to smoke with the captains and do a bit of trading. One of them brought a sea otter skin, for which the captains gave a few blue beads. But the party faced a question larger than beads or brants: where to set up winter quarters? The captains pondered the possibilities. The most important consideration was the availability of food, especially large mammals that would provide the necessary meat for a party of hungry explorers. Trading for provisions was not an option at their present site since it would take significantly more trade items than they had just to get roots and dried fish. Every effort had been made to question visitors about sources for meat. The universal response was that the south shore of the Columbia River was best for elks and upriver for deer. Since elks supplied considerably more meat than deer, were easier to kill at this season, and had better hides for clothing, the south side seemed best. Clark also thought the coast a more convenient situation to make salt, and it offered a better chance to catch incoming ships that could resupply them. Seeing local Indians lightly clothed and having thus far experienced mild weather, he reasoned that weather on the coast would be better suited to their threadbare condition. The captains were in favor of examining the area across the Columbia, but they felt the need to poll the party. Every member voted, including Sacagawea and York. Clark's notes on the vote, plus comments by Gass and Whitehouse, indicate that all were in favor of "Cross & examine" except for Shields, who preferred to go upriver. For a second choice the voters were divided between returning to the Sandy River (Shields's first choice) or to another spot upriver. Sacagawea wanted a place where she could find plenty of "Potas," probably meaning "potatoes" or wapato.

NOVEMBER 25, 1805. High winds and waves made it impossible to cross the Columbia, so the captains decided to head upriver to find a favorable spot to canoe over. Seven Clatsops joined the flotilla but soon turned their canoes into the waves and handily made the passage across. Everyone marveled at their seamanship. The explorers made at least one more attempt at crossing in their ungainly craft as they crept along the shore of Grays Bay but failed. Near nightfall they reached their encampment of November 7 and came ashore opposite Pillar Rock and within sight of Mount St. Helens at a distance to the east.

NOVEMBER 26, 1805. In spite of wind, the captains knew they were probably at the narrowest spot for crossing, so they turned the canoes into deep waters and worked their way toward the southern shore among their "Seal Islands," today's numerously named islands within the Lewis and Clark National Wildlife Refuge, Clatsop County, Oregon. Among the grassy islands the party counted great numbers of swans, geese, brants, ducks, and gulls. Now hugging the shoreline, they passed a Cathlamet village of nine huts near present Knappa, Clatsop County, where they purchased fish and wapato at what they considered an unreasonable price. The party eventually set up camp on the shore of Cathlamet Bay west of Svensen, Clatsop County. Clark called it a disagreeable day and a bad place to camp. Within a short time after landing three Indians came by to trade their wapato. Clark observed several scaffolds of canoes nearby on which the Cathlamets had placed their dead, but he did not examine the site.

NOVEMBER 27, 1805. It rained all night and continued into the morning. Eleven Indians in three canoes came to trade at daybreak but asked such exorbitant prices for their roots, skins, and meat that the captains refused to barter. As the party was about to depart, someone discovered that the Indians had stolen one of the axes. A quick search of the natives turned up the purloined prize hidden under the robe of the thief. The captains heatedly scolded him. The party passed the John Day River ("Ke ke mar que Creek" on expedition maps), Clatsop County, and rounded Tongue Point ("Point William," presumably after Clark), where huge swells convinced them to take to shore on the western side of the neck. The idea was to dry out a bit, but the effort proved useless because winds blew in, brought rain, and drenched the party once again. Moreover, one of the canoes split as they tried to get the boats out of the river.

NOVEMBER 28, 1805. More hard rain and winds all night soaked bedding and supplies, and the party had no way to keep dry. The canvas sails and tents they had used as shelters were now in tatters and useless against the driving rain. Several men went out on the point to hunt deer but were unsuccessful, as were those who drove south into the wooded country. Moreover, they could not get close enough to waterfowl to get a good shot, so the party had to live out the day on pounded fish that they had brought from Celilo Falls. Again Clark cried out, "O! how disagreeable is our Situation."

NOVEMBER 29, 1805. Determining that they would be unable to move, Lewis took Drouillard, Reuben Field, Shannon, Colter, and Labiche with him in the Indian canoe and set out along the southern shoreline. The captain also took up his pen and kept notes but made no map of his journey to find the party's winter encampment. No other member of his party was writing. Passing along the waterfront of the modern city of Astoria, Clatsop County, the captain turned into Youngs ("Meriwether") Bay and found shelter for the night in an abandoned Indian hunting lodge. The lodge was slight shelter against the night's intermittent downpours. His hunters brought in deer, brants, ducks, and a goose, a positive sign for winter prospects.

At the main camp Clark also sent out hunters while everyone else worked at drying out their goods over smoky fires doused by rain. The smoke burned their eyes more effectively than it dried their clothes. Along the shore Clark noticed beautiful pebbles of quartz and chert carried here by the Columbia River from upstream sources. He also enumerated the birds and crawlers within his view: California condors ("large Buzzard"), Steller's jays ("blue Magpie"), golden ("grey") and bald eagles, red-tailed hawks, ravens, crows, and wrens, plus snakes, lizards, bugs, worms, spiders, flies, and insects of various kinds: biters and stingers in abundance. The hunters returned unburdened by game to an unsatisfactory dinner of pounded fish shared by all. Some in the party were growing ill from lack of proper nourishment.

NOVEMBER 30, 1805. Lewis and party continued around Youngs Bay, weaving through the marshes and passing the Youngs ("Kilhow-â-nah-kle") and Lewis and Clark ("Netul") Rivers before ascending the Skipanon River for a couple of miles and having lunch. From here three men went out to the south and west to examine the country. Within two hours they returned to report a tangled woodland obstructed by lakes and marshes that inhibited their drive to the ocean, which they could hear breaking against the shore. Turning back, Lewis retraced his route to Youngs River, where he made camp a short distance upriver from its mouth. He was discouraged to have seen no elks in his outing for the day. He hoped to meet Clatsops whom he could question about their tales of abundant elks in the area. His disgust at the situation is apparent in the tone of his words: all this effort and no results. Like Clark on the preceding day he turned to counting birds: brants, geese, snow geese, sandhill cranes, great blue herons, double-crested cormorants, hawks, ravens, crows, gulls, and great varieties of ducks, including canvasbacks, mallards, and buffleheads or western grebes.

Clark and the rest of the party enjoyed a bit of sunshine in the morning after a night's respite from constant rain. While renewed drying began at camp, hunters dispersed but were disappointed in their quest. Seeing signs of elks but none to shoot, they could bring back only three hawks ("fat and delicious") and three coots for supper. The latter received descriptive scrutiny from Clark. Diarrhea and other intestinal complaints were becoming common among the party, as salt water soaked the pounded fish they had to eat. Sacagawea presented the captain with a small piece of bread that she had kept for her baby. Clark relished the taste despite it having gotten wet and turned a little sour. In a walk to the end of Tongue Point Clark observed rosebushes, California rhododendrons, Oregon ash, either alders or beeches, pines, and maples.

In his notebook journal (but not in his elkskin-bound field journal) Clark wrote a paragraph describing Chinookan burial practices. Lewis has nearly the same material in his entry for January 9, 1806; he may have been the original writer and Clark the copyist. They described the method of canoe burials in which a small canoe was sunk in the ground with the deceased's remains laid out wrapped in animal skins. A larger, overturned canoe was laid on top of the smaller one, and the two were lashed together. Various personal items were buried with the dead. The captains acknowledged their difficulty in describing the purposes of the practice because of their inability to communicate.

DECEMBER 1, 1805. Further frustrating Lewis, another group of hunters returned to report impenetrable woods and little sign of game. Hearing gunfire in the woods, the men hoped that the still absent Drouillard might have found the sought-after elks. After describing what was probably Richardson's red squirrel ("small grey squirrel"), Lewis turned to botanizing. He gave brief descriptions of salmonberry ("brier with a brown bark and three laves"), Pacific blackberry ("green brier"), bigleaf maple ("ash"), red alder ("black alder"), red elderberry ("large elder"), probably Lewis's syringa ("seven bark"), Oregon crabapple, and Pacific madrone, then ended his journalizing until the new year. Lewis collected a specimen of Pacific madrone on November 1, while salmonberry, bigleaf maple, red alder, and syringa specimens were obtained in spring 1806 on the Columbia River.

Having little success on Tongue Point, Clark joined several men for a hunting excursion to nearby marshy islands, but winds drove them back to their "Standing friend," dried fish. Other hunters also returned empty-handed, with "not even a duck," groaned Gass. Clark wearily counted the twenty-four days he had been in sight of the misnamed "Pacific."

DECEMBER 2, 1805. While Pryor, Joseph Field, and Gibson went hunting deer and elks, Clark joined York and two others seeking fish and fowl on the John Day River. Clark added himself to the list of the unwell, with complaints of cramps and diarrhea and a hardy distaste for dried fish, which he blamed for his distress. He hoped that Lewis might arrive with good reports of deer and elks; otherwise Clark considered moving to a better spot. In the evening the hunter Field carried the welcome news of an elk kill. Clark immediately sent six men with him to retrieve the meat. This would be the first elk shot on this side of the Rockies. Field had more good news: he not only found ample signs of elks but had also seen two gangs of them. The fishing party was unsuccessful in getting either fish or fowl.

DECEMBER 3, 1805. The party's spirits were lifted when the men sent to retrieve the elk returned with fresh meat. But Clark bemoaned the fact that when at last they had plenty of meat he was too sick to indulge. He tried elk soup along with a few wapato brought in by native traders, who got fishhooks in exchange. He felt a little better. Sacagawea broke the elk's shank bones, removed the marrow, and boiled the broken pieces for grease. Pryor and Gibson, who had gone with Field, returned in the evening having killed six elks. They got lost coming back to camp but had seen more elk signs. Later the captain found another tree suitable for his signature: "William Clark December 3rd 1805. By Land from the U. States in 1804 & 1805."

DECEMBER 4, 1805. Pryor and six men set out to retrieve the elks that he and Gibson had killed. They were to bring the meat to a convenient spot along the bay, where Clark would meet them to secure the bounty. Good news and fresh meat sharpened Clark's appetite and lessened his distress. But at the same time the flood tide for the day was two feet higher than usual, while hard winds and high waves together with the unstoppable rain kept him from joining the elk party. Now he had seven hunters agreeing that the region boasted abundant elks, so he began to think more positively of establishing winter quarters in the area. He also began to worry about Lewis and his party, from whom he had had no word since they left on November 29. Trying to warm themselves by the fires, the explorers' eyes suffered from the blowing smoke.

DECEMBER 5, 1805. If anything had been dried out, it was all for naught, as hard showers hit the camp and wetted everything anew, then drizzles kept up all day. Clark worried on paper and in his mind about Lewis, with "1000 conjectures" crowding his head. He was much relieved when Lewis and party returned safely with more good news. They had located an excellent spot for winter quarters and found elks enough to see them through to spring. Indeed, his party had killed six of them plus five deer, and two men had stayed behind to prepare and protect the stash. Elk meat had also revived the weakened members of the party. Things were looking up. Now if the wind would ease and rains slow a bit, perhaps they could get to Lewis's spot and build shelters that would ward off the worst effects of the Pacific Coast winter.

DECEMBER 6, 1805. Moving plans had to contend with the weather, so the only moving that took place was to pull back to a safe spot away from the rising waters of the Columbia River. Fair weather returned in the evening but too late for the party to take advantage of it and seek their winter camp.

DECEMBER 7, 1805. A fair morning bid the party into boats and gave them a chance to set out for Lewis's wintering spot. Coming around Youngs Bay they met Pryor's party who had gone after the elks that the sergeant had killed. Pryor explained that they had gotten lost, found the meat spoiled, and had brought back only the elks' hides. York had separated from the group and was somewhere behind. While the rest of the party went ahead, Clark delayed in one canoe until York arrived. Clark named the bay they were in for Lewis, "Meriwethers Bay," now Youngs Bay; then the party ascended the Lewis and Clark River about three miles to the place that Lewis had chosen. Clark called it the most likely spot in the area for a fort, being near the little river but situated well above high tide. Here they unloaded the canoes—each journalist noting that the site was two hundred yards from shore. The place, soon to see Fort Clatsop rise from a clearing, is about five miles south-west of Astoria, Clatsop County; it would be the party's home until March 23. A reconstruction of the fort stands at the site and is a national memorial.

DECEMBER 8, 1805. The captains having decided on the party's win-tering spot, Clark now looked to find a direct route to the coast and there establish an auxiliary camp for salt making. He wanted to blaze as direct a trail as possible and one easy to follow so no one would get lost in the deep woods that surrounded the main camp. Choos-ing five men, including Drouillard and Shannon, he set out for the sea. Alternately working their way through thick underbrush and swampy wetlands, they were forced to build a raft to cross the Ski-panon River or one of its tributaries. Nearby they scared up a gang of elks and followed them for miles over small hills and through immense bogs until they killed one, then camped for the night at the driest spot they could find. Bearberry and wild cranberries were in abundance in the area, which Clark noticed as he waded in water and mud up to his hips in pursuit of the elks. The men gathered what dry wood they could find, made fires for the night, wrapped themselves in elk skins, and bedded down north of and near pres-ent Seaside, Clatsop County. At the main camp Gass took eleven men in search of the elks left by Lewis, now guarded by two of his men. After finding them, the men carried two large loads of meat to the canoes and headed back to camp.

DECEMBER 9, 1805. Clark separated his party, sending Drouillard and Shannon in search of elks and taking the other three with him to find a route to the sea. Wading up to his knees through the marsh, he came to a stream too deep to cross on foot, so he retreated to the raft of the day before and set a new course through the waters. Along his new route he met three Clatsops who were returning to their village bearing freshly caught salmon; they invited Clark to join them. Finding a small canoe nearby, Indians and explorers crossed creeks and portaged others with two Clatsops shoulder-ing the canoe from place to place until they arrived at the village at the mouth of Neacoxie Creek, Seaside, Clatsop County. Here Clark found three or four houses of about twelve Clatsop families on the banks of the Neacoxie.

Intrigued by Clatsop architecture, Clark described the houses as being built with a southern exposure, set in the ground about four feet, and made of split pine boards. A small door provided entry and a ladder allowed descent to the interior, with a mat-covered floor. Raised beds, under which the owners kept their possessions, were placed against the walls, while fires glowed from the middle of the great room. Cuskala ("*Cus-ka-lah*," variously spelled), perhaps a chief, invited Clark into his lodge and treated him cordially, while his wife served fish and other items on mats and a soup made from "bread of the *Shele well* berries." Clark called the "Shele wele" (variously spelled) "common to this Country" and pleasant to taste. His name is Chinookan for salal, which Lewis described on February 8 and called "*Shal-lon*." Clark was impressed by Clatsop cleanliness and observed them frequently washing their faces and hands. The captain made an impression on the Indians as well when he shot a brant with his small rifle. Later he watched the Clatsops play games late into the evening, one in which a player passed a small bead or bone from hand to hand, singing all the while to distract onlookers, then offered bettors a chance to choose which hand held the object. Beads and other valuables were wagered on the outcome. Another game, which Clark could not quite figure out, had players rolling round wooden balls between two pins set at a distance. In his postexpeditionary notes Biddle provided a diagram of the game and some explanation. At end of day Cuskala gave Clark mats to sleep on near the fires, but biting fleas kept the captain up most of the night.

After a night of almost constant rain at the main camp, Ordway took eight men with him to retrieve the remainder of the meat left from the previous day, which they brought back at nightfall. The rest of the party set to clearing the land and building the fort. Four Indians came to the camp during the day.

DECEMBER 10, 1805. On a morning stroll along the coast Clark gathered seashells and watched Indians pick up sturgeons thrown on shore by retreating tides. Again, Clark astonished the Clatsops with his shooting, bringing down two brants and a duck with his rifle. They exclaimed that the captain had a very good musket, perhaps not understanding the greater accuracy of a rifled gun. Back at the village Clark could see Tillamook Head about four miles to the south. When he returned to Cuskala's lodge, he was offered more fish, roots, and soup. He tried to purchase a sea otter skin, but his offer of red beads stirred little interest. Blue and white were the desired colors. Fishhooks finally worked to get him some roots and berry bread. Cuskala and his brother joined Clark and his men part of the way to Fort Clatsop. Clark estimated the distance to the coast at seven miles, five in thick woods, over hills, and through swamps and the last two across an open, sandy prairie. Four of the men at the main camp complained of severe colds and various ailments. Gass, the best source for the fort's construction, reported that the foundation had been laid.

DECEMBER 11, 1805. Hard work, wet weather, and poor diets probably accounted for the party's physical problems. Pryor dislocated his shoulder, Gibson was down with dysentery, Joseph Field had boils on his legs, and Werner strained his knee. The rain continued, as did work on the fort, where a row of huts started coming up.

DECEMBER 12, 1805. Clark suffered a fitful night's sleep, as fleas infested everything and were impossible to get out of robes, blankets, and hides the party used for bedding. During the day all hands were employed at cutting timber and raising logs at the fort. The men had finished three rooms but had not yet topped off the huts. Gass thought that would be the hardest part, since suitable timber for roofing could not be found. Two men were assigned to find and fashion boards for the work. In the evening two canoes of Clatsops arrived bringing wapato, edible thistle, and a sea otter skin to trade. Fishhooks and Shoshone tobacco closed the deal. Clark recognized one of the men, Coboway, as a chief and presented him with a small medal and gave him the courtesy his station deserved. The captains would know him better in days to come. Clark was further impressed by the Clatsops' hard trading practices. He found them unwilling to close a deal until they were convinced they had made the best of the bargain. They particularly jacked up the price of wapato, which they had to purchase from upriver tribes at a premium. White beads were an acceptable exchange medium, but blue beads were best.

DECEMBER 13, 1805. After a breakfast of elk meat, Coboway and his Clatsops left the camp, but not before making a final trade, this time selling skins of Oregon bobcats and mountain beavers to the captains. They planned to use them for coats. Drouillard and Shannon returned from hunting having killed eighteen elks and butchered all but two, whose meat had spoiled. Word was getting out about trading possibilities at the camp. In the evening three Clatsops arrived with edible thistle roots, fish, and sea otter skins—now becoming the standard commodities—but the explorers turned them away. Construction of the fort was coming along nicely. Another line of huts had gone up, and the final lines of the fort were taking shape. Clark was especially pleased with the quality of wood in use, probably grand fir ("balsam pine"), which stood straight and split evenly. Gass agreed and found roofing with this timber much easier than he had expected. The day's hard showers did not deter progress.

DECEMBER 14, 1805. The captains dispatched Drouillard and Shannon with two other men to safeguard the hunters' catch until a larger party could get to it. Perhaps the captains also wanted to wait until the meat storage shed was completed, since they had already lost elk meat to spoilage. Unrelenting dampness had its effect on untreated meat. The party suffered as well. Indeed, no one had been dry since arriving at this camp. Although some of the ill were improving, York had come down with stomach pains and diarrhea. The Clatsop traders departed after selling a small sea otter skin and a robe. The last of the seven huts inside the fort was completed except for a bit of roof work.

DECEMBER 15, 1805. Clark, with sixteen men in three canoes, set out early to retrieve the elks killed by Drouillard and Shannon, who with two others were now guarding them. It would be a grueling day's work, as the men could get the canoes within only three or four miles of the kill site. Each man loaded up an elk quarter, worked his way through woods, underbrush, and wetlands to the boats, then turned around to do it all again. Clark even handled a load himself and then prepared a hardy elk dinner for the packers. Afterward they returned for a final haul. About half the men lost their way on the last trip and did not get back until late, while Ordway, Colter, Collins, Whitehouse, and McNeal spent a miserable, rainy night in the woods without fire. Those at the fort worked at finishing the captains' quarters and preparing the last of the roofing materials. Three Indians arrived at the fort with two large salmon.

DECEMBER 16, 1805. It rained all night. Clark's party covered themselves in elk skins, but the pelting showers soaked through everything, nor was there a dry place to lay down. What water did not get to them from above seeped in from below. They sat up most of the night—cold, wet, and miserable. Ordway's party joined Clark's in the morning. Together they loaded meat in the canoes, and a dozen men went to retrieve two more elks at another spot. When all came together again, Clark dispatched several men to get the last of the meat from another source and then moved on to the fort. With winds blowing and trees falling accompanied by rain, hail, and thunder, Clark called it "certainly one of the worst days that ever was!" Arriving at the fort, his party transferred the elk meat to the newly completed storehouse. Clark noted in his weather diary that they had returned with sixteen elks. Several men complained of injuries from carrying the heavy loads.

DECEMBER 17, 1805. All hands at the fort were at work on the structure, mostly chinking and daubing the spaces between the logs, building doors and chimneys, and generally doing finish work. They worked on through rain, hail, and snow. In the afternoon, the men who had been left behind to secure the last of the elks arrived, but with only two of the three they sought. They stripped the carcasses of useable meat and smoked it before hanging it in the storehouse. Perhaps still sleeping in his tent, Clark complained that it had become so rotten that the slightest touch would cause a tear and that it was useless to repel rain. Gibson's health was improving.

DECEMBER 18, 1805. The barefoot, thinly clad men continued work at the fort while rain, hail, and snow pelted them. They accomplished little under the circumstances, but one party brought planking from a nearby Indian fishing camp. Lewis entered lengthy zoological observations in one of his scientific notebooks. In detail he described "a bird of the Corvus genus," the gray jay, which he compared in size to the kingbird. In the same entry he also mentioned what appears to be pinyon jay, and then the entry falls off with a partial note on Steller's jay. In an undated entry from another scientific notebook, the captain wrote a longer passage about Steller's jay, perhaps completing the unfinished material in the first one, using the blue jay for comparison.

DECEMBER 19, 1805. With a fair day before them, Clark sent Pryor with eight men in two canoes to gather boards from an abandoned Indian house near Point Adams. Everyone else kept up work on the fort. Pryor and party returned in the evening, the canoes laded with boards. Two Indians visited for a short time. The men were generally in good health, but Ordway reported himself sick.

DECEMBER 20, 1805. Using the boards brought up by Pryor, the men continued covering the huts, plus they also worked to fill cracks between the logs. Indian traders brought their usual store of goods but demanded such high prices in files and fishhooks, and especially in blue beads and tobacco, that the captains refused to purchase anything.

DECEMBER 21, 1805. Work on the cabins continued. An Indian caught stealing a horn spoon was ejected from the camp. Two men set out toward the ocean in search of bearberry, which smokers mixed with their tobacco to obtain an acceptable flavor.

DECEMBER 22, 1805. While finish work on the fort went forward, Drouillard went out to set traps for beavers. The sick list grew as men complained of boils and bruises of many kinds. Ordway, Gibson, and York seemed to fare the worst. Although they kept the meat constantly smoked, a good deal of it spoiled.

DECEMBER 23, 1805. The captains moved out of the pouring rain and into their huts while work continued on the remainder, mostly getting the roofs covered and cracks filled between the logs. Two canoes of Clatsops came to camp selling wares. Clark purchased some well-made mats and bags of horsetail and cattail; he particularly admired the bags used for carrying fish. He also bought a mountain lion skin over seven feet in length and seashore lupine in exchange for a worn-out file, six fishhooks, and pounded fish. Although the fish was spoiled, the natives seemed to favor it. Clark gave a second-level Clatsop chief a string of seashells ("wampom") and sent a little pounded fish to the ailing Cuskala.

DECEMBER 24, 1805. Overnight rain, drizzles throughout the morning, and hard rain in the evening did not prevent the men from continuing work on the fort. The majority of the party was now in the huts. Cuskala came to the camp along with wit a younger brother and two young women. The young chief brought gifts of mats and roots to the captains but later wanted two files for the items. With no files to spare, the gifts were returned. Cuskala also offered the favors of the young women, but these were declined, which upset the Clatsops very much. Joseph Field fashioned a writing slab for each of the captains, and they gave him a handkerchief for his work. With the party's store of meat spoiled, they turned to the reliable pounded fish purchased at Celilo Falls. The enlisted journalists agreed that nothing interesting happened this day or the previous one.

DECEMBER 25, 1805. At daylight the captains were awakened by the boom of gunfire, hardy shouts of the men, and a holiday songfest—"a Selute, Shout and a Song," Clark called it. Christmas Day continued with celebrations and gift giving. The captains divided the last of the tobacco among the users and gave a silk handkerchief to each of the others. Lewis gave Clark a fleece shirt, drawers, and socks, while the latter received from Whitehouse a pair of moccasins, from Goodrich a small Indian basket, from Sacagawea two dozen weasel tails, and from the Clatsops some roots, probably edible thistle. With little food to make a feast, the party settled for poor, boiled elk meat, spoiled, dried fish, and roots—"a bad

Christmass diner," declared Clark. Whitehouse was more sanguine and echoed the words of his journalist comrades when he wrote that even without alcohol the party was content with the evening's meal. Having general good health was a greater blessing "than all the luxuries this life can afford, and the party are all thankful to the Supreme Being, for his goodness towards us," he concluded. During the day the last of the party moved into the huts.

DECEMBER 26, 1805. Rain, thunder, and wind as usual. Woodworker Joseph Field finished a table and seats for the captains. The party tried to dry wet goods at campfires but found little luck in keeping the gunpowder dry, as powder horns were soaked through from constant exposure to rain. Without proper ventilation, the cabins filled with smoke, and high winds drove smoke back into the rooms that had chimneys. The men set about adding chimneys to rooms without them and fixing the failing ones. Adding to the discomfort were fleas that invested the blankets, forcing the party into a daily routine of cleaning their covers or facing fitful, sleepless nights.

DECEMBER 27, 1805. Work was completed on the chimneys, which eliminated the smoke problem, and the remaining bunks were put in place. Reuben Field and Collins (and perhaps Potts) were sent to hunt, while Drouillard, Shannon, and Labiche prepared to set out hunting the next morning. Joseph Field, Bratton, and Gibson prepared for their excursion to the coast to make salt from ocean water. Willard and Weiser were assigned to help them carry kettles and other supplies for the task. All others were busy completing the fort's gates and pickets. Coboway and four Clatsops came to the fort bearing roasted edible thistle roots, seashore lupine roots, and salal berries. These items were prized by the Clatsops and given only sparingly. They were a welcome change of diet for the captains, who had been subsisting on spoiled elk meat. In recognition of this gift, Lewis presented Coboway with a sheepskin cap, while Clark gave his son a pair of earrings, a bit of ribbon, a small piece of brass, and a couple of fishhooks. The Indians seemed pleased with the exchange. Clark noticed a novel flying insect similar to a mosquito and showed it to Lewis for inspection or identification. It may have been a crane fly.

DECEMBER 28, 1805. The designated hunters set out in the morning, as did the men bound for the Saltmaking Camp at present Seaside, Clatsop County, Oregon. A changing cadre of men would remain at the site until February 21, 1806. Picketing the fort and finishing the gates occupied others left at the fort, except for York, who was ill from a severe cold and suffering from the strain of heavy labor.

DECEMBER 29, 1805. In spite of rain during the night and a hard wind from the southeast during the day, the party relished a relatively dry but cloudy day. Coboway and his entourage left the fort during the morning but took time to ask for trinkets and articles that the captains could not spare from their dwindling reserves. Clark did give Coboway a razor. It was probably someone in Coboway's party who reported during their stay that a whale was stranded on the coast southwest of the fort near a Tillamook village. The captains had been waiting for decent weather for Lewis to set out in search of it and secure some whale oil. While York was on the mend, Cruzatte came down with a severe cold.

In the evening a Wahkiakum chief along with four men and two women arrived at the fort in a large canoe bearing wapato and elk skins to sell. The chief gave Clark about half a bushel of the roots; the captain returned the favor with one of the small Indian peace medals and a strip of red ribbon for his hat. Apparently impressed with the hat, Clark added a drawing of it in his journal. The party purchased about a bushel and a half more of the roots, giving a few red beads, bits of brass wire, and a little checked cloth in exchange. As they were getting by on spoiled elk meat, the roots were a welcome repast. Clark noted that the Wahkiakums wore little more than lightweight fur skins and robes about their bodies, which were topped off with conical hats and adorned with ornamental beads. He also noticed that the Wahkiakums kept up a regular trade in wapato with the Clatsops, explaining that they were not willing to sell more to the party but saving it for their regular trading partners. The captain also scribbled opinions about coastal Indians in his notes for the day. He found Chinook women lewd and lascivious, the Wahkiakums short, ill-formed, and unattractive, and the Clatsops reserved. But worst of all was the flea-infested native garb, whose occupants were deposited around the fort when the Indians came for a visit. Despite all precautions, the party could not escape the tormenting swarms and every night were kept awake by the biting, stinging invaders.

DECEMBER 30, 1805. A sunny morning. Four more Wahkiakums arrived at the fort and offered roots for sale, but at such high prices that the captains declined. Nonetheless, the visitors remained all day with their tribal companions. Drouillard and a party of hunters returned in the afternoon to report that they had killed four elks nearby. Six men hurried off for the harvest and returned in the evening with the meat. The party enjoyed a sumptuous and much appreciated dinner of elk tongues and bone marrow. At nightfall the fort was completed, and camp routine was established. Under his entry of March 23, 1806, Whitehouse described the fort as built "in the form of an oblong Square, & the front of it facing the [Lewis and Clark] River, was picketed in, & had a Gate on the North & one of the South side." The captains let the Indians know that the practice would be to dismiss all visitors and shut the gates at sunset and not admit anyone again before sunrise. Putting the rule into place for the first time was not easily effected, as the Wahkiakums were reluctant to go, but they set themselves up in a nearby camp. Clark called this the best day so far because of the pleasant weather: spotty clouds, light winds, and few showers. The captain commented on the large size of a slug common to the area, the Pacific woods slug.

DECEMBER 31, 1805. Two or three Wahkiakums arrived by canoe and were followed in another canoe by three Watala men and a woman, all carrying the familiar wapato, edible thistle, dried fish, dressed elk skins, and mats made from horsetails and cattails. Again the asking price was much too high for the captains, especially for the elk skins. Nonetheless, Clark purchased wapato, two mats, and a small pouch of about three pipefuls of tobacco, for which he gave a large fishhook that the Indians desired. One of the Indians brought a musket for minor repair and gave a peck of wapato for the work. Clark added a piece of flint, a sheep skin, and blue cloth to the deal; the man seemed quite satisfied. The captain found these Indians more reserved and easier to deal with than those of the previous day. Having a sentinel keeping watch, Clark surmised, put the natives on better behavior, and they gave little resistance to being ejected when it came time to shut the fort's gates. Latrines were dug during the day and a sentinel's box was built. It was probably the red-headed Jack Ramsay, whom Gass had noticed on November 23, who visited this day. Apparently understanding more English than the Clatsops he accompanied, Ramsay nevertheless remained silent. Clark thought him at least half white but noticed that he displayed all the characteristics of the natives.

JANUARY 1, 1806. Lewis returned to his regular journal keeping this day, the first such writing since August 26, 1805, except for a few scattered entries. Beginning January 6 the captain typically wrote a short paragraph about activities at the fort, then more fully about the people, flora, and fauna of the Pacific Northwest. From this day's date Clark started copying Lewis's entries almost verbatim, perhaps to have a duplicate copy of Lewis's extensive scientific data. For some unknown reason he did not always copy Lewis's notes on the same date that they were entered. He occasionally added his own notes about the day's events. The enlisted men's journal entries grew shorter during the winter as the monotony of garrison duty set in.

As at Christmas, the captains were awakened by a volley of rifle fire and now with shouts of "Happy New Year." Although not as sumptuous as New Year's Days at home, their meager meal seemed to satisfy the group, and they looked to the next year's holiday to be enjoyed in the company of loved ones. Boiled elk, wapato, and fresh water were the day's offering, but returning hunters reported fresh kill nearby—two buck elks. The captains relished the marrow bone and tongue of such catches. Gass noted that on this day the fort received its official name of Fort Clatsop. Clatsops arrived with roots and berries to trade. Not obtaining the desired metal file for their offering, they nevertheless spent the night—probably outside the gates. Lewis penned his concern for the absent Willard and Weiser, who were sent with the saltmaking party but were expected to return quickly.

Clark made a list of the local Indians and their tribal leaders as he understood them at this point. His tribal groups can be connected to historic and modern tribes with some surety, but the names of a number of the individuals cannot be so identified. Many appear only on this list and nowhere else in the journals. The captains may never have met the men and probably garbled the information they received.

Clatsops: Coboway, Sha-no-ma, and War-ho-lote

Chinooks: Tahcum, Comcomly, Shelathwell, Nor-car-te, Chin-ni-ni

Chehalis: Mar-lock-ke, Col-chote, Ci-in-twar

Tillamooks: O-co-no

Cathlamets: Cul-te-ell

Wahkiakums: Scumar-qua-up

Clark also penned a list of ship captains who visited the coastal Indians. Again, identification of these persons is far from precise given the difficulties of Clark's understanding the Indians' renditions of the names. The list seems to include Hugh Moore, Ewen or Ewens, Swepeton, McGee or Magee, Winship, Jackson, Balch or William Bowles, Haley or Samuel Hill, Lemon, Davidson, Fallawan or Tallamon, and Callallamet.

Lewis prepared a set of orders for running the fort that included the following: establishing sentinels and a guard detail (cooks and interpreters were exempt), securing the fort at night and reopening it each day, maintaining the meat house, checking the canoes, gathering wood for fires, use and care of camp tools, and elaborate rules and precautions concerning the treatment of and interactions with visiting natives. In their weather diaries the captains noted the region's sudden shifts in the climate.

JANUARY 2, 1806. Twelve to fourteen men were sent out to retrieve the elks from the previous day's hunt and returned with the larder before noon. Lewis again penned worries about Willard and Weiser and others who had not returned to the fort from their outings. The trading Clatsops of the previous day departed after obtaining fishhooks and other small items for their roots and berries. Fleas continued to infest the party, so much so that Lewis lamented that they would have to put up with them throughout their stay. Although their numbers were dwindling, Lewis still counted several species of birds, including trumpeter ("large") and tundra ("small or whistling") swans, sandhill cranes, Canada ("large") and lesser Canada ("small") geese, snow geese ("white brant"), brants, double-crested cormorants, mallards, canvasbacks, and other unspecified ducks. Drouillard captured a river otter in his traps, and the captains observed that, while not as plentiful as those on the Missouri River, the fur of beavers, raccoons, and otters was extremely good in the area and upriver to the rapids.

JANUARY 3, 1806. After counting six dreary weeks, Clark was happy to report a morning of sunshine and fair weather—brief but welcomed. The captains particularly regretted the loss of the thermometer, which prevented them from having a reliable gauge for their belief that the weather here was milder than at the same latitude on the Atlantic coast. Coboway came by for a visit with six other Clatsops and brought roots, berries, dogs, and whale blubber to trade. Lewis presented the chief with satin breeches. The visitors had obtained the blubber from coastal Tillamooks and considered it excellent food, but Lewis was more interested in the dogs at this point. He noted that many in the party had learned to accept the taste of dog meat and that he personally considered it superior to deer or elk meat. Clark disagreed with Lewis on this matter of taste. Lewis also found the men strong and healthy from a dog-meat diet and thought that it provided the best nourishment for the party since leaving buffalo country.

The captains sent Gass and Shannon toward the saltmakers' camp in search of Willard and Weiser, who were supposed to have returned at least six days earlier. Reuben Field, Collins, and Potts, gone since December 28, returned in the evening and reported that they had ascended Youngs River about fifteen miles and had hunted a considerable distance to the east but had killed only one deer and a few birds, which barely sustained them. This news renewed the captains' determination to keep hunters working to supply their meager store of meat. Lewis counted more birds in the area, including the north-western ("small") crow, Steller's jay ("blue crested corvus"), gray jay ("smaller corvus with white brest"), winter wren ("little brown ren"), bald eagle, and California condor ("Buzzard of the columbia"), as well as an unspecified sparrow.

JANUARY 4, 1806. Noting the departure of Coboway and his tribes-men, Lewis reflected a bit on local Indians. He noted that the lin-guistically related Clatsops and Chinooks had been very friendly to the party and appeared to be a mild and inoffensive people but would readily pilfer if they thought it would go undetected. He found them great hagglers in trade, so much so that they were willing to spend a whole day bargaining for the smallest of items. He noted that sometimes an individual would refuse the first price just to bar-gain, even if he ended up with a lesser reward. To put his idea to the test, Lewis once offered a native a great deal for an inferior sea otter skin but was refused, only to have him come back the next day and sell the skin for a smaller price. He thought the locals had lit-tle sense of the value or utility of an object but were willing to trade hard for any bauble that caught their fancy. Lewis took a negative view of the trait and concluded that it derived from an "avaricious all grasping disposition."

Gass and Shannon made their way toward the Saltmaking Camp over low ground and through marshes to the coast, where they encountered a creek they could not pass without a boat. Here they spent the night just north of Seaside, Clatsop County, and dined on the tongue of an elk that Shannon had killed earlier in the day.

JANUARY 5, 1806. With relief the captains reported that Willard and Weiser had returned. It had taken them five days to find a suit-able spot for a saltworks, where they also found friendly Tillamook Indians who shared the blubber of a beached whale. The two had brought some of the meat with them, and Lewis declared it like hog fat in appearance and somewhat like the taste of beaver or dog meat when cooked. The other members of the saltworks party, Joseph Field, Bratton, and Gibson, remained at the new spot after erect-ing a comfortable camp and laying in a considerable amount of elk and deer meat. They quickly began boiling sea water for salt and found that they could get about three or four quarts a day. Lewis got a taste of the results and declared it "excellent, fine, strong, & white." The captain was much elated, since he had been without salt for some time; it made little difference to Clark. Lewis elaborated on his desire for salt in his diet, noting also that he did not miss bread and was open to about any source of meat, be it dog, horse, or wolf. He summarized his food philosophy in this way: "I have learned to think that if the chord be sufficiently strong, which binds the soul and boddy together, it dose not so much matter about the materials which compose it."

Another wayward explorer, Colter, also returned in the evening after a hunt of scant success. Gass reported that he and Shannon built a raft to cross the creek of the previous day, but the boat would carry only one man. Shannon went first, with the aim to push the boat back to Gass, but that failed, forcing Gass to go into the icy water to retrieve the craft in order to get to the other side. The two men continued on to Clatsop dwellings at modern Seaside, where they spent the night. At the fort, Clark gathered trade goods and readied to set out the next day with a small party in search of the whale reported by Willard and Weiser.

JANUARY 6, 1806. After an early breakfast Clark set out for the whale site with his party. The composition of the party is not entirely clear, but it seems that Charbonneau, Sacagawea (surely with her baby), Pryor, Frazer, McNeal, and Werner at least were on the trip, with perhaps thirteen in all. In fact, Sacagawea may have been an uninvited addition until she made clear her intention to see the ocean and the "monstrous fish." The captains said they "indulged" her. Clark began a makeshift field journal of his trip that goes through January 10. From internal evidence it appears fairly certain that Clark used this fragment as a first draft for his standard journal and may have copied the material into the regular notebook after returning to Fort Clatsop. (As with other multiple entries, the two are here blended into a single narrative.)

Lewis began a discourse on natives of the area—Clatsops, Chinooks, and Tillamooks. He characterized them as physically displeasing, especially in comparison to Indians of the Missouri. He found them talkative and inquisitive, with good memories and a cheerful nature. The Indian men talked openly and in the most private terms about native women and would prostitute their wives and daughters for trinkets. The women, as with other Indians whom Lewis knew, performed most of the domestic drudgery, but here the men participated in the work. Indeed, Lewis found that the women seemed to command a degree of authority in tribal and domestic affairs. The captain concluded with a maxim that in communities in which women participated in family subsistence, women and the elderly were treated better than in places where men were the sole providers. Thinking filial ties less strong naturally, Lewis praised "civilization" for the care it accorded women and the elderly. He noted that Missouri Indians would abandon their elderly, telling them that they had lived long enough and that it was time to pass on. But in the Missouri villages he also saw that the elderly and disabled were treated well. The captain attended to mundane matters during the day, such as hauling out and drying damp materials and counting the party's store of merchandise. He found trading goods reduced to a mere handful and fretted about the prospects for getting back with so little.

Clark and party took two canoes into the Lewis and Clark River toward Young's Bay, intending to find a Clatsop guide to take them to the whale site and Saltmaking Camp. Beset by high waves at the bay, the party retreated and abandoned the canoes at or near the Skipanon River, Clatsop County, Oregon, ready to go by land. The captain had passed this way on December 8, 9, and 10, 1805. Here they saw elks and were able to take one, butcher it, and carry it to their camp on Neacoxie Creek, Clatsop County. Gass and Shannon reached the Saltmaking Camp.

JANUARY 7, 1806. Drouillard's catch in his trap the previous night brought welcome food for the corps at the fort, and they ate "sumptuously" (according to Lewis) on the fat of a beaver during the day. The animal also supplied bait for catching others. Such a find induced Lewis to describe the intricate details of preparation of castoreum and how it worked to attract other beavers. He also gave attention to beaver behavior. Concluding that "nothing extraordinary hap-pened today," the captain noted that this was the first day without rain since the party had arrived at the Fort Clatsop location.

Clark and party continued their trek to the whale site at day-break. They found a tree trunk left by the saltmakers to cross a creek, then followed the Necanicum River, Clatsop County, Ore-gon, to its mouth at the coast, where they found a small Indian vil-lage occupied by a single family. Clark gave a local man a fishhook to get the party across the river. After the crossing, the captain dis-covered an unfamiliar fish, probably the big skate. Soon the party came to the saltmakers' camp at Seaside, Clatsop County, Oregon, near Tillamook Head, the party's "Clark's Point of View." Clark called the situation "a neet Close Camp, Convenient to wood Salt water and the fresh water of [the Necanicum River]." The camp was also near a Clatsop and Tillamook village of four houses whose inhab-itants had been very kind to the saltmakers. Clark hired a young Indian from there to guide his party to the whale, gave him a file for his services, and promised other small rewards after a success-ful return. They set out toward Tillamook Head, when the guide stopped, pointed to the hill, and uttered "Pe Shack," a Chinook jar-gon word for "bad." They had to ascend the hill.

Clark was apprehensive when he viewed the "emence mountain" reaching nearly straight up with its top obscured by clouds. See-ing a well-used Indian path, he thought the climb might be tolera-ble but soon found the going quite difficult, as the men had to pull themselves up by bushes, taking nearly two hours of hard labor to reach the top. From this point Clark estimated the height of Tilla-mook Head as "10 to 12 hundred feet"; its highest point is 1,136 feet above sea level. Clark noticed a stratum of "white earth" that his guide informed him the locals used to paint themselves. Recent research indicates that Tillamook Head was formed by seams of molten Grande Ronde Basalt lava that intruded into the Cannon Beach Member of the Astoria Formation. At the top they met four-teen Indian men and women carrying the oil and blubber of a whale. The explorers continued along a bad road and encamped at a small creek, perhaps Canyon Creek of Tillamook Head. Clark concluded, "all much fatiagued."

JANUARY 8, 1806. Worried about the supply of meat, Lewis sent Drouillard and Collins to hunt. He also worried about the absence of Gass and Shannon, who should have returned by now. He added guard duty to the cooks' routine, since the party's diminished numbers were putting a strain on the guards. Otherwise, the captain recorded that "nothing extraordinary happened today." Lewis continued his essay on coastal Indians. He found them fond of smoking and of doing so in a peculiar manner: they would inhale fully and deeply, holding the vapor as long as possible before exhaling, in order to get the full intoxicating effect. This activity had its effects on the bowels, or as Lewis put it, "they freequently give us sounding proofs of it's creating a dismorallity of order in the abdomen." Coastal Indians did not appear to know the use of alcohol and apparently had not received any from Euro-American traders. Lewis thought that fortunate.

On Tillamook Head Clark and party rose early and ascended to the highest part facing the sea, perhaps Bird Point. From there he "beheld the grandest and most pleasing prospects which my eyes ever surveyed." To the northwest he viewed Cape Disappointment, along the Columbia River he saw Chinook and Clatsop villages, and to the south and southeast he viewed the rocky coast for a great distance. The guide pointed to the mouth of Ecola Creek, the whale's location, and to four nearby Tillamook villages. Clark and company descended to an old Tillamook village. There Clark saw large canoes in which the Tillamooks had laid the coffins of their dead. He also noticed that hills near the village were slipping away. These landslides of the sandstone and mudstone of the Miocene-age Cannon Beach Member of the Astoria Formation occur when excess water saturates the soft rocks and deep soil. Nevertheless, the hills were covered with pines, firs, western redcedars, and red alders. The party moved on to Ecola (an expedition name from Chinookan, meaning "whale") Creek on the north side of Cannon Beach, Clatsop County, Oregon, where they discovered only the bony fragments of the once-great whale. The natives had stripped it of all its edible parts. Clark measured it at 105 feet, making it perhaps a blue whale. Returning to one of the villages, Clark found the natives busily engaged in boiling the blubber and extracting the oil. The captain was unable to purchase much of the whale meat or oil and found the natives stingy with their supply. With his scant supply of trade items he was eventually able to get three hundred pounds of meat and a few gallons of oil. In spite of the meager size of the purchase, he thanked providence for being kinder to him than he was to the biblical Jonah and for "having Sent this monster to be *Swallowed by us* in Sted of *Swallowing of us* as jonah's did."

The party crossed back over Ecola Creek and camped for the night on its north side in the north part of Cannon Beach. Tillamooks followed them into camp and gave Clark a chance to interview them through signs and gestures. The Tillamook ("Killamox") Indians lived south of the Clatsops in southern Clatsop, Tillamook, and northern Lincoln Counties, Oregon, along the coast. Their most northern village was shared with the Clatsops at Seaside. They belonged to a coastal branch of the Salishan language family, and in spite of the language difference, they shared many cultural traits with the Clatsops, who are Chinookan speakers. About bedtime Clark heard yelling on the opposite side of Ecola Creek and soon discovered that McNeal was not in camp and got disquieting news from the Indian guide about somebody's throat being cut. Clark sent Pryor and four men across for McNeal, who found him and brought him back to the camp. McNeal revealed that he had been lured away by promises of getting some fish. When things were sorted out they learned that there was a plot to kill McNeal for his blanket and clothes but that a Chinook woman gave an alarm that saved him. Clark put a sentinel and guard on alert for the night. Because of McNeal's blunder, the captain for a time seems to have renamed Ecola Creek, calling it "McNeal's Folly," but soon returned it to its first designation. Clark does not mention this name but Ordway and Whitehouse do. The captain was quite fatigued and weak from hunger. He confided that the trip back to the fort might be more difficult than the trip out but confidently wrote, "a deturmined [purcistance?] will . . . carry me through."

JANUARY 9, 1806. The men at the fort were mostly engaged in making clothing and moccasins from deer and elk skins. Lewis hoped that gunshots heard south of the fort were those of hunters Drouillard and

Collins shooting elks, especially since the party had been subsisting on poor, dried elk meat for several days.

The captain continued with his essay on local Indians. He noted that they buried their dead in small canoes, and then largely duplicated Clark's description of November 30. Then he turned to discussing the region's trade with Euro-Americans. He observed that locals knew a number of English words, including salty sailor language, and he learned that traders usually arrived about April and stayed for six or seven months. The traders brought outdated weapons, manufactured goods (particularly beads, especially the treasured blue ones), tobacco, and western cloth and clothing, while the natives provided skins of various animals, including elks, sea and river otters, beavers, foxes, and bobcats, along with dried salmon and cous. In his notes referencing the captains' journal entries for January 14, Biddle pointed out that New England traders used the elk skins to trade for more sea otter skins farther north, which they then took to trade in the East Indies.

Clark's party set out at sunrise and "Shudder at the dreadfull road on which we have to return . . . 35 miles" to Fort Clatsop. Along the way they met several Chinook and Clatsop Indians on their way to trade for oil and blubber from the Tillamooks. The explorers overtook one group of five men and six women taking back heavy loads of the stuff after a trading session. One of the women dropped her load while in a precarious position, so Clark tried to help by holding her bag as she righted herself. To his astonishment it was all he could do to lift it and estimated that it must have weighed over one hundred pounds. The party came to the saltworks late in the evening fully exhausted, while the Indians continued on. The Indian traders promised to come to the fort later and sell them oil and blubber. Clark encouraged them. They spent the night with the saltmakers at Seaside, Clatsop County, Oregon. At this point in his main journal, Clark copied almost verbatim Lewis's discourse on the local Indians from his journal entry of January 6, enabling us to understand that entries for this period must have been written later from Clark's whale-trip rough draft and from Lewis's own journal entries during Clark's absence. At the end of the copied material Clark added his own observations on the aged at the Mandan villages. He then concluded the day's entry with notes about the activities at the Saltmaking Camp.

JANUARY 10, 1806. Lewis was visited at the fort by a chief of the Cathlamets with eleven of his people in a large canoe; he gave his name as "Shâh-hâr-wâr-cap." He had missed the explorers on their way out since he was hunting at the time. The captain gave him one of the smaller Indian peace medals and other items while the chief presented Indian tobacco and a basket of wapato. The Cathlamets also brought dried salmon, wapato, dogs, and mats to barter; they were able to sell two dogs and wapato. Drouillard and Collins were successful in getting one elk only, and Lewis lamented that meat was becoming scarce. Clark left Gass with the saltmakers until Shannon returned from hunting, then ordered that both return to the fort. At sunrise he set out, waded the Necanicum River, and continued the route by which they had come out. They arrived at the fort at ten o'clock at night, and Lewis recounted the trip to the whale in his own journal, using the biblical story of Jonah in words almost identical to Clark's narrative. We may suppose that Clark copied the phrasing from Lewis, since it is not typical of Clark's writing. The biblical allusion is not given in Clark's rough draft journal. Clark's geologic notes about Tillamook Head may also have come from Lewis, who inspected and described a specimen brought back by Clark. Clark then picked up Lewis's discussion of the neighborhood's Indians from his entry of January 8 and also copied his notes on beavers from the entry of January 7.

JANUARY 11, 1806. Clark returned to writing in his regular journal and laid aside the field journal he used on the whale trip. He also resumed copying Lewis's entries almost verbatim. A small party went after an elk that was killed on January 9, which they brought back in the evening. An unsuccessful search for a missing canoe occupied several in the party for a good part of the day. Lewis considered it a significant loss since it was a light but sturdy boat capable of carrying a sizeable load. The visiting Cathlamets left during the evening on their way to barter with Clatsops for whale meat and oil. Lewis commented on this Indian trade that moved goods up and down the Columbia River and included items brought by white traders to the coast.

JANUARY 12, 1806. Giving Drouillard special recognition for his hunting skills, Lewis wrote, "I scarcely know how we should subsist were it not for the exertions of this excellent hunter." Later Biddle would provide in his book even more praise for Drouillard and add material not found in the captains' journals: "[He] is the offspring of a Canadian Frenchman, and an Indian woman, has passed his life in the woods, and unites, in a wonderful degree, the dexterous aim of the frontier huntsman, with the intuitive sagacity of the Indian, in pursuing the faintest tracks through the forest." In the afternoon the balance of Clark's whale-trip party came back to the fort, as did others who had been hunting unsuccessfully. Finding the men wasteful with freshly killed meat, the captains decided to stop dividing available food among the four messes and begin a new system with Drouillard's seven elks. Henceforth they would dry (jerk) the meat and distribute it in small quantities. The region's waterfowl were still in view.

JANUARY 13, 1806. Lewis took all available men to recover the seven elks killed the day before by Drouillard. They found the kill in good order and hardly touched by wolves, which Lewis noted as being scarce in the area. The elks' tallow, meager at best, was used to replenish the party's exhausted supply of candles. Lewis was pleased with his forethought in bringing along candle molds and wicks. The captain continued with his narrative about neighborhood Indians—this time discussing trade and enumerating Columbia tribes involved in the activity. White traders usually arrived at Cape Disappointment in April and stayed until October. Resident Indians pulled their canoes alongside the trading ships in Baker's ("Haley's") Bay and negotiated from the river, since there were no accommodations on shore for the purpose. Lewis described the bay as "spacious and commodious, and perfectly secure from all except the S. and S.E. winds" with fresh water and adequate timber to refit and repair ships. Indian groups near Cape Disappointment carried on direct trade with the Euro-Americans, while those upriver (in diminishing numbers) also participated. Upriver tribes, like the Watlalas ("Skil-lutes") were intermediaries between the downriver direct traders and upriver tribes who desired the manufactured goods.

JANUARY 14, 1806. One of the large pirogues broke loose during the night and was carried away by the tide. A search party found it and brought it back in about three hours. Lewis reflected that the loss of this pirogue would have been a serious setback since it would have taken three small canoes to replace it, and the party was short the necessary tools to build them. The captains then directed three of the pirogues be drawn up out of tide's reach; the fourth was secured near the fort's landing. The captains estimated that from Celilo ("Great") Falls or the Deschutes River to the Cascades of the Columbia ("Great Shute or Rapids"), Indians along the Columbia River annually prepared about thirty thousand pounds of pounded salmon for the coastal market. They could not determine if it was exclusively for seacoast consumption or whether it was also used in commerce with white traders. In spite of local Indians telling them that they used the commodity for trade with whites, the captains could not imagine that Euro-Americans would be interested in pounded fish. Clark ended his entry by copying Lewis's notes of January 9 on coastal trade, where the captain had mentioned other Indian exchange items. The captains marveled at the temperate climate and declared they had never experienced such a warm winter.

JANUARY 15, 1806. Lewis had a large coat made of bobcat skins and from an unfamiliar animal, the mountain beaver (which he described on February 26). He used finished robes that he bought from Indians for the coat, and it took seven of them to make the item. So incessant was the rain that hunters were confined to camp. The captain's brief description of the day's events ended with "no occurrence worthy of relation took place today." From there he filled space with a description of native hunting tools, including guns, bows and arrows, spears, deadfalls, snares, and pits. He found the guns of inferior quality, being largely discarded American and

British muskets repaired for this trade; they had no rifles. What few good weapons they had were worn and not properly maintained. When lacking ammunition, they shot gravel or metal shards that damaged the guns, which Lewis thought they did not understand or were unconcerned about. Use of bows and arrows was much more common; they were made from western redcedar and covered with elk sinew, and the bowstrings were also of elk sinew. Expedition hunters frequently found elks still carrying Indian arrows embedded in their flesh. Since hunting from boats was common, the Indians used arrows that would float and not be lost in water. Deadfalls and snares were used for entrapping wolves, raccoons, and foxes., while spears were used to take sea and river otters and beavers. Pits were used to capture elks and were quite large to accommodate the animal. The holes were cleverly disguised and placed at points frequented by elks.

JANUARY 16, 1806. Lewis seemed satisfied with the party's situation. With plenty of elk meat, a little salt, and dry, comfortable quarters, they seemed content to remain at the fort until the projected departure date of April 1. The captain found no advantage in traveling upriver earlier and several negatives, as the Indians informed him that they would find even less fuel for cooking on the treeless plains than they had on the outbound journey. Of course, the Rocky Mountains posed a great barrier, where snow would be upwards of twenty feet deep in places. It would be June before they could consider a crossing, hence the choice of April 1 for departure.

Lewis returned to his narrative of native customs. In fishing the Indians relied on straight nets, scooping or dipping nets, gigs, and hook and line. Common nets were used in taking salmon and trout in inlets and at the mouths of deep creeks. The scooping nets were used for smaller fish, while gigs and hooks were employed in all seasons to take any fish available. Nets and fishing line were made of dogbane ("silk-grass") or western redcedar bark, and hooks were of European manufacture. In earlier times the hooks were made from bones or other natural substances. Lewis described and drew a picture of a traditional hook in his journal. The enlisted writers talked about rain, "as usal."

JANUARY 17, 1806. Coboway and seven other Clatsops arrived for a visit and a trading session. They asked such high prices for their roots and berries that the explorers refused to buy. Nonetheless, the captains gave the chief a moccasin awl and thread, and he offered his own goods. One of Coboway's men was dressed in an elegant piece made from three sea otter skins. The captains (probably Lewis) tried to buy it but could not make a deal without the highly sought after blue beads, which the Indians called "Chiefs beads." The captains' stock of blue beads was small—not even enough to make the trade. Hunter Colter brought back a deer, a rare treat for the party, while Drouillard and Lepage went after elks and beavers.

Lewis continued his discourse on neighboring Indians, this time featuring their cooking and eating utensils, which consisted of wooden bowls, spoons, spits, and baskets. The bowls were shaped from a solid piece and Lewis thought them "extreemly well executed" and "neatly carved." The spoons were "not remarkable nor abundant." The spits were used for roasting meat and fish, while mats of rushes or cattails served as plates. Beargrass baskets were closely woven and watertight without the aid of glue. Beargrass was not found locally but came from high altitudes of snowy ranges, thus forming an article of commerce among the tribes. The threads were dyed in several colors and woven to create a variety of figures. The conic shape allowed the Indians to use them for carrying items or to wear as hats. The size varied from a small cup to five or six gallons. The Indians made them quickly and easily and sold them cheaply. Other nonwatertight baskets were made of cedar bark, dogbanes, rushes, cattails, and coarse sedges.

JANUARY 18, 1806. With few events at the fort to report, Lewis got right into his discourse on area Indians—this time about their housing. The rectangular, gabled plankhouse he described was typical of Chinookans on the Pacific Coast from southern Alaska to northern California, with variations in size and detail. Lewis measured them from fourteen to twenty feet wide and from twenty to sixty feet in length, accommodating up to three or four families. Supporting posts were first sunk in the ground, reaching upward from fourteen to eighteen feet. Then round beams were placed horizontally on top from one post to another the entire length of the house to form a ridgepole. Now other posts were placed on either side parallel to the center to serve as support for the roof and eaves. After that rafters were attached, as were ends, sides, and interior partitions. Finally finishing boards of cedar plank were secured to the outside and the roof was covered except for a hole in the center for smoke to escape. The house was sometimes sunk four or five feet into the earth, causing the eaves nearly to reach the ground. Inside a center space was dug out to serve as the fireplace and mats were spread around it for seating during the day and for occasional sleeping at night. Shelves were fixed along the inside walls where occupants placed their belongings. Clark's copy of Lewis's entry made changes to the size and structure of the houses.

JANUARY 19, 1806. Colter and Willard were sent toward Point Adams while Labiche and Shannon were sent up the Lewis and Clark River in search of elks and deer. Two Clatsop men and one woman brought sea otter skins for sale. The captains used the last of the party's blue beads, plus some small white ones and a knife, to purchase one of the hides. They also bought whale oil with a pair of brass armbands and a Clatsop hat with fishing hooks. The captains described the hats as similar to ones worn in the states in 1800, that is, like a top hat but with a lower crown and wider brim. Here the crown was larger at the top and the brim narrower.

Lewis returned to his examination of Indian customs and culture. He noted that extended families lived in the large plankhouses, shared their provisions, and appeared to live in harmony. Within the house a son rather than the father usually served as head of the household. Local families were generally monogamous, but polygamy was not against custom. Associated families formed bands with each, acknowledging the authority of a chief whose position was neither hereditary nor all powerful. Chiefs attained their position based on good character, ability, and service and were granted deference equal to the esteem in which they were held. Tribal laws, "like those of all uncivilized Indians," were based on local customs established over time. The captains felt encumbered in their inquiries by their inability to speak the language.

JANUARY 20, 1806. Three Clatsop men came to the fort for visiting and smoking but not for the usual trading. From them the captains learned that white traders did not barter for pounded fish but that it was bought and consumed by native populations. The captains had concluded as much. Gass disclosed that the Clatsops were allowed to spend the night in the fort, contrary to usual practice. Lewis enumerated local plants on which the Indians subsisted: edible thistle, western bracken fern, giant horsetail ("rush"), seashore lupine ("Liquorice"), and a "celindric root" that was unknown to the captain and tasted like a sweet potato to him. Its identity is unknown. On the eighteenth the captains had issued six pounds of jerked meat per person and by this evening all was gone. At this rate they calculated that Drouillard's seven elks would last only three days more, but no one seemed concerned. Having frequently reduced their provisions to almost nothing or even having gone hungry on occasion, the party hardly gave a thought to the situation. Confidence in the hunters' abilities bred a bit of indifference.

JANUARY 21, 1806. True to the party's confidence, Shannon and Labiche returned from their hunt having killed three elks. The captains arranged for a party to go after the kill the next day and planned to send Shannon and Labiche hunting again. Lewis filled the next several days' entries by describing plants he had noted on January 20, beginning with the edible thistle, which the natives called "shan-ne-táh-que" (variously spelled). It was nine to fifteen inches long, rose to three or four feet, and was about the size of a "mans thumb." When taken from the ground it was white and almost as crisp as a carrot, but when prepared like camas, it changed to black and became quite sweet. It flourished in deep, rich, dry loam that contained a good portion of sand. The captain wrote in detail of the plant's morphology using scientific terminology that may have come from one of his reference books. He collected a specimen on March 13.

JANUARY 22, 1806. Ordway, Gass, Whitehouse, and about a dozen others who were sent to bring back the elks killed the day before by Shannon and Labiche returned with the catch, but it was in poor condition. Reuben Field joined Shannon and Labiche in another hunting excursion. The captains had no word from other hunting parties, Colter and Willard in one and Drouillard and Lepage in another. The salt supply was exhausted. Lewis continued with his discourse on native plants, here the western bracken fern. The captain found it growing abundantly in open spaces of "deep loose rich black lome." On the roots there was a white substance that when roasted tasted similar to wheat dough. Lewis thought the food nutritious but found the flavor unpleasant ("pungency"), while Indians seemed to relish it. Again the captain provided detailed notes on the plant's morphology. Clark cut short his copy of Lewis's notes on the fern and instead copied his entry of January 24 on the seashore lupine.

JANUARY 23, 1806. Lewis sent Howard and Werner to the Saltmaking Camp for a supply of the condiment. Lacking animal brains for tanning elk skins for clothing, the explorers were also deficient in other possible substitutes, making the men's work difficult. Lewis discussed another of his enumerated local plants, the giant horsetail ("rush"). He described the bulb as about one inch in length and thick as a "man's thumb." The pulp was eaten raw or roasted, usually the latter, was found along the seacoast in sandy soil, and was favored by the Tillamooks. Lewis found its taste rather insipid. He gave attention to its morphology. In his entry Clark borrowed notes from Lewis's entry of January 24 to picture and describe a Chinookan digging tool. The sun came out for about two hours, but the day remained hazy nonetheless.

JANUARY 24, 1806. Drouillard and Lepage returned this morning bringing Coboway and six Clatsops with them. The hunters also brought two deer, the meat of three elks, and the hide of another. They had given the meat of another elk and three elk skins to the Clatsops as payment for their help in transporting the meat back to the fort from Point Adams. Gass observed that the Indians were barefooted despite snow on the ground; they were permitted to spend the night in the fort. The Indians had seen Drouillard shoot some elks and were impressed with American marksmanship and weaponry. Lewis thought that valuable, since it might keep them in check if they had hostile intentions toward the corps. Lewis's air gun also amazed the natives, who could not understand its repeating function and considered it "*great medicine.*"

Lewis finished his survey of native plants with notes on the seashore lupine ("liquorice"). He considered it much the same as the common wild licorice of the states. It liked a deep, loose, sandy soil and was abundant in the area. Indians roasted it in embers, then pounded it to separate and discard a tough center part while eating the rest. Lewis found even that part hard to chew but likened the flavor to the sweet potato. The wapato was not enumerated or discussed here because it did not grow in this area, but Lewis called it the most valuable plant in the Columbia valley, not only as a foodstuff but also as a trade item. Lewis closed his entry with a brief description and picture of a Chinookan digging tool made with a wood handle and a deer- or elk-antler spade and used to obtain edible roots.

JANUARY 25, 1806. Coboway and the other Clatsops left this morning. Colter returned to report that Willard was staying out to hunt from Point Adams to the saltworks camp. They had killed only two deer, which the Clatsops brought in the day before. In the evening Collins came back with one of the saltmakers and reported that they had made about one bushel of salt and that he and two others had hunted around the camp for five days without killing anything. They had subsisted on whale meat obtained from natives. Lewis named the local fruits and berries that he would discuss in detail over the next several days' entries: salal ("*Shal-lun*"), a variety of false Solomon's seal ("*Sol'-me*"), wild cranberry, Oregon crabapple, and bearberry ("*sac a commis*"). The captain ended the day's entry by noting that Indians south of the Tillamooks had distinct languages but that he had not been able to obtain examples of them. Winter had definitely arrived, with noticeable cold, a half inch of snow on the ground, and ice covering the canoes.

JANUARY 26, 1806. Lewis voiced the party's concern for Werner and Howard, who had been sent to the Saltmaking Camp on January 23 and were still gone. He thought that since neither was an able woodsman they might be lost. Even skilled outdoorsmen could get lost in this cloud-covered, heavily timbered country. Collins was to return to the saltworks the next day and was directed to carry small trade goods to exchange for food in case hunting was unsuccessful. The enlisted journalists all mentioned the snow and freezing cold, as did the captains in their weather diaries. Gass said it was the first freeze of any consequence.

Lewis intended to begin his descriptive narrative of the plants enumerated the day before, but he misidentified the plant of this day as salal, when he actually discussed the evergreen huckleberry (an expedition discovery), one not listed. Lewis later realized his error and described the salal on February 8; he came back to the huckleberry on February 11. The evergreen huckleberry is an expedition scientific discovery, and a specimen was collected on January 27. The captain noted its morphology and native uses. The Indians ate ripe berries straight from the bushes or would sun dry or kiln dry them for later use. Frequently they would pound them and bake them into large loaves of ten to fifteen pounds, then dip broken pieces into cold water and eat them. The bread kept well for a season and retained its moistness.

JANUARY 27, 1806. While Collins set out for the saltworks, Shannon appeared and reported that he and his party had killed ten elks. Labiche and Reuben Field had stayed with the elks. Two of the elks were at inaccessible spots, so Lewis opted to abandon them rather than send a party into very difficult terrain. He ordered all able-bodied men who could be spared to prepare to reclaim the remaining elks the next morning. The captain claimed to have cured (but probably had not) Goodrich of syphilis ("Louis veneri"), as he had Gibson earlier by using mercury. Lewis said that Goodrich contracted the disease from an "amorous contact with a Chinnook damsel." The captain could not discover that locals had any remedies for the disease but noted that through the use of simple medicines and diet an afflicted person might live a fairly normal, if somewhat shortened, life. He described decoctions that Indians of the Atlantic states used for the purpose and claimed them effective against gonorrhea, if not syphilis. In fact, the captain had observed few cases of gonorrhea and only slightly more of syphilis on the Columbia River. The captains thought this the coldest night they had experienced so far on the coast.

Returning to his essay on plants, Lewis reported on false Solomon's seal ("*solme*"). The plant under review could have been either of two varieties that have the same vernacular name. Giving a brief description of its morphology and habitat, the captain did not include his usual ethnobotanical notes.

JANUARY 28, 1806. Drouillard and Lepage set out on a hunting excursion, and about noon Howard and Werner returned from the Saltmaking Camp with a supply of the seasoning. They had been delayed by a poor road and bad weather. The saltmakers were still underprovisioned, subsisting on two deer for nearly the last week and without an elk in sight. The party sent to retrieve the elks that Shannon reported on the day before returned to the fort in the evening with only three of them. Ordway and Whitehouse counted fourteen in the retrieving party, including themselves. The accumulation of snow since the kill had covered the animals and altered the look of the country to such an extent that Shannon was unable to locate the rest of them. Whitehouse mentioned that his feet were severely frostbitten.

Lewis turned to his plant descriptions, this time wild cranberry and Oregon crabapple. He gave only a nod to the well-known wild cranberry and focused on the crabapple. In describing the plant he noted its similarity to the wild crabapple of the states. Local Indians made great use of the plant's hard wood, particularly to make wedges for splitting softer wood to build their houses and canoes and to ready their firewood. The explorers also used seasoned crabapple wood for wedges and axe handles.

JANUARY 29, 1806. Using the last of the whale meat that they had carefully rationed, the party turned to the elks recently acquired. Lewis revealed that "on this food I do not feel strong, but enjoy the most perfect health . . . a keen appetite supplys in a great degree the want of more luxurious sauses or dishes, and still render my

ordinary meals not uninteresting to me, for I find myself sometimes enquiring of the cook whether dinner or breakfast is ready."
Registering the monotony of camp life, Ordway lamented, "we do
nothing except git wood for our fires." The captain finished the
day's entry discussing bearberry ("*Sac a commis*"). Found around
Fort Clatsop in prairies and on woodland borders, the evergreen
shrub seemed to flourish even in poor soil, and its berries were little harmed by winter frost. Although natives much appreciated it,
Lewis found the berry tasteless and insipid. The captain provided a
detailed morphology of the plant but little ethnobotany. Clark copied Lewis's notes of this day and the next out of sequence.

JANUARY 30, 1806. Since "nothing transpired today worthy of notice,"
Lewis turned his attention to the dress and tools of the Clatsops. He
found little difference between their clothing and that of the Watlalas ("skillutes") on the Columbia River. They wore neither leggings or moccasins due to the mild weather and the constant need
to be in water. The Clatsop conic hat intrigued him so much that he
provided a detailed description of it in his journal. Made of cedar
bark and beargrass, it was tightly woven to shed rain and was kept
in place by a chin strap. Weavers worked-in variously colored figures such as whales, canoes, or harpooners, along with geometric
shapes. The Clatsops preferred a double-edged, double-pointed knife.
The blades on either end of a handle were of unequal lengths, nine
to ten inches on one end, four to five on the other. Clatsops carried the knives openly or sometimes under their robes. They used
them mostly to cut and clean fish. The captains pictured the conic
hat and knife in their journals.

JANUARY 31, 1806. A party of eight men, including Gass, started
up the Lewis and Clark River in search of elks but returned shortly
since the river was obstructed with ice. Joseph Field arrived in the
evening to report that he, Willard, and Gibson had been hunting
for several days to secure meat for the saltmakers. They were finally
successful in getting two elks about midway between the fort and
the camp. Gibson and Willard were behind tending the kill, while
Field came to fetch men to help get the meat to the saltmakers.

Lewis gave McNeal medicine for a case of syphilis ("pox"). Charbonneau brought the captain a bird he found near the fort. Lewis recognized it as the same bird he had seen on September 20 in the Rocky Mountains; it was the varied thrush. The captain added detail to his earlier description of the bird. He called it a "beautifull little bird" but had never heard it sing and incorrectly thought it might be songless. The captains reported on other birds in their weather diaries: swans, brants, geese, ducks, cranes, cormorants, jays, ravens, and crows.

FEBRUARY 1, 1806. Four men set out to help Joseph Field retrieve the elks for the saltmakers. Gass led a party of five men back on the Lewis and Clark River to get the elks that Shannon and party had killed some days earlier. The party opened their canisters of gunpowder and were pleased to find the contents dry and in good order, especially since some of the canisters had been submerged during boating accidents. Lewis was also pleased with his foresight in devising a method of securing powder in lead canisters that doubled as shot when melted down. Clark matched praise for his ingenuity. The captains were careful to distribute the canisters among the canoes in case of loss. Lewis concluded that their ammunition "is now our only hope for subsistence and defence in a rout of 4000 miles through a country exclusively inhabited by savages." Clark substituted "Indians" for "savages" but went on to write, "many bands of which are Savage in every sense of the word."

The captains were impressed by coastal Indian canoes, calling them neat, light, and maneuverable. Lewis said, "I have seen the natives near the coast riding waves in these canoes with safety and apparently without concern where I should have thought it impossible for any vessel of the same size to [have] lived a minute." They were usually built of western redcedar but sometimes of fir and were cut from a solid piece of timber. All had crossbars proportionate to their length that were used to hoist and manage the craft on land. The largest ones were upwards of fifty feet long and capable of carrying eight-to-ten-thousand-pound loads and twenty to thirty persons. When afloat the canoes were guided by a boatman at the stern while others worked in pairs with paddles over either side. All knelt, sitting on their heels. Lewis drew a picture of and described the ubiquitous and uniform paddle.

The captain wrote at length about and pictured four types of regional canoes, while Clark followed suit and added another. The first was a small canoe, perhaps the so-called shovel-nose canoe of the Chinooks, about fifteen feet long and able to carry one or two persons. The next, the high bow, was twenty-five to thirty-five feet long, perhaps the "Chinook" canoe that was actually made by the Nootkas of Vancouver Island, British Columbia, and traded south to the Chinooks. The third (and most common) was thirty to thirty-five feet long and capable of carrying ten to twelve persons. It could be portaged by four men. The final and largest canoe (with carved images) was not encountered until the party reached the Cascades of the Columbia. From there on it was common to most tribes but particularly to the Tillamooks and others along the coast. Its distinguishing feature was the "grotesque figures" carved and mounted on the boats. Clark added a description of another small canoe, from sixteen to twenty feet long and most common among the Wahkiakums and Cathlamets, who used it to navigate the marshy islands near their villages. Lewis also discussed the tools used in building the canoes: axes and chisels formed from files. The natives were very skillful in their use and could build a canoe with the tools in a few weeks.

FEBRUARY 2, 1806. The captains described the local Indian hand game, which was quite similar to that of the Hidatsas and Shoshones. Indeed, it was nearly universal among American Indians and consisted of tossing a small object from one hand to the other, then wagering about which hand held the piece. Lewis also mentioned a bowling game, but he had not been able to learn much about it. The captain found natives "excessively fond of their games of risk and bet freely every species of property of which they are possessed."

FEBRUARY 3, 1806. Rain washed away an early morning snow and by nine the sun was out. Drouillard and Lepage returned in the afternoon, reporting that Drouillard had killed seven elks several miles from the fort but that they were accessible by canoe. The captains sent Pryor and several men to retrieve the elks, but they had to delay several hours due to high winds. They eventually got underway but were forced back because of low water. The captains feared that the unattended elks would be poached by Clatsops. Later in the afternoon Gass and party also came in and brought the meat of four elks, a part of the kill from previous days. The sergeant left Reuben Field, Shannon, and Labiche to continue hunting. The four men who had been helping Joseph Field get meat to the saltmakers also returned. They brought back about a bushel of salt. Ordway and Whitehouse mentioned that they also brought whale meat and that "we mix it with our poor Elk meat & find that it eats verry well." The saltmakers were working day and night, as getting salt from seawater was a slow and laborious process. Lewis calculated that it would take three bushels to get them back to the salt cached at the mouth of the Marias River.

FEBRUARY 4, 1806. Pryor and five men set out again to retrieve Drouillard's elks. At the same time Drouillard and Lepage went hunting. The men at the fort were engaged in mending their clothes, Whitehouse reported. Lewis described the elks as being in better condition near the prairies, where they fed on grasses and rushes, than in the woody country around the fort, where they ate huckleberry bushes, ferns, and salals ("lorel"). The last species Clark, but not Lewis, identified as the "Shal-lon." Varied thrushes came by in small numbers. Lewis's observation of the day yielded a latitude for Fort Clatsop as 46° 10′ 16.3″ N; its location is approximately 46° 08′ 04′ N.

Lewis began his descriptions of five trees common to the region. The first was the Sitka spruce, a species new to science, which they encountered on November 4, 1805, and called "spruce pine." This was a tree of immense size, having a circumference from 27 to 36 feet and a height of 230 feet with limbs not starting until 130 feet. The wood was white and soft and split easily. Lewis, using his "slender botanicall skil," posted a scientific description of the tree, giving attention to its leaves, bud scales, and bark. In spite of repeated attempts, he had been unable to find cones of the tree.

FEBRUARY 5, 1806. Hearing hunters firing their guns and hooping for attention from the other side of the Lewis and Clark River, Lewis sent a party led by Gass to investigate. Along the way, the men found the long-lost small Indian canoe. The hunter turned out to be Reuben Field, who had killed six elks nearby. Field also had an Oregon ruffed grouse ("phesant"), which the captain described as similar to those in the states.

Lewis's "Fir No. 2" was neither a fir nor a spruce, as the captain supposed, but the western hemlock, one of the dominant species of Pacific Northwest forests. Rising to 160 to 180 feet with a diameter of 4 to 6 feet, it was next in size to the Sitka spruce. The captain again employed his botanical skills to draft a scientific description of the tree.

FEBRUARY 6, 1806. Ordway, Gass, and Weiser departed with Reuben Field and a party of about ten men altogether to bring in Field's elks. Having to spend the night away from the fort, Gass pointed out that even with four or five inches of snow on the ground they stayed tolerably comfortable with their blankets and elkskin coverings. Pryor returned in the evening with the meat of two elks and the skins of others from which the Indians had taken ("purloined") the meat. Clark commented, "I find that those people will all Steal."

Lewis's third fir tree, the grand fir ("balsam fir"), grew to a height of 80 or 100 feet with a diameter of 2½ to 4 feet. Confirming its vernacular name, the tree exuded a "fine clear arromatic balsam." Its wood was white and soft, with a thin, smooth bark of a dark brown color. His fourth fir may have been a depauperate form of the grand fir, which he compared to his number two, the western hemlock, in size and other features, but also to the grand fir, yet declaring that it yielded no balsam and little rosin. The fifth tree was the Douglas fir, with its thin, dark brown bark. Its wood was reddish white, somewhat porous, and tough. His final tree, number six, was the western white pine ("white pine"), a species new to science. He found little difference between it and the white pine of Virginia, except for its long cones, and he found it uncommon in the area. In fact, it is not now documented as occurring at the mouth of the Columbia River. Clark submitted that he had carved his name on one on the seacoast to the north and that he had seen some near Ecola Creek. To each of these trees Lewis added his technical notes, particularly describing the leaves.

FEBRUARY 7, 1806. In the evening Ordway and Weiser returned with a part of the meat of Reuben Field's elks. The rest of the party stayed with Gass to bring the rest of the meat in the morning to a point where they could be met by canoe to aid the haul. Gass called this rainy night away from the fort "disagreeable." Lewis declared the party's feast of bone marrow and elk brisket an "excellent supper" and "living in high stile." The captains noted that smallpox had claimed the lives of a great number of persons in the region. The most recent outbreak had been four years earlier and had taken several hundred persons, including four chiefs. They surmised that the disease probably accounted for the number of deserted Tillamook villages that Clark had seen along the coast. In fact, an epidemic in the 1770s may have been even more devastating than the more recent one. The captain's consideration of plants for the day included orange honeysuckles, blue elderberries, probably Lewis's syringa ("seven bark or nine-bark"), and mountain huckleberries. Only the last was given careful scientific examination and none received ethnobotanical scrutiny.

FEBRUARY 8, 1806. Rain that had been falling since the previous afternoon melted the last of the snow that had been covering the ground since January 24. Lewis decided that "the rigor of the winter have passed." The captains detailed Ordway and two men to join Gass and party to bring in the remainder of Field's elk meat. In the evening all returned with the meat of five elks. Pryor also made it back to the fort with Shannon and Labiche and brought meat from four elks. The captains were happy to dine on elk tongue and bone marrow.

Lewis, realizing his mistake of January 26 in describing the wrong plant for salal ("*Shal-lon*"), now provided a taxonomic description of it. It was a species that he had been calling a "loral," that grew abundantly near the fort, and that elks favored for food. In addition to his morphological description, Lewis noted that the shrub was an evergreen with a deep purple berry. He did not recount its many ethnobotanical uses, but he had collected a specimen on January 20. Clark alone added a drawing of its stalk and leaves in his journal.

FEBRUARY 9, 1806. Collins and Weiser took the recently recovered Indian canoe up the Lewis and Clark River on a hunting excursion. Drouillard returned in the evening but with only a beaver. He had seen a black bear, the first one observed in the area. Indians told the captains that the bears were usually plentiful but were now hibernating.

Lewis described a tree that he thought much like the Douglas fir (his number five of February 6). In fact, it was a Douglas fir, confirmed by the captain's drawing of its distinctive leaf. He also penned brief morphological notes on red alder ("black alder") but did not discuss its extensive ethnobotanical uses. In the Pacific Northwest it is second only to the western redcedar in its practical functions. Clark began copying Lewis's entry on the Douglas fir but switched to a description of the Sitka spruce; he also pictured its cone. Lewis's description is at February 4 and 18 and the drawing at February 18.

FEBRUARY 10, 1806. Drouillard found his beaver traps empty, Collins and Weiser returned unsuccessful in their hunt, and Willard arrived late in the evening from the saltworks. Willard had severely cut his knee with his tomahawk, and thinking he was of little use in the saltmaking operation returned to the fort. He told the captains that Bratton was ill and that Gibson was so sick that he could not walk alone or even sit up. Gibson requested help to get back to the fort.

Lewis returned to his botanical notes, describing first the bigleaf maple, which he found common along the Columbia River below the Klickitat River. He thought the tree resembled the white ash. This observation may account for Clark calling it an ash in his second entry on November 4. Lewis also wrote about the vine maple (new to science), which he considered similar to the white maple with which he was familiar from the East. He added morphological notes for both species and drew a picture of the vine maple's leaf, as did Clark. Neither supplied ethnobotanical notes for these species that were widely used by coastal natives. Lewis collected specimens of the trees, vine maple in late October 1805 and bigleaf maple on April 10, 1806.

FEBRUARY 11, 1806. Gass, Reuben Field, and Thompson set off on a hunting excursion, while Pryor and four men departed for the saltworks to bring the ill Gibson back to the fort. Colter and Weiser were also dispatched to the Saltmaking Camp to help out. Weiser was to replace Bratton if the man felt too sick to carry on there or to return if he wanted to stay.

Lewis described two plants: Pacific blackberry and evergreen huckleberry. The captains typically called the Pacific blackberry "green brier" and noted its habitat in moist areas near water. They found the evergreen huckleberry around the fort, a plant that Lewis took to be a variety of salal and mistakenly described as salal on January 26. He gave his customary morphology statement and added a line about native use. Area Indians ate the huckleberries when ripe but did not seem to collect them for drying and storage. Clark copied Lewis's material on the Pacific blackberry, then transcribed the longer description from his entry of February 13.

FEBRUARY 12, 1806. A Clatsop man brought three dogs to the corps as compensation for elks that he and his fellows had taken some time back. The dogs must have sensed their fate and bolted. White-house reported that the Clatsop sold one of the party a sea otter skin and seemed pleased with the bargain. He spent the night at the fort. Lewis's botany notes featured two plants new to science: Oregon grape and dull Oregon grape. He had collected a specimen of the latter at end of October 1805 and would get the other on April 11, 1806. Clark's copy of the scientific descriptions included drawings of the stems and leaves of the two, which are not found in Lewis's journal. Lewis had not seen the fruit or flower of either plant, nor did he discuss the plants' importance to natives. Both species were used for food, dye, and medicine.

FEBRUARY 13, 1806. The Clatsop man left in the late morning. Having completed drying their store of meat, Lewis thought they had enough to finish out the month. The party looked forward to large numbers of small fish that the Indians said would arrive in March. From the Indians' description Lewis supposed that the fish would be herring. In fact, it was a eulachon, a type of anadromous smelt, which Lewis described and pictured on February 24. Also from Indian information about traders, Lewis conjectured a white settlement to the north along the coast. Actually, there was probably no permanent European settlement in that area, but trading ships did winter at Nootka Sound, Vancouver Island, British Columbia.

Lewis entered a longer description of the Pacific blackberry in his journal, supplementing his notes of February 11. The captain discussed in more detail the habitat and morphology of the plant. He also penned scientific notes for the sword fern (*"large firn"*) and the deer fern (*"small firn"*), and both he and Clark added drawings of the leaf of the former. He also noted that the Indians ate the roots of both plants. The captain had collected a specimen of deer fern on January 20. Lewis ended his entry with brief notes on native grasses, calling them "generally coa[r]se harsh and sedge-like." He also mentioned bulrushes and cattails and noted that natives used the plants to make mats, bags, and other woven materials.

FEBRUARY 14, 1806. Lewis intimated the party's concern for the ailing Gibson and Bratton at the saltworks. The captain also worried about Pryor and a party who had been gone since February 11 in order to bring Gibson back to the fort. In the evening the party at the fort feasted on "a very fine fat beaver" that Drouillard had caught in one of his traps. Clark called it "a great delecessey." The captains outlined the contents of a map that Clark had completed showing the party's route. No extant map from the expedition fits the description given by the captains, but it may have been a preliminary piece for comprehensive postexpedition maps. In fact, the captains' accounts differ in details of the map's depictions. They stated that from the Three Forks of the Missouri River, Gallatin County, Montana, to their passage over the Rocky Mountains the route presented on the map had been established by celestial observations and direct survey. Moreover, the course and connections of rivers beyond their reach had been determined through information provided by Indians. In a bit of self-congratulation, the captains declared, "we now discover that we have found the most practicable and navigable passage across the Continent of North America." On this projected route they would do away with the long swing to the south that they took from the Great Falls of the Missouri River, Cascade County, Montana, and the route north along the Bitterroot Mountains to their Travelers' Rest campsite, Missoula County, Montana. Instead, they proposed that a more direct route by land might exist between those points. In fact, on the return Lewis and a small party would follow such an overland shortcut. From Travelers' Rest the "practicable" route would be the one they followed on their outbound trek over and out of the mountains to the Snake and Columbia Rivers and down those streams to the coast. Clark added a paragraph on western geography at the end of his entry. From Indian information they had learned of a river flowing from the south into the Columbia River. On the return trip they would find the Willamette ("Multnomah") River at modern Portland, Oregon. Trying to bring all this information together with their actual experience in the West, Clark speculated on a central point in the Rocky Mountains from which the principal rivers of the West originated. This conception grew out of the captains' pre-expedition notion of a "height of land" theory for western waters.

FEBRUARY 15, 1806. A robin's song reminded Lewis of spring. The bird had left the area before the party's arrival in November. Drouillard and Whitehouse set out hunting toward Point Adams. In the afternoon Bratton arrived from the saltworks saying that Pryor and party were carrying Gibson back to the fort since he too weak to walk on his own. Lewis observed that Bratton was in better health and recovering fast. Later in the evening Pryor arrived with Gibson. Lewis was relieved to find him not as ill as he had supposed but still exhibiting a fever and looking physically depleted. The captain thought his condition the result of a severe cold that he had caught while hunting through the swamps and marshes around the saltworks. He gave him potassium nitrate (saltpeter) to increase the flow of perspiration and urine and reduce his fever. He also had him drink sage tea, bathed his feet in warm water, and administered thirty-five drops of laudanum (tincture of opium) to help him relax.

The captains laid out a long list of the "quadrupeds of this country from the Rocky Mountains to the pacific Ocean." Of domestic animals, they named two: the horse and the dog. They counted nearly forty native wild animals, which they would describe more fully in later entries, much like their survey of regional plants. Here they took up Indian horses. They found horses abundant from the Rocky Mountains to the Cascades, many of whom were "lofty eligantly formed active and durable; in short many of them look like the fine English coarsers and would make a figure in any country." Lewis singled out the Appaloosa, a breed that they would see among the Nez Perces on the return trip. Otherwise, the horses appeared undistinguished, and the natives did not seem to practice selective breeding. Elegant horses could be bought for a few trinkets. Mules were found among the Shoshones, particularly those bands with ties to Mexico. The captains had seen horses and mules with Spanish brands.

FEBRUARY 16, 1806. Lewis worked on adjusting his octant by comparing it with his sextant, whose error had been previously determined. He found it off by 2°. Shannon, Labiche, and Frazer were sent hunting up Youngs River, Clatsop County, Oregon. The captains had no word from Gass and party. Bratton was still very weak and complained of lower back pain. Lewis gave him "barks," probably Peruvian bark (cinchona), to reduce fever. Gibson's fever was not responding to the captains' care, so Lewis administered a dose of Rush's pills, a powerful laxative, which he said he "found extreemly efficatious in fevers." The saltpeter of the day before was producing the desired perspiration, and Rush's pills took effect quickly, reducing Gibson's fever and providing the soldier a good night's sleep.

Lewis described the typical, small Indian dog and noted that the natives did not eat them or use them for any purpose other than hunting elks. The captain wrote that grizzly bears were generally found on the east side of the Rockies on the borders of the plains near timbered areas along waterways and less often on the west side. Lewis called it "the brown white or grizly bear." In his enumeration of animals the previous day, Lewis allowed that it was one species "with a mearly accedental difference in point of colour." On the return trip in May 1806 among the Nez Perces Lewis made his final determination and came to that conclusion. He noticed no difference between the black bear of the East and the one he encountered along the expedition's route. Clark followed Lewis's entry up to his descriptions of bears but moved that material to his entry of February 17. He also borrowed Lewis's description of the California condor from February 17 and recorded it in this day's entry, along with a drawing of its head.

FEBRUARY 17, 1806. Collins and Windsor took off hunting toward the prairies at Point Adams. Shannon, Labiche, and Frazer returned with the meat and hide of an elk. Apparently this was an elk wounded by one of the men in Gass's party, but none of that group was seen. Lewis continued giving Bratton Peruvian bark and started the treatment with Gibson, who seemed well enough to shift away from the harsher Rush's pills. Joseph Field arrived in the afternoon and reported that the saltmakers had about two kegs or three bushels of salt. Lewis thought it sufficient to last until the party reached their cache of the condiment at the mouth of the Marias River. Therefore the captain decided to send six men to accompany Joseph Field back to the saltworks the next day in order to collect the salt and kettles. Later in the day Gass, Reuben Field, and Thompson arrived, reporting that they had killed eight elks. They had quite a rough time, the sergeant explained, since they got caught in a hard rain with little covering, and their water-soaked, animal-skin clothing "made it the more disagreeable." Later still, Drouillard and Whitehouse returned, having taken one elk.

Shannon and Labiche brought a live California condor ("large carrion Crow or Buzzads of the Columbia"). Lewis deemed it to be the largest bird in North America. Even in poor condition it may have weighed twenty-five pounds and could have weighed ten pounds more in better form. Its most impressive feature was its wingspan, which Lewis measured at nine feet, two inches. Lewis examined it head to toe, counted its feathers, and noted its colors, presenting a thorough physical description. He thought it a handsome bird at a distance but one that flew clumsily. He added a drawing of the condor's head in his journal. Having called it a "buzzard" up to this point, Clark changed to Lewis's determination and declared it a "vulture" while adding the same caveats for the designation as Lewis. Shannon also had a golden ("grey") eagle, which Lewis recognized as the same as in the East.

FEBRUARY 18, 1806. As decided the day before, a party of five men under Ordway set out for the saltworks to collect the salt and equipment and close the operation. A second group of ten men under Gass went after the elks recently killed. Ordway returned in the evening, being unable to get to his canoe through the bay to the Skipanon River to reach the saltworks. Collins and Windsor also came back in the evening with the one deer they had killed. Deer meat was inferior to elk, and even that was poor but seemed to be improving, Lewis indicated. Eight Clatsops and Chinooks came for a visit and trading and remained until late in the evening before returning home. Lewis observed, perhaps with some envy, that the Indians were not constrained by high waves in managing their canoes. After they left Clark noticed that they had stolen an axe.

Ordway brought the captains a specimen of a pine tree that Lewis thought a new species and labeled "No. 7." But from his description and drawing of its cone, specialists have determined that it was the Sitka spruce, which Lewis called "No. 1" in his entry of February 4. The captain may have been fooled because of the effects of the brackish waters of its marsh habitat. He did notice similarities to his "No. 1." Since Clark had placed these notes in his entry of February 9, he instead filled this entry with notes on the Oregon bobcat ("*Tiger Cat*") from Lewis's entry of February 21. The transfer may have been prompted by Whitehouse showing him a robe made from skins of an Oregon bobcat that the Indians had sold him.

FEBRUARY 19, 1806. Ordway set out with his party (including Whitehouse) again to close down the saltworks. It was not a pleasant trip, as Ordway related that "the frozen rain beat in our faces verry hard." After wading through streams up to their waists, "benumbed & Chilled," where "Sand flew & waves rold," they were happy to spend the night in a deserted Indian lodge near a warm fire. Gass and his party returned with meat from eight elks and the skins of seven. Shannon and Labiche took the other skin and continued the chase. The elk skins were divided among the party to serve as baggage covering on the return trip. Sick men, principally Bratton and Gibson, were recovering but not as quickly as anticipated. Clark gave Bratton six Scott's pills, another strong laxative similar to Rush's pills, but they did not produce the desired effect.

Lewis came back to his review of trans–Rocky Mountain animals, the Columbian white-tailed deer ("common red deer") and Columbian black-tailed deer ("Black tailed fallow deer"), new to science. The captain had seen the former from Celilo Falls and believed it essentially the same as the common eastern deer except for its longer tail. Lewis noted that the "fallow deer" was peculiar to the coast and a distinct species having characteristics of both the mule and common deer. He reviewed these distinctive morphological and behavioral differences but declared its meat inferior to that of any deer he knew. Clark did not repeat the material on the deer but substituted Lewis's notes from February 21 about the fisher, red fox, and swift fox.

FEBRUARY 20, 1806. Collins returned from a day of unsuccessful hunting but brought cranberries for Bratton and Gibson. Lewis indicated that Gibson was recovering but that Bratton had a stubborn cough and sore back and appeared weaker. Apparently McNeal had not been treating his syphilis properly, and it was worsening. Ordway and party reached the saltworks about noon and dined on whale meat that they purchased from nearby Indians. In the afternoon Tahcum, a Chinook chief, and twenty-five of his tribe came to the fort. Meeting him now for the first time, the captains described him as a good-looking man of about fifty years of age and taller than typical for his people. The captains entertained him with food and ceremonial smoking and presented him with one of the smaller Indian peace medals, with which he seemed pleased.

In addition to a friendly visit, Gass mentioned that the Chinooks also brought native hats to trade. At sunset the explorers bid the group farewell and closed the fort's gates. Lewis explained that it was corps' policy not to allow visitors in such numbers to spend the night inside the fort. In spite of Chinook friendliness, the party had experienced having items stolen by them. Lewis warned of worse: "we well know, that the treachery of the aborigenes of America and the too great confidence of our countrymen in their sincerity and friendship, has caused the distruction of many hundreds of us." He thought that the men had become too complacent and trusting and needed to be reminded of Indian treachery and to be ever on guard. The captain gave scant attention to mule deer and elks, which he knew to be identical to those in the East. Likewise, gray wolves and coyotes were familiar animals. Clark placed the comments about gray wolves and coyotes at February 21.

FEBRUARY 21, 1806. This marked the final day of four days of high winds. Three Clatsops arrived for a visit. Lewis considered them "great begers" but gave one of them a few needles. Drouillard and Collins went after elks whose tracks Collins had seen the day before. Heavy rains had washed away the evidence, so they returned empty-handed. Drouillard saw a fisher, but it escaped him. Ordway and party returned from the closed saltworks, bringing all the equipment and about twenty gallons of salt. The sergeant revealed that the return trip was wet and exhausting and that he was sick. At the fort, they secured twelve gallons of the salt in two kegs to be used on the return trip. Lewis gave Willard and Bratton a dose of Scott's pills. The strong laxative worked on Willard but not on Bratton. Gibson continued to take Peruvian bark three times a day and was quickly recovering.

Lewis provided a detailed description of the Oregon bobcat ("tyger Cat"), including morphology, habits, and native use. He provided much the same information for the fisher ("*Black-fox*") and the red fox ("*Silver fox*"). Lewis thought the fisher was incorrectly named since it did not seek fish. In fact, there is disagreement among specialists about whether it eats fish or not. The "silver fox" is not a separate species but a color phase of the red fox, which Lewis used for comparison. He also mentioned the swift fox ("Kit fox") in passing.

FEBRUARY 22, 1806. Two Clatsop women came with two boys to sell their cedar-bark hats. Two of the hats had been made specifically for the captains from a previous order. The size and shape were just what the captains ordered, so they purchased them and the remainder ("at a moderate price," according to Gass) and distributed them among the party. Lewis was impressed by the ingenuity of their handiwork in crafting the waterproof hats and baskets as well as their woodworking skills. The women told Lewis that the "small fish," probably eulachons ("herring"), had begun to run. They also told him that Chief Coboway had gone up the Columbia River to purchase wapato to use for trade with the corps. Drouillard accompanied the visiting Clatsops back to their village in order to get the dogs that the Indians had promised as compensation for the party's elks they had taken. The ill members of the party—Gibson, Bratton, Ordway, Willard, and McNeal—were recovering. Ordway wrote, "I am full of pains." Lewis counted that this was the largest number of sick persons in the corps since leaving their camp at Wood River in Illinois. The general complaints were bad colds and fever and perhaps, Lewis reckoned, a touch of flu.

Returning to his catalog of animals, Lewis discussed the pronghorn ("Antelope"), which he found on the Great Columbian Plain as well as on the Great Plains but which were scarcer west of the Rockies. Locals used their hides for robes and hunted them when fish were not available. Having never seen a mountain goat ("sheep") up close, the captain wrote mostly of the animal's wool that served as native clothing. The well-known beaver and river otter he simply named.

FEBRUARY 23, 1806. Conceding that nothing worthy of notice happened this day, Lewis did mention that the sick were recovering, except for Ordway, who seemed to be the most ill. Ordway thought that he and three others "have the Enfluenzey." Since the men had been engaged in repairing and making clothing during idle winter days, the party was better supplied with moccasins and leather goods than at any other point in the trip, Lewis noted. Whitehouse missed few days of mentioning the party's tailoring work.

Lewis provided a long morphological description of the sea otter and considered its fur "the riches[t] and I think the most delicious fur in the world . . . it is deep thick silkey in the extreem and strong." For some time Lewis had thought that the infant sea otter was a different species, which he called "spuck" after a Chinookan word that the captain had mistook as a name for a separate animal similar to the sea otter. Lewis gave only scanty attention to minks but more to harbor seals. Again Lewis conceded an error in his identification by admitting that he had considered harbor seals to be sea otters at least since Celilo Falls on the Columbia River. "The Indians here have undeceived us," he confessed. Clark added the word "Phoca," the seal's scientific name, to his copy of Lewis's notes.

FEBRUARY 24, 1806. The sick men were recovering. Shannon and Labiche returned empty-handed from the hunt (or with a single elk, according to Ordway and Whitehouse) and informed the captains that elks had moved far away. Lewis called it "unwelcome information." As paltry as the elks were, they were the party's principal source of meat. In the evening Coboway and a dozen or so Clatsop men and women visited the fort. Drouillard had joined them and brought two dogs. The Clatsops were on a trading mission and carried sea otter skins, hats, sturgeons, and eulachons ("small fish") to sell. The party bought all the goods the Indians had and invited them to spend the night at the fort. The weather, being particularly harsh, induced this invitation, plus the presence of women among them convinced Lewis of their peaceful intentions.

Eulachons were being taken in large numbers in native nets about forty miles east at the Cowlitz River, Washington. Having heard about the run of the small fish, Lewis now had the opportunity to view them closely. The captain provided the first scientific description of the fish and offered a life-sized drawing of one in his journal. Probably consulting one of his reference books, Lewis grouped it with herring and similar species, a relationship that is not now accepted. He cooked them "Indian stile," by roasting a number of them together on a spit, and declared them "superior to any fish I ever tasted." The captains determined to send a small party upriver to procure more of this delicacy. Lewis also relished the Clatsops' sturgeons. Clark switched Lewis's scientific notes of February 24 and 25 to his entries of February 25 and 24, respectively. He placed his own drawing of a eulachon at February 25.

FEBRUARY 25, 1806. Due to heavy rains and blowing winds, the party stayed put for the day. The Clatsops, however, returned to their village. Willard was singled out among the sick men as not recovering. Frustrated by bad weather, Lewis despaired at not being able to take celestial observations. He retreated to his zoological catalog. Without describing the well-known raccoon, Lewis pointed out that Indians took them in snares and deadfalls but did not seem to value their hides. He gave more attention to a new scientific discovery, the western gray squirrel ("large grey squirrel"), discussing its habitat, morphology, food, native uses, and similarities with familiar squirrels. He provided much the same information on other unfamiliar species, Douglas squirrel or chickaree ("small brown squirrel"), Richardson's red squirrel ("small grey squirrel"), and Townsend's chipmunk ("ground squirrel"). The captain related that he did not find prairie dogs ("barking squirrel") or thirteen-lined ground squirrels ("handsome ground squirrel of the plains") on the Great Columbian Plain.

FEBRUARY 26, 1806. The captains sent Drouillard, Cruzatte, and Weiser in the Indian canoe up the Columbia River seeking sturgeons and eulachons. If unsuccessful, they were to buy fish and were provided with trade goods the natives valued for the purpose. At the same time Shields, Joseph Field, and Shannon set out up the Lewis and Clark River hunting elks while Reuben Field and others headed toward the prairies at Point Adams after the same animal. Lewis estimated that the party had only three days' supply of food and that mostly tainted dried elk meat. With some irony he underscored an afterthought: "*a comfortable prospect for good living.*"

The captain began his zoological studies of the mountain beaver by using a Chinookan descriptive designation, "*Sewelel,*" that he took for its Indian name. He also thought it might be a "brown mungo," a reference to the mongoose, an animal not native to North America. New to science, the mountain beaver is a rodent rather than a beaver, but Lewis incorrectly wanted to classify it under the genus *Mustela*, along with weasels, ferrets, and minks. The captain gave his customary appraisal of the animal, adding that Indians used its hide for robes. In fact, he never saw a mountain beaver but based his description on its hide and on information from expedition hunters who had a glimpse of it. Its fur he declared "very fine, short, thickly set and silky," and it made an excellent lining for his bobcat coat. He offered the locals a great price for a whole one but could not make himself understood. The captain also described the "*Braro*," which he took to be a distinct species; it is actually the badger, which he used for comparison. Lewis called it slow and clumsy, explaining that in a couple of instances he had outrun the animal and caught it. Clark moved the badger notes to his entry of February 27 and here placed Lewis's descriptions of species from his entry of that day.

FEBRUARY 27, 1806. Reuben Field returned with the sad news that he had not killed anything and that there were no elks toward Point Adams. Collins, from another hunting party, came in during the evening having killed a buck elk. Among the ailing, Willard alone remained sick. Otherwise, Goodrich and McNeal were recovering from syphilis ("pox"), as far as Lewis understood. The bushy-tailed woodrat, new to science, came under Lewis's scrutiny. The captain recalled that he had seen and described it in early July last year when he caught one at White Bear Islands. Now he provided more information. While Lewis said he had also seen it in western Georgia and north of Charlottesville, Virginia, Clark remembered it from southern Kentucky and southwestern Ohio. Those rats were probably the eastern woodrat. Lewis merely named the familiar meadow mouse (or meadow vole) and the western mole. The mountain lion ("Panther") received a bit more attention, but the captain knew it well.

FEBRUARY 28, 1806. Reuben Field and Collins had little time to rest, as they were sent on another hunting excursion this morning. Other hunters—Shields, Joseph Field, and Shannon—returned in the evening, having killed five elks, but two of them were at a considerable distance. Lewis ordered the men to return to hunting in the morning, while another party under Gass would retrieve the elks. Cuskala ("Kuskelar") and his wife came to the fort bringing eulachons, sturgeons, roots, and a beaver robe to sell. Finding the prices too high, Lewis bought a little sturgeon, for which he gave some fishing hooks. Cruzatte exchanged his capote (blanket coat) for a dog. The two Clatsops were permitted to spend the night.

The white-tailed jackrabbit ("hare") Lewis found on both the Great Columbian Plain and the Great Plains and here supplied detailed notes on its morphology, habits, and food. He was especially taken with its speed and ability to leap, which he measured at eighteen to twenty-one feet. The captain mentioned a "rabbit" that he thought to be the eastern cottontail, but specialists suggest that he was seeing Nuttall's, or the mountain, cottontail. He gave a quick nod to the ubiquitous striped skunk ("Pole-cat").

MARCH 1, 1806. Gass and a small party went after the elks killed by Shields, Joseph Field, and Shannon, who were already out hunting again. The sergeant returned in the evening with the meat of three of them. Thompson stayed with the three hunters in order to take care of the rest of the elk meat. Reuben Field and Collins returned disappointed from their hunt. Cuskala and his wife left about noon. The chief also had a slave with him—a boy about ten years old. He had obtained the boy from Tillamooks who had taken him prisoner from a coastal tribe to the southeast. Lewis explained that like other Indian nations the Clatsops adopted young slaves into their families and treated them almost like their own children. Modern research, however, indicates that the Chinookan slave system was not as benign as Lewis imagined. In fact, Clark revealed that Cuskala offered to sell the boy to him.

Lewis began his ornithological inventory, dividing birds from the Rockies to the Pacific under two headings, terrestrial and aquatic. He started with the Columbian sharp-tailed grouse ("Grouse or Prarie hen"), new to science, and a subspecies of the captain's familiar sharp-tailed grouse of the Great Plains. Again, he gave careful attention to the bird's morphology, food, and habits of flocking. In an aside, he noted that local Indians ate the roots of common cattail ("Cooper's flag"). He declared it pleasant to taste and nutritious, and with no need for preparation. Clark moved the cattail notes to March 2.

MARCH 2, 1806. Members of the party who had been sick were slow to recover due to their poor diet of lean elk. Then Drouillard, Cruzatte, and Weiser arrived bringing sturgeons, eulachons ("Anchovies"), and about a bushel of wapato. Gass said they got "thousands of the . . . small fish." Lewis cheered: "we feasted on Anchovies and Wappetoe." And Whitehouse revealed that they received some of the fish as gifts. Next in Lewis's list of birds was a new scientific discovery, the greater sage-grouse ("*Cock of the Plains*"), which was given the captain's customary careful attention along with comparing its flight to that of other birds. He considered its dark meat "only tolerable." Lewis drew the head of the bird in his journal, while Clark pictured it in full. Clark copied Lewis's material of March 3 on other grouse to this entry.

MARCH 3, 1806. Finding the canoes damaged due to effects of the tide, the captains had them moved to land. Recovering sick men were still coming along, but Lepage was newly ill. Lewis gave him a dose of Scott's pills but without result. The boredom of camp life was setting in, and Lewis declared, "every thing moves on in the old way and we are counting the days which separate us from the 1st of April and which bind us to fort Clatsop." In fact, the party could not hold out that long and quit the fort on March 23.

Lewis returned to his ornithological enumeration, describing three grouse and naming another, along with other species. The passage about grouse is somewhat confusing, and even with Lewis's thorough descriptions specialists disagree about the birds' identities. The "large black and white pheasant" is almost certainly the blue grouse, while his "small speckled pheasant" is the spruce grouse. His "small brown pheasant" is most likely the spruce grouse again, apparently a female. Absolute identifications may never be possible. Although he found the taste of the spruce grouse "not very well flavored," he enjoyed the meat of the latter, whichever bird it is. Lewis surmised that the area's crows were identical to the ones he knew, but in fact they were a new species, the northwestern crow. Also, the ravens around Fort Clatsop were a subspecies of the common raven. His "Large Blackbird" was Brewer's blackbird and not the blackbird he would have known in the East. Regarding hawks Lewis saw no difference between the ones here and those of the Atlantic Coast. Lewis's brief notes leave specialists to disagree on identifying the hawks. His "large brown hawk" may be the red-tailed hawk, Swainson's hawk, or the northern harrier. His "sparrow hawk" was the American kestrel, while the "hen hawk" may have been either the northern harrier or Cooper's hawk. Finally, the "large hooting Owl" was the great horned owl.

MARCH 4, 1806. With "not any occurrence today worthy of notice," Lewis did admit that the party "live sumptuously on our wappetoe and Sturgeon." The eulachons were so delicate that they spoiled quickly unless smoked or pickled. Discussing the Indian method of preparation, the captain noted that the natives were not above eating them slightly rank. Keeping sturgeons fresh was merely a matter of immersing them in water. The Clatsops had an intricate process of steaming sturgeons but could complete the whole procedure in about an hour. Lewis preferred the fish cooked in this manner to boiling or roasting.

Returning to his birds, the captain listed most of them without his customary descriptive detail since they were familiar species or ones that had been previously discussed, including mourning dove ("turtle dove"), robin, varied thrush ("Columbian robin"), black-billed magpie, pileated woodpecker ("large woodpecker or log cock"; new to science), northern flicker ("lark woodpecker"; new to science), red-breasted sapsucker ("small white woodpecker with a read head"), Steller's jay ("blue crested Corvus"), gray jay ("small white breasted [corvus]"), western meadowlark, sandhill crane, California condor ("vulture"), winter wren ("small redish brown [flycatcher]"), and perhaps Hammond's flycatcher.

MARCH 5, 1806. Visiting Clatsops brought fish and handmade goods for sale. The party bought most of what they offered. Late in the evening hunters returned from Youngs River with disappointing news that they had neither killed nor seen any elks. With only two days of provisions on hand (and that nearly spoiled), this was alarming news. The captains detailed Pryor and two men with a stash of trade items to take a canoe up the Columbia River and purchase fish. At the same time two other parties were to set out again in search of elks—one up the Lewis and Clark River and the other toward Point Adams. If elks were truly gone from the country, the captains conceived a plan to take the corps slowly up the Columbia River, using up the month while still remaining within the timbered country, hoping for better hunting. They considered it foolhardy to attempt to cross the open plains before April. They had already decided not to abandon Fort Clatsop earlier than April 1 unless lack of subsistence compelled it. The Youngs River hunters told Clark that they had found a considerable falls about six miles from the fort. It is present Youngs River Falls on the main western fork of the river. With an actual drop of about seventy-five feet, Clark's informants overestimated it by about twenty-five feet.

On less weighty matters, Lewis returned to his scientific inventory of birds, naming familiar winged ones: common snipe, spotted sandpiper ("small sand snipe"), probably song sparrow ("[s]parrow of the woody country"), probably Sprague's pipit ("little singing lark"), and long-billed curlew ("large brown Curloo"). Clark added to the list by borrowing from Lewis's March 6 list of "Aquatic birds."

MARCH 6, 1806. Fish-trading and elk-hunting parties set out in the morning, including Drouillard, Labiche, and Collins on the hunt. Coboway with two of his children came by at midmorning bearing well-prepared eulachons. Lewis considered them particularly welcome at the moment and gave the chief some small articles in appreciation. The captain declared him "much the most friendly and decent savage that we have met with in this neighborhood." Hall lost his grip on a log he was carrying and severely injured his ankle and foot. Fortunately, nothing was broken. Bratton remained weak, while others on sick call were recovering but slowly due to a deficient diet. The leaders bemoaned their inability to provide proper nourishment. Ordway, Gass, and Whitehouse noted that the enlisted men hauled out the canoes and began repairs should the party need to leave if hunting proved unsuccessful.

Lewis provided a quick list of "Aquatic birds," or those, he explained, that obtained their subsistence from the water: great blue heron ("large blue and brown heron"), osprey ("fishing hawk"), belted kingfisher ("blue crested fisher"), perhaps the western gull ("large grey gull of the Columbia"), double-crested cormorant, perhaps either the arctic loon or the common loon, and either the western grebe or the red-throated loon ("loons of two species"), snow goose, brant, lesser Canada ("small") goose, Canada ("large") goose, tundra or whistling swan and trumpeter swan ("small and large Swan"), mallard ("Duckinmallard"), canvasback, red-breasted merganser or common merganser ("red headed fishing duck"), bufflehead ("black and white duck"), unknown teal ("little brown duck"), American coot ("black duck"), pied-billed grebe and red-necked grebe or horned grebe ("two species of divers"), and blue-winged teal. Clark's entry carried material from Lewis's entry of March 7 on herons and gulls.

MARCH 7, 1806. Coboway spent most of the day at the fort, penned in by high winds. Hunters Drouillard and Labiche returned in the evening having killed but one elk. They had seen a scattering of elks about five miles up the Lewis and Clark River. Bratton was much worse, complaining of severe back pain and unable to sit up. The captains soaked flannel in alcohol, camphor, Castile soap, and a little laudanum and applied it to the area of pain. The patient got some relief in the evening. Gass, involved in repairing canoes, lamented the absence of tobacco. Of thirty-three members of the party, only seven abstained. Users substituted crabapple bark.

Lewis began his survey of the birds enumerated the day before but with less detail than usual. Among those cited were great blue heron, osprey, belted kingfisher, double-crested cormorant, and four species of gulls (Bonaparte's gull, perhaps a young glaucous-winged gull, western gull, and northern fulmar). The captains each drew a picture of the head of the northern fulmar ("white gull") in his journal, being particularly taken with its distinctive beak and its dominant nostrils. The northern fulmar was less common than other gulls in the area. And they recognized two species of loons. Their "Speckled" loon could be either the arctic or the common loon, while the second species may be either the western grebe or the red-throated loon. Clark gave a somewhat different account of a Sitka spruce than Lewis's of March 10.

MARCH 8, 1806. Hail and snow covered the ground this morning and the next. Bratton was much improved and felt little pain in his back. Collins returned with the good news that he had killed three elks about five miles from the fort near the prairie at Point Adams. He lost one of the elks in a pond but had butchered and secured the others. He also saw two large gangs of elks in the same area, so the captains dispatched Drouillard and Joseph Field after them. A party was also sent with Labiche to retrieve the elk that he and Drouillard had reported on the day before. Shields, Reuben Field, and Frazer returned in the evening from Youngs River having seen no elks. Ordway, Gass, and Whitehouse, but not the captains, reported that the three had lost a canoe. McNeal and Goodrich were directed to quit taking mercury since Lewis considered them recovered from a case of syphilis ("Louis veneri"). Clark called Willard "low Spirited."

Lewis penned detailed notes on the snow goose ("white brant"), comparing it to related birds and revealing its morphology. He gave the brant ("Brown or pided brant") similar attention and declared it precisely the same as the brant with which he was familiar in the East. Lewis found the lesser Canada ("small") goose sometimes difficult to distinguish from its larger cousin, the ubiquitous Canada goose.

MARCH 9, 1806. At daylight Ordway led ten men to get the elk meat that Collins had secured the previous day; they were back to the fort before noon. Drouillard and Joseph Field returned, unsuccessful in their elk hunt. Pryor and his party remained out on a trading assignment. Lewis attributed their delay to high winds that detained their canoe. Shields was at work making water-tight elk-skin storage bags. Clark hoped they would keep his papers dry. Bratton, who had seemed better the day before, was again complaining of severe back pain. Lewis supposed it was rheumatism and continued his medical treatment of applying a piece of flannel soaked in liniment to the sore spot. The soldier felt better in the evening. Three Clatsop men brought a dog, some fish, and a sea otter skin for sale. Ordway said the party bought some items. The captains let the Indians stay overnight.

Lewis considered the trumpeter swan ("large Swan") to be the same as the eastern one with which he was familiar. The "small swan" had a distinctive sound, which Lewis found impossible to describe, but it began with a sort of whistle, which caused the captain to coin the name "*whistleing swan*," its popular designation but now labeled the tundra swan. Although it was a quarter smaller than the trumpeter, the captain described the tundra as precisely the same in its habits, color, and morphology. The familiar mallards ("duckinmallard") were abundant in the area, as were canvasbacks, which Lewis extolled for their exquisite taste. The red-breasted merganser or perhaps the common merganser ("read headed fishing duck") was well known to the captain. Clark added notes on the bufflehead from Lewis's next entry.

MARCH 10, 1806. In the early afternoon the captains sent two hunting parties in different directions on the Lewis and Clark River. They had another party prepare to leave the next day for Youngs Bay in order to hunt in an area that they had not exploited. Returned hunters, named by Clark as Shields, Reuben Field, and Frazer, reported that a Sitka spruce (Lewis's fir "No. 1") had a girth of forty-two feet a few feet above its base. They estimated that it retained this circumference for about two hundred feet without tree limbs and may have been three hundred feet tall altogether.

Lewis described the bufflehead ("black and white duck"), with which he was familiar from the Atlantic Coast. His "brown duck" was probably one of several teals, while the "black duck" is the American coot. Both received the captain's notes on habits, food, and morphology. Lewis also noticed two species of "divers," the pied-billed grebe ("smaller species") and the red-necked grebe ("larger species"), and gave them some attention but declared them unfit to eat. Much less space was given to the familiar blue-winged teal, named as such.

MARCH 11, 1806. Lewis's attempts at astronomical observations proved fruitless due to cloud cover. Cloudy skies hampered him the next day as well. The trading party under Pryor sent out on March 5 returned with their canoe loaded with eulachons, sturgeons, and wapato. Viewing the hearty resource, Lewis commented, "we once more live in *clover*; Anchovies fresh sturgeon and Wappetoe." The traders had used only a small portion of their goods to buy the items from the Cathlamets, but high winds had kept them from crossing the river to the Wahkiakums to obtain more foodstuff and had delayed their return. Some dogs at the Cathlamets had chewed the rope securing their canoe, and it was set adrift. The men had borrowed their present canoe from the Indians and found the lost one along the way, secured it, and planned to recover it when they returned the Cathlamets' canoe. The captains sent Gass and a party after another canoe that had been left by Shields, Reuben Field, and Frazer while hunting. When he returned, Gass reported that the boat had been carried off by the tide. Drouillard, Joseph Field, and Frazer set off for Youngs Bay as was planned the day before.

Lewis turned to discussing "the reptiles of this country." He mentioned rattlesnakes but had not seen a regional one. He finally saw the northern Pacific rattlesnake on April 25, 1806, during the return trip. The captain found local garter snakes, perhaps the Pacific red-sided garter snake, to be identical to those he knew from the East. The western fence lizard ("black or dark brown lizzard") had been seen at The Dalles, Wasco County, Oregon, and also reminded him of lizards back home. Snails were common in the woody country along the coast and similar to those in the states but "at least five times their bulk," according to Lewis. He may have seen either the Oregon forestsnail or, less likely, the Pacific sideband. Lewis saw a rough-skinned newt ("water lizzard") above the Cascades of the Columbia and here wrote a detailed morphological description of it. The captain either remembered it, had a collected specimen at hand, or drew on notes not now available. Clark did not copy Lewis's notes on reptiles but instead transferred his discourse on the mule deer from the captain's entry of May 10, 1805, and also copied his material on the golden eagle from March 12, 1806. The reptile listing is found at Clark's entry of March 12. Again, there seems to be no ready explanation for Clark switching this material to different dates.

MARCH 12, 1806. Ordway took a party in search of the lost canoe but returned unsuccessful, as Gass had been on the previous day. The captains sent a hunter along the Lewis and Clark River, but by nighttime he had not returned. The corps could now count 358 pairs of moccasins (the enlisted writers counted 338) and a good portion of dressed leather, along with leather shirts, pants, and coats (capotes), ready for the homeward journey.

Lewis gave ample space to discussing the golden eagle ("Callamet Eagle"), describing not only its distinguishing features but also its significance to Native Americans. Its tail feathers were especially prized by the Mandans, Hidatsas, and Arikaras, and more so by Osage and Kansa Indians, who did not have access to the bird. They used the feathers as decoration on their pipes (calumets) for sacred or ritual purposes; hence the bird's colloquial name. They wove them into their hair and into their horses' manes and tails and ornamented their warbonnets with them. The captain gave but a line to bats, which were familiar to him. Lewis listed regional fish and shellfish, then discussed them individually in other journal entries. He also mentioned that locals practiced maritime whale hunting with harpoons, an activity generally considered to be restricted to Indians farther north. Clark added some lines from Lewis's March 13 entry about elk antlers.

MARCH 13, 1806. Lewis noticed some plants peeking through the ground during some uncommonly fair weather. In the morning Drouillard, Joseph Field, and Frazer returned, having killed two elks and a deer. While Drouillard went to a Clatsop village to try to buy some canoes, Pryor and two others made another unsuccessful search for the lost one. Collins, who was with Pryor, did manage to kill two elks. Ordway and a small group were sent after one of Drouillard's elks; the other elk and deer were too far away. Whitehouse and two others attempted to go to the Cathlamet village and trade for fish and other foodstuffs but high winds turned them back. Reuben Field and Thompson were still out hunting. Two Cathlamets came by for a visit and left in the evening. Facing a fair day for a change, Lewis took some astronomical readings. The captains noticed that some elks had not lost their antlers while others had grown new ones to a length of six inches. Finding the ones with new antlers in better condition, the captains concluded that inferior elks must retain their antlers longer.

Having finished his notes on events of the day, Lewis turned to his zoological inventory. Unlike the Indians, who seemed to relish the taste of the harbor porpoise, Lewis thought it disagreeable. The party found big skates ("Skaite") that had died and washed up on shore. The tide also brought in the starry flounder, which the Indians ate. The king (or Chinook) salmon ("common Salmon") came in for extensive morphological notes and a nod to its importance in local subsistence. Its roe was also a part of the native diet. It was probably the bull or Dolly Varden trout ("red Charr") that was compared in detail to the king salmon. Clark added notes on steelhead trout ("*Salmon Trout*"), cutthroat trout ("Speckled or Mountain *Trout*"), and mountain suckers ("*bottle nose*") from Lewis's entry of March 14.

MARCH 14, 1806. The captains dispatched a small party after Collins's elks, Gass included; they returned about noon with the meat. At the same time Collins, Joseph Field, Shannon, and Labiche went in search of the gang from which those elks were taken. The corps at the fort must have been elated when they heard some twenty rifle shots and hoped that the hunters had found the elks. Reuben Field and Thompson returned empty-handed, having gotten but a single brant, which they ate the previous evening. Late in the evening Drouillard arrived with some Clatsops, who brought an "indifferent canoe" and some small items for sale. The party bought the small items but could not bargain successfully for the canoe. The Clatsops demanded too much, and the party's slim store of merchandise would not allow the purchase. Lewis offered his uniform coat, but the seller refused. Clark indicated that the Indian trader wanted double the usual price for an inferior canoe. He also wrote that the Clatsops informed them that they had seen a Makah ("*Quinna-chart*") Indian who lived in the area of Cape Flattery, Clallam County, Washington, and had been told by him that four Euro-American trading vessels were in that area.

Lewis discussed the species that Clark had copied into his jour-

nal on the previous day: steelhead trout, cutthroat trout, and mountain suckers. The captain gave his usual morphological description
but made little note of the Indians' use of the fish. He added a bit of
writing about the range and habitat of the species. The mountain
sucker received the least attention since it was well-known from the
Missouri River and the mountains.

MARCH 15, 1806. Oregon oxalis ("sorrel") put forth its leaves, and
robins raised their songs. The Clatsop traders left early and hunters
Collins, Joseph Field, Shannon, and Labiche returned before noon,
having killed four elks. Labiche seemed to be the only hunter to find
elks and make the killing but having lost his gun sight he expended a
good amount of ammunition with scanty results. Although the elks
had scattered, the captains sent two parties of hunters after them.
The men returned in the evening with the skins and meat of several,
but one had turned putrid, because it had not been properly cleaned
of its internal organs. Ordway and Whitehouse (but not the captains) indicated that Drouillard and six men were sent to the Cathlamet village for another try at obtaining a canoe. Delashelwilt, a
Chinook chief, with his wife came to the fort for a visit. His wife,
"the old baud," brought six women to offer the men. Lewis claimed
that these were the same women who had given the men venereal
diseases in November. The men having finally recovered from their
bouts with the ailment, Lewis made them swear to abstain on this
occasion. Late in the evening Catel, a Clatsop, brought his family to
the fort along with a canoe and sea otter skin for sale. The captains
purchased neither. Bratton remained sick and weak. Another fair
day provided opportunity for astronomical observations.

In addition to his thorough description of the white-fronted goose
("third species of brant"), Lewis drew a picture of its head in his
journal, as did Clark. The captain's three species are the common
brant ("brown or pided brant"), the snow goose ("white brant"), and
this one. Clark copied Lewis's notes of March 16 on clams, periwinkles, and bivalves into this day's entry.

MARCH 16, 1806. The captains reported in their weather notes
that eulachons had ceased to run and had been succeeded by coho

salmon. Lewis wrote that the events of the day were not "worthy of relation," but he gave a few lines to routine matters, nonetheless. Drouillard and his party were still out on a trading mission to the Cathlamets, perhaps detained by high winds. Catel and company stayed at the fort, but he could not be persuaded to part with his canoe at a price the captains could afford. Lewis took stock of their merchandise and wrote, "two handkercheifs would now contain all the small articles of merchandize which we possess." The larger items included six blue robes and a scarlet one, five robes made from a large flag, a uniform coat and hat, and a few old pieces of cloth with ribbon trimming. With some uneasiness he continued, "on this stock we have wholly to depend for the purchase of horses and such portion of our subsistence from the Indians as it will be in our powers to obtain. a scant dependence indeed, for a tour of the distance of that before us." Ordway reported that the captains sealed some papers and letters and gave them to local Indians to be passed on to a visiting sea trader.

Retreating to his species list, Lewis wrote of clams, periwinkles, mussels, cockles, and bivalves. The natives sometimes ate the clams, although Lewis thought them rather small. Periwinkles and cockles were the same as on the Atlantic Coast, while local river mussels were similar to those that inhabited rivers in the East. Bivalves of the family Amoniidae appeared to be a new species to Lewis. In addition to a morphological description of the coho salmon ("*white Salmon Trout*"), the captain filled a page of his journal with a beautiful likeness of the fish. Clark filled a journal sheet with a similar expressive drawing. Clark also borrowed from Lewis's entry of March 17 to discuss jellyfish and kelp.

MARCH 17, 1806. Catel and family left in the morning, but Delashelwilt and his wife were still at the fort, along with the women they brought with them. They set up a camp outside the fort, from which Lewis said they were "determined to lay close s[i]ege to us but I believe notwithstanding every effort of their winning graces, the men have preserved their constancy to the vow of celibacy." The party was looking ahead to departing Fort Clatsop—preparing their boats and watching the weather. With April 1 as their target date, the corps had to be ready to leave earlier if bad weather threatened. In fact, Ordway pointed out that they would have left this day had they been ready. Without calm water and low winds the trip as far as the Cathlamet villages could be delayed and throw off their timing altogether. Drouillard and party returned late in the evening with Pryor's canoe and with another that they had purchased from the Cathlamets. Drouillard had to bargain away Lewis's uniform coat and half a carrot of tobacco for the boat. Hard bargainers would settle for nothing less than the coat for a canoe, which Lewis said "is an article of the greatest val[u]e except a wife, with whom it is equal, and is generally given in exchange to the father for his daughter." The captain insisted, "I think the U' States are indebted to me another Uniform coat." Still lacking one canoe, Lewis lamented that the Clatsops would not sell one at an affordable price. With the departure date closing in, Lewis was determined to get one and decided to take one from the Indians as payment for the six elks that were stolen during the winter if no other means was available. Indeed, Clark intimated that one of the interpreters (probably Drouillard or Charbonneau) and several of the men had proposed that very action. Lewis's notes on species included jellyfish ("sea-nettle") and kelp ("Fuci"), with some confusion about the latter. He closed his entry with a list of shipping traders who visited the mouth of the Columbia River in the spring and fall. This list nearly duplicates Clark's list of January 1. It is not clear which captain copied the other.

MARCH 18, 1806. Perhaps the confinement of camp life was affecting the corps, as several men were unwell, and Drouillard complained of a violent pain in his side. Clark bled the interpreter. The captains directed Pryor to prepare the two canoes that Drouillard had brought to the fort the day before. They were in need of bracing, corking, and paying. Pryor was able to complete most of the work, but rain hampered the drying. The Clatsop chief Coboway and two Cathlamets came for a visit and spent the night. The captains gave Delashelwilt a certificate of "good deportment" and a list of the corps' names, then sent him and his female band on their way. They also gave the list of names to other Indians and posted one at the fort.

The list also included a short narrative of their exploration and significant dates in crossing the continent. On the back of some sheets they added a map of their route, particularly showing the connections of the Missouri and Columbia rivers in the Rocky Mountains. Deciding that it was highly unlikely that officials in the East would ever receive a report of their mission by way of Indians and traders in the vicinity, the captains decided against leaving any. In fact, Captain Samuel Hill's ship *Lydia* entered the mouth of the Columbia in June 1806 and received from the locals at least one copy of the narrative and muster roll. That document has never been found.

Concluding that the party was already too small, the leaders also determined not to leave any of the men to return to the states by sea. They had already decided to split the corps into several smaller parties on the return trip to carry out multiple exploring goals. Resident Indians gave the captains names of twenty-four Indian nations south of the Tillamooks, but neither man added them to his journal. Clark wrote a brief note about one of the kelps that Lewis discussed the day before. Ordway and Whitehouse disclosed that the captains sent four men to a Clatsop village near the coast to take a canoe. The captains said nothing of this, but had sanctioned the idea the day before. In fact, Ordway revealed that since Coboway was at the fort, two men hid the canoe.

MARCH 19, 1806. With more rain and hail, work on the canoes was again delayed. A small party went after an elk killed the day before by Joseph Field and returned soon with the meat. The captains gave Coboway a certificate of his "good conduct" and expressed their appreciation for his goodwill while they resided in his neighborhood. The chief also received a copy of the party's muster roll. He left in the evening along with the two Cathlamets.

Lewis wrote one of his lengthiest entries describing Native Americans, here noting the physical features, clothing, and customs of the lower Columbia Indians, including Tillamooks, Clatsops, Chinooks, Cathlamets, and Wahkiakums. All were part of the Northwest Coast cultural group. Describing them as short and illy shaped, he also said they possessed "thick broad flat feet, thick ankles, crooked legs wide mouths thick lips, nose moderately large, fles[e]y, wide at the extremity with large nostrils, black eyes and black coarse hair." But for Lewis their most obvious physical trait was the deformation of their foreheads, and he allotted lengthy space to describe the process infants underwent to achieve the desired result. Lewis overstated the extent of the practice of head deformation when he attributed it to "all the nations . . . West of the Rocky mountains." Clark had described the phenomenon on October 17, 1805. Lewis attributed the natives' swollen legs to their habit of tying cords around their ankles and of constantly squatting, thus cutting off circulation. Male clothing consisted of animal-skin robes made principally of mountain beaver skins and the previously described hats (see January 30). Lewis declared that they wore no other articles of clothing, regardless of the season. They seemed very fond of Euro-American clothes except for shoes, which he had never seen them wear. The captains had quickly discovered that the favorite ornament of both sexes was blue beads, which they employed in numerous ways. Dentalium shells were also prized as adornments. The men sometimes wore bear-claw collars, while women and children fitted elks' teeth to clothing. Both wore bracelets of copper, brass, and iron.

The captains noticed that native men participated in domestic chores more frequently than other Indians with which they were familiar. There were notable gender distinctions, however: men built houses, constructed canoes, and made utensils, while women collected roots and prepared items made from rushes, flags, cedar bark, and beargrass. Native women wore robes similar to but smaller than the men's, which they loosely draped over their bodies, exposing their private parts. Their lower garments covered them sufficiently when standing but when moving or stooping "the battery of Venus is not altogether impervious to the inquisitive and penetrating eye of the amorite," wrote Lewis. Clark copied much of this last passage into his entry of November 7. Lewis concluded, "I think the most disgusting sight I have ever beheld is these dirty naked wenches." Clark echoed the sentiment and added, "The women Sometimes wash their faces & hands but Seldom."

MARCH 20, 1806. Rain and hard winds delayed preparations for departure. The captains had intended to send Drouillard and the Field brothers to hunt near Cathlamet Bay until the party caught up with them, but bad weather vexed that plan as well. Having provisions for several days yet, the captains were prepared to wait out the weather. Some men were still sick—Willard and Bratton were particularly weak. Lewis attributed the problems to the lack of proper food and believed that once they got underway everyone would improve. It had worked that way in the past, he recalled. Noting that Drouillard's and Pryor's guns were out of order, Lewis congratulated himself for the foresight in bringing spare parts from the Harpers Ferry arsenal. He also gave a nod to the ingenuity of Shields, the party's principal gunsmith. The enlisted men counted elks and deer killed during the stay at Fort Clatsop and came up with numbers varying from 131 to 155 elks, but all counted 20 deer. Reflecting on the past few months Lewis wrote, "Altho' we have not fared sumptuously this winter and spring at Fort Clatsop, we have lived quite as comfortably as we had any reason to expect we should; and have accomplished every object which induced our remaining at this place except that of meeting with the traders who visit the entrance of this river." He still hoped that some seaborne traders would arrive, so they could get additional merchandise for the trip home.

MARCH 21, 1806. Still delayed, the captains decided to send out Shields and Collins to hunt along the river near the fort. They returned empty-handed in evening. Now provisions were getting low, so the leaders directed Drouillard and the Field brothers to set out the next morning for hunting at Cathlamet Bay. Some Clatsops came by for a visit and left in the evening. Willard and Bratton remained weak as ever, with Willard now complaining of a violent pain in his leg. Bratton's condition caused some concern for the captains, who saw no improvement in the man's back pain. Lewis again attributed the men's ailments to rheumatism. Gass, in an uncommon entry, wrote of coastal Indians' dress and customs similar to Lewis's entry of March 19. The sergeant spoke negatively about the sexual practices of Chinookan women, especially their tendency to prostitute their young women. Otherwise, he complimented the Salish ("Flatheads") Indians of the Rocky Mountains on their chastity.

MARCH 22, 1806. Drouillard and the Field brothers headed for Cathlamet Bay while seven hunters spread out along the Lewis and Clark River in search of elks or deer. At midmorning some Clatsops and Tillamooks arrived with eulachons and a dog. The captains purchased the lot. At noon Coboway and three more Clatsops arrived. The captains gave their fort and its furnishings to the chief and expressed their appreciation for his hospitality. Clark mentioned that the Clatsops told him that several of their tribe had sore throats and that one had died as a result of it. The Indians left in the evening as hunters returned with nothing. Colter was still out. In spite of mild temperatures the rain would not let up, so work on the canoes suffered. The captains decided to seal the canoes with mud, begin their homeward journey, and finish the job along the way when fair weather permitted. They were determined to set out the next day.

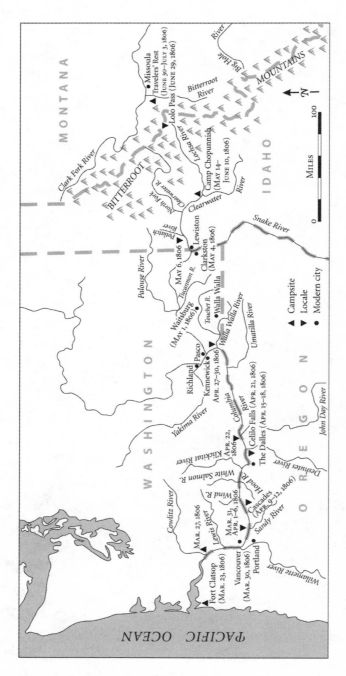

MAP 11. The expedition's route, March 23–July 2, 1806.

CHAPTER 10

Homeward Bound

March 23–July 2, 1806

MARCH 23, 1806. Colter arrived about nine thirty this morning having killed one elk but at such a distance that the captains decided not to send anyone after it. Such a diversion would keep them from getting around Tongue Point, Clatsop County, Oregon, the objective for the day. They would rely on the hunters Drouillard and the Field brothers, who were ahead of the main party, to supply them. In fact, there was some uncertainty about their departure because of rain and high winds, but the general opinion was that they could make it. About noon the rain ceased, the five canoes were loaded, and Lewis declared that the party "bid a final adieu to Fort Clatsop" about one o'clock. Clark, echoing Lewis's words of March 20, reminisced a bit about the stay at the fort: "at this place we had wintered and remained from the 7th of Decr. 1805 to this day and have lived as well as we had any right to expect, and we can Say that we were never one day without 3 meals of Some kind a day either pore Elk meat or roots." Ordway and Whitehouse copied the passage into their journals. A couple of weeks later Gass recalled the "wet and cold we had last winter" and that from November 4 to March 25 "there were not more than twelve days in which it did not rain, and of these but six were clear."

They had not proceeded more than a mile before Delashelwilt and a party of about twenty Chinook men and women caught up with them. Clark noticed Delashelwilt's wife and her "Six Girls" among the group. Learning that the corps was short a canoe the chief had brought one for sale. Since the party had taken one on March 18, the captains declined the offer. They reached Youngs Bay about three o'clock and began to work their way up the Columbia River along the southern shore. By seven they arrived probably at Mill Creek, Clatsop County, and set up camp at its mouth, having come about sixteen miles. Here they met the hunters, who had killed two elks but too far away to retrieve at the late hour.

MARCH 24, 1806. Ordway led a party of fourteen men after the elks that Drouillard with his hunters had killed. After they returned the full party had breakfast and set out at about nine thirty. They had some difficulty getting through Cathlamet Bay owing to shallow water. At one o'clock they arrived at the Cathlamet village they had visited on November 26, 1805, near Knappa, Clatsop County, Oregon. They purchased some wapato and a dog for the sick. Clark called the village "the dirtiest and Stinkingest place I ever Saw . . . and the inhabitants partake of the carrestick [characteristic] of the Village."

On one of the islands that dot the bay, the captains saw raised canoes for burying the dead. Clark thought the canoes were decorated with human teeth and the Indians told him as much, but close examination revealed them to be seashells. Lewis admired the Cathlamets woodworking skills and noticed intricate carvings on their doorposts. Moving on, the explorers lost the main channel until an Indian put them on the right course. This Cathlamet claimed the small canoe that the party had taken from the Clatsops on March 18. Lewis gave him an elk skin for the boat. The party camped at an old village of nine houses northeast of Brownsmead, Clatsop County, making another sixteen miles. Lewis got back to his bird watching, noticing red-breasted sapsuckers, double-crested cormorants, mallards, buffleheads ("butterbox"), and Canada geese. He related that he had not seen swans, snow geese, nor lesser Canada geese.

MARCH 25, 1806. After breakfast on a cold morning, the party got underway at seven along the south shore against a headwind and strong current. At the noon break for lunch some Clatsops came by with dried eulachons, sturgeons, and wapato, but the captains bought none. With the tide in their favor, they continued along the south side of Puget Island and arrived at a Cathlamet fishing camp, where they found several Cathlamets trolling for sturgeons. As the Indians demanded too high a price for their fish, the captains declined the purchase. Moving along the south side of the Columbia, the captains had difficulty in finding a suitable spot for the night's camp since the shoreline was swampy for some distance back. Late in the evening they located a place below the mouth of the Clatskanie River, Columbia County, Oregon, opposite their camp of November 6, 1805, at a point later called Cape Horn, about fifteen miles' travel for the day. Friendly Cathlamets offered them some seal meat, which Lewis found better than poor elk. Here too were Drouillard and the Field brothers, who had been separated since morning. In the area Lewis noticed red osier dogwoods ("red willow"), black cottonwoods, bigleaf maples ("resembles ash"), willows, probably Lewis's syringa ("sevenbark"), gooseberries, blackberries ("green bryer"), and perhaps salmonberries ("large leafed thorn"). For the salmonberry, see Lewis's discussion at April 8. He collected the type specimen two days later near the mouth of the Cowlitz River. In his weather diary he reported that elderberries, gooseberries, and honeysuckles were leafing out.

MARCH 26, 1806. Heavy rains and high tide forced Ordway and others to change spots during the night, while strong winds in the morning delayed departure until eight o'clock. Before leaving the captains presented one of the Indian peace medals to Wal-lal'le, a Cathlamet leader. He reciprocated with a large sturgeon. By noon they arrived at an old Indian village on the Oregon side opposite the lower end of Crims ("Fannys") Island. Here at lunch they met the principal chief of the Cathlamets, Sâh-hâh-wôh-cap (variously spelled) just returning from a trading trip. He presented fish and wapato to them, and the captains purchased more. Two Wahkiakums who had been pursuing the party also arrived with two dogs for sale. The two men wanted tobacco for the dogs, but the captains were unwilling to further diminish their scanty supply. In an aside Lewis related that the men who used tobacco were suffering from the lack of it. Chewers substituted crabapple bark, which Lewis thought bitter but which users found suitable. Smokers used the dried inner bark of red osier dogwood mixed with dried leaves of bearberry ("sacacommis"). During the break, hunters joined the party, having killed three eagles and a goose. The catch gave Lewis an opportunity to compare the bald and golden eagles by size, color, and physical details. Hummingbirds appeared, he wrote in his weather diary.

After lunch they continued along the Oregon shore, passing Crims Island and the open prairie that Clark named "fannys bottom" during a walk across the point. Probably naming it for his sister Frances, Clark may have been embarrassed by the humor in the name and gave it as "Fanny's Valley" on his map of the area. The party camped on one of the islands upstream from Crims Island in either Cowlitz County, Washington, or Columbia County, Oregon, about eighteen miles from their last camp. The hunters Drouillard and the Field brothers had gone ahead and did not make it back to camp by evening.

MARCH 27, 1806. Shortly after setting out the party was joined by upriver Watlalas ("Skillutes") who came for trading. At about ten o'clock they arrived at a Watlala village near Rainier, Columbia County, Oregon, and had breakfast. Here they found the unsuccessful hunters Drouillard and the Field brothers. The hospitable Watlalas gave the party dried eulachons, sturgeons, wapato, and camas and invited them to stay and hunt elks and deer. The captains declined since the weather was not dry enough to permit work on sealing the canoes. In discussing the Watlalas Lewis noted that their main village was on the lower side of the Cowlitz ("Cow-e-lis´-kee") River, Washington, and that in their "dress, habits, manners and language" they differed little from Chinooks and Clatsops. They had lately been at war with the Chinooks but had reestablished peace without completely restoring relations. Chinooks did not come this far upriver and the Watlalas did not visit the coast, so other tribes served as intermediaries. Watlalas are today identified as a part of a larger grouping called Cascades Indians. Lewis also identified a group of Salish-speaking Cowlitz Indians ("Hul-loo-et-tell") as living above the Watlalas on the Cowlitz River.

The captains sent two canoes ahead, led by Gibson and Drouillard, to hunt at Deer Island, Columbia County, where they hoped to halt and repair the canoes. Passing the Cowlitz River the captains saw several Watlala fishing camps on both sides of the Columbia River, whose inhabitants paddled out to visit and trade with them. With moderate prices from well-behaved Indians, the explorers purchased a good supply of fish and roots. Late in the evening, after traveling about twenty miles, the corps established camp in Columbia County, in the vicinity of Goble and opposite the Kalama River, Cowlitz County, Washington, but short of Deer Island. Upon landing the party was visited by eight men in a large canoe from whom they purchased dried berries. Near the camp in the bottomlands Lewis identified cottonwoods, willows, oaks, ash, and alders, while in the hills he saw the firs he had listed at Fort Clatsop. The night, like the day, Lewis wrote, "proved cold wet and excessively disagreeable."

MARCH 28, 1806. The corps set out early and by nine made five miles and arrived at Deer Island, where they found the hunters' camp with one man guarding the canoes while others were out hunting. Within an hour the hunters returned, having killed seven deer. The island lived up to its name, with the hunters reported seeing upwards of one hundred deer there during the morning. It also teemed with waterfowl—Lewis counted geese, ducks, large swans, sandhill cranes, canvasbacks, and mallards. Returning to his zoological studies, the captain described in detail a duck new to science, the ring-necked duck, which one of the hunters brought for inspection. He also noted the great number of snakes on the island and gave careful attention to the Pacific red-sided garter snake, a new subspecies. By midmorning the day turned fair, so damaged canoes were hauled out of the water, fires were built for drying them, and the sealing work was begun. By three o'clock everything was in order, and the canoes were returned to water, reloaded, and set to go. Instead of leaving, the captains decided to remain here, waiting for the hunters to return and taking advantage of the weather to dry other items. In the evening the hunters returned with the remnants of deer that had not been consumed by vultures and eagles. Joseph Field reported that one of the vultures, probably a California condor, had dragged a large buck some thirty yards before devouring it. Drouillard killed an Oregon bobcat ("tiger cat"). While at Deer Island the party was visited by ten Cathlapotles, a tribe they had met on November 5 on the way out.

MARCH 29, 1806. An early start took the party to the head of Deer Island, where they stopped for breakfast. Fourteen miles into the day they viewed a large inlet, probably Scappoose Bay on the south side of Sauvie ("wappetoe") Island, Columbia County, Oregon. On the island Lewis counted four tribes, which included the Katlamin-imins, or Kathlaminimins ("*Clan-nah-min-na-mun*"), three of whom had come to visit the explorers at Deer Island. All were Upper Chinookan speakers but cannot be positively connected to historic or modern groups. On the north side the Lewis ("*Cah-wâh-na-hi-ooks*") River (the boundary between Clark and Cowlitz Counties, Washington) entered the Columbia, and on its eastern side they came to the Nahpooitle village of the Cathlapotles, visited the year before on November 5. Lewis now wrote extensively about Cathlapotle language, dwellings, clothing, and customs and found them similar to those below "as far as we could discover." Rather than the bark skirts worn by women lower on the Columbia, however, here females had a kind of leather breechcloth they tucked between their legs and secured around their waists. Lewis considered it a "much more indecent article" than the piece worn by lower Columbian women. The captain saw great quantities of dried eulachons as well as sturgeons and wapato, the last being a principal trade item. The military man was impressed with an iron sword or scimitar ("syme-ters") the Indians carried and added a drawing of one in his journal. He called it "a formidable weapon."

The hospitable Cathlapotles gave them wapato and sturgeons to eat and sold them more wapato, camas, and twelve dogs. But Lewis also deemed them "great begers" and gave in to demands for small articles, with which they seemed satisfied. He also presented a chief one of the small Indian peace medals, while Clark gave him a blanket and an old flag. Clark moved much of this material into his next day's entry. Here he added a description of the women's technique of harvesting wapato. Holding a small canoe, they would wade into the water and loosen the plant with their feet, allowing it to float to the top to be gathered and tossed into the canoe. Clark also reported that Willard was quite well and Bratton improving. After a two-hour visit the party continued on some two miles to the night's camp in the vicinity of Ridgefield, Clark County, making about fifteen miles altogether.

MARCH 30, 1806. Again the party got underway early and were soon visited by three Katlaminimins, one of whom they had met the day before and who pleaded unsuccessfully for the explorers to visit his tribe on the southwest side of Sauvie ("Wappetoe") Island, Columbia County, Oregon. About five miles above Bachelor ("quathlahpahte") Island, Clark County, Washington, they halted for breakfast near their camp of November 4, 1805. Indians from villages on Sauvie Island joined the party, one of whom called their tribe "Mult-no-mah." For a few fishing hooks the party was able to purchase wapato and camas, but Lewis called the Multnomahs "great higglers in dealings."

After returning to water, the corps discovered a large canoe of Indians awaiting their arrival, who quickly became a part of the flotilla. Soon other canoes joined the fleet and stayed with the party until late afternoon. Lewis supposed that they came out of curiosity, and although he thought them friendly he noticed that they carried weapons. Ordway watched them in admiration and wrote, "I must give these Savages as well as those on the coast the praise of making the neatest and handsomest lightest best formed canoes I ever Saw & are the best hands to work them." Gass echoed the praise. The captain penned some observations about area Indians. He considered them larger and "better made" than the coastal Indians. He remarked on their fondness for steam baths and related a curious custom of bathing themselves with urine every morning. Just before sunset the captains located a camp for the night in Vancouver, Clark County, having made about twenty-three miles. Lewis took a walk and met Joseph Field, who had been unsuccessful in hunting elks. The captain attributed the soldier's failure to the noise created by walking through dry ferns, which scattered the game. From their camp, Lewis could see snow-covered Mount St. Helens and Mount Hood; the former he called "the most noble looking object of it's kind in nature." Clark, too, noticed a snow-covered peak to the southeast in Linn County, Oregon, which he called "Mt. Jefferson," a name it retained. Describing the valley between the Coast and Cascade Ranges in Washington and Oregon, Lewis believed that it could easily support a population of forty thousand to fifty thousand people.

MARCH 31, 1806. Setting out early again, the party landed on the north side near a spot they had passed on November 4, 1805. At that time on the south side they had counted twenty-five dwellings of Watlala Indians in the vicinity of the modern Portland International Airport, most of them constructed of straw and bark. The structures were now all gone except for one built of wood plank. A few inhabitants from there paddled over and informed the captains that others had gone upriver to the Cascades, which was their permanent residence. Three men in a canoe followed the corps as they set out again. Lewis noticed a distinction in their language, which represents the difference between Upper Chinookan (those below The Dalles, Wasco County, Oregon) and Lower Chinookan (Chinooks and Clatsops), while in dress, habits, and manners he found them much like the Cathlapotles. He also observed and commented on their burial vaults, which here reach their western limit on the Columbia River.

Staying on the north side, the party passed Government and McGuire Islands ("diamond island") and Lady ("whitebrant") Island and made camp above the entrance of the Washougal ("Seal") River, Clark County, Washington, a trip of about twenty-five miles for the day. Not learning a local term, the captains named the stream for the abundance of harbor seals at the river's mouth. They decided to spend several days here so Clark could examine the Sandy River on the opposite side, make celestial observations, and procure some meat. Drouillard brought the bad news that game was very scarce in the area. Troublesome mosquitoes, the first this spring, were not good news, either. The three Indian followers camped nearby and came in for a visit. Using sign language they informed the captains that Sandy River was a modest stream. In fact, it issues from near Mount Hood and did not answer Clark's conjecture that a sizeable stream must enter the Columbia from the south. He decided that he must return downriver and look for such a river, perhaps unnoticed behind Sauvie or Hayden Islands, Multnomah County. Clark may have written about these matters after this date, as they comprise a shorter version of Lewis's lengthier speculations on April 1. The corps remained here until April 6, near present Captain William Clark Park, Washougal, at a spot now called "Provision Camp."

APRIL 1, 1806. Trying to sort out the region's geography, the captains dispatched Pryor and two men in a small canoe to go up the
Sandy River on the Columbia River's south side as far as they could
and return by evening. The question at hand was whether the river
was the modest stream that Indians reported or a major affluent that
watered a vast interior. At the same time three hunters set out for a
large prairie at that Sandy River while other hunters dispersed on the
north side of the Columbia. Those remaining in camp were employed
at various tasks. Due to cloud cover Lewis could not make astronomical observations. The Sandy River hunters returned in the late
afternoon with four good elks and two inferior deer. They reported
abundant game in that area, while the north side hunters killed nothing and saw little. Lewis related a longer version of Clark's previous
notes on Indian information about the Sandy and the region's drainage to the south. The captains decided that another prominent river
must flow into the Columbia from the south and that the extensive
valley between the Cascade and Coast Ranges "must be watered by
some stream" other than the limited Sandy River. Indian informants
were of little further help on the matter, and Pryor's report yielded
not much more. Thus Clark's reconnaissance to come.

Several canoes of Indians coming downriver arrived at the corps'
camp during the day. Coming from the Cascades area, they brought
disheartening news of deficient food and depleted winter stores of
dried fish. Moreover, replenishing salmon runs were not expected
until May 2. In fact, they were here in search of food. Lewis was
shaken by the news and wrote, "This information gave us much
uneasiness with rispect to our future means of subsistence." He
knew that from Celilo Falls to the Nez Perces the party would find
no deer, pronghorns, or elks and that Indian horses and dogs would
be spare, malnourished, and unfit for consumption. With this disquieting information, the captains determined that they could not
await the salmon runs since it would detain them far too long to
reach the Missouri River before it was closed by ice. Moreover, the
Nez Perces were certain to be leaving the mountains for the Missouri headwaters in early May and taking with them the corps'
horses. Without their horses the party had little chance to getting
out of the mountains. They determined to leave as soon as possible.

APRIL 2, 1806. The captains resolved that the party would remain at Provision Camp at Washougal until they had obtained as much dried meat as possible to get them to Nez Perce territory. They also wanted to exchange their heavy boats for lighter native canoes or purchase them with elk skins or their scant merchandise. When they reached the point of overland travel they would trade those canoes for horses and dispatch a small party to race ahead and reclaim their horses from the Nez Perces. The horses would serve a dual purpose, as pack animals and meat on the hoof. Considering the prospect of eating horse meat, Lewis observed, "nor do we look forward to it with any detestation or horrow." Satisfied with the plan, the captains informed the party and sent out two hunting parties, including Gass, Windsor, Collins, Drouillard, and the Field brothers, one to the south side of the Columbia toward the game-rich Sandy River and another hunting in the immediate area. The north side hunters returned in the evening with dismal results. Those left in camp were set to preparing scaffolds for drying meat and gathering wood for fires. Lewis took time to do a bit of botanizing, noticing firs, cottonwoods, ash, and willows. Recognizing that huckleberries and salals were no longer to be found, the captain witnessed the transition between the moisture-loving vegetation region to be found downriver and the drier regions above. In the prairie around him he saw camas ("passhequo"), edible thistle ("Shannetahque"), western bracken fern, wild strawberries, sweet peas, silver-weed ("sinquefoil"), Mexican dock, and giant horsetail, among other plants. The last entry of Whitehouse's known journal writing ends this day. Indians continued to pour into the camp, bringing the same unwelcome news about the food situation to the east.

Most interesting was the arrival of several canoes of Watlalas, including some Clowewallas ("Cash-hooks") who resided "at a large river which discharges itself into the Columbia on it's South side some miles below us," reported Lewis. With this exciting news the captains had the Indians draw a charcoal sketch of the river on a mat. It was now clear that the river the natives called "Mult-no-mâh" (today's Willamette River, Multnomah County, Oregon) joined the Columbia behind Hayden and Tomahawk Islands ("image canoe Island") and that the party had missed it on both the outbound and homeward routes. Clark collected Thompson, Potts, Cruzatte, Weiser, Howard, Whitehouse, and York for a scouting mission, hired one of the Clowewallas as a guide, and set out at about eleven thirty to find the illusive stream.

Clark almost turned back when he viewed a large flotilla of Indians en route to Provision Camp. Worrying that Lewis and his small contingent might be in jeopardy, Clark hesitated but then remembered his cocaptain's standard precautions and carried on. They passed the village of their guide in northeast Portland but landed farther down at the village they had passed on March 31 at Portland International Airport. Here he viewed one hundred or more of the small canoes that native women used to gather wapato in swampy areas. The captain drew pictures of the canoe in his journal. Clark tried to purchase some wapato from the "Sulkey" occupants of one dwelling but was refused. He then resorted to tricks to get his way. He tossed a flammable piece of cord into a fire and used a magnet to whirl the needle of his compass. These actions had the desired effect, and the frightened Indians handed over wapato and begged him to put out the "bad fire." Calm returned when he passed his pipe and paid for the wapato. He then canoed around the south side of Hayden and Tomahawk Islands and entered the Willamette River. From here Clark had a grand view of prominent peaks: Mount Jefferson, Mount Hood, Mount St. Helens, Mount Adams (unnamed), and Mount Rainier. The captain found the Willamette gentle, with a smooth, even surface and sufficiently deep for the largest vessels. He continued ten miles upstream and made camp near St. Johns Bridge in northwest Portland at an uninhabited Clowewalla house, lately abandoned. There Clark viewed small canoes, mats, baskets, bowls, and trenchers lying about.

APRIL 3, 1806. Joseph Field returned to camp from the south side and reported that his hunting party had killed four elks. Lewis, concerned that he had few men to guard the camp with so many Indians crowding about, decided that he could spare Pryor and two others to go over and begin drying the meat. He ordered the hunters to keep up the chase. Impoverished and famished Indians from up the Columbia continued to arrive in the same desperate condition as previous visitors—some even scavenging for food scraps left around the camp.

Clark and party moved a short distance farther up the Willamette, to near St. Johns Bridge. Without getting a clear reading of the river's depth and not being able to view more than a short distance due to heavy fog, Clark determined that this great river "must Water that vast tract of the Country . . . as far S. as the Waters of Callifornia." In fact, the Willamette River lies entirely within the state of Oregon and emerges from the Cascade Range south and east of Eugene, Lane County. Satisfied with his reconnaissance, Clark turned the party back toward Provision Camp. The captain stopped at the village where the day before he had used tricks to get food, but the inhabitants were so frightened of him that he soon left. As the party paddled along the south side of the Columbia they met the same desperate Indians who had visited Provision Camp, but on the advice of their guide the explorers stayed clear of them. The little party stopped in northeast Portland at the village of their guide, giving Clark an opportunity to describe one long plankhouse of seven lodgings, each about thirty feet square. He drew a small diagram of the house in his journal. The captain tried to obtain information about the lack of inhabitants in a village that once must have supported a numerous population. Their guide's father brought a pock-marked woman to Clark to show the ravages of smallpox that had decimated the village. Clark persuaded another man to draw a sketch of the Willamette River with the names of Indian nations in the vicinity. The captain copied the map into his journal, and Lewis later added it to his own notebook. Among the Indian nations noted on the map were the Clackamas ("Clark a-mus"), Clowewal-las ("*Cush-hooks*" and "*Char-cowah*"), and Kalapuyas ("*Cal-lar-po-e-wah*"). Before leaving Clark bought five dogs. His party arrived at the Washougal camp about six o'clock, where he brought his journal up to date with events of the main party.

APRIL 4, 1806. Concerned about Gass's hunting party, the captains sent Ordway in search of the men. In a few hours all returned with bear meat and venison. Gass said that they had killed an elk and six deer but that the greater part of the meat was useless and was left in the woods. Collins, who had killed the bear, found a bed with three cubs and wanted to wait for the female to return, so he, Gass, and Windsor went back to wait out the mother bear. Indians from above and below came into camp. Those from above were following other hungry Indians to find food, while those from below seemed to have come out of curiosity. About noon the captains sent Gibson, Shannon, Howard, and Weiser in one of the small canoes about six miles ahead to hunt and wait for the main party's arrival. Drouillard and Joseph Field arrived late in the evening, reporting that they had killed and were drying the meat of two deer. The captains ordered them and perhaps Reuben Field to leave the next day to join Gibson and party in the hunt. With clear skies, Lewis got in a little astronomical observing. Clark's entry mimicked Lewis's, while Gass gave a brief account of Clark's excursion to the Willamette River.

APRIL 5, 1806. Joseph Field and Drouillard set out to join Gibson and his hunting party upriver. The captains dispatched Ordway and a small party to assist Pryor in bringing in the dried meat of four elks they went after on April 3. They were back by early afternoon but had prepared the meat so poorly that Lewis assumed it would spoil. The captain ordered that it be cut thinner and dried again. Also, the deerskin cases to hold the dried meat were not sufficiently finished and needed to be further dried. With plans to leave Provision Camp the next day, all the work had to be completed this day. A brief interval of sunshine hardly provided Lewis time for his observations, although he got a little peek through the clouds. Lewis counted woodpeckers, hummingbirds, geese, and ducks and also saw ticks and mosquitoes. The latter were not troublesome yet. Then he added purple martins, Steller's jays, ravens, crows, eagles, vultures, and hawks. Beetles, spiders, and flies also made his list. He noticed Nuttall's dogwood in the uplands and compared it to flowering dogwood. Clark provided a more extensive botanical discussion in his entry and evaluated the quality of the land. Ordway, too, assessed "the fertile valley of Columbia" and enumerated plants noticed by the captains. Gass reported that the wait for the mother bear proved fruitless, so they came back to the main camp this morning with the cubs. Clark said that visiting Indians gave wapato for the cubs to have as pets.

APRIL 6, 1806. With the canoes loaded and breakfast finished, the corps was underway again by nine. Lewis called it the "most perfectly fair day" that they had seen for some time and in his weather diary noted the leafing and greening of cottonwoods and willows. They stayed on the north side for a time but then switched to the south in order to find the hunters sent ahead. Noticing a physical feature from the previous year, Lewis was able to judge the Columbia's rise in spring flood, now some twelve feet higher. About ten miles from Provision Camp, they found the hunters, who had killed three elks this morning and were in search of two others they had wounded. The captains decided to camp here, gather wood for fires, and build scaffolding to dry the meat. With misstatements in Lewis's journal and errors on Clark's map of the area, it is difficult to determine the party's camp for April 6. From internal evidence it appears that the camp was the same as the one for the next two nights until they departed the morning of April 9. That camp was in Multnomah County, above Rooster Rock State Park, in the area of Shepperds Dell. Again, the captains decided to send hunters ahead to secure game until the main party caught up. They assigned the reliable hunters Drouillard and the Field brothers to head out in the morning. Lewis ended the entry with an extended version of Clark's reconnaissance of the Willamette River. He also copied Clark's drawing of native canoes and his depiction of a Chinookan plankhouse from the trip. Finally he commented on blindness he observed among Columbia River Indians and speculated that it might be caused by the sun's reflection on the water. Modern medical experts attribute it more likely to trachoma or gonorrheal conjunctivitis.

APRIL 7, 1806. While Drouillard and the Field brothers set out to hunt upriver, the rest of the party began drying the meat of the elks taken at this spot. They completed the task by evening, secured the meat in dried elk skins, and loaded it in the canoes, ready for an early start. The captains estimated that they now had enough dried meat to get them to Nez Perce territory. There they hoped to get some deer and perhaps a bear or two to see them through the mountains. Some Indians brought Drouillard returned in the evening to report that game had scattered from their hunting spot but that the Field brothers had continued on, hoping to have better luck higher up. Reuben Field killed a mountain quail and brought it in for inspection the previous night. Now Lewis provided the first scientific description of the bird, although Clark had copied Lewis's notes into his previous day's entry. Deeming it a beautiful bird, the captain preserved its skin and other parts for specialists in the East. The captains had the men practice shooting their rifles, make adjustments in the sights, and generally test the weapons. Clark found that his gun needed special attention with its rifling.

Several parties of Watlalas arrived from upriver. Lewis caught one of them stealing some lead and banished him from camp. All others left in the evening. Before they left, Clark convinced one elderly man to draw a map in the sand of the Willamette River. It conformed perfectly to the map he had received earlier during his reconnaissance of the river. The captain was particularly taken with the man's depiction of Mount Jefferson, which he exhibited with a large mound of sand. Obscured by hills on the south side, the captains had not seen it from the Columbia, but Clark got an unobstructed view of the peak from the mouth of the Willamette. The Indian mapmaker also provided information on natives along the Willamette and on the condition of the river.

APRIL 8, 1806. With high winds tormenting their canoes, the men had to undo the loading work of the day before. They got the boats unloaded just as lapping waves filled canoes with water and dashed one against the shore with such force that it split. Stuck in place, the captains sent Drouillard, Shannon, Colter, and Collins to hunt while others worked at smoking and drying meat. The hunters returned in the evening with little to show for the outing except for having sighted a black bear and some Columbian black-tailed deer. During the night an old Indian (Clark called him an "old amcinated retch") tried to sneak into camp to steal the party's belongings, but the guard caught him, whipped him with a switch, and drove him away at gunpoint.

Lewis took a ramble and corrected an earlier botanical identification. He apparently had been combining two different species that he called "large leafed thorn" (see March 25), but now, seeing the salmonberry in bloom, he detected the subtle differences. He may have been confusing the salmonberry with either thimbleberry or red raspberry. To clarify the distinction the captain penned a remarkable description of the plant. In his weather diary he discussed the phenological changes in local plants on this day and the next. On April 15 the captain collected a specimen of thimbleberry. Although Clark was following Lewis's account of expedition events, his entry is longer and more detailed. It is not the strict copying of earlier days. For instance, it was he who named the day's hunters but said nothing about the salmonberry. On the other hand, he copied Lewis's observations of April 6 about blindness among Columbia River Indians.

APRIL 9, 1806. Up early for reloading the canoes, the party was back on the river by seven. They caught up with the Field brothers, who had been unsuccessful in the hunt. During the day the party passed beautiful falls on the south side in Multnomah County, among them Multnomah and Horsetail. Lewis calculated one as falling three hundred feet and observed several others whose falling waters "become a perfect mist." Without delaying to admire the scenery, they proceeded on to a Watlala village on the north side about a mile below Beacon Rock and took breakfast. In one of the lodges Colter saw the tomahawk that had been stolen from the party on November 4 the previous year. He struggled with some Watlalas to regain it and was able to prevail. The Indians insisted that they had not stolen it but had bought it from others. The Watlalas were in the process of moving from what appeared to the captains to be a winter camp. Some were headed to the Willamette River while others moved upriver to Bradford Island, Multnomah County, Oregon. They not only carried their household goods but also carted away the framework and other parts of their lodges. Lewis described the plankhouses still standing as very similar to ones he had seen before. He noticed that the women inserted ornaments into their pierced nasal septa; otherwise he termed them much like other natives of this area. He declared these Watlalas very unfriendly, and only with difficulty was he able to obtain five dogs and some wapato. While they were here some Wishram-Wasco Indians arrived in two large canoes. They were on their way home from a trading trip downriver and were loaded with wapato, eulachons, and beads, which they obtained by bartering pounded salmon, cous, and beargrass. Remembering their kindness of the previous year, the captains smoked with them and treated them cordially.

By two o'clock the party was underway again. They passed Beacon Rock and purchased two dogs at another Watlala ("Clah-lel-lah," variously spelled) village, where Lewis found the inhabitants like the others, "sulky and illy disposed." Declaring them "great rogues," the captains kept them away from the party's baggage. The party passed Hamilton ("Strawberry") Island, where the rapids begin. Knowing that the north side would be difficult for the larger canoes, the party moved to the opposite side and negotiated the south side of Bradford ("Brant") Island. As it was getting late with the wind up, rainy, and cold, the captains decided to camp on the main shore near Bonneville, Multnomah County, after traveling about sixteen miles. Drouillard and the Field brothers in a small canoe could not navigate the waves, so they camped opposite the main party near North Bonneville, Skamania County, Washington. Lewis tried a little hunting after landing but without success. Seeing deer signs, the captains ordered Collins to go after them in the morning.

APRIL 10, 1806. While Collins set out for the hunt, Gibson, Shannon, Howard, and Weiser were directed to wait at the camp for him to return and in the meantime to collect pine rosin to seal leaky canoes. Now facing the rapids, the party set out at six in the morning, moved to the lower end of Bradford Island, Multnomah County, Oregon, and hauled the canoes with ropes for about a quarter of a mile over the obstacle. Having completed that task and without Collins or Gibson and party in sight, the captains left Pryor with the large tow rope to assist them in getting past the rapids. Meanwhile, the main party moved across the Columbia to the area of North Bonneville, Skamania County, Washington, and took breakfast near a Watlala ("Clah-clah'lah") village they had visited on October 31,

1805. Getting across the Columbia to this point was hard going, as the swift current worked against their best efforts. Here at one lodge Lewis was offered a "sheepskin," undoubtedly the skin of a mountain goat, a specimen of which he had been trying to obtain. The separate goat's head with horns still attached had been shaped as an ornamental headdress. The captain obtained the head for a knife and traded elk skins for the goat skin. Some villagers offered him the skin of a more mature goat but jacked up the price, detecting his interest. They tantalized Lewis further by telling him that they had lately killed two mountain goats from a herd of thirty-six. Nor were the captains able to obtain foodstuffs beyond some salmon.

By ten o'clock Pryor, Collins, and the Gibson party rejoined the main group, bringing along three deer killed by Collins. The party had little choice but to continue upriver on the north side, since the south side was impassable. Even on the north they were faced with a slow process since they could move only one canoe at a time, pulling with a single rope against the raging waters. Not marked on expedition maps, the party's camp was probably east of North Bonneville, near the community of Fort Rains and the party's camp of November 1. Although the boats were secured on shore, one of the small canoes got loose, went adrift, and dumped its contents into the Columbia. Indians below caught it and brought it back, so the captains gave them a couple of knives for their trouble.

APRIL 11, 1806. The corps had arrived again at the Cascades of the Columbia, a difficult stretch of the river that they had negotiated on October 30, 31, and November 1, 1805. With tents, baggage, and the party soaked from a ceaseless downpour that began the previous night, the captains decided to take the canoes overland first to the head of the rapids, hoping that the rains would end and allow them to carry the baggage over later. Clark led all able hands in the work, exempting Bratton, who was still too weak, three others who were injured, and a cook to prepare food for the haulers. A few men were also detailed to stand guard over the baggage against the threat of theft by Watlalas who crowded the camp. Lewis decried them as "the greates theives and scoundrels we have met with." By evening Clark had taken four of the canoes beyond the rapids with great difficulty and back-breaking work. Ordway provided the best short description of the process and noted the help of Indians. The men were so exhausted that the captains postponed taking the last canoe through the swirls. To add to their troubles, one Indian observing them from shore threw stones at the men. In spite of all precautions, the canoes were badly damaged by slamming against rocks. Indeed, Lewis declared the stretch much worse than in the fall when they first passed it.

Returning to camp, Shields lagged behind the others while dickering over the price of an Indian dog. The Indians took advantage Shields's separation and tried to steal the dog back, but he resisted, drew his knife, and prepared to fight. The Indians declined and ran off. In the evening some Watlalas stole Lewis's dog, Seaman, so the captain sent three men after the thieves with orders to shoot them if they showed any resistance. The soldiers caught up with them in a couple of miles, but rather than resisting they released Seaman and fled. At camp Thompson caught an Indian stealing a tomahawk but was able to recover it. With all this, the captains ordered the guard to keep all natives out of camp and relayed to the Indians that any caught stealing would be put to death. A chief of a Watlala division ("*Clah-clal-lahs*") explained that there were two bad men among the Watlalas who had instigated the trouble. He was mortified at their behavior. Sensing his sincerity, the captains presented him with a small peace metal, and the chief and Clark exchanged pipe tomahawks. Nonetheless, Lewis was certain that nothing but the party's numbers assured their safety, so they kept a careful guard. In fact, Lewis confided that the soldiers seemed disposed to kill some Indians.

In the evening the captains sent Drouillard and the Field brothers to Wind ("Curzatt's") River, Skamania County, to hunt until the main party arrived. Lewis commented on the Watlala "Y-eh-huh" village, Skamania County, that he had first seen on October 30. The inhabitants had lately moved to the south side and like the Watlalas had taken the main parts of their houses with them. His description of the houses matched his earlier notes of similar Chinookan dwellings in the neighborhood. Likewise, his characterizations of the men and women of the village were like his earlier accounts.

Lewis found that the Indians here were not as distressed as he had been led to believe. The captain also described burial vaults much like those Clark described on October 20 and 31, 1805. The captains met about a dozen Wishram-Wasco ("Elute") Indians coming from a trading trip below, now returning to their homes at the narrows in Klickitat County, Washington, and Wasco County, Oregon. They left their canoes here at the rapids and picked up those that they had left above on the downriver trip. The boats left behind were retrieved by Indians whom the Wishram-Wascos had gotten them from.

APRIL 12, 1806. Finding it still raining in the morning after a wet night, Lewis decided to lead a party around the rapids with the last canoe, a portage of over one mile. He took every man who could be spared and began the most difficult part, which was just a short distance above their camp. While they were trying to get around one large projecting rock, the canoe swung to the side, filled with water, and slipped from the men's hold, carrying canoe and tow rope adrift. The men's strongest exertions could not stop the loss. Now the captains were faced with trying to buy a canoe from the Indians at excessive cost. With breakfast finished, the party loaded up the baggage and set out. Clark stayed at camp, while Lewis stationed himself at the end of the portage. Those with short rifles—which may have had slings—were ordered to have them ready in case the party encountered pilfering Indians.

By five o'clock the transport was completed and Clark came up to the new camp below Stevenson, Skamania County, Washington, near the party's camp of October 30–31, 1805, having made only seven miles. About twenty well-mannered Watlala Yehuhs came across the Columbia and stayed with Lewis during the day. They condemned the behavior of other Watlalas. The captain noticed the black rocks of the Columbia River Basalt Group. He also sighted Douglas firs, western hemlocks, and western redcedars, and nearer the river, willows, cottonwoods, maples, hawthorns, cherries, currants, gooseberries, honeysuckles, huckleberries, bearberries, Oregon ash, and Oregon and dull Oregon grapes ("two species of mountain holley"). Clark added a few plants not listed by Lewis when he copied the captain's entry.

APRIL 13, 1806. With the loss of one of the large canoes (a pirogue), the men redistributed the crews and cargo into the remaining two large and two small canoes and set out about eight o'clock after a light breakfast of dog meat. They quickly discovered that the boats were overloaded, particularly the larger ones, which were not as steady as the others. Lewis feared that high winds would make them especially vulnerable. He therefore took the smaller canoes with extra men and passed to the south side, where the Watlala Yehuhs had relocated in order to purchase one or more canoes. He found a crowded village of eleven houses with a population that could muster "60 fighting men." The friendly villagers sold him two canoes for two robes and four elk skins. For some deer skins he also got four paddles and three dogs. Echoing his sentiments of January 3, Lewis acknowledged that dog meat had become a principal part of their diet and that most of the party considered it a favorite food. "Certain I am that it is a healthy strong diet and . . . I prefer it to lean venison or Elk and is very superior to the horse in any state." The captain continued along the south side with the new canoes, being afraid to risk the boats in the high winds to cross to Wind ("Cruzatts") River, Skamania County, Washington, where he expected to find Clark and the main party. Not seeing them on the north side, Lewis continued upriver until he was convinced that they were behind him. He stopped to wait for them to come in sight and prepared one of the dogs for lunch. Soon he noticed Clark's main party landing nearly opposite him and canoed over.

Clark had established camp in Skamania County, a few miles below Wind River near Collins Creek (not an expedition name), having come about twelve miles. Clark himself was out hunting with three others when Lewis arrived. Lewis learned that Drouillard and the Field brothers, who were supposed to be hunting at Wind River, were not there. When Clark returned the captains decided to send Pryor and two men back in search of the missing hunters. Although Clark had gone about one-half mile up Wind River, he was convinced that the three men were farther up. Pryor took an empty canoe along in hope that their hunt had been successful. Clark explained that he had been detained for several hours below the aptly named Wind River by high winds. When calmer water returned, he had set out again with the main party and established the present camp. Shields, who had been hunting nearby, returned to camp about six in the evening with two deer.

APRIL 14, 1806. By seven o'clock Pryor had returned with Droui-llard and the Field brothers, bringing along four deer that Droui-llard had shot. After breakfast the combined party set out along the north shore, facing a hard wind all day but one not strong enough to deter them. In describing the sediment and composition of Hood ("Labuish's") River as being similar to that of the Sandy ("quicksand") River, Lewis unknowingly associated the two principal conduits for Mount Hood mudflows (lahars) that flow into the Columbia River. He also noted the presence of ponderosa ("long-leafed") pine. As on the downriver journey in the Columbia Gorge, the party was cross-ing an ecological and climatic transition zone between the Doug-las fir–western redcedar zone to the west and the drier vegetation zone in the rain shadow of the Cascade Range to the east, typified by the dominance of the ponderosa pine. In this area Lewis also noticed the presence of the drowned forest of the Columbia. He tried to "account for this phenomenon" by conjecturing that the "narrow pass at the rapids has been obstructed by the rocks which have fallen from the hills into the channel." Indeed, he described from the north side the Bonneville landslide, which has been dated at around 1450 and which created the Cascades of the Columbia (see also October 30, 1805).

About one o'clock the party arrived at White Salmon River ("Canoe Creek"), the boundary between Skamania and Klickitat Counties, Washington. Here they found a large village of about twenty houses of the White Salmon ("We-ock-sock" or "Wil-la-cum") people, an Upper Chinookan language group. Lewis was particularly taken by the presence of about a dozen horses (Ordway counted more than double that number), the first he had seen since they left this area last fall. They purchased five dogs and various roots and berries from the villagers. Although friendly to the corps, the Indians related that they had recently returned from a war mission against the "To-wan-nah'-hi'-ooks," perhaps Paiute Indians, on the upper part of the Wil-lamette ("Multnomah") River. The horses Lewis observed were a result of that raid. After lunch they moved on while Clark and Charbonneau walked on shore. Clark essentially copied Lewis's entry this day except for a few notes about his excursion. Some six miles above the two men rejoined the water party and all made camp at Major Creek ("small run"), Klickitat County, Washington, above and opposite Mosier, Wasco County, Oregon. Not far from them was a large village opposite Memaloose Island ("sepulchre rock"). Ever the soldier, Lewis estimated that the *Smack-shops* (a term interlined by Biddle) could raise about one hundred fighting men. The "Smack-shops" were an Upper Chinookan–language people who apparently resided on both sides of the Columbia. The captains also called them "Chilluckkittequaws" (variously spelled); they have been classified as White Salmon or Hood River Indians (see also October 27, 1805). They visited the corps for a while in the evening.

APRIL 15, 1806. The party lingered while trying to barter for horses, but the villagers were not interested in the merchandise. Moving on, the party stopped at Memaloose Island ("sepulchre rock") to examine the graves, which were much like the ones seen below the Cascades on April 11. The island was about two acres in size and contained thirteen burial vaults. From here they proceeded along the north shore to another White Salmon Indian village below the mouth of the Klickitat ("Cataract") River, Klickitat County, Washington. Again they tried to purchase horses, but the Indians were interested only in a weapon that traders called an "eye-dag," apparently a type of dagger. The explorers had none so had to settle for two dogs. They were just as unsuccessful in getting horses from three other villages. By three o'clock they reached Mill ("Quinneette") Creek, at The Dalles, Wasco County, Oregon, and set up camp at the same spot they had camped on October 25–28, 1805, their Fort Rock Camp. They would be here until the morning of April 18. After landing Drouillard and some others went on a hunt and brought back a Columbian whitetail ("longtailed") buck. Indians in the vicinity came in to visit and trade, so the captains told them of their desire to obtain horses. It was agreed to meet the next day on the north side to barter. Lewis thought them better clothed than Indians below, with the men wearing leggings, large robes, highly ornamented shirts, and animal-skin girdles in the form of a loose apron. The women's clothes were much like those below the Cascades.

APRIL 16, 1806. At eight o'clock Clark and a small party crossed to the north side, carrying a good part of their scanty goods to trade with natives for horses. He had with him the "two interpreters," probably Charbonneau and Drouillard, plus Sacagawea and nine men, including Cruzatte, Goodrich, Frazer, Willard, McNeal, Weiser, and perhaps Werner. Anticipating their success, Lewis set Gass, Pryor, and others to work making packsaddles. He estimated that a dozen horses would be sufficient to transport the party's baggage. He also sent out hunters. Lewis "amused" himself by collecting "esculent plants in the neighborhood" that the Indians used. He also picked other unfamiliar plants, including poet's shooting star and a currant in bloom. Misidentified on the specimen sheet at the Academy of Natural Sciences, Philadelphia, poet's shooting star was not correctly named until 1999, based on studies in this area in 1929. It flowers only briefly in April and May and is mostly confined to area around The Dalles. Lewis called the golden currant "something like the yellow currant of the Missouri but is a different species." In fact, it was the same species that he had collected on July 29, 1805. This day's specimen of golden currant is housed at Kew Gardens, England.

In his weather diary the captain named local birds, including the western meadowlark, Say's phoebe, belted kingfisher, black-billed magpie, and blue grouse. Hunters Reuben and Joseph Field brought the captain a western gray squirrel and a blue grouse that he had described earlier (see August 1, 1805, and March 3, 1806). He gave the grouse another examination and a morphological description. Lewis declared their camp the last point on the river "at which there is a single stick of timber" until the Rocky Mountains. The captain obtained geographic information from Indian visitors who related that the Deschutes River did not water nearly as extensive a country as Lewis imagined. Again, Lewis surmised incorrectly that the Willamette ("Multnomah") must be the river that proved that hypothesis, but although extensive, it does not cover the watershed that the captain supposed (see April 3, 1806). Lewis added a bit of information into his journal about Clark's activities that he learned from men sent back to the main camp to get more trade goods.

After crossing the river to Klickitat County, Washington, Clark sent parties in different directions to notify natives to come for trading. Drouillard and Goodrich went toward one village, Frazer and Charbonneau to another. Indians came in and spent the day but yielded not a single horse. A lame chief of the Wishrams, which Clark inexplicitly called "Skillutes," a term usually applied to Indians at the Cowlitz River, invited the captain to his village some seven miles east, where he said the explorers could get horses. Clark and his party arrived late to the chief's village above the Long Narrows in Klickitat County, so he decided to spend the night and trade in the morning. After they were fed by the Indians, Cruzatte pulled out his violin and struck up a tune while the men danced, and the captain enjoyed a smoke with the principal Indian men. Clark may have been encouraged for the next day's trading session by the large number of horses he saw. He called the area the "Great Mart of all this Country," where Indians came from great distances to purchase fish at The Dalles and Celilo Falls and to trade their goods. The captain had a difficult night's sleep in a house crawling with mice and vermin. Clark was writing in two journals from April 16 to April 21, a first draft on letter paper and a finished version in his regular journal. He may have left his main notebook with Lewis and copied entries from the first draft into it later.

APRIL 17, 1806. Lewis dispatched more hunters and added hands to making packsaddles. Shields killed one deer in the hunt, and by nightfall workers completed the packsaddles—Gass counted twelve. The captain noticed that villagers were subsisting on roots and dried and pounded fish from the previous season. Salmon runs had not begun, and it was putting a strain on the corps' ability to trade for food. Lewis detected a change in the climate as the party neared the western edge of the Great Columbian Plain and the air became drier. Viewing "a rich virdure of grass and herbs," it exhibited for Lewis a beautiful scene, especially "pleasing after having been so long imprisoned in mountains and those almost impenetrable thick forrests of the seacoast." In the evening Willard and

Cruzatte brought a note from Clark informing Lewis about his lack of success in obtaining horses and suggesting that Lewis come on to the Wishram village above the Long Narrows while Clark went on Celilo Falls, even farther east in Klickitat County, Washington, in his search for horses.

Lewis sent Shannon with a return message telling Clark to double the price for horses and get at least five. With five horses and the small canoes, he felt they could make their way to "mussel shell rapid" between Benton County, Washington, and Umatilla County, Oregon, where horses were more numerous and cheaper. He also maintained that delaying at the present locations would be expensive, since they were compelled to buy both food and fuel. Ever the botanist, Lewis collected a specimen of wild hyacinth that was new to science, briefly described it, and indicated that local Indians ate its bulbs boiled, baked, or dried. Commenting on its pale blue color, Lewis declared it a "very pretty flower." Pursh's tag on the hyacinth specimen in Philadelphia gives April 20 as the date of collecting.

Clark was up early, laid out his trading goods on a prominent rock, and opened shop for the "Great numbers of Indian [that] Came from different derections." He made a bargain with one well-stocked chief for two horses, but the Indian dropped the deal. Clark came back with another offer for three horses but found the animals mostly unfit for service, so negotiations closed. Disgusted, he wrote, "they tanterlised me the greater part of the day." Just as Clark was leaving for Celilo Falls one Indian sold him two horses and another sold him one; then others came forward to trade. With promises of more horses to come, the captain decided to spend another night and bought three dogs and some cous to tide his party over. However, Clark was still skeptical of the Indians, who had disappointed him with such promises several times. Charbonneau did succeed in buying one "very fine Mare." Shannon arrived with Lewis's note.

From some visiting Indians Clark obtained geographic information and drew a grand map of the region in his notebook. Beginning at The Dalles and Celilo Falls, it depicted the Columbia River to just above the Snake River and then showed the connections of streams as far east as the party's Travelers' Rest campsite, Missoula County, Montana, and some distance north and south. Based on

Indian information from here and from earlier informants, Clark's map is a conjectural and sometimes erroneous depiction of river routes and connections. The captain changed houses for the night but found the mice and vermin ("with which those Indian houses abounded") just as annoying. His hosts had little food to offer and no wood for a fire on a cold night.

APRIL 18, 1806. The previous night Lewis was visited by a chief and a dozen others of the White Salmon or Hood River Indians ("Chilluckkittaquaws"). Most of them departed in the evening, but the chief and two others stayed over. Before he left this morning the chief promised to bring horses for sale once the party had crossed over to where he lived. After an early breakfast the party loaded up the canoes and set out for the north side. Reaching a rapid, the men unloaded the boats and made a portage around the obstacle, pulling the vessels as they went. From there they continued about five miles farther to a "bason" at the lower end of the Long Narrows, Klickitat County, Washington, where they camped. Lewis asserted that passing through the Long Narrows would be a much greater challenge than on the outbound journey. He was certain that he could not get boats either up or down the river under present conditions. After the canoes were unloaded and camp established, Lewis walked up to join Clark. He discovered that Clark had obtained four horses, for which he had paid more than double their former prices. Lewis had obtained one at the main camp, for which he gave a large kettle. The captains decided to make a portage around the Long Narrows with their five small canoes. The two large pirogues could go no farther, so they were cut up for fuel, since the Indians would give them nothing for the boats. Lewis and Clark returned to the main camp, leaving Drouillard, Werner, Shannon, and Goodrich in charge of the merchandise.

Clark was up early, built a fire, and laid out his trading goods as he had the day before. He had Frazer and Charbonneau collect the four horses purchased the day before and take them to the lower end of the Long Narrows, where he expected them to meet Lewis and the main party. They were to assist in transporting the main party's baggage. About ten o'clock Tenino ("Eneesher") Indians from upriver arrived and to Clark's "estonishment" would not sell their horses despite the previous day's promises. Nevertheless, Clark tended to the chief's ailments by dressing his sores; he also handed out small gifts to his children. The chief's wife, whom Clark called "a Sulky Bitch," complained of back pains. Hoping to get on her good side, the captain applied some camphor and warm flannel to her back. His ploy seemed to work. Making a new offer to the chief, Clark received two horses. Klickitat ("*Shad-datt's*") Indians from the Klickitat and Yakima Rivers regions were among the numerous Indians visiting Clark. The captain watched them in games of chance with the local Indians, one of which was similar to the ubiquitous hand game (see February 2, 1806). By three o'clock Ordway and three others arrived from the main party with additional supplies to add to Clark's store of trade goods. Ordway informed him that Lewis had arrived below the Long Narrows and wanted some dogs. Clark sent three. Within a couple of hours Lewis arrived, and Clark joined him on the return to the main camp.

APRIL 19, 1806. All able-bodied hands loaded what baggage they could carry and with the assistance of the four packhorses made the portage of about five miles around the Long Narrows, Klickitat County, Washington. By three in the afternoon they had accomplished the work and set up camp in the vicinity of Horsethief Lake State Park and the camp of October 24, 1805. Then they went back for the canoes and had them to camp by five. Lewis reported that the local Indians were overjoyed the night before at the first arrival of salmon. Although only one fish was caught, it was a harbinger of flush times ahead. Indeed, the captains were informed that within five days great quantities of the fish would arrive. According to custom the one fish was dressed and divided among the children of the village. Lewis said the practice was based on "a supersticious opinon that it will hasten the arrival of the salmon." Giving up two more kettles, the party was able to obtain four more horses after hard bargaining. Lewis's general disgust with the Indians came out: "these people are very faithless in their contracts. they frequently receive the merchandize in exchange for their horses and after some hours insist on some additional article being given them or revoke the exchange. they have pilfered several small articles from us this evening."

Knowing the natives' propensity to steal, Lewis had the horses hobbled and carefully tended. A negligent Willard let one of the horses wander off and got a severe reprimand from the captain. Lewis confessed that the tongue-lashing was harsher than usual. He had the horses picketed for better security. Not having been castrated, some of the horses were restless all night and demanded constant attention. Still without an adequate number of horses, Clark set out about five thirty with Pryor, Shannon, Cruzatte, and Labiche to the Tenino ("Enesher") village at Celilo Falls, Wishram, Klickitat County, hoping to obtain more. If he could get a sufficient number, they would abandon the canoes and go on by land. They arrived at about eight o'clock, but Clark found everyone in bed. The Teninos revived enough to have a smoke with the captain and to promise horse trading the next day.

APRIL 20, 1806. Lewis described the Teninos ("Enesher") and Wishrams ("Skillutes," for some unknown reason) as better clothed than when the party met them last fall. The men had leggings, moccasins, and large robes, while the women's clothing differed little from that of women at the Cascades and above. Most of the clothing came from Indians to the northwest in exchange for pounded fish, copper, and beads. Lewis knew of three principal Tenino villages at Celilo Falls, Klickitat County, Washington, where the inhabitants' large lodges housed several families each. The captain ended his ethnographic note in a critical tone: "they are poor, dirty, proud, haughty, inhospitable, parsimonious and faithless in every rispect, nothing but our numbers I believe prevents their attempting to murder us at this moment."

Giving credence to his words, the captain discovered that Indians had stolen six tomahawks and a knife during the night. And two spoons were taken during the day. Lewis informed the chief of the act. The chief's anger and harangue to his people failed to produce the items. Moreover, one of the strayed horses had been taken by its previous owner, had been gambled away, and was now gone. Lewis recovered his goods used for payment. During the day he obtained two indifferent horses for an extravagant price. Determining that he could get no more horses, the captain decided to leave in the morning. He would use two small canoes to carry baggage that could not be conveyed by horseback. With eight horses altogether, he had packs made up for seven and reserved the eighth for Bratton, who was still unable to walk. He bartered away one of the canoes with small rewards and so had the other cut up for firewood. With all the dried fish in the neighborhood, Lewis was especially displeased that he could not get a fair trade for any. He was able to get two dogs and some cous. Recalling previous difficulties, the captain had the horses hobbled and picketed near the camp. He ordered all Indians out of the camp at evening and told them that if any were caught attempting to steal anything he would beat them severely. Since the Indians left with a bad attitude, Lewis had the men examine their firearms.

Clark, ahead at one of the Tenino villages, laid out his goods for trade. Things quickly turned sour. The Teninos informed him that they would not sell any horses, except in exchange for kettles, which the party could not spare. Clark catalogued his goods for them: a blue robe, a calico shirt, a silk handkerchief, five containers of paint, a knife, a crescent-shaped decorated object ("wampom moon"), eight yards of ribbon, several pieces of brass, a moccasin awl, and six braces of yellow beads. To these he added his large blue blanket, coat, sword, and plume. Nothing worked. Having exhausted his time and patience and seeing that the main party would not arrive this evening, Clark packed up and retreated to his lodge of the previous night. He purchased a dog, some wood, a little pounded fish, and cous, built a fire, gathered the men, and ate. The captain had a smoke with the locals, then lay down with his men nearby, "haveing our merchendize under our heads and guns &c in our arms, as we always have in Similar Situations." Clark copied much of Lewis's entry into his draft and finished versions, indicating that these entries were written after reuniting with the main party.

APRIL 21, 1806. In spite of all his precautions, Lewis discovered that one of the horses had broken a five-elkskin-thick cord and even though hobbled had gotten away. He sent a party after the horse but told them to come back by ten o'clock, as he was "determined to remain no longer with these villains." In fact, the captain found that natives had stolen another tomahawk, but search as they might, the men could not find it. In his disgust, Lewis ordered all spare poles, paddles, and canoe parts put to the fire for warmth and to ensure that none would be left for the Indians. He gave a severe thrashing to one Indian caught stealing. Gass said it was the first act of that kind that had happened during the trip. Lewis told others that he would shoot the next person caught taking anything. He added that he would take the horses of the person who stole the tomahawk but that he would rather lose all his property than take anything from an innocent person. He emphasized that he had it in his power to burn the village and destroy its residents. Tension eased a bit when the chiefs seemed contrite, when Windsor returned with the lost horse, and when an Indian offered two horses. That man, perhaps a Nez Perce Indian, also offered to go with the corps as far as the Nez Perces.

With nine horses loaded and Bratton atop another the party set out about ten o'clock. The two canoes with four men (including Gass) had already gone ahead. The sergeant reported that the canoe party passed the Short Narrows with some difficulty. By one o'clock Lewis and party arrived at the Tenino village where Clark was with his men. Clark had found it useless to continue his attempts to gain more horses from "those unfriendly people." Here Lewis found the man who had sold him a horse that had run off. Lewis demanded that the man either return the large kettle and knife he paid for the animal or produce another of equal value. The man offered and Lewis accepted what he considered a very good horse. Having made the portage around the Short Narrows, the party halted for lunch on dogs they purchased at a nearby village. They then proceeded around Celilo Falls to their camp in Klickitat County, Washington, a little below the mouth of the Deschutes River on the opposite shore. One of the canoes joined the party there, while the other went ahead and camped on the Oregon side above the Deschutes River, having missed the others. The main party obtained some fuel and two dogs but at a high price. The Indian who was accompanying the party told Lewis that Indians ahead would be more hospitable. Lewis bought another horse in the evening "for a trifle," but it was barely able to carry a load.

APRIL 22, 1806. Again, in spite of being picketed and hobbled, two of the horses got loose during the night, but the man in charge was able to recapture them by morning. By seven o'clock the party set out, having sent the canoe ahead with Colter and Potts. On the way out Charbonneau's horse broke free, threw its load, and raced back to the village, where it tossed off its remaining saddle and blanket. An Indian quickly grabbed the blanket and hid it in his lodge. Charbonneau and another man were sent to retrieve the horse, saddle, and blanket. The blanket was not to be found. When Lewis learned of this he gathered a number of men to return to the village, get the blanket, or burn down their lodges. He had lost all patience. "They have vexed me in such a manner by such repeated acts of villany that I am quite disposed to treat them with every severyty, their defenseless state pleads forgiveness so far as rispects their lives." Labiche recovered the blanket before any harsh action took place. In the meantime Clark had climbed a hill near the camp, perhaps Haystack Butte, Klickitat County, Washington, directly opposite the Deschutes River, to gain a view of the country. From its height he observed Mount Jefferson and Mount Hood and scanned the course of the Deschutes River for some eighteen or twenty miles.

Apparently, at a halt the captains decided on procedures for the march ahead. Those men who were not managing horses would be divided into two squads, with one in advance and the other behind, alternating their positions each day. Following this procedure they moved on some eight miles to a Tenino village near Maryhill Museum, Klickitat County. Here they took a rest and had a meal of dogs purchased from the villagers. They also bought a horse. Lewis saw the canoes passing by on the opposite side, but high winds made it impossible for them to come across. Gaining another four miles after their meal, the party camped in the vicinity of the John Day Dam, Klickitat County. The Nez Perce guide suggested this spot since the next village was too far away to reach by evening. An Indian offered a horse for one of the canoes. Lewis signaled for Gass and Reuben Field to bring theirs over, but high winds prevented the crossing until it was too late. Charbonneau was able to buy a horse with a "red rapper," shirt, plume, tomahawk, and other items. Clark estimated that they had made fourteen miles "with the greatest exirtion."

APRIL 23, 1806. Charbonneau's success in obtaining a horse was short lived. He lost two during the night, having neglected to secure them. The captains sent Reuben Field and Labiche with Charbonneau to recover the lost animals. One of the animals was found close by while the other was given up as lost. At eight o'clock Gass and Reuben Field set out ahead in the canoe while the overland party got underway by eleven. During the delay some of the men made two more packsaddles. Staying longer to find the missing horse would have made it impossible to reach the next village this day, the captains concluded. Continuing on the north side for about twelve miles, the party reached a "Wah-how-pum" village at the mouth of Rock Creek, Klickitat County, Washington, where they camped for the night. These people were a Sahaptian-speaking group who are now classified as Teninos. These friendly folks sold the party four dogs, some firewood, and cous for a small amount of items, including pewter buttons, awls, and bits of tin, brass, and wire. They met a Nez Perce man with thirteen horses on his way home with his family. Clark remembered him from earlier. He offered to hire out some horses as pack animals for the corps, but the captains were interested only in purchasing them.

After settling in the captains invited the head men to join them for a smoke. Out came the expedition fiddle, and the men took to dancing. Then the Teninos entertained the party with their dance, which the captains described as different from any they had seen. The group formed a circle and began to sing while spectators joined in the chant. Inside the circle dancers in small groups stood shoulder to shoulder in a line and rocked from side to side. The event concluded with what the captains called a promiscuous dance, probably meaning a random or haphazard ending. After the dance all retired to their respective lodgings, and the captains had the horses hobbled and let out to graze. Charbonneau traded his shirt and two of Sacagawea's leather outfits for a horse. Villagers promised more horse trading in the morning.

APRIL 24, 1806. Up early, the men gathered the horses but found McNeal's missing. The captains hired an Indian to search for the animal, but it was noon or later before he returned with it and got a tomahawk for his effort. In the meantime workers fashioned four packsaddles, while the captains acquired three horses in barter from the Teninos. They also contracted for three horses from the Nez Perce man of the day before, who agreed to accompany the party along with his family. Finally, they sold the canoes for a few strands of beads after being "tantalized" with the promise that the Indians would exchange horses for the watercraft. Apparently the Indians saw that the party was to travel by land without the need of canoes and so thought they would be abandoned. Lewis decided to destroy the canoes rather than leave them under this circumstance. When Drouillard took his tomahawk to one, the Indians relented and offered the beads. With the whole corps now on land, they set out along a rocky, sandy road that made the going difficult and fatiguing. Most of the party complained of sore feet and legs. Lewis's left ankle was particularly sore; he got some relief from soaking it in cold water. Clark used the same treatment for his aching feet and legs.

Traveling about twelve miles, the corps reached a village of the "Met-cow-wes" they had met on October 21, 1805, on the outbound journey. They were probably Umatilla Indians, but some sources suppose they were Methows. Here they camped in Klickitat County, Washington, across the river from Arlington, Gilliam County, Washington. They bought three dogs and some cous, which they cooked over dry grass and willow sticks. Lewis noticed curlews, killdeers, and the western fence lizard (a species new to science). He also observed that the Indians had made a pet of a yellow-bellied marmot. The captains placed the newly acquired horses in a picket, while others were hobbled and turned out to graze.

APRIL 25, 1806. After collecting the horses the party got started by nine o'clock. Traveling about eleven miles, they reached a village of "Pish-quit-pahs" about two o'clock. These people have been identified as Yakamas (formerly called "Yakimas"), who were Salishan speakers, but here the corps was well within the historic territory of the Umatillas, a Sahaptian-speaking people and more likely candidates. When the party passed here in October 1805 the villagers were away, but now the captains counted some seven hundred people in about fifty mat lodges who gathered to greet the party. They purchased five dogs and some firewood from the natives and took lunch. The captains gave two peace medals to principal chiefs. Offering some old clothes, Lewis's long knife or short sword ("dirk"), and Clark's sword for horses, they got no takers. The captains described the Pish-quit-pahs as horseback hunters as well as riverine fishers and gave some attention to their mounts (which they praised), equipment, and riding skills. They noticed that the women dressed in skirts, leggings, and moccasins and that neither men nor women deformed their heads as much as those on the lower Columbia. The villagers wanted the travelers to spend the night, but the captains felt it necessary to move on.

The party set out about four in the afternoon, accompanied by twenty or so young Indian men on horseback. The captains described the hills bordering the river, Alder Ridge, as about 250 feet high with hard, black, craggy rock. This is basalt of the middle-upper Miocene Saddle Mountains Basalt Member of the Columbia River Basalt Group. Although the soil did not appear as fertile to the captains as that lower on the Columbia, they deemed it quite sufficient for horses. During the day the party killed six ducks, one of which—the northern shoveler—was unknown to Lewis. He preserved a specimen and gave it a lengthy description on May 8, when he had another one. He also saw lizards and rattlesnakes and a new species, the pigmy horned lizard, which he would describe more fully on May 29. At about nine miles upriver they established the night's camp, coming some twenty miles by the captains reckoning. Given the lack of clear geographic points it is difficult to locate the camp precisely, but it was probably within a few miles either side of the Klickitat-Benton county line, Washington. After encamping the captains were able to trade the items offered earlier for two "nags" from the Pish-quit-pah travelers, which they intended to ride, since the baggage was taken care of on the other horses. In the evening the Pish-quit-pahs asked for music and dance, so members of the party obliged with fiddle and foot.

APRIL 26, 1806. As the party moved on the country leveled out and the river hills decreased in size and stood back from the Columbia. Lewis commented on the variety of plants that characterized the shrub-steppe, xeric vegetation of the Columbia Basin, including sagebrush and rabbitbrush. Twelve miles into the day, they halted for lunch and dined on the last of the dogs bought the day before and some elk jerky. Here several families joined them, much to the party's annoyance, since the Indians' horses crowded in and broke the soldiers' order of march. The men were not ready to drive them away. Apparently the Pish-quit-pahs had returned home. After lunch the party continued for another sixteen miles, and the captains yielded their mounts to men with sore feet. The party camped a few miles above their camp of October 19, 1805, which would place them nearly opposite the mouth of the Umatilla River and in the vicinity of Plymouth, Benton County, Washington. Nearby the captains reported some Walla Walla (or Walúulapam) lodges, but these could have been occupied by Umatillas, Cayuses, or Walla Wallas. A young Indian boy from the village used a bone hook to catch a Columbia River chub, which both captains pictured in their journals. Lewis provided a description of this new fish species. An old tent provided some cover from the evening's rain for the captains.

APRIL 27, 1806. The absence of Charbonneau's horse detained the party until nine o'clock, when the animal was recovered. Continuing upriver along the shoreline, at about fifteen miles the party ascended the hills in the area of Switzler Canyon, proceeded about nine miles, and returned to the river near today's Yellepit Pond. Lewis ordered a break for the weary travelers, although they had not reached the intended goal of the Walla Walla village that their Nez Perce guide had set for them. While dining on a little boiled jerky the Walla Walla chief Yelleppit ("*Yel-lept'*," variously spelled) arrived with six men. The party had first met him on October 19, 1805, and had promised a longer stay on their return. Yelleppit invited the corps to his village to stay for several days. His promise of food and additional horses was an added inducement to the previous pledge. They followed him to his village in Benton County, Washington, opposite and below the mouth of the Walla Walla River, at a site probably now under Lake Wallula, making about thirty-one miles for the day. There Yelleppit exhorted the villagers to treat the visitors with food and fuel, then offered his own firewood and fish as an example. Others soon followed suit with firewood. The party purchased four dogs to add to the provisions and "suped heartily," said the captains. The Walla Wallas told the captains of a good road on the opposite side of the Columbia that led to the mouth of the Clearwater ("Kooskooske") River, at Lewiston, Nez Perce County, Idaho. On that level road they would find plentiful deer and pronghorns, with good water and grass. The captains calculated that taking this road would shorten their outbound trip by at least eighty miles. This good news persuaded the leaders to cross the Columbia the next day and follow that route.

APRIL 28, 1806. Yelleppit came early to the corps' camp, leading a "very eligant" white horse for Clark with the expectation that he would receive a kettle for his offer. Clark had to confess that all the expedition's extra kettles were gone, but the chief said he was willing to accept whatever the captain offered for the horse. The captain presented him with his sword, one hundred balls, gunpowder, and miscellaneous small articles. Yelleppit seemed pleased. Learning that they would not meet other Indians or be able to depend on the hunt in crossing to the Clearwater River, the captains directed Frazer to purchase as many fat dogs as he could acquire—he soon had ten. The captains asked Yelleppit for canoes to cross the Columbia, but he urged them to stay at least for this day, preferably for several, and he denied the request for canoes. The chief had sent word to the Yakamas ("Chym-nâp´-pos," variously spelled) to join them for a dance this evening, as he was determined to have the corps spend more time. Lewis got him to promise to furnish canoes if the party would stay the night. Using these boats they swam the horse herd over, hobbled them, and turned them out to graze. Finding a Shoshone woman prisoner among the Walla Wallas, the captains were able to converse with them through her with Sacagawea's assis-

tance. They explained their mission and spoke of trading possibilities with whites at the head of the Missouri River. Villagers brought
in a number of sick and lame, requesting medical attention from
the party. The most the captains could do was to administer a little
eyewash, which they had used on previous occasions. Clark also
splinted one man's broken arm.

Shortly before sunset the Yakamas arrived, numbering about one
hundred men and a few women. Joining the Walla Wallas, they circled the corps' camp and waited for the dancing to begin. Ordway
revealed that one chief requested one of the expedition's "meddi-
cine Songs" to learn, and he wanted to teach them one of his. For
an hour expedition men entertained the Indians with fiddle and
footwork. Then came Indian dancing at the corps' request. The captains counted several hundred dancers keeping time to the music
in a jumping motion while some of the men entered the circle and
swayed side to side. Some expedition men joined the Indian dancers, who welcomed their participation. Noticing one conspicuous
dancer, the captains learned that he was a medicine man and had
predicted the corps' arrival. By ten in the evening the music and
dancing ceased and everyone retired.

APRIL 29, 1806. With two canoes from Yelleppit the men began
transporting baggage across the Columbia. Some men went ahead
to collect the horses. The party now had a dozen dogs to see them
through the first part of their overland trip. Having gotten everything over, they were ready to go by eleven but were detained by
missing horses. By the time they had rounded them up their guide
declared it too late to reach a camping spot with water by nightfall,
so they made camp. They were situated on the north side of the Walla
Walla River about one mile from its mouth with the Columbia River
in Walla Walla County, Washington. Nearby a fish weir extended
across the river that was made from willow switches stitched together
and held up by crossed poles. Clark pictured it in his journal. At
this time fishers with skeins were getting only suckers ("mullets")
of one to five pounds. Lewis called the Walla Walla River a "handsome stream" of clear water about 4½ feet deep and 50 yards wide.
He noticed the Horse Heaven Hills across the Columbia in Benton

County, Washington, and was told by Indians that the Walla Walla had its source in today's Blue Mountains of northeastern Oregon. The captains also received garbled information on the geography of the country from informants, but it convinced them that they had been correct in determining that the Willamette River was the Columbia's major affluent coming from the south.

Near the party's camp was a Walla Walla village of twelve lodges whose occupants depended on the fish weir. The captains presented small peace medals to two chiefs and were given two horses in return. The captains responded with a few small items, and Lewis presented a chief with one of his personal pistols along with several hundred rounds of ammunition. Lewis found the Walla Wallas very well dressed, owing, he thought, to successful winter hunts. He noticed that most of the men styled their hair with two braids falling over the shoulder in front, while others sported a forelock at their forehead. The traditional livelihood of the Walla Walla Indians was tied to the resources of the Columbia River about the mouth of the Walla Walla River. The lower reaches of the Walla Walla River were the locus of their primary villages. Typical of Plateau Indians, the Walla Wallas fished for salmon in nearby streams or joined other area tribes at Celilo Falls for the annual salmon run and to trade for goods from distant points. They also harvested cous near their villages and gathered berries and hunted deer and elks in the Blue Mountains. By Lewis and Clark's time they had acquired numerous horses and were being influenced by Great Plains Indians' culture.

Several Indians came to Clark for medical aid. The captain wrote that he "administered as well as I could to all." One man brought a horse as payment for care for his wife. Clark thought she was suffering from a severe cold so gave her some simple medicine and wrapped her in flannel. He provided the usual eyewash for others. The Walla Wallas hoped for music and a dance from the party, but rain, wind, and cold prevented it. Ordway declared the Walla Wallas "the kindest and the most friendly to us than any we have yet Seen."

APRIL 30, 1806. Again the difficulty with scattered horses in spite of a picket and hobbles. The party purchased two more horses and several dogs and exchanged one of the more difficult horses for a better one from the Nez Perce man who followed the corps with his family. The man had a daughter with him who had just come into puberty and because she was menstruating was separated from others, sleeping at a distance and traveling at the rear of the family procession. Lewis also learned that while under this condition she was not permitted to eat with the family, touch any food utensils, or handle items of "manly occupation." Still hunting horses, this time Clark's gift horse from Yelleppit, Lewis lent his horse to the chief to search for it. Not long after Yelleppit left, the Nez Perce guide located the animal. The captains decided to leave Reuben Field to get Lewis's horse from the chief so the party could get underway. At eleven o'clock they set out, leaving "these friendly honest people the Wollahwollahs," wrote Lewis.

Traveling through a level, sandy plain in a northeasterly direction, the party reached the Touchet River, in Walla Walla County, Washington, after about fourteen miles. Here they camped, finding abundant wood for fires. These riparian forests stand out within the larger Columbia Basin dry zone. Lewis noticed cottonwoods, birches, and willows and an understory of woody species like hawthorns, currants, chokecherries, gooseberries, honeysuckles, rosebushes, probably Lewis's syringa ("seven bark"), and sumacs. He also observed basin wild ryes ("corngrass") and rushes in the bottoms. Drouillard killed a beaver and an otter, a portion of which they shared with their Indian companions. Lewis contended that the Indians would not eat dogs but ate heartily of the otter, which he considered inferior. He noted that they sometimes ate their horses, but only under grave conditions. The captain noticed the usual plant life of the shrub-steppe vegetation of the Columbia Basin and singled out "a short grass," probably Sandberg bluegrass. He also called attention to plants with edible roots that were an essential part of the native diet, particularly a plant that produced a root "somewhat like the sweet pittaitoe." The latter was probably cous, while the others were mostly other *Lomatium* species. Reuben Field arrived with Lewis's horse. The party now held twenty-three horses, most of them excellent young ones, but a number of them suffered bad backs. Lewis considered the Indians "cruel horse-masters" who rode their animals hard on poorly constructed saddles.

MAY 1, 1806. The horses were collected earlier this morning, enabling the party to get underway by seven. After they followed the north side of the Touchet River, in Walla Walla County, Washington, for about nine miles, the Nez Perce family man suggested they take what appeared to be an old, less-used path. He said they should spend the night and start on it the next day, as there was no water along that route for some distance. Worried about the shortage of water, Lewis wanted confirmation from the Nez Perce guide who was behind, so he directed the horses to be unloaded and set to graze while they waited. When the guide arrived he was much displeased with the other man and assured the captains that the route along the Touchet was much the best. The other man seemed to come around to this opinion. While the party halted, hunters sent out earlier returned. Drouillard had killed a beaver. Later Labiche got a deer. The guide said they would find abundant wood, water, and game from this point on to the Clearwater River. They resumed the march at about one o'clock, leaving behind the Nez Perce family, who had determined to spend the night and take the alternate route the next day. Adding another seventeen miles along the river, the party came twenty-six miles in all to their camp of the night, in the vicinity of Waitsburg, Walla Walla County. The captains compared the country they were passing through to the Great Plains of the Missouri River valley. After they settled in, three Walla Walla men from the last camp arrived bringing a steel trap left behind by the party. Lewis called this "an act of integrity rarely witnessed among indians" and declared the Walla Wallas the "most hospitable, honest, and sincere people that we have met with in our voyage."

MAY 2, 1806. As two hunters set out ahead, the rest of the party collected the horses except for the one from the Nez Perce man, who with his family was separating from the corps. In spite of being secured, the horse broke loose and tried to return to his former owner and herd. Joseph Field and one of the Walla Walla men finally located it about seventeen miles distant, on its way back. Continuing on the north side of the Touchet River in Walla Walla County, Washington, the party reached their next camp on Patit Creek, a short distance above its entrance into the Touchet, Columbia County, Washington, having come about nineteen miles. The three Walla Walla men stayed with them. Lewis observed them eating the inner bark of cow parsnip and tried some himself. He found it "agreeable and eat heartily of it without feeling any inconvenience." He knew it to be common on the Ohio River and branches of the Mississippi. Lewis saw camas in bloom along the river bottoms, observed the work of beavers and otters, and viewed deer at a distance. Sandhill cranes, curlews, and other birds common to the plains also appeared. Clark continued to copy Lewis's entries, making a few minor changes.

MAY 3, 1806. With little reference to lost or wandered horses, the party got an early start, at seven. The Nez Perce guide and three Walla Wallas left the party this morning. Moving cross country in Columbia County, Washington, at about twelve miles they reached the Tucannon ("Kimooemen," variously spelled) River near the Columbia-Garfield county line, Washington. The landscape was beginning to change. Lewis noticed a more fertile terrain with less sand, taller grasses, and fewer dryland shrubs. The party was passing from the drier shrub-steppe region of south central Washington to the steppe region characterized by perennial bunchgrasses. After halting for lunch at the Tucannon, they proceeded across the plains to Pataha Creek, Garfield County, where Lewis described the soil as "dark rich loam." Here he saw rich residual soils developed on the Columbia River Basalt and volcanic ash from Cascade volcanoes.

Continuing along Pataha Creek, the party met "We-ark-koomt," who they also called "Bighorn Chief" on account the horn of the animal that he wore. He had ten men with him. His name is generally given as "Apash Wyakaikt," which may be translated as "flint necklace." The captains acknowledged him as the head chief of a large band of Nez Perces. They also recognized that he had been instrumental in securing a friendly reception for the party the previous fall by going ahead proclaiming the corps' goodwill. He had now come some distance from his home to greet them. They all moved a couple of miles farther and set up camp out of the wind among some cottonwood trees on Pataha Creek, east of Pataha City, near U.S. Highway 12 and close to the point where the creek turns from a northerly to a westerly course. They had come about twenty-eight miles, enduring rain, hail, snow, and blowing winds a good part of the day. Fortunately the wind was at their backs. Having used the last of their dried meat at lunch and consumed almost all the rest of their dogs, they settled for a scant dinner. Apash Wyakaikt assured them that they would be able to reprovision themselves the next day at a nearby Indian village.

MAY 4, 1806. Both this day and the next the captains in their weather diaries noted a hard frost and thick ice on standing water. Again the party got an early start and soon reached Alpowa Creek, Garfield County, Washington, which they followed to its confluence with the Snake ("Lewis's") River in Asotin County, Washington, a few miles above the entrance of the Clearwater ("kooskooske") River into the Snake. Nearby they found the Indian village that Apash Wyakaikt spoke of the day before and halted for a breakfast of two lean dogs bought with difficulty from the "miserably poor" villagers. The party had visited this village on October 11, 1805. Coming through hills along this day's route, one of the party's horses slipped and took a tumble into Alpowa Creek but was not injured, nor were any supplies lost to the accident. The ammunition it carried was sealed in lead canisters, so it escaped harm. To his southwest Lewis viewed the Blue Mountains, which he had been sighting for several days, still covered with snow nearly to their base. He also noticed the forest vegetation coming out of the Blue Mountains, including ponderosa ("longleafed") pine, western larch, and grand ("balsom") fir. Given its rich soil, the area produced abundant camas and cous, which the Nez Perces were now collecting as they awaited the arrival of salmon.

The corps continued on to another village, where they met Tetoharsky, their erstwhile guide. The chief and others recommended that the party cross the Snake River at this point and ascend the Clearwater on its north side. They said it was a better and shorter route to Twisted Hair's village, where they would recover the horses they left with him last fall. The captains determined to follow this advice and secured three canoes for the purpose. They crossed the Snake to its north side west of Clarkston, Asotin County, and set up camp in Whitman County, Washington, about four miles from the mouth of the Clearwater. As the party crossed over, Apash Wya-kaikt returned to his village. Nez Perces crowded around the corps' camp until the explorers could hardly find a spot at their campfires to cook and keep warm. Among the Nez Perce villages the captains noticed small lodges set aside for menstruating women. They understood that men were not allowed close to those places and had to throw items to their women from a distance.

MAY 5, 1806. Off at seven o'clock along the Snake River, the party was soon at the Clearwater River and continued along its north side in Nez Perce County, Idaho. Passing small, temporary Nez Perce villages, the explorers were unable to buy provisions until they reached a large village at about one o'clock, where they secured two dogs and some roots. At one of the earlier villages a Nez Perce man gave Clark a gray mare in exchange for a vial of eyewash. It seems that while staying at Canoe Camp at the mouth of the North Fork Clearwater ("Chopunnish") River, Clearwater County, Idaho, the previous fall, Clark had doctored a man with leg pains, and the patient had extolled the captain's medical skills widely. Added to that was the benefit people received from the expedition's eyewash, so the corps' medicine was widely reputed and greatly admired. Lewis explained, "my friend Capt. C. is their favorite phisician and has already received many applications." Clark said that the natives had an "exolted oppinion of my Skill as a phician." The captains were not above using a little deception about their medical skills to obtain much-needed provisions, which they could not buy with their diminished trade goods. Lewis promised that they took care not to administer harmful items. At lunch a Nez Perce man threw a "poor half starved" puppy onto Lewis's plate and laughed as he mocked the captain for eating dogs. Lewis became enraged and threw the dog back at the man, hitting him in the face. The captain also drew his tomahawk and showed him what he would do if the man continued his insolence. The man left, and Lewis finished his "repast *on dog*."

After lunch they continued along the Clearwater about four miles to the Potlatch River ("Colter's Creek"). Here they encamped in Nez Perce County below the mouth of the Potlatch, having traveled about twenty miles. Nearby were two Nez Perce lodges. One contained eight families, while the other was one of the largest the party had seen, housing at least thirty families. It was 156 feet long and about 15 feet wide, built of mat and straw. It had a number of small doors on each side and was closed on the ends, and down the center ran a row of small fires. This was the village of one of four principal chiefs of the Nez Perces, as the captains understood it. He was known historically by the captains' name for him, "Cut Nose," in recognition of a facial lance wound he received in battle with the Shoshones. They gave his Indian name as "Nees-ne,-park-ke-ook" (more often, "Neeshneparkeeook"). The captains presented him with a small peace medal but were somewhat disparaging of him, finding that he showed little intelligence and seemed to have slight influence with his people.

The party's meager trade goods could not induce the Nez Perces to sell them food items other than some cous bread and dried roots, not nearly enough to assuage their hunger. The captains then opened the medicine chest, and soon Clark had more than fifty applicants, but the captains would not treat anyone without payment in horses or dogs. With the promise of a horse, Clark treated one woman with an abscess on her back by opening it, adding material to keep it open and draining, and applying a salve of resin, yellow wax, and lard ("basilicon"). Lewis prepared a potion of sulfur and cream of tartar to be taken each morning. The captains then halted their practice for the day. Indians were bringing dogs, but most were unfit for eating. On a different matter, the captains felt a need to explain themselves because an old man had told the Nez Perces that the explorers were evil and had come to kill them. They found a Shoshone man, perhaps a prisoner, at the village and through him and Sacagawea (unacknowledged) relayed the purpose of their trip. Apash Wyakaikt rejoined them in the evening and assisted in the mediation. It was eleven at night before all seemed satisfied. Clark largely copied Lewis's entry, as before.

MAY 6, 1806. The husband of the sick woman under Clark's care brought a young horse, which the men immediately killed and butchered. The captains got a second horse for medicating a young girl with rheumatism. With sore eyes a nearly universal complaint, Clark spent a good deal of the morning administering eyewash. Lewis obtained an elegant, strong, active, and well-behaved sorrel horse from Apash Wyakaikt and gave him a horse and small flag in return. The chief seemed satisfied with the exchange. The captains met three Coeur d'Alene ("Skeets-so-mish") Indians and found that they lived at the falls of a Columbia River tributary, the Coeur d'Alene River in northern Idaho. Lewis noticed a difference in their language (Salishan) but did not have time to take a vocabulary. In trying to locate the Coeur d'Alenes based on their knowledge of lands beyond their line of march, the captains confused the flow and placement of rivers and lakes in the region, and Clark's postexpedition maps added to the confusion. Lewis at this point renamed a river the party had been calling the Flathead for Clark ("in honour of my worthy friend and fellow traveller"), a name it still retains as the Clark Fork River. This act meant that he had to rename a tributary of the Columbia that he had earlier named for Clark. The Deschutes River was now designated "Towannahiooks" (variously spelled), from a Tenino term.

At three o'clock the party set out, accompanied by Twisted Hair's relative and Apash Wyakaikt along with ten or twelve other Indians. Drouillard and Colter got into a squabble over one of the horses, but the nature of the disagreement is unclear and barely mentioned. The party passed two small villages in their route along the Clearwater but were unable to obtain any provisions from the inhabitants. A little after dark one of the newly acquired horses broke loose and escaped, much to the regret of the hungry men. The location of the night's camp is not altogether clear, but it was on the Clearwater River, Nez Perce County, at or near the entrance of Pine Creek. Again, Clark largely copied Lewis's entry but added a description of Nez Perce burial practices that differed from his notes on these burials on October 11, 1805, and from his and Lewis's of the next day. Here he said that the Nez Perces buried the dead wrapped in robes in graves on stony hillsides. After filling the hole with earth and stones, they erected a stone arch over the spot. They also sacrificed the favorite horses of the deceased, the bones of which Clark saw on and around the graves.

MAY 7, 1806. The party collected their horses and got an early start in the company of Twisted Hair's relative as guide but absent Apash Wyakaikt and his group, who left the corps. After traveling about four miles their guide recommended crossing the Clearwater River near present Bedrock Creek in Nez Perce County, Idaho. He said that the going would be easier on the south side and game more abundant. The men unloaded the horses, found a canoe, and accomplished the crossing in about four hours. A man at a local village produced two lead canisters of gunpowder, which he said his dog had dug up. The explorers had buried them on October 7, 1805, near Lenore, Nez Perce County. Complimenting the man's honesty, the captains gave him a "fire steel," used to strike with flint and make fire. With this man's act in mind Gass made the following general comment on the Indians the party had met: "All the Indians from the Rocky mountains to the falls of Columbia, are an honest, ingenuous and well disposed people; but from the falls to the sea-coast, and along it, they are a rascally, thieving set." After the crossing, the party followed a difficult, stony road, then left the river and ascended hills that were level on top and thickly covered in grass, plants, and ponderosa pines. Lewis called it "a delightful pasture for horses" and "a beautifull fertile and picteresque country." The Nez Perce chief Cut Nose joined the party for a time while he was visiting local villages and gathering roots. A Shoshone man (perhaps the one of May 5) was with him and spent the night.

Their guide led them off the hills and down a steep path to Big Canyon ("Musquetoe") Creek, Nez Perce County, about five miles from where they crossed the Clearwater. They went up the creek about one mile and established camp on the east side near six recently abandoned Indian lodges, having traveled about twelve miles. Along the way Lewis noticed the work of the northern pocket gopher, which left little earth mounds from its diggings. Although the captain had observed its works, he had never seen the animal. Seeing deer and deer tracks in the neighborhood, the captains determined to spend the next morning hunting with the hope of getting some venison to supplement their horse meat. Viewing spurs of the Rocky Mountains covered with snow, the party was discouraged at information from Indians that it would be the first of June before they could pass through them. They thought longingly of the fat plains of the Missouri and relief from a constant diet of horse beef and roots. Lewis's and Clark's descriptions of Nez Perce burials differed from those of the day before, and Clark acknowledged the variety of patterns. Here they described bodies being wrapped in skins, laid on boards, stacked one on another, and placed in raised sepulchers. After copying Lewis's entry, Clark made comments of his own about deer decoys set out by Indians and manipulated in such a way as to attract deer without having to try to use horses in dense woods. He also described dress ornaments of the Nez Perces, drawn from Lewis's entry of May 13.

MAY 8, 1806. Based on the deer sightings the day before, expedition hunters turned out at first light. Without Lewis or Clark knowing it, some of the men stayed around camp. The captains chided them severely for their "indolence and inattention" to orders. By eight o'clock Shields was back with a small deer for breakfast. All the other hunters were in before noon. The reliable Drouillard had a deer, as did Cruzatte. Collins wounded another, which Seaman retrieved near camp. Altogether the party could count four deer and remnants of a horse in their larder. Shields also killed a northern shoveler, "a duck of an uncommon kind," according to Lewis, who preserved its head, beak, and wing and wrote a description of the bird. The captains learned from local Indians that they were quite distressed for food and had turned to eating boiled lichen that hung from ponderosa pines. They had also felled ponderosas to collect their seeds for nourishment. Lewis described the seeds as shaped like a large sunflower seed; he declared them nutritious and "not unpleasant when roasted or boiled." He noticed that Nez Perces also peeled the tree's bark to get at the edible inner layer.

Cut Nose and several Nez Perces joined the corps. The captains shared some of their provisions with the chief—venison, horse meat, the entrails of four deer, and four fawns that were taken with the does that the hunters killed. Although not eating the meat raw, the Indians gave it little preparation, boiling the fawns and eating them "hair hide and entrals." Lewis said that the Nez Perces would eat horses only under dire circumstances. He thought the reason more an attachment to the animal than a distaste for the meat. The Shoshone man was offended that he did not get enough to eat and refused to translate for the captains through Sacagawea. The captains ignored him, and he came around. Cut Nose and Twisted Hair's relative gave the captains a sketch of the principal rivers west of the Rocky Mountains. Clark made a copy of it.

By three thirty in the afternoon the party was underway again, accompanied by Cut Nose and others, but Twisted Hair's relative had left. They continued in an easterly direction parallel to the Clearwater River, going from Nez Perce to Clearwater County, Idaho. After a few miles they met Twisted Hair, to whom they had entrusted their horses the previous fall. He seemed to receive the explorers very coldly and spoke loudly and angrily to Cut Nose. The captains soon discovered a quarrel between Twisted Hair and Cut Nose and were delayed while the men argued. The captains eventually intervened and recommended that they establish camp nearby a few miles west or southwest of Orofino, Idaho. The two chiefs and their followers formed separate camps, and all appeared to be in bad moods. The captains learned that the arguments concerned the party's horses, that the cache with their saddles had been unearthed and taken away, and that their horses were scattered. Knowing that they had to establish a more permanent camp to await the receding of the Rocky Mountain snows, the captains wanted information on their horses to guide their decision about the camp's location.

With their Shoshone translator of Nez Perce still upset, the captains relied on Drouillard to speak to Twisted Hair through sign language and set up a meeting. Soon Twisted Hair joined the captains for a smoke and explained that after he had left the corps in the fall he collected the expedition horses. About this time Cut Nose and another chief, called "Broken Arm" or "Tun-nach'-e-moo-toolt" (variously spelled), returned from a war excursion. Apparently they were jealous that Twisted Hair was given charge of the horses. In consequence Twisted Hair ignored the animals, and they scattered. Regarding the saddles, he explained that they were threatened by rising water, so he took them out of danger and buried them at another spot but that some may have been lost in the original cache. He asked the captains to spend the next day at his lodge while he collected the horses and saddles. He also advised the captains to visit Broken Arm, as he was a chief of consequence. The captains accepted his explanations and told him that when he had returned the horses he would receive the guns and ammunition they had promised. They also promised to visit Broken Arm. Then Drouillard brought in Cut Nose, who smoked with the captains and Twisted Hair. Cut Nose announced that Twisted Hair was an evil man and two-faced. Indeed, instead of taking care of the party's horses he had let his young men ride them hard and injure them. That was the reason that he and Broken Arm curtailed use of the horses. Twisted Hair said nothing. Cut Nose agreed that the captains should visit Broken Arm. In fact, Broken Arm had sent provisions to the party, he said, but the bearers had taken the wrong route. It was ten o'clock at night before the conference ended and the captains could go to bed.

MAY 9, 1806. The captains sent out hunters with instructions to meet the rest of the party at Twisted Hair's village, then had the horses collected and set out. Moving southeasterly through Clearwater County, Idaho, they arrived at Twisted Hair's lodge after about six miles of travel. Nearby the captains again witnessed the separate lodges for menstruating females. Here the party waited while Willard and Twisted Hair took two horses to gather the explorers' saddles near their Canoe Camp of the previous fall at the mouth of the North Fork Clearwater River. At the same time Twisted Hair sent two young men in search of the corps' horses.

Waiting for these events to unfold, Lewis considered the country around him. In glowing terms he described watercourses flowing through fertile valleys with a mild climate and pure, dry air. He was certain the area could support an extensive settlement and produce abundant resources for "the comfort and subsistence of civillized man." To its inhabitants Lewis maintained that nature had liberally distributed all the necessities of life, which were "acquired with but little toil." Among the most beneficial plants, he named camas and cous, noted their habitats and forms, and explained the methods by which they were collected and prepared. He had collected a specimen of cous on April 29; he would press a camas specimen on June 23.

By two o'clock the hunters returned. Drouillard had killed a deer but lost it in the river, so the party was left with a few grouse that the hunters had acquired. Twisted Hair and Willard came in later, bringing about half the saddles plus some gunpowder and lead. Lewis lamented that his saddle was lost. About the same time the two Indians arrived with twenty-one expedition horses, the greater part of which were in good shape; five of them were still suffering from hard use during the winter. Lewis called their camp's situation "disagreeable" due to it being in the open country and exposed to the elements. The camp location is unclear, but it was southwest of Orofino, Clearwater County. A number of Nez Perces joined them, including Twisted Hair's relative, whom the captains thought "impertinent proud [and] supercilious." They mostly ignored him. Cut Nose and Twisted Hair seemed to have settled their differences and lodged together.

MAY 10, 1806. Snow was still falling and had gathered eight inches on the plains at six thirty, when the party got up. In their weather diaries the captains stressed the sudden transition in the weather since the day before, when it seemed almost summer-like. After a scant breakfast of roots, they set out for Broken Arm's village, some sixteen miles away over open plain. Drouillard separated from the party in order to hunt and did not get back in the evening. Wet weather brought a slippery road and caused horses to falter. By four o'clock they reached the chief's village on Lawyer ("Commearp") Creek, Lewis County, Idaho, southwest of Kamiah, and some four to five miles above the creek's entrance into the Clearwater River. The party remained here until May 13.

The "village" actually consisted of one 150-feet-long house of twenty-four fires and perhaps fifty families. Again the captains noticed separate lodges ("house of coventry") for menstruating women. Ever the military men, they calculated that the village could raise "100 fighting men." The party was greeted by an American flag the captains had left in the fall, hanging at Broken Arm's lodge. The captains met with chiefs and principal men, smoked with them, and explained their difficult food situation. Broken Arm brought out about two bushels of camas roots, some cous bread, and dried salmon. The sound of women pounding roots reminded Lewis of a nail factory. Thanking Broken Arm for his hospitality, the captains rather wished to exchange a horse in poor condition for a better one to slaughter. Instead Broken Arm gave them two fat, young horses as a gift and told them that the Nez Perces would provide them with as many horses as they needed. Lewis called it a "greater act of hospitality than we have witnessed from any nation or tribe since we have passed the Rocky Mountains." Given this hospitality, the captains instructed the men not to search lodges for food, as they had done in the past. In fact, Twisted Hair told them that the Nez Perces found that activity very offensive. Broken Arm also had a large tipi erected for the captains' quarters and a supply of wood laid out nearby. Being tired and hungry, the captains wanted to postpone further deliberations until they had eaten and rested, then to relate the objects of their mission.

About this time another chief, "Hohâstillpilp" (variously spelled), arrived with about fifty mounted men. He is known historically as "Hohots Ilpplip" or "The Bloody Chief" but more properly called "Red Grizzly Bear," a reference to his spiritual animal. He had come from his village about six miles away, so the captains invited him into the circle for a smoke and conversation. Rest for the captains would have to wait. They gave the two chiefs peace medals and explained the object's design and importance. Then as many as could moved into the captains' tipi, ate a little horse meat, and resumed their council for the rest of the evening. All seemed at ease, and Lewis was pleased that the party "have their stomachs once more well filled with horsebeef and the mush of the bread of cows [cous]."

MAY 11, 1806. Rising for an early breakfast, the captains found their tipi floor covered with "sleeping carcases," said Lewis. Soon another Nez Perce chief arrived—one of "great note." The captains described "Yoom-park´-kar-tim" (variously spelled) as a stout, good-looking man of about forty years of age and missing his left eye. His name apparently meant "Five Big Hearts," but the captains called him "One Eyed Chief." They presented him with one of the smaller peace medals, since they were reserving their last, large one with Jefferson's image for some later dignitary that Clark might meet on the

Yellowstone River. The captains surmised that the rank order of chiefs, from lesser to greater importance, stood in this fashion: Broken Arm, Cut Nose, Yoomparkkartim, and Hohots Ilpplip. Having all four together, the captains repeated their words of the day before, describing their mission, the government's position toward western Indians, the prospect of American trading houses in the area, the Americans' desire for peace among Indian nations, and the strength, power, and wealth of the United States. With the assistance of a Shoshone person, Sacagawea, Charbonneau, and others, the speech went through five languages. Lewis called it "tedious," and it lasted nearly half the day, but he thought the chiefs seemed pleased with the council. A son of a respected chief who had lately been killed by Atsinas presented the captains with a mare and a colt as a sign of his respect for the council. After the meeting the captains showed those attending the magic of magnetism and other curiosities like the telescope ("spye glass"), compass, watch, and air gun. In fact, the Nez Perces had learned of such things, since three of their people had visited the Hidatsas after the party left Fort Mandan.

During the afternoon Indians came applying for medical assistance. The captains gave them what medications they could spare. Lewis listed the ailments they were seeing: scrofula, ulcers, rheumatism, and sore eyes being the most common. Less common but now emerging as a complaint was the loss of use of limbs. One chief (apparently not one of the four named) had been afflicted with the condition for three or more years and was incapable of movement, yet the captains found him surprisingly healthy otherwise. The captains also indicated that in spite of living together in such close quarters, the Nez Perces' personal hygiene was superior to that of any Indians they had visited since leaving the Otoes on the Platte River. Twisted Hair brought in six more of the party's horses. By midafternoon Drouillard returned with two deer. Clark largely copied Lewis's entry but added a drawing of a Nez Perce fishing net (similar to Lewis's of May 18) and described some Indian fishing techniques.

MAY 12, 1806. After an early breakfast, Clark began his doctoring to a crowd of nearly fifty patients, most with eye problems. Nez Perce leaders met this morning to discuss the captains' comments of the day before. After the chiefs met, Broken Arm spoke to a gathering of the Nez Perces and informed them of the proceedings. He then invited all the men who agreed with the decisions to come forward and eat of a soup that he had prepared. Lewis found out that there was not a dissenting vote "but that all swallowed their objections if any they had, very cheerfully with their mush." Nonetheless, he reported that during the vote women cried, wrung their hands, and appeared distressed. After this the chiefs came to the captains' tent. Two young men presented each of the officers with a fine horse, while Lewis and Clark reciprocated with a flag, a pound of gunpowder, and fifty rounds of ammunition, plus some powder and balls for the young men. Cut Nose also gave Drouillard a horse. After these opening ceremonies, the chiefs asked to retire to the captains' tent, where they would give their reply to the previous day's proceedings. Considering the crowd seeking medical attention, it was decided that Clark would continue with his doctoring while Lewis met with the chiefs.

Hohots Ilpplip's father gave the Nez Perces' reply. He said that he had listened to the captains' advice about peace among the tribes. In fact, the previous summer they had sent a peace pipe to the Shoshones, who then murdered the three Nez Perce representatives—an act that precipitated retaliation by the Nez Perces. Killing forty-two Shoshones had satisfied their revenge, and now they were willing to make peace. Since the captains had not met with Blackfeet or Atsinas, the Nez Perces did not feel safe in venturing to the Missouri plains, but when American forts were established, they would come to trade for arms and ammunition. He also expressed their goodwill toward Americans and vowed to help them in spite of Nez Perce poverty. Also, they were willing to send some of their young men with the explorers to make peace but were unwilling to send a chief with the party until they had discussed it further. Lewis replied but did not record his words. The council was completed about two in the afternoon, after another smoke and the presentation of another fat horse to slaughter. Clark arrived and gave Broken Arm a vial of eyewash to administer. They gave Twisted Hair a gun, two pounds of powder, and one hundred balls of ammunition and promised another gun and more ammunition when they received the balance of their horses. The party was now short six horses. They gave ribbons, shells, and vermillion to the young men who presented them horses in the morning. Broken Arm and Clark exchanged shirts.

The captains told the chiefs that they wanted to form a more permanent camp where they could fish, hunt, and graze their horses and wait for the Rocky Mountain snows to recede. The chiefs recommended a place across the Clearwater River but said that there was no canoe available at the time to take them over, although they would have one by noon tomorrow. The captains were also looking for guides to lead them east to Travelers' Rest. Since Twisted Hair had several grown sons who were well acquainted with the mountain roads, they asked him to join them with his family at the new camp. He agreed to do so.

MAY 13, 1806. Clark spent the morning with patients, but by one o'clock the party had collected their horses, some sixty in all, and followed Lawyer Creek, Lewis County, Idaho, for about two miles, then turned nearly north toward the Clearwater ("Kooskooske") River to a spot on the river where they were to meet a Nez Perce with a canoe. That man did not arrive until after sunset, so they spent the night here at present Kamiah, Lewis County. A number of Nez Perces had accompanied them and stayed the night.

The captains admired Nez Perce horses. They found them active, strong, and finely configured, and they were amazed at the number of the animals, often fifty to one hundred for an individual. They also took account of Nez Perce looks and dress. The captains considered the men vigorous, active, and well formed. They had high noses, often of an aquiline shape, on agreeable faces. The men pulled out their facial hair but not the hair around the groin, which was more common with women. They appeared generally cheerful, with a fondness for gambling, shooting the bow and arrow, and horse racing. The captains called them expert marksmen and good riders. They seemed less interested in baubles than other Indians the captains had met but sought utilitarian items, such as knives, axes, tomahawks, kettles, blankets, and awls. Blue beads were an exception, and like others of the region they valued them highly. Men's clothing consisted of a long shirt, leggings, robes, and moccasins, much like the Shoshones. The women also dressed similar to the Shoshones, with beads, shells, and pieces of brass attached to their dresses and on earrings, necklaces, bracelets, and shoulder sashes. In their noses they fixed a single shell and used pearls and beads as earrings. Women also wore animal-skin bands on their heads, topped off with a cap of beargrass and cedar bark. Bear-claw collars were common for men. Men braided their hair on each side and let it hang in front. They gave special attention to a type of shawl made from the center portion of otter skins, about six inches wide, which hung over their heads to their knees. To it they attached pearls, beads, shells, cloth, and other items that the wearer desired. Lewis was especially taken with Hohots Ilpplip's tippet, which was formed of human scalps and ornamented with the thumbs and fingers of those he had killed in battle.

MAY 14, 1806. The party arose to a fair morning. The captains sent a few hunters to the opposite side of the Clearwater River and set others to hauling baggage across to the new camp they were to establish. By ten o'clock the baggage was transported, so the party took breakfast and then drove the horses across the river's 150 yards and swift current without incident. The captains considered their camp an ideal spot defensively, as it was an abandoned village sunk about four feet in the ground and surrounded by an earthworks. They constructed dwellings of sticks and grass facing outward at the wall and deposited their baggage in the center. They were told that they were in a good hunting area, close to the river for soon-to-arrive salmon, and adjacent to an excellent pasture for the horses. The party remained at this camp for nearly a month (May 14–June 10), longer than at any one place during the expedition except for Fort Mandan and Fort Clatsop. Although not named by the party, it has come to be called "Camp Chopunnish" or "Long Camp." The site is at Kamiah, Idaho County, Idaho, on the east side of the Clearwater about two miles below the mouth of Lawyer Creek on the opposite side. Not long after they arrived Broken Arm and Hohots Ilpplip arrived on the opposite shore with others and began to sing. The captains sent the canoe over for them and had a smoke. After

some time Hohots Ilpplip gave Lewis a "very eligant" gray gelding and the captain presented the chief with a handkerchief, four
pounds of gunpowder, and two hundred rounds of ammunition.

In the evening Collins, with Joseph Field and Weiser, brought
in two bears that Collins had killed. The male bear was large and
fat, while the female was moderate in size and meager. Lewis was
still trying to sort out the variations of color he was seeing in grizzlies. He thought they could be called the "white black grzly brown
or red" bear. He settled for "variagated" bear at this time. They
gave the Nez Perces, about fifteen people in all, half of the female
and the shoulder, head, and neck of the male. Lewis presented the
bears' claws to Hohots Ilpplip. The Indians quickly prepared a fire
and heated stones from the river. When the fire had burned down,
they spread the stones and laid on strips of bear meat, covering each
layer with pine boughs and topping it with more boughs, poured
on some water, and covered all with a layer of earth. After cooking for about three hours it was ready to eat. Lewis got a taste and
found it more tender than boiled or roasted meat, but the strong
flavor of pine ruined it for him. Later Labiche arrived, having also
killed a female bear and two large cubs along with several grouse.
Shannon also came in with grouse and two squirrels. Finding their
uncastrated horses too wild and unable to exchange them for mares
or geldings, the captains decided to castrate them. A Nez Perce volunteered to do the work and made the cut without first tying off the
bag. Lewis was not so sure of the technique but decided that they
would have a chance to judge its effectiveness.

MAY 15, 1806. Reuben Field, out hunting his horse, saw what was
probably a grizzly bear not far from camp. When he reported the
sighting several men went in pursuit of it but lost its tracks. Drouillard and Cruzatte hunted up the Clearwater River, while Shields,
Reuben Field, and Willard hunted in nearby hills. Shannon and
Labiche also set out for a hunt, and Gibson and Hall accompanied
them for a short distance to retrieve the meat of the bears that Labiche had killed the day before. They returned about eleven with the
supply. Lewis studied the bears' markings carefully and returned
to his consideration of color variations in the grizzly bear: "These

bear gave me a stronger evidence of the various coloured bear of this country being one specie only, than any I have heretofore had." He decided that if he tried to distinguish them by their colors and declare each variation a distinct species, he would have at least twenty.

Frazer, Joseph Field, and Weiser were complaining of severe headaches and Howard and York suffered with abdominal disorders ("cholic"). Lewis diagnosed the stomach problems as stemming from the change of diet. Broken Arm and twelve young men left the camp about eleven o'clock and crossed the river to their village. Hohots Ilpplip and three old men lingered until about five o'clock, when they also returned to their village. They came back later, unable to make the crossing. A party of fourteen Indian hunters passed the camp in early afternoon on their way to hunt deer. They carried the mounted skins of deer heads with them to use as decoys. The captains had the expedition horses brought together so they could get used to one another. Lewis noticed that some of the castrated animals were swollen, while others were still bleeding from the cut. The captain called their "little fortification" well secured from the elements. The party's baggage was protected in a good shelter. Ordway described it as a cellar, and around it the party formed their camp, with the idea that under an attack they could retreat to the cellar as a defensive position. A bower was also erected as a place to write and keep out of the intense afternoon heat. Looking around them, the captains could see three different climates within a few miles: the heat of the river bottoms, cooler temperatures and snow on hillsides, and four or five feet of snow in the Rockies. Clark's entry of the day largely copied Lewis's.

MAY 16, 1806. Drouillard's horse wandered during the night, but an Indian man and boy brought it back from a considerable distance. Hohots Ilpplip and other Nez Perces left the camp about noon; the captains gave them the head and neck of a bear, part of which they ate before leaving. Ordway reported that the party ate two of their unruly horses. The sick men of the previous day's note were improving. Sacagawea gathered a root ("fennel") that has been identified as Gairdner's yampah. Lewis found it a great food source and compared its taste to anise. He also discovered that it quieted the stomach disorders caused by eating cous and camas. Finding onions in great abundance, the party boiled them and added them to the roots and meat they cooked. The onions also eased their bloating.

Hunters sent out in the morning returned to camp before noon with little to show for their efforts except for a few grouse. Shields, hunting on his own, brought back a "black wood pecker with a red breast," reported Clark. Lewis's woodpecker was described fully by its namesake on May 27. Drouillard and Cruzatte returned about five o'clock. Drouillard had wounded some bears, but they all escaped. Shannon and Labiche came in a little after dark with a deer. They reported that game was scarce and that they were not able to extend their hunt because Lolo ("Collins") Creek, which runs into the Clearwater River below Camp Chopunnish, was too deep and rapid to cross. The Nez Perces had informed the captains that game was abundant beyond the creek. Pryor and Collins, who had gone hunting this morning, did not return. Lewis killed a Great Basin gopher snake near the camp and measured its length as three feet, eleven inches and counted 218 scuta on its belly and fifty-nine scales on its tail. He took a specimen of its skin.

MAY 17, 1806. With only flimsy covering to protect them, the rain that continued through the night into this morning soaked the party and their beds. Lewis's chronometer also got wet in spite of his precautions, and when he opened it he found it filled with water. He tried to dry it out and oil it properly but discovered rust in some parts. He set it going and hoped for the best. It rained moderately the rest of the day, and farther from camp snow fell. Pryor and Collins got back to camp about nine o'clock with the skin and meat of a black bear from Pryor and a report of Collins killing a grizzly. The bears were not in the best order. The men had secured the carcass of the grizzly, but it being too great a distance from camp Lewis decided to attend to it later. The ferocity of grizzlies convinced the captains to send hunters out in pairs. The captains were also rotating horses for the hunt so the animals would become accustomed to riders and to spare injury to any particular mount. No Indians visited the party this day—such an unusual occurrence that Lewis mentioned that it was the first time since October 1805. Watching the Clearwater rise from snowmelt in the Rockies, Lewis declared the mountains "that icy barier which seperates me from my friends and Country, from all which makes life esteemable—patience, patience." Clark, copying largely from Lewis, added that in consultation with Nez Perces he learned that it would probably be the middle of June before they could hope to cross the Rockies.

MAY 18, 1806. Twelve hunters, including the Field brothers, Drouillard, Lepage, Shannon, Collins, Labiche, Cruzatte, Shields, and Gibson, set out in different directions. Joseph Field was back by midafternoon, empty-handed and sick. Drouillard, Reuben Field, and Lepage returned a little before dark, also without success except for a hawk and part of a salmon taken from an eagle. The sight of an eagle prompted Lewis to hope for running salmon soon. These hunters had swept the countryside for ten miles to Lolo ("Collins") Creek and had seen neither deer nor bear and little sign of either. Potter and Whitehouse went with Collins to the bear he had killed on May 16; they brought it back in the afternoon. Again, Lewis was fascinated by the variety of colors in a single bear, "a mixture of light redish brown white and dark drown," bringing him to call it a "bey grizzle." Sacagawea spent the day gathering Gairdner's yampah ("fennel roots"), which Lewis explained the Shoshones' called "*year-pah*." That designation gave rise to its common name. Clark considered them palatable whether roasted, boiled, or dried.

In the afternoon three Indians who had been hunting near Weippe Prairie, Clearwater County, Idaho, visited the explorers' camp. Their hunt had been unsuccessful, so the captains gave them some meat. The Indians said they would save it for their hungry children. They left after a quick smoke. Nez Perces on the opposite side of the Clearwater erected a lodge, which Lewis thought was in anticipation of the coming of salmon. That anticipation was heartily shared by the party. The structure was in the form of a wharf projecting over the water where a fisher could stand with his net. Lewis drew a picture of the net in his journal, similar to Clark's of May 11. A native fisher tried his luck from the structure, but with little success, it seemed. An old man and woman arrived with medical issues: he complained of sore eyes, she of rheumatism. Clark

cleansed the man's eyes with eyewash and gave the woman cream
of tartar and sulfur.

MAY 19, 1806. With little success coming from expedition hunters, the captains sent Charbonneau, Thompson, Potts, Hall, and
Weiser across the river to buy roots to add to their scanty bear
meat. The men carried a few awls, knitting pins, and armbands for
the trade. The Field brothers were sent upriver in search of a horse
that Lewis had ridden on the outbound journey last fall. The animal had been spotted the day before among some Indian horses
but appeared to have gone feral. Thompson returned about eleven
o'clock, but instead of foodstuffs he brought with him "a train of
invalids," wrote Lewis. Sore eyes and rheumatism were the general
complaint, so the captains administered the usual remedies: eyewash and liniment. From her account of her illness and her appearance, the captains diagnosed one woman as "histerical" and gave
her thirty drops of laudanum. Clark called her "much hiped," perhaps meaning she was suffering from hypochondria or depression.
All appeared satisfied with the medical help. The "marketeers" got
back about five o'clock carrying five bushels of cous roots and a
large quantity of cous bread. The Field brothers came in late with
Lewis's horse, which was immediately castrated, along with two
others. Hunters Shields and Gibson returned having sighted deer
but without a kill. Horse races were the day's entertainment. The
captains agreed that the horses would be considered swift steeds
in Atlantic states. Clark mostly copied Lewis's entry.

MAY 20, 1806. It rained most of the night and until noon, when it
cleared for a short time and then resumed intermittently throughout the day. With inadequate covering, the captains lay in water all
night. As Drouillard and the Field brothers set out hunting, Shannon
and Colter came back, as unlucky as other hunters over the last few
days. They had wounded a bear and a deer, but with nightfall they
were unable to pursue. Snow in the morning had covered the animals' tracks and blood trails, so they gave up. Rain at camp became
snow on the plains. Labiche arrived with a mule deer buck that he
had killed on Lolo Creek. He left Cruzatte and Collins behind to

await his return. Later Lepage joined Labiche as he returned to his comrades. Frazer had gone to a Nez Perce village for trading and came back about five o'clock with a parcel of roots and bread. Finding that the natives were fond of brass buttons, the men stripped their clothes of them in order to obtain camas roots and bread. One of the hunters found a nest of sandhill cranes and saw that the young were coming out of their shells, the captains reported in their weather diaries. They also mentioned that young magpies had begun to fly. Clark wrote an abbreviated version of Lewis's entry.

MAY 21, 1806. Hunters Shields and Gibson went out and Collins came in, with few results. The captains set five men to building a canoe in order to fish and cross the Clearwater River. Some Nez Perces had promised to trade a horse for the craft when the party was through with it. Having been soaked on rainy nights, the captains had a lodge of willow poles and grass constructed to keep them out of the elements and to secure the party's baggage. Lewis declared it their most comfortable shelter since they had left Fort Clatsop. The captains divided the remainder of the party's trading merchandise among the men with the idea that they would use it to acquire as much camas as possible for the trip in the Rocky Mountains. Lewis was pessimistic about the prospects of obtaining dried meat here and unsure of the pending salmon run. For each man the supply amounted to an awl, a knitting pin, two needles, a few skeins of thread, about a yard of ribbon, and a half ounce of vermillion. Lewis called it "a slender stock indeed with which to lay in a store of provision for that dreary wilderness."

Lewis decided not to have the men gather cous on their own, since water hemlock of the area, a poisonous plant, could be easily mistaken for nontoxic cous. In the evening the party finished the last morsel of meat from the day before. They held in reserve a Nez Perce gift horse and relied on roots and their byproducts. Willard returned in the evening, having left Ordway and Goodrich at a village they had visited. He brought the usual offering: roots and bread. One of the party brought a young sandhill crane to camp. The birds were abundant in the area, Lewis noted. Clark's entry differed only slightly from Lewis's.

MAY 22, 1806. A clear morning for a change allowed the party to bring out the baggage to air and dry and also any damp roots or bread. Windsor and McNeal set out for a Nez Perce village about the time that Ordway and Goodrich returned with a supply of roots and bread. Ordway observed Nez Perce practices while at the village and noted that "the women do the most of the Slavery as those on the Missourie." He also saw Nez Perce men build and use a sweat lodge. Shannon and Colter were detailed to hunt in nearby mountains. A couple of Indian men came down the Clearwater River on a raft and visited for about three hours before returning to their village. Pryor was sent to find a potential spot for a new camp near Lolo Creek. Confined as they were by the river and creek, their hunting opportunities were cramped. Being able to cross Lolo Creek would give them access to a more advantageous hunting area. At lunchtime the men discovered that the Nez Perce gift horse had been taken away with the tribe's other mounts—probably in error, Lewis decided. Without that horse to butcher, a colt from the herd was selected. Lewis called its meat "fat tender and by no means illy flavoured." Three other horses were designated as rations for the Rockies, unless they were needed here. Lewis's horse that was castrated on the nineteenth had injured itself with its restraining rope, was swollen in the area of the operation, and could hardly walk. Lewis called the horse a "most wretched specticle." He had the infected area cleaned with a decoction of the bark, leaves, and roots of blue elderberry, a folk remedy he knew from home.

In the afternoon the party witnessed a number of Nez Perces chasing a deer that ran into the river near the camp. The captains and Gass were impressed by Nez Perce horsemanship. Gass described the details of Nez Perce saddles. Lewis, Clark, and others shot and killed the deer, so the natives could retrieve it. Their generosity was rewarded when they returned to camp to find that Drouillard, the Field brothers, Gibson, and Shields had just arrived with five deer. They also carried two steelhead trout they had purchased from Indians. Visiting Indians told them that the fish were not good at this season, a truth the explorers discovered. They also offered good news of excellent salmon runs on the Snake River but said it would be some time before the fish reached the Camp Chopunnish area.

The captains also learned that Shoshones had recently surrounded a Nez Perce lodge but were detected and driven away. Little Jean Baptiste Charbonneau was cutting teeth and suffering with diarrhea. When the diarrhea ceased he exhibited a high fever, with swollen neck and throat. Several ideas have been advanced about the child's illness, including mumps, tonsillitis, and an abscess on the neck. The captains gave him their usual medicines: cream of tartar and flour of sulfur. They also applied a warm poultice of boiled onions on his neck. Pryor returned late in the evening from his excursion to Lolo Creek but decided to go back and take a different route. Drouillard, who had been through the area, was pessimistic about finding a suitable location for a new camp. Clark again followed Lewis's entry.

MAY 23, 1806. Lewis recorded in detail the pursuit of a single deer by Seaman and mounted Nez Perces after Pryor wounded it. It was finally taken down by Pryor and shared with the Indian hunters. The captains' medicine seemed to be having an effect on Sacagawea's baby—at least he was feeling better this morning. They continued applying poultices of onions to his swollen neck, changing the wrap frequently during the day. Four Indians visited from the Snake River region after a two-day ride to the camp seeking eye medication. Clark applied eyewash and sent them home. Lewis observed that "our skill as phisicans and the virture of our medecines have been spread it seems to a great distance. I sincerely wish it was in our power to give releif to these poor afficted wretches."

By one o'clock Shannon, Colter, Labiche, Cruzatte, Collins, and Lepage returned but with little to show for their outing except a few blue grouse ("pheasants of the dark brown kind") and a Columbian ground ("whiseling") squirrel taken by Labiche. Lewis provided a lengthy description of the squirrel, a species new to science, on May 27. Confined as the men were between the Clearwater River and Lolo Creek, they largely hunted a game desert. Even to the south they found nothing. Clark also mentioned that the hunters brought in a great gray ("large hooting") owl, another new species. Lewis provided morphological notes on the bird on May 28. All the castrated horses except for Lewis's "poor unfortunate" beast appeared in good shape. In fact, the captain admitted that the horses cut by the Nez Perces were faring better than the ones cut in the party's traditional manner.

MAY 24, 1806. The baby Jean Baptiste was restless all night, and his jaw and neck were more swollen than earlier, but his fever had lessened. The captains gave him cream of tartar and continued the onion poultices. Bratton was not doing very well either. Although he was eating normally and had regained his weight, he was so weak that he was hardly able to walk and experienced great pain when seated. The captains had exhausted their medical remedies, so the day before they had followed Shields's suggestion to have him sweated. Shields dug a hole in which he set a fire until it was sufficiently heated, then the naked Bratton was lowered to a seat with a footrest. The hole was covered with arched willow poles, over which blankets were thrown. Bratton carried water into the hole to sprinkle on the bottom and sides and generate steam heat. After twenty minutes he was removed and dunked into cold water and then returned to the sweat hole for nearly an hour. He was then removed, covered with blankets, and allowed to cool gradually. During his time in the hole he drank large amounts of strong "mint" tea. Now, a day later, Bratton was walking and nearly free of pain.

The captains faced another medical issue when a canoe of three Nez Perces arrived about eleven o'clock. One of them was a chief "of considerable note," and his companions were anxious about his situation. He had lost the use of his limbs but complained of no particular pain, so the captains inferred that it was not rheumatism. Since his arms and legs were not withered, they rejected a "parelitic attack." They suspected that he may have eaten harmful roots. In an earlier encounter with him they had suggested a diet of fish or meat and cold baths every morning and offered their usual medicines, cream of tartar and flour of sulfur. He thought he had improved but was still incapacitated. Lewis sadly conceded, "we are at a loss what to do for this unfortunate man." They gave him a few drops of laudanum and a little portable soup.

It is not clear whether Drouillard, Labiche, and Cruzatte were sent out this day or the next with orders to get across Lolo Creek, if possible, and hunt toward Weippe Prairie ("quawmash fields"). Four others were sent across the Clearwater River to Broken Arm's village to trade some awls for roots. The men had fashioned the awls out of chain links from one of the steel traps. They came back in the evening with a good supply of roots and cous bread.

MAY 25, 1806. Lewis was happy to report that the captains' new shelter was "impervious to the rain" that fell all night until six o'clock this morning. Jean Baptiste was worse than ever. The cream of tartar (potassium bitartrate) did not have its desired effect as a purgative, so the captains gave the infant an enema in the evening. Turning back to the Nez Perce invalid, they decided to use the same sweat hole for him that had worked for Bratton. The chief was unable to use the seat to be lowered, so the captains suggested that his companions place him in one of their sweat lodges and give him plenty of the tea they had used with Bratton. They also confided to them that it might not work, since he had been so long in his condition. Lewis wished that he had the resources to use "electricity" on the patient. That remedy had gained some popularity in Lewis's time after Benjamin Franklin had experimented with it.

The Field brothers crossed the Clearwater River to hunt on that side while Drouillard, Labiche, and Cruzatte were hunting toward Weippe Prairie. Nez Perce informants had related that there were numerous bears and some deer on that side. Goodrich had been farther afield on a trading mission but returned with a few roots, since he found a near-empty village. Enticingly, he saw hanging in lodges "fat and fine" salmon, which the inhabitants said came from the Snake River. Gibson and Shields came in with a sandhill crane. They had wounded a female bear and a deer, but both got away. The bear had two cubs, said Gibson, one white and the other "black as jett." Four Indians stayed the night. Clark copied a good deal of Lewis's notes on the grizzly bear from his entry of May 15.

MAY 26, 1806. After a rainy night, Collins, Shannon, and Colter set out to hunt in the highlands northeast of Lolo Creek. The enema Lewis gave Jean Baptiste had the desired effect, the baby was clear of his fever, and his swollen neck was much reduced. The captains decided to continue with the onion poultices, nonetheless. Before the incapacitated chief and his companions left the captains gave them doses of their standard remedy—cream of tartar and flour of sulfur. They also gave them a bit of their portable soup and said to take him home. The Nez Perces ignored the last part of the instructions and spent another night at the explorers' camp.

About one o'clock the Field brothers arrived with Hohots Ilpplip, several other chiefs, and some young men. The soldiers told the captains that they had been unable to reach the hunting grounds to which they had been directed. They had passed Lawyer ("Commearp") Creek, Lewis County, Idaho, upriver on the Clearwater but then had been stopped at a large creek that was too deep and rapid to cross. That river may have been the South Fork Clearwater River, Idaho County, Idaho. They did bring back some cous roots and bread from a previously unvisited village and were able to buy the food at a good price. Given this information, the captains detailed Pryor and four men to go to that village for more food. Charbonneau and York were sent on a similar mission. The party's meat was again exhausted, so Reuben Field was directed to find the horse the Nez Perces had promised. The canoe the men had been working on was completed, put in the water, and appeared able to carry a dozen persons. One of the men brought tantalizing news that he had seen a salmon in the Clearwater River.

MAY 27, 1806. By ten o'clock Reuben Field returned with the Nez Perce horse. The men butchered it right away. Hohots Ilpplip told the captains that most of the horses they saw running loose in the area belonged to him and fellow Nez Perces and that the explorers were welcome to take any they needed for food. Lewis was struck by the man's generosity: "this is a peice of liberallity which would do honour to such as bost of civilization; indeed I doubt whether there are not a great number of our countrymen who would see us fast many days before their compassion would excite them to a similar act of liberallity." Pryor and his four men set out for the Nez Perce village where the Field brothers had such good luck trading for food. He came back in the evening with Gibson and Shields and with an ample supply of roots and bread; the others stayed behind.

The captains reported in their weather diaries that Indians considered the present mourning dove cooing a sign that salmon would soon arrive. Ordway, Frazer, and Weiser left this morning for the Snake River to acquire salmon. Locals said that they could reach the area of abundant fish in a half day's ride, but it would be a week before they returned. Ordway reported that they swam their horses across the Clearwater River, Idaho County, at Lawyer Creek, then followed it for about five miles, accompanied by three young Nez Perce men. After going west overland for a time they returned to Lawyer Creek and followed it to a Nez Perce village where they spent the night, making about twenty-six miles altogether. Unable to cross Lolo Creek, Drouillard, Cruzatte, and Labiche still killed five deer on the south side, which they brought to camp about four o'clock.

The baby Jean Baptiste was much better this day. Lewis described the swelling as "an ugly imposthume a little below the ear." The abscess would probably break through the skin. The Nez Perces who had stayed with their sick chief implored the captains to give Bratton's steam hole another chance. The captains had the hole enlarged so that the sick man's father could be lowered with the invalid. They were not able to get him to sweat as much as they desired, and he complained of much pain after being lifted out. Thirty drops of laudanum brought his pain level down. Lewis considered the father's act "a strong mark of parental affection." In fact, he further noticed that Nez Perces were generally attentive to their elders and treated women with more respect than did tribes of the Missouri valley. Those with the sick man were especially responsive to the chief's needs. Lewis thought this particularly impressive since the man had been in this condition for nearly three years.

Today Lewis began a naturalist survey of regional species that would extend until June 7. He wrote a lengthy note and the first description of the Columbian ground ("Burrowing") squirrel, detailing its morphology and behavioral traits. The captain preserved several skins of the animal, including the heads, legs, and feet. He gave the same careful attention in his entry to Lewis's ("Black") woodpecker, a scientific discovery named in his honor (*Melanerpes lewis*) by Alexander Wilson after the expedition, which he had noted previously but only now had an opportunity to examine closely. Clark copied Lewis's naturalist notes as well as his account of the day's events.

MAY 28, 1806. The captains sent Goodrich across the Clearwater River to Broken Arm's village. He came back in the evening with roots and bread, and with goat's hair to stuff their saddle pads. The Field brothers set out to hunt upriver on the Clearwater. At noon, Charbonneau, York, and Lepage returned, bringing with them four bags of cous roots and bread. Most gratifying was the sight of Collins, Shannon, and Colter bringing eight deer. The men had found a crossing spot on Lolo Creek that gave access to the rich hunting grounds of Weippe Prairie. Invalids were on the mend. The Nez Perce chief was able to use his arms and hands and admitted that he was feeling much better. And he sat up a good deal of the day. The captains consented for him to spend a few more days and continue the sweats. Jean Baptiste was also improving—he was free of fever, and his abscess had diminished and was perhaps ready to open.

Ordway's party's route is difficult to determine, since his account is vague. It appears that, following two Nez Perce guides (one perhaps being Twisted Hair), they continued westerly on or near Lawyer Creek, then traveled overland southwesterly to Deer Creek, descended it a way, and camped there for a rainy night near the Lewis-Nez Perce county line, Idaho.

Lewis described in some detail a bird that he had noticed earlier, Clark's nutcracker, and that Clark had called attention to on August 22, 1805. The bird was named for Clark by Alexander Wilson in about 1811. Lewis now had a specimen at hand and could give it a close inspection. He called it a "bird of the *corvus* genus," which he found only in the Rocky Mountains or nearby. The captain confessed that he may have confused the gray jay ("small *corvus*") at Fort Clatsop (see December 18, 1805) as the same bird but now could see that they were two distinct species. Hunters also brought the captains a "large hooting Owl," which Lewis found different from those on the East Coast. Indeed, the great gray owl, here described in careful detail, was a species new to science. Clark copied a good deal of Lewis's entry of the day into his own journal, but mostly he transcribed part of Lewis's notes of May 9 about cous and camas and his notes about a Nez Perce council on May 12.

MAY 29, 1806. There was little activity in camp this day, but the captains could report a good supply of meat and roots. Those on the sick list were doing better: Bratton was recovering his strength, Jean Baptiste was improving, and the Nez Perce chief was regaining more use of his arms and hands. The captains would have resumed the man's sweats this day but cloudy and rainy weather intervened. Lewis continued his naturalist survey, now describing a new species, the pigmy horned lizard, first noted on April 25. The captain compared it to a subspecies from Montana and the Dakotas, the eastern short-horned lizard, which he said the French *engagés* called the "prairie buffaloe." In fact, he wrote, "I cannot conceive how the engages ever assimilated this animal with the buffaloe for there is not greater analogy than between the horse and the frog." He preferred "horned Lizzard" as a name for both of them. Surprisingly, Lewis penned morphological notes on the common chokecherry, a species well known to him, and he collected a specimen this day and on August 10. Copying his fellow officer's entry, Clark also added Lewis's notes of the day before on Clark's nutcracker and jumped ahead to his entry of June 1 describing ragged robin and to June 2 with its admiring words about Nez Perce dexterity in roping horses.

Ordway reported a rainy night and a light breakfast for his excursion party. Frazer traded an old razor to an Indian woman for a two Spanish coins. Gass later related that the coins came from around the neck of a dead Shoshone whom the Nez Perces had killed in battle. The coins had probably worked their way north from Spanish settlements in New Mexico. The men descended Deer Creek to the Salmon River, then followed it southwesterly to Wapshilla Creek, Nez Perce County, Idaho. Going up Wapshilla Creek, the riders reached Wapshilla Ridge, then descended toward the Snake River, crossed Cottonwood Creek, and followed Big Cougar Creek southwesterly to rapids (perhaps Big Cougar Rapids or Cochrane Rapids) and a fishery on the Snake. Again, Ordway's vagueness does not lend certainty to his route. At the fishery the explorers were invited into an

Indian lodge and given roasted salmon and cous bread ("uppah"), and here they spent the night.

MAY 30, 1806. Lepage and Charbonneau set out for Nez Perce villages to undertake more trading for roots. Following Goodrich's success, Gass was sent after goat's hair to use as stuffing for the party's saddle pads. Gass's trip was cut short by an impassable river, and he returned without the padding material. Shannon, Collins, and Potts made their own trading excursion for roots using the merchandize that had been distributed to them on May 21 for the purpose. As they took the party's canoe across the Clearwater River, the boat was caught in a strong current just as they landed, was driven against shore-lined trees, filled with water, and sank. The men got free but the poor swimmer Potts had difficulty getting to land. They lost three blankets, a blanket coat, and what Lewis called "their pittance of merchandize." Counting the clothing a serious loss, Lewis sent Pryor with a party in a Nez Perce canoe to rescue the party's boat and what other items they could. He was pessimistic about recovering the canoe.

Those on the sick list continued to improve, so much so that the Nez Perce chief was the only one to get attention. The man took another "severe" sweat, which gave him even greater use of his arms and hands and the ability to move his legs and toes somewhat. Lewis was genuinely positive about his chances for recovery. Joseph Field returned in the evening in search of his horses that had wandered the previous evening and since had returned to Camp Chopunnish on their own. He left his brother behind at their overnight spot on Lolo Creek. They had killed three deer.

Lewis's naturalist notes this day focused on reptiles and amphibians. He mentioned the northern Pacific rattlesnake, two nonpoisonous snakes (perhaps the Great Basin gopher snake and the Pacific red-sided garter snake), the western fence ("common black") lizard, the pigmy horned lizard, the Pacific tree ("smal green") frog (a new species), the chorus frog ("common to our country which sings in the spring"), and the western toad ("large species of frog"). He also mentioned species familiar in the East but missing in the current survey, such as the copperhead snake. Most of the insects with which he was familiar in the East, such as butterflies, common flies, and caterpillars, were also found in the area of Camp Chopunnish, as were beetles he knew. He had not seen hornets, wasps, or yellow jackets, nor had he seen honeybees, but bumblebees were present. One of the men brought the captain an onion from the plains, either Tolmie's or Douglas's onion, which he compared to Geyer's onion, found near watercourses, and wild chive ("shive or small onion"), which he had noticed below Celilo Falls on the Columbia River. Clark copied the whole of Lewis's entry, with some minor modifications, into his own journal.

Ordway and his companions decided to spend the day at the Indian fishery, since natives had mostly left the place with all the salmon they had caught. The explorers hoped to be able to trade with others during the day. Friendly Nez Perces roasted salmon for the men to eat and later in the day some trading took place. The men were able to buy as much salmon as they thought they could get back to camp and set it out to dry. They remained here for the night.

MAY 31, 1806. Goodrich and Willard visited some Nez Perce villages during the day, and Willard came back with a bear skin he had bought for Clark. The Nez Perces told Willard that the skin of a "uniform pale redish brown colour" was not that of a grizzly bear ("*Hoh-host*") but that it was from the "*Yâk-kâh*," their term for the black bear. Now Lewis brought out different bear skins, laid them before the Indians, and asked them to identify to which bear each belonged. The captain was again trying to sort out color variations in bears. All those whose hair had white tips they designated grizzlies, the bear that was vicious, did not climb trees, and had long claws. Gass called the skins "white as a blanket." Those with short claws, not vicious, and climbers, they called black bears. Lewis was ready to accept the Indians' divisions but thought the "redish brown black" bear of this area not the same as the black bear he knew from the East and declared it a separate species. In fact, the "cinnamon bear" was at one time designated a separate species but is now considered a color phase or subspecies of the black bear.

The Field brothers brought in the three deer they had killed, as reported by Joseph the day before. The party watched some Nez

Perces pursue a deer to the Clearwater opposite their camp. One of the explorers killed it as it swam across, but it is not clear who got the animal. Having a large party of natives near the spot where the expedition canoe had sunk, Hohots Ilpplip (Clark said it was Broken Arm) and his men attempted to get the boat raised but were unsuccessful. Nez Perces returned another of the party's original horses. Only two of that herd were now missing, and the Nez Perces informed the captains that their guides on the outbound journey, Toby and his son, had taken them for their trip home. The corps could now count sixty-five mounts in their horse herd, which Lewis viewed as "in excellent order and fine strong active horses." Clark's journal entry was again a repeat of Lewis's. Neither captain mentioned that Clark completed a map in one of his notebook journals showing the Snake River and its connections with the Rocky Mountains and with the drainage of the Missouri River. The map was partly based on conversations with Nez Perces over the last two days.

Ordway reported that during the night Indians took some of the party's salmon that they had left out to dry. With little else to do here, the explorers, unaccompanied by their Nez Perce guides, began to retrace the route to the Salmon ("Toomonamah") River that they had taken on the outbound journey. At the Indian village where they had obtained the Spanish coins on May 28 a chief told them of a better way back to their camp and sent two boys to direct them. They left Deer Creek and went over "a very bad hill" (perhaps Hoover Point ridge), then east toward Maloney Creek, Lewis County, Idaho, which they crossed near its mouth at an oxbow of the Salmon River. From there they ascended another hill to the east and camped for the night near an Indian village in the vicinity of Keuterville, Idaho County.

JUNE 1, 1806. Charbonneau and Lepage returned in the night from what Lewis called a "broken voyage." They had ascended the east side of the Clearwater River for about eight miles to a Nez Perce village on the opposite side, near Kooskia, Idaho County, Idaho. Their lead horse, carrying most of their trade goods, slipped and fell into the river and swam to the opposite side. They convinced an Indian

to drive the horse back to their side. In swimming the river the animal lost a number of articles, and their trade paint was destroyed
by the water. The two men remained there the night of May 30 to
dry their goods. The Nez Perces, learning of their mission, tried to
get over to them on a raft carrying roots and bread, but they struck
a rock, capsized, and lost everything. Lewis summarized the outing: "the river having fallen heir to both merchandize and roots,
our traders returned with empty bags."

Drouillard set out this morning with Hohots Ilpplip to try to
recover some lost tomahawks. The captains had learned that the
items were in the possession of some Indians living on the plains not
far from Camp Chopunnish. One had been lost about May 7 on Big
Canyon ("Musquetoes") Creek, Nez Perce County, Idaho. Lewis wrote
that "Capt. C." left it there, while Clark (mostly copying Lewis) said
"Capt L." Ordway said it was Clark who lost it. The other tomahawk
was stolen from the party the prior fall. The captains also wanted
Drouillard to ask about Twisted Hair. They wanted to know about
guides to get them from Travelers' Rest to the Missouri River by a
less circuitous route than the one they had used coming out. Colter
and Willard were sent hunting beyond Lolo Creek toward Weippe
Prairie ("quamash grounds"). The captains expressed their anxiety
about the delayed return of Ordway and his party. Lewis wrote the
first scientific description of ragged robin in a lengthy morphological note and collected a specimen this day. After the expedition
Pursh named the plant scientifically for Clark (*Clarkia pulchella*).
Clark copied the material into his entry of May 29.

Ordway and party continued their journey back to the main camp
on the Clearwater River. They went almost due east from their overnight stop near Keuterville, Idaho County, following Cottonwood
Creek part of the way, then reached the South Fork of the Clearwater River south of Kooskia near Stites, Idaho County. Ordway
declared it mostly "a good road." They halted a short time to let their
horses graze and get something to eat for themselves at an Indian
village. Afterward they headed north, but with darkness approaching they decided to spend the night in another Indian village, perhaps Hohots Ilpplip's, still south of Kooskia.

JUNE 2, 1806. McNeal and York were sent on a trading mission to a Nez Perce village across the Clearwater River. Lewis admitted that he would use subterfuge in order to get necessary foodstuffs for the coming ascent of the Rocky Mountains. Mental preparations were also important: "to meet that wretched portion of our journy, the Rocky Mountain, where hungar and cold in their most rigorous forms assail the waried traveller; not any of us have yet forgotten our sufferings in those mountains in September last, and I think it probable we never shall."

The two men were given what little merchandise the party could gather. The captains supplied them with buttons cut from their coats, with eye water, "basilicon" (an ointment made from available substances), vials, and small tin boxes. It was enough to garner three bushels of roots and some bread. Lewis called it "not much less pleasing to us than the return of a good cargo to an East India Merchant." Collins, Shields, Shannon, and the Field brothers set out for hunting on Weippe Prairie. Lewis related that the corps' horses had become so wild that they could not be taken without the assistance of Nez Perce wranglers, who were masters at roping. In fact, since the party could not always get Nez Perce help, they had built a stockade to corral and have the animals accessible.

Drouillard returned this evening with Nez Perce chiefs Cut Nose and Hohots Ilpplip; the latter had accompanied him to retrieve some expedition tomahawks. Through the intercession of the chiefs, especially Cut Nose, he was able to obtain the items. The one that had been stolen was most prized, because it had been Floyd's before he died, and Clark wanted to return it to his friends. The man who had it said he had purchased it from the thief and was now himself about to die. It took some negotiating to get the item, since the man's family wanted to bury it with him. Drouillard gave the family a handkerchief and two strands of beads, while the chiefs offered two horses to be killed at the grave of the dying man, as was their custom. Lewis used the news to discuss Nez Perce burial customs. He explained that the custom of sacrificing horses to the deceased appeared to be common to all the tribes of the Great Columbian Plain. Cut Nose's wife had died a short time ago and the chief and his relatives killed twenty-eight horses in her honor. They typically buried their dead in the ground and placed stones on the grave. Between the stones they stuck little splinters of wood and then covered the site with a shelter of split timber. In another aside, Lewis admitted that the Nez Perce method of gelding was superior to their own practice. He saw horses castrated by the natives recovering quickly. Lewis's own horse was not doing as well (see May 22), and it was shot.

About noon Ordway, Frazer, and Weiser returned with seventeen salmon and some cous roots. They had followed the South Fork of the Clearwater River and the Clearwater River from their overnight camp south of Kooskia, Idaho County, Idaho, to Camp Chopunnish. Most of the fish were spoiled by the delay in getting back to the main camp. The good ones Lewis judged were as fat as any he had seen and could be cooked without grease. He called them "extreemly delicious." The captain recounted the men's journey in this day's entry, probably learned from access to Ordway's journal and from conversations with the men. Gass called it "a very disagreeable trip as the roads were mountainous and slippery." Clark followed Lewis's journal.

JUNE 3, 1806. All the patients on the sick list were recovering: Bratton was much stronger and walking with considerable ease; the Indian chief was gradually recovering the use of his limbs; and Jean Baptiste was nearly well—the swelling on his neck was almost gone, but it left a hard lump under his left ear. The captains continued applying the onion poultices for the infant. Broken Arm came into the camp about two o'clock in the afternoon and spent the night. Colter, Joseph Field, and Willard returned in the evening with five deer and a bear that Lewis had early designated as a "cinnamon" bear, now acknowledged to be a subspecies of the black bear. Ordway traded the worn-out horse he had taken on the excursion for a better mount. The Nez Perce who made the trade knew Ordway's horse and knew that when revived it would be better for buffalo hunting (his prime interest) than the one he traded.

The Nez Perces sent an advance party to the expedition's Travelers' Rest, near Missoula, Missoula County, Montana, to connect with the Salish ("Flatheads" or "Oote-lash-shoots") Indians and learn of events in that area. The captains thought that if Nez Perces could make it over the mountains then the corps could also. The Nez Perces disabused them of that idea, saying that the creeks were too high, that grass was not available for the horses, and that the roads were not safe. They advised the captains to wait up to two weeks. Still being anxious to move, the captains decided to relocate to Weippe Prairie, Clearwater County, Idaho, on June 10, hoping to lay up a stock of meat and then attempt the mountains about the middle of the month. The captains had given up hope of securing salmon on the Clearwater since the river was still unseasonably high and gave no indication of falling. Furthermore, they saw no salmon running and noticed that the Nez Perces' salmon came from the distant Snake River. The explorers had neither the merchandise to trade nor the time to give to such a distant trading venture. Clark copied Lewis with some minor changes.

JUNE 4, 1806. The three Nez Perce chiefs, evidently Broken Arm, Cut Nose, and Hohots Ilpplip, left Camp Chopunnish about noon and returned to their villages. Before they departed the captains renewed their request that they come with them to the Missouri valley, but the chiefs declined to go until the end of summer. And they gave no positive answer to Lewis's request that two or three of their young men accompany him to the Great Falls of the Missouri River and there wait for him to make a trip up the Marias River and possibly bring back Atsina or Blackfeet Indians. If the plan worked, the captain hoped to effect a friendly agreement between the Nez Perces and the others. If such a conciliation could not be obtained, then the young men would be so informed and know to remain on guard until Americans arrived in the area to establish a general peace.

Clark also put forth his plan to have one or two important Nez Perces accompany him in order to meet Shoshones near the party's Camp Fortunate or at the Three Forks of the Missouri. At one of those spots it was probable that they would meet chiefs of Shoshone bands with whom the Nez Perces were at war and could work out peace agreements. Again, the captains received no reply to this secondary plan. From these strategies laid out by the captains it is apparent that they had already determined the routes they would take on the return trip. Broken Arm invited the captains to his village for a conference and to give them a supply of roots for their mountain journey. Clark promised to visit him in a few days. Shields returned in the evening with two deer that he had killed at Weippe Prairie. Ordway and Gass mentioned rain in the morning and fair weather later in the day.

JUNE 5, 1806. Bratton must have been significantly improved, since he was allowed to go with Colter to visit and trade at an Indian village. They apparently obtained some bread and roots and returned later in the day. The Indian chief received another treatment in the sweat hole the party had devised. Although still weak, the chief continued to improve in the use of his limbs. Jean Baptiste was recovering quickly, and his inflammation was almost gone, but the area was still swollen and hard. The captains discontinued the poultice but applied a plaster of basilicon. Reuben Field, Shannon, and Labiche returned from their hunt bringing five deer and a black bear of the cinnamon variety. Gass noted that an Indian came with them and brought unwelcome news that he had tried to ascend the Rockies but was turned back by deep snow. The weather having warmed up for several days, the captains in their weather diaries called it colder this morning.

Lewis returned to his naturalist survey, now considering the grasses of the surrounding country. He noticed a grass called "maden cain" in Georgia, which is clearly the common reedgrass, based on the captain's excellent description. He also penned morphological notes on basin wild rye, which he remembered as similar to a plant called "Corn grass" in the South and "foxtail" in Virginia. A third species resembling "cheet" that was preferred by horses was some variety of brome. The final and most prevalent grass was similar to one called "blue grass" in many parts of the United States—it was Sandberg bluegrass; he collected a specimen on June 10. After applying detail and description to these grasses Lewis made a listing of other plants of the region: Canada wild rye, probably Lewis's syringa ("seven bark"), western wild and/or Nootka rose, honeysuckle, Pacific ("sweet") willow, red osier dogwood ("red willow"), ponderosa ("longleafed") pine, cattail, silver-weed ("sinquefield"), blue elderberry ("elder"), smooth sumac ("shoemate"), and probably Fremont goosefoot ("lamsquarter"), wild strawberry, black raspberry, peppergrass ("tonge grass"), western yarrow ("tanzy"), giant hyssop ("horsemint"), arrowleaf clotsfoot, a species of broomrape ("cansar weed"), and any of a number of species of the pea family. Clark largely followed Lewis's entry for the day.

JUNE 6, 1806. Frazer returned this morning after making a trip to retrieve some bread and roots left at Twisted Hair's lodge while on his excursion with Ordway to the Salmon and Snake Rivers. Twisted Hair came back with him but conversation with the chief was hampered by the absence of Drouillard and his skill in Indian sign language. The chief left in the evening. Lewis briefly revisited his naturalist work, describing for the first time in scientific detail the western tanager ("a beautifull little bird"). In the weather diaries the captains noted that does were producing their young.

Clark had taken Drouillard along with three other men to visit Broken Arm, fulfilling a promise he had made to the chief on June 4. The captain found several subordinate chiefs of Nez Perce bands at Broken Arm's village who had not heard the captains' speeches but now were anxious to hear the Americans' words. Clark repeated what the captains had said in earlier gatherings. Broken Arm told Clark that his band would not go into the Rockies until the latter part of summer. With regard to the captains' request to have some young Nez Perce men accompany the corps to the Missouri valley, the chief relayed that such a decision called for a general council meeting. He promised that such a council would happen in ten or twelve days at a spot on the plains at the head of Lawyer ("Commeâp") Creek, Lewis County, Idaho, and there two men would be selected. Clark seemed pessimistic about receiving help and decided that the corps would have to rely on help from the Salish near the party's Travelers' Rest campsite.

Broken Arm gave Clark some camas roots as a gift, but the captain confided in his journal that he preferred healthier cous roots. The chief told Clark that he had learned that a party of Shoshones had visited the Cayuse ("*Ye-E-al-po*") Indians and told them that they had heard of the captains' councils and were ready to make peace with them and the Nez Perces. Broken Arm declared that he was ready to smoke the pipe and make peace. He would send emissaries to the Shoshones to effect such a relationship. He brought out two pipes, one of which he would send to the Shoshones and one that he gave to Clark. Clark tied blue ribbons and a string of white beads ("wampom") around the stem and told the chief that it was a sign of peace.

Clark returned to camp in the evening. The men with him had made good trades for bread and roots with their "little *notions.*" In surveying the party's provisions the captains found that they had a sufficient supply for the trip into the mountains. Shortly after Clark's arrival the captains were visited by Hohots Ilpplip, two young chiefs, and several others, who spent the night. Lewis copied into his own entry Clark's notes on his visit to Broken Arm. He did not mention that Clark had met Twisted Hair on his way home from visiting Lewis and that the chief had informed him that he would not accompany the corps across the mountains because his brother was sick—Clark added "&c." Clark closed the present journal notebook with a list of Nez Perce terms for major tributaries of the Missouri River, even south of the Mandan-Hidatsa villages.

JUNE 7, 1806. The two young chiefs and other Nez Perces who had visited the party's camp the day before returned to their village on Lawyer Creek, Lewis County, Idaho. Gass, McNeal, Whitehouse, Goodrich, and Charbonneau went with them in order to buy some packing ropes in exchange for some fishing gear, old iron pieces, old files, and bullets. They were also to get bags to carry the party's bread and roots. All but Whitehouse and Goodrich came back in the evening. The returning men had obtained bread, roots, and the ropes but no bags.

Hohots Ilpplip, who must have left the camp earlier, came back leading a horse for Frazer, who had given the chief a pair of moccasin-like shoes ("Cannadian shoes"). Gass alone among the journalists mentioned that Frazer was learning the Nez Perce language and enjoyed talking with the Indians. Drouillard left on a hunting excursion to Lolo Creek in the evening. The captains had decided to quit hunting deer on Weippe Prairie so that when the party moved there on June 10 they would be able to find game. In fact, the explorers were already busily engaged in packing loads and preparing provisions for the move. Lewis turned to botany to close his entry, providing a detailed scientific description of bitter cherry; he had collected a specimen on May 29. Clark copied Lewis's entry for the most part but moved the description of the western tanager from Lewis's entry of June 6 to here.

JUNE 8, 1806. Drouillard returned to Camp Chopunnish without having killed any game. His horse got away during the night, but he found it shortly before reaching camp. The ill Nez Perce chief was recovering, could bear some weight on his legs, and was generally stronger. Jean Baptiste was nearly well. Bratton was so far along that he was no longer considered an invalid. Lewis congratulated him on the way he bore his illness with "much fortitude and firmness."

Cut Nose visited the corps this day, bringing ten or twelve warriors with him, two of whom were Cayuse ("Y-e-let-pos") Indians, whom Lewis mistakenly considered a band of the Nez Perces. The two tribes associated and intermarried and their languages are Sahaptian, but otherwise they are distinct. The captain also mentioned another tribe with which the corps was familiar but had not met, perhaps Palouses ("pel-late-pal-ler") or another band of Nez Perces. One of the Cayuses exchanged his horse for a poorer one from the corps' herd. He also received a tomahawk as a part of the bargain, the one Clark had received in an exchange with a chief of "Clah-clel-lâh" Indians (see April 11, 1806). The captains were also able to trade two indifferent horses for better ones without the need for additional tokens. Ordway mentioned that Indians helped get the party's sunken canoe out of the river, and Gass reported the return of Whitehouse and Goodrich.

Relaxing a bit in the evening, the men ran foot races with the Indians. The Indians proved very fleet, and one of them could keep up with Drouillard and Reuben Field, recognized as the party's fastest runners. After the races, the party divided up and played prisoner's base, a game in which each side tried to make prisoners by tagging opposing team players when they ran outside their area.

The captains applauded the games, which gave the men exercise before attempting the mountains. Lewis declared that the nonhunters were getting "reather lazy and slouthfull." Later the violin was brought out and men danced to the music, entertaining themselves and Indian guests. The evening also brought unwelcome news when one Indian informed the captains that the party would not be able to cross the mountains until the first of July. If they attempted the climb sooner, their horses would be at least three days without grass at the top. The captains decided that they would go with the more general opinion about mountain trail conditions and keep with their plan to leave about the middle of this month. Clark mostly copied Lewis's entry for the day.

JUNE 9, 1806. All the horses were brought up this morning and exchanges attempted with Nez Perces in order to obtain better mounts. Only one was traded. Later one of the men made a horse trade by adding an old leather shirt to the deal. Hohots Ilpplip and his companions left camp, headed for the plains near the Snake River where Nez Perce bands were to assemble. Broken Arm made a short visit and then followed Hohots Ilpplip toward the rendezvous. Cut Nose borrowed one of the party's horses to hunt young eagles on the Clearwater River in order to raise them for their feathers. He returned not long afterward with a pair of golden ("grey") eagles, nearly grown and well feathered. Ordway related that Cut Nose used a rope to climb a tree to the eagle's nest and get the birds. He also noted the social significance of the feathers, which were used in headdresses and painted to adorn the wearer. A young chief who had visited before came back and brought some young men with him; they spent the night. Having finished off the last of their meat the day before, the party lived on roots this day. Surveying the party prior to leaving Camp Chopunnish, Lewis made an optimistic appraisal: "our party seem much elated with the idea of moving on towards their friends and country, they all seem allirt in their movements today; they have every thing in readiness for a move, and notwithstanding the want of provision have been amusing themselves very merrily today in runing footraces pitching quites [quoits], prison basse &c." Seeing that the Clearwater River had been falling for several days, the captains were also optimistic that it indicated significant melting of snow in the mountains, but they also knew that the steep, rocky trails ahead would be wet, slippery, and dangerous. They hoped that in a few days the roads would dry and grass would flourish. Clark again copied Lewis's entry for the day.

JUNE 10, 1806. The party was up early collecting horses and readying for the move. A horse each of Cruzatte's and Whitehouse's was missing, but Cruzatte's eventually was found, and Nez Perces promised to bring the other to Weippe Prairie when it was located. At eleven o'clock they set out "with each man being well mounted and a light load on a second horse," wrote Lewis. Extra horses were in the train to serve as substitutes in case of accidents or to supply meat when game was not to be found. An optimistic Lewis declared, "we therefore feel ourselves perfectly equipped for the mountains." After ascending the hills out of the Clearwater River valley they traveled about three miles northeast to Lolo ("Collins") Creek, Clearwater County, Idaho, crossed it, and arrived at Weippe Prairie ("quawmash flatts"), where they set up camp near the western bank of Jim Ford Creek ("Village Creek" on an expedition map) and about two miles southeast of Weippe, Clearwater County, where they remained until June 15.

Along the way Lewis took note of the vegetation and listed Douglas fir, grand fir, Engelmann spruce, ponderosa ("long leafed") pine, western larch, and lodgepole pine; the undergrowth included chokecherries, thinleaf ("black") alders, redstem ceanothus ("redroot"), cascara, smooth sumacs ("shoemate"), black hawthorns ("perple haw"), serviceberries, gooseberries, snowberries ("wild rose honeysuckle"), and "two species of the wild rose" (Nootka rose and western wild rose). He collected specimens of cascara on May 29, black hawthorn on April 29, and redstem ceanothus on June 27. The captain also noticed a plant eventually named for him, Lewis's syringa, which he called "sevenbark." He had collected a specimen of it on May 6 and would again on July 4, when he found it in bloom. Based on the specimens, Pursh after the expedition honored the captain with the scientific name, *Philadelphus lewisii*. The captain also observed sandhill cranes and ducks in swampy areas around the camp. Gass was struck by the beauty of Weippe Prairie at this season, since camas ("com-mas") was in "full bloom with flowers of a pale blue colour."

Soon after arriving at camp the captains sent out hunters. Collins killed a doe that supplied the party with supper. In addition, the men killed several of the numerous Columbian ground squirrels, and Lewis found them "as tender and well flavored as our grey squirrel." A number of Nez Perces joined the explorers en route to Weippe Prairie. Lewis believed that they came along hoping to share in game taken by expedition hunters. The captain confided that as kind as the Nez Perces had been to them, he would have to disappoint them in this expectation since the party needed to conserve food for the difficult days ahead in the mountains. Clark copied Lewis's entry with some minor changes in wording.

JUNE 11, 1806. Hunters were out in force this morning, but only Shannon, Labiche, and Gibson were successful. Labiche killed a cinnamon variety of the black bear and a large buck, while Gibson also got a buck. Whitehouse returned to Camp Chopunnish in search of his horse. Five Nez Perces who camped nearby also went on a hunt but were wholly unsuccessful, so by midafternoon they returned to their village. Before they left one of the explorers was able to exchange a poor horse for a much better one with one of them. Hunters went out again in the evening with orders to expand their search since game was scarce near camp. They were to spend the night away and hunt remoter areas the next morning. Lewis wrote one of his lengthiest scientific discourses on camas ("quawmash"). His detailed description of the plant's morphology, floral development, and ecology shows his dedication to the scientific pursuits of the expedition and his impressive powers of observation. The captain also gave close attention to ethnobotany, denoting the plant's rich uses by the Nez Perces and other natives within its range. He concluded the essay by declaring that he found camas palatable but that "it disagrees with me in every shape I have used it." Clark, largely copying Lewis's entry for the day, added that when the party arrived among the Nez Perces "our men who were half Starved made So free a use of this root that it made them all Sick for Several days after."

JUNE 12, 1806. The hunters who had spent the night away from camp returned this morning, except for Gibson. Only Shields brought back a prize—two deer. Hunters returned for another night on the prairie. An Indian came by in the evening and spent the night with the party. Whitehouse returned in early afternoon with his horse. As the days warmed mosquitoes—"our old companions," groused Lewis—became more annoying. Cut Nose had told the captains that two young Nez Perces would join them at Weippe Prairie to accompany Lewis to the Great Falls of the Missouri and perhaps on to Washington DC, but no one had appeared yet. With camas in full bloom Lewis thought he could easily mistake the fields of blue flowers as "lakes of fine clear water." Clark again copied Lewis's entry. Gass gave a brief description of a woodpecker that was new to him—Lewis's woodpecker.

JUNE 13, 1806. The captains sent Reuben Field and Willard to a small prairie about eight miles ahead, perhaps Crane Meadow, Clearwater County, Idaho, to hunt and wait for the party's arrival. About noon seven hunters returned with eight deer. Ordway named the hunters: Gibson, Shields, Collins, Joseph Field, Drouillard, and Labiche. In fact, they had wounded several other deer and a bear but did not capture them. The captains had the meat cut thin, set in the sun, and preserved for the mountain trip to come. Less fortunate, Labiche and Cruzatte reported that turkey buzzards had gotten to a deer they had butchered and hung up to retrieve. The Indian from the night before exchanged his horse for one of the party's mounts that was suffering from its castration. He was given a small axe and a knife to boot. He hurried home after the bargain, bringing Lewis to conjecture that he feared the explorers might renege on the deal, as was customary with his people and considered fair. The captains continued work on their "Estimate of Western Indians" that they had completed at Fort Clatsop, calculating a total population of sixty-nine thousand. Clark copied Lewis. With warming weather came nagging mosquitoes, the captains complained in their weather diaries.

JUNE 14, 1806. The party kept up its purpose for being at Weippe Prairie—hunting in order to lay up a store of provisions before the ascent of the mountains. Colter brought in a deer at midmorning along with eight ducks' eggs, while other hunters returned empty-handed. Drouillard arrived late, also without anything. Packing got underway with a view to leave the next morning. Horses were made ready and hobbled for easy collecting. The captains had determined to make a forced march to Travelers' Rest, where they had stayed September 9–11, 1805, to rest there again for a few days. As on other occasions when the party was delayed by unfortunate circumstances, Lewis voiced his concerns on paper:

> we have now been detained near five weeks in consequence of the snows; a serious loss of time at this delightfull season for traveling. I am still apprehensive that the snow and the want of food for our horses will prove a serious imbarrassment to us as at least four days journey of our rout in these mountains lies over hights and along a ledge of mountains never intirely destitute of snow. every body seems anxious to be in motion, convinced that we have not now any time to delay if the calculation is to reach the United States this season; this I am detirmined to accomplish if within the compass of human power.

Clark shared his own apprehensions: "even now I Shutter with the expectation with great dificuelties in passing those Mountains." Otherwise his notes read largely like Lewis's.

JUNE 15, 1806. The party was late getting underway, since the horses had scattered and hard rain immobilized them for a time. By ten o'clock they were underway, having been at Weippe Prairie since June 10 and at nearby Camp Chopunnish since May 14. Ordway and Gass counted sixty-six horses in the train. After about 8½ miles they reached Crane Meadow, Clearwater County, Idaho, where the captains had sent Reuben Field and Willard. They found that the men had hung up two deer for them. The party's southeasterly route led them another 2½ miles to the upper reaches of Lolo ("Collin's") Creek, where they halted for a while for a meal and to graze their horses. Here they found the hunters and another deer. The two men had seen a grizzly and a black bear but were unable to get them. The rains had made the road slippery and caused several horses to fall, but without injury. Fallen timber also slowed their march and made the way extremely difficult.

The thick timberland that Lewis observed as they climbed eastward signaled a change from the dry forests of the lowlands to the moist forests of their mountain ascent and included western white pine and western redcedar. The captain called the soil good and compared its red cast to the soils of his native Virginia. He was seeing iron-bearing minerals of the Columbia Basalt, which in this wet climate weathers to a reddish-brown or brick-red hematite. As they continued on, Lewis noticed a hairy ("speckled") woodpecker, western kingbird ("bee martin"), and pileated woodpecker ("log cock or large woodpecker"). He also saw the nest and eggs of a hummingbird. The party followed Lolo Creek for about 10½ miles, crossed it, and camped on a small prairie on Eldorado Creek, Idaho County, Idaho, having come about twenty-two miles this day. Clark related this day's journey to his trip on the way out in September 1805. From a mountain vantage point he took a grand view of mountains and plains in various directions.

JUNE 16, 1806. With the horses easily gathered and a quick breakfast, the party was able to set out by six o'clock. Sometime during the morning Windsor broke his rifle near the muzzle. They followed Eldorado Creek, Idaho County, Idaho, for about two miles, passing beautiful camas meadows, then crossed the creek and ascended a ridge to the northeast, which led them to a branch of Fish Creek, misidentified as "hungry creek." Again fallen timber impeded their progress, so, finding good grass for the horses, the captains decided to lunch here, since they knew that good grazing would be unavailable farther on. The explorers noticed snow in the hollows and on the north sides of hills—in some places two to three feet deep. Given that, vegetation was behind that of the plains, so that glacier lilies ("dogtooth violet"), honeysuckles, huckleberries, and Rocky Mountain maples were just blooming or sprouting leaves. Lewis had collected glacier lily on May 8 and June 15. He worried about these conditions at such a low elevation and thought it did not augur well for the route ahead. Even so, the captains determined to continue on after a hasty lunch but found the road again covered with fallen timber, leading them through deep ravines and over high hills. It was covered with snow eight to ten feet deep but hard enough to bear the weight of the packhorses. Otherwise, it would have been impossible to proceed.

The party camped for the night at the spot where Clark had killed a horse on September 19, 1805, now memorialized as "Horsesteak Meadow," on Hungery Creek, Idaho County. The creek was small but running swiftly with water as cold as ice. Finding only a little grass for the horses, the captains decided to stay here for the night, knowing that grass ahead was a rare resource. They made about fifteen miles. Lewis noted that pines, larches, and firs were the principal trees, while he observed plants such as red columbine, tall bluebells, mountain thermopsis ("yellow flowering pea"), and licorice root ("anjelico," that is, angelica). He killed a grouse ("small brown pheasant"), perhaps a female spruce grouse.

JUNE 17, 1806. After collecting their horses, apparently with no problems, the party set out along Hungery Creek, Idaho County, Idaho, crossing it twice in seven miles. These were difficult and dangerous crossings due to the creek's depth and rapidity. Indeed, they avoided two other crossings by climbing a very steep hill. Beyond Hungery Creek the road led to a divide in the mountains. As they ascended, the snow reached depths of twelve to fifteen feet, even on the south sides of hills fully exposed to the sun. The weather was as severe as the road, which Lewis described in an icy tone: "here was winter with all it's rigors; the air was cold, my hands and feet were benumbed." Clark, in the lead, could find his way only by following trees that had been peeled of their outer bark by Indians to get at the inner bark for sustenance. The captains knew that it would take five days to reach resources at Colt Killed Creek on the Lochsa River, near Powell Ranger Station, Idaho County, if they were fortunate enough to find their way. Even the able woodsman Drouillard was not confident of their chances. They also knew that grass for horses would be unavailable given the deep snow. Lewis penned the gloomy prospects:

if we proceeded and should get bewildered in these mountains the certainty was that we should loose all our horses and consequently our baggage instruments perhaps our papers and thus eminently wrisk the loss of the discoveries which we had already made if we should be so fortunate as to escape with life. . . . under these circumstances we conceived it madnes in this stage of the expedition to proceed without a guide who could certainly conduct us to the fish wears on the Kooskooske [Lochsa River], as our horses could not possibly sustain a journey of more than five days without food. we therefore came to the resolution to return with our horses while they were yet strong and in good order and indevour to keep them so untill we could procure an indian to conduct us over the snowey mountains

Having agreed to this plan, the captains ordered the party to deposit all unnecessary baggage, including papers and scientific instruments, at a small, flat spit on the mountains they were ascending in Idaho County. They considered it safer to leave them here than to risk their loss in the descent to a grazing and hunting position. They also left cous roots and bread, except for a small proportion to sustain them for a few days. Hunters' kills would nourish them at lower elevations. After setting up scaffolds and securing covered items, the party began their descent about one o'clock. They followed Hungery Creek for about two miles and camped on its south side in Idaho County. Although dejected, the party was less downcast than the captains expected. Ordway wrote that the plan was "determined to our Sorrow." Lewis voiced his own regrets: "this is the first time since we have been on this long tour that we have ever been compelled to retreat or make a retrograde march." To add to their woes it rained most of the evening. Clark copied Lewis for the most part.

JUNE 18, 1806. During the night the horses had scattered, hunting for grass among the thick timber. It was nine o'clock before all were collected, with the exception of one of Drouillard's and one of Shields's. Shields and Lepage stayed behind to find them, while Drouillard and Shannon pushed ahead to Nez Perce villages to get the guides who had been promised or to find one who knew the way. The captains gave the men a rifle to offer as payment for guiding them to Travelers' Rest. If there was reluctance to accept, they were to offer two more guns immediately and ten horses when the party reached the Great Falls of the Missouri. With these anxieties before them, the captains had to deal with an accident by Potts. Clearing brush ahead of the party, he cut his leg severely with one of his large knives, and Lewis found it difficult to stop the bleeding. He finally stemmed the flow with a tight bandage and sewed up the wound. Colter's horse fell while crossing Hungery Creek and both rider and horse were carried down the creek a considerable distance, rolling over one another in the rocky stream. Somehow in the turbulence Colter retained his rifle and lost only a blanket. Incredibly, neither horse nor rider was injured.

By one o'clock the party got back to the place on Fish Creek, Idaho County, Idaho, where they had lunched on June 16. Here they halted and had lunch again. Seeing abundant signs of deer in the area, the captains assigned the Field brothers to stay and hunt and rejoin the party the next night at a new camp on Lolo Creek. After eating the party moved on toward Lolo Creek and camped about two miles above their camp of June 15, again on Eldorado Creek, Idaho County. They sent out hunters, who returned in the evening without success. Having seen steelhead trout in creeks but obtaining none, the captains ordered Colter and Gibson to prepare gigs for fishing the next morning. Hunters also noticed bear signs. This encouraged the captains to believe that the party could subsist on bears, deer, and fish until their guide arrived. And it would keep them from having to go back to Weippe Prairie. At least the grass here would sustain the horses. Clark, although largely copying Lewis, displayed a bit of optimism: "we are in flattering expectations of the arrival of two young chiefs who informed us that they intended to accompany us to the U. States, and Should Set out from their village in 9 nights after we left them on the 19th inst. if they Set out at that time Drewyer and Shannon will meet them, and probably join us on the 20th or 21st."

JUNE 19, 1806. Collins, Labiche, and Cruzatte, who went hunting early this morning, were back by noon with one deer. Fishermen Gibson and Colter were even less successful and reported few sightings as well. Their bone gigs had broken, but Lewis was able to find a piece of iron to fashion new ones. Still, they were able to take only a single fish, and it was a steelhead trout rather than the fat salmon they had hoped for. In the early afternoon the Field brothers arrived with two deer. Shields and Lepage were with them but had not been able to locate the lost horses they had gone after. More horses strayed. Frazer had seen Lewis's and Clark's horses along with a mule headed toward Weippe Prairie. He had pursued them for a time but gave up and came back. The captains decided to send out all available hunters in the morning to determine whether it was feasible to remain at their present location. If hunting was unsuccessful here they would have to return to Weippe Prairie, where game was not so scarce. They also wanted to give their anticipated guides time to reach them. Cruzatte brought Lewis several mushrooms, which the captain roasted and ate without salt, pepper, or "grease." He called them "truly an insippid taistless food" prepared in this way. The party's stock of salt was practically exhausted, except for a quart that Lewis had deposited on June 17 in the mountains and that he reserved for his trip on the Marias River. Clark, while largely following Lewis's entry, added details to his own journal, including notes on a short excursion. He commented on the abundant grass of the area, which would sustain their horse herd for as long as they needed to stay here.

JUNE 20, 1806. Expedition hunters set out early, but most of them returned without success by noon. Reuben Field had killed a cinnamon variety of the black bear, but its meat was mostly worthless. Later Labiche and Cruzatte returned—the former had killed a deer. The hunters assured the captains that in spite of their best efforts game was not to be found, and they did not see any possibility of sustaining the corps at this place. Seven steelhead trout caught this day added little to the party's larder. Still awaiting the return of Drouillard and Shannon with hoped-for Indian guides, the officers determined to go back to Weippe Prairie the next day, where they could replenish their stock of meat, now nearly exhausted. There they would also be able to know whether they could get guides to lead them over the mountains. Bratton's horse voted with its feet, probably headed for Weippe Prairie, guessed the captains.

The captains now contrived plans either to obtain a competent guide or to take action on their own. They knew that if they delayed until the snows receded enough for them to find a road, they would not be able to reach St. Louis before winter set in. Their alternate plan was to have one of the captains lead a group of four of the party's best woodsmen with three or four of the best horses into the mountains with sufficient supplies to last for several days. They would follow scrapings on trees left by past Indian travelers and leave their own tomahawk marks to guide the main party. Lewis observed that while snow was nearly ten feet deep on the trail, around trees it was much shallower, due, he surmised, to the trees' overhang and the warmth of the earth at the roots. This allowed Indian markings to be visible. The lead party would send runners back to keep the main force informed of their progress. Such communication would prevent delays on the road and better the chances of not running out of food.

Should the advance party not find a route, they would return to the main group and an alternate plan would be adopted. That plan, based on Nez Perce information, was to make a mountain crossing to the south by taking a long, circuitous route through southern Idaho, which by Lewis's estimates would require nearly a month of added time. The captains were also trying to assess various reports from Shoshones and Nez Perces and their own knowledge and perceptions of western geography to determine feasible routes over the Rocky Mountains. In fact, the captains' admitted that traveling on the hard-packed snow toward Lolo Pass at this time was not difficult, it was only finding a way and securing adequate provisions that made alternate plans necessary. Finally, they were more optimistic about the advance party plan than about attempting a trip far to the south.

JUNE 21, 1806. After horses were collected, the party got an early start for the return trip to Weippe Prairie. According to Lewis the party was mortified at having to retrace their route to the prairie, particularly along the difficult, dangerous route they had come up. Two horses succumbed along the way: Thompson's perhaps to distemper and Cruzatte's to a groin wound as it jumped some fallen timber. The party met two Indians bound for the mountains, leading the three horses and a mule that had escaped the explorers. These Nez Perces followed the corps to a grazing spot below on Lolo Creek, Clearwater County, Idaho, that the party had used on September 21, 1805. They told the captains that they had met Drouillard and Shannon on their way. Communication was clumsy, so the captains could not learn why the two expedition men had not returned with the Indians. Nonetheless, the officers pressed the Indians to guide them over the mountains but got a promise of only a two-day delay. The Nez Perces remained at Crane Meadow (see June 15), while the explorers pushed on to Weippe Prairie for hunting purposes. In fact, four hunters were sent ahead to get a start at replenishing the exhausted meat supply. Gass and the Field brothers stayed behind on Lolo Creek to hunt. The party reached the Weippe Prairie camp of June 10–15 by about seven in the evening, anxious to meet Drouillard and Shannon. Shields brought in a deer at dark. Clark copied Lewis's entry into his own journal.

JUNE 22, 1806. All hands who were able were on the hunt and the day's take was even greater than anticipated: eight deer and three bears. Gass and the Field brothers were less successful, having killed but a single grouse at their Lolo Creek camp. The captains sent Whitehouse back to the Camp Chopunnish locale to get some salmon, since the captains had learned from the two Nez Perce men that natives were taking them in considerable numbers now. Clark had found some beads in one of his coat pockets to serve as payment. Potts's injury to his leg on June 18 was causing him great pain and the area was inflamed. The captains applied a poultice of cous roots. Clark copied Lewis's entry.

JUNE 23, 1806. The captains were nervous that Drouillard and Shannon had not returned and at the same time concerned that the party's potential guides, whom they had left Crane Meadow, would give up on the explorers and set out for the mountains. So they sent Frazer and Weiser to try to convince the Nez Perce men to wait a day or two longer. If they were not able to persuade them to delay, then Weiser was to join Gass and the Field brothers in accompanying the Indians to Travelers' Rest, mark trees en route, and wait there until the main party followed their steps to that place. Hunters were out in force and benefitted from the does with new fawns, as the men could cry out like fawns and attract deer for the killing. The captains speculated that game were wary because the Indians hunted them so aggressively on horseback. Nevertheless, expedition hunters killed four deer and a bear. One hunter, Colter, did not return this evening.

At about four o'clock Drouillard and Shannon returned, bringing with them three Nez Perces who had consented to guide the party to the Great Falls of the Missouri for the price of two guns each. Whitehouse was also with them. The three Indians were familiar to the captains: one was a brother of Cut Nose, while the others had earlier given each of the captains a horse. The latter two were also the ones who had promised to join the corps by June 19. The captains counted them as "young men of good character and much respected by their nation." Clark, largely following Lewis, also reported that these Nez Perces brought both good news and disturbing reports about the captains' efforts to bring peace among the tribes. It seemed that Nez Perces and Walla Wallas ("Wallar-wallars") had made peace with the Shoshones but that Coeur d'Alenes ("Sheetsomis") and Atsinas ("Big bellie of Fort de Prarie") had killed a large number of Shoshones and Salish ("*Otte lee Shoots*"). Anticipating an early start the next day, the captains had the horses brought near to camp and secured for easy collecting.

Gass stayed at the Lolo Creek auxiliary camp while the Field brothers hunted, but they returned by late morning with nothing. The sergeant reported that the Nez Perces with them gave up and went on toward the mountains. About noon Frazer and Weiser reached the camp with the captains' plan. While Frazer remained here, Gass and the others set out to catch up with the two Nez Perces. They found the Indians on Eldorado Creek, Idaho County, Idaho, where the party had camped from June 18 to 21, and spent the night with them.

JUNE 24, 1806. With the horses close by and easily collected the party got an early start, led by the three Nez Perce guides. Colter, out all night, rejoined them and reported killing a bear. Given the bear's distance from camp and its poor condition, the captains did not think it worth retrieving. They arrived at Gass and party's temporary camp, found Frazer waiting for them, and learned that Gass, the Field brothers, and Weiser were in pursuit of the two Indians who had left for the mountains. After lunch the main party moved ahead and reached the spot where Gass's party with the Indians had overnighted and were waiting; it was the location of the main party's camp of June 18 to 21, on Eldorado Creek. While waiting, the Field brothers had killed a deer but had given so much of the meat to the Indians that little was left to share. The brothers had gone ahead to hunt on Hungery Creek, a place the main party expected to reach the next day. Gass had convinced the two Indians to wait by giving each a pair of moccasins. Clark copied Lewis's entry almost verbatim.

JUNE 25, 1806. Before turning in the previous night, the Indians had set fire to dry fir trees. The trees nearly exploded upward in flame. Lewis called them a "beautifull object," which reminded him of fireworks displays. The Nez Perces told the captain that the objective was to guarantee fair weather ahead. Lewis was a little concerned when one Indian complained of being unwell. Such notice by natives in the past had often been a pretext to quitting whatever task the person was not inclined to do. While the Nez Perces stayed behind with the sick one, the party moved ahead and reached the Field brothers, waiting for them at a branch of Hungery Creek, Idaho County, Idaho.

The party halted for lunch and the Indian guides caught up. Lewis took a moment to pursue his botanical interests and duties. The captain provided a morphological description of western spring beauty, noting that its roots were eaten by Shoshones and that the roots had the flavor and consistency of Jerusalem artichoke. He now realized that the plant he got from Drouillard on August 21 was this plant. Clark, largely copying Lewis, alone noted that it was Sacagawea who had collected the root. It is one of the few documented instances where she is credited with bringing a botanical specimen to the captains. The plant was new to science, and Lewis collected the type specimen two days later. After lunch the party followed their familiar route to Hungery Creek and camped about a half mile below their camp of June 16 and near the main party's camp of September 19, 1805. They faced rain most of the day. The Nez Perces stayed with them, so the captains were encouraged that they might be faithful to their pledge. Lewis gave the sick man a buffalo robe since he had little covering. Drouillard and Shields, who had been sent after horses this morning, appeared at camp with them in the evening.

JUNE 26, 1806. An early start, at six o'clock, got the party on the route they had followed previously to reach the mountainside in Idaho County, Idaho, where they had deposited excess baggage on June 17 before turning back. They took two hours here to gather and load the items and cook a hasty meal of boiled venison and cous soup. Having time, the captains measured the depth of the snow. From a mark they had left on a tree they saw that it had dropped from ten feet, ten inches, to about seven feet. The Nez Perces were anxious to be underway since it was a considerable distance to a camping place with sufficient grass for the horses. Now with the guides in the forefront, the party made their way upward over the "steep sides of tremendious mountains entirely covered with snow," according to Lewis. They "ascended and decended severall lofty and steep heights" and kept to the ridge of Lolo Trail between the North Fork of the Clearwater ("Chopunnish") and the Lochsa ("Kooskooske") Rivers.

It was late in the evening before they reached the Nez Perces' objective. They had passed no water during the afternoon's ride, so they were pleased to find a convenient spring and ample grass for the horses. One grass in particular, beargrass, Lewis noted as being abundant but not favored by the horses due to its wiry leaves. He gave it a few lines of botanical description. The captain had collected specimens on June 14, one of which is at Kew Gardens, England. Also on the way up someone had killed two spruce grouse ("small black pheasant") and a female blue grouse ("speckled pheasant"). Lewis took time to count their tail feathers, sixteen for the former and twenty for the latter, while he noted eighteen for ruffed grouse ("common pheasant"), with which he was familiar. The Nez Perces told him that neither species "drumed." Lewis had never heard either species make a noise. The camp was on Bald Mountain, Idaho County, northeast of their camp of September 18, 1805. Soon after they established camp another Nez Perce man joined them, hoping to accompany them to the Great Falls of the Missouri. From him apparently they learned that the two guides they had met on June 21 and who now accompanied them were "a party of pleasure" (as Lewis termed it) to the Salish. One of the guides lost two of his horses along the way and went in search of them. He returned with them before dark. Clark, mostly following Lewis, confided that he had suffered with a severe headache since the day before.

JUNE 27, 1806. Again an early start on the Lolo Trail, following the ridge to a point one mile short of the party's camp of September 17, 1805, west of Indian Grave Peak, Idaho County, Idaho, where the Nez Perces wanted to stop and smoke. The spot is now memorialized as "Smoking Place." Here Indians had raised a conic mound of stones some six to eight feet high, topped off with a pine pole of fifteen feet. From this height Lewis described his grand view "of these stupendous mountains. . . . we were entirely surrounded by those mountains from which to one unacquainted with them it would have seemed impossible ever to have escaped." Indeed, he confessed that without the assistance of the Nez Perce guides he doubted that the corps could have found its way to Travelers' Rest. The trees the explorers had marked on the way out and on which they expected to rely on the way back were too few and nearly impossible to locate. "These fellows are most admireable pilots," Lewis concluded.

After smoking and contemplating the scene "sufficient to have damp the sperits of any except such hardy travellers as we have become," the party moved on. At three miles into their march, they descended a steep mountain and crossed two streams, either Gravey, Horseshoe, or Serpent Creeks. From there they ascended a ridge and came to their camp of September 16, 1805, passed three small creeks, including Howard and Moon Creeks, and made their way to camp on Spring Hill, a little south of the Idaho-Clearwater county line and roughly midway between the camps of September 15 and 16, 1805. Its situation, about twenty-eight miles from the previous camp, was similar to that of the day before but with less grass for the horses, which had not been relieved of their packs or allowed to feed all day. Gass maintained that the party had climbed "some of the steepest mountains I ever passed." He also noted that the snow crust generally held the horses, but occasionally they would break through up to their bellies. The men, however, the sergeant related, had held off wearing their socks since they expected more snow.

The Nez Perces told the captains that the area abounded in mountain goats, but they saw none. They did see three mule deer but were unable to get a good shot at them. Without any meat, the captains issued a pint of bear grease to each mess to mix with boiled roots to make "an agreeable dish," according to the captains. Potts's swollen leg was improving and his pain had lessened. The captains applied a poultice of pounded roots and leaves of wild ginger to his wound and Potts gained additional relief. Wild ginger, not found at this elevation, must have been brought from lower regions. Lewis had collected a specimen of wild ginger on June 1, 1805, and had sent a specimen to Jefferson from Fort Mandan in April 1805, mentioning its medicinal properties. Near camp, Lewis noticed a stand of dogtooth violet, which he called "yellow lilly" at this point, probably due to its bright yellow petals in bloom. Clark, mostly copying Lewis, added that his headache was easing.

JUNE 28, 1806. Some of the horses had scattered during the night, but the men found them soon enough to get an early start after breakfast. Lewis judged the animals to be gaunt. The Nez Perce guides promised good feeding grounds at noon. Still following the ridge of Lolo Trail, the party passed their camp of September 15, 1805, and then bypassed Wendover Ridge, which they had ascended from the Lochsa River to reach that camp. By eleven o'clock they were at the place of abundant grass promised by the guides. Learning that no other grazing was within reach, the captains concluded to remain here. Having come thirteen miles, the party set up camp near Powell Junction, on Forest Road 500, Idaho County, Idaho, north of Powell Ranger Station and the party's camp of September 14, 1805. In spite of traveling on snow all day, Lewis conceded that it was better than negotiating fallen timber and rocky ground. Even though the horses sank into the snow, their footholds were more sure than on a dry but tangled trail. Not finding water nearby for the horses, the men melted snow for the purpose. Hunters went out but returned without luck. Clark killed a blue grouse, which Lewis called common to snowy regions of the mountains. Lewis noticed whortleberry on the heights and a species of grass, smooth wood-rush, that the horses favored. Clark again followed Lewis's writing.

JUNE 29, 1806. Before horses were collected and the party got under-way, the captains sent Drouillard and Reuben Field ahead to Lolo Hot Springs to hunt. The party moved through thick fog to the ridge of Lolo Trail, then after five miles descended to Crooked Fork, Idaho County, Idaho, near the entrance of Brushy ("Quawmash") Creek, on the opposite side. In descending the ridge, the party "bid adieu to the snow," in Lewis's happy words. Happy, too, was the sight of a deer that Drouillard and Field had left for them. This was an espe-cially welcome find since the party was now without grease for their roots and, most disappointing for Lewis, without salt. The explorers followed Crooked Creek upward to a point where they found the road they had followed in September 1805. At noon they arrived at Packer Meadows ("quawmas flatts"), in the vicinity of their camp of September 13, 1805. Here they halted to graze the horses, having traveled about twelve miles. Counting heads, the captains found that they had lost one of their packhorses and a riding horse. They sent Joseph Field and Colter after them.

After lunch the party continued their march to Lolo Hot Springs, crossing into Missoula County, Montana. Here they set up camp for the night. Several hunters were sent out, and Drouillard and Reuben Field returned without taking more deer. Later Colter and Joseph Field came back with the lost horses, also bringing a deer, which served as supper. Lewis spent a few lines of his journal describ-ing the area around the hot springs and enjoying a dip in the pool dammed up by Indian itinerants at the base of a hill (see Septem-ber 13, 1805). "I bathed and remained in 19 minutes, it was with dificulty I could remain thus long and it caused a profuse sweat," the captain related. Everyone seemed to take a turn at the refresh-ing bath. Lewis noticed that the Nez Perces would remain as long as they could in the scalding water, then run to an icy-cold creek and plunge in, return to the hot bath, and repeat the process several times, always ending in the hot pool. Lewis saw the tracks of barefoot Indians and supposed them to be natives fleeing from Atsinas or Hidatsas. Clark followed Lewis's entry but conceded that he could stay in the hot water no longer than ten minutes.

JUNE 30, 1806. Drouillard was again sent out to hunt, accompanied by Joseph Field. Fortuitously, just as the party was preparing to leave a deer wandered in, seeking a salt lick, and became the evening's dinner instead by the shooting skill of Reuben Field. The explorers now took up the road along Lolo Creek, Missoula County, Montana, toward Travelers' Rest. Along the way Lewis's horse slipped and fell, throwing the captain, and both slid some forty feet down a hill. The horse almost went over the top of Lewis, but the captain dodged a near disaster and both escaped unharmed. At noon they halted at their noon stop of September 12, 1805, at Grave Creek, after a thirteen-mile trek. They ate and let the horses graze while Shields took a deer. Probably while stopped Lewis noticed what may have been Richardson's red squirrel and wrote a short description of mountain lady's slipper ("lady's slipper or mockerson flower"), a rare species new to science. Before the party got underway Shields killed another deer, and during the remainder of the march the party picked up three others that Drouillard and Joseph Field had killed.

A little before sunset they arrived at the Travelers' Rest campsite of September 9–11, 1805, on the south side of Lolo Creek, south of Lolo, Missoula County, having made about nineteen miles since lunch. The captains decided to remain here for two days, restore the party, and make final plans for separate trips through Montana. They remarked on the stamina of the horses, which were still in good order but in need of some rest to fully recover. They found no evidence of Salish ("Ootslahshoots") in the area, but the Nez Perce guides were nervous nonetheless. They were also apprehensive about Atsinas and considered the Indian footprints of the day before as just cause for their worries. Lewis added a table of "courses and distances" to his journal and calculated a trek of 156 miles from Weippe Prairie to Travelers' Rest, June 24–30. Clark, recalling the Lolo Trail experience of 1805, added, "in passing of which we have experiensed Cold and hunger of which I shall ever remember," then penned a brief overview of the 1806 trip.

JULY 1, 1806. The captains finalized plans for the separation of the corps into groups to explore routes across Montana. It was an elaborate, bold, and somewhat risky plan. Lewis would lead a party to the Great Falls of the Missouri, leaving Thompson, McNeal, and Goodrich there to build carts for a portage of the falls while he and six others explored the Marias River to discover if any branch extended north of 50° latitude. The captain called for volunteers to accompany him on the Marias trek and from the many who stepped forward he chose Drouillard, the Field brothers, Werner, Frazer, and Gass. The remainder of the party under Clark would proceed to Camp Fortunate, Beaverhead County, Montana, the camp of August 1805. From there Ordway and a detachment of nine men would descend the Missouri River in canoes, link up with Thompson, McNeal, and Goodrich, and proceed to the mouth of the Marias River to join Lewis and party after their exploration of that river. In the meantime, Clark with the remainder would head overland to the Yellowstone River, build canoes, descend the river to its mouth, and there join Lewis's combined contingent coming down the Missouri. Pryor and two others would take the horses, leave Clark, and move ahead to the Mandan villages. From there they were to go to British posts on the Assiniboine River to find the trader Hugh Heney, whom the party had met at Fort Mandan (see December 16, 1804), and hire him to convince Sioux chiefs to accompany the captains to Washington DC. With the plan settled, the captains announced it to the party.

The Nez Perce guides informed the captains that they wanted to return home and not go farther with the explorers. Lewis and Clark told them that if they were determined to leave the party would supply them with meat for the trip, but the captains asked that they accompany Lewis on his trip to the Great Falls. It should take only two nights and would get Lewis's party on the right road. The Nez Perces agreed to this arrangement. The captains presented one young man, "who had been remarkably kind to us," wrote Clark, with an Indian peace medal. They tied blue ribbons about the hair of others. The Nez Perces told the captains that there were great numbers of mountain goats ("white buffaloe or mountain sheep") in snowy mountains to the west, where they inhabited inaccessible spots but were easy to kill. Again, stories of the goat but no good sightings. The lone Nez Perce who had joined the party on June 26 gave Lewis an excellent horse and assured the captain of his friendship toward Americans.

While hunters dispersed, Shields set to work on repairing the party's damaged guns. Hunters were able to take thirteen deer during the day, "large and in fine order," according to Lewis. Clark was more expressive: "this is like once more returning to the land of liveing a plenty of meat and that very good." Windsor had broken his gun near the muzzle, so Shields cut off the damaged end and Lewis exchanged it for a gun he had given one of the guides. The Indian seemed pleased with the trade and shot the new weapon several times. Lewis called him a good shot for an inexperienced rifleman. Lewis made a catalog of birds in the area, including mourning doves, Lewis's ("black") woodpeckers, common flickers ("lark woodpecker"), pileated woodpeckers ("logcock"), larks, sandhill cranes, sharp-tailed grouse ("prarie hen with short and pointed tail"), robins, sandpipers ("brown plover"), curlews, blackbirds, ravens, hawks, sparrows, and kingbirds ("bee martin"). In addition to the birds, the captain wrote a lengthy, detailed morphological description of the prairie dog ("*barking squirrel*"), along with notes on its burrows, food, and barking habits ("much that of the little toy dogs"). Lewis granted that "it's flesh is not unpleasant." This day and the next Clark wrote more independently of Lewis.

JULY 2, 1806. Hunters were not as successful as the day before—Collins brought in only two deer. Shields kept working on the party's guns and had them all in good working order by evening. With the separate trips laid out and everything ready to go, the captains anticipated departing in the morning. Communicating with the Nez Perces by signs, the only recourse since no one spoke the language, Lewis reiterated what Clark had written the day before about the Indians wanting to return home. The Nez Perce to whom Lewis gave the Indian peace medal insisted on exchanging names with the captain, whom he called "Yo-me-kol-lick," which Lewis said meant *"the white bearskin foalded."* As agreed to on June 23, the captains gave a second gun to each of the guides, along with ample gunpowder and ammunition. For entertainment in the evening, the Indians raced their horses while members of the party ran footraces against the natives with varying success. Lewis called the Nez Perces "a race of hardy strong athletic active men." Goodrich and McNeal were plagued with syphilis ("pox"), which Lewis said they had contracted from Chinook women while at Fort Clatsop (see January 31 and March 8, 1806). The disease was one of the reasons that he had detailed them to go with him to the Great Falls, since mercury was available there for medication.

Turning to botany, Lewis noted two species of clover in the vicinity: small-head ("small leaf") clover and perhaps thin-leaved owl-clover ("large"). Lewis had collected specimens of each the day before, and Pursh used the owl-clover specimen after the expedition to describe a new species. Lewis also collected a number of other new plants while at Travelers' Rest, notably a plant representing a new genus that Pursh christened *Lewisia rediviva*, bitterroot, in honor of the captain. Lewis went on to provide another catalog of area plants, including black cottonwoods, roses, serviceberries, honeysuckles, Lewis's syringas ("seven bark"), elderberries, alders, quaking aspens, chokecherries, and willows. He had collected a specimen of black cottonwood sometime in June. Now he noted that ponderosa ("long leafed") pines were the principal trees of the neighborhood and grew as well in the bottoms as on the hills, while firs and larches were confined to higher elevations. Abundant here also were the party's constant pests, mosquitoes.

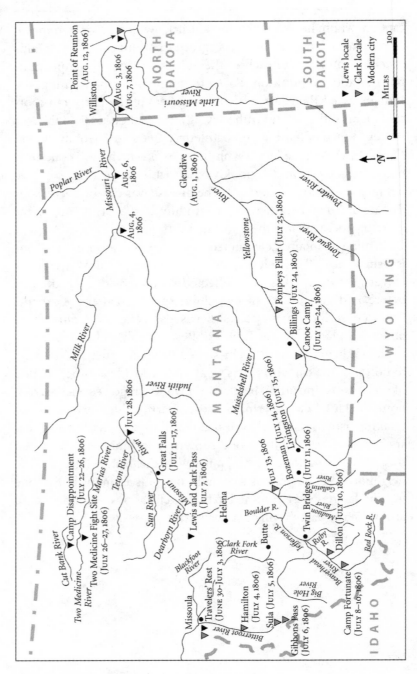

MAP 12. The expedition's route, July 3–August 12, 1806.

CHAPTER 11

Separation and Reunion

July 3–August 12, 1806

[From this point until the parties reunite on August 12, the captains' journal entries are presented separately, as Lewis heads for the Marias River while Clark seeks the Yellowstone River. The enlisted men's journals are linked with the party to which they were attached.]

Lewis on the Marias

JULY 3, 1806. With all plans completed for dividing the party into several groups for the return trip across Montana, Lewis and his men saddled their horses and "I took leave of my worthy friend and companion Capt. Clark and the party that accompanyed him. I could not avoid feeling much concern on this occasion although I hoped this seperation was only momentary." Lewis was leading a party of nine men and five Nez Perces with perhaps seventeen horses toward the Great Falls of the Missouri River. Three of the explorers, Thompson, McNeal, and Goodrich, were to remain there awaiting a detachment from Clark's group, while Lewis, Drouillard, the Field brothers, Werner, Frazer, and Gass made a reconnaissance of the Marias River.

They began the journey to the Great Falls by proceeding north along the west side of the Bitterroot ("Clark's") River for about seven miles, passing the point where the Bitterroot River joins the Clark Fork ("East branch of Clark's River") River. The Nez Perces recommended crossing the Clark Fork River about two miles above the junction of the two rivers. With little suitable timber nearby, the men spent four hours constructing three small rafts for the crossing, They ate a late lunch, then spent another three hours making the transfer in several shifts. The Nez Perces swam their horses over and used inflated deer skins to float and tow their baggage. The explorers drove their horses across after the Nez Perces. Lewis stayed behind until the last crossing with two men who were questionable swimmers. When these three entered the river the swift current carried them over a mile downstream before they reached the opposite side. It did not go smoothly. On approaching the shore the raft started to sink; Lewis grabbed a bush and swam ashore, while the two nonswimmers stayed aboard and made a landing as the raft went under. Lewis was carrying his chronometer for its safety but soaked it during his dunking.

Now re-formed, the party moved about three miles east to the night's camp on Grant Creek, near its junction with Clark Fork River, northwest of Missoula, Missoula County, Montana. Hunters went out and soon returned with three deer, which were divided with the Nez Perces. The guides pointed Lewis to the road that would lead them to their destination. By following the Clark Fork and Blackfoot Rivers, the latter of which they called "Cokahlarishkit" (variously spelled) or *"river of the road to buffaloe"* (as Lewis translated it), they would reach the Sun ("medicine") River and could descend it to the Great Falls. Since it was a well-worn and obvious path there was no need for the guides. In fact, they expressed their fear of attack by Blackfeet Indians (here called "Minnetares" by Lewis) and wanted to join friendly Salish ("Shalees"). They explained that once the explorers reached the Continental Divide the road forked and that they should take the left-hand road but that either would lead to the Missouri River. Lewis directed his hunters to turn out early, so they could supply the guides with a store of provisions "after their having been so obliging as to conduct us through those tremendious mountains." Mosquitoes pestered men and horses, so Lewis had a large fire built, hoping that the smoke would drive them away. The tormented horses were nearly frantic before evening cold scattered the pests.

JULY 4, 1806. Drouillard and the Field brothers were out early on the hunt but were back before noon empty-handed. Early, too, arrived a Nez Perce visitor who had been pursuing the party since shortly after their departure from that tribe. In fact, he was the man who had accompanied the party on their first attempt at crossing the Rocky Mountains. With the hunters returned, Lewis ordered the horses saddled, smoked a pipe with the Nez Perces, gave them a shirt, handkerchief, and some ammunition, and "bid them adieu." Learning that the Nez Perce men would return to their villages by the same route the explorers had used convinced Lewis that the Lolo Trail was the best route to the Great Columbian Plain. Knowing further that all the Indians on the west side of the Rockies who passed to the Missouri also used that trail was persuasive as well. As the explorers departed, Lewis described the Nez Perce guides' response: "these affectionate people our guides betrayed every emmotion of unfeigned regret at seperating from us; they said that they were confidint that the Pahkees, (the appellation they give the Minnetares [Blackfeet]) would cut us off." Gass was even more effusive: "it is but justice to say, that the whole nation to which they belong [Nez Perce], are the most friendly, honest and ingenuous people that we have seen in the course of our voyage and travels. After taking our farewell of these good hearted, hospitable and obliging sons of the west, we proceeded on."

Continuing along the north side of Clark Fork River the party crossed Rattlesnake and Marshall Creeks, Missoula County, Montana, within the limits of the city of Missoula. Passing through the narrow divide of Hellgate Canyon they reached the junction of the Blackfoot ("Cokahlahishkit") River with the Clark Fork. The captain calculated the width of the Blackfoot as sixty yards and that of the Clark Fork as one hundred yards below the junction. He found the waters of both murky, with beds of sand and gravel, but neither was navigable due to their shallowness and rapidity. They continued along the north side of the Blackfoot for about eight miles and camped in a "handsom bottom" in Missoula County, west of West Twin Creek, where they found abundant grass for their horses, having made about eighteen miles altogether. A welcome discovery was the lack of mosquitoes. Shortly before making camp Lewis killed a Richardson's red squirrel and an unidentified squirrel that was new to him. He preserved the skins of both.

JULY 5, 1806. Lewis's entries for the next several days consist of daily event notes in his course and distance table that typically reflect only the party's route of travel to assist in mapmaking. He returned to his usual narrative writing on July 11.

The party set out at six o'clock, soon passing West Twin and East Twin Creeks, flowing into the Blackfoot River at Twin Creeks, Missoula County, Montana. Counting creeks along the way, Lewis noted Union, Gold, and Belmont Creeks in Missoula County. At Ninemile ("high") Prairie, Missoula County, they halted to eat lunch. Here they encountered a herd of pronghorns and killed one. They were also seeing wild horses at a distance. Flies were now more bothersome than mosquitoes, Lewis noted in his weather diary. Passing more streams, Lewis honored Werner by naming one for him, the present Clearwater River, and another, Monture Creek, after his dog Seaman. The party camped on the west side of Monture Creek, Powell County, just upstream from its entrance into the Blackfoot River, having traveled about thirty-one miles. They found evidence of an Indian war party having camped here previously.

JULY 6, 1806. The party set out a little after sunrise and crossed Monture Creek, Powell County, Montana. They were following an ageless path carved out by countless natives, here made fresh by evidence of Atsinas ("Minnetares of Fort de prarie"). Blackfeet Indians ("Minnetares" in this entry) also frequented the area, and fear of meeting them kept the party on constant guard. Moving on, they entered an "extensive plains," Nevada Valley, which Lewis called "the prairie of the knobs" fir the number of hummocks scattered across it. By seven o'clock in the morning they had crossed the North Fork Blackfoot River with some difficulty, finding it wide, deep, and rapid. Lewis measured it as forty-five yards across, while Gass said it was "mid-rib deep to our horses." Lewis noticed great numbers of Columbian ground squirrels that he knew from the Great Columbian Plain, along with pronghorns ("goats") and deer. Hunters took a deer in passing, which the party shared at lunch. Soon afterward they crossed Arrastra Creek, Powell County, and then went over a steep hill and through thick woods to their camp on either Beaver or Poorman Creek, Lewis and Clark County, Montana, west of Lincoln, after twenty-five miles of travel. Here they saw the remains of thirty-two lodges, which Lewis supposed to be of Blackfeet origin.

Birdlife was abundant, and Lewis counted curlews, kingbirds ("bee martains"), woodpeckers, plovers, robins, doves, ravens, hawks, sparrows, and ducks. Vegetation was also in bloom, and he listed western blue flag, peppergrasses, sagebrushes, and two other, unnamed shrubs common to the area. The captain also collected several plants, including silverberry and bitterbrush, both new to science, the latter receiving its scientific name (*Purshia tridentata*) in honor of Lewis's botanical advisor after the expedition, Frederick Pursh. One of the specimens of silverberry is at Kew Gardens, England. The party killed five deer and a beaver this day.

JULY 7, 1806. On the road through a "level beautifull plain" by seven o'clock, the party moved from ponderosa ("longleafed") pine forests to lodgepole ("pitch") pines in the bottomlands. Now in Lewis and Clark County, Montana, they crossed Keep Cool, Spring, and Landers Fork Creeks, then left the Blackfoot River and ascended a hill in the Lewis and Clark Range of the Rocky Mountains, where they followed Alice Creek to the top. Along the way they stopped for lunch, perhaps eating one of the three deer and a fawn that hunters had killed. Lewis called the deer "remarkably plenty and in good order." Reuben Field had wounded but not captured a moose earlier in the day. At the summit the men passed "the dividing ridge betwen the waters of the Columbia and Missouri rivers." They had reached the Continental Divide at Lewis and Clark Pass, misnamed since Clark was never at this spot. From here Lewis could see Square Butte ("fort mountain") in Cascade County, Montana (see July 15, 1805). He calculated that it was about twenty miles away. As they descended they saw no buffalo but viewed the tracks and dung of many. After about thirty-two miles on the road, they made camp at nine o'clock in Lewis and Clark County about three miles south of the middle reach of the Dearborn River. While hunting Drouillard was bitten badly on his knee by a beaver that escaped; he killed two others.

JULY 8, 1806. Again Lewis's party got an early start, at six o'clock. From the top of a hill Lewis saw Haystack Butte ("Shishequaw mountain"), Lewis and Clark County, Montana, about eight miles away. They crossed the Dearborn River, which the captain may not have recognized as such since they were quite a distance from its junction with the Missouri River, where they had first seen and named it on July 18, 1805. In fact, he labeled it "torrant" river for a time, then crossed that out and substituted the original name when he discovered its identity. Traveling north and northeast through an open plain from the Dearborn River, the men reached Elk ("Shishequaw") Creek and halted for lunch. Reuben Field killed a buck and a pronghorn. His brother saw two buffalo—the first anyone had seen for some time. The party was seeing great numbers of deer, pronghorns, prairie dogs, and wolves, which caused Lewis to exclaim, "much rejoiced at finding ourselves in the plains of the Missouri which abound in game."

They followed Elk Creek to its confluence with the Sun ('Medicine") River, went down that stream for about eight miles, and established camp on a large island, between Lewis and Clark and Teton Counties and a few miles from the Lewis and Clark–Cascade county line, making about twenty-eight miles altogether. Lewis described the country as not particularly fertile and with a good proportion of gravel. Area gravel occupies river terraces and is mostly outwash that was deposited during the later part of Pleistocene glaciations. In the evening Lewis killed "a very large and the whitest woolf I have seen," a gray wolf.

JULY 9, 1806. A steady rain greeted the party as they set out this crisp morning along the south side of the Sun River. They tried to take shelter in some abandoned Indian lodges but gave up and moved on through the rain. Narrowleaf cottonwoods covered the bottoms of the Sun River, with its clear but rapid water. Despite the stream's speed Lewis thought it might be navigated. Joseph Field killed a very fat buffalo, which the party had for lunch. It was the first fresh buffalo meat they had eaten since July 16, 1805. They took as much of the remainder of the meat as they could carry on their horses. Under constant rain, the men were soaked to the skin, so

Lewis halted the party after eight miles and camped on the south side of the Sun River in the vicinity of Simms, Cascade County, Montana. They feasted on more buffalo in the evening.

JULY 10, 1806. Getting another early start, the party followed the Sun River along its south side, now seeing plains cottonwood in the bottomlands. Lewis also observed ripening gooseberries. If they needed confirmation, the men were further persuaded that they had returned to the Great Plains by the abundance of brittle and plains prickly pears on the high ground. The rain-soaked ground from the previous day's downpour made muddy work for men and horses. Fatigued mounts were given a rest after ten miles as the men halted for lunch. Unfavorable winds kept hunters from taking elks who had caught their scent, but later Lewis and Reuben Field killed three. Drouillard shot a grizzly bear that swam the river near the party. Butchering the elks and the bear kept the men occupied until dark, so that they had to hurry to catch up to Gass, who had gone ahead with packhorses to establish camp. They did not reach the sergeant until nine o'clock, meeting him on the south side of the Sun River, Cascade County, Montana, a few miles northwest of Great Falls, making about twenty-four miles. Lewis reported what Gass failed to mention—that he and Thompson were chased by a grizzly bear but that their horses were able to outdistance it.

JULY 11, 1806. Back in familiar territory Lewis dropped his course and distance tables and returned to his usual narrative of events. Before him stretched a beautiful plain with native grasses enlivened by recent rains. A pleasant, clear air carried "a vast assemblage of little birds," which "sung most enchantingly." Lewis dispatched hunters down the Sun River to find elks, while he led the rest of the party eight miles across the plains to White Bear Islands, opposite the Upper Portage Camp of June and July 1805. Hearing the roaring of buffalo bulls as they moved on, the captain attributed it to their mating rituals. The party's horses, unaccustomed to the animals and frightened by their bellowing, were skittish and hard to handle. At the islands, Lewis was once more amazed at the number of buffalo the Great Plains could carry. Here he estimated ten thousand buffalo within a circle of two miles. The men unloaded their horses and set up camp on the west side of the Missouri River, Cascade County, Montana, opposite the White Bear Islands. The hunters were there to greet them and had taken a buffalo cow but no elks. Lewis directed them to kill more buffalo, as much for their hides as for their meat. The men would use the hides to fashion bullboats like the ones they had seen at the Mandans. Within no time they had killed eleven shaggy beasts, and all hands assisted in the butchering. By three o'clock they had all the meat they needed as well as coverings for the boats, shelters, and gear; although the work was not completed, they retired for the night. They would have plenty of time to complete their tasks later, because Lewis had decided to give the horses a couple of days to rest. He also intended to cache unnecessary baggage while he made the trip up the Marias River.

JULY 12, 1806. The men rose early and by ten o'clock had finished work on the bullboats. In the meantime, two men who had been searching for scattered horses returned with only seven, while ten more of the best had either strayed or been stolen. Lewis sent two men on horseback to retrieve the others, if possible. About noon Werner returned with three that he had found near Square Butte. Gass said he had found those three horses, but Lewis wrote that the sergeant arrived after Werner having found none on a search up the Sun River. Lewis sent Joseph Field and Drouillard in pursuit of the remainder. Field got back before nightfall, but with no horses. Drouillard spent the night away from camp. Strong winds during the day prevented the party from crossing the Missouri until about five o'clock. They first transported the meat and baggage on bullboats, which Lewis declared "answered even beyond our expectation." They swam the horses across at sunset and set up camp on the east side of the Missouri River, north of White Bear Islands and south of Great Falls, Cascade County, Montana. It was a familiar setting with familiar pests: "quetoes extreemly troublesome," Lewis moaned. The captain thought the area had seen a wetter season than the previous year, since the grass was more luxuriant. He saw brown thrashers, passenger pigeons, and mourning doves fluttering about and golden currants ready to ripen.

JULY 13, 1806. The party moved south and formed a new camp at the site of the Upper Portage Camp of 1805—"my old station," Lewis recalled. He had the men uncover the cache that they had dug the previous year (see June 26, July 9 and 10, 1805) and found many of its contents destroyed by water. It was particularly unfortunate that all his botanical specimens were lost, but a map of the Missouri escaped harm. Trunks and boxes were opened and the contents set out to dry. Papers and other articles from inside were damp but salvageable. The stopper in one vial of laudanum had come loose, spilled its contents, and contaminated other medicines beyond recovery. The party's old friends, mosquitoes, tormented the men, and Lewis conceded that without his mosquito netting he would have been unable to write. The captain watched buffalo move to the southeast and killed one of their followers, a cowbird ("buffaloe picker") that he called a beautiful bird. Lewis noted his concern that Drouillard was still out.

JULY 14, 1806. Lewis had dug up the wheels that the party had used on wagons in transporting goods from Lower Portage Camp to Upper Portage Camp in 1805. He found them as well as the parts of the iron-framed boat in good order. Looking ahead to his excursion on the Marias River, he had meat cut into thin strips and dried in the sun. He also had some cous roots that he had brought from Nez Perce country pounded into meal. The captain matter-of-factly stated the obvious and spoke for the men when he wrote, "I find the fat buffaloe meat a great improvement to the mush of these roots." Regarding the damage done to the cached items by invading waters, Lewis had some goods taken to one of the White Bear Islands, placed on a high scaffold, and covered with skins for storage. He hoped the items would be safe from Indian discovery so that a detachment from the Clark's party could recover them. With the buffalo nearly gone, hunters took a couple of wolves from large numbers about the camp. Lewis counted twenty-seven of them at a buffalo carcass. Again, Drouillard did not return.

JULY 15, 1806. Lewis sent McNeal to the party's Lower Portage Camp, Chouteau County, Montana (see June 16, 1805), to check on the cache of the previous year and to determine if the white pirogue was safe. Everyone else was engaged in drying meat, dressing deer skins, and generally preparing for the days ahead. Drouillard arrived about one o'clock, reporting that after a diligent search for the last two days he had been unable to locate the lost horses. He followed their tracks to an abandoned Indian camp and from there to another spot to the west near the explorers' camp of July 7. His horse being fatigued and the Indians having a two-day start on him, Drouillard thought it useless to pursue them, so he returned. Lewis was relieved to have him back safely. Indeed, he had feared the worst and was about to send out a party in search of him. The captain thought the Indians who doubtless took the horses were a band of Salish ("Tushapahs") on a buffalo hunt.

Being elated at Drouillard's return, Lewis gave little thought to the lost horses, although they were seven of the best. Given the loss of his best horses, Lewis decided to adjust the number for his Marias excursion. Gass, Frazer, and Werner would go with the group to the Great Falls, while Lewis would take the Field brothers and Drouillard with him, along with six horses. The two extra horses would serve as relief mounts on the trip. The remaining four included two of the best and two of the worst. These he would leave with the party that would take the baggage around the Great Falls. Having made this decision, Lewis ordered the men to be ready to depart in the morning. In fact, he was ready to go this day, but McNeal was still out on one of the horses intended for the Marias trip.

McNeal had his own adventure on the way to the Lower Portage Camp, which he related to Lewis when he got back to camp just before dark. When he reached Box Elder Creek ("willow run"), along the party's portage route of 1805, he unknowingly came upon a grizzly bear, out of sight in bushes. When his horse discovered the grizzly it swung, threw McNeal straight toward the bear, and galloped off. The bear raised up on its hind legs, but McNeal recovered quickly enough to club the animal over the head with his rifle, breaking the gun at its breech in the process. The bear was stunned, fell to the ground, and began to rub its head, giving McNeal time to race off and climb a willow tree. The bear came to the tree and held the soldier there until evening before leaving. After about three hours McNeal climbed down, found his horse, which had wandered some two miles away, and rode back to camp. After writing this story, Lewis concluded, "these bear are a most tremenduous animal; it seems that the hand of providence has been most wonderfully in our favor with rispect to them, or some of us would long since have fallen a sacrifice to their farosity. there seems to be a sertain fatality attatched to the neighbourhood of these falls, for there is always a chapter of accedents prepared for us during our residence at them." The rest of the party, including Seaman, had their own complaints. Mosquitoes were thick in the air and as tormenting as ever. Seaman howled in despair at the bites, and the men could not keep the pests out of their mouths.

JULY 16, 1806. Lewis sent a man to retrieve the party's horses but was alarmed when he came back with only one of them. The captain then sent one of his best hands (unnamed) on that horse after the missing ones and was relieved when he returned with them about ten o'clock. Lewis took off immediately with his Marias-bound party. Drouillard and Reuben Field took the six horses across the Missouri River near White Bear Islands, moved downriver, and crossed the Sun ("Medecine") River, while Lewis and Joseph Field maneuvered the bullboats (see July 11) to the mouth of Sun River with their baggage. From here the four men rode to Rainbow ("handsom") Falls, Cascade County, Montana (see June 14, 1805), where they halted for lunch for about two hours. Lewis noted that he made a sketch of the falls, but no such drawing by him is known. From here they moved on to the Great Falls and set up camp for the night. Lewis found the falls greatly diminished since his visit in June 1805 due to low water on the Missouri. Nonetheless, he considered them "still a sublimely grand object." He viewed herds of buffalo and thinly scattered numbers of pronghorns along his passage to camp. Along with great numbers of geese, he also saw a cuckoo, the "rain crow" of the East, perhaps a yellow-billed cuckoo.

Gass and his party, which now included Werner, Frazer, Thompson, McNeal, and Goodrich, set to work on the wagons that they would use to portage the Great Falls. The sergeant reported that his party had received orders from Lewis to proceed to the Great Falls, use their four horses to portage around that obstacle, then move on to the mouth of the Marias. It was expected that a small party from Clark's detachment coming from the Three Forks would meet Gass and his men and assist in the portage. The captain also said that if he and his men had not arrived at the Marias by September 1, Gass and party were to continue on the Missouri River to link up with Clark at the mouth of the Yellowstone River. Lewis had further told the sergeant that "should his life and health be preserved," he would meet them at the Marias on August 5.

JULY 17, 1806. Lewis rose early and made another drawing of the Great Falls, but no such sketches by him are known to exist. After breakfast the men set out, following a generally northern course toward the Marias River. Their destination was the farthest point Lewis had obtained on the Marias on June 5, 1805. The captain commented that the wide, level plains had the appearance of an ocean, with not a tree nor shrub to be seen. He assessed the fertility of the land, compared it to the Great Columbian Plain, and found it wanting. He described it as light in color, mixed with coarse gravel, cracked and hard when dry, and soft and slippery when wet. The men were moving through the area of the Blackleaf Formation and Marias River Shale covered by glacial till of silt and clay, where richer portions are known as gumbo-till. The gravel arrived from glacial outwash and pebbles left behind after the more easily eroded part of the till disappeared. Clay and silt soil crack easily when dry, while gumbo-till becomes extremely plastic when wet.

Lewis noticed several ponds as they passed west of Floweree, Chouteau County, Montana, and watched avocets grouped around them raising their young. The ponds are glacial kettles and depressions that fill during heavy rains and dry up in summer heat. At five o'clock they arrived at the Teton ("*rose*") River, Chouteau County, and camped here, about ten miles northwest of Carter, having come about twenty miles. Buffaloberries were thick in the bottomlands. The captain had hoped to reach the Marias, but failing that he did not want to be caught on the plains without access to wood or water. Seeing evidence of a wounded buffalo, Lewis supposed it had been hunted by Atsina ("Minnetares of Fort de prarie") or Blackfeet Indians. The captain was particularly wary of these tribes and expressed his sentiments in strong language: "they are a vicious lawless and reather an abandoned set of wretches I wish to avoid an interview with them if possible. I have no doubt but they would steel our horses if they have it in their power and finding us weak should they happen to be numerous wil most probably attempt to rob us of our arms and baggage; at all events I am determined to take every possible precaution to avoid them if possible." While Lewis and the Fields made camp and loosed the horses to graze, Drouillard set out after the buffalo to confirm if it had been wounded by Indians. Soon the captain and Reuben Field went in opposite directions to reconnoiter the neighborhood. Lewis ascended the river hills and with his telescope determined that there were no Indians nearby, so he returned to camp in about an hour. Reuben Field had seen no traces either, and Drouillard could not find the buffalo. Now they dined on buffalo meat that Joseph Field had prepared, after which the other men resumed their searches while Lewis filled his journal with notes of the day's events. All came back to report no evidence of Indians.

Gass had nothing to report except a pleasant day absent of mosquitoes, which were driven away by high winds.

JULY 18, 1806. Lewis and his men got an early start a little before sunrise, again following a northern course through Chouteau and Liberty Counties, Montana. From a high point about six miles into their crossing, Lewis could see the Bears Paw ("North") Mountains and Sweetgrass Hills ("Tower Mountain" for one peak) to the north, and the Highwood ("South"), Big Belt, and Little Belt ("falls") Mountains to the south. They reached and followed a nearly dry Dugout Coulee ("Buffalo Creek") through Chouteau and Liberty Counties, found a stand of cottonwood trees along its banks, and halted there to eat lunch and graze the horses. Incredibly, for twelve miles along the way it seemed they passed a single, immense herd of buffalo that covered the whole plains about them. Ever-present wolves and coyotes accompanied the herd, waiting to take a straggler. The captain also counted pronghorns and wild horses. They reached the Marias River about six o'clock and made camp a few miles above the mouth of Dugout Coulee in a grove of cottonwoods; they had traveled about twenty-four miles. Lewis was convinced that the men were above the point he had examined in June 1805, so he directed Drouillard (who was with him in 1805) and Joseph Field to descend the Marias the next day to make certain that there was no major stream flowing from the north above his earlier excursion. Still fearing Atsinas and Blackfeet, the captain shared night watch duties with his men.

Gass took three men and visited the Lower Portage Camp in order to examine the party's cache of 1805. He found everything in good order, including the white pirogue. The men took some of the tobacco out of the cache, covered the items again, and returned to the White Bear Islands camp to await the men from Clark's detachment.

JULY 19, 1806. Drouillard and Joseph Field set out on their examination of the Marias River, as Lewis had directed the day before. They were back shortly after noon to report that they had reached the farthest point of Lewis's excursion of 1805, about six miles below the present camp. Since nothing was said about major streams coming from the north to the Marias, it must be assumed they reported none. The two men had killed eight deer and two pronghorns on the way out. Lewis completed his astronomical observations but gave no indication of his latitude or longitude position. Then the party set out. They followed the Marias River for about twenty miles, crossed Pondera and Willow Creeks, then passed from Liberty to Toole County, Montana, and established camp on the north side of the Marias a mile or so west of the county line. Lewis conjectured that Willow Creek came out of the Sweetgrass Hills, which he called "broken *Mountains*" due to their ragged shape. He noticed thick timber in the river bottoms—exclusively cottonwood—with underbrush of snowberries ("honeysuckle"), rosebushes, willows, and buffaloberries ("*grease de buff*"). Out on the plains he saw the ubiquitous prickly pears, and wildlife abounded. He listed pronghorns, wolves, geese, pigeons, doves, hawks, ravens, crows, larks, and sparrows.

Gass and his men busied themselves at the White Bear Islands camp with dressing skins as they waited for Clark's separated canoe party to arrive. At about three o'clock Ordway and nine men appeared, including Collins, Colter, Cruzatte, Howard, Lepage, Potts, Weiser, Whitehouse, and Willard. The combined party numbered sixteen men. Gass summarized Ordway's trip with Clark for July 3–13, and his leading his own detachment from July 13 to this day, while Ordway did the same for Lewis's party. (Ordway's material up to this day is found with Clark's entries below. From this point both Ordway's and Gass's entries are given with Lewis's until August 12, when all reunited.) In the evening they hauled the canoes out of the river to dry.

JULY 20, 1806. Lewis and party continued their survey of the Marias River up its north side in Toole County, Montana. Here the plains were rougher than usual and littered with small pebbles that irritated the horses' unshod feet. The hardened soil—"firm as brickbat," said Lewis—had sharp points that were as painful to the mounts as the stones. Bluffs along the Marias were two hundred feet high, Lewis reported, and were formed of earth that dissolved with rain and slipped into the river. Late Pleistocene glacial ice pushed the Marias southward from its preglacial course and cut a new path through Colorado Group shale that produced the rugged topography. When clay in this soil dries it becomes exceedingly firm, as the captain noticed. Lewis observed that buffalo decreased in numbers but not wolves, while elks increased, along with pronghorns and mule deer. Evidence of beavers and otters was readily apparent along the river. Giving space and time to a little botanizing, Lewis counted wild licorices, sunflowers, hemp dogbanes ("silkgrass"), and scouring rushes. He was doubtless pleased to report that mosquitoes had been less troublesome since the men left White Bear Islands.

Theorizing about the flow of rivers, Lewis reasoned that the South Saskatchewan River in Canada had subsidiary streams coming out of these plains even as far south as the Marias River. In fact, the drainage basin of the Saskatchewan River barely reaches south of the forty-ninth parallel north, the dividing line between the Canada and the United States. Moreover, the Milk River and its drainage blocks Saskatchewan and Marias subsidiaries from reaching one another.

During the heat of the day, the men took a break for four hours. Moving on, the party made twenty-eight miles total and camped about five miles southwest of Shelby, Toole County, and in the vicinity of the Pondera-Toole county line, on the opposite side of the river.

The Ordway-Gass combined party took a day off, as Ordway and his men were exhausted by the canoe trip from the Three Forks to the White Bear Islands. They also had more work to do on the wagons to be used on the portage. In the evening they placed harnesses on their horses and hitched them to the wagons to see how they would behave when hauling equipment around the Great Falls. The horses seemed to take to the work without difficulty in spite of being covered with mosquitoes and small flies.

JULY 21, 1806. Lewis set out at sunrise with his small band and proceeded up the north side of the Marias. Finding the going difficult since they were compelled to cross deep ravines, they moved to the south side of the river. In the crossing one of the packhorses lost its footing and soaked some of the captain's scientific instruments. The men delayed about a half hour for Lewis to inspect and dry the pieces. Apparently there was no damage. Later they crossed back to the north side and moved onto the plains and away from the river. Spying a large gang of elks, Lewis repeated that the buffalo were decreasing in numbers. At two in the afternoon, they arrived at the Marias fork, with Cut Bank Creek ("northern branch") coming from the north and Two Medicine River from the south, meeting on the Pondera-Glacier county line, Montana. Lewis was convinced that they should follow Cut Bank Creek to take them to the northern reaches of the Marias, and thus to the northern extent of the Missouri River and the limits of the Louisiana Territory. After lunch they followed Cut Bank Creek until dark, making about twenty-eight miles in all. Not finding any timber, they made camp where they could collect buffalo dung for fuel. They had no fresh meat at camp, since a buffalo they shot earlier had gotten away. The camp was on the west side of Cut Bank Creek, a mile or so southwest of Cut Bank, Glacier County.

After a troubling night with mosquitoes, Ordway and Gass and their men arose to learn that their horses were missing. Several men spent the day searching for them but could not find any. In the meantime, two canoes were loaded onto the wagons and pulled by hand for a distance. The sergeants gave no indication of their location for the night along the Great Falls portage, in Cascade County, Montana. They decided to spend one more day trying to find the horses before declaring them absolutely lost.

JULY 22, 1806. Lewis and his men continued along the west side of Cut Bank Creek across a broken country that the captain deemed of poor quality. They experienced here the same type of gravel that had irritated the horses' feet along the Marias, which made going painful and slowed them considerably. After seventeen miles on this terrain, the men halted for lunch and to graze the horses. "Not a particle of timber nor underbush of any discription is to be seen," Lewis wrote, so the men made a fire of buffalo dung and ate the last of the meat they had brought along, since a wounded elk got away. Above the town of Cut Bank, Glacier County, Montana, the creek makes a bend to the west; here the explorers crossed over and continued on the north side for a time before crossing back. Eventually Lewis reached a point where he could distinctly see that the creek came out of the Rocky Mountains south of his location. Seeing no need to continue looking for tributaries of the Missouri coming from more northern spots, Lewis decided to rest the horses and spend a couple of days taking astronomical observations to get a fix on his position. After traveling about twenty-eight miles the party camped at a spot that Lewis would name "Camp Disappointment" because he could not get a fix on his position. Here they would remain until July 26, on the south side of Cut Bank Creek, Glacier County, on the Blackfeet Indian Reservation, about twelve miles northeast of Browning.

As Lewis looked toward the Rocky Mountains and considered the course of the Marias River and Cut Bank Creek, he was sorry that the streams did not reach as far north as anticipated but hoped that the Little Muddy River, Williams County, North Dakota (see April 21, 1805), or the Milk River, Valley County, Montana (see May 8, 1805), extended to 50° north. In his notes Biddle related that the explorers had hoped to find rivers reaching that far in order to gain more territory for the United States. Lewis's party saw few buffalo or prong-horns and no deer this day. Lewis conjectured that Indian hunters had made game wary. One of the men wounded a buffalo, but the horses were too worn out to chase it down.

The Ordway-Gass party was up early in search of the four lost horses. About noon the animals were discovered at the Great Falls, brought back, and harnessed to the wagons carrying two canoes loaded with baggage, so that the men could renew the portage of the falls. About five miles into the trip one of the axles broke, so they removed the canoes, left a man to guard them, and returned to the river with the wheels to find wood to mend or replace the broken parts. After repairs were completed they loaded two more canoes, returned to the baggage site, and camped at an undisclosed location along the portage. Gass indicated that one of the newly loaded canoes was quite large and gave the men a bit of trouble in the passage.

JULY 23, 1806. Lewis sent Drouillard and Joseph Field to hunt and directed the former to observe the direction of Cut Bank Creek into the mountains as he hunted in that direction. Drouillard later reported that the creek came out of the mountains to the south-west. Both hunters returned without finding game or any indica-tion of such animals. The men resorted to rendering the grease from their tainted meat and mixing it with pounded meal of cous for something to eat. They reserved enough grease and cous meal to have one more serving the next day. On his hunt Drouillard saw evidence of an Indian encampment that had been abandoned for about ten days. Lewis was sure that it was the work of "Min-netares of fort de prarie," usually meaning Atsina Indians but here probably referring to Blackfeet, and that they were on Two Medi-cine ("main branch of Maria's") River seeking buffalo. Under this belief Lewis resolved to stay away from that river on the return to the mouth of the Marias to meet the Ordway-Gass party. Lewis was surprised to see the Columbian ground squirrel on the plains of the Missouri, as well as black cottonwood, the only cottonwood west of the Continental Divide and also found here. Fishing yielded only "one small trout," perhaps a cutthroat. Those troublesome mosquitoes were "uncommonly large" here, but the area about the party's camp provided excellent pasture for their horses. Lewis attempted to take astronomical observations during the day but clouds obscured his view.

After a hard shower of rain and hail during the night, members of the Ordway-Gass party harnessed their four horses, placed one large and one small canoe on the wagons, and set out again on the portage around the Great Falls. The wagon wheels supporting the large canoe broke down often, slowing the party and adding work to their hauling labors. Weiser cut his leg and was unable to walk, so he perched atop one of the wagons. Collins went ahead to Box Elder ("Willow") Creek to hunt. With a great deal of difficulty the men got the two wagons to the creek about sunset and camped there for the night. Collins had three buffalo waiting for them.

JULY 24, 1806. With a brief window of sunshine, Lewis tried to get a fix on his position, but the sky quickly clouded over again and spoiled his attempts. The frustrated captain decided to stay one more day, hoping for fair weather. Hunters were again unsuccessful, so with a little cous bread the men created a mush to mix with the pigeons they had recently shot. In fact, the hunters called hunting useless within six or eight miles of camp—they had not even seen an appearance of game. Wolves and coyotes, however, were evident around the camp. Lewis wounded a wolf, but it must have gotten away.

Ordway and Gass's party returned to the White Bear Islands camp with the wagons and loaded the last two canoes. Returning to Box Elder ("Willow") Creek, they were hit by a downpour that created a muddy road. One of the wagons with a small canoe was able to continue to Belt Creek ("Portage river"). Gass was unwell the night before and remained so during the day. He stayed in camp while others went after canoes. The injured Weiser, still limping, joined him at camp.

JULY 25, 1806. A cold, cloudy, blustery day again foiled Lewis's attempts to make astronomical observations. For breakfast the men ate the last of their cous mush and pigeon meat. Lewis sent Drouil-

lard and Joseph Field overland on a couple of horses to the southeast toward Two Medicine River to hunt buffalo. Lewis stayed with
Reuben Field, hoping to get one more shot at fixing his position, but
it continued to rain without a sunny opening all day. For lunch the
two men shot and ate nine pigeons that landed in trees near camp.
They fared better in the evening, when the hunters returned with a
deer. The hunters told Lewis that the Two Medicine River was about
ten miles away and that the river valley was heavily timbered. At
the Two Medicine they found Indian wintering camps and shelters
that looked to have been abandoned about six weeks. "We consider
ourselves extreemly fortunate in not having met with these people,"
the cautious captain wrote. He closed his entry in a discouraged
mood: "I determined that if tomorrow continued cloudy to set out
as I now begin to be apprehensive that I shall not reach the United
States within this season unless I make every exertion in my power
which I shall certainly not omit when once I leave this place which
I shall do with much reluctance without having obtained the necessary data to establish it's longitude—as if the fates were against me
my chronometer from some unknown cause stoped today, when I
set her to going she went as usual."

Members of the Ordway-Gass party at Box Elder Creek pushed
on to Belt ("portage") Creek and met those who had gone ahead
the day before. After setting up camp at Belt Creek, the men turned
back toward the previous camp for the remaining canoes and baggage. Two men stayed at Belt Creek—one to hunt and one to cook.
Hard rain and a muddy road "did not stop us from our urgent
labours," wrote Ordway. Horses tired in the mud, however, requiring the men's assistance and forcing frequent halts, but the explorers
got back to Belt Creek by evening. Leaving behind a heavy, damaged canoe, the party now had four canoes fully transferred with
one still to bring up from Box Elder Creek. Gass was mostly recovered from his illness. He concluded that with those canoes and the
pirogues they would recover ahead, the men would be sufficiently
equipped for the boat trip from the Marias River to a rendezvous
with Clark's party, coming down the Yellowstone River. Exhausted,
some of the men turned over a canoe and slept under it to be out of
the rain, while others tried to get comfort at the fires.

JULY 26, 1806. Hoping that the cloud cover would disappear, Lewis delayed until nine o'clock in getting underway on the return trip to the mouth of the Marias River. He finally gave up on getting a clear window for his astronomical observation and for a reliable fix on his position. "We set out biding a lasting adieu to this place which I now call camp disappointment," he conceded. The party traveled overland about twelve miles in a southeasterly direction to Two Medicine River, crossed to its south side, continued on another two miles, crossed Badger Creek, and soon passed from Glacier to Pondera County, Montana. Here they stopped to graze the horses. In a large, fertile bottomland thick with cottonwood trees, Lewis found Indian shelters that appeared to have been used during the last winter. The captain noticed that the three species of cottonwood that he had cataloged on the expedition came together here. In fact, Lewis made an acute ecological observation, because three major cottonwood species, typical of the Great Plains ("broad leafed"), the Rocky Mountains ("narrow [leafed]"), and the Pacific Coast ("common to the Columbia"), occur together here in the eastern foothills of the Rockies: plains, narrowleaf, and black cottonwoods. Reuben Field killed a deer while at this place, which may have served as lunch and a welcome relief from the mush of cous.

After lunch the men continued easterly along the south side of Two Medicine River. While Lewis and the Field brothers rode to the bluffs above the river, Drouillard stayed along the river bottom. Lewis's intention was to follow the Two Medicine to its junction with Cut Bank Creek, then head southeasterly overland to the Teton River and follow it down to the Marias. Within minutes of ascending the river hills, the captain spied several Indians with about thirty horses only a mile away. He saw them looking at Drouillard as he rode along the bank of the Two Medicine and oblivious to them. "This is a very unpleasant sight," an anxious Lewis wrote. He decided to try to make the best of the situation and approach them in a friendly manner.

Directing Joseph Field to hoist a flag, Lewis and the men moved slowly toward them. Suddenly Lewis saw the Indians become agitated. It seemed that, being so concentrated on Drouillard, they had not noticed the other explorers. Lewis estimated that their numbers probably equaled those of their horses, and if the explorers took flight the Indians might take up a chase, and their horses could easily outrun the soldiers' inferior ones. Moreover, if Lewis and the Field brothers got away, they would have to abandon Drouillard, who still seemed unaware of the situation. So Lewis and his men continued to advance slowly. When they were within a quarter of a mile of them, one of the Indians mounted his horse and rode full speed toward the soldiers. Lewis dismounted and beckoned for the man to come on, but the Indian paid no heed, whipped about, and raced back to his companions. Now all of them came forward on horseback, leaving the extra horses behind, while Lewis and his men continued to move toward them. Lewis counted eight Indians but supposed there were others out of sight since he saw more saddled horses. The captain told the Field brothers that he thought they were Blackfeet Indians ("Minnetares of Fort de Prarie") and "from their known character I expected that we were to have some difficulty with them." He further believed that if the Indians thought themselves strong enough, they would attempt to rob the explorers, "in which case be their numbers what they would I should resist to the last extremity prefering death to that of being deprived of my papers instruments and gun and desired that they [the Field brothers] would form the same resolution and be allert and on their guard."

Arriving within one hundred yards of the explorers, the Blackfeet except for one halted; Lewis ordered his men to do the same while he advanced slowly alone. When Lewis reached the man he offered his hand, which the Indian grasped; then the captain moved on to greet the others while the lone Blackfeet rider joined the Field brothers. The other Blackfeet came off their horses and asked to smoke, but Lewis told them through gestures that Drouillard had his pipe. Reuben Field set out with a young man to locate him. Lewis asked if they were "Minnetares of the North," and they affirmed their affiliation. It is now known that these men were members of the Piegan branch of the Blackfeet Indians, one of three divisions of that confederation, the others being Bloods and Blackfeet proper. They are an Algonquian-language people who had evidently moved west onto the high plains centuries before. In the eighteenth century they acquired horses and became bison-hunting nomads of the Great Plains. By Lewis and Clark's time they had become the dominant power on the northwestern plains, feared by Shoshones, Salish, and Nez Perces and reluctantly encountered by Lewis.

Even without the traditional smoke and without Drouillard's signing skills, conversations began. Lewis asked if there were any chiefs among them but was skeptical when they said there were three. Doubting their rank, Lewis nonetheless passed out gifts of a medal, a flag, and a handkerchief. The captain thought them more uneasy than he was at the encounter and, now assured that there were only eight of them, felt confident that the explorers could handle any difficulties. It being late, Lewis suggested that they move closer to the river and camp together for the night, since he had a great deal to say to them. On the way they met Reuben Field and the Indian coming with Drouillard. Finding one of the few places where they could descend to the river, they made camp in the bottom near three trees, probably cottonwoods. The campsite was in Pondera County, Montana, on the Blackfeet Indian Reservation, along the south side of Two Medicine River about four miles below the mouth of Badger Creek and some fourteen miles southwest of the town of Cut Bank. Known in modern times as the "Two Medicine Fight Site," the exact location is somewhat disputed due to the limitations of Lewis's notes and the similarity of the terrain in the area. The Blackfeet threw hides over a rough tree-limb shelter and invited the Americans in. Lewis and Drouillard joined them, while the Field brothers stayed by the fire.

With Drouillard's aid Lewis began a long conversation with the Indians. The captain learned that they were from a large band that was camped about a half day's march away in the foothills of the Rocky Mountains. He was also informed that within six days' travel there was a trading fort on the Saskatchewan River that provided them arms, ammunition, liquor, blankets, and various trade goods in exchange for animal skins. This was probably a North West Company post in Alberta, Canada. Now it was Lewis's turn, so he explained that he had met a great many nations all of whom I had invited to come and trade with me on the rivers on this side of the mountains, that I had found most of them at war with their neighbours and had succeeded in restoring peace among them . . . that I had come in surch of them [Blackfeet] in order to prevail on them to be at peace with their neighbours particularly those on the West side of the mountains and to engage them to come and trade with me when the establishment is made at the entrance of this river to all which they readily gave their assent and declared it to be their wish to be at peace with the Tushepahs [Salish].

Lewis found them fond of smoking, so he shared tobacco and conversation with them until late at night. He encouraged them to send one of their men to the band's encampment to invite chiefs and warriors to meet him at the mouth of the Marias, while he wanted those here to join him and his men on the trip to that place. The captain offered tobacco and ten horses if they would come along, but they made no reply. Ever cautious, Lewis took first watch as they bedded down, then woke Reuben Field at eleven thirty for the second shift. The Indians were asleep, but he directed Field to keep close watch on them and if any left camp to wake him because he feared they might try to steal the party's horses. Lewis lay down and fell into a deep sleep.

"A wet disagreeable morning," began Ordway's entry for the day. An Indian dog wandered into camp, and the men gave it some meat. Colter, Potts, and perhaps others worked at running canoes from their position on Belt Creek to their Lower Portage Camp of 1805, perhaps a three-mile trip. Others in the party returned to Box Elder Creek to pick up the last canoe. They had to assist the horses in moving the wagons, as the wheels sank nearly to the hubs in the mud. It was extremely exhausting work manhandling the awkward loads. Along the way Cruzatte killed a buffalo, so they took the best of the meat back to Belt Creek. Nearly spent, the men were nevertheless able to get the canoe off the wagon, loaded, into the creek, and floated down to Lower Portage Camp, where they still had the energy to help unearth the cache of 1805 and ready the white pirogue hidden nearby.

JULY 27, 1806. At daylight the Blackfeet men rose and gathered around the fire. Reuben Field slept nearby, and his brother, who was on guard duty, had "carelessly," in Lewis's words, left his gun unattended next to his sleeping brother. One of the Indians slipped behind the sleeping soldier and took the gun and one of Reuben's as well. At the same time two other Blackfeet grabbed Lewis's and Drouillard's guns. Seeing what was happening, Joseph yelled to his brother, who instantly jumped up, and they both ran after the thief. They caught the man and wrestled back their guns, and Reuben stabbed him in the heart. Blackfeet oral testimony later gave the man's name as "He-that-looks-at-the-calf" or "Sidehill Calf." The man ran a few paces, then fell dead. The men raced back to camp. In the meantime Drouillard saw the Indian take his gun and struggled with him to reclaim it, demanding, "damn you let go my gun." The noise and scuffle wakened Lewis, who reached for his own gun but found it missing. He drew his pistol, turned, saw an Indian running off with the rifle, and chased after him. Pointing his pistol, the captain yelled for him to drop the weapon, which he did, and Lewis quickly recovered it. Just then the Field brothers came up, prepared to shoot the man, but Lewis forbade it, since he was walking away and appeared to be no threat. Drouillard had also wrested control of his gun and wanted to kill the man, but again Lewis refused.

Having failed in their efforts to steal weapons, the Blackfeet went for the explorers' horses. Lewis shouted to his men to shoot the Indians if they tried to steal any. Drouillard and the Field brothers went after the main group, who were driving horses up the river, while Lewis pursued the man who had tried to steal his gun and another Indian, who were taking other mounts. The captain was so close to the Indians that they could not reach their own horses, but on foot they were driving off some of the explorers' steeds. Nearly out of breath, unable to run any farther, and seeing that they were about to take the horses to the highland above the river, Lewis called out that he would shoot them if they persisted. One hid behind a rock while the other wheeled about; Lewis shot him in the stomach. The man fell forward but raised up enough to fire on Lewis, who wrote that "he overshot me, being bearheaded I felt the wind of his bullet very distinctly." Without his shot pouch, the captain could not reload, and he thought it unwise to pursue them, so he turned back to camp. On the way he met Drouillard, who had heard the shot and raced to help Lewis, leaving the Field brothers to chase the other Indians. Lewis and Drouillard hurried back to camp to collect as many Indian horses as possible and recall the Field brothers, but they were too far away to respond. As soon as they reached camp, Lewis and Drouillard rounded up Indian horses, saddled some, and loaded packs on the rest. Soon the Field brothers returned leading four expedition horses. Rejecting one of their horses, the men selected four of the best Indian horses for the trip to the Marias, leaving nine Blackfeet horses behind.

While the men were preparing the horses, Lewis gathered up Blackfeet discards and tossed shields, bows, and arrows along with other items on the fire. Indeed, Lewis noticed that "they left all their baggage at our mercy." He took one of the guns they left behind and reclaimed the flag but tied the medal he had given an Indian about the neck of the dead man so the Blackfeet would know who the explorers were. Taking some buffalo meat the Indians had abandoned, they mounted and set out. Before leaving Lewis tried to account for the eight Blackfeet: the Field brothers pursued three who swam the river (one astride Lewis's horse); they saw two ascend the river's heights; Lewis chased two; and one could not be accounted for, but Lewis thought he had probably run off early in the skirmish.

Coming out of the river bottom the men set their course southeasterly toward the mouth of the Marias and their rendezvous with the Ordway-Gass party. Lewis's intention was to flee this area as quickly as possible in the belief that the escaped Blackfeet would return with a large party to attack them. Knowing where they were headed, the Blackfeet might go directly to the Marias, thus putting the other explorers in jeopardy. Haste was critical, so they pushed the horses "as hard as they would bear." At eight miles they passed a stream that Lewis named "battle river," Birch Creek, Pondera County, Montana, and by three o'clock they reached the Teton River, in either Teton or Chouteau County, Montana, having come about sixty-three miles by Lewis's estimate. They halted to eat and to rest and graze the horses. From here they took to the highlands above the Teton River and followed along its south side. By dark they had traveled about another seventeen miles. They halted again to rest for about two hours, killed a buffalo cow, took a small quantity of meat, and renewed their flight. Traveling by moonlight, they eased their pace but kept going until two in the morning, covering about twenty more miles, or perhaps one hundred miles altogether by Lewis's reckoning. They turned the horses out to graze and bedded down, "very much fatiegued as may be readily conceived." The camp was a few miles west of Fort Benton, Chouteau County. Lewis was pleased with his Indian horse and thought himself the winner in the exchange.

Gass and Willard set out with four horses, crossed to the north side of the Missouri, and headed for the mouth of the Marias River, while Ordway and the rest of the men followed along in the white pirogue and five canoes. On their way across the plains Gass and Willard viewed a land teeming with buffalo. During the crossing they killed a buffalo and a pronghorn and viewed wolf packs circling the herds. The sergeant watched wolves catch a pronghorn. Since the animal was too swift for a lone wolf to run down, they worked as a team to single out their prey and wear it out by alternating runners. The two men reached the Teton ("Tansy or Rose") River, followed it for about ten miles, and camped, probably within a few miles of Fort Benton. By noon the Ordway party was in the water and underway. Hunters on shore killed buffalo and deer as canoeists pushed through fast water and rapids. Ordway neither recorded his miles nor described the location of his camp this day.

JULY 28, 1806. After a sound sleep, Lewis rose stiff, sore, and barely able to stand from the previous day's hard ride. He woke up the other men, who had similar complaints, and they saddled the horses and set out. Lewis encouraged haste, telling the men that their lives and those of their fellow soldiers might depend of them reaching the rendezvous point as soon as possible. Drouillard and the Field brothers apparently wanted to follow the Teton River to its closest point with the Missouri, cross that river, and continue along it to opposite the mouth of the Marias. Lewis thought this would take too long and prevailed with an alternate plan to ride directly to the Marias, then continue between the Teton and the Missouri on a more direct route. If the Ordway-Gass party was not there, the captain proposed hiding their baggage above the Marias's entrance, then going upriver on foot until they met the canoes coming down or joined them at the Great Falls. If they were attacked on the way to the Marias, they would stand and fight and "sell our lives as dear as we could."

Implementing Lewis's plan, they rode easterly toward the Marias. When they came close to the Missouri River they heard a report of what they supposed was a gun. Hurrying on and approaching the spot where the Teton and Missouri nearly touch, they heard more rifle shots and "quickly repared to this joyfull sound and on arriving at the bank of the [Missouri] river had the unspeakable satisfaction to see our canoes coming down." Lewis and his men stripped their horses of supplies and gear, "gave them a final discharge," and joined Ordway's canoe party. All together except for Gass and Willard, they descended the Missouri to the location of their cache of June 9 and 10, 1805, between the Marias and Missouri. The cache had caved in and damaged most of the items buried there. Lewis particularly regretted the loss of two very large bear skins, while the men's furs and baggage were also harmed, but not so much. Gunpowder, corn, flour, pork, and salt were safe, but their parched meal was spoiled.

They canoed down to smaller caches at their camp of June 3–12, 1805, and found the contents unharmed. One small cache that hid three traps belonging to Drouillard could not be located. Gass and Willard joined the party at one o'clock carrying a load of freshly killed buffalo and pronghorn meat. With nothing to detain them, and despite a hard shower of rain and hail, they tried to launch the red pirogue but found it decayed beyond repair and useless. They removed all its nails and other ironware and abandoned the boat. Abandoning the horses as well, they set out with the white pirogue and five canoes against a headwind and managed fifteen miles on the Missouri before making camp on the south side of the river, below the mouth of Crow Coulee, Chouteau County, Montana. Hunters brought in a supply of fresh buffalo meat. Ordway added they "kept a Strict guard" that night.

Howard, in the Ordway party, and another hunter got an early start and killed two deer. By nine o'clock the canoe party saw Lewis and his men above them on the Missouri's banks, fired the swivel cannon in recognition, and saluted them with the discharge of small arms. An elated Ordway wrote, "rejoiced to See them . . . Capt. Lewis took us all by the hand." The sergeant then wrote a brief account of Lewis's experiences since his Marias group had separated from Gass's party on July 16, giving particular attention to the Blackfeet encounter. Gass reported on his and Willard's hunting successes and, like Ordway, recounted Lewis's activities, especially detailing the Blackfeet fight, after the two rejoined the party.

JULY 29, 1806. It was a miserable night for the men, since a violent storm brought thunder and lightning while rain and hail poured down on the unprotected explorers. Lewis lay in water all night, nor was there any relief during the day. He decided that as soon as the party got a break in the weather, they would halt to dry bodies and baggage. The captain sent the Field brothers with Colter and Collins ahead in the two smallest canoes to get meat for the men and elk skins to cover the canoes to provide protection from the elements. Nonetheless, they got an early start and moved swiftly with the current. Before noon they entered the White Cliffs of the Missouri, Chouteau County, Montana, so vividly described by Lewis on May 31, 1805. They continued until late in the evening and made camp where they had stopped on May 29, 1805, on the north side of the Missouri about a mile above Arrow Creek (the party's "Slaughter River"). Knowing the course and distances of the river, none of the journalists saw a need to keep standard mileage tabulations for this part of the return trip.

Lewis preserved skeletons of two females and one male out of nine bighorn sheep that hunters killed. Ordway and Gass said the trophies were bound for the "Seat of government." Nor did the captain waste the meat, which he found "extreemly delicate tender and well flavored." And he offered a few descriptive lines about the animal. He also mentioned immense herds of buffalo and an absence of elks. He speculated that the curlew had disappeared because it left for other climes after having raised its young. Finally, he decided that since his descriptions of the area from 1805 were sufficient, he would not now fill his journal with comments on the land. He did remark on the Missouri's muddiness, however, noting torrents of water carried by even the smallest rivulet, bringing "mud sand and filth from the plains and broken bluffs."

JULY 30, 1806. With unrelenting rain there was no need to stay in camp to try to dry soaked items, so the party got off to an early start. A strong current carried them forward and "the men anxious to get on they plyed their oars faithfully and we went at the rate of about seven miles an hour." They stopped several times during the day to kill bighorn sheep since Lewis wanted more skins and skeletons of the animal. He was pleased to obtain a male and a female for the purpose. Back on the abundant plains, the men killed seven more bighorns, two buffalo, an elk, two beavers, and a female grizzly with claws 6½ inches long. Ordway and Willard killed the bear, and Lewis kept the skin and claws despite its small size and poor condition. It was a day when "nothing extraordinary happened." The men camped either near or on "Goodriches Island," near the camp of May 25, 1805, and across the river from it in Blaine County, Montana. Gass had the party traveling seventy miles.

JULY 31, 1806. More rain seemed not to dampen the men's determination to get going "as fast as possible." By nine o'clock they fell in with a gang of elks, killed fifteen, and took their skins. The riverbanks abounded in game. The men killed fourteen deer on a leisurely hunt. Two bighorns and a beaver also fell to their guns, but there were few buffalo in sight. Late in the evening they found shelter from the persistent rain in some Indian winter lodges on the north side of the river. By throwing elk skins over the frameworks they had decent protection. Seeing such lodges all along the river, Lewis speculated that they were the work of Atsinas or Blackfeet. Lewis located the camp "about 8 ms. below the entrance of North mountain creek," today's Rock Creek, Phillips County, Montana. Gass said they had traveled another seventy miles.

AUGUST 1, 1806. Still canoeing under rain, the party kept up a good rate. Seeing a large grizzly swimming from an island to shore, Lewis and Drouillard shot and killed it. They hauled it aboard the white pirogue and continued downriver. Before noon they passed the mouth of the Musselshell River on the Petroleum-Garfield county line, Montana. By one o'clock, with no indication of a letup in the rain, Lewis decided to land at a bottom on the south side where there were a number of Indian lodges. He hoped for fair weather and for a chance to dry the bighorn skins, which were beginning to spoil. Now leaving bighorn sheep country, he knew there would be no way to replace the skins if he did not take care of them. The camp was on the south side of the Missouri, in Garfield County, in an area now inundated by Fort Peck Reservoir. The captain had fires built in the shelters to dry the skins.

After landing they got a break in the rain but overcast skies continued. A grizzly wandered near camp, raised up on its hind legs, perhaps to get a better look at the situation, and was downed by expedition firearms. It was a female, and they got several gallons of oil from it. Lewis contended that the carnivorous grizzly was fatter during the summer than the black bear because of the availability of food such as wolves. Black bears fared better in the winter, when grizzly food sources were not as plentiful. Lewis preferred the meat of black bears. More than that he favored elk meat, which was now "in fine order." He noticed that male elk antlers were at full growth, but the velvet remained. Elk does stayed in large gangs with their young and a few bucks, while mature males formed groups of two to eight apart from the females.

AUGUST 2, 1806. Greeted with a fair morning, Lewis decided to stay here another day to dry goods and gear. He had gunpowder and parched meal set out in the sun along with all the other items that needed drying. The day proved up to the purpose. By evening all was aired and dried, repacked, and ready to go in the morning. The Field brothers went ahead to hunt. Other hunters brought in several deer. Lewis commented that "nothing remarkable took place today," but all "were extreemly anxious to reach the entrance of the Yellowstone river where we expect to join Capt. Clark and party."

AUGUST 3, 1806. Not wanting to waste time, the explorers had the white pirogue and canoes loaded quickly and were on their way by six o'clock. Passing the canoe of Colter and Collins, who had hunted ahead, Lewis and his men shouted for them but got no response. A little later they overtook the other hunters, the Field brothers. With their anxiousness to get on, the men had decided to cook enough meat the night before so they could skip that task at noon and add twelve to fifteen miles to each day's advance. Seeing few buffalo, Lewis otherwise counted a variety of wildlife: elks, deer, wolves, bears, beaver, geese, ducks, magpies ("party coloured corvus"), a golden ("Callamet") eagle, bald eagles, and red-headed woodpeckers. They camped for the night on the north side of the Missouri River, below the mouth of Cattle Creek, Valley County, Montana, and about two miles above the party's camp of May 12, 1805. Ordway and Gass put the distance since the day before at seventy-three miles. The Field brothers came into camp later in the evening bringing the meat of "two fine bucks," having taken a total of twenty-nine deer since the previous day. Collins and Colter spent the night away.

AUGUST 4, 1806. It was still dark when the men set out at four o'clock in the morning. Ordway and Willard took the place of the Field brothers as hunters. By half past eleven the main party reached the entrance of Big Dry Creek, Garfield County, Montana, and by three o'clock they were at Milk River, Valley County, where they took a short break. One of the men killed a very large prairie rattlesnake, which Lewis measured at five feet, with 176 scuta on its stomach and 25 on its tail. In the evening they camped on the north side of the river in Valley County, some two miles above the camp of May 7, 1805. Gass estimated a trip of eighty-eight miles. During the night Lewis heard the cry of the common poorwill for the first time this season. Colter and Collins did not catch up again, while Ordway and Willard did not return until almost midnight. They had killed a grizzly and two deer and had had quite an adventure. In passing a bend near camp, they were pulled by the current into a cluster of submerged trees, which had broken loose, become stuck in mud, and now menaced boats. One of the shoreline trees caught Willard and threw him overboard, but he snagged it, held on tight, and did not go under. Since Willard was steering at the stern, Ordway was now adrift and was carried down about a half mile but finally got the canoe safely to shore. He raced back on foot to find Willard still clinging to a tree. There was no way to get the canoe back to the man, so Willard improvised a makeshift raft out of floating debris and worked his way through the maze of submerged trees to Ordway in the waiting canoe. Lewis was relieved that the man could swim "tolerably well."

AUGUST 5, 1806. Lewis decided to delay for Colter and Collins. In the meantime, hunters killed four deer near camp. By noon the two men were still out, so Lewis concluded they must have passed the party in the dark. Ordway said that he and Willard would have overshot the camp the previous night, but the sentry hailed them. Another long day on the river brought them to camp on the south side of the Missouri some four miles southwest of Wolf Point, McCone County, Montana. Ever the hunters, the Field brothers killed two large grizzlies in the evening. One of the bears measured nine feet from "the extremity of the nose to that of his tail," Lewis declared. It was nearly the largest bear he had seen. Lewis the naturalist could not resist listing again the abundant wildlife of the plains: buffalo, elks, deer, pronghorns, wolves, geese, and eagles. He saw few ducks or sharp-tailed grouse. Lewis noted that geese and pelicans were unable to fly because they were "sheding or casting the fathers of the wings at this season." Both species undergo synchronous molting, that is, changing their feathers all at once in a short time period.

AUGUST 6, 1806. During the night a violent storm came out of the northeast, bringing thunder, lightning, hail, hard winds, and heavy rain. The rain looked to overwhelm the small canoes, so with some difficulty Lewis had the boats unloaded before their contents got drenched. Luckily, the cargo escaped harm. The captain was soaked to the skin but found some protection in the white pirogue under an elkskin awning. He suffered a fitful night's sleep. After getting underway this morning, the party passed the Poplar ("Porcupine") River, Roosevelt County, Montana, and about ten miles beyond that high winds required them to delay until four in afternoon. They traveled another five miles before making camp on the south side of the river some ten miles east of Poplar, Richland County, Montana. Hunters killed a number of game animals during the day. Lewis remarked that they were so gentle that the men killed them with ease. The Field brothers went ahead.

AUGUST 7, 1806. Another miserable night in the rain, which continued nearly without interruption until ten o'clock in the morning. Nonetheless, they got the boats in the water and underway in the downpour, hoping to reach the mouth of the Yellowstone River this day. Lewis calculated it at about eighty-three miles ahead and thought the rapidity of the river together with the men's strength at the oars made the objective possible. By eight o'clock they passed Big Muddy Creek ("Marthy's River"), Roosevelt County, Montana, which had changed its point of entrance into the Missouri River and entered about a quarter of a mile lower than it had the year before (see April 29, 1805). Lewis got his first glimpse of "Coal birnt hills and pumicestone." The coal-bearing Fort Union Formation borders the Missouri River for about fifteen miles upstream, which Lewis must have missed until this point. The burnt hills and "pumicestone" (clinker) are produced by the burning coal beds. Vegetation was changing as well: elms, junipers ("dwarf cedar"), and ash trees now lined the bottomland.

At noon the men overtook the Field brothers. They had killed two grizzlies and had seen six others. Men on the pirogue had shot at another two on shore but had killed neither. Lewis pointed out that the bears lay in wait at the river's edge trying to catch unsuspecting elks or weak buffalo crossing the stream. At four o'clock the party arrived at the Yellowstone River. They found the camp of Clark and party; Lewis estimated that they had been gone for seven or eight days. Clark had arrived at here on August 3 and left the next day because the area was infested with tormenting mosquitoes. Lewis's men soon found Clark's note to the captain informing him of their arrival and departure from the point. Lewis wrote his own note to Colter and Collins telling them that all were ahead and to hurry on. With this done, Lewis pushed on, hoping to catch Clark by evening. About seven miles below they saw evidence of Clark's party—a Chinook hat owned by Gibson was solid proof that their fellow explorers were ahead. Anticipating a reunion, they hurried on but were disappointed at nightfall not to have met Clark's group. Camp was on the north side of the river in Williams County, North Dakota, a few miles south of Trenton. Gass estimated that they had come one hundred miles.

AUGUST 8, 1806. Still hurrying to catch up with Clark and party, Lewis and his men set out early. Facing a headwind, the explorers nevertheless made great strides with the help of the current and manpower at the paddles. By three o'clock they had moved within a few miles of the Little Muddy ("White earth") River, Williams County, North Dakota, but not any closer to Clark as far as Lewis could determine. Without knowing Clark's plan, Lewis determined to go ahead "as tho' he was not before me and leave the rest to the chapter of accedents." Finding a good landing spot and recognizing that the pirogue and one of the canoes needed repairs, Lewis decided to set up camp here on the north side of the river, several miles southwest of Williston, Williams County. He also knew that the men had not had a chance to mend or make clothing since the Rocky Mountains, so the stop would give them opportunity to dress skins for the purpose. With the rush to catch Clark set aside, the captain decided to hunt and dry as much meat as possible for the trip ahead. After tending to the boats to be repaired, he had poles erected for drying meat while the men otherwise busied themselves at dressing skins and making clothes. The party remained here until August 10. Even in the cold evening air mosquitoes did not give up their annoying bites.

AUGUST 9, 1806. With a fair day before them the men went about their work of dressing skins and making clothes. The pirogue was not yet dry, and the party had no pitch to repair it, so they used coal and tallow as a substitute. The Field brothers were sent across river and ahead to the Little Muddy ("White earth") River, Williams County, North Dakota, to try to find Clark's party and to hunt elks and buffalo. Lewis wrote that they returned in the evening without killing any game and without finding any trace of Clark, although Ordway and Gass had them taking an elk and a deer. They told Lewis there was not "a buffaloe to be seen in the plains as far as the eye could reach." Lewis expressed some anxiety that Colter and Collins had still not caught up: "I fear some missfortune has happened [to] them for their previous fidelity and orderly deportment induces me to believe that they would not thus intentionally delay."

AUGUST 10, 1806. A cloudy morning left Lewis worried that the men would not be able to complete boat repairs before rain set in, but the sky cleared and the repairs were completed by two o'clock. Those not working on the pirogue and canoe kept at dressing skins and making clothes. By four o'clock it clouded up again and began to rain, which put a stop to clothing operations. With no need to stay longer, Lewis had the boats loaded, and the party got underway again within an hour. They descended almost to the Little Muddy ("White earth") River and set up camp in McKenzie County, North Dakota, nearly opposite Williston, Williams County. Nagging mosquitoes kept the men from a sound sleep.

AUGUST 11, 1806. This day's early start was intended to allow the party to reach the Crow ("birnt") Hills in southeastern Williams County, South Dakota, early enough so Lewis could get a latitude reading there. He considered it the corps' most northern point on the Missouri River. The men promised to exert themselves to accomplish the objective. The captain instructed those in small canoes to watch for game, stop to hunt if feasible, and then catch up, but the men saw little game along the way. Lewis did see a buffalo crossing the river, shot it, and left it for the men in the small canoes to retrieve and prepare, but those men discarded it as unfit. His attempt to get a grizzly was likewise unsuccessful, since it caught the scent of them and ran off as they came to shore. As it was, Lewis was too late to his spot to get a reading. Seeing a herd of elks nearby, the captain decided to take Cruzatte and go after them.

During the hunting excursion Lewis killed one elk and Cruzatte wounded another. After reloading, the men took different routes through a thick stand of willows to find the wounded animal. Lewis found it and was just about to shoot when a bullet struck him. The captain described the incident this way: "a ball struck my left thye about an inch below my hip joint, missing the bone it passed through the left thye and cut the thickness of the bullet across the hinder part of the right thye; the stroke was very severe." He instantly thought Cruzatte had shot him; with his bad eyesight, he might have mistaken the deerskin-clad captain for the elk. Lewis yelled to him, "damn you, you have shot me." With no response and not seeing the man, he continued to call out. Still without a response and knowing that the gunfire came from a distance within earshot, he was now convinced that he had been shot by an Indian. Fearing that there might be more Indians nearby, Lewis dashed as best he could toward the boats, calling out all the while for Cruzatte to retreat as well. As soon as he got to the boats he ordered the men to arms, told them he was wounded—"but I hoped not mortally"—by an Indian, and instructed them to follow him back to the spot to defend Cruzatte.

Near the place of the event, Lewis's leg stiffened; he became consumed with pain and was unable to go on. He ordered the men to continue ahead, and if they were outnumbered to retreat in an orderly manner while keeping a supporting gunfire. When Lewis had hobbled back to the pirogue he added his pistol and air gun to the rifle he carried. Backed against the river, he knew that retreat was impossible, so he vowed to "sell my life as deerly as possible." He waited in "anxiety and suspense" for about twenty minutes, when the party returned with Cruzatte and reported no sign nor sight of Indians. Cruzatte denied hearing the captain's calls and said that if he had shot Lewis it was an accident. The ball was still lodged in Lewis's leather pants, so the captain was able to determine that it was from the type of rifle that Cruzatte carried. Lewis was certain that the man had not shot him intentionally but realized that he might now be ashamed and trying to hide the truth of his guilt. Lewis himself may have been embarrassed by the location of the lesion, calling it a wound in his thigh, while Ordway said "the ball passed through one Side of his buttock and the ball went out the other Side of the other buttock." Clark, meeting Lewis the next day, described it this way: "the ball had passed through the fleshey part of his left thy below the hip bone and cut the cheek of the right buttock for 3 inches in length and the debth of the ball."

Gass helped Lewis remove his clothes; then the captain dressed his own wounds as much as he was able. Lewis used rolls of lint to keep the wound open so new tissue could grow from the inside out and to promote drainage. There was serious bleeding, but neither bone nor artery had been cut. Lewis sent men to bring back the elk meat he and Cruzatte had secured. Hunters' canoes came up soon with another elk, and they set out. In the afternoon they passed Clark's camp of August 9 and 10 and found a note to Lewis. Clark explained that a note he left for Lewis at the mouth of the Yellowstone had been taken by Pryor. Pryor, Hall, Shannon, and Windsor had been sent ahead by Clark on July 24 on a separate mission but had been robbed of their horses. They built bullboats, descended the Yellowstone and Missouri Rivers, and caught up with Clark's party here, a number of miles above Tobacco Garden Creek, McKenzie County, North Dakota. Lewis and his men moved on and camped a little above the mouth of the White Earth River and below the Williams-Mountrail county line. Since it was painful for Lewis to move, he slept in the pirogue during an uncomfortable night and with a high fever.

AUGUST 12, 1806. From the previous day's appearance of Clark's camp, Lewis believed that his fellow explorer was not far ahead, so the party got underway early and with as much speed as possible. By eight o'clock the man at the bow of the white pirogue told Lewis that he saw a canoe and a camp of white men on the north shore. Lewis directed all the boats to pull over and found that it was the camp of two hunters from Illinois, Joseph Dickson (or Dixon) and Forrest Hancock. Dickson had lived in Pennsylvania and Tennessee before moving to Cahokia, Illinois, in 1802. Thereafter he met Hancock, who had hunted considerably in Missouri. The two started up the Missouri River in August 1804. Clark's entry of August 11, the day he met them, provides more information about the two hunters. Lewis gave them information about the country ahead and a list of distances to principal streams on the Missouri River and pointed out places with abundant beaver. He also gave them a file and some gunpowder and lead, which the hunters acknowledged they needed. The men visited about an hour and a half, then Hancock and Dickson decided to accompany the expedition party to the Mandan-Hidatsa villages.

Lewis's wounds had left him stiff and sore but without a great deal of pain. Moreover, there was less inflammation than he expected. Gass declared him in "good spirits." The previous night he had applied a poultice of Peruvian bark (cinchona) to the wounds—a general remedy of the time. While the party was with the Illinois hunters, Colter and Collins drew up to shore and explained their long absence, since August 3. Contrary to Lewis's fears, the men had not met with accidents but had concluded at one point that the party was behind them, so they halted for several days, waiting for them to catch up. Finally realizing their error, they hurried on and reached the party this day.

At one o'clock Lewis and Clark and the full Corps of Discovery reunited. Lewis exulted that he had "the pleasure of finding them all well." Ordway reported that the men fired their blunderbusses and small arms in celebration of the reunion, while Gass exclaimed, "thanks to God we are all together again." They met at the place where Clark had halted for lunch in Mountrail County, North Dakota, some six miles south of Sanish. Given his discomfort, Lewis explained that he would turn over writing duties to Clark until he recovered. In fact, this is the last journal entry known to have been written by Lewis. Fittingly and in spite of his pain, he closed off by writing a detailed morphological description of a "singular Cherry," the pin, or bird, cherry. It is a biogeographically interesting species that is more common in the East, with relic populations in the Black Hills of South Dakota and in the Colorado Front Range of the Rocky Mountains. The corps moved on and camped a few miles below the mouth of Bear Den Creek, Dunn County.

Clark on the Yellowstone

JULY 3, 1806. Clark and party collected their horses, about fifty in number, and set out about eight o'clock. The captain had with him Ordway, Pryor, Bratton, Collins, Colter, Cruzatte, Gibson, Hall, Howard, Labiche, Lepage, Potts, Shannon, Shields, Weiser, White-house, Willard, Windsor, York, Sacagawea, Charbonneau, and the baby Jean Baptiste. Clark especially wanted Sacagawea and Char-bonneau as interpreters with Crow Indians he hoped to meet, since they both spoke Hidatsa, a language similar to Crow. Moving in the opposite direction of Lewis's party, Clark's entourage proceeded south along the west side of the Bitterroot ("Clarks") River, crossing eight streams in eighteen miles and passing from Missoula to Ravalli County, Montana. Along the way the captain noticed ponderosa pines, lodgepole pines, cottonwoods, river birches, willows, and "2 species of clover," longstalk and small-head clover (see Lewis's entry, July 2, 1806). He also spotted a Columbian ground squirrel that was common at Weippe Prairie. They stopped at one creek, perhaps Kootenai Creek, for lunch and to let the horses graze. After eating they set out again, crossing ten creeks, eight of which were large with swift currents. After making about thirty-six miles for the day, the party settled in on the north side of Blodgett Creek, Ravalli County, about three miles north of Hamilton. There they found suitable grass for the horses, and Labiche brought in a deer. Potts was suffering from a rough ride on a hard-trotting horse, so Clark gave him some opium, and the man felt better.

JULY 4, 1806. Sending hunters ahead to provision the party, Clark and the rest ate breakfast, collected their horses, and by seven o'clock were moving south along the west side of the Bitterroot ("Clarks") River in Ravalli County, Montana. The party crossed a number of streams before they found a place to stop for lunch. One stream they crossed was so deep and rapid that several horses were swept downstream for some distance while others were drenched in the rushing waters that soaked expedition supplies. After getting across and regrouped, Clark saw the tracks of Indians he supposed to be Shoshones. Hunters killed two deer, but Clark missed his shot at some bighorn sheep. It being Independence Day, Clark had the party stop early enough to have a proper dinner in celebration. The captain called it a "Sumptious Dinner of a fat Saddle of Venison and Mush of Cows [cous]."

After dinner they moved on and reached a large creek, perhaps Rock Creek, Ravalli County, and ascended it for some distance trying to find a suitable place to ford the stream. At the crossing they again found difficulties with fast waters that surged over the backs of horses and soaked their loads. Clark noticed large boulders in the river, which remained from glacier deposits that had pushed into the Bitterroot Valley during Pleistocene glaciations or were carried downstream during flood flows. Reaching the mouth of the West Fork Bitterroot River, Ravalli County, the party camped on its north side for the night, having made thirty miles this day. The camp was about five miles northwest of the camp of September 6, 1805. Clark sent out two hunters and three other men to locate the best place to cross the West Fork the next day. The scouts returned with news of a possible place of passage, but it carried the risk of swamping horses. Clark decided to investigate the area himself the next day. Hunters brought in two deer.

JULY 5, 1806. Up at daylight, Clark started out with the three men of the previous day's excursion to investigate a place to ford the West Fork Bitterroot River. At the same time he sent Labiche after a buck he had killed late the previous evening. Clark was not satisfied with either place recommended by the scouts, but near one of Colter's spots he found a place that seemed practical for the attempt. Back at camp the party took breakfast, loaded up, and set out. Crossing the river between islands, all went well until the last channel, where Colter's horse lost its footing in deep water. Shannon found a better route, so Clark ordered all to follow it. Nonetheless, water ran over the backs of the smaller horses and supplies were generally drenched. Unfortunately, some important supplies were damaged, including Clark's trunks filled with sea otter skins, flags, "curiosities," medicines, and roots. The party took the previous year's road on the west side of the East Fork Bitterroot River for about a mile, then crossed to its east side, making an easy passing. At Warm Springs ("flour") Creek, Ravalli County, Montana, they halted to let the horses graze and to dry wet gear and supplies.

Clark noticed fresh signs of Indian horses and a fire by the road. He assumed it was a result of Shoshone activities. Shannon and Cruzatte each killed a deer and Shields got a bighorn sheep, but it was a meager specimen. Shannon left his tomahawk behind at the place he killed the deer, so Clark sent him back for it with orders to meet the party at the night's camp. Shields went ahead to hunt while the party delayed to dry wet items; it was four thirty before they got underway again. Coming out of the mountains the party reached Ross's Hole, east of Sula, Ravalli County, where the explorers had met the Salish ("flatheads") on September 4, 1805. Here they found Shields, who had been unsuccessful in his hunt. They crossed the East Fork Bitterroot River and followed Camp Creek for about two miles before making camp on its east side in Ravalli County, having come about twenty miles for the day. Several men were sent to examine the road ahead. Shields got back at dark to report a good road higher up Camp Creek, one that diverged from the western route of 1805 and appeared to be a shorter path to Camp Fortunate. Clark decided to try that route, figuring that it "can't be possibly be much wors" than the last year's road. Shannon got back about sunset with his tomahawk.

JULY 6, 1806. A chill during the night kept Clark awake, and he found frost on the ground this morning. Collecting their scattered horses, they started up Camp Creek, Ravalli County, Montana, crossed the Continental Divide at Gibbons Pass, moving from Ravalli to Beaverhead County, then went down Trail ("Glade") Creek toward the valley of the Big Hole ("Wisdom") River. Along the way the captain saw "handsom glades" of camas just starting to bloom. He also saw "old buffalow roads" and great numbers of "whistleing Squirrel," Columbian ground squirrels. Reaching a level plain, they found that the Indian trail scattered into several routes, making it impossible to follow. Sacagawea told Clark that she had been to this valley often and knew a passage through the mountains that would put them in the direction of Camp Fortunate. She was pointing them toward Big Hole Pass, at the upper end of the Big Hole Valley, Beaverhead County. Continuing in that direction, the party crossed Ruby Creek and ascended a "Small rise and beheld an open bountifull Leavel Vally," Big Hole Valley. Clark estimated the valley to be twenty miles wide and nearly sixty miles long, surrounded by snow-covered mountains. Going on a bit farther the party was assaulted by hard wind and rain for over an hour. They stopped awhile to let it pass, then proceeded on another five miles, possibly to Moose Creek at the western part of the Big Hole Valley and about seven miles southwest of Wisdom,

Beaverhead County, and made camp, coming perhaps twenty-six miles for the day.

JULY 7, 1806. Scattered horses necessitated a wide search that brought in all but nine of the animals. Clark ordered six men on horseback to range farther, but having circled the camp some six or eight miles they still came back empty-handed. Their thinking was that Indians had stolen the horses, since some of the best mounts were gone. Clark thought that they might have been taken by "Some Skulking Shoshones," but just in case they had wandered off he left Ordway, Shannon, Gibson, Collins, and Labiche to hunt for them and rejoin the others at Camp Fortunate. The main group would go on to that place and raise the canoes left there the previous year.

It was ten thirty before Clark's party started southeasterly across the Big Hole Valley, crossing a number of affluents of the Big Hole River, including Rock, Big Lake, Big Swamp, and Little Lake Creeks before arriving at the Big Hole itself and crossing it. After some miles on an "old road that frequently disappeared" they came to a boiling spring, Jackson Hot Spring, on Warm Springs Creek, east of Jackson, Beaverhead County. Clark considered it much too hot to touch, so he had Pryor and Shields each put a piece of meat in to see how long it took to cook. A piece the thickness of his three fingers was done in twenty-five minutes. The water has been reported with a temperature of 136°F, discharging 260 gallons of water per minute and emerging from a deep source of Tertiary sandstone and sandy limestone. After an hour and a half for dinner and to let the horses graze, the party crossed Warm Springs Creek and went southeasterly up Governor and Bull Creeks in Beaverhead County to reach Big Hole Pass. After passing over, the party made camp near the head of Divide Creek, the upper portion of Lewis and Clark's "Willards Creek," covering twenty-five miles for the day. Clark ended the day with a reflective note: "I now take my leave of this butifull extensive vally which I call the hot spring Vally, and behold one less extensive and much more rugid on Willards Creek [Grasshopper Creek] for near 12 miles in length."

Ordway split his party into two groups. He and Labiche found the horses' tracks and followed them until they were able to overtake the animals. Now near nightfall, they turned them around and went back to the camp on Moose Creek, apparently. There they found the other three men waiting for them. They hobbled the horses and settled in.

JULY 8, 1806. After gathering the horses the party resumed their march at eight o'clock. They followed Divide Creek, Beaverhead County, Montana, to a point west of Bannack, where the creek turns east to join Grasshopper ("Willards") Creek, which continues on to join the Beaverhead River. Clark and party turned south, following Grasshopper Creek through a gap that led them to Horse Prairie Creek ("West branch of Jefferons River"). Here the party halted for about two hours to let the horses graze and to have lunch. After eating they continued down Horse Prairie Creek to the Beaverhead River and to the site of Camp Fortunate, where the full party had reassembled on August 17, 1805. Here they made a new camp, having traveled about twenty-seven miles. Clark reported that he had traveled through "uneaven Stoney open plains and low bottoms very boggy." He was moving across Tertiary sedimentary deposits of volcanic rocks with boggy bottoms along the creeks.

The captain deemed the party's descent from Travelers' Rest "an excellent road" suitable for wagons after trees had been cleared. He calculated the distance as 164 miles. Reaching the site of Camp Fortunate, tobacco users in the party hurried to the deposit where it was buried. Clark divided the chewing tobacco among the users, reserving a portion for himself and also some to be taken downriver to Lewis's party. In his book Biddle noted the importance of tobacco to the men: "[It was] one of the severest privations [of the expedition]. . . . Some of the men, whose tomahawks were so constructed as to answer the purposes of pipes, broke the handles of these instruments, and after cutting them into small fragments, chewed them, the wood having, by frequent smoking, become strongly impregnated with the taste of that plant." Clark wrote that he found the remainder of the cached items to be in good condition except for a few dampened goods. In fact, most of the plants collected between the Great Falls and here may have been lost to mildew. Lewis's entries of August 20, 21, and 22, 1805, discuss this cache. Clark also found expedition canoes safe for the most part, except for one of the largest, which was damaged. It was too late in the day to deal with them.

Ordway's party got underway early. Without giving details about his route, the sergeant described how he and his men traveled south and intersected Clark's route into Jackson Hot Spring, Beaverhead County, where they halted for a short time. They found venison in the boiling water, probably left by Clark, and ate it. Ordway found the water as hot as Clark had described it. Continuing to trace Clark's steps, they crossed through Big Hole Pass, then followed Clark along Divide and Grasshopper Creeks. They made camp on a branch of Grasshopper Creek, in Beaverhead County, traveling about forty miles for the day. They hobbled their unruly horses and had only the "head of a goat" for dinner.

JULY 9, 1806. First thing, Clark had the canoes raised, washed, and brought on shore to dry and examine. While some men repaired and readied the canoes for launching the next day, others went searching for additional tobacco that was supposed to be buried at another cache. They were unable to locate it. Clark divided his party into those who would accompany him to the Yellowstone River and those who would canoe downriver to Lewis's party. Sacagawea brought Clark the root of a plant that the natives ate, most likely nineleaf biscuitroot. He described it as looking and tasting like a carrot but of a pale yellow color. Lewis had collected a specimen on May 6, 1806.

Ordway sent three of his men ahead to hunt while he and the other man went on with the extra horses. Soon Ordway overtook the hunters, who had killed a deer, so he halted while they roasted a quarter of it along with its entrails. By noon they reached Clark's party at Camp Fortunate.

JULY 10, 1806. A cold night was followed by a frosty morning. Water standing in a basin had a layer of ice three-quarters of an inch thick. Clark had the canoes set in the river and loaded for the trip. Ordway noted that one canoe "of no account" was cut up for paddles and firewood, leaving six canoes for the downstream trip. At the same time the horses were collected and saddled with packs that bore items bound for the Yellowstone River. After breakfast the two groups separated, with Ordway leading the canoe party and Clark in charge of the mounted group going down the east side of the Beaverhead ("Jeffersons") River "into that butifull and extensive Vally open and fertile." The captain considered the valley as extending from Rattlesnake Cliffs, Beaverhead County, Montana (see August 10, 1805), north to the South Boulder River ("fraziers Creek"), Madison County, Montana (see August 1, 1805), and from ten to thirty miles wide and perhaps fifty miles long. In passing Rattlesnake Cliffs later in the day, Clark saw a number of the reptiles—"they were fierce." Nevertheless, Clark sang the praises of the country by noting its numerous streams, quantities of beavers and otters, and great numbers of deer and pronghorns. He also saw fifteen bighorn sheep feeding along the mountainsides.

At noon the land party halted to let the horses graze and have a meal; Clark called in the boat party. Ordway reported that the canoes were moving steadily with the current as the river widened and deepened. Clark decided to join the boats with his Yellowstone-bound baggage for the trip to Three Forks. He put Pryor in charge of the six men and horses of the land party—the same number that would accompany him to the Yellowstone ("Rochejhone") River. He ordered Pryor to keep pace with the canoes and join them at camp this evening. As they moved on Clark noticed that they passed "Six of my encampments assending"; those would be the captain's camps of August 11–16, 1805. The combined groups made camp near their "3000 Mile Island" of August 11, 1805, on the east bank of the Jefferson River, Beaverhead County. Ordway estimated that the boat party made ninety-seven miles this day.

JULY 11, 1806. Clark sent four of the best hunters in two canoes ahead to hunt until the rest of the party caught up. By eight o'clock Clark's canoe group caught up with the hunter Collins, who had killed one deer, and at noon they passed a camp of Pryor's land party near Beaverhead Rock, Madison County, Montana (see August 8, 1805). Facing a hard headwind, the going was difficult in the twisting Jefferson River. At six in the evening they passed the Ruby ("Phalanthrophy") River and by seven were at the Big Hole ("Wisdom") River, Beaverhead County, where the party had camped on August 6, 1805. Here Clark found a bayonet left by one of the men the previous year and the canoe that had been deposited there (see August 7, 1805). Clark directed that the boat be stripped of its nails and that paddles be made of its wood. The party camped here again on the east side of the Jefferson River, opposite the mouth of the Big Hole, about two miles northeast of Twin Bridges. Pryor's mounted party had left a deer on shore for them and had gone on ahead to camp. In the evening two more hunters, Gibson and Colter, came in with a "fat Buck" and five geese. During the day Clark viewed great numbers of beavers, also deer, young geese, sandhill cranes, and other birds.

JULY 12, 1806. Stripping the canoe left from last year of its nails and usable wood occupied the men until seven o'clock. After breakfast they set out, the canoes hastened along by the Jefferson River's strong current. Heavy winds made for hard work keeping the canoes from running in to shore. At about two o'clock Clark's canoe was driven in to shore by a sudden squall and lodged under a log projecting from the bank. Howard was at the stern, got caught in the action, and was injured. As they extricated themselves they were pushed by the swift current into some driftwood, where the canoe nearly turned over. After removing some baggage, the canoe righted, and they proceeded on without any real damage. Seeing their situation, the men in the other canoes tried to race to their aid but found it difficult to reach them through the thick brushes lining the shore. Ordway indicated that Clark fired his rifle to bring attention to their plight. At three o'clock they halted for a meal at Boulder River ("Fields Creek"), which they had encountered on August 1, 1805. Willard and Collins came in with two deer. After eating they moved on and camped near the spot of their camp of July 31, 1805. Clark did not indicate on which side of the Jefferson River they camped, but his party was in either Jefferson County or near the Madison-Gallatin county line, Montana. Clark killed four young geese, and Collins killed two beavers in the evening.

JULY 13, 1806. Clark's canoe party got an early start and moved swiftly to the mouth of the Madison River, Broadwater County,

Montana, and their camp of July 27, 1805. They arrived about noon and found that Pryor's land party had come in about an hour earlier. Those men had killed six deer and wounded a grizzly bear. Clark had the horses driven over to a site below the entrance of the Gallatin River to graze. He also had all the baggage for the Yellowstone River party removed from the canoes and set aside for packing on the horses. After eating, Ordway's party set out by water down the Missouri with instructions for the trip and carrying Clark's letter to Lewis. Clark enumerated his own party when they set out overland at five o'clock in an easterly direction; it consisted of Pryor, Shields, Shannon, Bratton, Labiche, Windsor, Hall, Gibson, Charbonneau, Sacagawea, Jean Baptiste, and York. He also commented on the poor condition of the forty-nine horses and a colt, some of which were hardly able to walk.

Starting so late in the day, Clark's party traveled only four to six miles and camped on the north side of the Gallatin River, Gallatin County, Montana, about a mile from Logan. As they moved along Clark noted the "butifull leavel plain Covered with low grass" but called the soil indifferent and covered with white rocks. He was passing light-colored limestone beds of the Mississippian Madison Group. To the northeast he viewed the Horseshoe Hills, and he saw elks, deer, pronghorns, wolves, beavers, otters, eagles, hawks, crows, and geese in passing. Looking ahead to the east and north he saw several roads leading to a gap in the mountains, but Sacagawea recommended a pathway to the south. She advocated crossing Bozeman Pass, known to her from childhood,. Clark praised her at this point by penning a rare reference to her as a guide: "The indian woman . . . has been of great Service to me as a pilot through this Country."

Ordway and his nine men—Collins, Colter, Cruzatte, Howard, Lepage, Potts, Weiser, Whitehouse, and Willard—got a head start and put the six canoes into the Missouri River, bound for a rendezvous with Lewis's party at the Great Falls, Cascade County, Montana. Facing a stiff wind, the men landed before nightfall. Ordway, the only journalist in this detachment, did not provide enough information to locate accurately the camp for the night. They were on the Missouri River, probably in Broadwater County, Montana.

JULY 14, 1806. Clark sent Shields ahead at an early hour to hunt for breakfast. Not long after setting out, Clark and party found Shields with a "large fat Buck." Crossing and recrossing the Gallatin River, they kept a southeasterly route through the plains in Gallatin County, Montana, and followed buffalo roads leading to Bozeman Pass. Clark called it an "intolerable rout," since beavers had dammed streams along the way, causing the party to ride through a muddy mess that slowed their progress. Here again Sacagawea proved helpful by suggesting a more accessible road to the pass. Although Clark was seeing "old Signs of buffalow," he now viewed only elks, deer, and pronghorns. Sacagawea informed Clark that in earlier years buffalo were abundant in these plains, but the Shoshones were reluctant to hunt the animals except on brief and fearful excursions. Their stronger enemies, like the Blackfeet, made such caution necessary. They had to satisfy themselves with what game and fish they could catch in the mountains. After lunch the riders moved on easterly to the forks of the East Gallatin River, near Bozeman, Gallatin County, crossed Bozeman Creek, and found the buffalo road that Sacagawea recommended. They followed that road to Kelly Creek, several miles east of Bozeman, and made camp, having come about twenty-seven miles. Considering the use of canoes on these streams, Clark conceded that beaver dams impeded much of the way but that they could be navigated with small boats. During the day York brought Clark a "Tobacco worm," probably a tobacco hornworm.

Ordway's party got an early start also. Due to heavy winds they halted at noon and were unable to go on, so two hunters went after game. The wind settled in the evening, so they were able to make a little more progress before camping in some undisclosed location. One of the hunters, Collins, did not join the party at camp.

JULY 15, 1806. After collecting their horses, the party got on their way by eight o'clock. Going in an easterly direction, they followed Kelly Creek, then crossed Jackson Creek and went through Bozeman Pass in the Bridger Range, passing from Gallatin County to Park County, Montana. Continuing to the east, the party followed Billman Creek and reached the Yellowstone (*"rochejhone"*) River at Livingston, Park County, at two o'clock. Clark calculated that he had traveled eighteen miles from the fork of East Gallatin River to the Yellowstone on "an excellent high dry firm road with very incoiderable hills." From the Three Forks of the Missouri River to the Yellowstone, he put it at forty-eight miles. Here at the Yellowstone they spent about three hours to rest, graze the horses, cook, and have lunch. Staying on the northwest side of the river, the party followed an old buffalo road and crossed the Shields River, named after Shields of the party and retaining the name, in Park County. They continued on another three miles and camped on the north side of the Yellowstone in Park County. Stones and gravel along their path created a hard road and sore feet for horses. Otherwise, Clark counted the mounts in good condition. The rocky road was likely formed from alluvial and slopewash deposits.

The captain took a paragraph to describe the topography of the Yellowstone River valley. He saw it as coming out between the Gallatin Range to the west and the Absaroka Range on the east. He also viewed other mountains in his sweeping view from the valley floor: the Beartooth Mountains, Bridger Range, and Crazy Mountains. And he listed cottonwoods, willows, rosebushes, rushes, and honeysuckles along the river's banks, while noting "low grass" and "coarse grass" (probably blue grama, buffalograss, and other species) along with basin wild rye of the shortgrass prairie he had entered once more. He saw no trees large enough to build canoes that could carry more than three men, and all were scarcely suitable for his purposes.

Setting out at daylight, Ordway's men soon found Collins, who had killed three deer. While they halted to eat, Collins got another deer, Cruzatte a pronghorn, and Colter a mountain lion, a deer, and a rattlesnake. Probably picking them along the way, the sergeant found currants ample and ripe. After camping at a mosquito-infested site, Collins killed four elks.

JULY 16, 1806. Labiche was ordered ahead to get a "fat Elk or Buffalow" for the party, while the rest of the men rounded up the horses that had scattered; they did not get away until nine this morning. Not far into the trip, Clark spotted a buffalo bull and sent Shannon to kill it. In addition to its meat the men used the skins to make moccasins for the horses' feet, damaged by the rough road. Two horses' feet were worn smooth nearly to the quick. The buffalo-hide moccasins seemed to give them some relief. Keeping an eye out for trees large enough to build canoes, the party traveled about ten miles, crossed the Yellowstone River by way of an island, and found a place to graze the horses, rest themselves, and have lunch. The hunter Labiche was still out. About him Clark viewed the abundant wildlife of the plains—a gang of nearly two hundred elks and perhaps as many pronghorns. He chased a grizzly bear for a couple of miles before giving up. Not long after lunch Labiche rejoined the group with part of a fat elk.

The party recrossed the Yellowstone at a convenient point and made camp just below the mouth of Little Timber Creek, Sweet Grass County, Montana, called "Grape Creek" on an expedition map. Clark's course and distance tables registered twenty-six miles for the day. While Clark viewed immense numbers of elks on the opposite shore and a river bustling with young geese, one of the men, perhaps Labiche, brought a fish that was new to him. Clark provided enough detail to identify it tentatively as a mountain sucker; if he was correct, this was its first scientific description. The captain also wrote about the "perpendicular Straters . . . [of] a dark freestone." He was observing sandstone of the Livingston Formation and Eagle Sandstone but apparently not viewing perpendicular strata, which are unknown in the area. He may have been seeing near-vertical igneous dikes to the north. He also listed blooming plants, such as hemp dogbane ("Silkgrass"), sunflowers, and an unidentifiable species he called "Wild indigo." But still no cottonwoods large enough for canoes, so Clark resigned himself to continue the search. The rapidity of the Yellowstone made the use of unstable buffalo-hide bullboats impractical and unsafe.

Ordway's party made good progress until heavy headwinds forced them to lay by at the Gates of the Mountains (see July 19, 1805). Waiting for the winds to subside, the men made repairs to the canoes and then were able to pass through the gates in midafternoon. They viewed numbers of mountain goats and elks, and Collins got a fawn elk and two goats. They camped below Little Prickly

Pear Creek ("ordways river"), Lewis and Clark County, Montana. The sergeant here mentioned one of the few expedition place-names on his detached trip.

JULY 17, 1806. Without covering to protect them, the rain overnight "wet us all," Clark wrote. After collecting the horses the party set out, soon passing streams on opposite sides of the Missouri that Clark called "*Rivers across*," today's Big Timber Creek on the north and Boulder River on the south in the vicinity of Big Timber, Sweet Grass County, Montana. Within a few miles they reached a similar situation with Sweet Grass ("Otter River") Creek and Lower Deer Creek ("Beaver R"), near Greycliff. Below the entrance of Lower Deer Creek the party halted to eat and let horses graze. Again the hunt for trees suitable for making canoes was unsuccessful. Limber pines, Rocky Mountain junipers, and the ubiquitous cottonwoods were all too small.

As they continued along the Yellowstone, Clark noticed that buffalo and deer numbers were increasing, while elks were not as plentiful. The captain named a creek for Bratton of the party, "Brattens Ck.," now Bridger Creek. In a small bottom near Work Creek the captain saw an "Indian fort," which was built of logs and tightly formed in a circular pattern about fifty feet in diameter. The entrance faced the river and was guarded by defensive works. Sacagawea told him that war parties built such structures for safety from enemies who outnumbered them. Shoshones used them to guard against attacks by Hidatsas, Crows, and other better-armed adversaries. The party made camp on the north side of the Yellowstone a mile or two below the mouth of Hump ("Weasel") Creek, in either Sweet Grass or Stillwater County.

Making an early start on a clear morning, Ordway's party continued their boat journey down the Missouri River. Collins and Colter killed two mountain goats, removed the skins, and saved the skins and bones for the captains. Some of the canoes were nearly swamped due to heavy winds and high waves, so they delayed at Half-Breed Rapids for the winds to cease. By evening they were able to get underway again and camped about five miles below the rapids in a grove of cottonwood trees in Cascade

County, Montana. Along the way Ordway viewed large numbers of bighorn sheep.

JULY 18, 1806. About to set out, the men watched two buffalo bulls come near the camp. They got off several shots, but the bulls swam the river and collapsed on the opposite shore. The party continued their route along the Yellowstone, crossing White Beaver ("Muddy") Creek, Stillwater County, Montana, where Clark found golden and wild black currants ripe and delicious. To the southwest he could see the Absaroka Range, Beartooth Mountains, Granite Range, and other highlands in the vicinity of the Yellowstone Plateau. Far to the east he viewed the Pryor Mountains. Sand, gravel, and cobbles filled the bottoms of the Yellowstone River, while the "dark brown" earth was either organic-rich material or weathered soil of the dark-colored Tertiary-Cretaceous Livingston Formation. Beyond the river lay the "open wavering plains." Before noon Clark noticed smoke rising from the south-southeast and decided that it must be the work of Crow Indians, who may have detected them and wanted to meet to trade. Another possibility was that they were signaling friends to be on guard against the explorers.

Locating a good spot at noontime, the party stopped again to eat and graze the horses. Shields killed a "fat Buck," on which the party dined. They delayed here about three hours and then renewed their march. Shields got another animal, this time a buffalo, which caused the party to halt earlier in the day than usual. The meat turned out to be tainted and of little use. It was a day of accidents. Charbonneau's horse tripped in a badger hole and threw the interpreter over its head. The man was beat up a bit, with bruises on his hip, shoulder, and face. In attempting to mount his horse, Gibson fell on a snag, which penetrated nearly two inches into his thigh. Clark declared it a very bad and painful wound and dressed it appropriately. Somewhat out of order, the captain named a creek passed the previous day, Upper Deer Creek, as "*Thy snag'd* Creek." The party camped a few miles west of Columbus, Stillwater County, and above the mouth of the Stillwater River. Clark estimated that they had come twenty-six miles.

It was a clear, cool, windy morning for Ordway and party, and they had a gentle current to carry them forward on the Missouri. In spite of large herds of buffalo, it was three deer that Collins killed. The party passed the Smiths River, Cascade County, Montana (see July 15, 1805), and stopped nearby to camp and hunt buffalo. It turned out to be too late for hunting, but not too late for mosquitoes and flies to irritate the men's faces and eyes and cause swelling with their stinging bites.

JULY 19, 1806. Clark was up early to dress Gibson's wound. Excruciating pain kept the private awake during the night, and the discomfort extended from the puncture in his thigh to his hip and knee. Still not finding timber large enough to build a canoe and feeling the pressure of time to reach the mouth of the Yellowstone for the rendezvous with Lewis's party, Clark decided to make a litter for Gibson if he was not able to ride. The captain had the strongest and gentlest horse prepared with blankets and skins to give the most comfortable ride possible. It worked. They went on for about nine miles, passing the Stillwater ("Rose bud") River in the march, and then stopped to give Gibson some relief and the horses some pasture. Gibson's leg had become numb during the trip but was still extremely painful. Clark sent Shields to look for suitable trees for canoes and to hunt for wild ginger to make a poultice for Gibson's wound. Shields rejoined the party later without news of big trees or sight of wild ginger. The man had a bit of an adventure when two grizzlies chased him. He was able to get off some shots from horseback, but with no apparent results. But he did get away.

Reporting bluffs of a "darkish yellow earth" on the south side, Clark was viewing material formed principally of the Virgelle Member of the Upper Cretaceous Eagle Sandstone. He was tantalized that trees were gaining size as he traveled but large enough for only very small canoes. The captain was amazed that grasshoppers eaten every sprig of grass on the north side of the river and looked to be moving upriver. During travel in the after part of the day, Gibson's injury became so painful that he could not sit on a horse. Clark delegated Pryor and another man to stay with him in the shade of a tree for an hour or so and then come on to the camp for the night. About four miles farther on Clark found a place with big timber and good grass and set up camp on the north side of the Yellowstone River southwest of Park City, Stillwater County, having come about eighteen miles. They would remain here until July 24, at a spot that has become known as Canoe Camp. Not entirely satisfied with the size of the trees, Clark took Shields and went hunting for better ones. Returning at dark, he found Pryor with Gibson and the results of the efforts of the hunters (including Labiche)—seven elks and four deer. Clark had wounded a buffalo soon after the party arrived in camp, and during the day hunters had killed two deer and a pronghorn. Also while he was absent looking for trees, Charbonneau had spotted an Indian in the highlands to the south, perhaps from the same area that Clark had seen smoke on July 18.

Ordway's party had an uneventful morning. Hunters killed four buffalo and a buck deer, so the party took the best of the meat and continued down the Missouri. At three o'clock they arrived at the White Bear Islands camp and joined Gass's party. From this point both Ordway and Gass's entries are given with Lewis's, until August 12, when all reunited.

JULY 20, 1806. Clark placed new dressing on Gibson's wound and noted improvement. He sent Pryor and Shields ("good judges of timber") downriver six or eight miles to look for trees larger than they were finding near camp; they were to return by noon. He also sent Labiche, Charbonneau, and Hall to skin and take some meat from the elks that Labiche had killed yesterday. They returned with only one skin since wolves had ravaged the rest. Finally, he sent two men in search of wood suitable for axe handles; they found chokecherry limbs that would serve the purpose. Pryor and Shields were back by eleven thirty, having traveled nearly twelve miles without finding a tree any better than the ones near camp. Clark decided to work with what he had. He would make two canoes out of the largest trees, lash them together for stability, and be able to get all the party with baggage aboard. With the trees selected, Clark had the three axe heads sharpened, fitted to new handles, and put to work until dark overcame the axemen. From the trees the party would have canoes twenty-eight feet in length, sixteen to eighteen inches deep, and from sixteen to twenty-four inches wide. Other explorers were not idle. Some men were detailed as tailors to clothe a nearly naked party. Hunters brought in hides and meat: Shields killed a deer and a buffalo, Shannon a fawn and a buffalo, and York an elk. One of the buffalo provided especially good meat, some of which was sliced thin and set out to dry. Since the horses were suffering with sore feet and were fatigued from the hard march of the last several days, Clark decided to let them rest for a few days as the party prepared for river travel. There was also to be an overland detachment bound for the Mandans, and they would need well-rested mounts for the trip.

JULY 21, 1806. The party rose to find half their horses missing. Clark sent Shannon, Bratton, and Charbonneau after them. Charbonneau went up the Yellowstone, Shannon down, and Bratton searched the area about camp. Charbonneau and Bratton returned at midmorning with negative reports, while Shannon took a fourteen-mile trek downriver, not getting back until nighttime, but was equally unsuccessful. Shannon reported finding an Indian lodge on his trip. It was probably a Crow sun-dance lodge where the traditional ritual was performed. Clark began to become apprehensive that Indians had stolen the party's horses. He thought perhaps that the smoke he had seen in days past was related to this incident. In consequence of this idea, he put the party on alert and sent three men to guard the horses. For some unknown reason the horses were so frightened by the men that they scattered into the woods, and the men returned to camp.

While some of the men worked at building canoes, Clark sent two others after a "fat Cow." Within three hours they were back with the meat. Gibson's wound was healing—so much so that Clark anticipated he would be able to join the overland detachment to the Mandans. The captain was struck by the beauty and abundance of the plains but found the soil thin and stony. He was seeing the results of a semiarid climate, steep slopes, and winds combining to retard soil formation and stones from the Yellowstone River terrace gravel. Prickly pears abounded, as did great herds of buffalo, with wolves, their "constant attendants," trailing the shaggy beasts. Pronghorns

ical in form, about sixty feet in diameter at the base, with twenty poles some forty-five feet long leaning toward the center, and covered with bushes. The poles were topped off with eagle feathers, and also with carved or shaped wood items. For Clark the area was in a beautiful setting on the cottonwood island where wild rye, bluegrass, and sweetgrass covered the rich earth. He mentioned that Indians braided the sweetgrass and tied it around their necks for its pleasant, vanilla scent.

After lunch Clark decided to move on, since Pryor had not arrived. At Blue Creek ("Horse Creek" on expedition maps), near Billings, Yellowstone County, Clark met Pryor's party with the horses. Pryor had had a difficult time catching up. Unmounted horses, all trained to hunt buffalo, would go chasing every small herd they passed and delay the men while they gathered the runaways. The sergeant's solution was to send one man ahead to scare off buffalo, so the detachment could pass without incident. Once together, Clark had the horses driven across the river and Pryor's group ferried to the east side. Nonswimmer Hall asked to go with Pryor and the land party but pointed out that he did not have riding clothes. Clark honored the soldier's request and gave him a couple of shirts, a pair of leather leggings, and three pairs of moccasins. Moving easily now, the water party soon reached Dry Creek ("Pryers river"), coming in from the east at Billings. On the west side Clark killed "the fatest Buck I every Saw." Shields killed a deer, and "my man" York killed a buffalo bull for its tongue and marrow bones. Clark's language failed him in describing the abundant wildlife in view: "for me to mention or give an estimate of the differant Spcies of wild animals on this river particularly Buffalow, Elk Antelopes & Wolves would be incredible. I shall therefore be silent on the Subject further. So it is we have a great abundance of the best of meat." Making nearly seventy miles, the river party camped a little below Dry Creek. Nearby the captain noticed "yellowish Gritty Stone" and dark rocks. He was seeing the Virgelle Member of Eagle Sandstone and outcrops of Clagett Shale.

JULY 25, 1806. The party put in three hours on the Yellowstone before Clark called a halt to shoot a fat buffalo and have breakfast. They delayed an hour and a half, giving Shields time to kill two deer. Not long after returning to the river a rain storm came up accompanied by heavy winds, which drove them to shore. They built a makeshift shelter and started a fire to keep dry. The rain stopped about noon, but the wind continued until after two o'clock. Back on the water for another two hours, the party arrived at a rock formation that Clark called "Pompy's Tower" after the baby Jean Baptiste, nicknamed "Pomp." In his history Biddle changed the name to a classical reference, "Pompey's Pillar," now altered to "Pompeys Pillar," near the village of Pompeys Pillar, Yellowstone County, Montana. The sandstone formation is composed of the uppermost Cretaceous Hell Creek Formation. Clark estimated it to be two hundred feet high and four hundred paces around at the base. Indians had carved animal figures on the rock face, so Clark engraved his name and the date as well. Clark's inscription, since deepened and protected, remains the only surviving physical evidence of the expedition on the route. Clark climbed to the top and had an extensive view of the Yellowstone valley. A stream just coming into the Yellowstone from the west Clark christened "Baptiests Creek," today's Pompeys Pillar Creek. After his jaunt he penned a positive assessment of "this delightfull prospect of the extensive Country around, and the emence herds of Buffalow, Elk and wolves in which it abounded."

Seeing a herd of forty bighorn sheep, Clark fired on them and killed two. The canoes landed so the captain could retrieve them, which proved difficult, as he had to crawl through narrow crevices along almost inaccessible cliffs. Unsuccessful in getting his sheep, he killed two more along the way but did not get the large buck he sought. Clark was also able to pry loose the "rib of a fish" that was cemented onto the face of the rock he was climbing. He described it as about three feet in length, although a part of the end appeared to have broken off. The captain had probably found the fossilized rib from a terrestrial dinosaur. After getting the bighorn on board the party moved on and camped earlier than intended due to heavy, dark clouds and the appearance of violent winds. They camped just below the entrance of Sand Creek ("Shannons River," after Shannon of the party), which meets the Yellowstone from the south in Yellowstone County, a few miles east of Pompeys Pillar. The wind and rains came as predicted, but it was buffalo that kept the party awake. "The bulls keep Such a grunting nois which is very loud and disagreeable Sound that we are compelled to Scear them away before we can Sleep."

JULY 26, 1806. Canoeing the swift Yellowstone River, the party passed Cow Gulch, given as "Halls creek" on expedition maps after Hall of the party, and "handsome Islands" covered with cottonwood trees, eventually arriving at the Bighorn River, flowing in from the south and forming the Yellowstone-Treasure county line, Montana. The party made camp on the Bighorn's east side in Treasure County, having come about sixty-two miles. With Labiche, Clark walked up the Bighorn for about seven miles to Tullock ("Muddy") Creek. He penned a rather long description of the river, calling it darker and muddier than the Yellowstone. It gains these characteristics by flowing across a large exposure of shales of the Colorado Group. Clark had been informed by Hidatsas and others that the river came out of the Rocky Mountains near the Platte River and passed by the Bighorn ("Coat Nor or Black") Mountains. The main branches of the Platte rise in the Colorado Rockies and some tributaries of those streams are relatively close to the upper Bighorn River in Wyoming. Clark considered the area inhabited by a "great number of roveing Indians," principally the Crow Indians. The captain got back to camp after dark. Although he had killed a deer, he was so tired that he went to bed without eating.

JULY 27, 1806. Before leaving camp Clark marked his name on a cottonwood tree with red paint. Here the Yellowstone was wide, four to six hundred yards, and dotted with islands and sandbars. And it was crowded with buffalo and elks at its edges. Clark declared the elks so tame that the party could come within twenty or thirty paces without alarming them. Pronghorns, bighorn sheep, and deer were less numerous. At fifteen miles they passed Akali ("Elk") Creek, Treasure County, Montana, coming in from the north, and then halted at Muggins ("Little wolf" or "Winsors") Creek, where hunters killed four buffalo, had breakfast, and saved as much meat as possible. With some regret Clark took "leave of the view of the tremendious chain of Rocky Mountains white with Snow in view of which I have been Since the 1st of May last." The captain killed a "large fat buck elk" near camp and was close to being bit by a rattlesnake. The camp was near the mouth of Big Porcupine Creek ("Little Wolf River") and about eight miles west of Forsyth, Rosebud County, Montana. They had traveled about eighty miles. Clark described the Yellowstone below the Bighorn as being much like the Missouri River, except its islands were more numerous and the current swifter. Above it was "yellowish white" and much clearer than the Missouri. He also penned brief notes of the river's plant life, topography, and geologic features.

JULY 28, 1806. "Glideing down this Smooth Stream," the party passed many islands and a number of small streams. At six miles they passed Big Porcupine Creek ("Little Wolf river"), west of Forsyth, Rosebud County, Montana, coming in from the north. Noting other streams along the way, Clark and party eventually came to Rosebud Creek on the south side of the Yellowstone River, which the captain called "Little Big Horn River." It is not the historic "Little Bighorn," a tributary of the Bighorn River passed on July 26. Leaving the Cretaceous Hell Creek Formation behind, Clark began to notice "Straters of Coal in the banks on either side." He was now entering an area underlain by the coal-bearing (lignite) Tertiary (Paleocene) Tullock Member of the Fort Union Formation. The party camped at the upper end of a small island after traveling about seventy-three miles. The camp was on the north side, perhaps opposite the mouth of Graveyard Creek, Rosebud County, or just east of the Rosebud-Custer county line. Confusingly, on one of the expedition maps Clark labeled the stream "Mar shas kap River," a term the captain got from either the Mandans or Hidatsas and meaning "rosebud." In spite of abundant elks along the banks Shields killed two deer and Labiche killed a pronghorn during the day. Clark saw a bobcat lazing on a log in the river.

JULY 29, 1806. Rain in the night was accompanied by thunder, lightning, and violent northeast winds. The winds slowed the party's pace along the Yellowstone River in Custer County, Montana.

Late in the evening they arrived at Tongue River, as Clark called it and as it is known today; at its mouth is Miles City. Clark also added another name for it that he had learned from the Mandans or Hidatsas, "*Lazeka*," meaning "tongue." A little below the mouth of the Tongue River the party made camp on the Yellowstone's north side after a trip of about forty-four miles. Someone caught three catfish and a softshell turtle in the evening. Clark got his first mule deer since returning to the plains either this day or the next.

JULY 30, 1806. After an early start the party was slowed by shallow ("Shoals") waters on the Yellowstone at twelve miles into the trip. The shoals continued for about six miles, finally ending in a very shallow part that compelled the men to move the canoes by hand, fearing that hidden rocks would wreck the boats. Clark called it the worst place on the river, and he named it "Buffalow Sholes," having seen so many of the animals in the river bottoms at this point. The shoals are in Custer County, Montana, near the mouth of Muster ("dry") Creek on the north side, where the party stopped for breakfast. Clark compared the Yellowstone at this point to the Missouri River, where seemingly dry creeks could carry immense amounts of water and mud from the plains in a downpour.

After breakfast they moved on and at twenty miles below Buffalo Shoals they passed a rapid with relative ease, having found a good channel on the north side. Clark called it "Bear rapid," since a bear was sitting on a rock in the middle of the rapid as he passed. The rapid is in Prairie County just below the mouth of Custer Creek, Clark's "York's dry R." after his slave, coming from the north. A violent storm forced them to shore just below the rapid, where they took shelter in an Indian lodge. When the rain and wind ceased the party moved on for another seven miles to the entrance of a large stream, Powder River. Clark's named it "red Stone" after the red clinker in the river. He also called it "War har sah" on an expedition map, an Indian name presumably learned from the Mandans or Hidatsas meaning "powder." Not finding a good campsite at Powder River, the party crossed to the north side and camped below the mouth of Crooked Creek, Prairie County. They had come about forty-eight miles. Before crossing, hunters in the party killed two fat buffalo cows and took as much meat as the canoes could handle. Gibson was now walking, so he took a stroll in the evening and killed a pronghorn.

JULY 31, 1806. Bellowing buffalo kept Clark awake a good part of the night. One group crossed the river near camp and had the captain worried that they might damage the canoes. Fortunately his fears were not realized. Setting out at sunrise, the party soon passed through a rapid that Clark named "wolf rapid" after an animal seen nearby. It is near the mouth of Conns Coulee, about four miles southwest of Terry, Prairie County, Montana. Observing the Little Sheep and Big Sheep Mountains to the northwest, Clark presumed them composed of colored earth and coal with little rock. Various members of the Fort Union Formation are exposed in those hills, which include shale with coal beds. As they proceeded on the party passed Cherry Creek on the north, which Clark called "little wolf or *Sa-a-shah* River," the latter being a name he got from the Hidatsas, meaning "wolf." On an expedition map Clark labeled it "Shabonas River" after Charbonneau. Beyond that they landed at O'Fallon Creek on the south about a miles west of Fallon, Prairie County. Without naming it in his journal, Clark called it "Oak Tar pon er River" and "Coal River" on an expedition map. Its modern name honors Benjamin O'Fallon, Clark's nephew, and was bestowed some years after Clark's travels. Given the confusion between Clark's journal and maps, it seems that a stream that the captain labeled "Gibsons deep river" on an expedition map is Cabin Creek, Dawson County. As the party was landing to set up camp for the night Clark saw a huge grizzly feasting on a dead buffalo. The men fired two shots at it, but it walked away. On coming to shore the captain got off two more shots, but to no effect. It was bleeding profusely but darkness prevented following its trail. Camp was in Dawson County, about seven miles southwest of Glendive. The party made about sixty-six miles.

AUGUST 1, 1806. The party found it slow going due to high winds and choppy water. With rain pelting them unrelentingly all day, Clark sighed, "My Situation a very disagreeable one. in an open

Canoe wet and without the possibility of keeping my Self dry." The country was much the same as he had been passing for some days back: the Yellowstone was muddy and dotted with sandbars, while trees such as limber pines, Rocky Mountain junipers, and green ash hugged the shorelines of streams flowing into the Yellowstone. At two o'clock they had to pull over on an island near Thirteenmile ("Buffalow Crossing") Creek, Dawson County, and wait for buffalo crossing the river. While the party waited more than an hour viewing the crowded passage, Clark estimated that the herd passed over an island nearly half a mile in width with a quarter mile of the river on either side. Taking four men with him, Clark and his hunters killed four fat cows and took what meat the small boats could carry. Making about forty-five miles, the party camped on an island near the north side in Dawson County, Montana. On the opposite side in Wibaux County, Cottonwood Creek enters the Yellowstone.

AUGUST 2, 1806. The party was glad to get underway and rid themselves of the pestering mosquitoes. The Yellowstone was its usual self—wide, muddy, island strewn, and tree lined. On the northwest side the country rose to a low plain and extended for a great distance, while to the southeast Clark saw high, rugged hills where bighorn sheep ranged. At about eight o'clock the captain saw a grizzly ("of the large vicious Species") rise to full height on a sandbar, then plunge into the river and swim toward them, perhaps picking up the scent of meat on the canoes. Riflemen put three shots into it, and it swam away, badly wounded. In the evening another bear came close to the canoes and Clark shot it in the head. The men hauled it on shore and it proved to be "an old Shee" bear with teeth worn smooth, but the largest female bear Clark had seen. For fifteen or twenty minutes Clark watched two wolves pursue a doe elk, which finally tried unsuccessfully to escape into woods. Another large herd of buffalo almost stopped the party again, but canoeists were able to slip between two gangs. After about sixteen miles the party came to Charbonneau Creek, McKenzie County, North Dakota. Clark may have initially called it "Jo. Fields" Creek, after Joseph Field of the party, but then changed it to "Ibex Creek." His maps and journal entries shift between the names. The party settled into camp with their old enemies the mosquitoes just above the mouth of Charbonneau Creek. They made about eighty-six miles.

AUGUST 3, 1806. Mosquitoes harassed the party throughout night and no one got much sleep. "Those tormenting insects found their way into My beare [bier netting] and tormented me the whole night," Clark revealed, allowing him less than an hour of decent sleep. The party passed Charbonneau ("Jo. Field's") Creek, McKenzie County, North Dakota, just two miles ahead, where Clark saw bighorn sheep in bluffs above the creek. He went after them but mosquitoes were so thick that he could not get a clear sighting to shoot, so he returned to the canoes. Later he spied ewes, yearlings, and lambs with a ram nearby and sent Labiche to get the bighorn male. The soldier soon came back with the specimen; it was smaller than others that Clark had examined, but he decided to keep it anyway. Clark now had skins and bones of a ram, a ewe, and a yearling of the species. This all happened early in the morning, since the party reached the mouth of the Yellowstone at the Missouri River, McKenzie County, at about eight o'clock, having come some eight miles. They set up camp at the meeting of the two rivers, where they had also camped on April 26, 1805. Clark shot a large buck elk, had it skinned, and had the hide laid out to dry. The captain had the canoes unloaded and everything spread out to dry. A great many articles were wet, and nearly all the meat was spoiled and useless. The tainted meat was thrown in the river. More regrettable was the loss of several skins that were to serve as clothing for the remainder of the trip.

Clark finished the day's entry with an overview of his trek from the Rocky Mountains to the mouth of the Yellowstone, a trip he calculated to be 837 miles. In fact, much of the entry is in Lewis's hand, obviously inserted by him after the captains reunited on August 12. Also from internal evidence it appears that Clark wrote all his entries from this date to August 12 after the reunion on that date. Here they described the nature of the Yellowstone and the country through which it passed. The particulars can be found in Clark's daily entries during the time under review. The captains provided their conceptions of the sources and flows of western waters. "This delighfull river from indian information," Lewis wrote, adding that it had its most distant sources in proximity with the Rio Grande ("North river"). In fact, the Rio Grande rises in south central Colorado, hundreds of miles southeast of the sources of the Yellowstone. The men also believed that its western sources were connected with the Willamette ("Multnomah") River, which heads in western Oregon. The Yellowstone River rises in northwestern Wyoming in the Absaroka Range. The captains also heard from Indians that a good road followed the Yellowstone to its farthest source and from there it was but a short distance to Spanish settlements. Those settlements in New Mexico were a good deal farther than Lewis imagined. They also learned that there was a considerable falls on the river, today's Falls of the Yellowstone in Yellowstone National Park, Wyoming, south of where Clark struck the river. And like all rivers that come out of the Rocky Mountains, the captains proclaimed, the Yellowstone abounded in beavers and otters. They also believed that a trading post on the river would attract Shoshones, who would fear visiting a post on the Missouri that might bring them into conflict with the better-armed Blackfeet. It might also attract Indian nations of the Snake and Columbia Rivers.

AUGUST 4, 1806. Men working at converting animal hides to clothing were so aggravated by mosquitoes that they could not stay at the task. Hunters in the river bottoms were also tormented. The only escape seemed to be on open sandbars under high winds, which drove the pests away. Nights were particularly agonizing with nothing to shield them from the bites but worn blankets. The baby Jean Baptiste was particularly tormented, since his face was repeatedly bitten and much swollen. Given this nearly unendurable situation and the lack of buffalo nearby, Clark decided to move the party to a better camp. So the canoes were reloaded, Clark tied a note to Lewis on a pole to let him know of the move, and at about five o'clock in the afternoon the party set out down the Missouri. They camped on a sandbar on the northwest side of the Missouri, but due to Clark's lack of course and distance material and his abbreviated descriptions of the terrain it is difficult to determine the campsite's location.

It was a few miles below the mouth of the Yellowstone, probably in Williams County, North Dakota.

AUGUST 5, 1806. This camp proved no better than the last— mosquitoes were as troublesome as before. Clark suffered a sleepless night, as his enemies found holes in his netting and swarmed in to bite him. The party got underway as early as possible. Irritants all night, the mosquitoes even got in the captain's way as he tried to shoot a bighorn sheep. They were so thick on his rifle that he could not get a clear shot and missed his aim. By ten o'clock the wind had come up enough to drive the pests away, and the party found a sandbar that looked promising for a camp. Here hunters killed two buck elks and a deer and saved the best meat. Finding no signs of buffalo, the captain decided to move to another spot for the night's camp and better hunting opportunities. At four o'clock they set out again. Within a few miles Clark spied a grizzly on a sandbar and sent a hunter after it. The bear plunged into the river as the hunter approached, but he was able to kill it. It turned out to be one of the largest female bears that Clark had encountered, which made hauling it to shore very difficult. With a light breeze to drive away mosquitoes, the party established camp on the south side of the Missouri above Little Muddy River in McKenzie County near Williston, Williams County, North Dakota.

AUGUST 6, 1806. Before midnight, high winds, sharp lightening, and loud thunder came up, while hard rain doused the party for about two hours. After setting out in the morning Clark spotted a female bighorn sheep and had Labiche shoot and skin it. Later a grizzly plunged into the river and, perhaps mistaking them for a buffalo, headed for the canoes. Clark had the party be still and waited until the bear got with forty yards of them before turning. Riflemen tried to shoot it, but the bear was able to get to shore in spite of being badly wounded. Going on an undisclosed distance, the party pulled over to the south side of the Missouri beyond the mouth of the Little Muddy ("White earth") River, McKenzie County, North Dakota., to dry animal skins and the party's bedding. It seems that the party then went some distance father and made camp on the north side in Williams County. In the area Clark saw where Indians had been digging for Indian breadroots within the previous week. Clark took a walk in the evening and killed five deer while a man with him killed two. Four others were killed during the course of the day but only two were worthy of keeping. Clark attributed their poor condition to mosquitoes, who so tormented the grazing animals that they could not feed in peace.

AUGUST 7, 1806. Rain after daylight soaked the party again. They waited out the rain until eleven o'clock, when it eased for a short time. They loaded up and got underway but rain followed them off and on throughout the day. About six o'clock they landed on a sandbar on the south side and set up camp, where they remained until August 9. With little help from Clark, the camp is difficult to locate other than to note that it was above Tobacco Garden Creek, McKenzie County, North Dakota (see August 9).

AUGUST 8, 1806. Shields and Gibson went out early for a hunt. At eight o'clock Pryor, Shannon, Hall, and Windsor came by river to the camp in the bullboats they had constructed from buffalo hides. Pryor and party had separated from Clark on July 24 on an overland mission to the Mandans. With no journalist among them, we have only Clark's account of Pryor's review of their journey. The night of July 25–26 they camped in a spot that provided good grazing for their horses; it was probably several miles west of Hardin, Bighorn County, Montana. The next morning all their horses were gone, and Indian tracks were obvious around the camp. The men tracked the Indians for a distance, but with no chance of catching them, they returned to camp. Being in the country of the Crows— notorious horse thieves—they are the most likely culprits.

Pryor's men loaded all the baggage they could carry and headed back to the Yellowstone, which they reached at Pompeys Pillar, missing Clark's group by a day. There they killed a buffalo bull and constructed two bullboats such as they had seen among the Arikaras and Mandans. Although one bullboat could carry six to eight men, Pryor thought it prudent to have their guns and ammunition divided between two boats for safety. On the night of July 26 Pryor was bitten through his hand by a wolf, which then went after Windsor, but Shannon shot it. Pryor's hand had now nearly healed. On an expedition map Clark labeled one small river in honor of the sergeant, "Pryors river," now Pryor Creek, Yellowstone County. At the mouth of the Yellowstone Pryor found Clark's note for Lewis and, thinking that Lewis was ahead, brought it with him. Clark did not seem concerned, as he was certain that Lewis would recognize that Clark had gone on. Pryor, anxious to catch up with Clark, had left his saddlebags and papers at the last camp. Clark sent the sergeant with Bratton to retrieve the items, which they did and returned in the evening. With horses gone, Clark knew that he had little to barter when they reached the Mandans and Hidatsas, so he sent the recently returned Shields and Gibson downriver in a bullboat to kill as many animals as possible. The captain knew he could use the hides for trading at the villages. Shannon was sent across the Missouri with the same orders.

AUGUST 9, 1806. The party loaded and launched the canoes and traveled about six miles to link up with hunters Shields and Gibson, who had gone ahead the night before. They had acquired five deer, two of which Clark considered in good order. The party stayed a bit to have breakfast, then moved on a few miles. Getting off the boats here, Clark walked through an open bottom and killed three deer, which he judged of poor quality. He was in the vicinity of two creeks on either side of the Missouri bearing the same modern names, Tobacco Garden ("Pumic Stone") Creek, McKenzie County, North Dakota, and Tobacco Garden ("Halls Strand") Creek, Williams County. Completing his trek, he found the canoes had been waiting for him downriver for nearly two hours. Sacagawea had picked gooseberries and brought some to Clark. They would be either hawthorn or bristly gooseberries, here at their southern limits on the Missouri River in North Dakota. She also gave him golden currants, which the captain said the engagés called "Indian Current." Late in the evening the party located a camp for the night some miles above Tobacco Garden Creek, McKenzie County. Clark took a walk and killed an elk. He thought it the largest buck and fattest animal they had killed on the expedition trip. He had the meat brought back to camp, cut up, and readied to dry the next day.

AUGUST 10, 1806. The elk meat of the day before was hung on poles to dry, and hunters spread out across country to secure more. Only Shields was successful; he got a mule deer and a pronghorn. A hard wind from the east blew in on the party all day, and they got a bit of rain. Clark worked at finishing his maps of the Yellowstone River. He also copied Lewis's morphological notes on the pin cherry from his entry of August 12, again showing that Clark was writing his entries some days after the fact. Near camp the men dug up a great number of Indian breadroots, which they boiled and ate with their meat. Clark noted that Indians dried the root, pounded it, and used it in soups. He thought it insipid.

AUGUST 11, 1806. After an early start the party stopped at ten o'clock on a sandbar for breakfast. They delayed here a couple of hours to dry elk meat. Underway again, Clark spotted a canoe near the shore and had the party pull over to that spot. There they found the camp of two hunters from Illinois, Joseph Dickson (or Dixon) and Forrest Hancock. Lewis would encounter them the next day. Dickson had lived in Pennsylvania and Tennessee before moving to Cahokia, Illinois, in 1802. Thereafter he met Hancock, who had hunted considerably in Missouri. The two had started up the Missouri River in August 1804, spent the winter with the Teton Sioux, and got into a scuffle with the Indians that resulted in a rifle wound for Dickson. Clark also learned that they had met the keelboat party (see April 7, 1805) from Fort Mandan near the Kansas River carrying the Arikara chief, perhaps Too Né, on his ill-fated journey to Washington DC (see October 12 and November 6, 1804). They also gave the disquieting news that the Mandans and Hidatsas were at war with the Arikaras and that the Assiniboines were also fighting the Mandans. This internecine warfare would dash the captains' objective to bring peace among tribes of the Missouri valley. Clark also feared that it would end their plans to take Mandan, Hidatsa, and Arikara chiefs to Washington. He still had hope of bringing about a reconciliation. The party camped in McKenzie County, North

Dakota, across from Little Knife River ("Goat pen creek"), Mountrail County (see April 15, 1805).

AUGUST 12, 1806. After setting out, Shannon confessed that he had lost his tomahawk, so Clark sent him after it. Taking one of the bullboats, the young man landed on shore and started back to the previous night's camp. The party stopped for breakfast at an island ("Jins") a few miles south of Sanish, Mountrail County, North Dakota, now under Lake Sakakawea. They also wanted to wait for Shannon and Gibson to catch up. Clark sent Shields and Labiche to hunt, while others set about repairing the other bullboat, which was damaged by a six-inch-diameter tear. A piece of elk skin served to patch the hole, and the craft was water worthy once more. Shields and Labiche were unlucky in their hunt.

At noon Lewis and party arrived. Clark was alarmed when he learned of Lewis's injury. Lewis assured him that the wound was slight and that it would heal in less than a month. Clark recorded the events that led to the injury, either from Lewis's journal (see August 11) or from the captain's testimony. Then Clark wrote a lengthy reconstruction of Lewis's trip from Travelers' Rest to this point, again probably from a combination of Lewis's journal and his firsthand account. At two o'clock Shannon and Gibson arrived with Shannon's tomahawk and the meat of three elks they had shot. At three o'clock, with the entire corps reunited and with Dickson and Hancock accompanying them, the party set out, leaving behind the two bullboats, which had served their purpose. They camped below the entrance of Bear Den ("Shabonos") Creek, Dunn County, North Dakota. In the evening Clark washed Lewis's wounds, which had become quite painful.

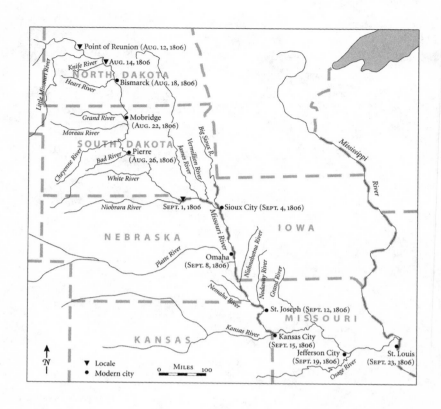

MAP 13. The expedition's route, August 13–September 23, 1806.

CHAPTER 12

Hurrying Home

August 13–September 23, 1806

AUGUST 13, 1806. Clark exclaimed that "all hands were on board" as the party set out at sunrise with a stiff wind at their backs. It was an unremarkable day and in brief words the captain announced passing the Little Missouri River at eight o'clock and arriving at Snake Creek ("Myry river") at sunset, where they camped on the north side, in McLean County, North Dakota, northeast of Riverdale. With the help of heavy winds, a swift current, and strong oars, the party made eighty-six miles. Along the way Clark and Drouillard went hunting. Drouillard wounded an elk but was unable to get it. The captain also spotted Indians in bullboats and native items at a hunting camp but was unable to make contact. He supposed they were Hidatsas on a hunt. He happily reported fewer mosquitoes in the evening.

AUGUST 14, 1806. Not long after setting out the party arrived at the northernmost Hidatsa village, Menetarra ("Minetares Grand Village"), Mercer County, North Dakota, and viewed Indians gathering for their arrival. The men saluted them with several shots from the blunderbusses, to which the natives replied with small arms fire. The party then landed opposite Mahawha village ("*Mah-har-ha's*") and met White Buffalo Robe Unfolded, chief of that village, and Black Moccasin, chief of Metaharta village ("Little Village of the Menitarre") to the north. They all seemed extremely pleased to see the explorers. In fact, Black Moccasin broke down and cried incessantly. Clark later learned that his son had been killed by Blackfeet Indians a short time back. After a brief meeting with the Hidatsas, the fleet drifted down to Chief Black Cat's Mandan village, Ruptáre, in McLean County, where Clark intended to establish camp, but blowing sand altered the plan. Ruptáre villagers flocked to the party and seemed as pleased as the Hidatsas to see them. Clark walked to Black Cat's lodge, ate with him, and had the customary smoke. The captain found that Ruptáre had been altered since 1805 and that it was much smaller. He learned that a quarrel had taken place, and some villagers had moved across the river and built lodges there.

Wanting to gather the various village leaders for a conference, Clark sent Charbonneau to the Hidatsas and Drouillard to Mitutanka village ("lower Village of the Mandans") to ask René Jusseaume (see October 27, 1804) to join them as a Mandan interpreter. When Jusseaume arrived Clark repeated his former invitation for Black Cat to join the captains on their return to the United States, along with principal chiefs of the other villages. Black Cat showed some interest but feared that the Sioux, who had lately killed some of his countrymen, might kill him also. Clark promised protection both going and returning and generous rewards if he made the trip. Nothing of consequence was accomplished. The party then crossed the Missouri and made camp in Mercer County some distance north of Mitutanka village and south of Stanton. Chief White Buffalo Robe Unfolded met Clark here and said he had corn for the party if the captain would send some men to collect it. Gass and two men went back with the chief and soon returned with a load of corn. Only Ordway reported that Lewis fainted when Clark was dressing his wound in the evening, but he seemed to have recovered quickly. Clark's division between his entries of August 14 and 15 is difficult to determine, so an arbitrary separation has been made.

AUGUST 15, 1806. Le Borgne, or One Eye ("Great Chif of all the Menitarres"), came to camp along with several other prominent men of different villages. Clark assembled them at a convenient spot and passed the pipe. He reminded them of his words in 1804 and renewed the request to have leaders return with the captains to the United States. Again, he offered safety both going and returning and substantial gifts to participants. Le Borgne replied first, saying that he would very much like to meet the president ("great father") but feared obstinate Sioux, who would certainly kill him and would not listen to reason. He recalled that the captains had told him that they had made peace with the Sioux but since that time eight of his people had been killed by them, and they had stolen many horses. Nonetheless, he had listened to the explorers' council and made peace with the Cheyennes and some Rocky Mountain tribes, but to no avail. They had acted in the same way as the Sioux. He would be glad to go east but was certain he could not trust the Sioux.

Black Cat sent over a messenger and asked Clark to come to Ruptáre, across the Missouri. Clark crossed over and met the chief, who presented nearly twelve bushels of corn to the captain, despite the village's poverty. After the customary smoke, Black Cat repeated the familiar refrain: it was too dangerous to pass through Sioux country. Black Cat had called his head men together to find a volunteer for the trip but none accepted, so a young man was designated to go. Clark knew the man and objected because of his age and known bad character. In fact, Gibson (who was along) told Clark that he was the very man who had stolen his knife. Clark demanded its return, and the young man sheepishly complied, with scant apologies for the theft. The captain then rebuked the leaders for suggesting such a person for this important trip. Their only reply was fear of the Sioux. Clark crossed back to his camp.

Upon arriving at camp Clark learned that one of the secondary Mandan chiefs, Little Crow of Mitutanka, was interested in returning with the party. Taking Charbonneau with him, Clark walked down to the village and found that he wanted to go but must first get advice from his people. Clark had a smoke with him and returned to camp. In the evening many Indians came to the camp to trade, and village chiefs sent corn for the explorers. The captain learned from Charbonneau that not long after they had left the Knife River villages in 1805 a party of Hidatsas had killed some Shoshone Indians and lost two of their own men, one of whom was the son of Black Moccasin. The Hidatsas had also killed two Arikaras and there had been friction between the Hidatsas and the Mandans, but it was resolved peaceably. Colter came to Clark in the evening requesting a discharge from the corps so that he could join Dickson and Hancock in a trapping enterprise back to the interior. Clark agreed that it would be advantageous for Colter and consented as long as no one else requested release from the party. All agreed to the conditions and wished Colter well in his new venture. In fact, friends gave him a number of small articles and provided him with gunpowder and lead. Ordway later wrote that the three men were planning to be out two years but were "determined to Stay untill they make a fortune."

AUGUST 16, 1806. Clark sent Pryor to Mitutanka to collect corn that the Mandans had offered the party. Pryor came back with a heavy load and reported that they offered more corn than the party's canoes could carry. Clark sent his thanks to Chief Big White. Indians were visiting all day to trade, but there was also some thievery going on. At ten o'clock a number of village chiefs came to the camp for another conference. After the traditional smoke, Clark had the chiefs assembled in a large circle around the party's swivel cannon. It having served its usefulness, Clark intended to give the cannon to Le Borgne in order to gain his goodwill and compliance in his plans, but first he wanted to speak to the assemblage. He criticized them severely for their hostility toward Shoshone and Arikara Indians so soon after the captains had called for peace during their previous stay with them and after they had promised as much.

Cherry Grows on a Bush of the Hidatsa Menetarra village spoke first. He repeated the familiar excuse for not joining the explorers on the return trip: fear of Sioux attacks and reprisals. In fact, he told Clark that Hidatsa attacks on the Sioux and Arikaras were in response to killings of his own people. Le Borgne also responded and promised adherence to Clark's call for peace and rejection of bad advice. With a great deal of ceremony Clark then presented the swivel cannon to Le Borgne and told him that as often as he fired it, it should remind him of the wise words of the "great father." Then the cannon was fired and handed over to the chief.

In the evening Clark settled accounts with Colter and discharged him from service. He then walked to Mitutanka to visit Little Crow and find out when he would be ready to travel. Clark was astonished to learn that the man had changed his mind and refused to accept a flag that the captain had brought along as a gift. It seemed that some undisclosed jealousy had developed between Little Crow and Big White. Clark called on Jusseaume to use his influence to get one of the Mitutanka leaders to accompany the corps. The Frenchman was able to get a commitment from Big White as long as he could also take his wife and son and if Jusseaume would come along with his wife and two children. The captains agreed to the demands. Ordway called the children "verry handsome" and noted that one had had some schooling with the Northwest Company, a Canadian fur trade operation. In his weather diary Clark reported watching the aurora borealis this evening.

AUGUST 17, 1806. As further enticement to keep his pledge to travel with the corps, Clark gave Big White gunpowder and lead. Clark directed that the two largest canoes be lashed together for stability for Big White, Jusseaume, and their families. Hidatsa chiefs came by to bid the party farewell, and at two o'clock they set out, leaving Colter and companions going in the opposite direction. Before leaving Clark settled with Charbonneau for his services; he was no longer needed, as no Hidatsa chiefs were descending with the corps. After adding the cost of a tipi and a horse he provided for the expedition, the interpreter's payment came to $500.33⅓. In his book Biddle added some assessment of Charbonneau and Sacagawea that is not found in the journals: "This man has been very serviceable to us, and his wife particularly useful among the Shoshonees. Indeed, she has borne with a patience truly admirable, the fatigues of so long a route, incumbered with the charge of an infant, who is even now only nineteen months old." Clark offered to take Charbonneau downriver, but he declined, since he had no prospects there. Saying his goodbyes to Charbonneau, Sacagawea, and the baby, Clark asked to take little Jean Baptiste with him. Father and mother refused at this time but said that after a year, when the baby was weaned, they would bring him to Clark to raise.

The party descended the Missouri River to Big White's Mitutanka village while Indians trailed along by land. After landing Clark walked up to his lodge and found him surrounded by friends and relatives, the men smoking and the women wailing. While his wife and children loaded up the canoe and Jusseaume and his family got aboard, Big White had another smoke and passed out gifts of gunpowder and lead that he had received from Clark. Well-wishers followed him to the river—many weeping as he got aboard. Clark turned to bid farewell to Le Borgne and other chiefs, but they insisted he take one last smoke. In the final ceremony, these men pledged efforts toward peace and asked Clark to send Arikaras to them to work to that end. They voiced no such entreaties to the Sioux, whom they still considered determined enemies. Le Borgne, the grand chief at the Knife River villages, viewed Big White as taking his place in conversations with the president and said he would anxiously await his return to learn of all he had experienced. He asked Clark to take care of this great chief. With a salute of gunfire, the flotilla set out. They stopped briefly at Fort Mandan, so Clark could view the post. Most of the structure had been burned by some unknown accident, but he found a rear section intact and some front pickets still standing. The party made camp near an old Arikara village near Hensler, Oliver County, North Dakota. They had come about eighteen miles.

AUGUST 18, 1806. The party delayed getting underway, as hard winds made the river too choppy for safe passage. They got going at eight but still encountered high waves and strong winds. Seeing an Indian running along the shore and beckoning to them, Clark landed the canoes. The man was the brother of Big White and had apparently missed his departure. There were affectionate gestures between them and Big White gave him a pair of leggings. Back in the boats, the party moved on. At about two o'clock the party reached hunters who had gone ahead and found they had killed three deer. They halted on a sandbar and had the meat for lunch. During the meal Big White gave Clark "extroadinary Stories of their tredition." After lunch the party made it to the Heart ("*Chiss-che tor*") River and made camp a little south of Bismarck, Burleigh County, North Dakota, having come about forty miles altogether. Four more deer were killed near camp.

Now settled at the campfires, Clark sat down with Big White to listen to and record some of his "extroadinary Stories" and the reasons the Mandans had left villages that the chief had been pointing out along the Missouri. Big White related that a grapevine grew down into the earth where the Mandans had a village, and they saw light coming from above. Some of the people climbed the vine toward the light and at the surface found buffalo and other animal creatures and a land abundant in vegetation. They gathered grapes and took them back to their people, who thought them so good that they decided to return to the surface. Many men, women, and children made the climb, but one "large big bellied" woman broke the vine and ended access to the top. All who did not make the climb remained below. After death, Mandans on the surface return to that original village. Big White said that he was born at a village across from the camp and that at one time the Mandans had seven villages in the area of the Heart River. Smallpox and attacks by Sioux, Arikaras, and Pawnees had decimated the tribe, so that they were reduced to two villages and eventually had to move to the Knife River to put space between them and their aggressors.

AUGUST 19, 1806. Weather attacked the sandbar camp of the explorers with persistent winds and blowing sands that cut at the party. Clark sent hunters ahead but had to wait until four in the afternoon to get the boats underway. With a small window of calm weather, the party made only ten miles before landing under signs of rain and more strong winds. Hunters met them with four elks and twelve deer. The camp was in Burleigh County, North Dakota. Jusseaume gave Clark some covering for shelter, and the Indian women draped it over a quickly constructed frame. The captain indicated that it was the only covering he had had to keep out rain since leaving the Columbia River. Clark noted that Lewis's wounds were healing, while Gass mentioned that "we are all in good spirits."

AUGUST 20, 1806. Rains of the day before continued, with a violent storm this morning drenching everyone but Clark and the Mandan guests, who were dry under makeshift covering. It cleared off a little after sunrise and they were on their way again. Nevertheless, winds beat up the river and made bailing water from the canoes a constant task. They party passed familiar points such as the Cannonball River on the Morton-Sioux county line, North Dakota, and Beaver Creek ("Wardepon River"), Emmons County, North Dakota. Clark was amazed at the transformation of the river in the short space of less than two years: "I observe a great alteration in the Corrent course and appearance of this pt. of the Missouri. in places where there was Sand bars in the fall 1804 at this time the main Current passes, and where the current then passed is now a Sand bar—Sand bars which were then naked are now covered with willow Several feet high. the enteranc of Some of the Rivers & Creeks Changed owing to the mud thrown into them." Buffalo and elks were declining in numbers, but wolves were seen in abundance. Making about eighty-one miles (Clark said "only"), the party again camped on a sandbar, in Campbell County, South Dakota, some miles below the entrance of Spring Creek. Ordway and Gass complained of mosquitoes at the camp.

AUGUST 21, 1806. Clark echoed Ordway's and Gass's complaint of mosquitoes that continued to bite at them into the morning. The captain sent Ordway ahead to find ash trees suitable for making much-needed oars. The men were busy checking their weapons, but the party still got underway at five o'clock in the morning. At eight the party met three Frenchmen coming upriver from the Arikara villages, one of whom may have been Rivet, who had been an expedition *engagé* in 1804–5. They were on their way to the Mandans with plans to return to St. Louis in the fall. One of the three, a young man, decided to leave that enterprise, so Clark accepted him as a guest of the corps and a hand at the oars. The Frenchmen passed along information that included notice that seven hundred Sioux had passed through the Arikara homeland on their way to attack Mandans and Hidatsas but that no Arikaras had joined them. The captains also got the same sad news that they had from Hancock and Dickson, that an Arikara chief, perhaps Too Né, had died before returning home (see October 12 and November 6, 1804). After spending about an hour with them, the explorers gave them some gunpowder and lead and moved on.

Near noon they party arrived at the most northern of the Arikara villages. They had visited these people October 8–12, 1804, at their villages near the mouth of the Grand River in Corson and Campbell Counties, South Dakota. The explorers saluted them with gunfire and received friendly bursts in reply. They landed at another village, where Arikaras from both places joined to greet them. Gathering chiefs around him, Clark took the traditional smoke of Mandan tobacco provided by Big White. The captain told the assemblage that he had been to the Mandans and Hidatsas and the results of his meetings with them. He pleaded again for peace among the nations, asked that Arikara chiefs accompany him to Washington DC, and promised substantial gifts if they agreed to go. An Arikara man in his thirties, Grey Eyes, who was absent during the 1804 meeting, was now introduced to Clark as the tribe's "principal chief." Kakaw-issassa, whom the captains had acknowledged as principal chief in 1804, told them that Grey Eyes was more prominent than he.

Clark told the Arikaras that he was sorry to learn that they had allowed their young men to join the Sioux in attacking the Mandans and Hidatsas, which had provoked retaliations. Nevertheless, he said that the Mandans and Hidatsas were still willing to make peace and pointed to Big White's presence as an example of the northern tribes' desire for reconciliation. Grey Eyes replied to Clark, saying that he wanted to follow this wise advice but that some young men went their own way in the attacks and had since been banished from the villages. He blamed the Sioux for corrupting them. He said that several of the chiefs wanted to visit Washington but would first wait until the chief (perhaps Too Né) who had gone last year had returned. Grey Eyes promised that any Mandans or Hidatsas who visited them would be safe.

With all suffering on a hot day, a visiting Cheyenne chief invited everyone to join him in his lodge out of the sun. The Cheyennes had come to trade with the Arikaras and had set up nearly 20 lodges in the area, but when all arrived they would have nearly 120 lodges altogether. After entering the chief's spacious lodge Clark offered him an Indian peace medal, but the chief declined, fearing that some evil was associated with it. Gass called the Cheyennes "a silly superstitious people." Clark explained the medal's purpose of acknowledging the man's authority, so he accepted and gave the captain a buffalo robe and quantity of buffalo meat. Big White then spoke of his desire for peace, the reasons for the misunderstandings between the tribes, and his wish to establish friendly relations. There were promises of friendship all around, another smoke was had, and they parted "on the best terms," according to Clark. Later Clark joined Grey Eyes at his lodge and was informed that none of his chiefs were willing to go with the corps. Again, he said they wanted to wait until their other chief returned. Grey Eyes also disparaged the Cheyennes and said they were afraid to go.

As Clark was returning to his boat an Arikara chief, perhaps Kakawissassa, of the village on Ashley Island, joined the party, and all canoed to his home. Arriving a little before dark, the men were greeted by the villagers, but all was not as friendly as anticipated. A secondary chief whom Clark had hoped would join them turned on Big White in a threatening manner. Clark tried to intervene by explaining that the other Arikara chiefs had accepted Big White warmly and that the captain had the Mandan chief under his protection and would defend him with his life. He also scolded the Arikara chief for Arikara attacks on the Mandans and Hidatsas. That seemed to disarm the situation, and the chief invited Clark and Big White into his lodge for a smoke. After the usual pleasantries, Clark and Big White went to Kakawissassa's lodge, where they received a large supper of corn, beans, and squashes, served in wooden bowls. Kakawissassa also presented a quantity of tobacco seeds and promised good relations with Big White's people. Like his kinsmen, he blamed Sioux Indians for the mischief. Conversations continued late into the night, after which Clark and his Indian companion returned to the canoes and their Ashley Island camp.

AUGUST 22, 1806. Rain soaked the party all through the night, and they woke to sopping bedding. Ordway, at least, slept in the village. About eight Clark received a request to visit the Arikara village near their camp on Ashley Island, Campbell and Corson Counties, South Dakota. There the chief, perhaps Kakawissassa, said he would not be joining the party for the trip back. He intended to stay at his village and make sure his young men did not cause trouble with neighboring tribes. An interpreter and trader at the village, Joseph Garreau (see March 16, 1805), informed Clark that he had been visiting with Arikara chiefs and said that none intended to go east with the explorers. Again, they were waiting for their chief to return from his own trip. Ordway wrote that "they are all afraid to go down with us." All Clark could do was insist they keep their promises and end attacks on others.

While preparing to leave, the party was visited by some Cheyennes who came to smoke with the captains and detained them for a while. Clark used some space to characterize the Cheyennes. He found them "portly," with much the same complexion as the Mandans and Arikaras. While he saw the men as large, he called the women homely and coarse featured. He gave some attention to their clothes and adornments, essentially typical of Plains Indians: the men had buffalo robes, breechcloths, and moccasins and used shells, beads, and brooches for jewelry. They also wore bear-claw collars and otter-skin shawls thrown over their backs. The women wore simple leather dresses of two pieces sewn together with a string over the shoulders to hold it up. The piece fell to midleg and was often adorned with beads, shells, and elk teeth ("which all Indians are very fond of") and painted with figures. They let their hair flow loosely and wove ornaments into the lengths. Clark estimated the Cheyennes at from 350 to 400 men and inhabiting nearly 150 lodges. They were rich in horses and dogs, the latter used for hauling light baggage. They claimed to be at war with no one except the Sioux. They encouraged Clark to send traders to them.

While the party was visiting with the Cheyennes a French *engagé*, perhaps Roi, who had been with the party up to the Mandan villages, came forward, admitted that he had spent his wages, and wanted to return with the party. Clark agreed to take him along. The party moved on, firing guns in salute as they departed. They soon passed the Grand ("*We ter hoo*") River, Corson County, and landed for a time to dry their bedding and clothes. Clark sent five hunters ahead to Grouse Island and then moved beyond that place to make camp in Walworth County, South Dakota, about six miles southeast of Mobridge. Clark ended the day's entry on a positive note: "I am happy to have it in my power to Say that my worthy friend Capt Lewis is recovering fast, he walked a little to day for the first time. I have discontinud the tent in the hole the ball came out."

AUGUST 23, 1806. Setting out early, with high winds and a choppy river, the party passed the Moreau ("Sar-war-kar-na-har") River, Dewey County, South Dakota, by ten o'clock. Before noon they were forced ashore by wind and waves and stayed there until about three in the afternoon. During the delay Clark sent Shields and the Field brothers ahead to hunt. After a small shower the winds quieted, and they were on the river again. Catching up with the three men, the main party found that the hunters had killed three elks and three deer, but none were in good condition. They took what meat they could. A violent storm forced them to shore again, but it was brief, and they quickly returned to the canoes. Clark noticed grapes, chokecherries, and currants along the way. He thought one currant a new species, but it was the wild black currant previously seen. The captain chose a spot for the night that he considered relatively free of mosquitoes, but Gass thought otherwise and called the pests "very troublesome." Making about forty miles, the party camped in Potter County, South Dakota, near the mouth of Swift Bird Creek, Dewey County.

AUGUST 24, 1806. Even an early start did not guarantee a full day at the oars, since wind and waves forced them to shore at about two o'clock, where they stayed for several hours. When calm conditions returned, they got back in the canoes and moved on. During the morning they passed "La-hoo-catts" Island, later Dolphees Island between Dewey and Potter Counties, South Dakota, now submerged by Lake Oahe. Near here Clark observed strata of "Soft White Stone containing very fine grit." He was seeing a layer of bentonite contained within the Upper Cretaceous Pierre Shale. Hunters saw numerous deer, mostly mule deer, but killed none, and buffalo were few. The party camped in Dewey County near a trading post of Jean Vallé's and their camp of October 1, 1804, where they first met him. They traveled about forty-three miles.

AUGUST 25, 1806. A stiff breeze faced the party at they set out on a clear, cool morning. Shields, Collins, Shannon, and the Field brothers took two small canoes ahead to hunt at "Ponia," later Cheyenne, Island, just below the mouth of the Cheyenne River, Sully County, South Dakota, near the party's camp of September 30, 1804. It is now under Lake Oahe. Clark commented on stands of cottonwood and willow trees as the party approached the Cheyenne River, gaining its thickest stands on the northeast side of the bend above the river. They landed at the Cheyenne River for several hours for the captains to take astronomical observations and to send hunters up the stream. These men brought in two deer, and the party moved on about noon. Passing Cheyenne Island, they found Shields and Collins, who had killed two deer ("only," said Clark). Later they canoed by an old camp of "Troubleson Tetons" that they had passed on September 30, 1804, in Stanley County. They made camp in Hughes County across from and below Chantier ("No timber") Creek, Stanley County. Clark had been viewing the remains of Arikara villages that had been destroyed by the Sioux along this stretch of the river from Dolphees Island to this place. With a still day on the river the party made forty-eight miles despite the time at the Cheyenne River. Hunters Shannon and the Field brothers did not rejoin the men, but Drouillard brought in a deer he killed near camp.

AUGUST 26, 1806. Shannon and the Field brothers returned to camp at sunrise. They had killed only two small deer and had eaten one. The party proceeded on. As they passed it, Clark called attention to the spot where they had their troubles with the Teton Sioux in late September 1804 and to the entrance of the Bad ("Teton") River, Stanley County, South Dakota., all near Pierre, Hughes County. Clark sent hunters after some mule deer, but they were too elusive for the men. The captain saw evidence of Tetons having been in the area, but none were to be seen. Stopping at noon to eat (but without cooking, according to Ordway), they found a level spot with great quantities of wild plums, not yet ripe. They halted at Chapelle ("Smoke") Creek, Hughes County, to make repairs on the white pirogue. Here they found abundant but unripe riverbank grapes. Back on the river they passed Loisel's Fort aux Cedres on what was later named Dorion Island No. 2 (see September 22, 1804). The fort remained in good condition and had not deteriorated much since the captains inspected it in 1804. They moved on another ten miles or so and set up camp across from the one of September 21, 1804, and a few miles above Medicine Creek ("Tylors River"), Lyman County, having come about sixty miles, a good part of it against the wind. Knowing that they were back in Sioux country, the party was extra vigilant. Arms were inspected, and they were "deturmined to put up with no insults" from the Indians, Clark promised. Lewis's condition was steadily improving; he was up and walking.

AUGUST 27, 1806. Against a stiff breeze, they reached Medicine Creek ("Tylors river") and landed on a nearby sandbar so hunters could resupply the party's store of meat. Hunters returned in three hours without having killed anything. They reported the ground torn up by the recent passage of buffalo, but none were here now except for unfit bulls not worth their time or ammunition, and deer were also scarce. Also they saw the first signs of wild turkeys. Entering the Big Bend, or Grand Detour, of the Missouri River in Lyman County, South Dakota, a hunter killed a fat buck elk just in time to feed hungry men nearly out of meat. As they moved on they saw more buffalo, and later in the evening the bellowing of bulls convinced them that cows must be nearby. Five men were sent in two canoes in search of the animals and were able to get two cows, a bull, and a calf. Coming out of the bend they found an island suitable for camp between Lyman and Buffalo Counties near where they camped on September 19, 1804. They made forty-five miles. Lewis overexerted himself on a walk, and Clark reported him as "very unwell all night."

AUGUST 28, 1806. Lewis seemed no better this morning as the party got underway. Moving at a good rate they reached the "3 rivers of the Scioux pass" (Campbell, Wolf, and Crow Creeks, Buffalo County, South Dakota) at nine o'clock. A short time later the captains sent the Field brothers in search of mule deer or pronghorns, after their skins and skeletons. The brothers were directed to rejoin the party at the "pleasant Camp" of mid-September 1804. Drouillard and Labiche were dropped off a few miles below with the same orders. Clark recalled that the camp was so named due to the abundance of buffalo, elks, pronghorns, mule deer, western white-tailed ("fallow") deer, common deer, wolves, and prairie dogs and for the delicious grapes and plums found in the neighborhood. In fact, the captain had earlier called it "Plomb Camp." Several of the men joined Jusseaume's wives and Big White and ventured out to pick plums; they came back with more than the party could eat in two days. The camp was near Oacoma, Lyman County, about thirty-two miles from the previous one. The captains had already decided to stop here to collect animal skeletons.

By noon the party arrived at the appointed spot and established camp for the night. More hunters, including Pryor, Shields, Gibson, Willard, and Collins, were sent up American Crow ("Corvus") Creek, at Oacoma, with the same hunting objectives as the other men. Bratton and Frazer were sent after prairie dogs, while all were directed to get a magpie. Nonhunters were busy making clothing from animal skins. Drouillard and Labiche got back in the late afternoon—the latter killing one common deer only. All other hunters returned later but without the desired results, although they did bring four common deer and two buffalo. Butchers took the best of the meat. Clark admitted that two prairie dogs were also procured, and Ordway added a porcupine to the list. Still in want of mule deer and pronghorn specimens, the captains decided to delay until ten o'clock in the morning to give hunters time to obtain the desired specimens. Shannon and Collins were to go to the opposite side, while Labiche and Willard would drop down on this (western) side of the Missouri to rejoin the party below the White River. Reuben Field was to take a small canoe, trail along after them, and retrieve any meat they might secure.

AUGUST 29, 1806. Hunters spread out under the orders of the day before, while a couple of men went after some prairie dogs at their nearby village of tunnels. They were unsuccessful at luring any out of their holes. Gathering up all loose baggage, the canoes were reloaded, and the party got underway again by ten o'clock. They passed the White River, Lyman County, South Dakota, by noon, then halted at Bull ("Shannons") Creek, a couple of miles farther on, where they had camped on September 14, 1804, now under Lake Francis Case. Clark called the White River "nearly as white as milk." Here they were joined by Labiche, Shannon, and Willard, who had killed two common deer but no mule deer or pronghorns, the desired species. Leaving Drouillard to hunt, the boat party moved on, delaying only to obtain some buffalo meat. Hunters killed two bulls, but they were in poor condition. Ordway indicated that the men were saving all the buffalo horns they could since they made excellent knife and fork handles. Clark, on the hunt, climbed a nearby hill and made this observation: "from this eminance I had a view of a greater number of buffalow than I had ever Seen before at one time. I must have Seen near 20,000 of those animals feeding on this plain. I have observed that in the country between the nations which are at war with each other the greatest numbers of wild animals are to be found." He killed two deer on his way back. After lunch they moved about three miles, to a camp formed by Collins and the Field brothers, and camped for the night, having traveled altogether about twenty miles. The camp was in Lyman County, a little below the camp of September 13, 1804. But still no mule deer or pronghorn specimens. Joseph Field told Clark he had wounded a female mule deer but could not pursue it, so the captain decided that Field would go after it in the morning.

AUGUST 30, 1806. Clark's first words of the day were "Capt. Lewis is mending Slowly." As planned, Joseph Field stayed behind to find the wounded mule deer of the day before. His brother and Shannon took one of the small canoes to go a short distance ahead and wait for him. Clark joined three hunters in search of fresh meat. Approaching a thick plum orchard, the men scared out two large buck elks and killed both of them. They took the best of the meat to the boats and also loaded up several quarts of plums. It was two hours before they were back on the river.

Moving along, Clark spied several Indians on horseback atop hills to the northeast. The party landed on the southwest side to try again to get some prairie dogs, and from here Clark saw a group of about twenty Indians on a hill opposite them. Using his telescope ("Spie glass"), Clark thought he detected a Frenchman among them, based on his clothing. Then some eighty to ninety Indian men came from the woods on the opposite shore about a quarter of a mile below the party. Armed with fusils, the Indians fired their weapons in salute and the explorers returned the greeting. Without a clear view, the captains feared they might be Tetons but hoped they were Yanktons, Poncas, or Omahas, more amicable tribes. Not wanting to put the entire party at risk, Clark took "three french men who could Speak the Mahar [Omaha] Pania [Pawnee?] and some Seious [Sioux]" in a small canoe to a sandbar near the opposite shore. It seems likely that Clark had Cruzatte and Labiche with him, while the other could have been Jusseaume or Lepage.

Three young men from among the Indians swam to the sandbar, and Clark had his interpreters speak to them in Ponca and Omaha, but they understood nothing. They did understand Sioux that Clark directed to them and said they were Tetons and that their chief was Black Buffalo (see September 25, 1804). Clark remembered him very well from the 1804 encounter as one with whom the party was "near comeing to blows." Clark told the young men that the Tetons had not followed the captains' councils, that they had treated the explorers poorly at the last meeting and others since then, that he was not willing to visit with them now, and that if any tried to come over they would be killed. The captain found a man who spoke Ponca, and as one of his men was fluent in that language, he made sure his message was delivered and understood. He also said that no traders would be coming to them and that he would advise any passing through their territory to trade above to be well armed in order to "whip any vilenous party who dare to oppose them." Moreover, he let them know that the Mandans and Hidatsas were now sufficiently armed to address Teton aggression. Clark returned to his men and had the party's weapons inspected and prepared. When the Tetons got to the other side, Clark wrote that they "blackguarded us" and said they would kill any in the party who came across.

Clark was concerned for Shannon and the Field brothers, who were out hunting, but was relieved when they appeared, bringing with them three mule deer. All in place, the party set out again. As they came close to the opposite shore, the Tetons on that side became somewhat agitated. While some scattered, one Teton came to the river's edge and called for the explorers to come ashore. Clark ignored the invitation, although he recognized the man to be the Teton chief Buffalo Medicine, whom he had met in 1804. The party moved on about six miles and camped on a sandbar in the middle of the river between Gregory and Charles Mix Counties, South Dakota. It was not a happy place, as it was totally exposed to the wind and they had to bed down on wet sand. Yet it provided protection from possible attack by either Tetons or mosquitoes.

AUGUST 31, 1806. Clark opened his journal with the words "all wet and disagreeable this morning." Starting before midnight, the wind had shifted and brought in rain, thunder, and lightning. The men had to hold down the pirogue and canoes to prevent them being blown away. Even with that, the canoes lashed together for Jusseaume's and Big White's families broke loose with Willard and Wiser inside, and they were carried across the river. Clark sent Ordway and some men to rescue them, and it was all they could do to keep their boat upright. It was two o'clock in the morning before all were back and safe. The rain did not let up until daylight. There was a general inspection of arms before the party set out. They passed Little Cedar Island ("Island of Cedar") between Gregory and Charles Mix Counties, South Dakota, by midmorning, and by four o'clock they reached Old Baldy, Boyd County, Nebraska, first noted on September 7, 1804, with its ubiquitous prairie dogs. Having come about seventy miles, the party camped in Charles Mix County, between the camp of September 5, 1804, and the mouth of Chouteau ("Goat") Creek.

SEPTEMBER 1, 1806. After a night being harassed by mosquitoes the party got underway at the "usial hour." Thick fog soon compelled them to delay for about half an hour. The Field brothers and Shannon, in search of deer, landed on an island at the mouth of Ponca Creek, Knox County, Nebraska. By nine o'clock the canoes reached the Niobrara River ("River *Quiequur*"), which they had passed on September 4, 1804. A couple of miles below the Niobrara nine Indians came to the riverbank and tried to wave the party ashore. Clark, thinking they were Tetons, paid no attention to them other than to shout some words that were not heard or understood. Remembering that one canoe with the hunters was behind, the captain decided to land beyond the Indians' view to make certain the men came through safely. Soon after landing they heard gunfire upriver and worried that the hunters were being attacked by the Indians. Taking fifteen men with him, Clark dashed to a point where he could see what was happening "with a fill deturmination to Cover them if

possible let the number of indians be what they might." Lewis hobbled to shore with the rest of the party and took a defensive position.
When Clark reached a point where he could see upriver, he spotted
the hunters' canoe about one mile from him and the Indians near
enough that he could meet them. Clark greeted them with a hand-
shake and asked what they were shooting at. They admitted that
they were simply practicing their marksmanship on a floating keg
that the explorers had thrown overboard. Back at the boats the captains learned that they were Yanktons, so they invited them to have
a smoke. There they met Big White and smoked several pipefuls.

Clark told them he was happy to discover that they were Yanktons rather than Tetons and took them by the hand once more. The
nine Yanktons were armed with only five fusils and four bows with
quivers of arrows. One of the Yanktons replied that since the previous meeting their people had kept the promises of peace. Clark
asked if any of their chiefs had gone downriver with Pierre Dorion
Jr. They said that one chief and a number of brave men had gone.
Clark tied a ribbon in each man's hair and gave them some corn,
while Big White presented the principal man among them with an
elegant pair of leggings. With the return of the hunters, the party
set off again after telling the Yanktons to return to their band (on
Emmanuel Creek, Bon Homme County, South Dakota) and remind
their people to keep the peace.

At about two o'clock the party reached the upper point of Bon
Homme Island, presently inundated by Lewis and Clark Lake. Clark
mentioned the "antient fortification" nearby that he had seen on September 2, 1804, which were actually natural, windblown formations.
He had described and sketched them in 1804 and now made more
sketches and additional notes. The captain sent hunters in search
of meat while he walked along the northern shore. Heavy, head-
high grass and thick vines forced him to take to the plains above
the river in order to make his way. Hunter Labiche brought elk
meat to the island shortly before they set off. Drifting to a sandbar
opposite where they had met the Yanktons in 1804, they established
camp near the Calumet Bluff, Yankton County, South Dakota, having come about fifty-two miles altogether. Having camped opposite
here on September 1, 1804, Clark commented on their bringing the

two years together. Mosquitoes troubled the party until about ten o'clock, when strong winds blew them away.

SEPTEMBER 2, 1806. With their usual early start, the party passed the James River ("River Jacque"), Yankton County, South Dakota, by eight o'clock. Clark saw a structure that had been built since the party passed here in 1804 and speculated that it had been built by Robert McClellan, who used it as a trading post for the Yanktons during the winter of 1804–5. The party would meet McClellan (whom they already knew) on September 12 and may have received this information at that time. With meat supplies getting low, Clark took eight hunters and pursued buffalo for several miles before eventually killing two. He found them in good order, had them butchered, and had the men carry as much meat as possible back to the canoes. On the hunt Clark noticed American linden and slippery elm, a significant observation since the trees reach their distributional limit in this area. He also saw bur ("white") oaks and green ("white") ash on his hunt. Besides seeing greater prairie-chickens, two turkeys were killed—the latter fascinated Big White's family, who had never seen one. High winds and rough water delayed departure until nearly sunset, so that they added only two miles, for a total of twenty-two for the day. The camp was a few miles below the mouth of the James River in either Yankton or Cedar County, Nebraska. Camping on an open sandbar exposed them to the wind, which helped drive tormenting mosquitoes away. Clark closed out the day by noting, "Capt L. is mending fast."

SEPTEMBER 3, 1806. Although winds across the sandbar drove off mosquitoes, they added the irritant of blowing sand, which made for a miserable night. The party passed the mouth of the Vermillion ("redstone") River, Clay County, South Dakota, by eleven o'clock. At about four thirty in the afternoon they spied two boats with several men coming upriver and all came to shore after gunshot greetings. Ordway counted "18 hands" in the boats. Here the captains met James Aird, whom Clark described as "from Mackanaw by way of Prarie Dechien and St. Louis," with a license to trade for one year with the Sioux. He had two boats loaded with trade goods for that purpose. Aird had been a trader in Mackinac since at least 1779 and was one of the earliest settlers of Prairie du Chien, in modern Wisconsin. Suffering from a cold with chills, he nonetheless greeted the captains cordially and brought them up-to-date on stateside news.

Clark stayed up late into the night querying Aird about national politics and Indian affairs. Aird told him that the house of Jean Pierre Chouteau in St. Louis had burned, and he had lost a good deal of his furniture. The captain expressed his regret at the misfortune. Aird also told him that James Wilkinson had been appointed governor of Louisiana at St. Louis. He further told of the stationing of three hundred American troops a short distance up the Missouri River from its mouth. This deployment was brought about because of tensions between the United States and Spanish governments in the area around Natchitoches, Louisiana, and Nacogdoches, Texas, which were quieted when Wilkinson negotiated an agreement to establish a "neutral ground" east of the Sabine River. There was other unsettling news as well. The U.S. frigate *President* had been fired on by Spanish gunboats near Algeciras, Spain, in the fall of 1804, and the British warship *Leander* had fired on the American merchant ship *Richard* off New York City on April 25, 1806, killing one seaman. Two Indians (perhaps Kickapoos) had been hanged in St. Louis for the murder of a white man. Finally, Clark heard the disquieting news of the duel between Aaron Burr, Jefferson's vice president, and Alexander Hamilton, a Federalist leader and Washington's secretary of the treasury. It took place on July 11, 1804, in Weehawken, New Jersey, and resulted in Hamilton's death, Clark learned. On more immediate matters, the captain tallied the day's miles at sixty, but the site of the night's camp is unclear, other than it was some miles above Sioux City, Iowa. Clark also gave a good report on Lewis's condition.

SEPTEMBER 4, 1806. It was a wet morning and the party was thoroughly drenched. Clark bargained for tobacco from Aird and was able to purchase four carrots, for which he agreed to pay an amount equal to that charged by "any Merchant of St. Louis." In fact, the trader sold as much as the party wanted and threw in a barrel of flour. The men gave him what corn they could spare, about six bushels. All were pleased with the exchanges, Clark noted. Trading having ended, the party set out at about eight o'clock, and moving along swiftly they reached the Big Sioux River by eleven, at the line between Union County, South Dakota, and Woodbury County, Iowa. By noon they were at the Floyd River, Woodbury County, and stopped to visit Floyd's grave. Lewis with some others discovered that it had been opened and left partially uncovered, so they recovered it, returned to the canoes, and proceeded on. Moving on a few miles to the party's outbound camp of August 13–20, 1804, their "Fish Camp," they established a new camp in either Woodbury County or Dakota County, Nebraska, having traveled about thirty-six miles. The captains had all the wet baggage unloaded and set out to dry. It was reloaded before nightfall in order to get an early start the next day. During the day Clark noticed black walnut trees but was wrong in his conjecture that this was their northern limit on the Missouri River. Biting mosquitoes allowed little sleep during the night.

SEPTEMBER 5, 1806. Mosquitoes drove them out of bed and out of camp early this morning. Here the river narrowed, became more crooked, and ran more swiftly. Snags and sawyers impeded the party's travel and compelled the close attention of canoeists. Clark called a formation in Thurston County, Nebraska, the "blue Stone bluff," due to the late afternoon shading of shale of the Lower and Upper Cretaceous Dakota Group. Below that and below their camp of August 9, 1804, they set up camp in Monona County, Iowa, a few miles south of Onawa, having come about seventy-three miles. Ordway said the camp was on a sand beach with the intent to avoid mosquitoes. They had seen no game worthy of attention, but Clark counted pelicans, geese, ducks, eagles, and hawks. In his weather diary he mentioned that he heard the song of the whip-poor-will. "Capt. Lewis still in a Convelesent State," wrote Clark.

SEPTEMBER 6, 1806. Ordway's hope to be rid of mosquitoes during the night was in vain. Clark called them "excessively troublesom." Seeing a herd of elks after they got underway, Clark sent out several hunters, but they returned empty-handed. The captain then sent two small canoes ahead to hunt while the main party delayed rather than face a hard headwind. They soon reached "Pelecan Island" (now gone) a little above the Little Sioux River ("Petite River de Seeoux"), Harrison County, Iowa, and met a trading boat of René Auguste Chouteau's led by one of several possible Missouri River traders. The leader had laid out his goods to dry and sent out hunters, who were able to bring in an elk. Ordway counted twelve Frenchmen in the trading party. The captains purchased a gallon of whiskey from him and passed a dram to each of their party. Clark and Gass recalled that it was the first spirituous liquor they had tasted since July 4, 1805. The men were able to trade leather shirts for linen ones and beaver hats for woven headgear.

The captains got some additional information about troop movements and learned that Wilkinson was about to leave St. Louis. Lewis and Clark urged the traders to treat the Teton Sioux with contempt. The two groups parted ways at one o'clock under swivel gun salutes from both parties. Moving on, the explorers met their hunting parties, but they had been unsuccessful in their pursuits. The Field brothers remained out hunting as they party established camp on a sandbar in either Harrison County, Iowa, or Burt or Washington County, Nebraska, between the Little Sioux and Soldier Rivers. They had come about thirty miles. Clark reported that the Indians on board were nervous and that the children cried.

SEPTEMBER 7, 1806. Worrying that the Field brothers might be behind them on their hunting excursion, Clark directed Ordway and four men to stay in camp until noon, waiting for the brothers. If the main party met the hunters ahead, they would fire a signal shot for Ordway to come on. As it was, the main party had gone about eight miles when they saw the two men's fire and signaled Ordway as planned. The brothers had killed nothing and were a little worried at the boat party's delay in reaching them. Underway again, the party came to shore a short distance above the Soldier River, and the captains sent out hunters. They were able to get three elks, which the party ate heartily. After Ordway and his men arrived they shared in the "Sumptious Dinner." At about four o'clock the reunited group moved on against a headwind until dusk, making about forty-four miles for the day. They camped a few miles below their camp of August 4, 1804, on a sandbar in either Harrison County, Iowa, or Washington County, Nebraska, near Blair, Nebraska.

SEPTEMBER 8, 1806. Early on the party passed an old trading post they had seen on August 4, 1804, probably established by Mackay in 1795, south of Blair, Washington County, Nebraska. By eleven o'clock they were at the party's "Council Bluff," near Fort Calhoun, Washington County, where they had met Otoe and Missouria Indians and camped from July 30 to August 3, 1804. The captains walked up to the bluffs to examine the terrain and concluded again that because of its commanding position it would make an excellent place for a fort or trading post. With everyone eager to get underway and reach the Platte River, the men plied steadily at their oars and paddles, eventually making seventy-eight miles for the day. They reached their Camp White Catfish of July 22–27, 1804, near the Mills-Pottawatomie county line, Iowa, and made camp here again. Clark was amazed that the Missouri River did not appear to contain any more water than it did one thousand miles above, in spite of receiving the outpourings of at least twenty rivers and numerous creeks. He attributed the phenomenon to the river's incredible rate of evaporation.

SEPTEMBER 9, 1806. Getting an early start, the party soon passed the mouth of the Platte River, the dividing line between Sarpy and Cass Counties, Nebraska, first reached on July 21, 1804. Clark reported the river "turbelant as usial," with sandbars choking its entrance into the Missouri, speeding the current of the main stream downriver and adding numerous and dangerous snags, making headway difficult. Having made seventy-three miles ("only," wrote Clark), the party arrived at their "Bald pated prarie" of July 16, 1804, and camped in either Nemaha County, Nebraska, or Atchison County, Missouri, northeast of Peru, Nebraska. During the day Clark counted tall timber in river bottoms, probably cottonwoods and sycamores, while in sheltered ravines he saw oak, ash, elm, walnut, and hickory trees. Clark noted that the men were becoming restless and anxious to get home. He declared Lewis "entirely recovered" from his injury, able to walk, even to run, as well as ever, but "the parts are yet tender." Warm nights allowed the captains to sleep under thin blankets, and their persistent pests, mosquitoes, were less troubling.

SEPTEMBER 10, 1806. Facing only a moderate headwind the party made good progress in the early hours. By afternoon they met a certain "Mr. Alexander La fass" and three Frenchmen from St. Louis who were bound for the Platte River to trade with Pawnee Indians. Clark called La Fass "extreemly friendly," offering whatever he had. The captains accepted a bottle of whiskey, which they gave to their men. He related news that Wilkinson had moved his troops down the Mississippi and reported that Zebulon Montgomery Pike was leading an expedition toward the Arkansas River. In fact, Pike had set out in July 1806 leading a small party to cross the Great Plains toward the headwaters of the Arkansas. He followed the river to its upper reaches, saw but did not climb Pike's Peak, was captured by Spanish authorities, and was eventually returned to the United States in 1807. The captains visited with La Fass about an hour and then set out again, only to meet within three miles another trading party of seven men from St. Louis in a large pirogue. They were headed for a trading venture with the Omaha Indians. Joseph La Croix ("La Craw"), an Englishman and associate of James Aird, apparently led this group. The captains spent only a short time with him and wrote nothing of their talks. Now encountering a narrowing river filled with snags and sawyers, the boatmen had to constantly stay on the alert against accidents. Having come about sixty-five miles, the party camped on a sandbar in either Richardson County, Nebraska, or Holt County, Missouri, above the Big Nemaha River near Rulo, Nebraska.

SEPTEMBER 11, 1806. Heavy clouds and stiff headwinds delayed the party until after sunrise. They now moved along steadily, but the river was rapid and crowded with snags, slowing safe passage and allowing progress of only forty miles. Passing familiar streams like the Big Nemaha River, Richardson County, Nebraska, and the Wolf River, Doniphan County, Kansas, they came to at the Nodaway River on the Holt-Andrew county line, Missouri. They stopped above the

Nodaway River to let six hunters out, but the men returned with only two deer in spite of abundant deer signs. Proceeding on, they established camp below the Nodaway on an island in either Andrew or Buchanan County, Missouri. Clark was happy to report that mosquitoes were fewer, but he could not account for the decrease. Wolves howled during the night and coyotes kept up their yapping. The barks of the coyotes were so like domestic dogs' that three-quarters of the men supposed the sounds were coming from dogs accompanying nearby trading parties.

SEPTEMBER 12, 1806. An early morning thick fog blew off before daylight, so the party got underway at sunrise. Only seven miles into the day, they met more traders coming upriver, now in two pirogues from St. Louis headed for the Pawnees at the Platte River or the Omaha Indians farther up. After a short visit, the explorers moved on in the face of a steady headwind. At the "St. Michl. Pra-rie" of July 7, 1804, the party met Robert McClellan, a man already known to the captains from shared army service, and Joseph Grave-lines, whom they had hired at the Arikara villages in October 1804, kept on at Fort Mandan, and had accompany an Arikara chief (per-haps Too Né) to Washington DC in the spring of 1805. Pierre Dorion Sr., the Sioux interpreter, was also with the traders; the captains had met him in June 1804. McClellan had wine for the captains and "as much whiskey as we all could drink," wrote Ordway.

Gravelines had instructions from Jefferson and was carrying a letter from the president to the Arikaras explaining the sad news that their chief had died in Washington during his visit. Jefferson wanted to assure the Arikaras that there had been no foul play in the chief's death. Gravelines was also carrying gifts that had been given to the chief, which were now to be presented to the tribe. Dorion was accompanying Gravelines in order to establish relations with the Teton Sioux and to arrange for at least six of their princi-pal men to visit Washington in the spring. The captains expanded these instructions to add chiefs from other Sioux bands for the trip to Washington, bringing the number to nearly a dozen. Both men had also been urged to gain what information they could about Lewis and Clark. In fact, Ordway reported that the explorers learned that people in the states feared the party had all been killed or perhaps captured by the Spanish. A cloudy, wet evening convinced the captains to remain at St. Michael's Prairie, Buchanan County, Missouri, near St. Joseph. They sent two canoes ahead with ten hunters.

SEPTEMBER 13, 1806. McClellan shared another dram of whiskey with the men as the party set out at sunrise. In conversations with Clark that Biddle penned in his notes under this date, the captain related that some of the men had been weaned from liquor while others had not. In time the former "relapsed into their old habits." By eight o'clock they reached the camp of the hunters sent out the day before but found them empty-handed. With high winds and dangerous snags impeding their journey, the captains decided to halt here for a time. They sent a small canoe to hunt below. Hunters near camp brought in a turkey and negative reports about getting any deer. Clark was feeling unwell, so he took some chocolate that McClellan had given him. By noon he was feeling better.

The party returned to the river, found their hunters had killed four deer, and delayed again until everyone reached the main party. With all hands in place by five o'clock they set out again but traveled a short distance only before landing for the night. The camp was about eighteen miles below the previous one and in either Buchanan County, Missouri, or Doniphan County, Kansas. Clark mentioned that Shannon left his powder horn, pouch (with powder and ammunition), and knife behind and did not notice or mention it until nighttime. There is no report that he was sent after the items, nor any record of recrimination for the negligence. Clark cataloged the trees common to the area: cottonwoods, sycamores, ash, mulberries, elms, walnuts, hickories, hornbeams, pawpaws, haws, and willows. He also observed grapevines and perhaps hog peanuts in the underbrush and watched turkey vultures, crows, hawks, and owls on the wing or in trees. The next day one of the captains would collect a specimen of raccoon grape, the last dated specimen from the expedition.

SEPTEMBER 14, 1806. The captains considered this part of the Missouri River to be a haunt of Kansa Indians, who regularly waylaid and robbed passing traders. The captains were determined that they would not let the Indians take advantage of them, had their men on the ready, and promised to fire on them "for the Smallest insult." By two o'clock they passed a Kansa village in northeast Leavenworth County, Kansas, near Fort Leavenworth. Here they met three large boats bound for trade with the Yankton Sioux and Omahas. These boats belonged to Joseph La Croix, perhaps Charles Courtin ("Coutau"), and a "Mr. Aiten" of St. Louis. The traders on board were generous with the explorers and "pressed on us Some whisky for our men." They also offered biscuits, pork, cheese, and onions, along with other items from their store of goods. The captains queried them extensively and asked for the latest stateside news. The traders expressed their concerns about the Kansa Indians ahead, who might try to rob them. After about two hours the two groups parted company and moved on in opposite directions. Clark counted thirty-seven deer along the river, and hunters were able to get five, but they were in poor condition. Gibson shot one from his canoe, Ordway reported. After traveling about fifty-three miles, the party found camp on an island near Leavenworth, Kansas. The captains gave each man a dram of whisky and listened as the soldiers sang songs "in greatest harmoney" until eleven o'clock.

SEPTEMBER 15, 1806. An early start put the party against a stiff breeze. The river nevertheless by eleven o'clock had carried them to the mouth of the Kansas River, Wyandotte County, Kansas. They landed about a mile below its entrance, and the captains climbed a hill that formed a "Commanding Situation," an ideal spot for a fort. This hill, in downtown Kansas City, gave a perfect view of both the Kansas and Missouri Rivers. The men gathered pawpaws ("Custard apple"), which they had become fond of, and saw rattlesnakes in their search. They took one for its skin. Hunters Shannon and the Field brothers went after a large elk, shot it, found it in excellent order, and put its meat to good use. With unfavorable winds the party made only about forty-nine miles and camped a short distance above the Little Blue River ("Hay Cabin Creek") in Clay County, Missouri. Clark thought it unpleasantly warm, especially for persons accustomed to the cool weather of the north. If not for the winds on the river, he was certain that the party would be extremely uncomfortable. Clark called the bottomlands they passed "Charming" and thought the uplands well timbered. The captain declared mosquitoes less tormenting on this lower portion of the Missouri, especially compared to the area between the Platte and Yellowstone Rivers.

SEPTEMBER 16, 1806. With an excessively hot day, the men let the river carry them, and they relaxed at oars and paddles. The party met a large pirogue with eight Frenchmen at ten o'clock headed for trade with the Pawnees, and an hour later they encountered a large boat and two canoes with about twenty Frenchmen, led perhaps by Joseph Robidoux of St. Louis, bound for the Pawnees, Omahas, and Otoes. The captains were suspicious of the man's authorization to be trading in the area since he was so young, and his papers did not seem to carry the proper signatures. They were also suspicious of his loyalty to the United States and cautioned him against degrading the relationship of the American government with native people. Traveling about fifty-two miles, the party camped on an island between Carroll and Lafayette Counties, Missouri, a few miles up the Missouri River from Waverly, Lafayette County. Ordway reported that one of the men caught a catfish in the evening that may have weighed one hundred pounds.

SEPTEMBER 17, 1806. In the early part of the day the party passed a village of the Little Osage Indians. Clark renewed his comments of June 15, 1804, when he noted the dangers of the Missouri River in this vicinity. Passing through a swift, narrow channel at Malta Bend, Saline County, Missouri, for more than two miles, the explorers found a river littered with snags and crowded in by falling banks. Navigators carefully negotiated their way through the obstructions. At eleven o'clock they met an old acquaintance of Lewis's. James McClallen (or McClellen, and apparently unrelated to Robert McClellen), a former captain in the U.S. artillery, was on a government assignment leading a large boat of fifteen hands, an interpreter, and a clerk (perhaps a black man). Clark reported that he "was Somewhat astonished to See us return and appeared rejoiced to meet us. . . . this Gentleman informed us that we had been long Since given out by the people of the U S Generaly and almost forgotton, the President of the U. States had yet hopes of us." From McClallen the captains received the latest news from the states and queried him until nearly midnight. The party also received biscuits, chocolate, sugar, and whiskey from him and in exchange gave him corn and their thanks for his "civilities." Ordway reported that he "gave our party as much whiskey as they would drink."

McClallen's mission, as he told Clark, was "reather a speculative expedition to the confines of New Spain." He was to proceed to the Platte River and set up a trading establishment with the Pawnees and Otoes. He carried a speech for the Indians from Governor Wilkinson and gifts to help him gain their support. After securing the friendship of the Pawnees and purchasing mules and horses from them, he was to convince some of the principal chiefs to accompany him to Santa Fe, where he would establish trade in that area. He carried gifts for Spanish officials to smooth the negotiations and merchandise he hoped to sell for Spanish gold and silver, "of which those people abound." If the Spanish government accepted his plans, he proposed to set up a trading post in the Louisiana Territory convenient to traders from New Mexico. Clark called his plan "a very good one if strictly prosued." In fact, McClallen's movements after meeting Lewis and Clark are not entirely clear, but he did not make his way to New Mexico, and regular trade with Santa Fe did not begin until 1821.

The party made some thirty miles altogether and camped about four miles above the Grand River, which meets the Missouri between Carroll and Chariton Counties, Missouri. The camp would have been above in Saline County. The captains sent five hunters ahead in two small canoes with orders to hunt below the entrance of the Grand River and meet the main party there in the morning.

SEPTEMBER 18, 1806. Before separating McClallen gave the captains a letter, but neither the addressee nor the contents are revealed in the explorers' journals. They gave him a keg of corn. By seven o'clock the party passed Grand River, and a short distance below they caught up with the hunters. They had killed nothing. With little else but some biscuits to eat, the party pulled ashore at ten o'clock to gather pawpaws, which they found in abundance along this stretch of the river. Pawpaws were their only source of nourishment besides the biscuits, which when divided amounted to but one per person. This was to last them for another 150 miles, according to Clark's calculation. The captain called the party "perfectly contented and tell us that they can live very well on the pappaws." Potts and Shannon, however, complained of sore eyes, which Clark surmised were caused by the sun glaring on men without head covering. The day was excessively hot. Biddle later reported in his notes that Potts, "originally a dark complexioned man," being nearly naked in the summer heat had turned "as dark as any [Indian]." At the Chariton River, Chariton County, Missouri, they experienced a gentle Missouri River, much more so than on their ascent in 1804. With little appearance of deer, Clark also saw only a bear in the distance and three turkeys closer to shore. The party made about fifty-two miles and camped on an island nearly opposite the Lamine River, Cooper County, Missouri, a few miles above Boonville.

SEPTEMBER 19, 1806. Getting underway shortly after daylight, the party moved along swiftly as the men bent to their oars and paddles. In fact, they stopped only once, to gather more pawpaws. All agreed to forego hunting in favor of making miles in order to reach settlements that Clark calculated to be about 140 miles below, with the possibility of arriving there the next night. Nonetheless, Ordway noted that one man killed a deer. The men wanted to get to the Osage River by evening and make the small French village of La Charette, Warren County, Missouri, the next night. Indeed, after about seventy-two miles they arrived at the Osage River at dark on the Cole-Osage county line, Missouri, and camped at their spot of June 1–3, 1804. The complaint of sore eyes by Potts and Shannon the day before had now spread among the party. Clark reported that three men had inflamed eyes that were swollen and painful. Unable to fully account for the distress, he again blamed it on direct sunlight or bright reflections off the river. Modern judgments suggest that it may have been caused by the pawpaws. Handling the fruit can cause dermatitis, and the infection could transfer to the men's eyes when they wiped sweat from their faces. Gass's journal effectively ends on this day, but he penned a short comment within this entry about reaching St. Louis on September 23.

SEPTEMBER 20, 1806. Three men were so disabled by their eye infections that they were unable to work at the boats. To make things work, the captains abandoned the canoes that Clark had lashed together as a single boat in July on the Yellowstone River and redistributed the men among the remaining boats. By noon they were at the Gasconade River, and a little below that they met five Frenchmen headed for trade with the Osage Indians. Lewis and Clark did not tarry long, as their men were anxious to get home. A shout of joy went up when the men first sighted a cow along the riverbank. In early afternoon, having come about sixty-eight miles, they reached the little French village of La Charette, Warren County, Missouri, since washed away by the Missouri. Another grand shout rang out, and the men raised their oars and paddles in salute. They asked the captains for permission to fire their guns, and when it was granted they fired three rounds and gave out more hearty cheers. Traders along the shore answered in kind.

Landing on shore, the party was received "very politely" by Scot tradesmen whose identity is not clear. Headed for trade with the Osages and Otoes, the traders gave Lewis and Clark beef, flour, and pork and prepared them a welcome supper. With rain on the way, the captains gladly accepted a bed in one of the traders' tents for the night. Less obliging was a local citizen who charged the captains eight dollars for two gallons of whiskey. Clark called it an "imposition." Ordway termed it "extorinatable." Otherwise, the explorers were warmly welcomed by French and Americans who seemed astonished that they had survived and returned. Clark was impressed by the traders' boats. He described them as of the "Skeneckeity form," that is, resembling boats built in Schenectady, New York, and used on the rivers of western New York and the upper Saint Lawrence. Clark measured them at thirty feet in length and eight in width, with a pointed bow and stern, a flat bottom, and six oars. Clark considered them well suited for working the shallow waters and sandbar-infested rivers ahead. The captain learned of discontent among the American settlers over land grants promised them by the Spanish government, which were now in limbo under the new American administration. It was a contentious issue that Lewis and Clark later had to face as U.S. administrators.

SEPTEMBER 21, 1806. It took a little time to get the party together, since La Charette residents had invited a number of the men to lodge with them and the explorers were slow getting back to the boats. Nevertheless, by seven thirty the party was underway and soon met twelve canoes of Kickapoo Indians going upriver to hunt. Later in the afternoon they encountered two large boats, also headed upriver, probably to trade. Seeing domestic livestock on shore elated the party and encouraged their rowing efforts. By four o'clock they were in sight of St. Charles, so the men pushed even harder to reach the village. Soon they viewed Sunday strollers walking along the shore, saluted them with gunfire, and landed at the lower end of the town, having come about forty-eight miles. Here they were met by many villagers and received invitations to board with old friends and new acquaintances. Clark found them "much delighted at our return and seem to vie with each other in their politeness to us all." He noted specifically Basil Proulx, perhaps Pierre-Antoine Tabeau, and François Duquette and named two or three other unidentifiable persons.

SEPTEMBER 22, 1806. Staying comfortably in the homes of St. Charles residents while it rained hard, the captains delayed getting the party underway. The captains stayed at the home of Basil Proulx, an early inhabitant of St. Charles, where Clark busied himself with letters to friends in Kentucky. By ten o'clock the rain ceased, the party came together, and they set out down the Missouri River again. They soon reached Fort Bellefontaine, Saint Louis County, Missouri, at the mouth of Coldwater Creek, where they received a gun salute of seventeen rounds from field artillery pieces and a hearty welcome from the occupants, many of them known to expedition soldiers. The cantonment was established in 1805 by Wilkinson and was the first U.S. fort west of the Mississippi. There they met Colonel Thomas

Hunt, a Revolutionary War veteran, and Lieutenant George Peter, in charge of an artillery company. Apparently, Wilkinson was away and his wife, Ann Biddle Wilkinson (a distant relative of Nicholas Biddle), was ill ("in delicate health") and not able to greet the visitors. Within a few months she died. Most of the party was quartered for the night within the post.

SEPTEMBER 23, 1806. Before departing Fort Bellefontaine the captains took Big White to the post store and outfitted him in American clothes. Then they had breakfast with the garrison commander, Colonel Hunt, and set out. Within a few miles they reached the Mississippi River. Ordway revealed that the party stopped briefly at their camp of 1803–4 at Wood River, Illinois. From there they descended the Mississippi River to St. Louis, and in honor of the grand arrival the party fired their weapons as a salute to villagers who poured out to welcome them home. Ordway said that the "people gathred on the Shore and Huzzared three cheers." The sergeant ended his journal this day with these poignant words: "much rejoiced that we have the Expedition Completed and now we look for boarding in Town and wait for our Settlement and then we entend to return to our native homes to See our parents once more as we have been So long from them."

Learning that the day's mail had already been dispatched, Lewis wrote a quick note to John Hay, postmaster at Cahokia, asking him to hold the mail until he could get expedition letters to him by noon the next day. Clark met an old acquaintance, William Christy, who had been a neighbor in Kentucky and now had a tavern in town. He generously provided space in his storerooms for the party to stow their baggage. Jean Pierre Chouteau offered lodging for the captains at his home, and in the evening they visited René Auguste Chouteau and other local friends.

The next day the captains were up early, writing letters to government officials, to family, and to friends, including Lewis's summary of the expedition to Jefferson. They sent Drouillard in haste to get the letters to Cahokia, to postmaster Hay, and to the world. The captains spent the rest of the day examining their baggage and purchasing new clothes, which they gave to a tailor to finish.

On the evening of the twenty-fifth they attended a dinner and ball at Christy's tavern, where eighteen toasts were drunk, the final one to "Captains Lewis and Clark—Their perilous services endear them to every American heart." Clark closed his journal on September 26 with a brief entry and the final words, "we commenced wrighting."

Afterword

Contrary to some Americans' fears, the Corps of Discovery was not captured by the Spanish, nor were they killed; they arrived safely home, as we know. But what of their lives after the great adventure? About Lewis and Clark there exists much information, but for most members of the corps we know little. Most lived obscure lives before and after their brief season of glory. Indeed, for some even the details of their expedition experience are meager. Clark made some attempt to keep up with his comrades in arms, but separation in time and distance made this nearly impossible. Two decades after the expedition he drew up a list of thirty-four members of the corps and tried to account for each. Eighteen he either knew or thought to be dead and for five of the remainder he had no knowledge at all. We know only slightly more today.

After the expedition Lewis did not return to a satisfying personal life. His attempts to find a wife failed and he came back to a job in St. Louis alone. Clark in the meantime had married, and his bride probably took the emotional place that Lewis had previously filled. This separation from Clark was intensified by Lewis's distance from Jefferson, who on occasion scolded him for not writing and wondered when he would finish the book about the expedition. Never deeply religious, Lewis had no reserves of spiritual commitment to fall back on and find solace when problems mounted and demons set in.

In recognition of their accomplishments Lewis and Clark were given posts of standing and responsibility. The president appointed Lewis governor of Upper Louisiana, with its capital at St. Louis, and he placed Clark in charge of Indian affairs for the same district. The governorship was to be the just reward for a national hero, but in contrast to his success as an explorer Lewis encountered a multitude of frustrations in the job. Perhaps he was not meant to be a desk-bound administrator. He did not help matters when he left the office unattended while he lingered in the East after the expedition. Lewis was also burdened with an enemy in his office, an administrative assistant with a political appointment who was writing negative reports about Lewis to officials in Washington.

Notable among Lewis's difficulties as governor were attempts to return the Mandan chief Big White to his home. Expedition sergeant Pryor, now an army ensign, led the first attempt to restore the chief, in 1807. He was turned back by an attack from some Arikara Indians who were angered by the death of their own chief in Washington. In the fight Shannon, another member of the corps, suffered a wound that cost him a leg. It was not until 1809 that a private fur trading company, receiving a substantial payment under Lewis's signature, succeeded in getting Big White back to his people. Washington officials refused to honor some of Lewis's expenditures in this effort. A new executive in the White House was less obliging than Jefferson might have been. This was, in a sense, the final insult for Lewis in the unhappy ordeal of his governorship. Personal financial problems also loomed. It appears he took to drinking heavily in this period and was in a state of severe depression when he set out for Washington to straighten out his affairs. On the journey he died at Grinder's Stand, a way station on the Natchez Trace in Tennessee, on October 11, 1809, apparently by putting a pistol to his head and breast.

While some historians have suggested that he was murdered, available evidence strongly supports the belief that he committed suicide. In fact, he had attempted twice earlier to kill himself along the way. His eventual fate inevitably attracts the attention of amateur psychoanalysts seeking the roots of his emotional problems. But knowledge of his childhood is scant and there is no evidence of psychological turmoil during the expedition. On the trail he functioned effectively as a cool and capable leader under numerous trying circumstances. Moreover, neither Clark nor Jefferson, the persons who knew him best, seemed to have doubted his suicide. Clark's reaction was to write, "I fear, O! I fear the weight of his mind has over come him." And Jefferson later noted that he was subject to "hypochondriac affections," perhaps meaning that he suffered bouts of depression. Suicide remains the most acceptable explanation for his death.

Jefferson had expected Lewis to prepare a full account of the expedition after his return. Although the captain had begun efforts in that direction, he had written not a single word for publication. To Clark now fell the task of bringing the results of their labors into print. Having small confidence in his own literary abilities, Clark arranged with Nicholas Biddle, a Philadelphia literary figure, to become the expedition's ghostwriter. Using the captains' journals and that of Sergeant Ordway, and in extensive consultation with Clark and with Shannon, Biddle produced a narrative account of the expedition in two volumes. Final publication was further delayed until 1814 by the failure of the initial publisher. Two years later Clark himself was still trying to get a copy.

Clark was to survive his friend by nearly thirty years. He is so established in history as joint commander of the famous expedition that it is easy to forget that the greater part of his career was spent in St. Louis as a federal agent of Indian affairs. The captain was an effective and conscientious officer in that position, promoting the best interests of his Indian wards and gaining the respect of his white contemporaries. All the while he had to balance a changing disposition in Washington toward Native Americans as Jeffersonian paternalism was succeeded by Jacksonian pressures. Western travelers were eager to visit Clark's home, to view his museum of frontier curiosities, and perhaps to hear him recount expedition adventures. He was married twice, first to Julia Hancock of Fincastle, Virginia, for whom Clark named the Judith River in Montana in the summer of 1805. He died on September 1, 1838, at the St. Louis home of his eldest son, Meriwether Lewis Clark.

For most other members of the Corps of Discovery the end of the expedition meant a return to their previous obscurity. Many of them dropped completely out of sight. Patrick Gass, promoted to sergeant to replace the deceased Floyd, produced his own account of the expedition. Heavily edited by a Virginia bookseller, Gass's book beat that of his leaders into publication, coming out in 1807. First in print and last to die, Gass survived until 1870, longer than any other member of the party whose fate is known. John Colter gained some independent fame for his later adventures. He is best known for his exploration and description of today's Yellowstone Park, but his tales of hot springs and geysers led to jokes about "Colter's Hell." His escape, naked, from the Blackfeet Indians near the Three Forks of the Missouri has become a western legend. Settling in Missouri, Colter died in 1813 of jaundice.

That expert hunter, interpreter, and woodsman Drouillard returned to the wilderness interior on fur trading ventures. He died in 1810 at the Three Forks at the hands of the Blackfeet, his foes in the Two Medicine River incident. Pryor was in and out of military service; he participated in the Battle of New Orleans in 1815. Afterward he became a trader among the Osage Indians, married an Osage woman, and died among that tribe in 1831. Shannon received a government pension for the loss of his leg. He later studied law and practiced his profession in Kentucky before moving to Missouri to become a state senator; he died in 1836.

Journalist and top sergeant Ordway apparently returned to his home in New Hampshire, later settled in Missouri, and was dead by 1817. Information about the trustworthy Field brothers, Joseph and Reuben, is vague. Joseph apparently died less than a year after the return of the expedition, while Reuben settled in Kentucky and died by 1823. York received his freedom in 1811 and operated a freight business for a time in Tennessee and Kentucky; he may have died in 1832 on his way to see Clark in St. Louis. About the rest of this "band of brothers" we know little—their stories long lost and forgotten, like those of so many other common foot soldiers.

Charbonneau lived on among the Mandans and Hidatsas, much of the time, thanks to Clark's affection for him, working as a government interpreter and agent. A train of notable visitors used his interpreting services at the Upper Missouri villages through the years. After Clark's death in 1838, accounts of the man quickly faded, and he was dead by at least 1843, but of unknown causes or whereabouts. His child and the baby of expedition, Jean Baptiste, became a fur trader and a noted guide. Clark cared for him as a child as he had promised, seeing to his upbringing and education. As a young man Jean Baptiste joined Prince Paul Wilhelm of Württemberg, who was on a scientific journey in America, and returned with him to Europe. He came back to America in 1829, afterward associating with some of the most famous frontiersmen of his day. In the 1840s he served as alcalde of the San Luis Rey Mission in California, then followed the gold rush north. He died in 1866 in southeastern Oregon while traveling to another gold discovery.

Of the fate of Sacagawea there are two versions. One story, now discredited, has her living to the 1880s on the Wind River Shoshone Reservation in Wyoming, with Jean Baptiste joining her and dying there also. In truth, there is little doubt that she died of fever at Fort Manuel in South Dakota in December 1812. Despite her limited but useful contributions to the expedition, geographic landmarks have been named for her; markers, monuments, and memorials have been placed in her honor; and numerous literary and artistic works have given her a prominence that competes even with that of the captains.

The journey was over—the expedition not simply completed, it was magnificently accomplished. The Lewis and Clark expedition is one of the great stories in American history. Everyone knows of the two captains' trek across the continent with their band of intrepid explorers. And who has not heard of Sacagawea, the young Shoshone woman who accompanied the party with her newborn baby strapped to her back? The journey is filled with tales of high drama: of tense encounters with natives; of hair-raising river crossings and precipitous mountain trails; of hunger, thirst, and bodily fatigue. Less well known are the scientific endeavors—the constant activities of observing, considering, collecting, and recording. The records are marvels of geographic revelations, natural history studies, and ethnographic investigations. The expedition remains for all time a story of endurance, discovery, and achievement.

The expedition was preeminently a geographic endeavor. Jefferson made clear at the outset that the discovery of a practical route across the continent was the principal objective of the mission. In fact, the explorers were seeking the elusive all-water route across the continent, the fabled Northwest Passage. By following the Missouri River to its headwaters, then crossing mountains and deserts to the sea, Lewis and Clark were able to lay out the general topographic features of the West and minutely delineate their avenue of travel. The men proved that an easy path to the western ocean did not exist and that the crossing of the continent would be lengthy and difficult. Yet, in reaching the coast, the expedition laid an important claim to the Oregon Country. This claim, plus the purchase of the Louisiana Territory, played an important part in the eventual settlement of the West.

Lewis and Clark's vision of the West was colored by images before the exploration. The leaders' geographic preconceptions hindered some of their work, but they were willing to reorder their ideas in the face of topographic realities. Nonetheless, they persisted with some unchanged notions about certain incorrect theories. They returned, for instance, still believing in a "height of land," from which flowed many of the great streams of the West. During their trip the captains may have relied not only on a geography of sight but also on a geography of imagination. More important, however, was their actual field work. The men displayed an amazing ability to make accurate decisions in the face of the unknown—sometimes without the aid of helpful Indian advice. Keen geographic intuition and wilderness lore served them well on several occasions, the correct determination at the Marias River being only one example.

An important part of the captains' geographic assignment included mapping the unknown. All the attention given to securing the most accurate maps of the West before the explorers' departure fixes cartography as a principal purpose of the expedition. The men were exploring new possessions acquired under the Louisiana Purchase; thus mapping became important in determining the boundaries and dimensions of the new lands. Moreover, accurate maps of lands beyond the purchase would serve as devices to further American territorial ambitions. To know the lands was ultimately to possess them.

Clark was the principal mapmaker. He is the author of all but a few of the nearly two hundred maps from the expedition. Clark's maps are masterfully executed and are models of field cartography. Working with crude and unreliable instruments and with no apparent training, Clark did an exceptional job, and his drafting abilities have been universally admired. Later generations of explorer-mapmakers followed his example. Clark's mapping accomplished two major objectives: he skillfully plotted the route of the Corps of Discovery and he provided a view of peripheral areas based on the best native information available. Clark's great map of the West, published with the first account of the expedition in 1814, alone justified his efforts. It was the beginning of a new generation of accurate maps of the American West—maps that were based on actual field sightings and acute topographic inference. It has been called a cartographic achievement.

Lewis's scientific studies in Philadelphia before the expedition proved profitable on the trip. Especially noteworthy were the captain's accomplishments in the biological sciences. Lewis, and occasionally Clark, was the first to describe in detail a wide range of characteristic plant and animal species of the West. Previous discoveries and reports of species before them do not detract from their contributions to understanding the range, habits, and physical characteristics of many known species, such as the grizzly bear, buffalo, and beaver. Because of various mischances the results of their work did not see full publication for a century after the expedition, so that Lewis's priority of discovery was not adequately recognized until the last few decades.

Jefferson has been criticized for not sending a naturalist on the expedition. However, there were few trained naturalists in America at the time and Lewis was nearly their equal. Moreover, not many available naturalists could have stood up to the rigors of wilderness travel. Lewis was blessed with those qualities most important in a naturalist: an unquenchable curiosity, keen observational powers, and a systematic approach to understanding the natural world. For example, when Lewis counted eighteen tail feathers on the western blue grouse he recalled that the familiar ruffed grouse had exactly the same number. One has only to look at Lewis's discourses on the animals of the West to understand that Jefferson did not err. The captain's botanical writings are equally impressive, especially his precise ecological distinctions.

Among expedition accomplishments must be counted the health and well-being of the party. Lewis and Clark were their own physicians. For twenty-eight months they doctored themselves and their party. Starting out in the company of "robust, healthy young men," the captains nonetheless had to face ordinary human ills—abscesses and boils, dysentery, malaria, pleurisy, and rheumatism. Injuries and accidents were recurring events—bruises and dislocations from spills and falls, frostbite, and snakebites. Contagious diseases troubled the party as well; colds and venereal disease were not uncommon ailments. The captains' choice of bleeding and purging as routine remedies was the period's accepted practice. Lewis also had some medicinal knowledge, gained partly from his mother, who grew and dispensed vegetable drugs. During the continental crossing Lewis occasionally concocted a strong brew of local plants for his own and others' relief.

More important than the captains' limited medical knowledge was the care and concern they accorded their men. As Jefferson would observe, Lewis was "careful as a father of those committed to his charge." At the end of the trip Lewis could happily report that they had returned in good health. In fact, during the entire expedition Floyd was the only member of the party to die, and his death from a ruptured appendix could not have been averted under the best medical care of the day.

In line with Jefferson's lengthy instructions regarding Indians, the captains spent much time in carrying out these responsibilities. In councils under brush arbors and around campfires where the pipe of peace was passed, the captains worked hard to establish good relations between the natives and the young republic they represented. We should not discount the important effects of the individual friendships and mutual admiration that developed, be it a Hidatsa chief's regard for Shields's handiwork in iron, Lewis's praise of Yelleppit's hospitality, the Nez Perces' admiration for Clark's medical knowledge, or the simple joys of dancing to Indian drum and expedition fiddle.

The explorers established peaceful contact with most of the Indian tribes that they met. Meetings with Indians were generally cordial and mutually beneficial. Presents were exchanged and information was shared. At times, indeed, the party's success and well-being depended upon the goodwill and assistance of the natives, who provided them with food, horses, and guidance through unknown and difficult country. Indians were often helpful in describing the way ahead and providing information about distant lands. In fact, there was only one episode of violence between the explorers and Indians during the whole twenty-eight months; some other moments of extreme tension ended without bloodshed. Yet even the difficulties with the Sioux and the Blackfeet did not result in bitterness, though later relations between these tribes and whites caused friction, war, and death.

Working among a diversity of tribes, linguistic groups, and cultural settings, from nomadic horsemen and buffalo hunters of the Great Plains to riverine villagers and salmon catchers of the Pacific Coast, the captains faced a formidable task. Simply to pass through this multitude of humanity was job enough, but to catalog, study, and understand them all appears impossible. And so it was to some extent. These tribes had their own views of such matters as trade relations, intertribal associations and conflicts, and internal tribal politics. Many of the subtleties of these attitudes were not noticed or were misunderstood by the American leaders. The captains were not totally unbiased observers, able to obtain accurate and systematic cultural information, but they did rise above cultural relativism and were not nearly as ethnocentric as some of their contemporaries. As well as they could for their time and circumstance the captains took a detached, descriptive, and scientific view of Native Americans. Lewis and Clark were transitional figures between the hit-and-miss ethnographers of the early nineteenth century and the trained ethnologists of later decades.

A final and essential legacy of the expedition is the diaries that were so meticulously written and carefully preserved during the transcontinental crossing. The journals of Lewis and Clark are a national treasure. Besides describing the natural resources and native peoples of the West, the diaries also contain myriad scientific observations. Moreover, they are a genuinely interesting account of expedition events in themselves. Had the captains and four enlisted men not kept daily journals of their activities—recording events, observations, and impressions in more than one million words—many of their important discoveries might be lost. Recognizing that they were charged with an incredible array of responsibilities, one stands in awe of the range, depth, and constancy of the men's journal-keeping labors.

The expedition is enshrined in the imagination of Americans as a heroic feat of geographical exploration, which it was, but not as the major contribution to science that it was intended to be. Only in the twentieth century has the breadth of Lewis and Clark's accomplishments in so many areas been truly appreciated. Continued attention to the achievements of the Corps of Discovery can only increase the esteem it so richly deserves. It remains for all time our American epic of discovery.

Index